AGING

Scientific Perspectives
:: and Social Issues ::

SECOND EDITION

Brooks/Cole Series in Social Gerontology

Vern Bengtson, *University of Southern California*
Series Editor

Health and Aging
Tom Hickey, *University of Michigan*

Environment and Aging
M. Powell Lawton, *Philadelphia Geriatric Center*

Last Chapters: A Sociology of Aging and Dying
Victor W. Marshall, *University of Toronto and McMaster University*

Aging and Retirement
Anne Foner, *Rutgers University*
Karen Schwab, *Social Security Administration, Washington, D.C.*

Role Transitions in Later Life
Linda K. George, *Duke University Medical Center*

AGING

Scientific Perspectives
:: and Social Issues ::

SECOND EDITION

Edited by

Diana S. Woodruff
Temple University

James E. Birren
Ethel Percy Andrus Gerontology Center
University of Southern California

Brooks/Cole Publishing Company
Monterey, California

Brooks/Cole Publishing Company
A Division of Wadsworth, Inc.

Printed in the United States of America

10   9   8   7   6   5   4   3

Library of Congress Cataloging in Publication Data
Main entry under title:

Aging: scientific perspectives and social issues.

   Bibliography: p.
   Includes index.
   1. Gerontology—Addresses, essays, lectures.
I. Woodruff, Diana S.   II. Birren, James E.
III. Ethel Percy Andrus Gerontology Center.
HQ1061.A4835   1983   305.2'6   82-19768
ISBN 0-534-01253-1

Project Development Editor: Marquita Flemming
Manuscript Editor: Jonas F. Weisel
Production Editor: Richard Mason
Interior and Cover Design: Vicki Van Deventer
Illustrations, Figures 2.4, 6.1, 6.2, 8.1, 8.2, 8.4, 8.5, 9.2, 9.3, 15.1: Joan Carol
Typesetting: Linda Andrews

Preface

Since the first edition of *Aging: Scientific Perspectives and Social Issues* was published in 1975, the field of gerontology has expanded tremendously in the form of research, published material, and public interest. The National Institute of Aging was created by the federal government in 1975; this was followed by the White House Conference on Aging of 1981 and the World Assembly on Aging sponsored by the United Nations in 1982. The scientific study of aging has received increasing impetus from the large cadre of first-rate scholars who have started to expand their research interests into the field of aging and work along with those already trained and engaged in aging research. Aging as a social issue has been accepted as a fact of life, but there are many stereotypes that need to be replaced by increased knowledge.

The population pyramids that were a unique feature of the chapter on demography in the first edition have graced the front pages of publications such as the *New York Times,* and the information contained in these figures, which indicates that the aged are becoming an increasingly large percentage of the population, is now common knowledge. In colleges and universities, social and natural science departments are now considered deficient when they do not include scholars with some expertise in gerontology. Business schools and colleges regularly consider the impact of aging on the population when they include course-work and research on retirement and the role of the older consumer. Geriatrics is no longer neglected in medical schools, and the training of specialists in the health care of the aging will soon be a requirement in many professions. Indeed, many institutions of higher learning in the United States now belong to the Association for Gerontology in Higher Education, an association that did not exist when the first edition of *Aging* was published. Research and teaching in gerontology has not only expanded in the United States but is generating worldwide concern. In developing nations, as well as in developed countries, aging is an important social issue.

With this dramatic growth of the field we felt it was important to revise *Aging.* Many new developments in gerontology were making the first edition obsolete. When we planned the second edition of *Aging,* we sought our colleagues' advice on how we should change the book. We asked professors who had used the text to identify new areas that needed to be covered and areas that could safely be deleted. This second edition reflects our experience and the experience of others who have used the text. We found, for example, that the topic of personality and aging was not adequately

v

covered in the first edition, and we have now added a chapter on that subject. Sexuality and aging is another area where there is currently a great deal of information that was not treated in sufficient detail in the original *Aging*. Other topics significant enough to merit chapters in the second edition are "Ethnicity and aging"; "Retirement, employment, and aging"; and "Aging and physical and mental health." Although some topics must be omitted in such a broad and diverse discipline, we feel that the second edition, even more than the first, covers most of the significant subjects in the field of aging.

Aging: Scientific Perspectives and Social Issues is an introductory text for students interested in the processes and problems of aging and for individuals providing services to the elderly. The material in this volume is original and represents current perspectives on aging. Although we deal with biological, psychological, and sociological concepts, we have not assumed that our readers have had any previous exposure to those disciplines, and thus we have outlined basic concepts underlying each discipline's approach. For those interested in further exploration of any of the topics covered in this volume, we have provided extensive references at the end of each chapter.

The book's organization reflects the pattern we have found to work best with our students. We first set forth a broad overview of gerontology, and then we gradually narrow the focus from sociological to psychological to biological perspectives. This scientific knowledge best prepares the student to deal with the broad social issues of human aging that are discussed in the concluding chapters.

The first chapter provides an overview of the history of the scientific study of aging and discusses some of the ways in which the various approaches presented in the rest of the volume are related in contemporary gerontology. The focus then moves to sociological perspectives of aging, with Chapters 2 through 5 including descriptions of the demographic and social aspects of aging, and discussions of ethnic minority aging and aging and the family. Chapters 6 through 10 are devoted to recent psychological research on the aged individual. Cognitive processes such as intelligence, learning, and memory are covered in this section along with a consideration of personality and aging, physiology and behavior relationships, and sexuality. Biological perspectives are next presented in Chapters 11 through 13 with a discussion of aging at the molecular, cellular, and physiological levels. From this microscopic perspective we turn to social issues such as health care (physical and mental), housing and environment, retirement and employment, economics, political behavior, and public policy. Much research still needs to be done; we hope some readers of this book may elect a career of research on aging, or perhaps others may be stimulated to be trained in a helping profession that cares for older persons.

As in the first edition, the contributors to this second edition have all been associated in some capacity with the Andrus Gerontology Center at the University of Southern California. Many of us have moved on to other academic institutions or to facilities in which we work with the aging. However, we all share a common experience in having worked at the Center and having interacted with other professionals in that exciting atmosphere. Although the authors worked together in one setting, the reader will find that the chapters adhere to no single theoretical orientation; nor is there a common data base. Written by academicians who have been trained in many disciplines, this book reflects a broad range of perspectives and scientific approaches. We share, nonetheless, a mutual interest in and dedication to understanding the complex processes of aging and a strong common bond developed as we interacted at the University of Southern California.

As we stated in the preface to the first edition, the originator of the concept of this book is James E. Birren, Executive Director of the Andrus Gerontology Center and Dean of the Leonard Davis School of Gerontology.

Clearly this volume has a multidisciplinary approach to aging. At the Andrus Gerontology Center some view the processes of aging through a microscope; others use a stethoscope, a polygraph, or a questionnaire; still others become involved as participant-observers. In this book we attempt to share these views of aging, and we also try to apply our various perspectives to demonstrate how this knowledge can help improve the quality of life for contemporary and future generations of old people.

Diana S. Woodruff
James E. Birren

Contributing Authors

Dr. Vern L. Bengtson, *Andrus Gerontology Center, University of Southern California*

Dr. James E. Birren, *Andrus Gerontology Center, University of Southern California*

Dr. Nan Corby, *Andrus Gerontology Center, University of Southern California*

Dr. Neal E. Cutler, *Andrus Gerontology Center, University of Southern California*

Dr. Mary Beard Deming, *Andrus Gerontology Center, University of Southern California*

Dr. Paul Denny, *School of Dentistry, University of Southern California*

Dr. Herbert A. deVries, *Andrus Gerontology Center, University of Southern California*

Dr. David Haber, *Institute of Gerontology, University of Columbia, Washington, D.C.*

Dr. Ira S. Hirschfield, *Levi Strauss Foundation*

Dr. Paul A. Kerschner, *American Association of Retired Persons–National Retired Teachers Association*

Dr. Frances S. Kobata, *Department of Senior Citizens Affairs, County of Los Angeles*

Dr. Steve McConnell, *U.S. House of Representatives, Select Committee on Aging*

Dr. Sharon Y. Moriwaki, *Department of Labor and Industrial Relations, State of Hawaii*

Dr. Margaret Neiswender Reedy, *Veterans' Administration Medical Center, Long Beach, California*

Dr. Victor Regnier, *Department of Architecture, University of Illinois*

Dr. K. Warner Schaie, *Department of Individual and Family Studies, Pennsylvania State University*

Dr. Bruce Sloane, *School of Medicine, University of Southern California*

Dr. Robert E. Solnick, *La Paz Psychological Group*

Dr. Judith Treas, *Andrus Gerontology Center, University of Southern California*

Dr. David A. Walsh, *Andrus Gerontology Center, University of Southern California*

Dr. Robin J. Walther, *Southern California Edison Company*

Dr. Ruth B. Weg, *Andrus Gerontology Center, University of Southern California*

Dr. Diana S. Woodruff, *Department of Psychology, Temple University*

Contents

AGING
Scientific Perspectives
:: and Social Issues ::
SECOND EDITION

CHAPTER 1

Aging: Past and Future

James E. Birren and Diana S. Woodruff

Research on aging is primarily a development of this century. Although many thought-ful people in the past raised basic questions about the nature of aging, it was not until this century that we had the research methods to investigate the many facets of aging. Increasing numbers of biological and social scientists are drawn to this new field of knowledge. Also new professions have been created to provide services to a large population of elderly adults (for example, psychologists, gerontologists, geriatricians, geropsychiatrists, and many others).

The newcomer to the field often raises provocative questions: How long am I likely to live? What will I be like when I am old? Will there be dramatic extensions to length of life in the near future? What can we do to slow down the rate of undesir-able aspects of aging and maximize the advantages? Some of these questions can be answered from what is now known about aging. Since the subject matter is so broad, it is very difficult to have a clear perspective about aging. Researchers tend to specialize on a narrow topic within their own scientific or professional discipline. Chapters in this book were written by psychologists who specialize in cognition, learning and memory, and psychophysiology and by biologists who do research on cellular mech-anisms and human physiology. Information about aging is so extensive that we cannot hope to cover all the scientific perspectives or social issues in one book. We have, however, provided the reader with the highlights of the biological, psychological, and social facts about aging.

There are few topics in this century that have more vast implications than aging. We are living longer and better than humankind has ever lived. In the 19th century few people lived long enough to retire. More has been added to the average length of life in this century than was added from prehistoric times through the last century.

Growing older is a biological, psychological, and social process. Furthermore, one should be aware of the distinction between the consequences of disease that may be associated with advancing age, and the accompaniments of normal aging, which even relatively healthy older adults will undergo. Senile dementia, for example, is a disease associated with the later years of life. It is a process that affects the nervous system of perhaps 5%–6% of older persons. Similarly, the consequences of heart disease and an endocrine disease such as diabetes should be separated from the changes typically seen in an otherwise healthy person who is advanced in age. This distinction is important, because much of what passes as typical human aging is really a consequence of disease.

Gerontology and geriatrics are new fields. Undoubtedly their rapid development has been spurred by the rapid increase in the older population. In the early part of this century White House Conferences on Children were convened, but now we have grown used to expecting a White House Conference on Aging every 10 years. Long planning went into the White House Conference on Aging of December 1981, and over 2000 delegates debated issues concerning aging of individuals and society. Increasingly other countries of the world are expressing interest in the various aspects of aging. The United Nations convened the World Assembly on the Elderly in 1982. Many states now have departments on aging, whose function is to plan, sponsor, and monitor programs for elderly persons. One might say that aging is perhaps receiving more attention as a social issue than as a scientific question. However, the United States Congress created a National Institute on Aging in 1975 to support fundamental research into the many processes of aging. In addition, the National Institute of Mental Health has created a Center for the Study of Mental Health of Aging. In fact, a wide range of government agencies now support research on aging, including studies of health care, nutrition, and retirement.

Clearly, the scientific and social aspects of aging are highly interrelated. They are, in fact, so interrelated that it is difficult to separate them; some perhaps would like to slow down basic research because some findings may have far-reaching implications for human aging. However, within our lifetime, if basic research were to cut in half the devastating consequences of senile dementia, it would make a remarkable contribution to the well-being of humankind.

Many scientists studying basic mechanisms of aging received university training because of the foresight of scientists who planned long-term investments in basic research. Future generations will derive many benefits from our developing a broad foundation of knowledge. The promotion of health, the development of educational programs for the elderly, the increased utilization of the skills of older persons, and indeed, the development of generations of competent, healthy older adults with an interest in utilizing their skills to best advantage requires basic research knowledge and training of professionals who will apply such knowledge to the well-being of older persons.

AN HISTORICAL VIEW OF AGING

Early thought about aging

Gerontology, the science of aging, began as an inquiry into the characteristics or qualities of long-lived people. Much speculation and many myths were devoted to explaining why certain individuals were favored with long life.

Myths about aging and death in literature are usually structured around one of three basic themes: antediluvian, hyperborean, and rejuvenescent. The antediluvian theme (Gruman, 1966) emerges from myths that are based on the belief that people lived much longer in the past. This theme is exemplified in the book of Genesis, where the life spans of ten Hebrew patriarchs are recorded: Adam lived for 930 years, Seth for 912 years, Noah for 950 years, and so on. To take another example, the Trobrianders and the Ainu in North Japan believed their forefathers were able to rejuvenate themselves by shedding their skins like snakes.

The hyperborean theme, originating with the Greeks, arises from the belief that in some distant place there is a culture or society whose people enjoy a remarkably long life. "According to the traditions of ancient Greece, there dwells hyper (beyond) Boreas (the north wind) a fortunate people free from all natural ills" (Gruman, 1966, p. 22). "Their hair crowned with gold bay-leaves they hold glad revelry; and neither sickness nor baneful eld mingleth among that chosen people; but, aloof from toil and conflict, they dwell afar" (Pindar, quoted in Gruman, 1966, p. 22).

A third theme found in many legends is the rejuvenescent theme, which is often expressed by a fountain whose waters are purported to rejuvenate. Americans are familiar with the legend of Juan Ponce de Leon, whose search for the fountain of youth led to the accidental discovery of Florida in 1513. The earliest account of Ponce de Leon's adventure was published in 1535 in the general history of the Indies by Oviedo, who served as a Spanish official in the New World. He wrote that Ponce de Leon was "seeking that fountain of Biminie that the Indians have given it to be understood would renovate or resprout and refresh the age and forces of he who drank or bathed himself in that fountain" (Beauvous, quoted in Gruman, 1966, p. 24). Drinking from or bathing in a fountain is not the only expression of the rejuvenescent theme in history. For example, the Chinese, in the third century B.C. advocated gymnastic techniques for increasing the length of life.

Present hopes of rejuvenation extend beyond the fountain. Recently in Switzerland medical researchers have ground up and homogenized sheep embryos and injected the material into an elite circle of human clients. Certain hormones and other substances not present in the adult animal are said to be in the embryo. Rat embryos that had undergone the same procedure were injected into old rats, which lived slightly longer than normal. Such efforts often capture the imagination of novelists. The popular *Methuselah Enzyme* by Fred M. Stuart is an adaptation of this embryo homogenate theme, and Aldous Huxley develops a closely related theme in *After Many a Summer Dies the Swan.*

The scientific era

The advent of the scientific mode of thought in the 1600s caused a break with earlier traditions that relied on magic or speculation to explain naturally occurring phenomena. The scientific method advocated the systematic observation of phenomena in order to discover the underlying laws governing behavior. As Francis Bacon stated, "The end of our foundation is knowledge of causes, and secret motions of things; and the enlarging of the bounds of human empire, to the affecting of all things possible" (Bacon, as quoted by Gruman, 1966, p. 80). Bacon's implication for gerontology was that by undertaking a systematic study of the processes of aging one might discover the causes of aging. Bacon thought that poor hygienic practices had the most significant effect on the aging process.

Early empirical period. One of the great American heroes in the early 1700s was Benjamin Franklin. Franklin was a versatile thinker with serious interests in many fields, including aging. Like Bacon, he hoped that science would be able to discover the laws governing the aging process and that it might, ultimately, discover a way to rejuvenate people.

> I wish it were possible, from this instance, to invent a method of embalming drowned persons, in such a manner that they may be recalled to life at any period, however distant, for having a very ardent desire to see and observe the state of America a hundred years hence. I should prefer to any ordinary death, the being immersed in a cask of Madeira wine, with a few friends, till that time, to be then recalled to life by the solar warmth of my dear country. But since in all probability we live in an age too early and too near the infancy of science, to hope to see an art brought in our time to its perfection, I must for the present content myself with the treat, which you are so kind as to promise me, of the resurrection of a owl or a turkey cock [Franklin, quoted in Gruman, 1966, p. 84].

Franklin also explored the possibility that lightning might influence the resurrection of deceased animals and people. It was thought at the time that, because electricity had a stimulating effect, it would have a direct influence on the life span. Even today some people try to sell static-electricity belts under the pretense that they will prolong life.

Although Bacon and Franklin were among those who anticipated the scientific method, a Belgian named Quetelet is considered the first gerontologist (Birren, 1961). Quetelet was born in Ghent in 1796 and received the first doctorate in science from the University of Ghent in 1819 in mathematics. After earning his degree, he became interested in probabilities and subsequently developed the concept of the average man around which extremes were distributed. The result of Quetelet's pioneering work was a curve that we now accept as representing a basic distribution of most human traits. The curve indicates that there is an average or central tendency around which are distributed higher and lower measurements. In his book published in 1835, *On the Nature of Man and the Development of His Faculties,* Quetelet lists the averages and the extremes he measured for various traits, such as hand strength and weight. Quetelet also published records of variations in the death and birth rates and included some data on the psychology of aging. Specifically, he looked at the age of French and English playwrights and began to analyze their productivity in terms of how old they were. Such notions have been followed up in the more recent work of Lehman (1953), who found that the focus of artistic production changed with the age of the producer. Young poets typically write lyric poems, while many older poets write sagas and epics.

The use of the Gaussian curve to describe human characteristics represented a conceptual revolution. Quetelet introduced the idea that the traits of man varied in degrees. Variations in human traits could also be related to natural causes in keeping with the scientific approach. Quetelet broke with earlier thought and tradition by examining longevity. Before the 1800s longevity belonged to the domain of theology and was not considered fitting matter for natural science. For Quetelet, however, little was beyond knowing if one attended to scientific observation and statistical relationships.

Sir Francis Galton was perhaps the next most prominent investigator in the field of aging. Like Quetelet, he was a member of the upper class. He was also a cousin of Charles Darwin. In his own right he was a well-known statistician who was responsible for developing the first index of correlation. Galton's fundamental contribution to the study of aging is the data he collected at the International Health Exhibition in London in 1884. Over 9337 males and females aged 5 to 80 were measured on 17 characteristics, including Quetelet's measure of strength of grip, vital capacity, visual accuracy, and reaction time. With these data Galton demonstrated that many human characteristics showed differences with age. Hearing for high tones was one of the variables that showed a lower capacity with age. Galton developed a series of whistles that he could tune by varying their volume and their frequencies. He found that with increasing age subjects could no longer hear the higher frequency whistles. The data would seem to confirm English folklore that old farmers could no longer hear the very high frequency sounds of flying bats.

Later empirical period. At the turn of the century a number of individuals began to study various aspects of aging. Minot (*The Problems of Age, Growth and Death,* 1908), Metchnikoff (*The Prolongation of Life,* 1908), Child (*Senescence and Rejuvenescence,* 1915), and Pearl (*Biology of Death,* 1922) were among the major biologists interested in explaining the phenomenon of aging.

Some of the hypotheses of these early scientists were unsound or incomplete. Metchnikoff, for example, was impressed by the observation that yogurt eaters of Middle Europe apparently lived long lives. He attributed their longevity to the possibility that yogurt cleanses the gastrointestinal tract of bacteria, which, he thought, causes an increasing toxicity of the organism with age. Metchnikoff's hypothesis was faulty, however; some of the gastrointestinal bacteria are actually important. If, for example, a rat's gastrointestinal flora are destroyed, the rat will suffer from vitamin deficiency because the flora synthesize the vitamins needed for normal functioning.

Pearl was an epidemiologist and biostatistician at Johns Hopkins University. Studying longevity in families, he found that people who had long-lived parents and grandparents tended to live longer than the average of the population. This seemed to be evidence of a genetic factor in longevity. As a result of Pearl's findings, people thought that heredity was the sole key for determining how long we live. If you picked the right grandparents, so to speak, a longer life was guaranteed you. This reasoning, however, represents a violation of one of the major features of the aging process—namely, multiple determination. Getting old is the result of the interplay of biological, social, psychological, and ecological forces. Imagine that you had grandparents who lived into their 80s. Nevertheless, your personal lifestyle might lead you to be 30% overweight, to smoke, and to drink alcohol heavily. These factors could eliminate the genetic advantage of having long-lived grandparents, and you would probably have a shorter life span than the average.

Another book on aging that appeared in 1922 was *Senescence: The Second Half of Life* by G. Stanley Hall, a psychologist specializing in childhood and adolescence who published the first book in this country on the topic. His concern with his own retirement led him to write *Senescence*. Up to this point psychologists had regarded old age as the regression of development. Hall noted:

> As a psychologist I am convinced that the psychic states of old people have great significance. Senescence, like adolescence, has its own feelings, thoughts and wills, as well as its own physiology, and their regimen is important as well as that of the body. Individual differences here are probably greater than in youth [Hall, 1922, p. 100].

One of Hall's innovations was a study of old people's religious beliefs and fears of death by means of a questionnaire. Hall found that people did not necessarily show an increase in religious interest as they grew older; he also discovered that the old in his sample had not become more fearful of death. Gerontologists today keep rediscovering the fact that the aged are afraid of the circumstances of dying but are not more fearful of death itself. Death, as an abstraction, is more a young person's fear.

A contemporary of G. Stanley Hall was a physician named Osler, an internist at Johns Hopkins University. At that period medicine had the tradition of looking for a single cause of a disease or disorder. Osler was impressed by a preponderance of arteriosclerosis, or hardening of the arteries, in old individuals. His contribution to gerontology was the discovery that aging was closely related to the state of blood vessels in the body.

Whereas the Americans in the 1920s stressed the relation between calcification of arteries and the cardiovascular system in the aging process, Pavlov and his students in Russia emphasized the importance of the central nervous system. From his now classic conditioning experiments with dogs, Pavlov found that old animals conditioned differently from young ones and that their responses showed a different course of extinction. Pavlov's research and conclusions on the aging process are reflected in the following quotation from a summary of Russian studies on aging:

> On the basis of all the material at our disposal, we can say that the inhibition process is the first to succumb to old age, and after this, it would appear that the mobility of the nervous processes is affected. This is evident from the fact that a large percentage of our aging dogs ceased to tolerate the previous more complex conditioned-reflex system. The responses become chaotic, the effects fluctuate in an entirely irregular fashion, and good results can be obtained only by simplifying the scheme. I think that this can very legitimately be ascribed to the fact that mobility decreases with the years. If we have a distinct effect in a large system, this means that one stimulus does not interfere with another and does not spread its effect to the next nerve process. When a nerve process is delayed, however, the remaining traces of each stimulus become prolonged and influence the succeeding ones, i.e., we have a chaotic state and confusion [Nikitin, 1958].

In one of his statements, Pavlov presents a fundamental issue of gerontology that has persisted to the present. This issue involves the differentiation between a normal process of senescence (aging) from that of age-related disease. He states, "In our dogs, we were able to observe both normal physiological and pathological old age" (Nikitin, 1958). Some physicians maintain that only disease or pathology can lead to the demise of an otherwise perfect organism and that it is meaningless to say that someone dies of "old age." Others who oppose this disease model of aging claim that there is a normal pattern of aging, apart from disease. Normal patterns of aging could be the result of genetic or environmental determinants. To distinguish the inevitable from the avoidable through manipulation of the environment is the concern of many researchers today.

Growth of gerontology

The 1930s laid the groundwork for many of the developments in gerontology. Medicine became increasingly interested in the degenerative diseases because dramatic progress was being made in controlling the early-life killers, the infectious diseases. Studying chronic disease, however, involves examining the physiological changes of the aging host to that disease. In 1933 *Arteriosclerosis: A Survey of the Problem,* edited by E. V. Cowdry, was published. This volume considered the relationship between aging and the blood vessels, of which arteriosclerosis is in part a manifestation. The Josiah Macy Jr. Foundation sponsored a conference with the National Research Council and the Union of American Biological Societies at Woods Hole, Massachusetts, July 25-26, 1937. The National Research Council further sponsored a conference of its committee on the biological processes of aging on February 5, 1938. The rapid acceptance of another volume edited by Cowdry (1939, 1942), entitled *Problems of Ageing,* was evidence that the ideas presented in it were timely.

Several influential organizations held conferences on aging in 1940 and 1941. Among these were the American Orthopsychiatric Association, Medical Clinics of North America, the American Chemical Society, and the National Institutes of Health. The Josiah Macy Jr. Foundation provided a grant to aid the Public Health Service in conducting a conference in Mental Health and Later Maturity, and the National Institutes of Health sponsored a conference on this subject on May 23-24, 1941. Many of the topics of that conference are still contemporary concerns, such as the psychiatric significance of aging as a public health problem, intellectual changes with age, psychotherapy in the practice of geriatrics, and industrial aspects of aging personnel. In opening the conference, the surgeon general made the following observations, which indicate how many of our current concerns in aging were anticipated and appreciated at that time.

> The aged are people whereas aging is a process. However, in order to solve the urgent clinical and sociologic problems introduced by the greatly increasing numbers of older people in the country, we need to know more of the processes and the consequences of aging. Not the least important of many questions are those concerned with the mental changes introduced by senescence. Without health, the increasing millions past the meridian represent a potential disastrous economic and social menace to the commonwealth. Thus the maintenance of mental and physical health into true senility is an objective worthy of our most conscientious and extensive efforts. . . .
>
> Senescence is not a disease, nor is it all decline. Some functional capacities increase with the years as others diminish. This is particularly notable with certain mental activities. It is thus of the greatest importance that far more precise information as to the changes in mental capacities which occur with aging become available if we are to employ wisely and utilize the vast reservoir

of elderly persons only too anxious to be of use. There is no greater tragedy for the aged than the unnecessary sense of uselessness which society now imposes upon them prematurely [USPHS, 1972, p. 2].

Several basic concepts of gerontology were developed in the 1930s. One was that problems of aging are complex and are best studied in an interdisciplinary context. A second concept was that aging represented an interactive process of biological predisposition and the environment. As noted earlier, impetus for the study of aging came from the fact that the focus of medicine was shifting from infectious diseases to chronic diseases, which by their nature are involved in the physiology of aging. Another impetus was the fact that the proportion of persons over 65 was expanding. During the 1930s the number of individuals over 65 increased 35%, as contrasted with an increase in the general population of only 7.2%.

A detailed description of the growth of the field in this period is beyond the scope of this chapter, but some examples are appropriate. In 1940 the Surgeon General, Thomas Parran, appointed a National Advisory Committee to assist in the formation of a unit on gerontology within the National Institutes of Health. This culminated in the creation of the National Institute of Aging, which was signed into law in 1974. In 1946 staffing was started at the Gerontological Unit of the National Institutes of Health and the Nuffield Unit for Research into Problems of Aging at the University of Cambridge. These units attracted many scientists who are now prominent in the field of aging. An international congress of gerontology was founded and held its first meeting in Liege. The Gerontology Society in America, founded in 1945, encouraged discussion among professionals of all disciplines.

The growth of gerontology is perhaps best reflected in the literature. In 1835 the subject had no more than a mere handful of publications, such as the material by Bacon and Franklin. From about 1835 to the early 1900s, there was not much increase. At the turn of the century five or six books were published, and, except for some interruption due to World War II, this rate continued until 1949. The literature generated between 1950 and 1960 equaled the production of the preceding 115 years. It appears, then, that research and interest in aging are showing an exponential growth curve.

THE IMPACT OF AGING ON SOCIETY

One of the themes running through this book is the impact on society of the increasing number of individuals surviving into old age. There is a greater proportion of aged in our society today than ever before, and the aged population continues to grow. Life expectancy for the average male born today is about 68 years, and for the average female it is 76 years. This represents a gain of over 25 years from the average life expectancy in 1900.

Until the 20th century only aristocrats, poets, and philosophers wrote about longevity. Aging was not a topic of concern to the common man who had to expend all of his energy just to stay alive. In the past, the aged were few in number and were considered unique and remarkable rather than burdensome. A large proportion of elderly in society is thus a very recent phenomenon.

The changing age structure of our population is detailed in Chapter 2. Declines in the mortality rate, the birth rate, and the immigration rate are presented as the societal forces that have led to an aging of the population. Aging, in turn, affects society, and some of the issues concerning demographers are the impact of increasing numbers of elderly on the *dependency ratio* (defined as the number of people in the dependent segment divided by the number in the supportive or working population), the effect of large concentrations of elderly in the cities, and the implications of sex difference in longevity. Projections suggest that the number of people over the age of 65 will continue to grow and thus have continued impact on society.

Chapter 4 develops the notion of continuing change with regard to the aged in society, and the author expands on the discussion of *cohort* (a group of individuals born in the same 5-year period). Since people born around the same time share many common social and historical experiences and hence, perhaps, a common perspective, and since rapid change is characteristic of our society, Bengtson suggests that new cohorts of the aged may be different from previous cohorts. Furthermore, future aged cohorts may retain many of their particular characteristics as younger cohorts. Thus, the radical hippie generation of the late 1960s may be the older radicals of the 2020s.

In Chapter 19, Cutler reemphasizes the importance of the increasingly large aged cohort for politics; the implications of this phenomenon for policy makers are also discussed in Chapter 18. It is essential that programs for the aged be structured flexibly so they can meet the needs of future, as well as present, cohorts of elderly.

Some of the more positive findings from this cohort analysis must also be taken into consideration. Future cohorts of the elderly will most likely be more fortunate than the contemporary aged. Proportionately fewer individuals in future elderly cohorts will be foreign born, and hence they will be more acculturated in American society. Perhaps they will suffer less from culture and future shock and find it easier to be involved in society. Future cohorts of elderly will also be better prepared for retirement, less economically deprived, and better educated. Moreover, legislators will have had more experience in planning for the elderly and will be able to avoid some of the earlier policy pitfalls.

Schaie, who was one of the first to recognize the importance of cohort differences, suggests in Chapter 7 that one has to be aware of these differences in order to have a sophisticated understanding of human aging. Since the present aged are educationally deprived, as compared to younger cohorts, Schaie discusses the need for alleviation of educational obsolescence. Although contemporary cohorts of aged need remedial education to bring them to the educational level of younger people, future cohorts of elderly will be better educated. Since people with more education tend to seek out continuing education in greater numbers, future cohorts of aged will have an impact on society as they may demand educational opportunities throughout life. Furthermore, at a time when zero population growth is becoming a reality, schools and colleges will need to fill their enrollments. Classroom space and teachers could serve the needs of the elderly. A life-span approach to education is contrary to the current emphasis on early childhood education, but it would benefit both the educational institutions and the aging if the classrooms were opened to students of all ages.

Treas makes clear the impact of aging on society in Chapter 5 by pointing out the tremendously different experience of contemporary marriage and family life as compared to that experience at the turn of the century. In 1900 one spouse died, on average, before the last child left home. Today, a married couple can expect 15-20 years together after the last child is launched. The myth of three-generational families is dispelled. Although more and more individuals are surviving to reach grandparent-hood, they neither desire nor undertake to live with their children and grandchildren.

More of the elderly live in urban centers than in rural areas. In Chapter 16 Regnier describes the impact of the urban neighborhoods on the aged and the means for effec-tively planning facilities to serve the elderly in these neighborhoods. Although most elderly live in the community, some are institutionalized or live in housing designed specifically for them.

The fact that there are greater numbers of aged in society has sensitized academi-cians to the issues of aging and raised researchers' consciousness of aging as a problem for scientific investigation. In a more affluent society where individuals are living longer, scientists are trained and encouraged to undertake, among other things, re-search on the basic processes in aging. This research, in turn, may have great impact on the future age structure of society. If cures for cardiovascular disease alone were to be discovered, ten years might be added to the average life expectancy. Cellular level engineering to extend the human life span (Chapter 11) has overwhelming ethical and social implications. Improving the health of the aged through nutrition (Chapter 12) and exercise (Chapter 13) could lead to added vigor in the elderly and perhaps greater participation in social roles. If psychologists devise means to help the aged function as efficiently as the young in learning and memory (Chapter 8), or if they discover some of the secrets of brain function and can alleviate depression in old age (Chapter 9), aging might become quite a different experience in the future.

INTERACTION: THE NEED FOR A MULTIDISCIPLINARY APPROACH

The rates of biological, psychological, and social aging may be different in the same individual. Although the biological rate of aging—the efficiency of the bio-logical organism—may contribute to the pace of psychological and social aging, a person may feel and behave on a psychological level somewhat apart from how well his body functions. Social norms prescribe that individuals should "act their age"; again, while these prescriptions may be related to biological and psychological phe-nomena, they can also stand apart from them. Furthermore, social and psychological events can affect the rate of biological aging. We have only to compare photographs of our presidents when they take the oath of office and when they finish their terms to witness the dramatic biological consequences of environmental stress.

We take a multidisciplinary approach to aging in this volume because aging is a multifaceted phenomenon. Although aging can occur independently at the various biological, psychological, and social levels, these components generally interact. There are countless examples in this volume of the interactive nature of the aging process. We tend to think of aging as simply a biological process, but in this book it becomes clear that social and psychological factors can affect biological processes at least as pro-foundly as biology affects behavior, socialized activity, and social policy.

For example, age changes in brain biochemistry may be related to the greater incidence of depression observed in old people; thus, a chemical reaction in the brain has significant psychological consequences. From a sociological perspective we can observe that many of the admissions to mental institutions are old, depressed patients and also that the suicide rate increases dramatically with age. These phenomena may be the psychological and social outcomes of age changes in biochemistry.

On the other hand, as pointed out in many of the chapters, the aged suffer a number of losses that might predispose them to be depressed and that might, in turn, affect brain biochemistry. As discussed in several chapters, retirement leads to loss of role, loss of status, and loss of income. Deaths of friends and spouse are another type of loss faced by the aged. Since in general women outlive their husbands, they are most likely to face widowhood and the unfortunate psychological and social losses that accompany it. The loss of physical vigor and the decline in health are yet other causes for depression—especially in white males who commit suicide in old age at higher rates than any other group.

Thus, independent mechanisms may operate in the aged to predispose them to depression. Independent biochemical changes may occur to initiate depression in old age, independent physiological losses may cause this mood change, or social and psychological losses may serve to depress elderly people. Each of these phenomena might lead to depression, but more likely they interact to present the complex and difficult-to-treat depressions found in the aged. Thus, to intervene and alleviate depression in old age, we might prescribe drugs to affect brain biochemistry, we might recommend moderate exercise or a better diet to affect health and vigor, we might suggest psychotherapy to provide emotional support in time of grief, and we might devise new social roles for old people in programs such as Foster Grandparents so that they feel needed in society.

INTERVENTIONS IN AGING

Depression is only one of many aging problems that have attracted interventions at all levels. Indeed, a major theme recurring throughout this volume is intervention. What intervention strategies can we devise on the biological, psychological, social, or policy level to improve the lot of the aged in society today and future generations of elderly? Concern is also expressed for the need to improve health in old age and to add life to years rather than merely adding years to life.

Quality of life and life satisfaction represent one of the sociological perspectives presented in Chapter 4. Bengtson and Haber discuss the need to intervene on a social level to affect the vicious cycle of society's attitudes toward the elderly. On a societal level the aged are considered incompetents to be moved aside to make way for the young. They are relegated to lower status, they are deprived of their jobs and sources of income through forced retirement, and they are provided with few alternative roles. When told that they are burdensome and unneeded, the aged themselves begin to believe that they are unfit to take part in society and that they are incompetent. Incompetence thus becomes a self-fulfilling prophecy: once they accept the fact that they are incompetent, they fail more frequently and accept failure and defeat as part of the process of growing old. Surprisingly, the aged themselves are often the most rigid adherents to negative stereotypes about old age. Believing they are incompetent, the aged may become less effective in their actions and confirm the social stereotype.

Many chapters in this book present research findings that suggest that the old are not incompetent or that we can intervene to help the aged perform more effectively.

We must look at the possibility of intervention at a societal level through the use of mass communication and the potential for intervention with the aged themselves in terms of changing their self-image. The images of aging on television already appear to be changing for the better, and television can sometimes be a means of educational intervention. Not only do many elderly have limited mobility and little access to transportation, but also they tend to view television more frequently than most other age groups. Therefore, television provides a means of bringing education to the aged in a form with which they are already familiar.

Education is also a means to provide the aged with information about health care and nutrition. Many chapters deal with medical interventions for the elderly, and we do have a great deal of information about how to maximize health in old age. In Chapter 12 Weg discusses normal aging processes and disease in old age and presents a number of suggestions about how those of all ages can improve their chances of having a healthy old age and how the already aged can maximize their health. Among the important aspects are the maintenance of a balanced diet (which many old people do not receive due to poverty and/or because, living alone, they do not prepare proper meals) and the avoidance of stress (which leads to pathologies such as strokes, heart attacks, and ulcers). In Chapter 10 Solnick and Corby discuss sexuality and attitudes toward sexuality in old age, the potential intervention of alleviating anxiety about sexuality in old people, and the importance of eliminating some of the negative stereotypes and stigmas we seem to have about sexuality in the aged.

Chapter 13, deVries's discussion of exercise physiology and aging, is addressed entirely to the issue of health interventions. The author views many of the observed physiological declines as resulting from disuse rather than the aging process; he finds that when old people exercise, they not only regain some of their physiological capacity, they also actually feel better.

Chapters 6, 7, 8, and 9, which deal with aspects of the psychology of aging, are all concerned with interventions to help older individuals think better as well as feel better. In describing research on learning and memory, Walsh discusses models used by psychologists to explain these phenomena. With these models he presents a rationale for some of the strategies investigators have used to help older people learn and remember better. Among these strategies are helping the aged to form associations, making material meaningful to them, presenting material at a slower pace, and making sure the aged are comfortable and relaxed in the learning situation.

Comfortable living for the elderly is addressed from another perspective by Treas in Chapter 5 on aging and the family. She points out the greater longevity of people who are married and considers ways to intervene in what is becoming a growing social problem—widowhood. Women outnumber men in increasing numbers over the life span so that the women who survive to the age of 80 outnumber men by an almost 2:1 ratio. Since living with someone normally enhances life satisfaction and health, Treas considers some alternative living arrangements as an intervention for happiness in old age.

Alternatives to retirement are presented in Chapter 17 on economics. Walther suggests that part-time employment is an intervention that would provide the aged with greater economic independence. She also discusses some of the considerations economists must make when they advise policy makers on the design of programs for the elderly. Programs must be both equitable and efficient, and Walther points out some of the difficulties in structuring intervention programs to meet these constraints.

The potential of political action as a source of intervention to improve the lot of the aged is presented in Chapter 19. Increased political awareness on the part of the elderly can be used as a powerful force to bring about change. Older people tend to vote in greater numbers than do younger cohorts; they may place themselves in a position to affect their future, while younger, more apathetic voters often ignore the political process. Groups such as the American Association of Retired Persons and the National Retired Teachers Association, which have a combined membership of over 7 million, have active lobbyists in Congress and are acknowledged as a political force. More activist-oriented groups such as the Gray Panthers are also forming to demand equal rights for the elderly.

In Chapter 11 on the cellular biology of aging, Denny presents research that could lead to the most far-reaching of all interventions—the extension of the upper limit to which people have been known to live. We are at a point in gerontological research where this type of genetic intervention is no longer a prospect for science fiction. As biologists begin to break the genetic code of life, we may actually realize the dream expressed through the earliest recorded myths: the dream of conquering, or at least postponing, death.

Is this the final goal of gerontological research and its social implementation? Most of us working in the field of aging think not. We generally aim to affect the quality rather than the quantity of life; it is our hope that our work and the material in this book will contribute to understanding the processes of aging and improving the quality of life for older people living today and in the future.

AGING IN THE FUTURE

We are experiencing a rapid increase in the number of aged persons in our society. What effect will this increase have on the future of gerontology, and how has it already influenced our ideas about aging?

It is apparent that social and economic adjustment will be necessary to meet the needs of the elderly. There is a growing feeling among many old people and psychologists that retirement should not be determined by age alone. Other criteria, such as ability and motivation to do useful work, should be considered. With the increasing predominance of females in the older age groups, part-time employment opportunities that would utilize their skills would be ideal. As a result of the decline in birth rates and the increased spare time of the elderly, older people will be coming back for more education at all levels. The materials used in higher education, however, are geared to the young. The skills young people learn might be superfluous to the older individual; conversely, the knowledge and experience the older person brings to the classroom could be utilized. It appears that modification of the university curriculum will be necessary.

Some adjustments have already been made in social and economic conditions of older adults; Social Security and pension plans are products of the 20th century.

Planners who design housing for the elderly have been incorporating special features that enable the old to continue living independently and safely. Recreational facilities are expanding their programs to incorporate the old.

With about 25 million individuals over the age of 65, the old represent a significant voting bloc. They have already become politically active, forming such organizations as the National Council of Senior Citizens, the American Association of Retired Persons, the Gray Panthers, and others.

Thus, Cutler predicts that age will be a salient factor in the politics of the not too distant future. He bases this prediction on five sources of evidence. First, the size and proportion of elderly in the population will continue to grow. Second, as people grow older, they tend to participate more and are more interested in politics than the young. Third, people with more education tend to participate more in politics, and future cohorts of the aged will have attained higher levels of education. Fourth, future cohorts of the elderly are individuals who, in their youth, participated in new forms of political action, and this behavior may continue into old age. Finally, people in general are becoming more conscious of older people and of aging, and this consciousness-raising has already begun to lead aged cohorts to become more politically active.

The goal of political groups for the elderly has been to bring public attention to their needs as well as to create a new image of the older person as active and interested in continuing his or her involvement with society. Is a new type of old person emerging in America? Researchers in many disciplines who study aging have a considerable amount of evidence to indicate that the present generation of old people is different from previous generations of the aged, and perhaps from future aging cohorts. This makes it very difficult to state with certainty how current trends will influence the future of gerontology. If the growth in the number of people in the older age groups continues, it is possible that men and women will be having second and even third careers. Such a possibility will be created by the accelerated rate of change, making jobs and skills antiquated within a person's lifetime.

Discovery of cures for age-related diseases, such as cardiovascular disease, would significantly alter the expenses and difficulties associated with aging. Unraveling the genetic and the environmental influences on the aging process would enable us to intervene more effectively in modifying some of the less desirable features of getting older.

Though these are great expectations for the future, the importance of the present should not be minimized. Not only has a new kind of old person emerged in America, but a new social movement as well. If our era has been characterized by major upheavals in sexual mores, political standards, and racial equalities, it is clear that the changes brought by the growth and influence of our elderly will be felt in science and in society for many generations to come.

REFERENCES

Birren, J. E. A brief history of the psychology of aging. *Gerontologist,* 1961, *1* (2), 67–77.

Bottig, K., & Grandjeau, E. The effect of organ extracts on behavior of old rats. In A. Welford & J. Birren (Eds.), *Behavior, aging, and the nervous system.* Springfield, Ill.: Charles C Thomas, 1965.

Cain, L. Age states and generation phenomena: The new old people in contemporary America. *Gerontologist,* 1967, *7* (2), 82–92.

Child, C. M. *Senescence and rejuvenescence.* Chicago: University of Chicago Press, 1915.

Cowdry, E. V. (Ed.). *Problems of ageing.* Baltimore: Walhams and Wilkins, 1939.

Gruman, G. J. *A history of ideas about the prolongation of life: The evolution of prolongevity hypothesis to 1800.* Philadelphia: American Philosophical Society, 1966.

Hall, G. S. *Senescence: The second half of life.* New York: Appleton and Co., 1922.

Kiser, C., & Whelpton, P. Social and psychological factors affecting fertility. Summary of chief findings and implications for future studies. *Milbank Memorial Fund Quarterly,* 1956, *36,* 3.

Leaf, A. Every day is a gift when you are over 100. *National Geographic,* 1973, *143* (1), 93–118.

Lehman, H. D. *Age and achievement.* New Jersey: Princeton University Press, 1953.

Metchnikoff, E. *The prolongation of life.* New York: Putnam and Sons, 1908.

Minot, C. *The problems of age, growth and death.* New York: Putnam and Sons, 1908.

Nikitin, V. N. *Russian studies on age-associated physiology, biochemistry and morphology: Historical sketch and bibliography.* Kharkov, USSR: A. M. Gorkiy Press, 1958.

Pearl, R. *The biology of death.* Philadelphia: J. P. Lippincott Co., 1922.

Rossett, E. *Aging process of population.* New York: Macmillan, 1964.

Thompson, W., & Lewis, D. *Population problems.* New York: McGraw-Hill, 1965.

U. S. Public Health Service. *Proceedings of the conference on mental health in later maturity* (Supplement 168, U. S. Public Health Reports), Washington, D. C.: U.S. Government Printing Office, 23–24 May 1941.

PART **I**

SOCIAL SCIENCE
PERSPECTIVES

CHAPTER **2**

Demography of the Aged

Mary Beard Deming and Neal E. Cutler

Basic demographic information is of the utmost importance for gerontologists. The trends that have resulted in the dramatic increase in the number and proportion of older persons in the United States are a major reason for the expansion of interest in gerontology. The tools of demography are essential for understanding past and future changes in the size and growth of the older population. The demographic perspective is not limited to population size and growth but also includes composition and geographic distribution. Changes in these population aspects are explained, in part, by changes in fertility, mortality, and migration. In this chapter we apply these descriptive and analytical concepts to the older population to illustrate their use for gerontologists. In addition, we present some descriptive demographic data, which is valuable in understanding the nature and position of older persons in contemporary society. Frequent references to other chapters in the book indicate the importance of relating population trends to other aspects of aging in society.

Before discussing the descriptive demographic data and the concepts underlying this information, we must note what *demography*—the science of population dynamics—can and cannot do. First, demography tends to be a macro-level science, that is, it typically focuses at the level of society rather than at the micro-level of the individual, which, for example, is the typical realm of psychology. Thus, demography generally focuses on large and broad statistical groups within and across populations. Demographic descriptions of these collectivities or groups are usually given by summary statistical measures such as the mean, median, or percentage of a group that has characteristic X or characteristic Y. Thus, demographic information represents descriptive statistical generalizations; there will be variations within the group and individual exceptions to the generalizations.

A second major point is that demographic analysis is limited to the kinds of inferences that can legitimately be made from past and present information regarding

Funding for this research was provided, in part, by the National Institute on Aging, Grant 5 P01 AG 00133.

population dynamics. In this sense demography cannot "predict" the future; however, it can "project" the future of a population, given certain data describing past and present population structures and processes and certain assumptions about the likelihood or probability that these structures and processes will continue into the future. Such population projections can be quite accurate when detailed information about a particular population is available. In fact, projections for the older population tend to be more accurate than projections for the population as a whole.

The population of primary concern for students of gerontology is the category of persons aged 65 and older. Age 65 has traditionally been used to define the beginning of "old age" in demographic and gerontological studies mainly because that has been the age of full retirement benefits in the Social Security system. Although comparisons using the "65 and older" definition are useful, we shall also present data for younger and older age groups. Furthermore, since the population aged 65 and older is not homogeneous, we shall present some data to illustrate the variation in demographic and socioeconomic characteristics of age subgroups of this larger old-age population.

SIZE AND GROWTH OF THE OLDER POPULATION

Past and present

The number of elderly in the United States has increased dramatically since 1900, representing a larger share of the total population for each succeeding decade. The number of persons aged 65 and older in the United States for each decade since 1900 is presented in Table 2-1. The table also shows the percentage of the total population aged 65 and over and the percentage increase for this older group for each decennial year from the previous one. For comparison, the corresponding increase of the total population has also been included.

Most noticeable is the rapid growth in numbers of the older population from 3 million in 1900 to 20 million in 1970 and to 25 million in 1979. This eight-fold increase in nearly 80 years was much greater than the increase in the total population, which nearly tripled from 76 million in 1900 to 221 million in 1979 (United States Bureau of the Census, 1980). Three factors account for this rapid increase in the population aged 65 and older: the high fertility of the period 65 or more years ago (in the late 19th and early 20th century), declining mortality during the 20th century, and the high level of immigration prior to World War I. The influence of these factors is discussed in greater detail in the next section.

The proportion of older persons in the population has exhibited an uninterrupted growth from 4.1% in 1900 to over 11% in 1980. Thus, not only has the older population dramatically grown in terms of the number of persons, but the relative size of the older population in the United States has almost tripled.

An efficient way to show this change in the proportion of elderly is to use an age-sex population pyramid, which graphically depicts the composition of the total population by age and sex. For our purposes this distribution is best presented in 5-year age intervals (on the vertical axis) expressed as percentage of the total population (on the horizontal axis). Figure 2-1 shows the age-sex pyramids for the United States in 1900, 1940, and 1970. Without regard to the absolute numbers, we can graphically see how the age composition of our population has changed during this

TABLE 2-1. Population aged 65 and over in the United States, for each decennial year with projections to 2020: 1900–2020

Year[a]	Population aged 65 and over		Percentage increase from preceding decade	
	Number (in thousands)	Percentage of total population [b]	Age 65 and over	Total population [b]
1900	3,099	4.1	–	–
1910	3,986	4.3	28.6	21.0
1920	4,929	4.7	23.7	14.9
1930	6,705	5.4	36.0	16.1
1940	9,031	6.8	34.7	7.3
1950	12,397	8.2	37.3	14.5
1960	16,675	9.2	34.5	18.7
1970	20,087	9.8	20.4	13.4
Projections:				
1980	24,927	11.2	24.1	8.4
1990	29,824	12.2	19.6	9.6
2000	31,822	12.2	6.7	6.9
2010	34,837	12.7	9.5	5.7
2020	45,102	15.5	29.5	5.4

SOURCE: United States Bureau of the Census, *Current population reports,* Series P-23, no. 59, Demographic aspects of aging and the older population in the United States, May 1976; Series P-25, no. 704, Projections of the population of the United States: 1977 to 2050, July 1977.

[a] As of July 1 each year.

[b] Projections are from Series II, which assumes that women average 2.1 births at the end of the childbearing years.

century. In 1900, when fertility and mortality rates were still quite high (32 births and 17 deaths per 1000 population), the population pyramid closely approximated a triangle. By 1940, this form was undergoing certain changes, so that the pyramid begins to take on the shape of a pear. This change reflects the effects of lower fertility during the post-World War I economic depression years. Further evidence of the effect of changing fertility rates is seen in the 1980 population pyramid and will be discussed in the following section.

The older population is itself "aging," as shown in Table 2-2. A declining proportion of the population aged 65 and older is in the age group 65–69, while the proportion aged 75 and older is increasing. Of the total older population, those 75 and older increase from 29% in 1900 to 38% in 2000. More than half of the population aged 75 and older is now 80 and older. The aging of the older population helps to explain some of the changes in the demographic and socioeconomic status of the entire age group 65 and older.

Future

The older population is expected to more than double from 20 million in 1970 to 45 million in 2020 (Table 2-1). Growth will be much slower in some decades (7% in the 1990s) than in others (29% in the 2010s), reflecting fluctuations in fertility since the 1920s. Projections of the proportion of older persons in the total population are more difficult to make because of uncertainties in future fertility. If fertility follows the birth expectations of young married women, then 16% of the total popu-

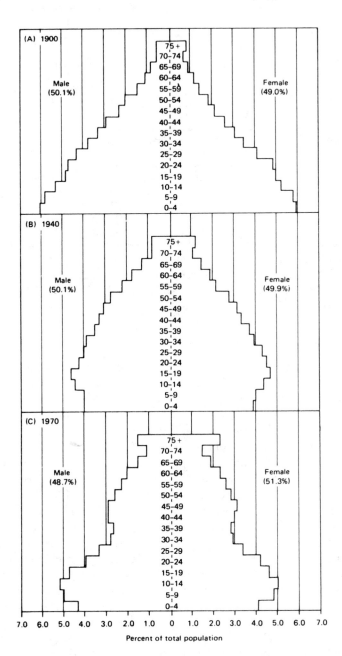

Figure 2-1 (A) (B) (C). Age-sex population pyramids for the United States: 1900, 1940, 1970. (*United States Bureau of the Census,* Census of population: Characteristics of the population, *Washington, D.C.: U.S. Government Printing Office, 1940, 1970.*)

TABLE 2-2. Percent distribution of the population aged 65 and over in the United States by age for selected years: 1900–2000 [a]

	1900	1930	1950	1970	1979	Projections 2000
65 years and older	100.0%	100.0%	100.0%	100.0%	100.0%	100.0%
65–69	42.3	41.7	40.7	35.0	35.3	28.9
70–74	28.7	29.3	27.8	27.2	26.7	25.9
75–79	29.0	29.0	17.4	19.2	17.3	20.1
80 and over			14.1	18.6	20.7	25.1

SOURCE: United States Bureau of the Census, *Current population reports,* Series P-23, no. 59, Demographic aspects of aging and the older population in the United States, May 1976; Series P-25, no. 870, Estimates of the population of the United States, by age, race, and sex: 1976 to 1979, January 1980; Series P-25, no. 704, Projections of the population of the United States: 1977 to 2050, July 1977.

[a] As of July 1 each year.

lation will be aged 65 and over in 2020. This is shown as Series II in Table 2-1. If fertility is relatively high (Series I, assuming 2.7 births per woman), we can expect about 13% of the population to be aged 65 and over in 2020. However, if fertility is slightly lower than current levels (Series III, assuming 1.7 births per woman), the older population will be 18% of the total population.

BASIC DEMOGRAPHIC PROCESSES

Three demographic processes basic to the understanding of population dynamics are of particular importance in understanding the demography of aging: fertility, mortality, and migration. Thinking of aging, one may consider only mortality (or rates of death from various causes). Yet if our goal is to understand the dynamics of population changes that have produced a population containing an increasing proportion of older persons, then the complete set of factors must be understood.

Fertility, or the childbearing behavior of a person or group, adds new individuals to a population each year. The size of each new *cohort*, or group of persons born at the same point in time, varies with the number of women in the childbearing ages and the number and spacing of children they choose to have. *Mortality* subtracts members from a population each year. Death rates are relatively high in the first year of life, rapidly decline in early childhood until ages 10–14, and then increase gradually until they reach their maximum at old age. *Migration,* or shifts in usual place of residence, may either add or subtract members from a population, depending on the direction of movement. The highest rates of migration are for young adults. Since married couples with small children are frequent migrants, there is a secondary peak for very young children. In general, the elderly have the lowest rates of migration.

Variations in these three demographic components of change have shaped the current age structure of the United States. The age structure may be viewed as a series of different birth cohorts, each experiencing and contributing to historical changes in fertility, mortality, and migration. Projections of future population take into account the current age structure, the history of different cohorts, and likely changes in these demographic processes. These three processes continually interact, even though we discuss each one individually.

Fertility

Fertility is the most important determinant of the size and proportion of the number of older persons. Past fertility determines the number of persons aged 65 and older, while current fertility determines their proportion of the total population. The role of past fertility is clear when we trace any current age group back to the size of the group when it was born. Thus, for example, from the population pyramids in Figure 2-1 we see that the 70-74 age group (1970) was aged 40-44 in 1940 and aged 0-4 in 1900. The initial size of the cohort determines how large the population group could possibly be 60-70 years later. Of course, the rate of mortality is important in determining just how many members of the cohort survive beyond the sixth decade of life. Changes in fertility, then, are important for understanding the changing age composition of the population during this century.

Figure 2-2 shows the "crude birth rate" (the number of births per 1000 population) in the United States since 1900. We can see the results of these birth rates in the 1970 population pyramid. The high birth rates of the late 19th century and the first few decades of the 20th century explain the high rates of increase in the numbers of older persons through the 1980s. The drop in the birth rate in the 1920s and 1930s, resulting in small cohorts in the ages 30-49 in 1970, will slow the increase in the older population in the 1990s and the first decade of the 21st century. The bulge in the

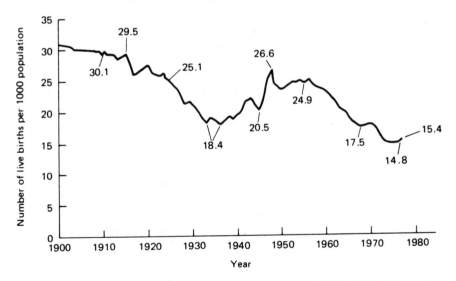

Figure 2-2. Crude birth rates for the United States: 1900-1977. (*United States Public Health Service, National Center for Health Statistics,* Vital statistics of the United States 1975, Volume I—Natality, *Washington, D.C.: U.S. Government Printing Office, 1978; Advance report: Final natality statistics, 1977.* Monthly Vital Statistics Report, *1979, 27(11), Supplement.*)

1970 population pyramid for the cohorts aged 10-14 and 15-19 represents the "baby boom" births of the 1950-1960 decade. Following this cohort as it ages, we see that by the 2010-2020 decade there will be a significant increase in the number of persons aged 65 and older. Although the older population is expected to increase by 15 million in the 40 years between 1970 and 2010, it will increase a remarkable 10 million in the following 10 years. Thus, the baby boom of the 1950s will produce a "gerontic boom" in the years 2010-2020!

The changes in the proportion of older persons, unlike changes in numbers, are affected by variations in the numbers of people in other age categories. Current fertility determines the number of people in younger age groups. As a result, current fertility has a stronger influence than past fertility on the proportion of persons aged 65 and over in the total population. When fertility was high, as in 1900, the proportion of older persons was small. Because fertility rates have dropped significantly in the United States during the last 20 years (down to 14.8 births per 1000 population in 1976), as illustrated in Figures 2-1 and 2-2, the proportion of older persons has increased.

The effect of fertility is best illustrated with the projections in Table 2-1. Note that the same number of older persons (Column 1) can represent different proportions of the total population (Columns 2 and 3) under different fertility assumptions. Under conditions of high average fertility (2.7 births per woman), the population aged 65 and over will be only 12.7% of the total in 2020, a figure that is little higher than the 11.2% in 1979. However, if average fertility for the next 40 years is only 1.7 births per woman, the number of "new people" will decrease, and the number of older persons will represent 17.8% of the total population. The differences in the two projections can have distinct ramifications on public policy and the ability of social, economic, and political institutions to serve the needs of the older population. As we shall see, the differences resulting from these fertility assumptions are greater than differences due to alternative mortality or migration assumptions.

Mortality

Once fertility has set the stage by imposing certain limits on the size of each new birth cohort, differentials in mortality rates begin to determine a population's composition. Mortality rates at each age determine how many cohort members will reach old age.

The historic decline in mortality has contributed to the increase in the number of survivors to old age. Human populations have been improving in average life expectancy since the days of the Babylonian and Roman empires. But these improvements have been slow in coming, at least until the last two centuries. Consider, for example, the change in average life expectancy at birth since 1000 B.C. At that time it was approximately 18 years; in 1977 the average life expectancy at birth in the United States was 73 years. This increase of 55 years took almost 3000 years to achieve, but in this century alone average life expectancy at birth in the United States increased by 26 years—from 47 years in 1900 to 73 years in 1970, as shown in Table 2-3. Note however, that similar dramatic advances have not been made in average life expectancy at age 65, where there has been a gain of only 4 years since 1900—from 12 to 16 in 1977.

TABLE 2-3. Average life expectancy at birth and at age 65 in the United States, for various years: 1900-1977

Age	1900	1939	1949	1955	1959	1970	1977
At birth	47.3	63.7	68.0	69.6	69.9	70.9	73.2
At age 65	11.9	12.8	12.8	14.2	14.4	15.2	16.3

SOURCE: United States Public Health Service, National Center for Health Statistics, *Vital statistics of the United States: 1970, Vol. II–Mortality, Part A*, Washington, D.C.: U.S. Government Printing Office, 1974, Tables 5-1 and 5-5; Final mortality statistics, 1977, *Monthly Vital Statistics Report*, May 1979, *28*, Table 3.

Another important fact shown in Table 2-3 is the slower rate of increase in average life expectancy at birth since 1939. The largest increment (16.4 years) occurred between 1900 and 1939. Since then, however, the increase in average life expectancy at birth has only been 7.2 years. The trend is clearly toward a much slower rate of increase in average life expectancy, especially since 1949.

Table 2-4 indicates that other developed countries exhibit similar averages in life expectancy at birth. But the same cannot be said for many of the developing nations, particularly those in Africa and Southeast Asia. In most countries of these regions, the average life expectancy at birth stands in sharp contrast to those of the developed nations. As Table 2-4 shows, average life expectancies in selected African and Asian countries remain below 60 years (some even below 50 years).

To determine the impact of mortality on the proportion of older persons in the population, we need to see which age groups have benefited the most from the general decline in mortality. Referring to Table 2-3, we find that the improvement in life expectancy at birth far outpaces the relatively small gains made in life expectancy at age 65. The dramatic age differences in the improvement of life expectancy can be seen by looking at the probability of survival to specified ages in the United States. This measure is similar to life expectancy, but is expressed as the percentage of a birth cohort that is expected to survive from one age to another. In 1900 only 39% of those born could be expected to survive to age 64. By 1970, this figure had increased to 72% or a gain of 33 percentage points. Of the population aged 65 and older in 1900, the probability of survival to age 80 was 33%. By 1970 this proportion had increased to only 49%, a much smaller gain than the figures at birth.

The decrease in infant mortality has been by far the most significant factor in increasing life expectancy in the United States since early in the century. The reduction and virtual elimination of infectious diseases as a cause of death in the United States, combined with major improvements in postnatal infant care, have primarily benefited the youngest age groups. As recently as 1935, the United States had an infant mortality rate (deaths under 1 year of age per 1000 live births) of 55.7. By 1970, the infant mortality rate had dropped to 19.8, and further reductions have brought this figure down to 14.1 in 1977 (United States Public Health Service, 1979b).

When infant mortality is substantially reduced, the effects of fertility can have a greater impact. Of the number of babies born in 1980, a smaller number will die within the first year of life, thus increasing the number of new members of the population. As infant mortality declines (other things being equal), the number of new

TABLE 2-4. Life expectancy at birth by sex, and population aged 65 and over for selected countries and years

Country	Year	Life expectancy at birth		Population aged 65 and over		
		Male	Female	Year	Number (thousands)	Percentage of total
North America						
United States	1975	68.7	76.5	1977	23,493	10.9
Canada	1970–1972	69.3	76.4	1977	20,691	8.9
Haiti	1970–1975[a]	47.1	50.0	1978	193	4.0
Mexico	1975	62.8	66.6	1978	2,212	3.3
South America						
Argentina	1970–1975	65.2	71.4	1978	2,102	8.0
Brazil	1960–1970	57.6	61.1	1977	3,678	3.2
Venezuela	1961	– 66.4 –		1977	391	3.1
Asia						
China	1970–1975[a]	60.7	64.4	–	–	–
Japan	1976	72.2	77.4	1977	9,561	8.4
Iran	1973–1976	57.6	57.4	1976	1,185	3.5
Syria	1970	54.5	58.6	1978	356	4.4
USSR	1971–1972	64.0	74.0	1973[b]	32,974	13.1
Europe						
Austria	1976	68.1	75.0	1976	1,136	15.1
Denmark	1975–1976	71.1	76.8	1976	691	13.6
France	1976	69.2	77.2	1978	7,343	13.8
Hungary	1974	66.5	72.4	1977	1,383	13.0
Netherlands	1977	72.0	78.4	1977	1,532	11.1
Sweden	1972–1976	72.1	77.8	1976	1,262	15.4
England and Wales	1974–1976	69.6	75.8	1976	7,057	14.3
Africa						
Ethiopia	1970–1975[a]	37.0	40.1	1978	790	2.7
Ghana	1970–1975[a]	41.9	45.1	1970	311	3.6
Kenya	1969	46.9	51.2	1969	391	3.6
S. Africa	1970–1975[a]	56.6	59.4	1970	876	4.0
Uganda	1970–1975[a]	48.3	51.7	1969	366	3.8
Zambia	1970–1975[a]	44.3	47.5	1977	133	2.5

SOURCE: United Nations, *Demographic yearbook: 1978*, New York: United Nations, 1979, Tables 4 and 7.

[a] Estimated.

[b] Age 60 and over.

members of the population increases relative to the number of older members, and the proportion of older persons declines.

With infectious diseases and the diseases of early childhood now well controlled, it is primarily the aged who remain vulnerable to such degenerative diseases as heart disease, cancer, and stroke. This fact is seen in Table 2-5, which shows the death rates for the ten leading causes of death in the United States in 1900 and compares these with the rates and ranking for 1970. Although influenza, pneumonia, and tuberculosis are no longer major causes of death, the degenerative diseases have taken their place. This latter group of diseases is concentrated among the older population. Because more people are living to older ages within the total population, health problems associated with the degenerative diseases have become a major concern. By 1969, diseases of the heart, cancer, and stroke together accounted for three out of every four deaths of persons aged 65 and over. See Chapter 12 for a discussion of the diseases of old age.

TABLE 2-5. Death rates for the ten leading causes of death in 1900 with comparable rates for 1970 in the United States

	Rate (deaths per 1000 population)		Rank	
Cause of death[a]	1900	1970	1900	1970
Influenza and pneumonia	202.2	30.9	1	5
Tuberculosis	194.4	2.6	2	–
Gastroenteritis (diseases of stomach and intestine)	142.7	0.9	3	–
Diseases of the heart	137.4	362.0	4	1
Cerebral hemorrhage and other vascular lesions	106.9	101.9	5	3
Chronic nephritis (kidney diseases)	81.0	3.7	6	–
All accidents	72.3	56.4	7	4
Cancer and other malignant neoplasms	64.0	162.8	8	2
Diseases of early infancy	62.6	21.4	9	6
Diphtheria	40.3	0.0	10	–

SOURCE: Public Health Service, National Center for Health Statistics, *Vital statistics of the United States, 1970, Volume II—Mortality, Part A,* Washington, D.C.: U.S. Government Printing Office, 1974, Table 1-5; *Monthly Vital Statistics Report,* 27 June 1974, *22* (13), adapted from Tables 7 and 8.

[a] Eighth Revision, International Classification of Diseases, Adapted, 1965.

For the curious reader we note that the diseases ranked seventh through tenth as causes of death in 1970 were not in the ten leading causes of death for 1900. These diseases for 1970, listed in rank order from seven through ten respectively, were as follows: diabetes mellitus (18.9 deaths per 1000), arteriosclerosis (15.6), cirrhosis of the liver (15.5), and bronchitis, emphysema, and asthma (15.2).

To emphasize further the relative importance of the degenerative diseases in mortality rates, we can estimate what effect their eradication would have on life expectancy. Given current death rates in the United States, and applying the analytic tool of life-table estimates (Barclay, 1958; Dublin, Lotka, & Spiegelman, 1949), the elimination of tuberculosis would yield a gain of only 0.04 years in life expectancy at birth and even less than that at age 65. However, if diseases of the heart were completely eradicated today, life expectancy at birth would increase by 5.9 years and by 5.1 years at age 65 (United States Public Health Service, 1975).

The dominant role of heart disease, stroke, and cancer is further emphasized by data on the lifetime probability of dying from these diseases. For the newborn there is approximately a 61% chance of eventually dying from major cardiovascular diseases, a 15% chance of eventual death from cancer, and about a 5% chance of death due to accidents. Except for accidents, however, the concentration of deaths from these degenerative causes is in the oldest age groups of the population. Note in Table 2-6 that the median age at death in 1970 from influenza and pneumonia was 74.5, indicating their heavier toll on the older rather than the younger population.

TABLE 2-6. Median age at death from selected causes, United States: 1970

Cause of death	Median age at death
Major cardiovascular-renal disease (heart diseases and stroke)	75.6
Malignant neoplasms (cancers)	67.5
Influenza and pneumonia	74.5
Accidents (all kinds)	39.9

SOURCE: Adapted from United States Public Health Service, National Center for Health Statistics, *Vital statistics of the United States: 1970, Vol. II–Mortality, Part A*, Washington, D.C.: U.S. Government Printing Office, 1974, Tables 1–26.

The cause-specific mortality rates of persons in the United States and in other relatively developed countries are quite different from those in underdeveloped parts of the world. Those countries with the highest life expectancies in general (illustrated in Table 2-4) are the countries with low infant mortality but relatively high mortality from the degenerative diseases of heart, cancer, and stroke. Data from the United Nations *Demographic Yearbook: 1977* (1978) show, for example, that in 1975 Sweden had an infant mortality rate of 9 (per 1000) and a heart-disease related mortality rate of 403 (per 100,000 population). In 1974 Mexico, on the other hand, had an infant mortality rate of 48, but a heart-disease related mortality rate of only 71. For the United States in 1975, the corresponding rates were 16 and 333. Thus, the increasing contribution of degenerative diseases to death rates in developing countries is, in a sense, an index of the growth of the older population.

A number of demographic analyses have shown that general declines in mortality rates do not contribute to a rise in the proportion of the population aged 65 and over unless those declines are concentrated in the older age groups (Coale, 1956; Hermalin, 1966). Because of the relatively low level of mortality at the ages below 50, future substantial reductions in mortality can only occur at the ages above 50. "Substantial" reductions are not anticipated, but death rates in the middle and older adult ages (35 years and over), which account for about 90% of deaths, declined much more rapidly from 1973 to 1975 than from 1960 to 1973. This decline was due largely to reduction in mortality from major cardiovascular diseases. As a result, recent estimates and projections of the older population have had to be revised upward. For example, the latest projection of the population aged 65 and over, shown in Table 2-1, is 4% greater in 2000 and 5% greater in 2020 than the last previous projection (Siegel, 1969).

Although future declines in mortality will probably contribute to an aging of the population, rather than to a "younging" of the population as in the past, fertility will continue to be the most important determinant of the proportion of older persons. Variations in the proportion of older persons under alternative mortality assumptions are less than variations in the proportion under alternative fertility assumptions. Table 2-7 illustrates these effects with the three assumptions of fertility used by the

Census Bureau and with three mortality assumptions: (1) Census Bureau projections of slow and steady reduction in future mortality, (2) death rates declining twice as rapidly as the Census Bureau projects, and (3) death rates of 1976 reduced by one-half in 2050. Assumptions 2 and 3 are viewed as unrealistic, but useful for illustrative purposes. Consider the third mortality assumption. The percentage aged 65 and over would increase to 11.9%–13.6% (depending on the fertility assumption), as compared with the Census Bureau's projection of 11.3%–12.9%. By 2020, the percentage would increase to 14.1%–19.6%, compared with the lower Census Bureau projections of 12.7%–17.8%. Greater differences can be seen from the fertility assumptions (between columns) than from the mortality assumptions (within columns).

TABLE 2-7. Percentage of the population aged 65 and over in 2000 and 2020 under alternative fertility and mortality assumptions

Year Mortality assumption	*Series I* *(High)*	*Series II* *(Medium)*	*Series III* *(Low)*
		Fertility assumption	
2000			
1. Census Bureau projection	11.3	12.2	12.9
2. Twice the decline of the Census Bureau	11.6	12.6	13.3
3. One-half of 1976 rates by 2050	11.9	12.9	13.6
2020			
1. Census Bureau projection	12.7	15.5	17.8
2. Twice the decline of the Census Bureau	13.6	16.5	18.9
3. One-half of 1976 rates by 2050	14.1	17.2	19.6

SOURCE: Jacob S. Siegel, *Current population reports,* Series P-23, no. 78, Prospective trends in the size and structure of the elderly population, impact of mortality trends, and some implications, January 1979, Table 12.

It is important to emphasize the interactions among fertility and mortality in Table 2-7. Low fertility in combination with low mortality results in the highest proportion of older persons in the United States in the future. Table 2-4 also illustrates the interactions. Countries with low mortality and low fertility (in Europe) have the highest proportion of older persons. Countries with high fertility and lower life expectancies (in Asia and Africa) have the lowest proportion of older persons.

Immigration

Immigration is the third demographic factor affecting population composition. Like fertility, past levels of immigration tend to increase the number of older persons in subsequent years by increasing the size of the original birth cohort. Like mortality, current levels of immigration tend to lower the median age of the population. Since migrants are typically young adults, the proportion of older persons is reduced. Note that *emigration,* or movement away from a country, would have the opposite effect on the age composition.

Early immigration during the late 19th and early 20th centuries was concentrated among younger males. Eventually assimilated, they married and had families. During this period the number of immigrants was high, thereby having a distinct effect on the age and sex composition of our population. From 1881 to 1930, the United States received almost 27.6 million immigrants, most of whom were 15–39 years old (United States Bureau of the Census, 1975a). Immigration continues, but the average annual number of alien immigrants has declined from 879,000 in 1901–1910 to 332,000 in 1961–1970, and the net effect on the total population and its composition is decreasing over time (Irwin and Warren, 1972).

The age distribution of the foreign-born population reflects these trends in immigration (United States Bureau of the Census, 1975b, 1979e). As a result of the sharp curtailment of immigration after World War I, the foreign-born population tends to be concentrated in the older ages. In 1970, about one-third of all foreign-born persons was aged 65 years or over, and about 15% of the population aged 65 and over was foreign-born. Since Europeans dominated the migration streams early in the century, one of every three persons of foreign stock (foreign-born plus native persons of foreign or mixed parentage) from Denmark, Germany, Ireland, Norway, and Sweden was aged 65 or older. By contrast, less than 10% from Cuba, China, Japan, and Mexico was aged 65 or older, since these countries contributed immigrants more recently.

With the present annual statutory ceiling of about 400,000 immigrants (with some legal exceptions in times of war or special international crises), the population projections into the 21st century are minimally affected by immigration. The projections in Table 2-1 assume that 400,000 immigrants enter the country annually. If immigration is eliminated in the Series II projection, then 16.4% of the population would be aged 65 and over by 2020, as compared with 15.5% in Series II. The median age of the population in Series II would be only slightly higher (37.8 years) without immigration than with immigration (37.0 years).

The foregoing discussion has presented a wealth of information to emphasize the important changes in age composition and the growth of the older population in the United States since the turn of the century. We have stressed the past importance of fertility in determining the size and proportion of older people in the American population. Although fertility has been the key to setting limits on the potential size of the older population, reduction in mortality, especially in infant mortality, has helped to make the effects of fertility even more pronounced (Sauvy, 1954). As we have seen, large-scale reductions in already low mortality rates are unlikely to change the age composition of the population appreciably. But the reduction of deaths from (or at least better treatment for) the major degenerative diseases can provide immeasurable benefits to the physical and psychological well-being of older people. Although past immigration has tended to make the population younger, the recent lower annual number of immigrants indicates that immigration will play a very minor role in determining the future age composition of the population. Attention to all of these basic demographic factors is of utmost concern to anyone interested in gerontological issues.

SOME DEMOGRAPHIC CHARACTERISTICS OF
THE PRESENT OLDER POPULATION

Throughout this discussion we have attempted to illustrate the basic demographic processes of fertility, mortality, and migration with descriptive data concerning the past, present, and in some instances future old-age population. We now present additional demographic data to provide a better understanding of the current socioeconomic status and lifestyle of older people in the United States. These data describe such characteristics as the distribution of older persons within the United States in terms of urban versus rural residence and in terms of various regions and states within the country. We also consider the economic and educational status of older persons as well as general patterns of living arrangements found among contemporary older persons. As a final prefatory note to this discussion we emphasize that these data are not meant to be a complete description of contemporary older persons. We present only the highlights of available information. Additional data are presented in other chapters in this volume; still additional information can be obtained from the many census documents and other publications cited throughout this chapter.

Birth cohort

In this context we again refer to the *birth cohort*. As suggested earlier, a birth cohort may be defined as all the individuals born in a particular period of time—a month, year, decade, or other unit of time. Thus, all persons born on September 23, 1975 in the United States constitute a birth cohort, although this is a much too narrow definition to be useful for any demographic research purpose. All persons born in 1970-1975 is a more useful birth cohort for purposes of description and analysis as would be all persons born in the 1970-1979 decade or the 1940-1949 decade.

The importance of the concept of the birth cohort can be seen from a number of different, but complementary, points of view. First, by referring to a group or category of individuals as "the cohort of 1940-1944," we recognize the fact that this set of individuals was born in a particular historical time, raised in a particular historical milieu, and from the moment of birth represents a particular configuration of demographic characteristics. Thus, the cohort of 1940-1944 will have different characteristics from the cohort born in 1930-1934. Clearly, the demographic characteristics of these two cohorts as well as the social, economic, and political circumstances of socialization and maturation were quite different. All people age, and at any particular point in history the survivors can be identified as the old people in the population system. Yet the demographic composition of the category of "old people" differs from time to time, and these differences can be traced to the birth cohort of the particular group of old persons.

Second, cohort analysis is important for anticipating the future needs and demands of the older population. Of course, one way to estimate future contributions, problems, and issues of the older population is to observe and study the aging process among today's old people. Although much study needs to be done to understand the individual and the societal aspects of aging, we should also be in a position to anticipate future needs as well.

We can describe the old persons who will be alive in the near future, since these persons represent the aging of birth cohorts who are already alive. For example, suppose we are interested in comparing the people who will be 65-74 years of age in the year 2000 with those who will similarly be 65-74 years old in the year 2030. By simple subtraction we can determine that the old people in the year 2000 are the survivors of the birth cohort of 1926-1935; similarly, we can determine that the old people in the year 2030 will represent the birth cohort of 1956-1965.

Once we have identified the old people for any given year in terms of their birth cohort, the task of "predicting" the future old-age situation becomes substantially easier. In this example, the birth cohorts of 1926-1935 and 1956-1965 have already been born; no new members of these two cohorts can affect the predictions. With fertility completed and immigration a negligible factor, the projection of future cohorts of older people requires "only" two additional kinds of information. The first is a description of the cohort; census data can be used to describe the number of people in each cohort, according to their geographic distribution and their economic and social characteristics. The second factor is the expected survival of the members of the cohorts; this, of course, is the more tricky part of the problem. Although demographic analysis cannot predict with absolute certainty which individuals or types of individuals within a cohort are likely to survive, we can make a series of estimates given what is already known about mortality. Therefore, given such factors as sex and race differentials in mortality, including expected changes over time, we can roughly determine the composition of the cohort when it reaches the sixth decade of its own life cycle.

Thus, the concept of a birth cohort and the demographic techniques of cohort analysis can be quite important to gerontological analysis (see Chapters 7 and 19). One can better understand the processes of aging with the realization that old people at any given point in time partly reflect the characteristics and experiences of their own particular birth cohort. A description of the future composition of the older population can be drawn because many of tomorrow's cohorts of older persons have already been born. When gerontologists consider the various social and economic aspects of the "problems of aging," and how the institutions of society are going to meet those problems, their consideration can be enlightened by an analysis based on the concept of cohort. Indeed, one point of view that has been espoused by social philosophers as well as demographers (for example, Mannheim, 1928; Ryder, 1965) is that history and social change can be viewed as a succession of birth cohorts traveling through society. Each cohort has its own unique set of birth characteristics and its own social, economic, and political life history or collective biography. For gerontologists each cohort represents a different context in which society confronts aging, and in which the aged confront society.

Dependency ratio

The questions concerning the relative sizes of different birth cohorts lead to the question of economic dependency of older persons on family or on younger members of society. The measure that demographers use to summarize the relationship between these two classes of individuals is the *dependency ratio*. Arithmetically, the dependency ratio is simply the number or proportion of individuals in the dependent segment of the population divided by the number or proportion of individuals in the supportive or working population. Distinguishing these two groups conceptually has been more problematic.

The dependent population typically has two components: the young and the old. Babies, children, and most adolescents typically do not support themselves. Thus, at the individual level they are supported by their parents and families; from a more social system point of view, these youngsters are supported by the working population. Similarly, the retired population is no longer working but is supported by the working population. Of course, the recipients of pensions are supported in part by their own contributions to the pension system. In the case of Social Security, however, increased payments or benefits are greater than previously contributed shares. In such a case, the younger working population is paying its Social Security payments to support the current recipients of benefits.

We focus here on older dependents. Several ratios of dependency developed by the United States Bureau of the Census (1976) are provided in Table 2-8. The first two are "familial" dependency ratios, which relate one generation defined by age at a given date to another generation that is likely to include their children approximately 20-30 years younger. The burden of supporting the aged has more than doubled since 1900, and it will likely peak in 2000 and again in 2020 or 2030. By 1975 there were 49 persons aged 80 and over for every 100 persons aged 60-64, and 174 persons aged 65-84 for every 100 aged 45-49.

The next three types of ratios are "societal" dependency ratios, which relate older dependents to younger productive persons. The first two are based on the age

TABLE 2-8. Selected old-age dependency ratios for the United States: 1900-2020 [a]

	Familial dependency ratios		Societal dependency ratios		
	80 and over	*65-84*	*65 and over*	*60 and over*	*Nonworkers 65 and over*
Year	*60-64*	*45-49*	*18-64*	*20-59*	*Workers 20-59*
Estimates					
1900	0.21 [b]	0.86 [b]	0.07	0.13	(NA)
1930	0.22 [b]	0.90 [b]	0.09	0.16	(NA)
1960	0.36	1.44	0.17	0.27	0.28
1970	0.43	1.54	0.17	0.29	0.29
1975	0.49	1.74	0.18	0.29	0.29
Projections [c]					
2000	0.73	1.44	0.19	0.28	(NA)
2020	0.45	2.35	0.24	0.40	(NA)

SOURCE: United States Bureau of the Census, *Current population reports*, Series P-23, no. 59, Demographic aspects of aging and the older population in the United States, May 1976, Table 6-10.

NA Not Available.

[a] As of July 1, except as noted.

[b] Figures are census data for April 1.

[c] Series II projections from the United States Bureau of the Census.

structure alone, assuming that all persons aged 60 or 65 and over are dependents, and all persons aged 18–64 or 20–59 are working. These are actually measures of age composition rather than of economic dependency, since some persons over 65 work, and many between the ages of 18 and 65 are in school, keeping house, disabled, or not working for some other reason. The growth of the older population is reflected in the increase in these ratios during the century. If we assume later labor-force entry (age 20) and earlier retirement (age 59), the dependency ratio reaches 0.29 in 1975.

The last measure more closely approximates economic dependency by relating nonworkers aged 65 and over to workers aged 20–59. By 1975 there were 29 non-workers for every 100 workers.

Note that in the first decades of the next century, the baby-boom children of the late 1940s and 1950s will have reached retirement age, and thus become part of the numerator of the dependency ratio. At the same time, a lowered birth rate, such as we have now, means a relatively smaller work-force population in this same period—comprising the denominator of the dependency ratio. The implication of this pair of demographic facts is a continual increase in the dependency ratio.

This increase in the societal dependency ratio is influenced not only by the demographic facts of relative cohort sizes, but by what might be called the "social definition" of old age and dependency. The first two societal dependency ratios presented in Table 2-8 illustrate the impact of these social definitions; that is, the differences between them signify different average retirement ages—65 and over, and 60 and over, respectively. Although the legal retirement age in the national Social Security system has been age 65, during the 1960s changes in Social Security law allowed people to choose early retirement, as early as age 62. A number of private and governmental pension systems also allow early retirement. The consequence of these early retirement opportunities has been a gradual decline in the proportion of older persons in the labor force; the economic consequences of this are discussed later in this chapter. Consequently, the difference between the dependency ratios using ages 65 and over, on the one hand, and 60 and over, on the other, is a difference based not only on the demographic numbers of older persons, but also on the social definition of old age and dependency. To the extent that people leave the labor force, on the average, at earlier and earlier ages, then the dependency ratio for those aged 60 and over will indeed come to be the more accurate description of the United States in future years.

In the past couple of years, however, a number of factors have emerged to suggest that the social definition of old age and dependency may begin to lower the dependency ratio. In 1978 the Congress passed legislation (the Age Discrimination in Employment Act Amendments of 1978) that raised the mandatory retirement age from 65 to 70 and eliminated it altogether in federal employment. In the past few years inflation has eroded the value of Social Security and other retirement income resources, so that many older people have expressed a desire to retire later rather than earlier (Harris, 1975). In general, older persons are more healthy now than they were just a few decades ago; similarly, more and more persons have jobs that are less physically demanding than was the case a few years ago.

All these factors suggest that the trend toward earlier retirement may begin to reverse itself. To the degree that older persons want to continue working, that legal obstacles to their continued employment continue to be removed (mandatory retirement, age discrimination in employment), and that social and economic policies are formulated to provide employment opportunities for older workers (Chiles, 1980; Cutler, 1981), a reversal in the trend toward increasing dependency ratios may be noticeable within the next 20 years.

The dependency ratio can be computed for any nation or for any group within a nation, even for different retirement systems (Torrey, 1979), yielding a quick summary of the relationships between dynamic elements within the population system. To the degree that money represents a scarce resource in any society, and to the degree that the old are to be supported by the society to which they have contributed, the dependency ratio is a useful summary statistic for measuring changes in the population. These changes can have substantial implications for the social, economic, and political systems.

Residential distribution

A first part of the description concerns information on where the older population resides. Of the total older population in 1970, the largest number (14.6 million, or 73%) lived in urban areas. Of these urban elderly, the majority (55%) was located in heavily urbanized areas, and 6.8 million of these were in central cities. Only 4.3 million older people lived in suburbs. In this respect the elderly differ from the population as a whole, in which suburbanites outnumber central city residents. Clearly, older people are disproportionately concentrated in central cities—a fact that makes urban problems of congestion, transportation, living costs, crime, and housing of paramount concern to those interested in the health and well-being of older persons.

In terms of the proportion of elderly in an area's total population, however, the highest concentration of elderly is in small rural towns (places of 1000–2500 total population), where they are 13.6% of the total. Next highest in proportion are the elderly living in urban places of 2500–10,000 population; here the elderly represent 12.2% of the population. This residential pattern implies that the smaller the area, the greater the concentration of older people. There is an exception to this pattern, however. Farm areas have one of the lowest proportions of elderly people. This is in part explained by the post-World War II movement of older people from unproductive and burdensome farms to nearby small towns (Youmans, 1967) and by the more recent general migration of older people to cities in the South and West. The other exception to the pattern, suburbia (with only 7.8% elderly), is explained by the high cost, excessive size, and transportation necessities of suburban housing relative to the finances and needs of older people (Taeuber, 1972).

Another important distributional characteristic of the older population concerns the states in which they are concentrated. Numerically, the states with the largest populations also have the largest numbers of older people. California, New York, Pennsylvania, and Florida account for nearly one-third of the total older population of the United States. Ten states accounted for 56% of all older people in 1975, as shown in Table 2-9. Note, however, that these ten states vary widely in the percent increase of their populations during the 1960–1970 and 1970–1975 periods. Florida experienced the most dramatic increase in both periods.

TABLE 2-9. Population aged 65 and over: Number and percentage of total in 1975, percent change 1960–1970 and 1970–1975, in ten leading states in the United States

Rank	State	Number (thousands) 1975	Percentage of state total 1975	Percent change 1960–1970	Percent change 1970–1975
1	California	2,056	9.7	30.2	14.8
2	New York	2,030	11.2	15.6	4.0
3	Pennsylvania	1,377	11.6	12.2	8.7
4	Florida	1,347	16.1	78.2	36.8
5	Texas	1,158	9.5	32.6	17.2
6	Illinois	1,153	10.3	11.7	5.9
7	Ohio	1,066	9.9	10.7	7.4
8	Michigan	815	8.9	17.4	8.8
9	New Jersey	767	10.5	23.8	10.6
10	Massachusetts	672	11.5	10.7	6.0
	United States	22,400	10.5	20.6	12.2

SOURCE: United States Bureau of the Census, *Current population reports,* Series P-23, no. 59, Demographic aspects of aging and the older population in the United States, May 1976, Tables 4–1 and 4–2.

Some states with high percent increases such as California, Texas, and New Jersey still have lower proportions of older persons than the national average. A low percentage of older persons is due to high fertility, the in-migration of persons under age 65, or the out-migration of persons aged 65 and over. States in the South and West typically have a low proportion of older persons. A high percentage of older persons results from low fertility, heavy out-migration of young persons, substantial in-migration of older persons, or heavy immigration of foreign-born persons prior to World War I. Parts of the Midwest and the Northeast exemplify this pattern.

Percent change figures can often be misleading when comparing two or more populations, since the denominators (or base population), upon which the percent change is based, can vary widely. Thus, California's 1960–1970 net increase of 416,000 older persons represented a 30.2% increase, while the net increase of 432,000 older people in Florida represented an increase of 78.2% for that state. Conversely, Arizona's similar large increase rate of 78.8% in that decade represented only 71,000 additional older people. The percent increase figures may be the same, but the absolute numbers can be quite different.

Given such variations in numbers and percent changes among the states, we need to consider estimates of net migration of the 65-and-over population for a better understanding of where older people are located and where they are going. These estimates are derived from the 1960 and 1970 population censuses. Simply stated, by applying region-by-region survival ratios (Barclay, 1958) to the population aged 55 and over in every region (or state) in 1960, we derive the expected population from this age cohort still alive ten years later in 1970 (the cohort aged 65 and over). This expected figure can then be compared with the actual older population in the region given by the 1970 census, the difference being the estimated net migration for that cohort during the decade.

Using this method, the net migration figures for the major geographic regions of the United States were derived, and they give us the best picture of the geographic mobility and changing distribution of the older population in the country. The South, particularly the southern Atlantic states, and the West are attracting great numbers of older migrants, while almost all northeastern and east north-central states are losing older people through net out-migration (United States Bureau of the Census, 1971).

Underlying these regional trends are some interesting state-level differences and contrasts. For example, Florida's net in-migration of over 366,000 older people during the 1960–1970 decade stands in sharp contrast to the net out-migration of almost 203,000 older people from New York. Similarly, where Illinois experienced a net loss of 105,000 older people from 1960 to 1970, Texas and Arizona had net in-migration of 52,700 and 46,000 older persons, respectively, during the decade. In the same period California had a net gain of almost 143,000 older in-migrants.

Out- and in-migration together affect population size. Obviously the net in-migration contributes to a state's total increase in population. Also, a state or region can experience a net out-migration of older people despite an increase in its older population. The loss from migration represents the difference between the expected increase and the actual number of older people at the end of the period under consideration. Illinois is a case in point: despite a 11.7% increase in its older population during the 1960–1970 decade, it had a net out-migration of 105,000 older people during that time. Its total older population increased, but not by as much as was expected. Out-migration was the reason.

These migration trends, if they continue, will lead to an increasing concentration of older people in the southern and western states. As each state's population composition changes, adjustments in public policy and service delivery systems will be necessary to meet the heavier needs of larger proportions of older people. States such as Florida, Arizona, Texas, and California are particularly challenged to be aware of these trends and to adjust their programs for such needs as adequate housing, health care, leisure activities, and mass transit for the elderly.

Our review of the migration trends of older people must include a note of caution in order to put these trends in proper perspective. Although some states show high rates of in- or out-migration of older people, the group aged 65 and over is less mobile than all other age groups. Table 2-10 presents an interesting portrait of the differences in residential mobility between younger and older persons. The data show the rates for moves in the period March 1975–March 1978 as collected by the Bureau of the Census (1978). Almost two-thirds of the population aged 25–29 experienced some kind of move in this period—that is, at least living in a different house at the end of the period—as compared with about 14% of the population 65 and over. However, the relative distance of residential change for older persons is similar to that for the younger population. Of these who did change residence, almost 62% of the older persons stayed in the same county (8.4 of the 13.6), while the comparable figure for the younger population was 58% (36.7 of the 63.4).

Even if we consider only the age group 65–74 of the older population, the migration rates remain low. For the same period (1975–1978), only 5.8% of the population aged 65–74 moved to a different county, while 8.9% moved to a different house in the same county—that is, a total of only 14.7% for this age group. Although the migration rates of older persons are relatively small, old-age residential migration is selective and is bringing increasing numbers of older persons to certain regions and states. In the

TABLE 2-10. Percent distribution by mobility status for selected age groups in the United States: March 1975–March 1978

Mobility status	Total population [a]	Age 25–29	Age 65 and over
Total	100.0%	100.0%	100.0%
Same house (nonmovers)	64.5	34.0	86.3
Different house (movers)	34.2	63.4	13.6
Same county	20.5	36.7	8.4
Different county	13.7	26.7	5.2
Within the state	7.4	14.8	2.9
Between states	6.4	11.9	2.3
Movers from abroad	1.3	2.6	0.1

SOURCE: United States Bureau of the Census, *Current population reports,* Series P-20, no. 331, Geographical mobility: March 1975 to March 1978, November 1978, Table 6.

[a] Three years old and over. Mobility over the three-year period is determined only for persons born by March 1975.

following sections it should be noted that national level data fail to reflect the resulting variations in the demographic, social, and economic structure of regional, state, and local areas.

Sex composition

The sex composition of a population is best summarized by the sex ratio. As usually expressed, the sex ratio is the number of males per 100 females in a population or population subgroup. Thus, if there were an equal number of males and females, the sex ratio would be 100. If there were 500 males per 100 females, the sex ratio would be 500. If there were only 50 males per 100 females, then the sex ratio would be 50. In most modern societies, the general sex ratio is less than 100, since women tend to outlive men.

The particular importance of the sex-ratio measure is that it allows demographers to describe different population groups. One basic kind of comparison of particular relevance to gerontologists is the changing sex ratio over the life cycle: the later the stage in the life cycle, the smaller the number of males relative to the number of females. Equally, historical projections of sex ratios can also indicate the nature of changes in the population system. Table 2-11 indicates the changing sex ratio for different age groups in the current population. As can be seen, the 1979 sex ratio decreases with increasing age. Since 1900 the sex ratio of the older population has continually decreased.

The fact that different age groups within the total population have different and changing sex ratios is closely connected to one of the basic demographic processes described earlier: mortality. Although mortality eventually affects everyone, certain causes of mortality are more likely to affect males than females. Of the four leading causes of death in 1977, only cerebrovascular diseases (stroke) affected females more than males. The ratio of the male death rate to the female death rate was 1.28 for diseases of the heart, 1.35 for malignant neoplasms (cancer), 2.65 for all accidents, and only 0.84 for cerebrovascular diseases (United States Public Health Service, 1979b).

TABLE 2-11. Sex ratios for the United States by age group in 1979 and for the population aged 65 years and over in selected years: 1900–2020

Sex ratio by age 1979		Sex ratios for the population aged 65 years and over	
Age	*Sex ratio[a]*	*Year[b]*	*Sex ratio[a]*
Under 5	104.7		
5–17	104.2	1900	102.0
18–24	101.6	1930	100.4
25–44	97.3	1960	82.6
45–64	92.4	1970	72.0
65–74	77.0	1979	68.4
75–84	60.4	2000	66.6
85 and over	44.7	2020	69.3

SOURCE: United States Bureau of the Census, *Current population reports,* Series P-23, no. 59, Demographic aspects of aging and the older population in the United States, May 1976, Table 3–1; Series P-25, no. 870, Estimates of the population of the United States, by age, race, and sex: 1976 to 1979, January 1980, Table 1; Series P-25, no. 704, Projections of the population of the United States: 1977 to 2050, July 1977, Table 11.

[a] Males per 100 females.

[b] As of July 1 each year.

Not only do females have lower death rates at each age than males, but their life expectancy has increased faster than that of males throughout this century, as shown in Figure 2-3. Because racial as well as sex factors are strongly associated with differential life-expectancy rates, the data are presented by both categories. As these data indicate, whites have a greater life expectancy than nonwhites; within both racial groups, females can expect to live longer than males.

Two other demographic factors influence the sex ratio at different ages. The first is the sex ratio at birth. The sex ratio at birth typically favors males. In 1979 there were 105 boys for every 100 girls under 5 years of age. The second is the balance of males and females among the migrants to a country. In the 1960s female immigrants outnumbered males; at the beginning of the century 70% of immigrants were male.

The past history of births, deaths, and migration explains changes in sex ratios by age over time. Table 2-12 presents sex ratios by age for the United States from 1900 to 1979. Various trends can be noted. The first is that during the 20th century the number of males per 100 females in the total population has been steadily decreasing—as can be seen from the "all ages" row in Table 2-12. A second, and more dramatic, trend is that in both 1960 and 1970 the proportion of males to females among adults over the age of 45 decreased substantially. The decline in the sex ratio at age 65 and over continued through 1979. The higher mortality of males and the aging and mortality of male immigrants who arrived early in the century are leaving a larger proportion of women in the older ages.

A third important trend is seen by comparing the age pattern of sex ratios across time. Considering the figures for 1900 and 1979, we again see the dramatic change that has occurred during the century. In 1900 all but one of the age groups had sex ratios over 100 (that is, more males than females). Notably, the age group under 15 and the group aged 65 and over had identical sex ratios of 102 in 1900. The increasingly strong

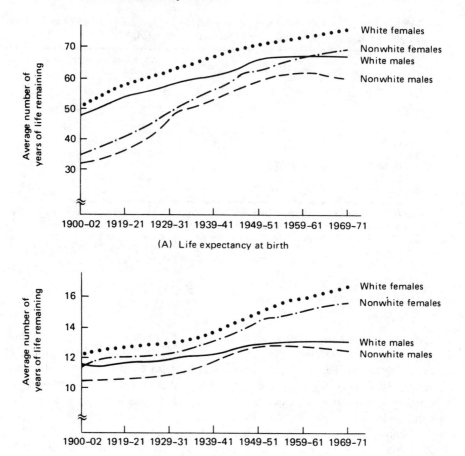

Figure 2-3 (A) (B). Average life expectancy at birth and at age 65 in the United States. (*Adapted from United States Public Health Service, National Center for Health Statistics,* Vital statistics of the United States: 1970, Volume II—Mortality, *Washington, D.C.: U.S. Government Printing Office, 1974.*)

influence of sex selectivity in mortality is clearly indicated by the figures for 1979. Note that the sex ratio under age 25 remains above 100. It is not until the population is in its late 20s that higher mortality eliminates the initial advantage that males have at birth. By 1979 there is a clear decline in the sex ratios with increasing age. Most dramatic here is the sex ratio comparison between 1900 and 1979 for the age group 65 and over: from 102 to 68, a drop of 34 males for every 100 females in the older population in about 80 years!

Furthermore, projections to the year 2000 indicate that the sex ratio will remain below 70. If such is the case, by the year 2020 the boom in the older population is likely to present an even greater degree of widowhood among older women—with attendant social, economic, and housing problems.

TABLE 2-12. Sex ratios for broad age groups, by race in the United States for various years: 1900-1979 (males per hundred females)

	1900	1930	1960	1970	1979
All races					
All ages	104.4	102.5	97.8	95.8	95.0
Under 15	102.1	102.8	103.4	103.8	104.3
15-24	98.3	98.1	101.4	102.3	102.4
25-44	109.1	101.7	96.9	96.9	97.3
45-54	113.9	109.4	97.2	93.2	94.3
55-64	106.5	108.3	93.7	89.8	89.8
65 and over	102.0	100.4	82.6	72.1	68.4
White					
Under 15	102.4	103.2	104.0	104.5	104.9
65 and over	101.9	100.1	82.1	71.6	67.8
Negro and other races [a]					
Under 15	100.0	99.0	100.0	100.0	101.8
65 and over	102.9	105.7	90.1	79.8	74.4

SOURCE: Adapted from United States Bureau of the Census, *Census of population: 1970, general population characteristics,* Washington, D.C.: U.S. Government Printing Office, Final Report, PC(1)-B1, Table 53; United States Bureau of the Census, *Current population reports,* Series P-25, no. 870, Estimates of the population of the United States, by age, race, and sex: 1976 to 1979, January 1980, Table 1.

[a] "Negro and other races" classification is affected by incorrect inclusion of some persons of Spanish surname.

The age pattern of sex ratios for black and other races is similar to the pattern for whites. As shown in Table 2-12, the sex ratio is lower under age 15 but higher at age 65 and over for black and other races. As shown in Figure 2-3, the gap between male and female mortality is somewhat smaller for black and other races, resulting in a higher sex ratio at older ages.

Race composition

Like the white population, the population of black and other races has increased dramatically—from 278,000 in 1900 to 2,327,000 in 1979—as shown in Table 2-13. There are racial differences in growth and composition, however (see United States Bureau of the Census, 1979d). The older population of black and other races has grown more rapidly than the older white population: 34% since 1970 compared with 22% for whites. They will continue to increase faster (58%) than whites (26%) throughout the rest of the century. While 11.7% of the white population is age 65 and over in 1979, only 7.7% of other races is in that age group. As a result of these patterns, black and other races are underrepresented in the older population. Although they constitute 13.7% of the total population, they make up only 9.4% of the older population.

These patterns are explained by race differences in fertility, mortality, and migration. The fertility of black and other races followed the same pattern of increases (during the post-World War II period) and decreases (during the Depression and in recent years) as the fertility of the white population. However, black fertility has consistently been higher than white fertility: by an average of 2.6 children per woman in the middle of the 19th century to about one half a child per woman in recent years.

TABLE 2-13. Population aged 65 and over in the United States by race, estimates and projections for selected years: 1900–2000

Year	Number aged 65 and over (in thousands)		Population 65 and over as a percentage of the total population		Black and other races as a percentage of	
	White	Black and other races	White	Black and other races	Total population	Population 65 and over
Estimates						
1900 [a]	2,814	278	4.2	3.0	12.3	9.0
1930	6,244	400	5.7	3.1	10.4	6.0
1960	15,304	1,256	9.6	6.1	11.4	7.6
1970	18,330	1,735	10.3	6.8	12.5	8.6
1979	22,331	2,327	11.7	7.7	13.7	9.4
Projections						
2000	28,155	3,667	12.9 [b]	8.8 [b]	15.9 [b]	11.5

SOURCE: United States Bureau of the Census, *Census of population: 1970, general population characteristics,* Washington, D.C.: U.S. Government Printing Office, 1972, Final Report, PC(1)-B1 United States Summary, Table 53; United States Bureau of the Census. *Current population reports,* Series P-25, no. 870, Estimates of the population of the United States, by age, race, and sex: 1976 to 1979, January 1980, Table 1 and Series P-25, no. 704, Projections of the population of the United States: 1977 to 2050, July 1977, Tables 7–9.

[a] Persons with age not reported are distributed proportionately by age.

[b] Projections are from Series II, which assumes that women average 2.1 births at the end of the childbearing years.

These fertility differentials have contributed to the more rapid increase in the older population of black and other races and to a younger age structure with a smaller proportion aged 65 and over.

Both racial groups, but especially black and other races, benefited from the control of infectious diseases and the principal childhood diseases. In 1910 these diseases accounted for 37% of all deaths to black and other races and 26% of all white deaths. By 1974 these causes accounted for only 3% of deaths to both groups. Beginning during World War I, geographic mobility to northern and urban areas provided access to better educational institutions and health services. As a result, life expectancy increased more rapidly than among whites during the 20th century. The life expectancy of black and other races was 16 years less than that of the white population in the early 1900s, but it was only 6 years less by 1974. More rapid mortality decline contributed to the more rapid growth of the population of black and other races in recent decades.

The patterns of migration of racial groups to the United States have been very different. With the end of the slave trade at the time of the Civil War, black and other races contributed little to the growing number of immigrants to the country. As a result, black and other races declined as a percentage of the total population and of the older population until 1930 (Table 2-13). Although immigration 60–80 years ago explains some of the current increase in the older white population, the current increase in the older population of black and other races is almost entirely due to changes in fertility and mortality.

The racial composition of more recent migration streams reflects the changing national origins of immigrants. Black and other races increased from 4.4% of net civilian immigration in the 1950s to 13.6% in the 1960s (Irwin and Warren, 1972). Census Bureau projections assume that 41% of annual net immigrants (including the armed forces) will be of black or other races, based on data on national origins for the year ending June 30, 1975 (United States Bureau of the Census, 1977a). These trends will increase the size of younger age groups and reduce the proportion aged 65 and over. As these immigrants age over time, however, they will add to the growing size of the older population.

By the end of the century, the older population of black and other races is expected to number 3.7 million. Past trends in fertility and mortality will result in more rapid growth than for the white population. Somewhat higher current and projected fertility and the immigration of young adults will keep the percentage aged 65 and over below that of the white population. Although blacks and other races will make up 15.9% of the total population by the year 2000, they will be only 11.5% of the older population.

Marital status and living arrangements

The characteristics of the older population in terms of marital status and living arrangements reflect the demographic trends of recent decades, especially concerning male/female differentials in mortality rates. Most older men are married and living with their spouses (75%); only 37% of older women fall into this category (see Chapter 5). The increasing prevalence of widowhood among older women (52% in 1978) is primarily a function of the higher death rates of older men and the fact that men are typically older than their wives. Men also have higher remarriage rates than women. As a result, they are more quickly reclassified as married.

Table 2-14 shows that the effects of mortality on family status are much stronger with increasing age and that the changes are greater for women than for men. Between ages 65–74 and age 75 and over, more men are likely to be widowed, but a majority are still married and living with their wives. Among women, the percentage married and living with their husbands drops from 46% for those 65–74 to 22% for those 75 and over; the percentage widowed increases to 69% in ages 75 and over.

This situation, in turn, helps to explain the much higher percentage of older women living alone (40% in 1978). This has substantially increased from 1965, when 29% of older women lived alone. For both older men and women there has been an overall decrease since 1960 in the proportion living in families, particularly with relatives other than spouses. It should be noted that, although housing and living arrangements may be separate, there is often frequent and close contact among relatives. Isolation and loneliness among older persons cannot be assumed on the basis of living arrangements alone.

Although there has been some recent discussion of a trend toward increasing "pairing" of older unmarried individuals as a way to pool economic resources and to provide companionship, census data do not bear this out. No significant change has occurred since 1960 in the proportion of older persons reported as living with unrelated individuals. To the degree that the census data in Table 2-14 accurately

TABLE 2-14. Percent distribution of the noninstitutionalized population aged 65-74 and 75 and over by marital status and by living arrangements, March 1978

	Males		Females	
	65-74	*75+*	*65-74*	*75+*
Marital status				
Total	100.0%	100.0%	100.0%	100.0%
Single	5.7	4.8	6.6	5.7
Married, spouse present	78.1	68.3	46.1	21.6
Married, spouse absent	3.0	2.1	2.2	1.3
Widowed	9.7	23.0	41.2	69.3
Divorced	3.5	1.8	3.9	2.1
Living arrangement				
Total	100.0%	100.0%	100.0%	100.0%
In families	85.0	76.6	61.8	50.0
Living alone	12.8	21.3	35.8	47.6
Living with unrelated individuals	2.2	2.1	2.4	2.4

SOURCE: United States Bureau of the Census, *Current population reports,* Series P-20, no. 338, Marital status and living arrangements: March 1978, May 1979, Table 1; Series P-23, no. 85, Social and economic characteristics of the older population: 1978, August 1979, Table 2.

represent changes in living arrangements, the proportion of people living with unrelated individuals remains around 2% for both sexes, the same proportion as in 1960. In 1978, less than 1% of households headed by males aged 65 and over were considered "two-person unmarried-couple households."

Educational attainment

The cohort perspective is especially useful in considering the educational attainment of the older population. Educational opportunities for each new cohort of students have expanded, as have educational aspirations and achievement. Since education is typically completed before age 65, reasonable projections of the educational attainment of the older population can be made. Younger cohorts will bring their educational status with them as they age.

The present population aged 65 and over compares poorly with the population aged 40-64 in educational attainment. Table 2-15 provides a breakdown by years of school completed for five-year age groups between 40-44 and 75 and over in 1977. The data indicate that 58% of the population aged 65 and over had some high school education, as compared with 30% of the population aged 75 and over. Of those who had some high school education, a larger percentage of the population 40-44 (73%) than of those aged 75 and over (54%) had completed four years. Variation in educational attainment within the older population is evident in Table 2-15.

Expected changes in educational attainment within the older population are seen in Table 2-16, based upon age-cohort projections through 1990. The change toward an increasingly better educated older population will be gradual through the year 1990, when 67% of all persons aged 65 and over will have had at least some high school education. Also by 1990, the proportion of older people having some

TABLE 2-15. Percent distribution of the population by age, by years of school completed for the United States, March 1977

Age	Total	No school	Elementary 1-8 years	High school 1-4 years	College 1 year or more
			Years of school completed		
40-44	100.0	0.6	11.7	57.8	29.9
45-49	100.0	0.7	16.6	56.0	26.7
50-54	100.0	0.7	17.8	57.7	23.8
55-59	100.0	1.0	22.7	54.6	21.7
60-64	100.0	0.8	30.0	50.9	18.3
65-69	100.0	1.2	37.1	43.4	18.3
70-74	100.0	2.1	44.0	37.6	16.3
75 and over	100.0	3.7	52.8	30.0	13.5

SOURCE: United States Bureau of the Census, *Current population reports*, Series P-20, no. 314, Educational attainment in the United States: March 1977 and 1976, December 1977, Table 1.

TABLE 2-16. Projections of the percent distribution of the population aged 65 and over by years of school completed for the United States: 1980-1990

Year	Total	Less than high school	High school 1-4 years	College 1 year or more
			Years of school completed	
1980	100.0	46.1	38.9	15.0
1985	100.0	39.1	44.7	16.2
1990	100.0	33.0	49.4	17.6

SOURCE: United States Bureau of the Census, *Current population reports*, Series P-25, no. 476, Demographic projections for the United States, February 1972, Table 5.

college education will have increased to over 17% and those with only an elementary school education will have dropped from half to one-third of all older people. Remember that the cohort aged 65 and over in 1990 represents the cohort aged 45 and over in 1970. Because most people have completed their education by age 45, these projections can be viewed as minimum figures. Further improvements will continue beyond 1990 as the rather well-educated adolescents of the 1960s and 1970s become the old people of the 21st century. The 2010-2020 "gerontic boom" will be a well-educated group of people.

Economic characteristics

The labor force participation of older males has steadily decreased from 46% in 1950 to 22% in 1975; the rates for females have been quite low and appear to have declined to 8% in 1975. This decline is reflected more recently in the participation rates of males aged 55-64. Females aged 55-64 have not shared this pattern, as their rates have increased to 41% in 1975. General decline in labor force participation is projected for these age groups through 1990. Table 2-17 shows these relationships. This reflects the increase in voluntary retirement programs, the availability of early retirement benefits in Social Security and some private pensions, and the decline in self-employment.

TABLE 2-17. Labor force participation rates for persons aged 55-64 and 65 and over by sex, selected years: 1950-1990

	Males[a]		Females[a]	
Year	55-64	65 and over	55-64	65 and over
Estimates				
1950	86.9	45.8	27.0	9.7
1955	87.9	39.6	32.5	10.6
1960	86.8	33.1	37.2	10.8
1965	84.7	27.9	41.1	10.0
1970	83.0	26.8	43.0	9.7
1975	75.8	21.7	41.0	8.3
Projections				
1980	74.3	19.9	41.9	8.1
1985	71.6	18.0	42.2	7.8
1990	69.9	16.8	42.3	7.6

SOURCE: United States Department of Labor, *Employment and training report of the president: 1976,* Washington, D.C.: U.S. Government Printing Office, 1976, Table A-2; United States Department of Labor, *New labor force projections to 1990,* special labor force report 197, Washington, D.C.: U.S. Government Printing Office, 1976, p. A-2.

[a] Percentage of the noninstitutional population in the labor force.

In line with this low and decreasing labor force participation among the elderly is the relatively low median income of the older population, as shown in Table 2-18. In 1977 the median income of families in which the head of the household was 65 or over was $9,110, just 57% of the median income for all families in that year ($16,009). However, the families headed by older persons are smaller than families headed by persons under 65, so that fewer persons have to share the family income. The per person income of families headed by persons aged 65 and over ($4,090) is 75% of the per person income in all families ($5,478). Only female-headed families with older heads have higher median incomes than all families of this type.

TABLE 2-18. Median income of families and unrelated individuals, by age of family head or unrelated individual: 1977

	Age of family head or unrelated individual	
Family type	All ages	Aged 65 and over
Families	$16,009	$ 9,110
Male head	17,517	9,156
Married, wife present	17,616	9,108
Other marital status	14,518	10,376
Female head	7,765	8,777
Unrelated individuals	5,907	3,829
Male	7,831	4,123
Female	4,840	3,762

SOURCE: United States Bureau of the Census, *Current population reports,* Series P-60, no. 118, Money income in 1977 of families and persons in the United States, March 1979, Tables 4 and 6; Series P-23, no. 85, Social and economic characteristics of the older population: 1978, August 1979, Table 25.

The gap in median income between unrelated individuals aged 65 and over and all unrelated individuals is smaller. Note also that the median income of older unrelated individuals falls below the per person income in families headed by older persons. Thus, older persons living alone or with nonrelatives are disadvantaged compared with those living in families, especially if they happen to be women.

The summary measures of median income and per person income fail to describe the distribution of the population by income. Of particular concern is the poverty status of the older population. Although the population aged 65 and over is 11% of the total population, older poor persons are 13% of the total population below poverty. About 14% of persons 65 and over in 1977 lived in families or as unrelated individuals with incomes below the official poverty level. The proportion of older poor persons has actually declined since 1970, when one-fourth were in poverty. Figure 2-4 illustrates the composition of the older population by poverty status and family status. Of all family status groups, female unrelated individuals are most likely to be living in poverty. These women constitute one-half of all the older persons in poverty, although they are only one-quarter of the total older population.

The economic situation of older people remains a major problem, despite contemporary increases in benefits from Social Security, private pension plans, Medicare, and other income maintenance and in-kind transfer programs. Food, housing, and health care costs are rising far more quickly than are the economic resources of older people, especially those not in the labor force, those located in city centers, unrelated individuals, women, and black and other races. Indeed, the combination of relatively fixed incomes and substantial annual inflation adds to the economic plight of these older persons.

CONCLUDING REMARKS

The simple fact that there are now more older people in the United States than in previous years is but a small part of the overall story. When we look for the "causes" of increasing numbers of older persons, we must look to the high fertility rates of previous decades coupled with dramatic reductions in infant mortality. Another "cause" of a growing older population is a declining younger population, which is one result of a reduction in current fertility and population growth rates. Thus, the same absolute number of older persons becomes a larger proportion of the population when fewer babies, children, and adolescents are part of that population.

The growing number and proportion of older persons have many effects upon society, and a discussion of the demography of aging is not the place for a full consideration of the social policy implications of aging. Yet some of the demographic facts and indicators discussed here directly suggest the kinds of problems with which the leaders of society must work.

The dependency ratio draws our attention to the potential political implications of a changing proportional mix of age groups in society. As long as only a relatively small number of old people are drawing pensions and a large number of younger working people are contributing to those pension systems, the financial problems may be minimal. But the changing population composition, as suggested by the trends in the dependency ratios, predicts a future time when a larger number of old people will

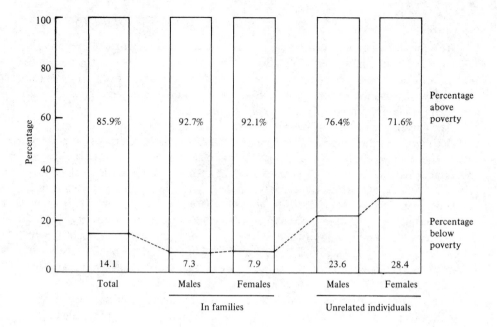

(A) Persons aged 65 and over: Composition of family status groups by poverty status: 1977

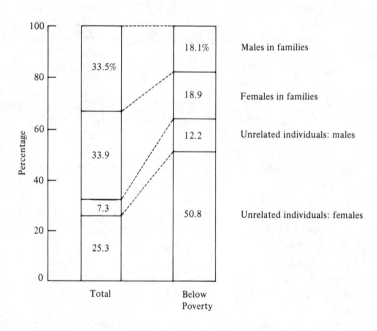

(B) Persons aged 65 and over: Composition of poverty status groups by family status: 1977

Figure 2-4 (A) (B). Characteristics of the population aged 65 and over by poverty and family status. (*United States Bureau of the Census,* Current population reports, *Series P-60, no. 119, Characteristics of the population below the poverty level: 1977, March 1979, Table 3; Series P-23, no. 85, Social and economic characteristics of the older population: 1978, August 1979, Table 2*)

have to be supported by a society with a decreasing proportion of younger workers. Clearly such a situation has public policy and political implications, as well as social and economic ones.

The combination of fixed incomes, regularized trends in inflation, and a growing older population implies a range of economic security problems and issues. Certainly not only the aged are affected by difficult economic times. Yet, as our discussion and a number of other analyses have indicated, the old are disproportionately represented among the poor in the United States. Furthermore, old age acts to accentuate other inequalities in the social and economic system, such that when age is combined with minority, racial, and ethnic status, the problems of poverty, disease, labor-force discrimination, and other dislocations become greater for the individuals concerned.

The higher mortality of older males has resulted in a substantially greater preponderance of females in the older population. Thus, a substantial number of old people are widows who live alone; public policy in the domain of housing for the elderly must take into consideration some of the unique demographic aspects indicated by old-age sex ratios. Moreover, this kind of information has implications for medical care, transportation, income maintenance, and tax policy.

Finally, our consideration of the changing educational composition of the population, when combined with the concept of the birth cohort, implies that future cohorts of older persons will be much better educated than past and even contemporary cohorts of older persons. Thus, many of our social and political stereotypes of the elderly, even to the degree that such stereotypes are based on informed observations of old people, will be out of date. (See Chapter 7 for the psychological implications of cohort differences in education and Chapter 19 for estimates of the political influence of future cohorts of the elderly.) Tomorrow's cohorts of old people will represent today's cohorts of substantially educated, socially conscious, and politically active and experienced people. Although we cannot predict with certainty that the cohorts that were involved in civil rights and student protest activities will be "senior activists" when they reach their 60s and 70s, we should at least seriously consider such a possibility.

Therefore, demographic analysis can provide the descriptive parameters of tomorrow's older population, and thereby offer insight into some of the economic and social problems that are likely to be precipitated by the predicted age changes in the composition of the population. At the same time, however, demographic analysis predicts that tomorrow's older persons will be, perhaps, in a better position in terms of education, skill, and experience to deal with these problems on the basis of both individual and collective action.

REFERENCES

Barclay, G. W. *Techniques of population analysis.* New York: John Wiley and Sons, 1958.

Chiles, L. C. Chairman's opening statement for *Work after 65: Options for the 80's.* Hearing before the United States Senate Special Committee on Aging, Part 1, April 23, 1980. Washington, D.C.: U.S. Government Printing Office, 1980.

Coale, A. J. The effects of changes in mortality and fertility on age composition. *Milbank Memorial Fund Quarterly,* 1956, *34*, 79–114.

Cutler, N. E. The aging population and social policy. In R. H. Davis (Ed.), *Aging: Prospects and issues* (2nd ed.). Los Angeles: University of Southern California Press, 1981.

Dublin, L. I., Lotka, A. J., & Spiegelman, M. *Length of life: A study of the life table* (Rev. ed.). New York: Ronald Press, 1949.

Harris, L. *The myth and reality of aging in America.* Washington, D.C.: National Council on the Aging, 1975.

Hermalin, A. I. The effect of changes in mortality rates on population growth and age distribution in the United States. *Milbank Memorial Fund Quarterly*, 1966, *44*, 451–469.

Irwin, R., & Warren, R. Demographic aspects of American immigration. In C. F. Westoff & R. Parke, Jr. (Eds.), *Demographic and social aspects of population growth*, United States Commission on Population Growth and the American Future, Vol. 1 of Commission Research Reports, pp. 167–178. Washington, D.C.: U.S. Government Printing Office, 1972.

Mannheim, K. The problem of generations. In Paul Kecskemeti (Ed. and trans.), *Essays on the sociology of knowledge*, pp. 276–322. London: Routledge and Kegan Paul, 1928 (1952).

Ryder, N. B. The cohort as a concept in the study of social change. *American Sociological Review*, 1965, *30*, 843–861.

Sauvy, A. *General theory of population.* Paris: University of France Press, 1954.

Siegel, J. S. Prospective trends in the size and structure of the elderly population, impact of mortality trends, and some implications. In *Current population reports*, Series P-23, no. 78. Washington, D.C.: U.S. Government Printing Office, January 1979.

Taeuber, I. B. The changing distribution of the population of the United States in the twentieth century. In S. M. Mazie (Ed.), *Population, distribution, and policy*, United States Commission on Population Growth and the American Future, Vol. 5 of Commission Research Reports, pp. 29–107. Washington, D.C.: U.S. Government Printing Office, 1972.

Torrey, B. B. *Demographic shifts and projections: The implications for pension systems.* Working Papers. Washington, D.C.: President's Commission on Pension Policy, 1979.

United Nations. *Demographic yearbook: 1977.* New York: United Nations, 1978.

United States Bureau of the Census. *Census of population: Characteristics of the population.* Washington, D.C.: U.S. Government Printing Office, 1940 and 1970.

United States Bureau of the Census. *Current population reports*, Series P-25, no. 460. Preliminary intercensal estimates of states and components of population change, 1960 to 1970. Washington, D.C.: U.S. Government Printing Office, June 1971.

United States Bureau of the Census. *Census of population: 1970, general population characteristics*, Final Report, PC(1)-B1 United States Summary, Washington, D.C.: U.S. Government Printing Office, 1972a.

United States Bureau of the Census. *Current population reports*, Series P-25, no. 476. Demographic projections for the United States. Washington, D.C.: U.S. Government Printing Office, 1972b (February).

United States Bureau of the Census. *Historical statistics of the United States, colonial times to 1970, Bicentennial Edition, Part 2.* Washington, D.C.: U.S. Government Printing Office, 1975a, Series C138–142.

United States Bureau of the Census. *Current population reports*, Series P-23, no. 57. Social and economic characteristics of the older population: 1974. Washington, D.C.: U.S. Government Printing Office, 1975b (November).

United States Bureau of the Census. *Current population reports*, Series P-23, no. 59. Demographic aspects of aging and the older population in the United States. Washington, D.C.: U.S. Government Printing Office, 1976 (May).

United States Bureau of the Census. *Current population reports,* Series P-25, no. 704. Projections of the population of the United States: 1977 to 2050. Washington, D.C.: U.S. Government Printing Office, 1977a (July).

United States Bureau of the Census. *Current population reports,* Series P-20, no. 314. Educational attainment in the United States: March 1977 and 1976. Washington, D.C.: U.S. Government Printing Office, 1977b (December).

United States Bureau of the Census. *Current population reports,* Series P-20, no. 331. Geographical mobility: March 1975 to March 1978. Washington, D.C.: U.S. Government Printing Office, 1978 (November).

United States Bureau of the Census. *Current population reports,* Series P-60, no. 118. Money income in 1977 of families and persons in the United States. Washington, D.C.: U.S. Government Printing Office, 1979a (March).

United States Bureau of the Census. *Current population reports,* Series P-60, no. 119. Characteristics of the population below the poverty level: 1977. Washington, D.C.: U.S. Government Printing Office, 1979b (March).

United States Bureau of the Census. *Current population reports,* Series P-20, no. 338. Marital status and living arrangements: March 1978. Washington, D.C.: U.S. Government Printing Office, 1979c (May).

United States Bureau of the Census. *Current population reports,* Series P-23, no. 80. The social and economic status of the black population in the United States: An historical view, 1790–1978. Washington, D.C.: U.S. Government Printing Office, 1979d (June).

United States Bureau of the Census. *Current population reports,* Series P-23, no. 85. Social and economic characteristics of the older population: 1978. Washington, D.C.: U.S. Government Printing Office, 1979e (August).

United States Bureau of the Census. *Current population reports,* Series P-25, no. 870. Estimates of the population of the United States, by age, race, and sex: 1976 to 1979. Washington, D.C.: U.S. Government Printing Office, 1980 (January).

United States Department of Labor. *Employment and training report of the President: 1976.* Washington, D.C.: U.S. Government Printing Office, 1976a.

United States Department of Labor. *New labor force projections to 1990, special labor force report 197.* Washington, D.C.: U.S. Government Printing Office, 1976b.

United States Public Health Service, National Center for Health Statistics. *Monthly vital statistics report,* 22 (13). Washington, D.C.: U.S. Government Printing Office, 1974a (June).

United States Public Health Service, National Center for Health Statistics. *Vital statistics of the United States: 1970, Volume II–Mortality, Part A.* Washington, D.C.: U.S. Government Printing Office, 1974b.

United States Public Health Service, National Center for Health Statistics. United States life tables by causes of death: 1969–1971, *United States decennial life tables for 1969–1971,* Vol. 1, no. 5. Washington, D.C.: U.S. Government Printing Office, 1975 (May).

United States Public Health Service, National Center for Health Statistics. *Vital statistics of the United States: 1975, Volume I–Natality.* Washington, D.C.: U.S. Government Printing Office, 1978.

United States Public Health Service, National Center for Health Statistics. *Monthly vital statistics report,* 27 (11) Supplement, Advance report, final natality statistics, 1977. Washington, D.C.: U.S. Government Printing Office, 1979a (February).

United States Public Health Service, National Center for Health Statistics. *Monthly vital statistics report,* 28 (1) Supplement, Advance report, final mortality statistics, 1977. Washington, D.C.: U.S. Government Printing Office, 1979b (May).

Youmans, E. G. *Older rural americans: A sociological perspective.* Lexington: University of Kentucky Press, 1967.

CHAPTER **3**

Ethnic Minority Aging

Sharon Y. Moriwaki and Frances S. Kobata

The needs and problems of ethnic minority elderly were first brought to the attention of the nation at the 1971 White House Conference on Aging. Since that time, minority aging has had greater visibility. Research, advocacy efforts, and service programs have emerged. Although some of the research focuses on aging patterns across cultures, much of the current effort focuses on needs assessments, particularly as they relate to services and service delivery. Perhaps because of the disproportionately poorer life conditions experienced by this segment, and thus the urgency of determining needs and attitudes toward services, development of theoretical paradigms—although much needed—has lagged. Although progress has been made, the field is still highly fragmented and inconclusive. The only consistent conclusion is that the minority elderly comprise many subgroups with diverse lifestyles. In itself, this poses one of our greatest problems in understanding the aging process. To date, no conceptual framework has been developed to analyze the differences and similarities between and within groups of minority older persons.

This chapter attempts to piece together the fragmented and inconclusive data available on ethnic minority elderly. Although we make generalizations from existing sources on the subject, we caution the reader to avoid rigidly applying these generalizations; rather, one should keep in mind intra- and intergroup diversity and variation. We raise issues here that may stimulate further exploration of the complex world of the minority elderly. The first section presents a brief demographic profile of the ethnic minority elderly groups on which data are available. The following section examines whether ethnicity does make a difference in human behavior. In the third and fourth sections we explore the relationship between ethnicity and "minority" status and experiences in America. The fifth section provides a framework for understanding the influence of ethnicity as a support network for the elderly. This is followed by an overview of current programs that have been developed to serve minority elders. The final section summarizes implications for future research, training, and service.

WHO ARE THE ETHNIC MINORITY ELDERLY?

For the purposes of this chapter, ethnic minority elderly are those who belong to groups whose language and physical and cultural characteristics make them visible and identifiable—people of color. These are blacks, Hispanics (Mexican Americans/Chicanos, Puerto Ricans, Cubans, and Latin Americans), Native Americans, and Pacific/Asians (Japanese, Chinese, Pilipino,[1] Korean, Guamanian, Samoan, other Pacific Islanders, and the newer immigrants from Southeast Asia).

With the increase in interest in ethnic minority elderly during the past decade, the lack of useful demographic data about ethnic elders in American society has become apparent. For example, we lack ethnic-specific data on the elderly, not only on morbidity and life expectancy, but on other essential characteristics such as income, housing conditions, and chronic and limiting health conditions. The census has been the primary data base for most agencies planning for minority elderly; however, it has been under attack from many sectors for its undercounting of minority subgroups and misclassifications of individuals (P/AERP, 1978; Rogers & Gallion, 1978; Siegel, 1968).

Although the Bureau of the Census has made serious efforts to obtain greater accuracy in its 1980 enumeration, at the time of this writing, we are still left with the inaccurate counts of the 1970 census. At that time there were approximately 2.8 million ethnic minority elderly aged 60 and older. According to the census, the ethnic minority elderly groups, from largest to smallest, are black, Hispanic, Native American, Japanese, Chinese, Pilipino, Hawaiian, and Korean (see Table 3-1). Although small in

TABLE 3-1. Ethnic/racial minorities 60 years and older, 1970

Ethnic group	Population	Percentage of ethnic group population
Black	2,330,242	10.3
Hispanic	326,621	3.6
Native American	63,809	8.0
Japanese	61,711	10.5
Chinese	40,287	9.3
Pilipino	36,667	10.9
Hawaiian	6,089	6.1
Korean	3,270	5.0
All other	14,175	6.0
Total	2,882,871	8.4

SOURCE: U.S. Bureau of the Census. *Characteristics of the population—Volume 1, Part I.* Washington, D.C.: U.S. Government Printing Office, 1970.

numbers (about 10% of the total population aged 60 and older), this segment has brought increased attention to its needs because of its rapid growth. For example, between 1960 and 1970, the white population increased by 22%; however, the nonwhite population increased by 38.9% (see Table 3-2). Furthermore, the increase was

[1]*Pilipino* is used throughout this chapter to refer to persons whose mother country is the Philippine Islands. Since there is no *F* sound in the Pilipino language, the Pilipino community prefers that the spelling be with a *P*.

greatest for those in the most vulnerable age categories (aged 75 years and older), increasing by 99.2% for nonwhite minorities as compared to 73.4% among their white counterparts.

TABLE 3-2. **Comparison of white and nonwhite elderly population, 1960–1970**

| | White | | | Nonwhite | | |
Age	1960	1970	Increase	1960	1970	Increase
Total population 60+	21,478,576	26,193,850	22.0	1,840,558	2,556,250	38.9
60–64	6,519,629	7,834,302	20.2	592,268	814,629	37.5
65–69	5,668,320	6,290,291	11.0	518,443	693,050	33.7
70–74	4,312,863	4,985,511	15.6	348,273	463,245	33.0
75–79	2,759,955	3,581,952	29.8	217,392	288,106	32.5
80–84	1,420,987	2,120,102	49.2	97,219	163,821	68.5
85+	796,822	1,381,692	73.4	66,963	133,399	99.2

SOURCE: U.S. Bureau of the Census. *Characteristics of the population – Volume 1, Part I.* Washington, D.C.: U.S. Government Printing Office, 1970.

Further justification for addressing the needs of ethnic minority elders is seen in their lower income levels. Although the problem of living on drastically reduced incomes is encountered by the elderly in general, particularly after age 65, the problem is even more severe for minority elders. For example, the proportion of the total population (including families and unrelated individuals) who had incomes below the poverty level in 1975 was 12.3%. In contrast, among those 65 years and older, 15.3% were living below the poverty level. For black elderly, however, 36.3% over 65 had incomes below the poverty level (census data cited in NCOA, 1978, p. 44).

The mean annual incomes of those aged 65 and older who were working in 1974 was less than half of those aged 45–64, or $6,505, compared to $10,964. The income for black elders aged 65 and older was even lower at $3,694 compared to whites at $6,794. For both black and white alike, women over 65 had incomes disproportionately lower than men. Thus, even for those working, incomes were not adequate for the minority elderly.

The lower incomes of minority elderly can be viewed as a result of discrimination in the labor force during their younger years. In 1975, for example, 16% of minority men and 39% of minority women aged 45–64 worked part-time or full-time for less than 27 weeks. Additionally, the unemployment statistics for the same year indicate that for all age groups, minorities were more likely to be unemployed; the unemployment rate of males aged 45–54 was 4.4% for white, as compared to 9.0% for minorities. Although those aged 55 and older were less likely to be in the labor force and looking for work, the unemployment rate was still higher for minority elderly males: 6.1% for minorities, as compared to 4.1% for their white counterparts (U.S. Department of Labor, 1979).

In short, the demographic profile of the ethnic minority elderly, based on the fragmented data available, reflects a segment of our population with poorer life conditions and limited access to resources and opportunities.

WHAT IS ETHNICITY?

To determine whether knowledge of ethnic background is important in understanding behavior and attitudes toward aging, we should first define *ethnicity*. Ethnicity is a complex social variable that involves three components: culture, social status, and support subsystems (Moriwaki, 1976). Together they influence the individual's self-concept and, in turn, interact with the individual's present life circumstances to produce a unique pattern of adjustment to aging.

Novak (cited in Solomon, 1977) answers the question "What is an ethnic group?" in rather lyrical terms.

> It is a group with historical memory, real or imaginary. One belongs to an ethnic group in part involuntarily, in part by choice. . . . Ethnic memory is not a series of events remembered, but rather a set of instincts, feelings, intimacies, expectations, patterns of emotion and behavior; a sense of reality; a set of stories for individuals—and for the people as a whole—to live out [p. 21].

Ethnicity, then, provides some understanding of the behaviors and attitudes of the ethnic elderly by identifying the culturally conditioned beliefs, values, and attitudes of their heritage. First-generation immigrants have a world view and language derived from a country different from the one in which they are now old. They learned early how their parents and other community members treated each other and how they treated their elders. For example, the elderly were a symbol of order and predictability for the Japanese immigrants. They came primarily from small farming villages in southwestern Japan, where ancestor worship was important in tying genealogy to their land. The aged directed ceremonies and were highly respected, since they would soon become ancestors who would watch over the family.

This example emphasizes the importance of understanding the culture in which ethnic elders were socialized. Their initial world view seems to be what is best remembered in old age. The problem for many of the immigrant elderly, however, stems from their growing old in an environment much different from that of their beginnings. Kalish and Moriwaki (1973) suggested that the Japanese and Chinese elderly tried to maintain the values and customs of the old country because they expected to make their fortunes and then return to their homelands. They transplanted their values, language, and rules of behavior. They also transmitted these to their children in order to facilitate their adjustment on returning home. But streets in the new country were not lined with gold, and the Asian immigrant grew old in a foreign land with children socialized in a different country and at a different time.

Two ethnic groups, however, did not follow the pattern of immigration, arrival, prejudice, and acceptance: the American Indian, who was already here, and the black, who was captured and brought unwillingly to toil on the Southern plantations. The histories of these two groups differ from the other ethnic minorities, and, consequently, the elderly of these groups have had different cultural experiences. Pinckney (1969) discussed the situation of black Americans. When they were uprooted from their native lands and randomly sold to Southern plantation owners, they were unable to keep intact their tribal customs and organizations. Few aspects of Negro life today, with the possible exception of religion, stem from their past native culture.

WHAT IS A MINORITY?

The National Urban League's approach that "Today's aged Negro is different from today's aged white because he is Negro . . . and this alone should be enough basis for differential treatment" focuses on the minority situation and ethnic stratification as the means for acquiring resources in the larger social network. Minority status connotes categorical and differential treatment. According to Louis Wirth (1945):

> We may define a minority as a group of people who, because of their physical or cultural characteristics, are singled out from the others in the society . . . for differential and unequal treatment, and who therefore regard themselves as objects of collective discrimination. The existence of a minority in a society implies the existence of a corresponding dominant group with higher social status and greater privileges. Minority status carries with it the exclusion from full participation in the life of the society [p. 47].

Statistical underrepresentation does not, in itself, account for groups being considered minorities in the sociological sense. It is not even a necessary condition (Rose, 1964). Those groups that have unequal access to power, that are considered in some way unworthy of sharing power equally, and that are stigmatized in terms of assumed inferior traits or characteristics are minority groups (Mindel & Habenstein, 1976). The salient variables in defining minority status are the patterns of relationships, the distribution of power, and the assumed differences in character traits.

Any discussion of aging as a social process in America would be incomplete without some attention to the experiences of the minority elderly, who make up a small but significant segment of the total aging population. Each of the many ethnic minority subpopulations in the United States has a unique history. Each has developed its own method of coping with the inevitable conflicts between traditional and adopted lifestyles. As Kent (1971) points out in referring to these groups:

> Each of the groups is a minority and exhibits many of the characteristics associated with minority status. Each encounters discrimination; each has developed coping behavior that, together with a physical separation, has given rise to distinctive subcultures. The unity among these groups lies in the fact of minority position . . . the diversity between groups lies in the distinctive patterning of life [p. 26].

The vulnerabilities and strengths resulting from shared experience have led to negative and positive consequences for adjustment to aging.

THE MINORITY EXPERIENCE

An examination of the minority experience will provide insights into some of the situational factors affecting the attitudes and behavior of ethnic minority elders.

Significance of the minority experience

Most research on aging has been based on limited samples, primarily of middle-class whites, from which overgeneralizations have been made. Only recently has the field of minority aging emerged and focused concern on the life histories and current conditions of this segment of the population. To understand more fully the aging process in general and the effects of minority experiences on aging, Moore (1971) suggests examining what is inherent in the minority situation—rather than focusing on minority status per se. She presents five characteristics of the minority situation that are relevant to aging:

1. Each minority group has a *special history*.
2. The special history has been accompanied by *discrimination*.
3. A *subculture* has developed.
4. *Coping structures* have developed.
5. *Rapid change* is occurring.

On a more personal level we can examine the impact of the minority experience as leading to a certain self-consciousness and uncertainty about one's status (Kramer, 1970). This self-consciousness may remain as a telltale trace and reveal minority member status when other signs have faded: "I think the thing that irks us most is the teasing uncertainty of it all. Did the man at the box office give us the seat behind the post on purpose? Is the shopgirl impudent or merely nervous? Had the position really been filled before we applied for it?" (Jessie Fauset, in Davie, 1949, p. 439).

"Teasing uncertainties" include being turned away from housing in more desirable neighborhoods with oft-repeated, "Sorry, it was just rented" or "It was just sold." Doors to certain clubs, organizations, and institutions are closed. The world of the minority elderly has been shaped by such individual experiences as well as by group responses that have been passed along in the stream of culture. The social and psychological consequences of repeated rejection, denial, segregation, and exclusion extending over the life cycle into old age have not been sufficiently studied or explored. The lack of data severely impedes our understanding of the implications of long-term societal neglect and its effect on the aging minority member's adjustment to aging.

Historical kaleidoscope: A collective experience

The history of the United States has been a history of diverse groups. As most new national groups arrived from abroad, they were likely to encounter hostility for one or two generations. Eventually, however, their members were able to move out of the slums, acquire better paying jobs, and achieve social respect and dignity. This has not been true of such nonwhite groups as blacks, Asians, Hispanics, and Native Americans. Many of today's elderly are immigrants from other countries. At least 1.6 million are persons of minority backgrounds (Butler & Lewis, 1977; Maykovich, 1972). Kent (1971) goes on to say that this diversity has long been a source of pride in America. Few nations have been so varied, and even fewer have permitted or encouraged the preservation of variant cultural patterns in which subcultures abound, creating a variety of patterns of aging. According to Butler and Lewis (1977), two major and distinctly separate issues need to be kept in mind when considering the minority elderly: the unique culture of each group, which affects its lifestyle; and the effect that living in a majority culture has had on their lives.

The historical memory of each group has been unique. Conquest, prolonged conflict, and annexation are antecedents linking the history of the Native Americans and the Mexicans; dehumanizing enslavement and its special institutional forms in America are unique to the blacks; varied immigration and migration patterns of the Asian and Hispanic peoples have resulted in a cycle of recruitment, exploitation, and exclusion.

Our country was being settled at the very time the racial cleavages began to be drawn. Kramer (1970) and Simpson and Yinger (1965) recount in some detail the consequences of deculturation of the American Indian and blacks through conquest and enslavement. "The humiliation of a people without a culture is perhaps more exquisite than that of the man without a country, whatever his sensibility. The real issue is, nevertheless, the particular—and peculiar—history that impels each . . . toward self-validation" (Kramer, 1970, p. 189).

A variation on the theme of historical memory is the cyclic pattern of immigration and migration of the Asian and Hispanic groups over the years. The period prior to and immediately following the turn of the century saw a new phase, particularly on the West Coast. Racial cleavages were extended to immigrants from Asia: initially with the influx of the Chinese, later to the Japanese and Pilipinos, and more recently to the newer immigrants from Southeast Asia and Cuba. As each new group grew in number and began to compete economically, restrictive legislation was enacted to exclude further immigration from these countries. Federal legislation in 1882 and 1892 sealed off further immigration from China; the enactment of the Alien Land Laws of 1913 and 1920, combined with the Alien Exclusion Act of 1924, virtually brought to a halt all immigration from Japan. Curtailment of Pilipino immigration followed in 1935. Throughout the 1920s and 1930s, a massive repatriation effort was directed against the Mexicans (Daniels & Kitano, 1970; Simpson & Yinger, 1965). These campaigns for restriction and exclusion have made today's minority elderly a unique cohort isolated not only from its counterparts in their countries of origin, but also from the contact that a continuing flow of immigrants from their homelands would have afforded. Newcomers entering the United States following the lifting of restrictions in 1965 have been members of a younger generation, who grew up in a different era with values unlike those of a half-century ago. Such circumstances have created a subculture of men and women who belong to a vanished era.

Since social interaction requires mutual intelligibility, the frustration of not being able to bridge the gap of experience increases the sense of alienation and isolation among the minority elderly. Solomon (1972) cautions that it is unrealistic to assume that the black aged constitute a homogeneous group, as though they had all had the same life experiences. On the other hand, Golden (1976) cites Jackson as arguing that race is indeed a reality and that black old people should not be treated as though they were the same as white old people. Jackson believes racism has adversely affected the black's preparation for old age. In essence, all minority groups can share these sentiments.

The historical events recounted earlier are not in the too distant past for many of the ethnic minorities of today. For some they have become an ethnic memory, for others the experiences are still vividly imprinted on their minds and souls, and for yet others life continues to bring daily reminders of separateness.

One outcome of minority status is a lifestyle of hypervigilance (suspicion, caution, and guardedness)—a form of cultural paranoia that many minorities have adopted as a mechanism to deal with the external world. At issue is whether this adaptation has been positive.

Discrimination and stereotypes

The literature abounds with analyses of the patterns of prejudice, discrimination, segregation, and even annihilation; yet viable solutions for eliminating such practices are far from being realized for many of today's elderly. One of the dangers of institutionalized discrimination is that it pervades the entire system so that those with racial prejudices find validation for their prejudgments (Allport, 1958; Daniels & Kitano, 1970; Kramer, 1970; Rose, 1964; Simpson & Yinger, 1965). Discrimination in its most common forms has been experienced in housing, employment, educational or recreational opportunities, churches, health care, or other social privileges. All groups have received their share of discriminatory practices in varying degrees of intensity. According to Butler and Lewis (1977), our historical gifts to minority citizens have been poverty, poor housing, and lack of medical care and education.

A concomitant feature of discrimination is the emergence of stereotypes, which grow out of our need to justify hostilities, to order our complex world, or to simplify the categories we assign to groups. Labels such as the "inscrutable Oriental" or the "happy-go-lucky black" and epithets of "lazy," "filthy," or "sneaky and sly" have had deleterious effects on the self-concept of minority groups. Although stereotypes are not always negative, in most instances the attributes assigned to groups classify them as inferior.

Assumptions based on inaccurate stereotypes are frequently made about particular groups; when acted upon, such assumptions can lead to further alienation of basic human rights. For example, it has been a common belief that "Asians take care of their own." This myth fails to take into account the many elderly Chinese and Pilipino men, who were denied opportunities to establish families because of the Exclusion Acts, for whom such a care system does not exist. The stereotypic notion that problems do not exist because Asians look after their own has resulted in these groups being deprived of adequate attention and resources. Needless suffering goes unnoticed and unattended.

Status changes

The effects of minority status on the elderly are influenced by time. Assimilation occurs with succeeding generations, which affects the group's status or position in society. Societal attitudes may also affect the minority situation. Moore (1971) notes that discriminatory practices and stereotypes are now being attacked and displaced. Changes in status occur not only with each succeeding generation but also as a result of international events.

The racial distance studies by Bogardus (1959) reflect changing attitudes toward ethnic groups over a 30-year period. He reported on the status of 30 ethnic groups in 1926, 1946, and 1956. His data reflect the relationship between international events and the status of entire national groups. For example, the Japanese were highest on the social distance scale during World War II (1946), but their perceived distance was lower after their defeat and the shift toward democracy (1956).

NATURAL CARE AND SUPPORT SYSTEMS

One outcome of discrimination and stereotyping is the selective association within minority groups; this gives rise to subcultures, and more particularly, to informal ethnic networks that buffer against discrimination, prejudice, and the unfamiliar customs, language, and institutions of the dominant host society. The ethnic group acts as the reference and membership group with which people identify and through which they find self-worth. Our identity or self-image depends on how we define ourselves in terms of the values and attitudes that have been learned and accepted; but it is also modified by how we are treated by others, particularly by those who are significant in our lives.

Although many commonalities related to minority experience exist among different ethnic groups and subgroups, their heterogeneity cannot be overemphasized. In general, there is no definitive research that addresses such issues as the minority elders' interpretation and expectation of care and support in their later years. Historically, the family, church, and community have usually been viewed as their major support systems.

Family

The world of the minority elderly has, to a large extent, been limited to the ghettos, barrios, reservations, and enclaves cut off from interaction with the dominant group. This has been true for those in the rural areas of the South and Southwest, where reverence and attachment to the land placed a value on the extended family and on the role assigned to older members (Maldonado, 1975).

Familial support and expectations vary by ethnic group, social class, and subculture. The literature on minority groups provides strong evidence that the role of the nuclear and extended family is still viable for many ethnic communities (Alvarez & Bean, 1976; Bell, Kasschau, & Zellman, 1976; Bengtson, 1976; Kitano & Kitamura, 1976; Price, 1976; Solomon, 1976). For each minority group the family has played an important role in transmitting cultural values, beliefs, customs, and practices and has given relative stability and sanctuary in a hostile world. Subcultural identities are maintained and preserved through the values of filial piety among Asians; the idealized role of the extended family, including relatives and *compadres* (godparents) among Mexican-Americans; the extended or augmented families that provide support and maintain continuity in the black community; and the kinship system and its lines of descent among the Native Americans.

In discussing the traditional Japanese family, Kitano (1969) describes filial responsibility as "a reciprocal obligation from parent to child and child to parent." Within this cultural framework the elders would expect their children to assume total responsibility for parental needs in old age. Other first-generation minority elders with similar traditions are likely to have the same expectations of their children. This is true for the Mexican-American culture, where the family, *curanderos* (folk healers), and church provided needed support (Andrulus, 1977; Padilla, Carolos, & Keefe, 1976; Trinidad, 1977). Reliance on the extended family for support and guidance is also fundamental to the black elderly. A recent exploratory study found that regardless of marital or employment status, the family was the primary source of support (Anderson, 1978). However, it is still not uncommon to hear elderly blacks say that they pray to God they will not become an economic or social burden to their children.

Church

Ethnic churches have played a major role in most of the minority communities, since they were usually the first institutions to be established. Kramer (1970) states that for many immigrants religion was the only experience they could carry unchanged from their old home to their new life. The church, which was the only institution that was completely transferable, was a source of comfort to the first generation when they experienced the stress of uprooting and isolation.

As a primary social institution in the minority community, the church offers psychic support to its members in general and to the elderly in particular. A study of mental health services for Spanish-speaking/surnamed populations (Padilla, Ruiz, & Alvarez, 1975) noted that individuals with emotional or "spiritual" problems were more likely to seek out or be referred to clergy than mental health professionals for comfort and reassurance.

Kitano (1969) cites a similar religiosity among the Issei (first-generation Japanese immigrants), whose average age is now in the middle 80s. They attend both Buddhist and Christian churches in large numbers and appear to be seeking reassurance in the face of aging and death. For the black elders, the church and religion are pervasive forces in the community (Jackson & Wood, 1976; Solomon, 1976; Swanson & Harter, 1971). Plumpp (1972) proposed that since the black church is the only institution for instilling a sense of self-determination, it can be a major force for change. Further corroboration comes from Solomon (1976), who sees the church as the most stable organization in black communities, and thus the most viable mechanism for service delivery.

Community

Institutional structures in minority communities have functioned to help their members cope with the alien society as well as with the vicissitudes of life in a new country. As Kramer (1970) suggests, "The fact that they live in communities provides them with the social support that permits constructive action."

Identifiable and visible minority communities as we know them today had their origins in the ghettos of the first generation. The uprooted immigrants and displaced groups formed ethnic enclaves to meet their needs in an alien society. Within the boundaries of these communities, which are to some extent physically segregated and socially isolated, a social system parallel to that of the host society evolved. The support subsystem, as described by Moriwaki (1976), served as a buffer against acts of discrimination and the strange language and customs of the dominant society. Kramer (1970) and Kitano (1969) noted that in the process of developing a subculture as a reaction to external pressure from a hostile society, cultural insulation served to strengthen the cohesiveness of the community and to perpetuate the distinctive values, beliefs, and norms of the group. Similar language, food preferences, and common experiences were further sources of communal strength and cohesion. But a price is exacted, for in adapting to a subculture, participation in the larger society is impeded. For the elderly Japanese, despite their alienation from American society, integration within an ethnic community—where values are affirmed—compensates for loss and mitigates the likelihood of alienation (Maykovich, 1972). The emergence of a minority community, especially for immigrants, is not a re-creation of the original community or village in the old country but an adaptation to minority status (Kramer, 1970).

Solomon (1976) points out the difficulty of specifying what constitutes the black community. Geographic boundaries alone do not define a community. The involuntary and forced limits on residential options have created ghetto centers rather than integrated communities where major functions are carried out by social organizations over which one has some control. According to Solomon, an important ingredient in defining community is the presence of a degree of personal intimacy among the residents of a particular physical space. The incorporation of children into other than nuclear families, especially those headed by older women, as well as the taking in of relatives, suggests that intimacy and a feeling of community do exist.

The Japanese and Chinese communities (Little Tokyos and Chinatowns), by contrast, developed an elaborate network of associations and institutions to support their members. The early immigrants, who are today's elderly, viewed themselves as sojourners who always expected to return to their homeland, however long their residence in the United States. This orientation strengthened ethnic solidarity, leading to exclusive association with kinship groups (Kramer, 1970). As discrimination and prejudice intensified, the ethnic community provided a certain degree of refuge and security. In time, associations to perform familial and welfare functions developed: *kenjin-kais* (Japanese prefectural organizations), benevolent societies, ethnic churches, language schools, athletic leagues, and merchants' associations. This created a community within a community, where cultural values were reinforced to encourage in-group solidarity. For the Japanese, the social organization was severely dislocated with the wartime evacuation in 1942. Following the war, re-created communities have emerged, and they increasingly feel the strain of no longer being able to fulfill all the needs of their members (Kitano, 1969).

Although community support and cohesiveness may range from total support to little more than the comfort that comes from being with people who look and talk like oneself, such support is still significant to the minority elderly after a lifetime of prejudice and discrimination on "the outside" (Moore, 1971).

The language patterns of ethnic elders are crucial but often overlooked aspects of minority communities. Among the major subcultural groups, a significant number are handicapped by their inability to speak English. Asian- and Spanish-speaking elders are particularly vulnerable because of their lack of proficiency in the dominant language, which contributes to their sense of estrangement and isolation.

At the same time, the shared language has contributed toward the preservation of their subculture and the maintenance of segregated communities. Numerous works have been written on the role of language in the formulation of the world view (Giglioli, 1972; Hall, 1959; Kramer, 1970; Lynd, 1958; Sotomayor, 1977). Through this function of language the attitudes of individuals and groups and, by extension, their personalities and behaviors, are shaped (Sotomayor, 1977). If we apply this principle to the minority elderly, we find a mosaic of experiences viewed through multiple lenses, and this pattern contributes further to their heterogeneity.

Changing cultures and changing values

The strength of the community as a reference group—a source of values and criteria for evaluation and control of behavior—provides durability and continuity. However, changes taking place at all levels of society threaten the more traditional family characteristics and the role of the elderly. These changes impinge on the lives of all elderly to varying degrees, and their impact may bring into question the viability and relevance of many traditional values, beliefs, and supports thought to be inherent elements of ethnic groups and communities.

What will be the prognosis for these subcultures in succeeding generations? Kramer (1970) notes that the hard core of the minority community is its lower middle-class. Those of higher status move out and become peripheral to the community by virtue of increased contact with the majority group, while those of very low status move to the periphery because of increased dependency on the larger society for basic sustenance. Compounded by social isolation, these factors produce the phenomenon of a middle-class minority community. Many would argue that given present racial cleavages, economic mobility alone will not obliterate ghettos, barrios, and the like. A continual re-creating process, different with each succeeding generation yet still identifiable, is more likely to be taking place. Regional differences as well as rural and urban differences exist among the various groups. Some of the major changes occurring are sources of stress, resulting in dislocation from familiar surroundings, increased isolation, and changing roles.

With the increased mobility and economic independence of the younger generations, there has been a gradual but consistent upward and outward movement from formerly insulated ethnic communities. Beginning with the major thrusts in migration of the blacks and Mexican-Americans during and immediately after World War II, the trend has continued for the Native Americans and other Spanish-speaking/surnamed groups. Not all migration to urban centers included taking the aged family members, although for many the uprooting did occur. This caused a sense of alienation for those elders cut off from familiar surroundings and knowledge appropriate to an agrarian society. For those left behind, especially in the South and Southwest, the vulnerabilities of old age have increased and given rise to greater dependence on surrogate families made up of friends, neighbors, and churches.

The same pattern of upward and outward mobility has transformed many tightly knit enclaves of the Asian communities, especially among the Japanese and Chinese. With each succeeding generation of American-born offspring of immigrants, acculturation has modified the structure of the institutions and organization of the ethnic communities in which the traditional supports were predictable and forthcoming. Remnants of formerly insulated ethnic communities are still visible in parts of major cities such as Los Angeles and San Francisco, but the predominance of older members in these communities is evident. A more recent phenomenon is that of the new immigrants arriving from Southeast Asian countries, replicating in many ways the earlier patterns of settlement based on language, culture, and ethnicity.

Rapid changes affect intergenerational relationships as well. Among many minority families, it is not uncommon to find members who are virtually cut off from any meaningful communication with one another. For example, the monolingual elderly (Chinese, Japanese, Spanish-speaking, and Native American), who, in most cases, did not master the English language, experience a communication gap with their grandchildren. The traditional role of transmitting cultural values, beliefs, and rituals is denied them, resulting in a sense of mutual loss. Solomon (1970) also points out an important fact that gives cause for concern: very often, the younger generation of blacks holds stereotypes of elderly blacks in somewhat the same manner that whites have stereotyped all blacks.

While the distance is widening between the younger generation and the elderly, an equally disturbing gap is occurring because of the socioeconomic mobility of the middle generation. Their hold on the newly acquired status of "middle class" is precarious, according to Solomon (1970), because it strains the material resources that were once shared with dependent parents. The black elderly may, in fact, have had a more secure family status when things were worse for black people.

The kinship supports and supportive networks of ethnic communities are precarious at best in the face of rapid change. How supportive are ethnic communities and how supportive will they be in the future? Some observers are questioning the assumption that ethnic communities are strongholds for the preservation of values and culture; and, further, whether they are capable of maintaining the well-being of all members (Kitano, 1973; Kramer, 1974).

A countervailing force, especially among Mexican-Americans, is the affirmation of cultural and linguistic identification as a way of easing the internal stress caused by external political and socioeconomic derogation. A rebirth of ethnic pride is emerging as a strategy for a renewed sense of self-acceptance and self-worth (Sotomayor, 1977).

On a more conceptual plane, Solomon (1976) proposed a model for empowerment of the powerless to ameliorate historical inequities. Empowerment is a process by which the powerless and stigmatized collective becomes engaged in identifying those obstacles or power blocks that have kept them from developing the skills, knowledge, and resources necessary for effective performance in social roles. Problem solving is seen as a critical strategy. Removing the stigma of the powerless role and becoming instead a causal force in effecting change instills a sense of empowerment for many who have historically not known power. Perhaps this sense of empowerment can be used to recreate the strength of ethnic communities, while eliminating the dysfunctional aspects of insulation and restriction.

SERVICE PROGRAMS FOR ETHNIC MINORITY ELDERLY

Earlier sections explored the complex world of the ethnic minority elderly. It is clear that the dynamics involved in shaping the lives of the ethnic minority in this society are carried into old age. Given their experiences of isolation and insulation in ghettos, barrios, and reservations—where a strong reliance on self and family have been the major supports in times of need—we can understand their discomfort, distrust and even fear in venturing outside the traditional communities when needs and problems arise.

Most programs and services for the elderly are designed primarily to meet the needs of the majority society. They thus reflect a response to only one facet of the heterogeneous older population. Additionally, service delivery and utilization issues cannot be separated from the ethnic minority experience in America. Both are intricately woven and oftentimes confound planners and social service agencies when they try to design appropriate and acceptable programs that will be utilized by the minority elderly.

The passage of the Older Americans Act in 1965 established the "aging network," a partnership of federal, state, and local public and private agencies, which provides a range of programs and services to respond to the needs and concerns of older Americans. At the local level, programs have proliferated to meet their needs for nutrition, transportation, housing, recreation, education, volunteerism, employment, and information. However, in most cases, minority older persons are conspicuously absent in these programs.

Subsequent amendments to the act have drawn attention to the needs of those older persons with the greatest economic and social need. In this regard questions relating to equity have been raised. Specifically, are ethnic minority elderly receiving their fair share of public benefits? Despite these legal mandates to serve those who are most needy, current programs are grossly underutilized by those who can benefit most—namely, the poor and disadvantaged elderly, among whom the ethnic minorities are disproportionately represented (Cuellar, 1980; Guttman, 1980).

Attempts are being made to ameliorate some of these problems through the development of culturally relevant programs, especially on the West Coast and in Hawaii. These programs can serve as models for successfully integrating the ethnic minority elderly in meaningful participation. Although only a few have been created, and though they are limited to large metropolitan areas, programs are emerging that are designed with the older minority person in mind. For example, some nutrition programs serving ethnic elders have responded to their preferences by preparing ethnic menus, using ethnic utensils, and creating a cultural ambience at their sites. Other evidences of the emergence of programs responsive to ethnic minority elderly are the day centers dealing with the frail who live with their families, nursing homes within ethnic communities, and special housing developments that carry out the cultural theme in their design of facilities as well as in programming (that is, care-giving by bilingual and bicultural staff, observation of ethnic holidays and traditions).

Program utilization

Results from the study conducted by the San Diego State University Center on Aging (San Diego State University, 1978), which examined the needs of seven elderly minority groups—black, Hispanic, Samoan, Japanese, Chinese, Pilipino, and Guamanian—reflected more similarities than dissimilarities in needs and attitudes toward services. All groups had the same needs for income, health, housing, transportation, and so on. Thus, the critical question is not whether minority elders have needs, but rather how programs should be designed so as to enable them to use the services they need.

Colen and Soto (1979) examined characteristics of existing programs in California to determine their impact on minority elderly participation. Programs were deemed to be successful in this regard if they reached a significant number of the minority population represented in the locale of the program. They found that the keys to success were to involve the minority community in planning programs and to capitalize on the formal and informal networks indigenous to the community (for example, churches, family associations, politicians, community leaders). Ethnic media, especially newspapers, radio, and television, which provide information in the language most familiar to the elderly, were also helpful in informing and encouraging the use of programs.

Examination of successful ethnic programs (Cuellar, 1980; Moriwaki, 1980) indicates that ethnic elderly do use services when they are in need, but several common elements must be present:

1. They are located in the ethnic community and are easily accessible.
2. They have an informal and personalized climate.
3. They have client-oriented staff that assists elders to get all the services needed.
4. They have bilingual and/or indigenous outreach workers, who are culturally sensitive and concerned about the people and the community they serve.

IMPLICATIONS FOR RESEARCH, TRAINING, AND PROGRAMS

The issues presented here have yet to be untangled and understood. They are important for enabling us to provide appropriate services and facilitate optimal functioning and well-being among ethnic minority elderly. With the goal of quality care for our elderly—minority and majority alike—the need is great for valid research, training, and appropriate services.

Research

Researchers of minority aging sought to obtain valid data on ethnic minority elderly through the development of "community-based" research projects (Moriwaki, 1981). Traditionally, research has focused on white, middle-class subjects and has been under the control of researchers, who found subjects to test the theories and to answer the questions that most interested them—primarily in order to develop knowledge. Change began in the mid-1970s when the National Science Foundation sought to increase knowledge of minority elders. It awarded funds to the Andrus Gerontology Center to examine policies affecting minority elderly. At the request of the black and Mexican-American communities being studied, the Center formed a Community Advisory Board for the project and hired ethnic staff. The board assisted in developing interview instruments, gathering data, interpreting project findings, and disseminating results to aid their communities. Because the board's involvement increased the validity, reliability, and usefulness of project results, the Center has since extolled community involvement in research (Bengtson, 1974). The important elements here are the community's involvement and control and the partnership between the researcher and the researched.

These efforts were enhanced through the cross-cultural study of eight ethnic minority elderly groups at the San Diego State University Center on Aging (San

Diego State University, 1978). More recently, Cuellar (1980) has developed a "proto-type research process" for conducting research to compare various groups of minority elders. He has detailed 22 tasks from initial formation of a minority elderly research planning committee, through instrument design and data collection procedures, to final report writing and dissemination of results. An ideal design, it is very time-consuming and requires the commitment and expertise of all individuals involved. Perhaps for these reasons not enough of the large and potentially significant research projects have included minority elderly and the community-based approach.

Training

The current status of curricula in aging that address minority concerns is perhaps dampened by the lack of adequate research (Moriwaki, 1978). At best, we have minority students being recruited for careers in gerontology and one or two special courses related to minority groups. What is needed is a curriculum founded on a solid knowledge base and accompanied by practical experience. This would allow students to develop more responsive models and to test them in the ethnic community. Such experiences will enable students to learn and to apply their sensitivity, understanding, and skills to guide clients effectively toward maintaining their dignity and well-being in old age. In their assessment of mental health issues of the minority elderly, Kobata, Lockery, & Moriwaki (1978) presented some cases in which minority elderly clients were harmed, rather than helped, because professionals lacked an understanding of their clients' cultural backgrounds.

To train our future professionals, we must closely tie research to training and service, so that new theories and modalities can be assessed in terms of their benefits to the current and future elderly who live in changing ethnic communities. Problems in research on the ethnic elderly stem from their feelings of mistrust and of being exploited because the purpose and potential benefits of the research are not usually explained (Kalish & Moriwaki, 1973). This has been somewhat ameliorated by the community-based research projects cited previously. However, if results could be tested in demonstration programs serving minority elderly, more cooperation would also be forthcoming.

Service programs and policies

Programs and delivery models to serve the ethnic minority elderly should be encouraged by funding sources as well as by service providers themselves. We must support and build upon those culturally relevant programs that have proven to be effective. This will entail having administrators of ethnic and community-based agencies look objectively at their programs to delineate aspects that are effective as well as ineffective. They must also begin to work with other service providers and researchers to examine in-depth the inter- and intracultural and geographic differences and similarities among ethnic minority elderly, particularly as they relate to designing effective programs and delivery of services.

Ideally, the culturally relevant component suggested could be integrated into the "aging network," but administrators must be made aware of and become sensitive to the needs and preferences of ethnic elders. Indigenous, bilingual/bicultural workers and other informal support networks have been particularly successful in increasing program utilization. Results from various studies indicate further the viability and importance of the family and informal social networks. Use of such structures in providing services and support may well improve the access to and use of much-needed services by ethnic minority elders. Current policies, such as SSI and other income-tested programs, should be reexamined, particularly regarding their negative impact on ethnic families who want to keep their elders at home. Incentives for buttressing these informal networks, particularly in caring for frail elders, should be tested and established.

At a time when national trends portend decentralization and mainstreaming of the elderly into age-integrated services in the interest of efficiency and cost-effectiveness, advocates of the ethnic minority elderly express grave reservations (San Diego State University Center on Aging, 1981). Currently the focus is on services based on age rather than on need. The frail elderly, defined as those 75 years and older, are to receive comprehensive services, while the "young-old," aged 60-74, are to use the existing age-integrated, adult service system. If this notion is adopted as a national aging policy, what will be the impact on the ethnic minority elderly, who not only have lower life expectancies but have been underrepresented even in the age-segregated existing programs? The proposed policy will once again thrust them into competition with all other age groups for scarce resources. This will further alienate those who have historically been on the outside.

Advocacy organizations within the minority communities have also been concerned with these national developments. Although recently established, they have demonstrated themselves as viable structures for stimulating the development of ethnic-sensitive programs and for ensuring that minority elderly receive their fair share of public resources. A limited list of such organizations is presented in Appendix A. Future exploration of the functions of these supports as well as the conditions necessary to maintain and utilize them will be crucial to the life conditions of ethnic minority elderly.

SUMMARY

This chapter has presented a framework for understanding the ethnic minority elderly. It discussed several lenses—culture, social status, and support group—through which to view and understand the behaviors, attitudes, and needs of ethnic minority elderly. However, service providers and future professionals must be open to societal and individual variations as well as to alternative and creative strategies for enhancing the well-being of our current and future ethnic minority elders.

REFERENCES

Allport, G. W. *The nature of prejudice.* Garden City, New York: Doubleday, 1958.
Alvarez, D., & Bean, F. D. The Mexican American family. In C. H. Mindel & R. W. Habenstein (Eds.), *Ethnic families in America: Patterns and variations.* New York: Elsevier, 1976.
Anderson, P. Support services and aged blacks. *Black Aging,* 1978, *3*(3), 53–59.

Andrulis, D. P. Ethnicity as a variable in the utilization and referral patterns of a comprehensive mental health center. *Journal of Community Psychology*, 1977, *5*, 231–237.

Bell, D., Kasschau, P., & Zellman, G. *Delivering services to elderly members of minority groups: A critical review of the literature.* Santa Monica, Calif.: Rand Corporation, 1976.

Bengtson, V. *Families, support systems and ethnic groups: Patterns of contrast and congruence.* Paper presented at the Gerontological Society, New York, 1976.

Bengtson, V., & Corry, E. Academic research and social concern. Paper presented at the 27th Annual Meeting of the Gerontology Society, Portland, Oregon, 1974.

Bogardus, E. *Social distance.* Yellow Springs, Ohio: Antioch Press, 1959.

Butler, R. N., & Lewis, M. I. *Aging and mental health: Positive psychosocial approaches.* St. Louis: C. V. Mosby, 1977.

Colen, J. N., & Soto, D. L. *Service delivery to aged minorities: Techniques of successful programs.* Sacramento, Calif.: California State University School of Social Work, 1979. (Funded through AoA grant.)

Cuellar, J. *Minority elderly Americans: A prototype for area agencies on aging.* San Diego, Calif.: Allied Home Health Association, 1980.

Daniels, R., & Kitano, H. H. L. *American racism.* Englewood Cliffs, N.J.: Prentice-Hall, 1970.

Davie, M. R. *Negroes in American society.* New York: McGraw-Hill, 1949.

Giglioli, P. P. *Language and social context.* New York: Penguin, 1972.

Golden, H. M. Black agism. *Social Policy*, 1976, *7*(3), 40–42.

Guttman, David. *Perspective on equitable share in public benefits by minority elderly.* Washington, D.C.: Catholic University of America, 1980.

Hall, E. T. *The silent language.* Greenwich, Conn.: Fawcett, 1959.

Harris, Lou, & assoc. *Fact book on aging: A profile of America's older population.* Washington, D.C.: National Council on Aging, 1978.

Jackson, M., & Wood, J. L. *Aging in America: Implication for the black aged.* Washington, D.C.: National Council on Aging, 1976.

Kalish, R. A., & Moriwaki, S. The world of the elderly Asian American. *Journal of Social Issues*, 1973, *29*(2), 187–209.

Kent, D. P. The elderly in minority groups: Variant patterns of aging. *Gerontologist*, 1971, *11*(1), 26–29.

Kitano, H. H. L. *Japanese Americans: The evolution of a subculture.* Englewood Cliffs, N.J.: Prentice-Hall, 1969.

Kitano, H. H. L. Japanese-American mental illness. In Sue S. & N. N. Wagner (Eds.), *Asian-Americans—psychological perspectives.* Palo Alto: Science & Behavior Books, 1973.

Kitano, H. L., & Kikumura, A. The Japanese American family. In C. H. Mindel & R. W. Habenstein (Eds.), *Ethnic families in America: Patterns and variations.* New York: Elsevier, 1976.

Kobata, F. S., Lockery, S. A., & Moriwaki, S. Y. Minority issues in mental health and aging. In J. E. Birren & R. B. Sloane (Eds.), *Handbook of mental health and aging.* Englewood Cliffs, N.J.: Prentice-Hall, 1980.

Kramer, J. R. *The American minority community.* New York: Thomas Y. Crowell, 1970.

Lynd, H. M. *On shame and the search for identity.* New York: Harcourt, Brace & World, 1958.

Maldonado, D., Jr. The Chicano aged. *Social Work*, 1975, *20*(8), 213–216.

Maykovich, M. K. *Japanese American identity dilemma.* Tokyo: Waseda University Press, 1972.

Mindel, C. H., & Habenstein, R. W. *Ethnic families in America.* New York: Elsevier, 1976.

Moore, J. W. Situational factors affecting minority aging. *Gerontologist,* 1971, *11*(1), 88–93.

Moriwaki, S. Y. Ethnicity and aging. In I. M. Burnside (Ed.), *Nursing and the aged.* New York: McGraw-Hill, 1976.

Moriwaki, S. Minority curriculum: Disappointing. *Generations,* Summer 1978, 29–30.

Moriwaki, S. *Implementing culturally relevant programs for Asian/Pacific elderly—a conceptual paper.* Paper presented at the Institute for Human Resources, Tahoe, Calif., July 24, 1980.

Moriwaki, S. *Community-based research and its relationship to practice.* Paper presented at the National Pacific/Asian Mini-White House Conference on Aging, San Francisco, Calif., 1981.

Pacific/Asian Elderly Research Project. *Understanding the Pacific Asian elderly—census and baseline data: A detailed report,* Los Angeles, Calif., 1978. (Funded through AoA grant.)

Padilla, A., Carlos, M. L., & Keefe, S. Mental health service utilization by Mexican-Americans. In M. Mirranda (Ed.), *Psychotherapy with the Spanish-speaking: Issues in research and service delivery.* Los Angeles: Spanish Speaking Mental Health Research Center, 1976.

Padilla, A. M., Ruiz, R. A., & Alvarez, R. Delivery of community mental health services to the Spanish-speaking/surnamed population. *American Psychologist,* 1975, *30,* 892–905.

Pinckney, A. *Black Americans.* Englewood Cliffs, N.J.: Prentice-Hall, 1969.

Plumpp, S. *Black rituals.* Chicago: Third World Press, 1972.

Price, J. A. North American Indian families. In C. H. Mindel & R. W. Habenstein (Eds.), *Ethnic families in America: Patterns and variations.* New York: Elsevier, 1976.

Rogers, C. J., & Gallion, T. E. Characteristics of elderly Pueblo Indians in New Mexico. *Gerontologist,* 1978, *18*(5), 482–487.

Rose, P. I. *They & We.* New York: Random House, 1964.

San Diego State University Center on Aging. *A cross-cultural study on minority elders in San Diego.* Grant number AoA 90–A–317. San Diego: Campanile Press, 1978.

San Diego State University Center on Aging. *Proceedings of the 9th Annual Institute on Minority Aging* (in progress).

Siegel, J. Completeness of coverage of the nonwhite population in the 1960 census and current estimates, and some implications. In D. M. Heer (Ed.), *Social statistics and the city,* Cambridge, Mass.: Harvard University Press for the Joint Center for Urban Studies of the Massachusetts Institute of Technology and Harvard University, 1968.

Simpson, G. E., & Yinger, J. M. *Racial and cultural minorities.* New York: Harper & Row, 1965.

Solomon, B. *Better planning through research.* Paper presented at Fourth National Institute on Minority Aging, Center on Aging, California State University at San Diego, 1977.

Solomon, B. Ethnicity, mental health and the older black aged. In *Ethnicity, mental health and aging.* Summary of Proceedings of a 2-day workshop. Los Angeles: Andrus Gerontology Center, University of Southern California, 1970.

Solomon, B. Social and protective services. In Richard H. Davis (Ed.), *Community services and the black elderly.* Los Angeles: Andrus Gerontology Center, University of Southern California, 1972.

Solomon, B. B. *Black empowerment: Social work in oppressed communities.* New York: Columbia University Press, 1976.

Sotomayor, M. Language, cultures, and ethnicity in developing self-concept. *Social Casework,* 1977, *58,* 195–203.

Swanson, W. C., & Harter, C. L. How do elderly blacks cope in New Orleans? *Aging and Human Development,* 1971, *2,* 210–216.

Trinidad, L. L. The Spanish-speaking elderly. In B. L. Newsome (Ed.), *Insights on the minority elderly*. Washington, D.C.: National Center on Black Aged, Inc. and University of the District of Columbia, 1977.

U.S. Bureau of the Census. *Characteristics of the population* (Vol. 1, Pt. 1). Washington, D.C.: U.S. Government Printing Office, 1970.

U.S. Department of Labor, Employment and Training Administration. *Employment-related problems of older workers: A research strategy* (R. & D Monograph 73). Washington, D.C.: U.S. Government Printing Office.

Wirth, L. The problem of minority groups. In R. Linton (Ed.), *The science of man in the world crisis*. New York: Columbia University Press, 1945.

APPENDIX A

Minority Organizations/Resources
(Limited Selection)

Center on Aging
San Diego State University
San Diego, CA 92120

National Association for Spanish-Speaking Elderly
(Associacion Nacional Pro Personas Mayores)
3875 Wilshire Blvd., Suite 401
Los Angeles, CA 90005

National Caucus and Center on Black Aged
1424 K Street, N.W., 5th Floor
Washington, DC 20005

National Indian Council on Aging
P. O. Box 2088
Albuquerque, NM 87103

National Pacific/Asian Resource Center on Aging
Colman Bldg., Suite 210
811 First Ave.
Seattle, WA 98104

CHAPTER **4**

Sociological Perspectives on Aging

Vern L. Bengtson and David Haber

Sociological inquiry in gerontology focuses on changes in social structure that accompany the aging of individuals. Sociologists examine how people, groups, and whole populations develop, change, or remain the same over time, and they explore the social consequences of individual aging and of generational succession, as reflected in individuals and in groups.

Sociological investigation in aging begins by contrasting two levels of social influence in society: (1) *microsocial,* which is the immediate interpersonal environment of individuals as they interact with family, friends, neighbors, and associates in activities of daily living, and (2) *macrosocial,* which comprises the political, economic, religious, and cultural forces, often unseen or unnoted, affecting large groups of individuals. Both levels change with the passage of time, as evidenced in the unfolding biographies of individuals and in the developing histories of societies and groups. Both are affected by changes in the characteristics of aging populations within the society.

The microsocial and macrosocial levels can be helpful in understanding the complex problems and issues relative to social aging. The social perspective is particularly relevant to contemporary societies, where public attention has focused on problems apparent when unprecedented numbers of our population survive into their sixth, seventh, eighth, and even ninth decade of life. Less often discussed in the mass media are the potentials that the new phenomenon of longevity can afford the aged of today and tomorrow—a theme that should not be neglected in sociological perspectives on human aging.

Rebecca Gronvold, of the University of Southern California, collaborated in the revision of this chapter and should be given proper credit for her extensive assistance. The original version of the chapter, which appeared in the 1975 edition of this book under a slightly different title, was co-authored by Dr. David Haber of the District of Columbia University. I wish to acknowledge Professor Haber's contributions to the original text and outline, which are apparent in this revision.

This chapter will focus on five fundamental questions relevant to sociological investigation of aging in contemporary societies:

1. What are the manifestations of aging, as viewed from analyses of social organization and behavior?
2. What are *age status systems* and *age norms,* the two basic processes in analyzing the social contexts of aging individuals?
3. What are the unique sociological perspectives on time—that is, the *cohort* and the *generational analytic approaches*—that are encountered so often in social gerontology?
4. What are the characteristics of the emerging elderly population in American society? How is this population different from, and similar to, the elderly of past and future historical periods?
5. How is aging perceived as a social problem in contemporary society, and to what extent is this social problem capable of amelioration by policymakers, practitioners, and researchers?

SOCIOLOGICAL DEFINITIONS OF AGING

From the perspective of sociology, social aging consists of passage from one socially defined position to another in the course of growing up and growing old. Such passage is usually marked by the occurrence of socially acknowledged events— for example, the entrance into, or exit from, roles or social positions (spouse, worker, parent of a dependent child). We live out our lives in a complex network of roles, each of which has acknowledged obligations, rights, and expectancies. Our definitions of growing up and growing old are given substance by events of role taking and role exiting, as we construct our individual life biographies within a social context that places expectations on our behaviors and roles.

Some of the events marking "growing up" or "growing old" are directly linked to specific chronological age by laws or other formal definitions of eligibility or obligation: voting, drinking liquor, marrying without parental consent, and retiring and receiving Social Security benefits. Other events are less linked to specific chronological age; their advent is socially noted, however, and there often are informal expectations concerning when they should occur in life. The "best age" to marry or opinions as to whether a candidate for president is too old or too young reflect informal expectations about the timing of passages from one social position to another.

Chronological age: Definitions of functions and events

Chronological age is based on calendar time; to a great extent it reflects a purely arbitrary definition of the passage of certain events in the course of life. Though there is not always a link between chronological age and human behavior, in most societies— and certainly in contemporary American society—chronological age dominates the structuring of functions and events for approximately the first two decades of an individual's life (Cain, 1964; Neugarten, Moore & Lowe, 1965). During this early period the anticipated sequence of interests, skills, and cognitive development is usually more ordered and predictable than in later stages of life, when there are fewer specific expectations and less formalization of events. The predictability of the youthful years is greatly reinforced by the formal system of grade sequence within most public schools.

Chronological age expectations become apparent again at about age 65, which is frequently the age arbitrarily chosen for retirement. The selection of 65 as the age for the right to receive old-age insurance benefits was a congressional decision of the mid-1930s (Cain, 1974). Legislative provision for retirement came about because of economic and demographic factors: namely, the reduced need for the manpower, skills, and knowledge of the older worker in an increasingly industrialized society. Age 65 has since come into wide, generalized use as the accepted time of retirement from work.

It should be noted, however, that patterns of retirement and labor-force participation are changing. Of all those aged 65 and older in 1978, about 20% of the men and less than 10% of the women are still in the labor force, that is, are presently working or seeking work (see Table 4-1). By contrast, in 1900 over two-thirds of the men aged 65 and older were still in the labor force. Similarly, there have been trends for earlier retirement. A 1978 national survey found that almost two-thirds of retired employees reported they had retired before age 65; the median age of retirement in this sample was 60.6 years (Foner & Schwab, 1981).

TABLE 4-1. Labor force participation for the population 55 years old and over: 1950–1990

Age	1950	1955	1960	1965	1970	1975	1980	1990
Male								
55–64	86.9	87.9	86.8	84.7	83.0	75.8	74.3	69.9
65 and over	45.8	39.6	33.1	27.9	26.8	21.7	19.9	16.8
Female								
55–64	27.0	32.5	37.2	41.1	43.0	41.0	41.9	42.3
65 and over	9.7	10.6	10.8	10.0	9.7	8.3	8.1	7.6

SOURCE: United States Bureau of the Census, *Current population reports*, Series P-23, no. 59, Demographic aspects of aging and the older population in the United States, January 1978, Table 6-5.

The legal age of retirement has also changed during the past few years. Changes in Social Security legislation during 1964–1966 made early retirement possible at age 62. In 1978, Congress passed the Age Discrimination in Employment Act Amendments, which raised the legal age of retirement from 65 to 70 and eliminated mandatory retirement for federal employees. The trend toward early retirement may be slowing (Cutler & Deming, 1982; Harris & Cole, 1980).

Though arbitrary chronological age markers, such as age 65, may be associated with specific events, and though they may be more prevalent in the early and then again in the later stages of life, they nonetheless have broad social and personal significance in our society in all stages of the life cycle. Eight-year-old Johnny is deemed precocious because of his accomplishments compared with other children of his age;

some people cannot trust anyone over 30; for other people life begins at 40; most people use the age interval around 65 as a general reference point in distinguishing between middle age and old age (Neugarten, Moore, & Lowe, 1965). An important consideration with chronological age markers is that they do provide social regulation of the aging process, however arbitrary they might be, and no matter how much controversy they generate.

Social age: Expectations and status

Not only are the significance and the timing of events chronologically regulated; they are also subject to a complex array of biological, psychological, sociological, and cultural influences (Bengtson, 1973). Four of the sociological influences on an individual's aging are socioeconomic status or work context, ethnicity, birth cohort and consequent historical experiences, and gender (Bengtson, Kasschau, & Ragan, 1977).

For instance, several studies (Neugarten, Moore, & Lowe, 1965) have shown that an individual's socioeconomic status can influence the age at which major events occur in his or her life. In general, the lower one's socioeconomic class level, the sooner one reaches major events in his or her life course. Women from lower socioeconomic classes. Working men from lower socioeconomic classes leave school earlier and begin and begin work earlier than their counterparts of the middle and upper socioeconomic class. Working men from lower socioeconomic classes leave school earlier and begin work sooner than men from higher socioeconomic brackets. The careers of unskilled or blue-collar workers may be terminated early as they are replaced by more vigorous younger men or by machine labor. This quicker timing of major events in the lower socioeconomic class may also lead to its members perceiving themselves as "old" at earlier chronological ages than members of the middle and upper classes.

Another sociological influence on the aging process is the occupational context in which an individual's work is performed, or from which he or she is retired. Caplow and McGee (1958) reported that mathematicians frequently refer to their colleagues as old when they are still in their early 30s. Historians, however, are often considered to be young even in their late 40s. Many analysts of human behavior have observed that careers that require longer education or apprenticeships tend to peak at later ages (Dennis, 1966; Pelz & Andrews, 1966). For example, the profession of medicine requires both a lengthy education and a period of internship, so that a doctor may not reach the highest achievements of his or her career for another 10–15 years. Similarly, in the business world many years of experience are usually required to produce top executive ability. In some vocations certain activities may not even be attempted until a later age is reached.

Retirement patterns, too, vary according to previous occupational lifestyle (Bengtson, Chiriboga, & Keller, 1969). Though few studies have investigated this issue, considerable continuity appears to exist between previous occupational style and retirement patterns. This phenomenon was manifest in comparisons between retired teachers and steelworkers (Bengtson, 1969).

A third major sociological factor that has significance in the timing of events and patterns of aging is ethnicity. Although this issue has only recently attracted concerted research effort, it is becoming clear that there are contrasting patterns of needs and adaptations to aging among blacks, Chicanos, Anglos, and "white ethnics" in contemporary American society (Myerhoff, 1979; Bengtson, 1979; Cuellar, 1974). For example, in questions to elderly subjects about the major advantage of being their age, Mexican-American respondents were most negative in their perception of old age, Anglo respondents were most positive, and blacks were intermediate. In the preliminary analysis Mexican-Americans were most likely to perceive the stigma attached to old age, while blacks tended to respond with a feeling of pride at having survived to such an age (Bengtson, et al., 1977). Such results are consistent with the findings of Sterne, Phillips, and Rabushka (1974) on the contrast between ethnic groups in patterns of aging and perception of needs. These studies point to the importance of considering the sociocultural context in assessments of the aging process (Bengtson, 1979).

A final observation on sociological influences and aging: these influences may be inconsistent from one social institution to another, on an individual or societal level. For example, 50-year-old graduate students with successfully employed adult children may consider themselves young in an occupational career sense, even though their family goals are already accomplished. At the societal level, a familiar example of age-status inconsistency is that young adult males are eligible to lose their lives for their country but are not eligible to drink liquor. Cain (1974) suggests this "age-status asynchronization" is due to the building of law on a case-by-case and statute-by-statute basis rather than from broad, inclusive concepts.

THE AGING INDIVIDUAL IN A SOCIAL CONTEXT

The microsocial perspective examines the complex ways in which individuals internalize the demands of society—that is, how individuals come to accept their social context, including the series of age-related positions they must enter, occupy, and exit. As the social context becomes internalized, it also becomes self-imposed.

A social psychology of the life cycle is built on at least four basic assumptions. First, the age structure within a society is an essential dimension for understanding human behavior. Four decades ago, Linton (1936) noted the universal significance of age structures for the study of social organization. Since that time many studies have supported the idea that all societies provide unique rights and responsibilities for members of different age groups, and that the relations between age groups are governed by sets of rules and expectations (Riley, Johnson, & Foner, 1972).

Second, biological events and social-psychological processes are not always clearly related to each other. Neugarten, Wood, Kraines, & Loomis (1963), for example, found that menopause is not the major determinant of behavior in the lives of older women, as had once been assumed. Similarly, it has recently become well established that the decreased capacities of age do not necessarily produce depression (Palmore, 1974). Biological models of the life course are inadequate by themselves to account for individual behavior and attitudes because social definition exercises considerable influence.

Third, social-psychological processes are important throughout the life cycle. In recent decades studies have begun to focus on the continuities and changes in social influences over the entire life course, rather than only in childhood. For example,

Brim (1966) notes that socialization during childhood works on fundamental motivations and values, such as the controlling of primary drives. After childhood, social influences bear more on overt behavior, such as the acquisition of knowledge and abilities in order to perform one's work competently (Bengtson, 1973, p. 19). In old age neither the motivations nor the behaviors of individuals appear to be subjected to specific and direct socializing influences. Although this could be a time of opportunity and experimentation with alternative patterns of behavior, it often creates social problems for the elderly, which we shall discuss later.

Fourth, the social-psychological perspective does not view later life as merely a continuation of behavioral patterns in earlier years. Strauss (1969, pp. 89-93), for instance, views the developmental process as a "transformation of identity," a radical change of behavior and identity from earlier times. For example, an individual in early middle-age entering the role of "boss" for the first time deals with new sets of problems and develops new perspectives. Attitudes toward such things as production schedules, company policies, worker efficiency, labor unions, and authority must be changed in relation to the person's new position in the company. Similarly, leaving the "boss" role after age 65 again involves a transformation of identity. Some of today's elderly must reluctantly give up their life's work and, in its place, are expected to substitute less important activities, including card playing, bingo, and other games that contribute little in the way of a positive self-image. The awareness of a new constellation of expectations and behaviors occurs with each new role or status, producing a distinctive reconstruction, or transformation, of one's identity (George, 1980).

Age-status systems

Researchers in social psychology have found the concepts of age-status systems and age norms to be important to a social perspective on aging. An *age-status system* is the sequence of roles available to an individual—such as son, daughter, brother, sister, friend, student, husband, wife, intern, father, mother, neighbor, professional colleague—through the life course. It is "the system developed by a culture to give order and predictability to the course followed by individuals" (Cain, 1964, p. 278).

Every new role or status may signal the beginning or ending of a major stage of an individual's life. The most significant characteristic of an age-status system is that major stages or periods of the life course emerge, contract or elongate, and eventually terminate. Studies over the last several decades in America, for example, reveal trends toward a longer period of postparenthood (Neugarten, Moore, & Lowe, 1965); or "the empty nest," as sociologists often call it. Aries (1962) reminds us that childhood did not always exist as a major period of the life cycle. This acceptance of the idea of an early stage of life with its own distinctive needs and unique characteristics appeared only after the growth of industrialization reduced the need for child labor, causing the child to remain longer in a sheltered status. The stage of adolescence appeared in the early part of this century, as middle- and upper-class young people were encouraged to remain in school for at least 12 years, and even longer, in order to prepare for increasingly complex kinds of work.

The end of the life cycle is increasingly emerging as another distinctive period of life. In addition, as more people reach old age (Brotman, 1977), and as longevity slowly increases (Sachuk, 1970), many policymakers, researchers, and practitioners are starting to distinguish between the old and the very old (Neugarten, 1974)—that is, those aged 65–74 in contrast to those above 75 or 80.

Age norms

The distinctive sets of norms associated with particular periods of the life course are assigned to specific age ranges not only by social scientists but also by a vast majority of people. A sample of middle-class, middle-aged people, for instance, achieved a high degree of consensus regarding the appropriate or expected age for retirement (Neugarten et al., 1965). A wide variety of other age-related characteristics in adulthood are located with an identifiable range by a large percentage of people (see Table 4-2).

TABLE 4-2. Consensus in a middle-class, middle-aged sample regarding various age-related characteristics

	Age range designated as appropriate or expected	Percentage who concur	
		Men (N = 50)	Women (N = 43)
Best age for a man to marry	20–25	80	90
Best age for a woman to marry	19–24	85	90
When most people should become grandparents	45–50	84	79
Best age for most people to finish school and go to work	20–22	86	82
When most men should be settled on a career	24–26	74	64
When most men hold their top jobs	45–50	71	58
When most people should be ready to retire	60–65	83	86
A young man	18–22	84	83
A middle-aged man	40–50	86	75
An old man	65–75	75	57
A young woman	18–24	89	88
A middle-aged woman	40–50	87	77
An old woman	60–75	83	87
When a man has the most responsibilities	35–50	79	75
When a man accomplishes most	40–50	82	71
The prime of life for a man	35–50	86	80
When a woman has the most responsibilities	25–40	93	91
When a woman accomplishes most	30–45	94	92
A good-looking woman	20–35	92	82

SOURCE: Neugarten, Moore, & Lowe. Age norms, age constraints and adult socialization. *American Journal of Sociology*. © 1965. Used by permission of University of Chicago Press.

It is not so much the age norms characterized by a high degree of consensus, but the systematic deviation from norms that has entranced generations of sociologists. Three such intriguing variations found in Neugarten's study are pertinent to our subject: (1) norms are perceived as more binding for others than they are for oneself; (2) as people grow old, they ascribe more importance to age norms; and (3) the discrepancy between the binding force of norms for oneself versus others is considerably greater for the young person than the old person.

Turk's study (1965) appears to be directly applicable to the finding that all norms are more binding for others than for oneself. He rejects the prevalent definition of norms as ideas on how one should personally behave. Instead he finds norms to be expectations about how others should behave. This interpretation is consistent with Neugarten's data: all age groups regard norms as a more coercive force for others than for themselves. However, Turk's study does not address the issue of why aging people ascribe increasing importance to the personally binding force of age norms. The concept of adult socialization is useful in this regard (Neugarten et al., 1965). As people grow old, they are more likely to experience the consequences of having not fulfilled previous age-related expectations. They may feel a stigma from having not married during the appropriate time span. They may be disappointed at feeling it is too late to begin study for a profession they wish they had pursued. The personal belief in the relevance and validity of age norms, therefore, increases over the life course.

None of these ideas, however, appears to be adequate for explaining why the young are likely to minimize the coercive nature of age norms for themselves, while the old are likely to maximize the validity of norms for all age strata. One useful possibility for explaining this discrepancy is the *generational stake*: the expectations that one generation has of another (Bengtson & Kuypers, 1971). While the parental expectation for the young is continuity and similarity, the personal goal of the young is frequently the freedom to experience, create, and re-create—to divest oneself of the parental "stake," or investment, in the younger generation. The young are likely, therefore, to see age norms as much less constraining and relevant for themselves than for older people. Old people, however, have a stake in continuing that which has been found desirable or deemed appropriate. They are more likely, therefore, to maximize the validity and relevancy of norms.

A final attribute of age norms to be mentioned here is the sanctions—rewards and penalties—for approved and disapproved behavior that are applied to major stages of the life cycle. An example of internalizing a sanction is the man who engages in a period of job experimentation until he feels that "it's time" to settle into a particular career. Age norms can "operate as prods and brakes upon behavior, in some instances hastening an event, in others delaying it" (Neugarten et al., 1965, pp. 22-23). Individuals who feel that their timing is early or late for a particular major event may "move back toward the norm on the next event" (Neugarten & Datan, 1973). For example, a man who postpones marriage until the completion of a long preparatory period of education may wish to have children shortly thereafter. Age-related activity can be controlled by external sanctions as well. Perhaps the most common example of how other people informally enforce conformity to age norms is the sharp rebuke, "Act your age!"

SOCIOLOGICAL PERSPECTIVES ON TIME

Time is not merely the steady accumulation of equal units as measured on clocks and calendars. Time can also be interpreted as a sequence of socially defined and regulated experiences through history. Modern sociologists employ the terms *cohort* and *generation* to express concepts of sociological time as seen in the macrosocial level of societies and groups. A *cohort* refers to those who are born during the same period of specific calendar time or who enter into a specific social institution, such as school or work, during the same precisely demarcated intervals. A *generation* refers to a group of people who are conscious of having shared similar sociocultural experiences, sometimes regardless of chronological age boundaries (Bengtson & Cutler, 1976; Berger, 1960).

Cohort analysis was devised by demographers in order to compare groups of people born during specific intervals of calendar time, usually consisting of five- or ten-year intervals. Those who were born in each period of time share the experience of particular cultural and historical events, as well as membership in a cohort of a particular size and composition. For instance, the cohort of people born between 1945 and 1955 was the first to experience living under the threat of nuclear destruction, followed by forced participation in an unpopular Asian war. It is often observed that these historical conditions have had an effect on the consciousness and behavior of many members of this birth cohort (Kenniston, 1968; Fendrich, 1974).

Not only are cohorts affected by the events occurring around them, but demographic characteristics of cohorts can influence the social institutions with which they came into contact. The sheer size of the 1945–1955 cohort (the "baby boom") compared with those of previous decades resulted in the opening or expanding of maternity wards, the construction of new schools, increased demands for housing, and an expansion of the labor supply. Similarly, the decline in birth rate that characterized the succeeding cohorts has just recently begun to create its own dislocations: the slowing down or closing of maternity or pediatric wards as well as the dwindling occupancy of nursery and elementary schools. Furthermore, some demographers predict that as the trends toward zero population growth and increased longevity continue, the relative size of future cohorts of elderly may force institutional changes at least as great as the ones caused by the baby-boom cohort.

Demography describes an age cohort quantitatively and includes such facts as size, geographical distribution, socioeconomic distribution, average age at marriage, and death rate. Cultural and historical events—such as the threat of nuclear war, racial upheaval, the advent of space exploration, and economic depression—are qualitative aspects of an age cohort, and they are most important when considered from the perspective of generational analysis.

Generational analysis is useful in studying the contributions of age groups to social change. Although the concept of generation has to be described in various ways by social analysts over a long period of time, Mannheim (1952) was one of the first to write systematically about generations. A generation consists of a group of individuals in a generalized period of historical time who share experiences of the same qualitative nature and, most importantly, who share an awareness or consciousness of themselves as distinctive because of such experiences. Mannheim also conceived of generational units, subunits that can arise within a generation that may be contrary to the dominant cultural trends. Generational analysis employs the concept of age cohorts and historical experience in constructing the base information for more far-reaching implications in terms of social change.

Leonard Cain's (1967) analysis illustrates the interlocking use of both cohort and generational analyses. Cain compares the cohort born during the decade just before the turn of the century with the cohort born during the decade just afterwards. His data reveal cohort differences on such characteristics as labor-force participation, fertility rates, education, and sexual attitudes. He also made comparisons of sociocultural factors existing during the two decades and used them in a more far-reaching, generational analysis. The generation born just after the turn of the century was a more favored generation than those born just ahead of them. This advantaged generation had less to cope with in the way of crises and more to benefit it in terms of economic, technological, and educational resources. Specifically, this generation did not have to fight in World War I, fared well through the depression, and, beginning with the high-paying defense positions during World War II, has enjoyed an exceptional period of prosperity. Furthermore, they had fewer children to support and spent less time at work and more time in school. Cain implies there were differences in certain ideological stances or value systems between the two groups. In general, the more favored group followed a trend away from institutionalized religion and the Protestant Ethic and toward greater affluence and leisure time and a certain loosening of sexual attitudes. Since these and other differences emanated from the two groups, Cain suggests that a distinctive generation may be identified with each cohort. In order to examine intriguing questions such as whether the elderly constitute a potential generation unit, see Dowd (1980) and Laufer and Bengtson (1974).

THE NEW OLD PEOPLE IN AMERICAN SOCIETY

Although some sociologists and social psychologists of aging focus their attention on growing old over the life cycle or on the relationships between generations and cohorts, much of the current research in social gerontology restricts its scope to the state of being old. From a scientific standpoint this perspective can be helpful for counteracting the long-standing bias of social scientists and funding sources that human behavior ceases to be interesting after childhood. However, from a purely pragmatic standpoint, the current focus on the state of old age is practically guaranteed to continue because of a very dramatic, extrascientific phenomenon: the tremendous population growth of the elderly. The remaining pages, therefore, will focus not on the individual as he or she ages, but on the characteristics of those who are already considered old. (References to the old, the aged, or the elderly are to the population of people aged 65 and over, in accordance with the common parlance and practice of population experts.)

Between 1900 and 1980 the elderly population in America increased from 3.1 million to 22.5 million people. This sevenfold increase among the aged during this century is significant even when compared to the upsurge in numbers of those under age 65. One way to compare the dramatic population changes of the old with the young is to note that the proportion of the entire population over 65 rose from 4% in 1900 to just over 11% in 1980. If the birthrate decline of the past two decades continues, the percentage of older people will rise significantly in the next century as well (see Table 4-3).

Life expectancy at birth has increased more than 20 years since the turn of the century. Most of this increase is attributable to a reduction in infant and childhood mortality. Life expectancy for those already 65 has increased by 3.7 years during the same period—from 11.9 years in 1900-1902 to 15.6 years in 1974 (U.S. Bureau

TABLE 4-3. Population percentages for the United States: 1900–2050 [a]

	1900	1930	1940	1950	1960	1970
Young (under 15)		29.4	25.1	26.9	31.1	28.5
Work force (15–64)		65.2	68.1	65.0	59.7	61.6
Old (65+)	4.1	5.4	6.8	8.1	9.2	9.9

	1980	1990	2000	2020	2050
Young (under 15)	22.5	22.7	21.9	20.7	20.2
Work force (15–64)	66.3	65.1	65.9	63.8	62.2
Old (65+)	11.2	12.2	12.2	15.5	17.6

SOURCE: United States Bureau of the Census, *Census of the population: 1970. Vol. 1 Characteristics of the population,* pt. 1, Table 53; U. S. Bureau of the Census, *Current population reports,* Series P-25, no. 702, "Projections of the population of the United States: 1977 to 2050," July 1977.

[a] Projections based on Series II, 2.1 births average per woman at end of childbearing years.

of the Census, 1978). If cardiovascular disease were eliminated, life expectancy at age 65 would increase by 5.1 years (U.S. Public Health Service, 1975).

Life expectancy also appears to be sex-linked. In 1900 women were outliving men by five years; by 1975 the difference had widened to eight years. If this trend continues, some demographers predict that two out of three aged persons in the year 2000 will be women (Atchley, 1980). It is not likely that the current trend toward equal working roles for men and women will offset this discrepancy in longevity; there is a tendency for females to outlive males within equivalent sociocultural settings, such as exist in monastic life, as well as under controlled experiment with animal species.

A rough, broad sketch of the contemporary American population reveals a variety of differences between the elderly and people under the age of 65. Old people are most likely to live in the city, as are younger people; they are also more likely to live in the city center rather than the urban fringe or suburbs, where more younger people are found (Brotman, 1972). Older people are slightly more likely than younger people to live in small towns and rural areas. The aged are considerably more likely to be functionally illiterate. Not only are they more likely to have stopped before completing high school, but more likely to be without much education at all. Old people are twice as likely to be poor. They are also twice as likely to have one or more chronic physical conditions than are people in the age strata between 15 and 44. The aged spend three and one-half times as much on health care as do those under age 65 (Brotman, 1977). More older women are widows than wives. The 8% of the older population who are blacks and other minority status are likely to be even worse off than their aged colleagues in terms of income level, education, and health. Perhaps most pervasive of all, the elderly population almost categorically suffer from diminished resources of all kinds, particularly finances, health, physical ability, and even their eligibility to work.

The contemporary older American can also be differentiated from the elderly of other epochs. Though we have less information about older persons in 1900 than we do about the aged today, a rough comparison can still be made. Around the turn of the century older people were considerably more rare, both in absolute numbers and in proportion to the rest of the population. The elderly did not go into retirement; the majority were expected to continue whatever work and lifestyle they had been following. In this respect the elderly of 1900 were not as likely to be differentiated from the remainder of the population as are older people today. The elders in a rural multigenerational family were respected for their useful information and skills just as they are today. As rapid industrialization drew families into the city, the shortage of existing housing led to similar three-generational households and comparable respect in an urban context; economic necessity more than filial piety created multigenerational households. However, the older person may have been more appreciated in a time when the community itself was an important and satisfying social resource. Today's more mobile society tends to build relationships according to work-related or interest-related activities, not necessarily restricted to the home community.

Accumulating facts about the future elderly does not guarantee clear-cut predictions about their relative position in tomorrow's society. For example, we know that old people of the future will be better educated than today's aged population, because an increasingly larger percentage of America's young people—the future elderly—are entering school. Yet we are also aware that the educational level of those under age 65 increases even more rapidly than does each new cohort of old people. This means that either the educational disparity between young and old will continue to widen for some time to come or, in a society that requires constant renewal of knowledge, the growing numbers of older people taking advantage of continuing educational opportunities over their life course will reduce this gap.

We also know that reduced birthrate, a slight increase in longevity, greater numbers of people reaching traditional retirement age, and the recent advent of plans calling for retirement earlier than 65 contribute to what demographers call an increasing *dependency ratio,* as discussed in Chapter 2. This demographic tool reveals the proportion of people who are economically dependent on the work-force population. From 1930 through 2050, the dependency ratio for the older population is expected to follow a general linear trend upward, with increasing proportions of people dependent (Cutler & Harootyan, 1975). If this forecast is accurate, some demographers predict that within the next half-century, for every 2.2 employed persons, there will be 1 person dependent on Social Security.

Sex ratios tend to decline with increasing age. There has been a dramatic decline in the sex ratio in the 65 and over age group: in 1900 there were 102 men per 100 women, while in 1979 there were 68 men per 100 women (United States Census Bureau, 1978). As noted earlier, if the tendency for women to outlive men increases over the life span (see Table 4-4) and if the age median for women over 65 continues to rise as it has during the past several decades, the ratio of elderly women to elderly

TABLE 4-4. Population of males per 100 females, United
States: 1970

Age	Males per 100 females
All ages	95.0
Under 5	104.7
5–17	104.2
18–24	101.6
25–44	97.3
45–64	92.4
65–74	77.0
75–84	60.4
85+	44.7

SOURCE: United States Bureau of the Census, *Current population
reports,* Series P-25, no. 870, Estimates of the population of the United
States by age, race, and sex: 1976 to 1979, January 1980, Table 1.

men may increase to 2:1 by the year 2000. If the social tradition of women marrying men older than themselves persists, the percentage of elderly women widowed
and living alone will be startling. Alternatives to this prospect might be to reverse the
social custom of men marrying women younger than themselves or to adopt new
forms of social institutions, such as communal or polygamous living arrangements in
which women can find companionship with each other as well as share the more
scarce resource of the older man.

AGING AS A SOCIAL PROBLEM

The identification and interpretation of social problems are in large measure
shaped by the particular sociocultural context in which they are made. The identification of the aged as a social problem is a product of such factors as rapid industrialization, its resulting social changes, and 20th-century American values (Kuypers &
Bengtson, 1973). Even the existence of the American Gerontological Society, which
has identified old age as a social problem, contributes to this bias. All factors considered, however, there is an enormous amount of evidence to document that modern
society is singularly unprepared to meet the basic needs of its rapidly expanding older
citizenry. Some of that evidence follows, demonstrating three ways in which the aged
can be viewed as a social problem.

Poor health

As gerontologists are wont to observe, the popular portrayal of the decrepit
oldster is grossly misleading. Major contributions to art, music, literature, and science
are made by people in their 70s and 80s or beyond (Lehman, 1953). Bertrand Russell
was writing important philosophical ideas until his death at nearly 100. Painter and
sculptor Pablo Picasso continued his contributions to the artistic world well past his
90th year. Investigations of more everyday types of work reveal that nonagenarians are
active in the Foster Grandparent program and Operation Green Thumb (Brotman,
1969). A more general view of the capabilities of those 65 and over discloses that less
than 4% require institutionalized care, and of those who are noninstitutionalized, 80%

are mobile (Brotman, 1972). If a more flexible and imaginative labor market existed, there would undoubtedly be many more elderly, even up to advanced ages, contributing their personal resources to their communities.

Although most older people are unlike the stereotypical image of a superannuated human being, they are not likely to be as healthy as people under 65. Though poor health is not necessarily associated with old age, older people in general suffer from a greater prevalence of chronic conditions. Such serious conditions as arthritis, rheumatism, high blood pressure, and heart disease tend to increase with age after 50. Among the elderly 20% have at least two chronic conditions, and 33% have three or more; nearly 40% suffer restrictions on their ability to perform major activities, such as ability to work or keep house; around 5% reside in institutions resulting from multiple chronic conditions (Hickey, 1980). In all, approximately 80% of all older persons have one or more chronic conditions (Ward, 1980).

Older persons are not only more physically disadvantaged by their health, they are also likely to spend more on their health care. Those over 65 spend more on drugs, usually for their chronic impairments, are more likely to see a physician, and tend to have more and longer hospital stays (Brotman, 1977). In 1970, 25% of the country's hospital beds were occupied by the elderly, though they constituted only 10% of the population.

Age is also a factor in the length of time spent in the hospital per visit. In 1976, the average length of stay per hospital visit was five days longer for persons aged 65 and older than for adults 17–44 years old. All these factors result in health-care expenditures of the elderly three and one-half times greater than those of the under 65 age group ($1745 per year versus $514). In 1977, Medicare covered only 44% of this total. The remainder of the costs were paid either from Medicaid, out-of-pocket expenses, or private insurance (Table 4-5). Note the significant increases in the 11-year span from 1966 to 1977.

TABLE 4-5. **Per capita expenditures for personal health care: 1966 and 1977**

Age and year	Total cost	Direct out-of-pocket cost	Government	Private health insurance	Philanthrophy and industry
Under 65					
1966	$ 155	$ 79	$ 30	$ 42	$ 3
1977	514	164	150	187	13
65 and over					
1966	445	237	133	71	5
1977	1745	463	1169	101	13

SOURCE: D. K. Harris & W. E. Cole, *Aging in mass society: Myths and realities.* Cambridge, Mass.: Winthrop Publishers, 1980, Table 17.4, p. 357.

Although the general older population is clearly more physically disadvantaged than younger people, the health status of the very old is more impaired than that of those under the age of 75. For example, 40% of those between 65 and 74 have some type of impairment, while 60% of those over 75 have similar difficulty. Nearly 25% of the very old are totally disabled (Atchley, 1972). In 1977 about 25% of the population 85 years and over were institutionalized (Atchley, 1980). In fact, the median age of the nursing home population in 1977 was 80 years old (Hickey, 1980).

In addition to the increasing prevalence and severity of health problems with age, the numbers of the very old are increasing as well. Between the 1960s and 1970s, the population of the very old (75 years and over) increased at six times the rate of those between the ages of 65 and 74 (United States Bureau of the Census, 1978). These age groups will both continue to increase, but at a slower pace than in the past (Cutler & Harootyan, 1975). The obvious consequence of dramatic increases in the numbers of the very old will be a heightened demand for an improved health delivery system for the aged as well as a health-care plan to cover the spiraling costs.

Poverty

Many people experience a rising level of income over their life course; this reaches a peak shortly before age 65 (Riley & Foner, 1968) and is followed by a 50% reduction in income on their first day of retirement (Hendricks & Hendricks, 1980). Although earnings and economic productivity have increased steadily since the turn of the century, the income levels provided by retirement programs have lagged considerably behind. Retirement income not only is based on lower wage earnings of the past but is also especially vulnerable to the higher prices that accompany inflation. In addition to private programs, public programs are a major source of retirement income, providing 80% of the aggregate income of elderly persons (Atchley, 1980). Public programs, unfortunately, suffer from the same problems of comparatively low, fixed payment levels. The magnitude of the discrepancy between income and need makes the aged poor an identifiable social problem.

The percentage of the elderly who are poor varies considerably, depending on the source of the definition. The terms *poor* and *poverty* are often used interchangeably as well. According to the measure of adequate income provided by the Bureau of Labor Statistics, 75% of the aged live below standard (Binstock & Levin, 1976); Atchley suggests that 60% of the aged are poor (1972, p. 148); in an overall view of the various living situations of the American population, the U.S. Bureau of the Census reports that 13%, or 3.2 million, of the elderly (65 and over) were below the poverty level in 1977 (United States Bureau of the Census, 1979). The median income of families with heads of households 65 or over was $9110 in 1977, compared with the median income for all families in that year of $16,009. Elderly Americans living alone, older women, and older blacks and other minorities are particularly prone to experiencing poverty (Atchley, 1980).

Some data suggest cautious optimism: the proportion of the elderly population (aged 65 and over) below the poverty level has declined in the last few years. Between 1959 and 1969, the number of poor elderly persons had increased to the point that one-fifth (20%) of all the poor were individuals 65 years old or over. That trend has reversed itself, and the proportions of poor elderly have dropped to 13% as of 1977 (United States Bureau of the Census, 1979). The turnaround in the proportion below the poverty level for the elderly population has been attributed to increases in Social Security benefits, more comprehensive coverage in other private and public pensions, and the implementation of the Supplemental Security Income Program (SSI) in 1974 (Harris & Cole, 1980).

However, in addition to the elderly poor defined by census categories, there are other large groups that should be taken into account. If the "near poor" threshold (25% above the poverty level) is used to measure the poor elderly, then approximately 2.3 million additional persons need to be added to the census figure for 1977. There are also many elderly persons whose income is raised above the poverty level because they are living with others (for example, children). Another hidden group of elderly poor not figured into the census count are those who are institutionalized.

Consequently, in addition to the 3.2 million formally recognized as "poor elderly," there are approximately 7 million elderly Americans who live below or very close to the poverty level, if the "hidden poor" and the "near poor" are combined with the census figures (Harris & Cole, 1980).

The sharply reduced income levels that beset individuals at retirement are not compensated for by a diminished economic need nor by a decrease in the motivation to consume. In fact, the consumption pattern of the affluent elderly is markedly similar to that of affluent youth. It is only the less fortunate members of the older age stratum that must spend more than $4 out of every $5 on the staple items of housing, food, transportation, and medical care. The proportion of these items in an elderly person's budget are approximately: 28.9% for housing, 21.4% for food, 12.8% for transportation, and 8.3% for medical care (Harris & Cole, 1980). When the income cannot be stretched sufficiently to meet all of these needs, psychological needs are sacrificed first. Despite the prevalence of leisure time during retirement, for example, the aged person spends less on recreation than the job-oriented young person. Stringent financial conditions force a shift in the consumption patterns of the elderly population that would appear to be detrimental to their psychological well-being.

There is an obvious reciprocal relationship between the economic plight of the aged and their health problems. The reduced economic resources of the aged encourages both a crisis-oriented approach to health care (Suchman, 1966) and an inadequate diet (Guthrie, Black, & Madden, 1972). The neglect of preventative health care increases the already higher probabilities of disabling illness. Poor health, in turn, aggravates the economic strains associated with old age. These related problems too often have pathetic consequences for an aged individual.

Social loss

Even those older persons with adequate physical and financial resources are inevitably faced with the problem of social loss. Essentially every older adult loses some rights and responsibilities attached to social roles, that is, specialized positions within social groups. Men and women retire from work, losing such roles as coworker, union member, manager, or fund chairman. By the time of retirement, most people have already shed such parenthood roles as cook, confidant, disciplinarian, school visitor, and committee member. The deeper losses are those brought about as friends

TABLE 4-6. Rates of interaction by age and sex

Sex and age	Number interviewed	Percentage of numbers interviewed	
		Large number of roles	High daily interaction
		(I)	(II)
Both sexes	211	41.7	47.9
50–54	36	61.1	72.2
55–59	34	61.8	58.8
60–64	34	58.8	58.8
65–69	31	38.7	45.2
70–74	50	22.0	34.0
75 and over	26	7.7	15.4
Males	107	42.0	46.7
50–54	19	68.4	78.9
55–59	18	61.1	50.0
60–64	19	47.4	52.6
65–69	12	50.0	50.0
70–74	25	20.0	32.0
75 and over	14	7.1	14.3
Females	104	41.3	49.0
50–54	17	52.9	64.7
55–59	16	62.5	68.8
60–64	15	73.3	66.7
65–69	19	31.6	42.1
70–74	25	24.0	36.0
75 and over	12	8.3	16.7

SOURCE: From *Growing old: The process of disengagement* by E. Cumming and W. E. Henry. ©1961 by Basic Books, Inc., Publishing Co., N.Y.

and spouses and other family members die, sometimes leaving the aged individual entirely alone. With every loss of role and relationship, the number of contacts diminishes (see Table 4-6). Often financial and physical restraints make it increasingly difficult to continue other social roles, such as club or political membership, or substitute activities that might fill the expanding amount of free time.

Elderly people also experience a reduction in normative control; that is, the norms available to govern their behavior become increasingly less well defined or disappear altogether (Kuypers & Bengtson, 1973). For example, people in careers lose much of their social identity and patterns of interaction when they retire from work. Many women lose their social function and source of emotional support when their children are launched and their husbands are outlived. The expectations that do exist for the elderly are general, vague, and often inappropriate. Havighurst and Albrecht (1953), for example, found little evidence of explicit norms for old age. Instead, the prescriptions for this period of life are rather general and vague standards about family, social, and religious activities, characterized by a tapering off in intensity over time. Clark (1967) observed that older people often resort to norms of middle age, such as independence and providing for one's own needs.

The consequences of this reduction in normative control for the elderly person are subject to some disagreement. Advocates of the *disengagement perspective,* for instance, argue that since people inevitably decline in both economic productivity and social interaction, the weakening of the pressures of normative constraint is not only consonant with this natural process, but beneficial as well. Devotees of the *activity perspective,* on the other hand, claim that active middle-age roles and norms are still appropriate in old age, although to a lesser degree (for succinct and more detailed summaries of both these frameworks, see Bengtson, 1973; Dowd, 1980; Marshall, 1980). There is some evidence, however, that if either orientation became accepted to the exclusion of the other, there might be deleterious effects on many older people. For example, if an aged individual maintains the expectations of middle age (activity orientation) in the face of biological decline, he or she may be a likely candidate for psychiatric problems (Clark, 1967). On the other hand, if compulsory retirement leads to a reduction of normative constraint (disengagement orientation) for an unwilling 65-year-old, the probable result will be uncertainty and alienation (Martin, Bengtson, & Acock, 1974). This potential for diversity among the aged poses the question of whether explicit and specific norms for old age will develop. If so, they will likely develop within reference groups, of which the elderly were members in their earlier years.

A *reference group* is the group whose perspective is used by an individual as a source of social identity and standard for behavior. During an individual's life, his reference group may be either a present or an anticipated one, either real or symbolic. The rhetoric that older people constitute a subculture with a sense of group consciousness and political awareness—and therefore a potential reference group for its members—seems premature (Ragan & Dowd, 1974; Rose, 1965). The reference group for older people, regardless of whether functional or chronological criteria are used to define old age, so far continues to be that of the former years. As Binstock cogently states:

> Even if the disadvantaged aged see their problems as age-related problems, they see them in other contexts as well. A full life cycle of socialization, experiences and attachments—family, schooling, ethnicity, occupation, income, residence, peer and other associations—presents a multitude of sources for group identification and perceptions of special interest (Binstock & Levin, 1976, p. 15).

Perhaps a prerequisite to determining whether the reference groups of older people are other older people would be to assess general attitudes toward old age, particularly those endorsed by old people themselves. More than a decade ago, Kogan and Wallach (1961) questioned 268 male and female subjects on their attitudes toward various life-stage concepts. Half of the subjects were university students; the other half were adults with a mean age of 71. The study found a generally negative evaluation of the elderly, old age, and death, although old people were less negative than young people. What changes in the image and self-image of the elderly have taken place since then? In the continued presence of health and economic losses, how likely are the aged to adopt negative stereotypes of themselves? How likely are they, consequently, to eliminate being elderly as a desirable source of social identity and standard for behavior? These are only a few of the many questions with far-reaching implications for the future of the elderly in America.

There is no question that the elderly often occupy a difficult position in American life (Dowd, 1980). Some are able to maintain a positive self-image and to adapt well to the changes of age; many are not. A great deal of human talent and energy is now being wasted, and a great deal of unnecessary suffering exists. Even if we did not each have a vested interest in the issues of aging and old age, there are important implications to the denial of benefits to a sizable and increasing number of elderly. For as de Beauvoir (1973) has written, "By the way in which a society behaves toward its old people, it uncovers the naked, and often carefully hidden, truth about its real principles and aims" (1973, p. 131).

REFERENCES

Aries, P. *Centuries of childhood.* New York: Random House, 1982.
Atchley, C. *The social forces in later life: An introduction to social gerontology.* Belmont, Calif.: Wadsworth, 1972.
Atchley, C. *The social forces in later life* (3rd ed.). Belmont, Calif.: Wadsworth, 1980.
Beauvoir, S. de. *The coming of age.* New York: G. P. Putnam & Sons, 1973.
Bengtson, V. L. Cultural and occupational differences in level of present role activity in retirement. In R. J. Havighurst, J. M. A. Munnichs, B. L. Neugarten, & H. Thomae (Eds.), *Adjustment to retirement: A cross-national study.* Assen, Netherlands: Van Gorkum, 1969.
Bengtson, V. L. *The social psychology of aging.* Indianapolis, Ind.: Bobbs-Merrill, 1973.
Bengtson, V. L. Ethnicity and aging: Problems and issues in current social science inquiry. In D. E. Gelfand & A. J. Kutzik, (Eds.), *Ethnicity and aging.* New York: Springer, 1979.
Bengtson, V. L., Chiriboga, D. A., & Keller, A. B. Occupational differences in retirement: Patterns of role activity and life-outlook among Chicago teachers and steelworkers. In R. J. Havighurst, J. M. A. Munnichs, B. L. Neugarten, & H. Thomae (Eds.), *Adjustment to retirement: A cross-national study.* Assen, Netherlands: Van Gorkum, 1969.
Bengtson, V. L., & Cutler, N. E. Generations and intergenerational relations: Perspectives on age groups and social change. In R. Binstock & E. Shanas (Eds.), *The handbook of aging and social sciences.* New York: Van Nostrand Reinhold, 1976.
Bengtson, V. L., Grigsby, E., Corry, E. M., & Hruby, M. Relating academic research to community concerns: A case study in collaborative effort. *Journal of Social Issues,* 1977, *33*(4), 75–92.
Bengtson, V. L., Kasschau, P. L., & Ragan-Robinson, P. K. The impact of social structure on the aging individual. In J. E. Birren & K. W. Schaie (Eds.), *Handbook of the psychology of aging.* New York: Van Nostrand Reinhold, 1977.
Bengtson, V. L., & Kuypers, J. A. Generational differences and the "developmental stake." *Aging and Human Development,* 1971, *2*(1), 249–260.
Berger, B. How long is a generation? *British Journal of Sociology,* 1960, *2*, 10–23.
Binstock, H., & Levin, M. A. The political dilemmas of intervention policies. In R. H. Binstock and E. Shanas (Eds.), *Handbook of aging and the social sciences.* New York: Van Nostrand Reinhold, 1976.
Brim, O. Socialization after childhood. In O. Brim and S. Wheeler (Eds.), *Socialization through the life cycle.* New York: John Wiley and Sons, 1965.
Brotman, H. Income and poverty in the older population in 1975. *Gerontologist,* 1977, *17*, 23–26.

Cain, L. Life course and social structure. In R. E. L. Faris (Ed.), *Handbook of modern sociology*. Chicago: Rand-McNally, 1964.

Cain, L. Age status and generational phenomena: The new old people in contemporary America. *Gerontologist*, 1967, *2*, 2.

Cain, L. The growing importance of legal age in determining the status of the elderly. *Gerontologist*, 1974, *14*, 167–174.

Caplow, T., & McGee, R. *The academic marketplace*. New York: Basic Books, 1958.

Clark, M. The anthropology of aging: A new area for studies of culture and personality. *Gerontologist*, 1967, *7*, 55–64.

Cuellar, J. *Ethnographic methods: Studying aging in an urban Mexican-American community*. Paper presented at the annual meeting of the Gerontological Society, Portland, Oregon, October 1974.

Cumming, E., & Henry, W. *Growing old: The process of disengagement*. New York: Basic Books, 1961.

Cutler, N. E., & Harootyan, R. A. Demography of the aged. In D. Woodruff & J. E. Birren (Eds.), *Aging: Scientific perspectives and social issues, 2nd ed.* Monterey, Calif.: Brooks/Cole, 1982.

Dennis, W. Creative productivity between the ages of 20 and 80. *Journal of Gerontology*, 1966, *21*, 1–8.

Dowd, J. *Stratification and aging*. Volume in V. L. Bengtson (Series Ed.), Brooks/Cole Series in Social Gerontology. Monterey, Calif.: Brooks/Cole, 1980.

Fendrich, J. Activists ten years later: A test of generational unit continuity. *Journal of Social Issues*, 1974, *30*, 2, Pt. 2.

Foner, A. & Schwab, K. *Aging and retirement*. Volume in V. L. Bengtson (Series Ed.), Brooks/Cole Series in Social Gerontology. Monterey, Calif.: Brooks/Cole, 1981.

George, L. K. *Role transitions in later life*. Volume in V. L. Bengtson (Series Ed.), Brooks/Cole Series in Social Gerontology. Monterey, Calif.: Brooks/Cole, 1980.

Guthrie, H., Black, K., & Madden, J. Nutritional practices of elderly citizens in rural Pennsylvania. *Gerontologist*, 19, *12*(4), 1972, 330–335.

Harris, D. K., & Cole, W. E. *Aging in mass society: Myths and realities*. Cambridge, Mass.: Winthrop, 1980.

Havighurst, R., & Albrecht, R. *Older people*. New York: Longmans, Green, 1953.

Hendricks, J., & Hendricks, C. D. *Aging in mass society: Myths and realities*. Cambridge, Mass.: Winthrop, 1980.

Hickey, T. *Health and aging*. Volume In V. L. Bengtson (Series Ed.), Brooks/Cole Series in Social Gerontology. Monterey, Calif.: Brooks/Cole, 1980.

Kenniston, K. *Young radicals: Notes on committed youth*. New York: Harvest, 1968.

Kogan, N., & Wallach, M. Age changes in values and attitudes. *Journal of Gerontology*, 1961, *16*, 272–280.

Kuypers, J. A., & Bengtson, V. L. Social breakdown and competence: A model of normal aging. *Human Development*, 1973, *16*(3), 181–201.

Laufer, R. S., & Bengtson, V. L. Generations, aging and social stratification: On the development of generational units. *Journal of Social Issues*, 1974, *30*(3), 181–295.

Lawton, M. *Environment and aging*. Monterey, Calif.: Brooks/Cole, 1980.

Lehman, H. *Age and achievement*. New Jersey: Princeton University Press, 1953.

Linton, R. *The study of man*. New York: Appleton-Century-Crofts, 1936.

Mannheim, K. The problems of generations. In P. Kesskemeti (Ed.), *Essays on the sociology of knowledge*. London: Routledge and Kegan Paul, 1952.

Marshall, V. *Last chapters: A sociology of aging and dying*. Volume in V. L. Bengtson (Series Ed.), Brooks/Cole Series in Social Gerontology. Monterey, Calif.: Brooks/Cole, 1980.

Martin, W. C., Bengtson, V. L., & Acock, A. C. Alienation and age: A context-specific approach. *Social Forces*, 1974, *53*(2), 266–274.

Myerhoff, B. G. A symbol perfected in death: Continuity and ritual in the life and death of an elderly Jew. In B. Myerhoff and A. Simic (Eds.), *Life's career: Aging.* Beverly Hills, Calif.: Sage, 1979.

Neugarten, B. Age groups in American society and the rise of the young-old. *Annals of the American Academy of Political and Social Science,* September 1974, 187–198.

Neugarten, B. & Datan, N. Sociological perspectives on the life cycle. In P. Baltes and K. W. Schaie (Eds.), *Life-span developmental psychology: Personality and socialization.* New York: Academic Press, 1973.

Neugarten, B., Moore, J., & Lowe, J. Age norms, age constraints, and adult socialization. *American Journal of Sociology,* 1965, *70,* 710–717.

Neugarten, B. L., Wood, V., Kraines, R. J., & Loomis, B. Women's attitudes toward the menopause. *Vita Humana,* 1963, *6,* 140–151.

Palmore, E. (Ed.). *Normal aging: Volume II.* Durham, N.C.: Duke University Press, 1974.

Pelz, D., & Andrews, F. *Scientists in organizations.* New York: John Wiley and Sons, 1966.

Ragan, P., & Dowd, J. The emerging political consciousness of the aged: A generational interpretation. *Journal of Social Issues,* 1974, *30,* 2, Pt. 2.

Riley, M. W., & Foner, A. *Aging and society, Volume I: An inventory of research findings.* New York: Russell Sage Foundation, 1968.

Rose, A. M. The subculture of the aging: A framework for research in social gerontology. In A. M. Rose and W. A. Peterson (Eds.), *Older people and their social world.* Philadelphia, PA.: F. A. Davis, 1965.

Sachuk, N. M. Population longevity study: Sources and indices. *Journal of Gerontology,* 1970, *25,* 262–264.

Shanas, E., The family as a social support system in old age. *Gerontologist,* 1979, *19,* 169–174.

Sterne, R. S., Phillips, J. E., & Rabushka, A. *The urban elder poor: Racial and bureaucratic conflict.* Lexington, Mass.: D. C. Heath, 1974.

Strauss, A. L. *Mirrors and masks: The search for identity.* San Francisco: Sociology Press, 1969.

Suchman, E. Health orientation and medical care. *American Journal of Public Health,* 1966, *56,* 97–105.

Troll, L., & Bengtson, V. L. Generations in the family. In W. Burr, R. Hill, I. Reiss, and I. Nye (Eds.), *Handbook of contemporary family theory.* New York: Free Press, 1979.

Turk, H. An inquiry into the undersocialized conception of man. *Social Forces,* 1965, *62,* 518–521.

United States Bureau of the Census. *Census of the population: 1970.* General population characteristics. Final report, PC(1)-B1 United States Summary. Washington, D.C.: U.S. Government Printing Office, 1972.

United States Bureau of the Census. *Current population reports,* Series P-25, no. 704. Projections of the population of the United States: 1977 to 2050. Washington, D.C.: U.S. Government Printing Office, July 1977.

United States Bureau of the Census. *Current population reports,* Series P-23, no. 59. Demographic aspects of aging and the older population in the United States. Washington, D.C.: U.S. Government Printing Office, January 1978.

United States Bureau of the Census. *Current population reports,* Series P-60, no. 119. Characteristics of the population below the poverty level: 1977. Washington, D.C.: U.S. Government Printing Office, March 1979.

United States Bureau of the Census. *Current population reports,* Series P-25, no. 870. Estimates of the population of the United States, by age, race and sex: 1976 to 1979. Washington, D.C.: U.S. Government Printing Office, January 1980.

United States Bureau of the Census. *Current population reports,* Series P-60, No. 125. Money, income and poverty status of families and persons in the United States: 1979 (Advance Report). Washington, D.C.: U.S. Government Printing Office, 1980.

United States Public Health Service, National Center for Health Statistics. *United States Decennial Life Tables for 1969–71* (Vol. 1, no. 5). United States life tables by causes of death: 1969–71. Washington, D.C.: U.S. Government Printing Office, May 1975.

Ward, R. *The aging experience.* New York: J. B. Lippincott Co., 1979.

CHAPTER **5**

Aging and the Family

Judith Treas

Few people, lay or professional, will quarrel with the notion that family ties are particularly important for the aged. Indeed, we rely, rightly or wrongly, on the family bonds of affection and obligation to make up for the shortcomings in society's provisions for the well-being of our older citizens. Kin can function as important resources for the elderly, meeting health or financial needs with services, gifts, and monetary contributions. They can provide affection and companionship at a time when the older person's social network may be circumscribed by infirmities and budget restrictions. Although we recognize friendships to be transient—dependent on common interests and geographic proximity—we tend to view familial relationships as enduring and, hence, suited to sustaining the individual throughout the life cycle.

This chapter focuses on family relations in the second half of life. First, we shall consider the extended kin network—that is, the relationships of older persons to their children, grandchildren, aged parents, siblings, cousins, in-laws, and other peripheral kin by blood or marriage. Though sometimes characterized by infrequent interaction or low affect, extended kin display cohesiveness transcending generational, geographical, and socioeconomic differences. Second, we shall turn to the family centered on husband and wife: the conjugal family of parents and dependent children sharing a common household, lifestyle, and social status. Predictable changes accompany the maturation of the family—notably, a contraction in household size. We shall examine marital relations and individual adjustments in middle and old age from a family life-cycle perspective, which stresses the family alterations typically experienced in the course of aging.

LIVING ARRANGEMENTS OF OLDER PEOPLE

Some critics argue that historical changes in the family are responsible for many problems faced by the aged today. They point to a past when grandparents were contributing members of three-generation households, enjoying the fortunes and company of kin and respected by all as repositories of acquired wisdom. Indeed, today the media frequently present stories of lonely and destitute old people, who have been abandoned by kin in rest homes or downtown hotels and who are stripped of their feelings of personal worth and usefulness. Some historians and demographers, however, now question whether multigenerational households have ever been the norm, if only because in the past so few people survived to old age (P. Laslett, 1971). To be sure, the aged in earlier eras were more likely to live with kin. At the turn of the century, 58% of those married and aged 65 and older lived with offspring, as did 65% of the unmarried (Dahlin, 1980). Social researchers, however, find little evidence that the lot of older people today would be substantially improved by their incorporation into extended households.

As Table 5-1 demonstrates, most older people do not live alone or even with nonrelatives. Most live in families, although such families typically consist of only an aged husband and wife. Since they usually have a surviving spouse, older men enjoy family living more often than their female counterparts. Because more women are widowed, they live alone more often—especially at advanced ages. Black men and white women

TABLE 5-1. Living arrangements of those aged 65 and older by race, Spanish origin, age, and sex, 1978

	65-74 years		75 years and older	
	Men	*Women*	*Men*	*Women*
White				
In families	86.5	61.6	77.8	49.3
Primary individual[a]	12.6	37.2	21.7	49.8
Other[b]	0.9	1.2	0.5	0.9
Black				
In families	71.0	63.5	65.6	56.3
Primary individual[a]	19.8	34.5	24.6	43.2
Other[b]	9.2	2.1	9.8	0.5
Spanish origin				
In families	85.1	72.5	—[c]	69.8
Primary individual[a]	15.5	25.0	—[c]	26.7
Other[b]	—	2.5	—[c]	3.5

SOURCE: U.S. Bureau of the Census. *Current population reports,* Special Studies Series P-23, no. 85, Social and economic characteristics of the older population, Table 2, 1979.

[a] A household head living alone or with nonrelatives only.

[b] Includes lodgers, resident employees, and those living in group quarters such as convents or rooming houses.

[c] Base less than 75,000 persons, so no results reported due to their low reliability.

are somewhat less likely to live in families than are their counterparts in other race and origin groups. Spanish origin women are more likely than other older women to live with kin. Admittedly, few older people live in multigenerational households. A 1975 national survey found only 12% of those married and 17% of those unmarried sharing households with offspring (Shanas, n.d., Table 6-1A). In 1970, not even 3%

of households encompassed parents, children, and grandchildren (U.S. Bureau of the Census, 1973a, Table 17).

Those older people who share housing with offspring may be either heading their own households or living as guests in their children's homes. The latter option is exercised largely by those who are widowed, ill, impoverished, and/or very old. Contrary to common belief, the widow is not much more likely to move in with kin than is the widower. In 1970, only a third of those whose spouses had died lived with relatives (U.S. Bureau of the Census, 1973b, Table 2). The rarity of residentially dependent parents is suggested by the fact that less than 5% of households in 1970 contained a parent or parent-in-law of the head (U.S. Bureau of the Census, 1973a, Table 2).

Neither is it common for the aged to head households containing younger generations. Only 3.3% of all household heads aged 65 and older in 1970 had dependent offspring under 18 in their homes, although the figure was closer to 10% in black and Spanish-surname homes where late childbearing has been more usual. Occasionally, grown children who are single or just starting married life live with their parents. Thus, of older husbands heading households, one in six had offspring in residence. However, grandchildren seldom live in their grandparent's home. Only 3% of families headed by older people included grandchildren. Again, subcultural variations exist: 13% of black families with older heads contained grandchildren (U.S. Bureau of the Census, 1973a, Table 17).

It would be wrong to conclude from the living arrangements of older people that they have been spurned by kin. Most older people have chosen to live apart—that is, alone or with their spouses. This preference for privacy is not limited to the aged: the young, single or married, are also less likely to share housing with their middle-aged parents today than was the case 40 years ago (Beresford & Rivlin, 1966). The independent living arrangement of the aged couple or widow is but one aspect of a broader trend toward smaller and more private households; in 1870 the average household had 5.7 persons, but today the average is less than 3 persons. This trend may owe less to the demise of the extended family than to declines in fertility, servants, and boarders (B. Laslett, 1973). For the aged, however, trends toward solitary living have been attributed to rising income permitting the old to purchase desired privacy in housing (Michael, Fuchs, & Scott, 1980) and to fertility declines, which have limited the numbers of grown offspring with whom housing might be shared (Kobrin, 1976).

There is nothing to indicate that the morale of older people suffers from such private living arrangements. In 1975, older unmarried women living with children were about as likely to report themselves as "often lonely" as were their counterparts living alone (Shanas, n.d., Table 8-12A). Another survey of 11,153 individuals aged 58-63 found that those married men and single women living with kin were actually less likely to report themselves "happy" (Murray, 1973, p. 18). Other research revealed that for married couples in retirement, the morale of both husbands and wives was inversely related to the propinquity of offspring (Kerckhoff, 1966a). Widows have been shown to identify readily sources of potential friction in intergenerational living; they point to lifestyle differences, conflicts over authority or household division of labor, and the irritating boisterousness of grandchildren (Lopata, 1973, pp. 114-123). In short, the aged today live apart from offspring because it is their preference to do so, and this arrangement seems to have no ill effects on well-being.

INTERGENERATIONAL RELATIONS

Many older people manage to maintain both their own homes and involvement with kin—a pattern aptly characterized as "intimacy at a distance." For example, 89% of parents aged 65 and over report having seen one of their children in the last month (Shanas, n.d., Table 7-1A). This reflects the accessibility of kin; three-quarters of older parents have a child who lives less than 30 minutes away (Shanas, n.d., Table 6-11A).[1] Of course, not all children are in close contact with parents. Daughters keep in touch more than sons, unmarried offspring more than married ones, own children more than sons-in-law and daughters-in-law, and nearby children more than distant ones.

Clearly, interaction with aging parents depends not merely on bonds of affection but also on financial constraints to visiting, other responsibilities, and competing social or recreational interests. Visiting with relatives is more common in the working class. If distance is taken into account, however, the middle class visit most—because they have the economic wherewithal and because they typically move away to pursue economic opportunities, not to escape from kin (Adams, 1968). Retirement sometimes permits middle-class parents to move nearer to their children (Litwak, 1960), and parents in ill health seem more likely to have children residing nearby (Shanas, 1962, p. 119).

In addition to socializing together, families typically exchange help along generational lines, and most people turn to their kin with their troubles. Help may take the form of financial assistance, gifts, services, or advice and counseling. Some help is routinely given (for example, child care, chauffeuring, shopping, or housekeeping), and other aid may be extended periodically on ceremonial occasions or during crises. For instance, relatives may make funeral arrangements, help pay a hospital bill, or attend sick kin.

There is little support for any stereotype of the aged as abjectly dependent on or brazenly demanding of the resources of the kin network. Indeed, high expectations for children's filial involvement are associated with low morale (Seelback & Sauer, 1977). Older people endorse self-reliance: they are more likely than the general public or the offspring of the elderly to feel that older folks should provide for themselves after retirement and less likely to assign responsibility to children (Shanas, 1962, pp. 133-134). Older people either represent a more independent generation or come to hold such views only with age—as they measure their own capacities, their potential as an economic burden, and the willingness and ability of others to help. Data from the Cornell Study of Occupational Retirement suggest that, although four-fifths of older people expect their children to keep in touch by visiting or writing, fewer believe that children are obliged to take care of them; only a minority feel children should live nearby or frequently entertain parents (Streib & Thompson, 1965, p. 478). Apparently, older people value personal affection and respect from children more than concrete aid, but most are loathe to intrude on their children's lives. An accounting of help received by the grandparent generation of a three-generation sample showed that, although a third of the older people acknowledged economic assistance, they were

---

[1] Only 3% of the noninstitutionalized population over 65 is without spouse, children, or siblings, although the proportion is doubtless higher among the 6% requiring institutional care. About 21% in 1975 had no living children (Shanas, n.d., Table 5-2A).

more likely to report getting help during illness (61%), help running their households (52%), or emotional gratification (62%) (Hill, 1970, p. 67).

Instead of being passive recipients in the family aid network, older people commonly contribute to relatives, especially children. Although declining health and finances may sometimes make the aged dependent on kin for support and services, older family members seem to give to the limits of their resources. Sons are apt to receive monetary aid, while daughters get services such as child care (Sussman, 1953). Parents are also more likely to furnish housing for married daughters than for married sons, perhaps because of the legendary antagonism between wives and mothers-in-law. In general, the working class may rely more on an exchange of services; middle-class kin are better able to provide financial help, a form of assistance transcending geographic separation (Adams, 1968).

Adjacent generations maintain the closest relations. Visiting and mutual assistance occur infrequently between grandparents and grandchildren (Hill, 1970), and in one study nearly half of the Chicago widows sampled did not feel close to any of their grandchildren (Lopata, 1973). Generally, it is the middle-aged, not the aged, person who has young grandchildren. Involvement with this youngest generation is so varied that Neugarten and Weinstein (1964) can distinguish five styles of grandparenting: formal, fun-seeker, distant figure, substitute parent, and reservoir of family wisdom. The latter two styles are rare, for few grandparents assume motherly care of, or patriarchal authority over, grandchildren. Although some grandparents, especially younger ones, foster playful relations, most exercise greater reserve, maintaining a benevolent concern but perhaps only fleeting contact. Grandparenting is not universally enjoyed, and a third of grandparents interviewed by Neugarten and Weinstein found the role uncomfortable, disappointing, or unrewarding.

Siblings also evidence less solidarity than parents and children. Indeed, a principal link between adult siblings is often the aged parent. Apparently, siblings assume greater importance in the lives of the never married and the childless widowed (Shanas, n.d., Table 7-10A), and sisters form stronger attachments to one another than do brothers (Adams, 1968).

THE FUTURE OF INTERGENERATIONAL EXCHANGES

Do these familial exchanges meet the interpersonal needs of the elderly? In reviewing all the evidence on contemporary kin relations, Peterson (1970, p. 516) finds considerable support for the thesis that family "relations do not offer substantial intimacy or emotional support to aging persons." Some aged have no family. Some families are characterized by outright conflict, as evidenced by vindictive disinheritance of kin by some aged will-makers (Rosenfeld, 1979). For many older people, contact with kin is too infrequent to provide companionship. Money and services may be exchanged with only minimal affect and interaction. Even if families fall short of providing day-to-day social contact for the aged, younger kin may be sources of generative gratification and vicarious accomplishment. As Bengtson and Kuypers (1971) point out, many parents view offspring as social heirs who extend their personal histories and validate their lives. Given this involvement, it is not surprising that older people feel their children should move away from them if better economic opportunities beckon (Peterson, 1970; Streib, 1958). This "developmental stake" in descendants encourages parents to minimize generational differences and, as compared to their children, to perceive greater closeness, understanding, and communication between family members (Bengtson & Kuypers, 1971).

Although families may remain a source of emotional satisfaction, social change may alter the capacity of families to respond to the day-to-day needs of aging kin. Today the provision of services to frail and dependent elderly relations constitutes a major challenge for families. Demographic, social, and economic changes are undermining the family's role as the self-sufficient mainstay of support systems for the aged (Treas, 1978). First, lengthening life spans have swelled the ranks of aging parents, and long-run declines in fertility have acted to reduce the number of siblings who can shoulder the responsibility for aging mothers and fathers. Second, rising labor-force participation of middle-aged women has meant that these family "kinkeepers" have new responsibilities that cut into time to perform housekeeping services, run errands, or furnish custodial care for the aged who can no longer care for themselves. Lastly, economic transformations have reduced the financial interdependence of generations. On the one hand, the declining importance of inheritance for the socioeconomic fortunes of offspring has reduced the aged's clout in compelling attentions from heirs. On the other hand, Social Security, Medicare, and other public provisions for older Americans have reduced their dependence on the generosity of kin.

These factors argue that fewer and fewer families will be willing and able to go-it-alone in meeting the everyday needs of aging kin for housekeeping, nursing, and custodial care. Increasingly, professional service-providers are called on to meet the needs once filled by family members. For a quarter of the noninstitutionalized bedfast elderly in 1975, for example, housework and meal preparation were performed by nonrelatives—an increase over 1962, when nonrelations did housework for 15% of the bedfast elderly and made meals for 20% (Shanas, n.d., Table 4–10A).

To be sure, families will continue to have a role in helping the aged. A study of grandmothers, mothers, and daughters found that all three generations prefer family members over friends or formal service-providers for confidantes, food shopping, or financial management. However, younger generations are more favorably disposed toward formal supports for housework, meal preparation, and personal care as well as for help in meeting expenses (Brody, Davis, & Johnsen, 1979). This division of labor between family members and others may represent a necessary adaptation to the changing demands of family life.

THE LATER FAMILY LIFE-CYCLE

Thus far our discussion has focused on the influence of extended kin in the lives of older people. It is worth noting, however, that the conjugal family undergoes predictable changes in composition, organization, and function as its members age. Under the rubric of the family life cycle, these changes represent a modal pattern of family experience. Deviations from this pattern or variations in timing of experience are important determinants of the social context of aging for the individual.

From an historical perspective the most striking feature of family life in later years is the prolonged period that a couple may expect to spend together after their children have left home. It is estimated that mothers born in 1920 will be at an average age of 52 at the marriage of their last child, as compared with an age of 56 for those women born in 1880. This decline is due to the mothers' early conclusion of childbearing and their offspring's propensity to marry young (Glick & Parke, 1965). More noteworthy is the fact that eight in ten mothers will share this "final launching" with their husbands; among the earlier generation, only half of the couples survived to see their last child wed. Declines in mortality have meant couples may anticipate a decade or two together without children in the home.

Although we recognize that family life-cycle schema are inapplicable to some (for example, the never-married, the childless, and the divorced), we find it useful to consider those family situations that are customarily experienced by the majority of middle-aged and aged. These include a child-launching phase during which offspring assume economic independence, a childless preretirement period, a retirement stage, and ultimately widowhood. Despite the association of stage and age, there is considerable diversity in the timing and duration of each phase of the family life-cycle (Neugarten & Moore, 1968), and the impact of any stage on the individual may depend on the scheduling of family events.

Consider childbearing patterns. Couples who complete their families at young ages will still be in the prime of life when the last child leaves home; the parents of "change of life" babies may have a dependent child in the household when they are ready to retire. Adolescent children are expensive to support, and increasingly parents are called on to subsidize the prolonged schooling or early marriages of offspring. If heightened economic responsibilities coincide with peak earnings of the breadwinner, there is no threat of a deterioration in family living standard. However, as Oppenheimer (1974) has noted, the father whose relative earning power declines as family needs rise faces a serious problem, and this pattern of "life-cycle squeeze" unfortunately typifies the lower paying occupations. A crisis of the family exchequer may be averted by moonlighting, overtime, or the wife's return to work, just as an earlier generation met rising expenses by taking in boarders (Modell & Hareven, 1973). Those couples who in their late 50s or 60s must still support children, especially when the breadwinner's income fails to keep pace, have little opportunity to save for retirement.

A considerable body of research evidence suggests that sudden life changes (a residential move, divorce, or a financial windfall, for example) can precipitate declines in health and morale (Holmes & Holmes, 1970). Chance creates a staggering accumulation of change in the lives of a few individuals. (Most of us have known someone beset like Job with a rapid succession of calamities.) The intersection of physical, economic, social, and family life-cycles ensures that most older people experience patterned (and possibly disconcerting) episodes of heightened change. Retirement, for instance, usually is accompanied by a drop in income, sometimes involves relocating in a retirement community, and may result from a disability.

The child-launching stage brings a welcome reduction in economic responsibilities and a release from household chores and child supervision. Although this postparental period presents opportunities for increased marital intimacy, travel, and new leisure activities, it is thought to be a troubled time for some women. A few years ago the "empty nest" phenomenon gained national attention with well-publicized accounts of First Lady Betty Ford's own bout with depression, a demoralization associated with grown children and a busy husband. Most women, of course, make the transition to the empty nest with little difficulty, and a national survey found empty nest women average higher morale than do counterparts with children still at home (Glenn, 1975). Some women, however, seem to experience a crisis of purposelessness when their days of active mothering are behind them. Pauline Bart (1971) reports that maternal role loss is characteristic of middle-aged women hospitalized for depression and that emotional illness serves to reinvolve children in their mother's life.

Physiological aging compounds the empty nest syndrome. Youth, beauty, and sex appeal—qualities so valued in women—are regarded as virtually synonymous in our culture; it is hardly surprising that wrinkles and sagging flesh represent to middle-aged women the loss of important assets. Menopause, so shrouded in myth, also signals the end of youth. Husbands, for whom the middle years may mean the zenith of a career, are sometimes too involved in work to be very supportive. In fact, some husbands may be preoccupied with crises of their own—crises instigated by declining sexual potency or the realization that they must reconcile youthful ambition with their more modest accomplishments.

The usual prescription for the problems of the empty nest is the substitution of new roles for lost ones. Women are encouraged to find a job, return to school, get involved in community affairs, or take up a hobby. Actually, few mothers wait until the nest is empty to reenter the labor force. Family economic need is greater when the children are still at home; also, as they get older, qualify for day-care centers, go to school, and assist with chores, children require less care and supervision. By working after the children are launched, a woman may be contributing to retirement savings, demonstrating career commitment, or just keeping busy. Women workers, however, tend to retire earlier than men; this comes in response to reduced economic need, husband's retirement, or declines in health and energy that make it more difficult to keep house while holding a job (Treas, 1979). Relatively little is known about how women adjust to their retirement. Since women's lives have traditionally centered on the home, their labor-force withdrawal has been viewed as unproblematic and even welcome.

As we might anticipate, household changes (such as the children's dispersal or the husband's retirement) are associated with changes in marital interaction. Unfortunately, researchers have achieved little consensus on the question of whether the last half of marriage affords couples more or less satisfaction than earlier years; some have discerned growing marital disenchantment (Pineo, 1968), while others find an upswing in contentment among middle-aged and older couples (Rollins & Cannon, 1974; Stinnett, Carter, & Montgomery, 1972). However people may view their own marriages, the later years are not considered the best time in most marriages; only 8% of respondents in a 1972 Gallup poll believed married couples are happiest after the children have left home (Blake, 1974, p. 38). Despite this dim view of late-life marital relationships, the old are less likely than younger couples to divorce. Although the old have been affected by the rising divorce rate, their rates of marital dissolution have not increased as rapidly as those of the young. The lower divorce rates of the old may reflect happier marriages, more aversion to divorce, fewer alternative partners, or greater investment in the ongoing relationship. The marriages of the old are also select matches so solid as to have avoided divorce in early years.

Qualitative changes in marital interaction are apparent. For one thing, companionship seems to replace romance and passion (Feldman, 1964). Although an end to sexual activity is not inevitable, coital frequency decreases after the middle years. When marital sex ends, it is usually due to the husband's wishes or declining capacities (Pfeiffer, Verwoerdt, & Wang, 1970); however, as Masters and Johnson (1966, 1970) have pointed out, boredom, fatigue, overeating, preoccupations, illness, or heavy drinking may cause temporary impotence, which is reversible if not compounded by grave anxieties about declining virility. The physical changes of menopause need not hamper sexual pleasure either, although some women benefit from hormone therapy. For both men and women, sexual capacity in old age depends on previous adjustment and continuing sexual stimulation; long periods of abstinence in old age are associated with declining sexual prowess. Despite physiological changes that may lengthen necessary arousal time or reduce orgasmic intensity, the greatest obstacle to full sexual enjoyment may well be the widely held misbelief that sexuality is not a normal aspect of old age.

Older couples focus conversations on different topics than their younger counterparts. For example, they discuss children less often than those whose offspring remain at home. The talk of elderly marrieds has been found to be limited to conventional topics: church, home upkeep, and particularly health (Feldman, 1964). To be sure, aging may reorder the conversational concerns of older couples. Some interactional differences between middle-aged and aged couples, however, may reflect cohort differences in preoccupations. Unfortunately, there is a lack of longitudinal data following couples over time—data that could clarify many issues of aging and marital adjustment.

Available evidence contradicts the notion that couples grow apart; middle-aged husbands and wives were found to be more alike in personality than were newlyweds (Murstein, 1961). Gutmann (1975) has speculated that a sex-linked division of labor in parenting encourages men to suppress dependency needs in order to be good providers and protectors, while women give up aggression to better meet their affective roles. The postparental phase, it follows, allows men to become more "feminine" and women more "masculine." Some evidence suggests that women acquire more power with age. In Hill's (1965) study of three generations, interviewers reported that grandmothers dominated the interview more often than wives in the two younger generations, despite the fact that the grandfather was more often reported to have the final word in decision making. Neugarten and Gutmann (1968) report the results of a Thematic Apperception Test (TAT) in which respondents were asked to fantasize a story based on the picture of a conventional group consisting of an old man, an old woman, a young man, and a young woman. Interestingly, passivity and familial attachment were often attributed to the old man, while the old woman was commonly described as aggressive and demanding. These age-sex role descriptions were reported most frequently by older respondents; since TAT results are often interpreted as projections of respondents' own needs and traits, it seems age may well bring a convergence (or even a reversal) of gender-linked personality characteristics.

Relatively little is known about interpersonal adaptations demanded by retirement of the family's principal breadwinner. A husband's retirement may occasion change in task allocation as he helps more around the house. Infirmities sometimes require major shifts in household division of labor as couples work out ways to accomplish basic housekeeping (and perhaps new nursing) responsibilities. Incorporating a newly idle husband into the daily household routine is commonly thought to be stressful for a wife. A study of wives of retired teachers revealed complaints about too much togetherness, too little personal freedom, and too many demands on time—disadvantages sometimes offset by satisfactions in feeling needed (Keating & Cole, 1980). Several studies suggest wives may become increasingly disillusioned with their spouses' retirement. For one thing, retirement often fails to fulfill women's expectations of more time in which to pursue their interests (Kerckhoff, 1966b). Retirement typically requires a downward adjustment of living standard due to the decline in income, but it may take some time before any inadequacies of retirement provisions are recognized. Also, the longer a man is retired, the more likely he and his wife are to suffer poor health. For whatever reason, women with husbands retired five or more years are more likely than wives of more recently retired men to wish for later retirement on the part of their spouses (Kerckhoff, 1966b). A positive relation was also found between the length of the husband's retirement and the proportion of wives saying they were sorry their husbands stopped working (Heyman & Jeffers, 1968).

WIDOWHOOD

The conclusion of the family life-cycle involves marital dissolution and the new role of widowhood for the surviving partner, usually the wife. The increase in the percent widowed, shown graphically in Figure 5-1, illustrates the gradual attrition from the married population. After age 65, less than half of women are living with a spouse. Because widowhood touches most aging families and demands such dramatic adaptations in the lives of survivors, this last stage of the family life cycle warrants special consideration.

Some psychological preparation for widowhood usually occurs before bereavement. The death of friends' spouses may precipitate mental rehearsals for one's own potential loss, as does the declining health or terminal illness of one's mate. As we have suggested before, timing may influence the impact of a life-cycle event (such as widowhood) on the individual. The young widow, whose loss is typically sudden and unanticipated, is thought to be more shaken by the death of a spouse than is the older woman who has had more ample time to ready herself psychologically and economically (Heyman & Gianturco, 1974).

Despite anticipatory socialization, bereavement is typically a trying time of numbness, and it is subsequently followed by uncontrollable episodes of longing and sorrow interspersed with depression; weight loss, insomnia, and irritability are common conditions (Parkes, 1965). Although symptoms usually abate in a few months, one in five widows reports that she has never gotten over her grief (Lopata, 1973,

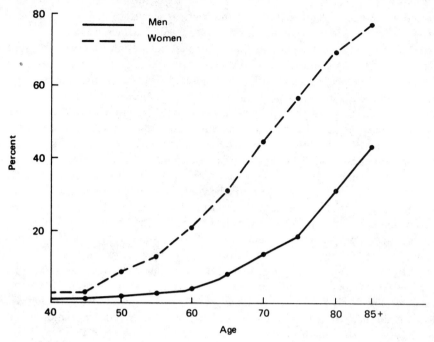

Figure 5-1. Widowed as a percentage of the population by age and sex, 1970. (United States Bureau of the Census, *Census of Population: 1970, Marital status*, Table 2.)

p. 51). Indeed, the widowed are more likely than those married to report themselves unhappy (Gurin, Veroff, & Feld, 1960). As we might expect given the known association of life changes and illness, the widowed represent a population of high health risk; they have higher rates of mental illness (Gove, 1972), mortality (Gove, 1973), and suicide (Bock, 1972).

Exactly what life changes occur with the death of one's spouse? Lopata's (1973) study of Chicago-area widows represents a pioneering effort to provide some answers to this question. Clearly, widowhood means the loss, reorganization, and acquisition of social roles. In ceasing to be a wife, a woman can no longer function as her husband's nurse, confidante, sex partner, or housekeeper, but she may have to assume unfamiliar roles such as financial manager, handyman, or worker. Other social relations may also be disrupted. Intimacy with in-laws seems not to survive the husband's death; only a quarter of Chicago widows saw their husband's relatives with any frequency (Lopata, 1973, p. 57). The widow may find that she is avoided by friends who are discomforted at her grief, that she is a "fifth wheel" in couple-oriented interaction, and that she can no longer maintain old social contacts because her entertainment budget is limited or because she does not drive. New activity patterns, friends, and gratifications eventually supplant old ones; half of Lopata's (1973, p. 75) widows had so adjusted to their new lifestyles as to see compensations in widowhood (for example, independence or a reduction in work load).

Those who would undertake to help the newly widowed adjust would be well informed by Lopata's (1973, p. 270-274) suggestions. Companions who can listen sympathetically to the widow's grief, relieve loneliness, and share activities are most valuable. Building the widow's competence and confidence at problem solving is top priority; while help with immediate crises is desirable, well-meaning advice that encourages dependency is not. Major decisions (such as investments or change in residence) are best postponed for a year or so, until the widow's outlook and lifestyle adjust to the change in her marital status.

Children may facilitate the mother's adjustment in three ways: by assuming responsibilities previously borne by the father, by replacing the father as a focus of the mother's attention and ministration, and by maintaining supportive interpersonal relations. Although sons are reportedly most helpful at overseeing funeral arrangements and finances, daughters (who give services and visit frequently) are regarded as emotionally closer to the mother. Apparently, oldest and youngest children are especially obliged to help, for first and last children who shirk filial responsibilities are subject to the most maternal criticism (Lopata, 1973, p. 101-103).

NEW MARRIAGES AND MARITAL ALTERNATIVES

Although loneliness is reportedly the greatest difficulty faced by widows (Lopata, 1973, pp. 66-72), remarriage is not a commonly employed recourse. Marriage rates for older people are low, despite variations by sex and previous marital status. Many senior citizens seem to view remarriage as improper; about a third of those over 60 in a rural sample frowned on such matches, although younger respondents were more tolerant of these older unions (Britton & Britton, 1967, p. 67). Nevertheless, children's opposition or Social Security penalization of widows who remarry may discourage many from seeking new partners. Happily, late marriages seem to enjoy considerable success, especially when buttressed by motivations of love or companionship, adequate income, and offspring's approval (McKain, 1972).

Older people encounter some difficulties in finding new mates. Since limited mobility, energy, and budgets restrict courtship activities, it is not surprising older people tend to marry longtime acquaintances (McKain, 1972). Men are six times more likely than women to marry after 65. Due to sex differences in mortality and widowhood, there are three single women for every unmarried man in the population over 65. Older men, however, are not restricted by social norms to marrying older women: 20% of grooms over 65 attracted brides under 55 in 1970, while only 3% of older brides wed men under 55 (Treas & VanHilst, 1976). Certainly, this behavioral evidence buttresses survey findings that women are seen as "old" sooner than men (Neugarten, Moore, & Lowe, 1965).

Although older men have an easier time than older women finding partners, they also may have more to gain from marriage. Widowhood may be a more devastating experience for men; because so few husbands can expect to survive their partners, they may not undergo the mental rehearsals for life alone which are typical of older wives. Widowers seem to suffer from greater social isolation than widows, a condition leading us to predict the higher suicide rates of widowed men (Bock, 1972). Not only do widowers lose a companion, they also experience a greater decline in kin inter-action (Berardo, 1967), presumably because the wife typically maintains contact with relatives. Husbands tend to be more enthusiastic than wives about their marriage —reporting greater happiness, fewer marital problems, and less blaming of spouse (Gurin, Veroff, & Feld, 1960, pp. 84–116); it follows that men may be more favorably disposed toward remarriage, given their more satisfactory experiences within the insti-tution. At least among women, Lopata (1973, pp. 90–91) found that widows who had been satisfied with previous unions were more receptive to the notion of remarrying.

Despite the benefits that married living confers, there are obvious demographic constraints on the numbers of older people who can pair off in traditional unions. Alternatives to conventional marriage may offer solutions to the unmet needs of some older people, just as foster grandparent programs can furnish affectionate intergenera-tional contacts. A retirement magazine has featured an article entitled, "Should Retired Women Live Together?" On the basis of her own experience, the author answered yes, pointing out the economy and companionship in sharing a home (Conk-lin, 1974). Cavan (1973) speculates that many marital innovations (heretofore limited largely to bohemian youth) could work for the aged if their disapproval could be over-come. Nonmarital cohabitation, polygyny, group marriage, communes, and homo-sexual companionships are examples. As Gebhard (1970, p. 94) reports, a sizable minority of older women already acknowledge unconventional liaisons; of those aged 51-60, 40% of divorcees and 25% of widows reported postmarital coitus. Nonmarital cohabitation is rare among the aged, nonetheless. In 1976, only 2% of all unmarried men aged 65 and older lived alone with a woman to whom they were not related. Only 0.5% of aged single women lived alone with an unrelated man (Glick, 1979).

CONCLUSION

The family is the focus of many of the life changes associated with aging, such as the dispersal of offspring and the loss of a spouse. The family is a source of life change, but it is also a resource for change. The kinship aid network, the intergenerational investments of emotion, and the reciprocal support of marital relations all may miti-gate the stressful personal disorganization that can accompany life's transitions. The family may fall short of meeting the needs of some older people, and its inadequacies may be even more apparent if the broader society fails to provide adequately for older citizens. Nevertheless, the American family shows remarkable solidarity in the face of a mobile and changing world.

REFERENCES

Adams, B. N. *Kinship in an urban setting.* Chicago: Markham, 1968.

Bart, P. Depression in middle-aged women. In V. Gornick & B. K. Moran (Eds.), *Women in sexist society.* New York: New American Library, 1971.

Bengtson, V. L., & Kuypers, J. A. Generational difference and the developmental stake. *Aging and Human Development,* 1971, *2,* 249–260.

Berardo, F. M. *Social adaptation to widowhood among a rural-urban aged population.* Washington Agricultural Experimental Station Bulletin 689. Pullman, Wash.: Washington State University College of Agriculture, December, 1967.

Beresford, J. C., & Rivlin, A. M. Privacy, poverty, and old age. *Demography,* 1966, *3*(1), 247-258.

Blake, J. Can we believe recent data on birth expectations in the United States? *Demography,* 1974, *11*(1), 25-44.

Bock, E. W. Aging and suicide: The significance of marital, kinship, and alternative relations. *Family Coordinator,* 1972, *21*(1), 71-79.

Britton, J. H., & Britton, J. O. The middle aged and older rural person and his family. In E. G. Youmans (Ed.), *Older rural Americans.* Lexington, Ky.: University of Kentucky Press, 1967.

Brody, E., Davis, L., & Johnsen, P. *Formal and informal service providers: Preferences of three generations of women.* Paper presented at the 1979 annual meeting of the Gerontological Society, Washington, D.C., November 25-29, 1979.

Cavan, R. S. Speculations on innovations to conventional marriage in old age. *Gerontologist,* 1973, *13*(4), 409-411.

Conklin, F. Should retired women live together? *NRTA Journal,* 1974, (25), 19-20.

Dahlin, M. Perspectives on the family life of the elderly in 1900. *Gerontologist,* 1980, *20*(1), 99-107.

Feldman, H. Development of the husband-wife relationship. Preliminary report. *Cornell studies of marital development: Study in the transition to parenthood.* Ithaca, N.Y.: Department of Child Development and Family Relationships, New York State College of Home Economics, Cornell University, 1964.

Gebhard, P. Post-marital coitus among widows and divorcees. In P. Bohannan (Ed.), *Divorce and after.* Garden City, N.Y.: Doubleday, 1970.

Glenn, N. D. Psychological well-being in the postparental stage: Some evidence from national surveys. *Journal of Marriage and the Family,* 1975, *37*, 105-110.

Glick, P. C. The future marital status and living arrangements of the elderly. *Gerontologist,* 1979, *19*(3), 301-309.

Glick, P. C., & Parke, R. Jr. New approaches in studying the life cycle of the family. *Demography,* 1965, *2*, 187-202.

Gove, W. R. The relationship between sex roles, marital roles, and mental illness. *Social Forces,* 1972, *51*, 34-44.

Gove, W. R. Sex, marital status, and mortality. *American Journal of Sociology,* 1973, *79*(1), 45-67.

Gurin, G., Veroff, J. & Feld, S. *Americans view their mental health.* New York: Basic Books, 1960.

Gutmann, D. Parenthood: Key to the comparative psychology of the life cycle. In N. Datan & L. Ginsberg (Eds.), *Life span developmental psychology.* New York: Academic Press, 1975.

Heyman, D. K., & Gianturco, D. T. Long term adaptation by the elderly to bereavement. In E. Palmore (Ed.), *Normal aging II.* Durham, N. C.: Duke University Press, 1974.

Heyman, D. K., & Jeffers, F. G. Wives and retirement: Pilot study. *Journal of Gerontology,* 1968, *23*(4), 488-496.

Hill, R. Decision making and the family life cycle. In E. Shanas & G. F. Streib (Eds.), *Social structure and the family: Generational relations.* Englewood Cliffs, N.J.: Prentice-Hall, 1965.

Hill, R. *Family development in three generations.* Cambridge, Mass.: Schenkman, 1970.

Holmes, T. S. & Holmes, H. Short-term intrusions into the life style routine. *Journal of Psychosomatic Research,* 1970, *14,* 121-132.

Keating, N. C., & Cole, P. What do I do with him 24 hours a day: Changes in the housewife's role after retirement. *Gerontologist,* 1980, *20*(1), 84-89.

Kerckhoff, A. C. Family patterns and morale in retirement. In I. H. Simpson & J. C. McKinney (Eds.), *Social aspects of aging.* Durham, N.C.: Duke University Press, 1966a.

Kerckhoff, A. C. Husband-wife expectations and reactions to retirement. In I. H. Simpson & J. C. McKinney (Eds.), *Social aspects of aging.* Durham, N.C.: Duke University Press, 1966b.

Kobrin, F. E. The fall of household size and the rise of the primary individual in the United States. *Demography, 1976, 13,* 127–138.

Laslett, B. The family as a public and private institution: An historical perspective. *Journal of Marriage and the Family,* 1973, *35*(3), 480–492.

Laslett, P. *The world we have lost.* London: University Paperbacks, 1971.

Litwak, E. Geographic mobility and extended family cohesion. *American Sociological Review,* 1960, *25,* 385–394.

Lopata, H. Z. *Widowhood in an American city.* Cambridge, Mass.: Schenkman, 1973.

McKain, W. C. A new look at old marriages. *Family Coordinator,* 1972, *21,* 61–69.

Masters, W. H., & Johnson, V. E. *Human sexual response.* Boston: Little, Brown, 1966.

Masters, W. H., & Johnson, V. E. *Human sexual inadequacy.* Boston: Little, Brown, 1970.

Michael, R. T., Fuchs, V. R., & Scott, S. R. Changes in the propensity to live alone: 1950–1976. *Demography,* 1980, *17*(1), 39–56.

Modell, J. & Hareven, T. K. Urbanization and the malleable household: An examination of boarding and lodging in American families. *Journal of Marriage and the Family,* 1973, *35*(3), 467–479.

Murray, J. Family structure in the preretirement years. *Retirement history study report no. 4.* Washington, D.C.: U.S. Department of Health, Education, and Welfare, 1973.

Murstein, B. I. The complementary need hypothesis in newlyweds and middle-aged married couples. *Journal of Abnormal and Social Psychology,* 1961, *63,* 194–197.

Neugarten, B. L., & Gutmann, D. L. Age-sex roles and personality in middle-age: A thematic apperception test. In B. L. Neugarten (Ed.), *Middle age and aging.* Chicago: University of Chicago Press, 1968.

Neugarten, B. L., & Moore, J. W. The changing age-status system. In B. L. Neugarten (Ed.), *Middle age and aging.* Chicago: University of Chicago Press, 1968.

Neugarten, B. L., Moore, J. W., & Lowe, J. C. Age norms, age constraints, and adult socialization. *American Journal of Sociology,* 1965, *70,* 710–717.

Neugarten, B. L., & Weinstein, K. The changing American grandparent. *Journal of Marriage and the Family,* 1964, *26,* 199–204.

Oppenheimer, V. The life-cycle squeeze: The interaction of men's occupational and family life cycles. *Demography,* 1974, *11*(2), 227–246.

Parkes, C. M. Bereavement and mental illness: A clinical study. *British Journal of Medical Psychology,* 1965, *28,* 1–26.

Peterson, J. A. A developmental view of the aging family. In J. E. Birren (Ed.), *Contemporary gerontology: Concepts and issues.* Los Angeles: University of Southern California Gerontology Center, 1970.

Pfeiffer, E., Verwoerdt, A., & Wang, H. S. Sexual behavior in aged men and women. In E. Palmore (Ed.), *Normal aging.* Durham, N.C.: Duke University Press, 1970.

Pineo, P. Disenchantment in the later years of marriage. In B. L. Neugarten (Ed.), *Middle age and aging.* Chicago: University of Chicago Press, 1968.

Rollins, B. C., & Cannon, K. L. Marital satisfaction over the family life cycle: A re-evaluation. *Journal of Marriage and the Family,* 1974, *36*(2), 271–282.

Rosenfeld, J. P. *The legacy of aging: Inheritance and disinheritance in social perspective.* Norwood, N.J.: Ablex, 1979.

Seelbach, W. C., & Sauer, W. J. Filial responsibility expectations and morale among aged parents. *Gerontologist,* 1977, *17*(3), 492–499.

Shanas, E. *National survey of the aged.* Final report, grant no. HEW OHD 90-A-369. Unpublished manuscript, n.d.

Shanas, E. *The health of older people: A social survey.* Cambridge, Mass.: Harvard University Press, 1962.

Stinnett, N., Carter, L. M., & Montgomery, J. E. Older persons' perceptions of their marriages. *Journal of Marriage and the Family,* 1972, *34*(4), 667–672.

Streib, G. F. Family patterns in retirement. *Journal of Social Issues,* 1958, *14*(2), 35–45.

Streib, G. F., & Thompson, W. E. The older person in a family context. In E. Shanas & G. F. Streib (Eds.), *Social structure and family intergenerational relations.* Englewood Cliffs, N.J.: Prentice-Hall, 1965.

Sussman, M. B. The help pattern in the middle class family. *American Sociological Review,* 1953, *43*, 22–28.

Treas, J. Family support systems for the aged: Some social and demographic considerations. *Gerontologist,* 1978, *17*(6), 486–491.

Treas, J. Women's employment and its implications for the status of the elderly of the future. In S. B. Keisler, J. N. Morgan, & V. K. Oppenheimer (Eds.), *Aging: Social change.* New York: Academic Press, 1981.

Treas, J., & VanHilst, A. Marriage and remarriage rates among older Americans. *Gerontologist,* 1976, *16*(2), 132–136.

U.S. Bureau of the Census. *Census of population: 1970.* Family composition. Final Report PC(2)-4A. Washington, D.C.: U.S. Government Printing Office, 1973a.

U.S. Bureau of the Census. *Census of population: 1970.* Persons by family characteristics. Final Report PC(2)-4B. Washington, D.C.: U.S. Government Printing Office, 1973b.

PART **II**

BEHAVIORAL SCIENCE PERSPECTIVES

CHAPTER **6**

Personality and Aging

Margaret Neiswender Reedy

There are many popular stereotypes about how personality changes as we grow older. Some common notions are that as individuals age they become more irritable, demanding, critical, fault-finding, and set in their ways. This chapter explores the validity of these commonly held notions by presenting the theoretical and empirical literature on personality and aging. Specifically, this chapter addresses the following topics: (1) definitions and problems in studying personality and aging; (2) theories of personality development; (3) empirical research on personality stability and change; (4) cohort and sex differences in personality; (5) personality, stress, and disease; (6) psychopathology of later life; and (7) personality, adaptation, and life satisfaction. As we shall see, there is evidence for both personality continuity and change with aging. Also, aging both affects and is affected by personality. That is, personality change is the result of age-related processes, but also the quality of life during aging is affected by the kind of personality an individual has.

DEFINITIONS AND PROBLEMS
IN STUDYING PERSONALITY AND AGING

For the developmental psychologist, *personality* can be most usefully defined as the predictable way in which an individual perceives himself or herself and responds to others and the events of life. The predictability of personality implies that personality traits may be stable or that they may change in predictable ways. Within this definition personality becomes a broad concept that includes such other concepts as ego strength, competence, self-concept, self-esteem, and self-acceptance, as well as intrapsychic processes and overt behaviors.

Many theoretical and methodological problems arise in the study of personality and aging. These have been reviewed by Neugarten (1968). A major problem is that researchers do not agree on their definitions of personality traits, nor on the instruments they use to measure these traits. Also, samples of subjects have been extremely varied from one study to the next, and, within one study, subjects of different ages may also vary along a number of different dimensions such as intelligence, health status, or socioeconomic level. Unless these extraneous factors are controlled, research findings about age differences are confounded by these variables.

Other problems include the use of measuring instruments of unknown or questionable reliability and validity for older persons and the use of tests that are not meaningful or relevant to assessing personality in older adults. Furthermore, it is not clear that personality constructs (for example, aggression/dominance) have comparable meanings in youth, middle age, and old age. Finally, in most studies, investigators of personality and aging have attempted to assess age-related changes without investigating the impact of specific life events (such as retirement, widowhood, or remarriage) on personality change. Given all these problems, it is not surprising the empirical research on personality and aging is replete with inconsistent and contradictory findings.

THEORIES OF ADULT PERSONALITY DEVELOPMENT

Theories of personality development center around the notion that normal personality development, successful adjustment, mental health, or maturity involves mastering a series of stresses at various points in life. These stresses have been called *psychosocial crises* (Erikson, 1959) or *developmental tasks* (Havighurst, 1972). According to these developmental theories, mental health does not involve the "absence of problems, difficulties and frustrations, but rather an ability to deal with problems and events of daily life in a satisfying and effective manner" (Birren & Renner, 1979). Theories of personality development, then, give us some ideas about how adulthood is organized; describe the major concerns, events, and transition points in adulthood; and reveal some of the forces leading to stability and change in personality during adulthood. Frameworks for understanding adult personality development can be divided into four basic types: psychodynamic and ego psychology theories, social psychological theories, cognitive theories, and empirical descriptive models (Stevens-Long, 1979).

Psychodynamic and ego psychology theories

The early dominance of psychoanalytic thought in the development of personality theories led to the notion that personality is established early in childhood and that adult personality does not change. However, three important theorists—Jung, Buhler, and Erikson—proposed life span models of personality change. Jung (1933) proposed a stage model of adult development. In this model he describes an increase in introversion in middle and old age. He also suggests that old age is characterized by an urgency to reevaluate and integrate life experiences.

Buhler (1935; Buhler & Massarik, 1968) described stages in personality development corresponding to a biological model of growth, culmination, and decline. Her model was developed from the autobiographies and biographies of over 400 individuals and emphasizes changes in motivation and goals at different stages of life. For Buhler, adolescence and young adulthood are characterized by the goals of creative expansion and tentative self-determination. Central concerns during these years are to select an occupation and establish an intimate relationship with another person. In the adult years from 25 to 45, stability, continued creative expansion, and maximum self-determination are central goals. Although stability is the major characteristic of these years, there is continuing family and occupational development. Upholding internal order is viewed as the goal of the middle years from 45 to 66. The middle years are a time of self-assessment and reevaluation of past goals. This reevaluation can lead to the decision to make major life changes. Finally, the major goal of the aging individual is seen as being self-limitation. Self-limitation involves the realization of declining energy and the focusing of goals and interests within the boundaries of available strength. The later years are viewed as a time for introspection and reviewing life experiences, leading to a sense of fulfillment or failure in life. The aging individual must also come to terms with the possibility of increasing physical, economic, and interpersonal dependency. In Buhler's view, life satisfaction in old age is related more to an individual's assessment of whether life goals have been fulfilled than to biological decline or dependency. For Buhler, a sense of personal productivity, morality, self-actualization, and luck are all avenues by which the aged individual can realize a sense of fulfillment in life.

Erikson (1959, 1963) described eight stages of personality development across the life span, building on Freud's psychoanalytic theory of development. However, in contrast to Freud and Buhler, who viewed personality development as more biologically determined, Erikson viewed development as consisting of the progressive resolution of conflicts between individual needs and social demands. His model emphasizes the cultural and social influences on personality development. In Erikson's model, the last four stages characterize the years from adolescence to the end of life, and each stage is characterized by a key psychological task or conflict. Failure to resolve the key psychological task successfully at each stage at least partially makes it impossible to move on to the next stage of development.

According to Erikson, the central task for the adolescent involves achieving a sense of ego identity. To avoid identity diffusion, the individual must try out and experiment with adult roles, begin to discover his uniqueness, and clarify his attitudes and values. Achieving intimacy is the key psychological task for the young adult. In order to achieve intimacy and avoid isolation, commitment to another person is essential. Failure at this stage leads to self-absorption, isolation, and fearfulness of others. The task for the middle-aged person is to achieve a sense of generativity, which involves occupational and/or family productivity. Generative middle-aged individuals are those who have produced something of value for future generations through occupational accomplishments or by helping to develop creativity and productivity in younger individuals. An individual who fails at the task of generativity feels a sense of stagnation, boredom, and self-preoccupation. The key task for the older adult is to achieve ego integrity. Ego integrity involves accepting responsibility for the kind of life one has had, realizing that it could not have been much different, and accepting one's life as having been meaningful and worthwhile. Failure to achieve ego integrity results in despair, a sense of the meaninglessness of life, and a sense that the time left to live is too short.

Peck (1968) has elaborated Erikson's framework for the developmental tasks of middle and old age. Peck delineates four subtasks of the middle years, including (1) valuing wisdom versus physical powers (focusing on intellectual values and effective decision-making or on body strength and physical achievements); (2) socializing versus sexualizing in relationships (focusing on people as friends or people as sexual objects to be conquered; (3) emotional flexibility versus impoverishment (being able to shift emotional investments or emotional rigidity); and (4) mental flexibility versus impoverishment (being flexible in establishing new goals or dominated by past habits). The three subtasks of old age, according to Peck include (1) ego differentiation versus work-role preoccupation (viewing oneself as a complex, flexible person or limited to one major role activity); (2) body transcendance versus preoccupation (valuing social and mental activities or valuing body attractiveness); and (3) ego transcendance versus preoccupation (leaving a legacy or ego-centered with no lasting record of one's existence).

The models of personality development proposed by Jung, Buhler, and Erikson have been most influential in describing important dimensions of adult development and personality change. These models are based on clinical observation, case studies, and interviews. They have not been confirmed by empirical research, mainly because operational definitions and measuring instruments for psychoanalytic or ego concepts are lacking. Furthermore, although these models sensitize us to normative personality issues, they do not help us to understand individual differences in development, nor the ways development proceeds differently by sex, ethnicity, social class, or culture.

Social psychological theories

Social psychological theories of adult personality development generally maintain that there are no general personality dispositions. Personality and behavior are seen as being situation-specific, and personality is believed to result from socialization experiences and social roles. Two of the best known social-psychological theories for understanding adult personality development come from the works of Ahammer (1978) and Brim (Brim & Wheeler, 1966). Ahammer has promoted a social learning theory of adult personality development. According to this theory, new stimulus conditions (events in the environment such as marriage, occupation, or parenthood) demand new responses and therefore lead to personality and behavior change. In this model the process of socialization, which refers to learning the skills, attitudes, values, and roles characteristic of a particular sociocultural milieu, is responsible for development and change in personality during adulthood. In a similar vein Brim and Wheeler have argued that adult personality change can be understood in terms of the changing demands society places on individuals as they move through the age-graded structure of our culture. Since society's expectations for appropriate behavior change with age (see Chapter 4), individuals acquire new roles, attitudes, and beliefs as they age. In this was individuals gain new personality and behavioral dispositions as they move from youth to middle to old age.

Clearly, social psychological theories can account for considerable personality change in adulthood. They can also be used to support the notion of personality continuity and stability in the adult years. For example, Ahammer has suggested that adults tend to be resistant to personality and behavior change and experience demands for change as aversive events. Thus, people are attracted to other people and environmental settings that do not demand much change. In this sense personality may remain stable for relatively long periods of time because interpersonal and/or environmental settings (for example, marriage, occupation, or friendships) remain fairly constant, either because the present situation is experienced as pleasurable or because the individual resists changing an unpleasant situation.

Cognitive theory

Cognitive theorists have emphasized the internal nature of personality development during aging. Thomae (1970) has described a cognitive theory of personality and aging that involves three basic assumptions. First, according to this view, the perception of change in the self leads to behavioral changes in an individual. Second, beliefs, concerns, and expectations determine self-perceptions, so that change in self-perception results from changes in beliefs and expectations. Third, adjustment to aging is related to how efficiently the individual is able to maintain and restructure the balance between cognitions (self-perceptions based on roles and activities) and motivations (expectations, needs, or concerns). To the extent that self-perceptions, expectations, beliefs, and concerns remain stable or are changing across the life span, this cognitive theory is able to support both the idea of personality change and stability in adulthood.

Empirical-descriptive models

Three empirically based frameworks describing adult personality development have been recently proposed by Roger Gould (1972); D. J. Levinson, Darrow, Klein, M. H. Levinson, & McKee (1974); and Vaillant (1977; Vaillant & McArthur, 1972).

Gould examined major life concerns at different phases of life by administering a questionnaire to a large group of white, middle-class individuals aged 16–60 and to a group of psychiatric outpatients. Gould has described ambivalence and leaving home as the central concerns of adolescence; establishment as the central goal of young adulthood; reassessment, turmoil, and uncertainty about the future as key concern in mid-life; and freedom and flowering as the most salient characteristics of individuals moving into their 60s. Notably, Gould characterizes the middle years as an unstable period, accompanied by personal discomfort, introspection, a sense of the finiteness of life, and an existential questioning of values and goals.

The Harvard Grant Study by Vaillant (1977; Vaillant & McArthur, 1972) reports data from a 40-year longitudinal study of 268 men who were among those in the Harvard classes of 1939–1944. This study reveals the nature of personality development in adult men under the most favorable circumstances. Based on clinical interviews, Vaillant and McArthur conclude that middle age is a time of reassessing and reordering the past, self-appraisal, and depression, as well as a time for a renewed sense of personal vitality. Vaillant and McArthur also report that from young adulthood to middle age there is an increasing tendency to use mature rather than immature defense mechanisms. This suggests that, in spite of the turmoil experienced during the middle years, there is an increasing ability to handle stress and change. Also, their data suggest that crisis and turmoil need not necessarily be experienced as negative. The Harvard men seemed to be able to accept the turmoil and depression of their middle years, and the best adapted of these men described the period from 35 to 49 as the best period of their lives. Additionally, these middle-aged men experienced an increasing sense of competence and mastery as well as a greater sense of autonomy and authority.

Finally, the longitudinal study conducted by Levinson and his associates (1974) has described the psychosocial development of men from college age through mid-life. This developmental framework is based on interviews with 40 men from four occupational groups including blue-collar and white-collar workers, business executives, and academicians. Like Erikson, Levinson maintains that the developmental periods he describes are determined both by the nature of man and the nature of society. According to Levinson, the major task of the adolescent years is leaving the family. The individual is trying to separate himself physically and psychologically from his family of origin. The major goal of the 20s is to get into the adult world. This involves exploring the possibilities available, developing an initial life structure, and choosing an occupation and a mate. The 30s are viewed as a time for settling down and for making deeper commitments to work, family, and valued interests. In addition to this desire for stability and security in the 30s, there is also a desire to be free and unfettered of commitments. The middle or late 30s is characterized by a desire to become one's own person, to function independently of authority figures, and to end relationships with mentors. The mid-life transition period, which occurs in the early 40s according to Levinson, results from the experience of disparity between achievements and aspirations. The major issues during this period involve a sense of bodily decline, an increasing sense of personal mortality and aging, and a greater openness to formerly devalued parts of the self—especially those typically associated with the opposite sex. Finally, the middle-to-late 40s are seen as a time of restabilization, when a new life structure emerges following the reassessment and reevaluation of the previous period.

Although they involved different samples, methods of data collection, and methodology, all three descriptive studies offer quite similar descriptions of personality development in adulthood. Table 6-1 shows the relationship between the models proposed by Buhler, Erikson, Gould, and Levinson. Like Buhler and Jung, all the descriptive models suggest that the middle and later years are a time of heightened introspection and that there is an increasing awareness of personal mortality and the finiteness of time in middle age. Similarly, Neugarten (1968) describes a shift in the perception of time in the middle years, so that individuals begin to think in terms of years left to live rather than in terms of years lived. Similarities between the models are also evident in conceptualizations of personality development in old age. For both Buhler and Erikson, the central task of the later years is to achieve a sense of fulfillment and acceptance of one's self and the life one has lived. Butler (1963) has described a normal process of life review through which this sense of integrity may be achieved. The life review can be accomplished by story telling, reminiscence, or the writing of autobiographies. According to Butler, the life review may be related to the development of candor, serenity, and wisdom in old age. Through the life review the

TABLE 6-1. Stages and personality development in adulthood

Buhler (1935, 1968)		Erikson (1959, 1963)		Gould (1972)		Levinson et al. (1974)	
Age range	Central task	Age range	Central task	Age range	Central task	Age range	Central task
13–24	Creative expansion and tentative self-determination	13–19	Identity versus identity diffusion	16–18	Ambivalence	16–20	Leaving home
				18–22	Leaving home	20–29	Getting into the adult world
		20–35 (approx.)	Intimacy versus isolation	22–28	Establishment		
25–45	Stability and continued creative expansion			29–32	30s transition	30–34	Settling down
		35–50 (approx.)	Generativity versus stagnation	33–40	Adulthood	35–39	Becoming one's own person
				40–43	Mid-life transition	40–42	Mid-life transition
45–65	Self-assessment and upholding of internal order	50+	Integrity versus despair	43–50	Mid-life	43–50	Restabilization
65+	Self-limitation, life-review, and fulfillment or failure			51–60	Flowering		

individual can integrate life experiences, tie loose ends together, and interpret and find meaning in existence. Since a life review through story telling and reminiscence may not naturally occur in our society, artificially structured opportunities for life review may be needed. Birren, Reedy, and Schroots (1980) studied the effects of a 10-session guided autobiography class on the self and ideal self-concepts of a group of older persons. The results of their preliminary study suggest that the process of writing one's autobiography leads to a greater sense of personal integration, as measured by a greater congruence of the real and ideal self-concepts.

IS ADULT PERSONALITY CHANGING OR STABLE: EMPIRICAL RESEARCH

Although hundreds of studies have been conducted during the past two decades to explore age differences in personality traits, the findings have been notably inconsistent from one study to the next. The following paragraphs describe the major findings of empirical research giving evidence for personality change and stability.

Research evidence for personality change

Increasing attention to the inner self, or introversion, is perhaps the best-documented finding in the developmental study of personality (Botwinick, 1978; Neugarten, 1977; Schaie & Marquette, 1972). Neugarten (1968) described a shift toward increasing "interiority" with advancing age based on projective data obtained on individuals aged 40-90 as part of the classic Kansas City studies of adult development conducted by the University of Chicago Human Development Committee. This increased interiority, or decrease in ego energy, among older adults reflects a shift from outer to inner concerns. These researchers found a decline with age on all measures of ego energy both cross-sectionally and longitudinally. Specifically, older adults, compared to middle-aged adults, projected less conflict, vigorous activity, intense emotion, and nonpictured characters into their responses to ambiguous Thematic Apperception Test pictures. A number of other research studies have also found an increase in introversion with age (Calden and Hokanson, 1959; Chown, 1968; Gutman, 1966; Heron & Chown, 1967; Sealy & Cattell, 1965; Slater & Scarr, 1964). These other studies, however, were cross-sectional, so that age changes were confounded with generational differences. Since the correlations between age and introversion are statistically significant but small (Chown, 1968), it appears that age alone does not account for this increase in introversion as people age.

A number of cross-sectional studies suggest that there may be an increase in desurgency with age (Botwinick, 1978; Cattell, 1950; Fozard, 1972; Sealy & Cattell, 1965). Desurgency reflects the tendency to be serious and sober rather than zestful and happy-go-lucky. This finding of increased desurgency with age is consistent with the findings for increased introversion, since an individual who tends to be introverted would be more likely to be desurgent rather than surgent.

There also seems to be an increase in cautiousness with age (Botwinick, 1978). In laboratory studies older adults tend to avoid taking any action, even if taking action involves little risk. For example, when making a decision in which one choice of action offers a 90% chance of success and a 10% chance of failure, and the other choice is an alternative of inaction, the older person will choose inaction (Botwinick, 1966). However, if the choice of taking no action is removed from the decision-making situation, age differences in cautiousness disappear (Botwinick, 1969) This suggests that when older people are forced to take some risk, they take just as much risk as younger subjects do. The tendency to avoid making decisions and a preference for not being wrong appears to begin before old age. Gergen and Back (1969) studied age differences in responses to a political survey. They found that middle-aged individuals (40-59) were more likely than young adults to give "no opinion" responses. Furthermore, this tendency to have no opinion was even more pronounced among the old.

Level of education appears to be an important variable affecting the relationship between age and cautiousness. Botwinick (1966) found that a high level of education seems to reduce the tendency toward cautiousness in later life. Cautiousness in the old, which appears to be more marked among elderly with little education, has been interpreted as resulting from a greater need for certainty with advancing age. This greater need for certainty may be related to an increasing fear of failure or to decreasing self-confidence in one's abilities. Cautiousness in old age is a way of avoiding failure and maintaining self-esteem. When viewed in this way, cautiousness in the elderly becomes an adaptive mechanism in that it helps protect the older person's ego.

An increase in conformity and passivity also seems to occur with advancing age. In the Kansas City studies researchers found a shift from active to passive mastery from mid-life to old age (Neugarten & Gutmann, 1958). Whereas individuals in their 40s described a pictured male figure as energetic, aggressive, and achieving, 60-year-olds described the same male figure as passive and conforming. Other studies, reviewed by Chown (1968), have also found a shift from active to passive mastery with aging. Gutmann (1964, 1969, 1974) studied four other cultures, including the Navajo in Arizona, the Lowland and Highland Mayans in Mexico, and the culturally isolated Druze of Israel. He found this same shift from active to passive mastery in all four cultures, suggesting the possible universality of this aging change.

This greater tendency among the aged toward passivity, conformity, and inaction also emerges in studies of social conformity (Klein, 1972). Older adults are more likely to be swayed by group opinion in making perceptual judgments, especially as the difficulty of the judgments increases. In Klein's research, greater conformity among the old occurred in a variety of situations, including visual and auditory judgments, arithmetic problems, and social attitudes. Thus, it appears that social conformity is a generalized tendency among older adults. Klein hypothesized that conformity in the elderly might be due to a greater need for certainty or to a sense of incompetence. In one phase of his study Klein manipulated the experimental situation to increase the elderly subjects' perceived level of competence. He found that when he did so, their tendency to conform decreased.

Taken together, the studies of introversion, cautiousness, and conformity suggest that there is an increasing tendency to turn inward with age and that there is greater cautiousness. This cautiousness appears to reflect an increased need for certainty and desire to avoid failure. In this sense, cautiousness in old age appears to be an adaptive mechanism serving to maintain self-esteem. Since most of the research that investigates the traits of introversion, desurgency, passivity, cautiousness, and conformity is cross-sectional, it is possible that the age differences found do not reflect age changes but are due to generational differences in values, experiences, socioeconomic status, and/or education. Although cross-cultural research suggests the possible universality of a shift from active to passive mastery (Neugarten, 1977), it also appears that these personality dispositions, if they do increase with advancing age, may be reversible (Klein, 1972).

Research evidence for stability

Although age differences in the personality dimensions of introversion/extroversion, surgency/desurgency, activity/passivity, cautiousness, and conformity have been identified, what is perhaps most remarkable about research in this area is that relatively few age-related changes in personality have been consistently identified (Botwinick, 1978; Neugarten, 1977; Schaie & Marquette, 1972).

Little research evidence supports the popular notions that rigidity or conservatism increases with age (Botwinick, 1978; Chown, 1961; Cutler, see Chapter 19). Cross-sectional studies do suggest a greater tendency toward rigidity in older persons. Older persons are more likely to persist in using inappropriate solutions or to appear dogmatic in their attitudes (Botwinick, 1978). However, since measured intelligence is a more important predictor of rigidity than age (Chown, 1961), the greater rigidity of the elderly in cross-sectional studies can be understood in terms of the lowered measured intelligence and fewer years of education among today's elderly. It is likely that an intelligent older person will be flexible, rather than rigid, and that future generations of elderly will be increasingly less rigid. In relation to the stereotype of increasing conservatism with age, the results of one investigation of political attitudes (Douglass, Cleveland, & Maddox, 1974) clearly show that sociocultural and generational factors explain most of the important political differences between age groups. Age appears to bear little relationship to political attitudes or candidate preferences.

Generally, the cross-sectional and longitudinal research on personality and aging suggests that personality remains fairly stable in adulthood. Given that dramatic changes in life circumstances do not occur, people become more consistently themselves, more like what they have always been, as they grow older (Neugarten et al., 1964). Four major studies point to the continuity and stability of personality in adulthood.

The Kansas City studies revealed stability in the "socioadaptational" aspects of personality as individuals moved from their 40s into their later years. Based on questionnaires and interview data obtained over a 10-year period, Neugarten (Neugarten et al., 1964) concluded that styles of coping, achieving life satisfaction, and goal-directed behavior remained consistent from mid-life to old age. The University of Chicago researchers concluded that the way individuals relate to others and to the world generally remain the same as individuals age and that there are a variety of ways in which a relatively stable personality can successfully adjust and adapt to the changes in roles and status that accompany aging.

In the Berkely study of personality differences in adaptation to retirement, Reichard, Livson, and Peterson (1962) extensively interviewed 87 men aged 55–84.

Compared to the middle-aged men, the older men were observed to be less defensive in their relations with others and more candid and self-disclosing on sensitive topics. In general, however, the researchers found evidence for consistency of personality from middle to late life. Based on personality ratings, five personality types were identified. There was no tendency for age to be related to personality types.

Whereas these first two studies emphasize the stability of personality from mid-life to old age, a longitudinal study by Woodruff and Birren (1972) gives evidence for the stability of personality over a 25-year-period from young adulthood to middle age. Out of a large group of college students who completed a personality inventory in 1944, 54 of these individuals were located and retested in 1969. Comparing the 1955 and 1969 responses provided information about objective age changes in personality. Also, at the 1969 testing, these now middle-aged individuals were asked to complete the inventory describing how they thought they were in 1944. By comparing this retrospective view with their actual self-descriptions in 1944, subjective age changes could be examined. The results showed that objective age changes from young adult-hood to middle age were small, supporting the concept of stability of personality during adulthood. However, subjective age changes were large (see Figure 6-1). As middle-aged people, the subjects projected a negative image of themselves as young adults. They tended to see themselves as having changed in a positive way over the 25 years much more than they actually had changed. Subjects subjectively experienced a discontinuity between their young adult and middle-aged selves, which did not exist objectively.

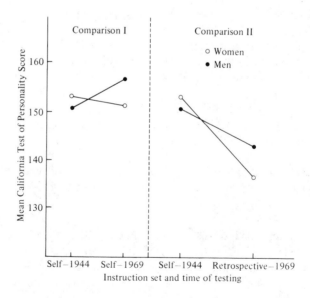

Figure 6-1. California Test of Personality scores in 1944 and 1969 for the 1924 cohort in the self and retrospection conditions. (*Woodruff & Birren, 1972*)

Schaie and Parham (1976) administered a personality and attitudes questionnaire to a large sample aged 21–84. The testing was done twice, with seven years intervening between testings. Using a cross-sequential design to analyze the data, these researchers were able to identify maturational and sociocultural trends as well as cohort differences in personality. Schaie and Parham found stability rather than age change for most of the personality factors. They found evidence for increases with age for two dimensions of personality: excitability and humanitarian concern. This finding of increased excitability conflicts with other research pointing to decreases in surgency with age (Botwinick, 1978). Thus, although research suggests changes in selected aspects of personality with age, including a shift from active to passive mastery and increases in introversion, conformity, and cautiousness, the findings generally point to the stability of personality during aging.

COHORT AND SEX DIFFERENCES IN PERSONALITY

There is considerable evidence for the existence of cohort differences in personality (Botwinick, 1978; Neugarten, 1977; Schaie & Marquette, 1972; Schaie & Parham, 1976; Woodruff & Birren, 1972). In the study described in the previous section, Woodruff and Birren (1972) tested high school and college students as well as middle-aged people and found large cohort differences in self-description. Schaie and Parham (1976) emphasized the importance of cohort differences over maturational changes in understanding personality development. These researchers found their older cohorts (aged 57–77) to be less morally constrained and more candid in relations with others compared to younger cohorts. The middle cohorts (aged 43–56) were uniquely characterized by greater dominance and assertiveness as well as vulnerability and sensitivity to criticism. Finally, the youngest cohorts (22–42) were characterized by greater flexibility, restraint in their relations with others, and concern with honesty and morality. These researchers also noted shifts in personality over time due to sociocultural influences. Sociocultural trends in personality, which affected all cohorts over the seven-year period, included increases in conservatism and practicality and a decrease in trust of others.

Whereas the importance of generational differences in personality has been well emphasized, the developmental nature of sex differences in personality has not received much attention (Botwinick, 1978; Stevens-Long, 1979). Some research suggests that a sex role reversal may occur in middle or old age. The observed shift from active to passive mastery may be more characteristic of the aging male than the aging female. Two decades ago, Neugarten and Gutmann (1958) collected data using projective tests and observed that men seemed to be less aggressive and domineering with age and more in touch with their needs for nurturance and affiliation. By contrast, women appeared to move toward greater assertiveness and dominance from middle to old age. More recent studies have identified a similar shift (Lowenthal, Thurnber, & Chiraboga, 1975).

Gutmann (1975) has suggested that this shift in sex roles and tendency toward a "normal unisex of later life" may result from the increased freedom and decreased need for traditional sex roles in the postparental years. He suggests that in the postparental years, women no longer need to suppress their aggressive impulses to nurture and care for children. Further, older men do not need to suppress affiliative and nurturing tendencies in order to succeed as breadwinners. Another explanation for the finding of a sex role reversal is methodological. Because of differential dropout rates in longitudinal studies, better educated subjects remain in the study over the years and are less likely to show traditional sex role differences (Urberg & Labovie-Vief, 1976). Also, some cross-sectional research does not give evidence for this sex role reversal. A study by Ryff and Baltes (1976) revealed similarity between middle-aged and older men and women in personality traits. In this study middle-aged men and women both emphasized more masculine traits such as ambition, competence, and courage compared with their younger counterparts. Older men and women both emphasized accomplishment, freedom, and happiness.

With the current cultural emphasis on male involvement in parenting and female participation in work outside the home, this sex role reversal in later life may be less likely to occur as today's young adult women and men grow older. A cross-sectional study by Reedy (1977) suggests that traditional sex differences in personality are less likely to characterize young adult men and women compared to middle-aged and other individuals. Reedy studied the personality needs of 102 married couples aged 20–80. All subjects were well educated. For five of the personality needs studied—including autonomy, affiliation, dominance, abasement, and nurturance—no significant differences were found for young adult men and women, whereas traditional sex differences in these needs emerged for the middle-aged and older men and women. Thus, although no sex differences in these needs were evident in young adulthood, middle-aged and older women were found to be more affiliative, nurturing, and self-abasing, but less autonomous and dominant compared with their male counterparts (see Figure 6-2). The evidence from this data is that, at least in a well-educated sample, the women's movement and the emphasis on androgenous roles may be having its impact on the personality need structures of young adult men and women. If traditional sex differences in personality are less characteristic of the current young adult cohort, there may be less potential for a sex role reversal in middle or later life for these individuals.

PERSONALITY, STRESS, AND DISEASE

Although many factors such as individual constitution, exercise, nutrition, and marital status appear to mediate the relationship between life stress and physical health, increasing evidence suggests that lifestyle and personality play an important role in health and longevity (Woodruff, 1977). Anecdotal evidence suggests that certain personality traits characterize very long-living individuals. In particular, long-lived people seem to be happy, self-confident, and relaxed. Gallup and Hill (1960) interviewed individuals who had lived close to 100 years and found that the majority described themselves as easygoing, cheerful, and self-confident. They felt their lives had been well spent, they enjoyed people and beauty in the world, and they were able to tolerate frustration.

By contrast, a number of investigators have postulated that certain personality characteristics are related to the development of life-shortening diseases. Individuals

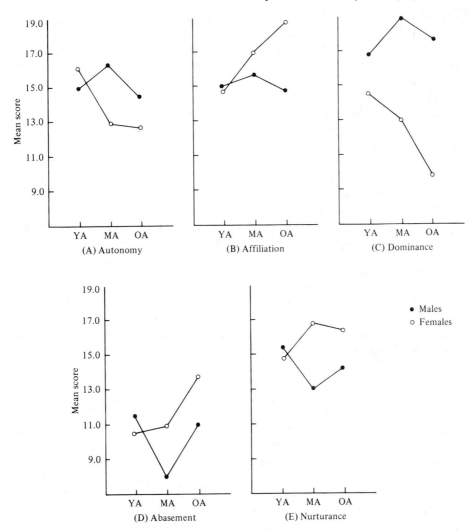

Figure 6-2 (A-E). Sex differences for five personal needs in young, middle-aged, and older adults. (*Reedy, 1977*)

with hypertension have been characterized as obsessive or compulsive, lacking in self-assertion skills, aggressive, tense, and anxious (Brod, 1971; Sainsbury, 1960). Several studies (Bakker, 1968; Caffrey, 1969; Nowlin, Williams, & Wilkie, 1973) of middle-aged and older individuals have found that anxiety, apprehension, and sensitivity to other people's approval and disapproval is related to the development of coronary artery disease. A study of elderly male patients by Brown and Ritzman (1967) revealed that coronary disease patients were more likely to report excessively high levels of stress, tension, and worry in describing their lives than patients without coronary disease. More importantly, 83% of those with coronary disease described themselves as competitive, aggressive, and status-conscious, compared with only 17% of their counterparts without coronary disease.

Perhaps the most influential studies of the relationship between personality and disease are those by Friedman and Rosenman (1974), who have published some 50 articles and books on the Type A and Type B behavior patterns and coronary heart disease. The Type A personality pattern involves a style of life that is characterized by excessive competitive drive, achievement orientation, aggressiveness, time urgency, impatience, restlessness, and easily aroused hostility (Eisdorfer & Wilkie, 1977; Woodruff, 1977). The Type A person does not take time for lunch, is constantly trying to do two or more things at once, and often interrupts to answer questions before they have been fully asked. Directly opposite to Type A behavior, Type B behavior is nonaggressive, patient, easygoing, and relaxed. Type B individuals are characterized by traits similar to those Gallup and Hill found among the near-centenarians they interviewed.

Friedman and Rosenman began a large-scale prospective study in 1960 involving men aged 39–59. These men were classified as Type A or Type B, and a variety of physiological measures were obtained. Follow-up data revealed that the Type A men were twice as likely to develop clinical coronary heart disease and to suffer a fatal heart attack as the Type B men (Rosenman, 1974). Other risk factors in heart disease including weight, diet, and moderate smoking were also found to predict the development of heart disease. However, Type A was as powerful a predictor as these other factors. Also, these risk factors did not predict heart disease in Type B individuals, suggesting that the Type B personality provides an immunity to heart disease.

Significantly, Type A people without clinical evidence of heart disease have been found to show biochemical changes similar to those found in coronary heart disease patients. Furthermore, these biochemical changes have been found to vary directly with the intensity of Type A behavior. For example, blood cholesterol levels increased in a group of accountants from January to April. Time urgency and cholesterol peaked on April 15th, and by May or June the levels of both had dropped. Smoking, exercise, and diet were not found to have changed over the time period studied. Although most of the research on Type A and heart disease has involved middle-aged men, Type A women appear to show similar biochemical changes and to be equally predisposed to develop heart disease (Kenigsberg, Zyzanski, Jenkins, Wardwell, & Licciardello, 1974). As more women pursue demanding careers that encourage Type A behavior, the incidence of heart disease in women is likely to increase.

In addition to the Type A behavior pattern, individuals who have a lifestyle in which change, unpredictability, and ambiguity are central characteristics appear to be more susceptible to heart disease. Research by Theorell and Rahe (1974) revealed that a significant increase in life changes—alterations in the people, activities, or environments that an individual experiences—over a six-month to one-year period were positively related to the incidence of heart attacks. Holmes and Rahe (1967) developed the Social Readjustment Rating Scale, which lists 43 life events such as retirement, death of spouse, and change in residence. Each life event is assigned a "life crisis unit" score, reflecting how stressful the event is. There is considerable evidence that the greater the number of life crisis units an individual experiences, the more likely he or she is to develop an illness (Holmes & Masuda, 1973).

This increase in susceptibility to illness following life changes may be influenced by a number of factors including degree of preparation and anticipation, the "on-timeness" of the events, the extent to which the individual has control over the event, previous experience in dealing with particular life changes, and resources for coping (Eisdorfer & Wilkie, 1977; Lowenthal & Chiraboga, 1973). Since women may be more prepared for widowhood (Lopata, 1973), they may adjust more easily to it. Some studies (Gerber, Rusalem, Hannon, Battin, & Ankin, 1975; Parkes, Benjamin, & Fitzgerald, 1969) have found higher mortality rates and more health problems among widowers in the six months following the death of the spouse compared to their married counterparts. Some evidence suggests (Woodruff, 1977) that widowers fare less well than widows following the death of a spouse; rates of physical and mental illness, accidents, and suicide are all higher for single men compared with single women. Preparation and anticipation also appear to ease the transition for elderly who are moving into an institution or who are being relocated from one institution to another (Boureston & Pastalan, undated). Neugarten (1970) has suggested that life events that occur "off-time" rather than "on-time" are experienced as more stressful. For example, when grandparenthood, retirement, or widowhood occur earlier in life than expected, these events are experienced as more stressful and are more likely to precipitate changes in physical and mental health. Younger individuals who are widowed appear to suffer from more prolonged or delayed grief (Stevens-Long, 1979).

A sense of control is also an important element in adjustment to stress and life change. In a study by Langer and Rodin (1977), residents in a nursing home who were given some sense of control and who were encouraged to make their own decisions were found to have higher morale and to be less depressed than those who were not given a sense of personal control over their lives. Resources for coping with change also appear to mediate the relationship between life changes and physical and mental health. The presence of a *confidant,* that is, a person in whom one can confide during a time of crisis or stress, has been found to decrease the incidence of depression in individuals who had recently been widowed or retired (Lowenthal & Haven, 1968).

PSYCHOPATHOLOGY AND AGING

Psychopathology in later life may be viewed as the failure to adapt to the life changes, stresses, and losses that typically characterize the later years. Based on his review of the literature, Pfeiffer (1977) concluded that approximately 15% of the aged in the United States suffer from at least moderate psychopathology. The incidence of psychopathology is higher in those elderly who are of advanced age, in poor physical health, or who are unmarried as a result of widowhood, separation, or divorce. Approximately 2%-3% of older people live in institutions as a result of psychiatric illness. The majority of institutionalized elderly with psychiatric illness reside in nursing homes, rather than in private or public mental institutions, and receive social and custodial, rather than psychiatric, care (Kahn, 1975). Although the elderly represent 30% of the public mental hospital population, they are dramatically underrepresented in outpatient care, where only 2% of patients seen are aged. There are several reasons why relatively few elderly seek or receive outpatient psychiatric treatment. First, a certain amount of mental illness may be more expected and tolerated in the elderly. Second, older people may be more reluctant to seek help. Third, counselors and therapists may be reluctant to treat the elderly because they mistakenly believe that the aged will not benefit from counseling (Busse & Pfeiffer, 1977). Finally, therapists and counselors may lack adequate training to deal with the psychological problems of the aged.

There are two general types of psychiatric disorders. *Functional disorders* are disorders that occur despite intact brain function. The most common functional disorders of later life include depression, paranoia, and hypochondriasis. *Organic disorders* are disorders that occur because of impaired brain function. The organic brain syndromes, which include senile dementia, vascular dementia, and delirum, are the most common organic disorders of later life. Both organic and functional disorders are relatively common in the elderly, and organic and functional disorders can coexist within the same individual.

Functional disorders

Depression. Depression is the most common functional disorder among the aged. It has been estimated that approximately 2%-10% of community-residing individuals over the age of 65 are significantly depressed (Gurland, 1976). Depressive reactions may be thought of as appropriate and inappropriate. Feelings of sadness, grief, and mourning are normal and appropriate depressive reactions to loss. Inappropriate or psychiatric depressive reactions are generally more intense reactions to loss, which are characterized by affective, cognitive, behavioral, and physiological symptoms. These include intense sadness; feelings of guilt and hopelessness; negative perceptions of the self, the environment, and the future; problems in attention and concentration; withdrawal; psychomotor retardation; decreased appetite; insomnia; weight loss; and decreased libido (Beck, 1967). Unfortunately, since these changes are commonly thought of as "normal" in the elderly, depression in the aged is often not diagnosed or is misdiagnosed as organic brain syndrome (Copeland, Kelleher, Kellett, Fountain-Gourlay, Cowan, Barron, & Degruchy, 1974; Gurland, 1973).

Depressive affect may be so prevalent among the aged for several reasons. First, biochemical changes that occur with age may make older people more predisposed to depression. Research has shown that both the aged and depressed patients show decreased levels of norepinephrine and increased levels of monoamine oxidase in the brain (Zarit, 1980). Second, it has been proposed that depression follows losses and stresses. Since older people are more likely to experience major losses, they are more likely to become depressed (Paykel, 1974). Busse (1961) has suggested that whereas depressions in younger adults are based more on shame, guilt, or self-hate, the depressions of later life stem from the loss of loved ones or from loss of self-esteem due to financial, physical, or social role losses. Although no systematic research has investigated the efficacy of approaches to treating depressions in the elderly, Beck's (1967) cognitive behavioral therapy of depression and Lewinsohn's (Lewinsohn, Munoz, Youngren, & Zeiss, 1975) behavioral model appear to be very promising approaches.

These approaches focus on increasing self-esteem by altering perceptions of the self, the world, and the future; increasing pleasant activities; and increasing social skills.

Suicide. Thoughts of suicide are a primary characteristic of severe depression. Along with the high incidence of depression among the elderly, more suicides are committed in old age, especially among white males. In 1970, 23,000 people in the United States committed suicide, and 7000, or approximately 30% of these were people over age 65 (U.S. Public Health Service, 1974). The suicide rate increases steadily with age for men; for women, the suicide rate reaches a peak in middle age, and the rate is always lower than it is in men. Alcoholism, organic brain syndrome, and terminal illness (in addition to depression) increase suicide risk in the elderly. Older people are more likely to be successful in a suicide attempt than the young. Whereas the ratio of attempts to successes in the young is approximately 7:1, the ratio among the aged is approximately 1:1 (Pfeiffer, 1977).

Paranoia. Paranoid reactions are probably the second most common psychiatric disturbance among the elderly (Pfeiffer, 1977). Paranoia is characterized by suspiciousness and ideas of persecution. Whereas in young people paranoia often reflects severe psychiatric disturbance, paranoid reactions among the old have less serious psychiatric implication. Paranoia and suspiciousness are more common in older people with various kinds of sensory deficits, especially hearing impairments. Also, whereas depression is more likely to occur in an elderly individual who has experienced the loss of a close relationship, paranoid ideation is a more common reaction among elderly who have been loners, living relatively isolated from others for most of their lives (Berger & Zarit, 1978).

For the older person who is isolated from others, either because of sensory impairments or lack of a social network, paranoid states can compensate for this sensory or interpersonal deprivation. Precipitating factors in the development of paranoia in later life generally involve an acute stress, so that the individual feels he is no longer adequate or in control (Berger & Zarit, 1978). Symptoms of paranoia in the aged can be treated by the use of medication when appropriate; development of a therapeutic, supportive relationship with the individual; use of prosthetic devices to decrease sensory isolation; development of social skills and a social network; and a relatively stable, familiar environment.

Hypochondriasis. The third most frequent psychiatric disorder among the elderly is hypochondriasis. Hypochondriasis involves an excessive preoccupation with one's health in the absence of significant physical pathology (Pfeiffer, 1977). Hypochondriasis is more common in women and occurs with increasing incidence with age. In old age it has been explained as an escape from a feeling of personal failure (Busse & Pfeiffer, 1977). Thus, becoming sick may be more acceptable to the elderly person than assuming the role of failure. For example, the individual who has devoted his or her entire life to work or to raising a family may seek refuge in being a sick person after retirement or after children leave home. For some individuals, it may be easier to justify one's failure to reinvest in new goals and interests by taking the role of a sick person.

Organic disorders

Approximately 5% of the aged suffer from organic brain dysfunction. Incidence of organic brain impairment increases with age. Whereas about 3% of individuals aged 60-70 show evidence of organicity, about 20% of those aged 90-100 show signs of organic impairment. Symptoms of organic brain disease include impairments in abstraction skills, ability to assimilate new information, short- and long-term memory, and visual motor coordination. There may also be disorientation in relation to time, place, and people. With gradual onset and mild impairment, only the abilities to abstract and assimilate new information may be affected. When impairment is severe, individuals may not be able to recall their age or the names of their children; self-care skills may be lost, so that the individual is no longer able to dress and may be incontinent. Behavioral changes such as depression, loss of interest, apathy, panic, anxiety, agitation, and bewilderment may accompany organic impairment.

Chronic brain syndrome, or dementia. Two basic types of brain syndrome occur in later life (Sloane, 1980). Dementia, or chronic brain syndrome, refers to brain dysfunction that is irreversible. Two major types of dementia have been identified. Senile dementia is associated with diffuse brain cell loss of unknown etiology as well as other specific changes in the brain (Drachman, 1980; Sloane, 1980; Zarit, 1980). The course of the disease is generally progressive, although the disease process may stop at any point. Vascular dementia, in contrast to senile dementia, is due to localized death of brain tissue resulting from arteriosclerotic disease. The onset of the impairment is generally sudden, but some improvement in function may gradually return. Compared to senile dementia, the course of the disease is less even, and multiple cerebrovascular accidents may lead to a stepwise increase in impairment. The degree of cognitive and intellectual impairment in dementia is related to the extent of brain impairment, the rapidity of onset, the initial personality and intellectual resources of the individual, and the supportiveness of the environment. For example, community-residing elderly with organic brain syndrome generally do not show the decrements in self-care abilities that their institutionalized counterparts do.

Acute brain syndrome, or delirium. The second major type of organic brain disease found in the elderly is acute brain syndrome, or delirium. Delirium is reversible and is due to the temporary malfunctioning of a significant proportion of brain cells. Malnutrition, vitamin deficiency, infections, inappropriate medications, broken bones, posttrauma surgery, accidents, extreme sensory deprivation, alcohol, and a variety of diseases can cause an acute brain syndrome. Approximately 10%-20% of elderly individuals with organic brain syndrome have the reversible form (Pfeiffer, 1977). Individuals may have both chronic and acute organic impairment at the same time.

In the treatment of delirium, function is generally restored if the cause of the acute impairment can be alleviated or eliminated. In the treatment of dementia, the goals are to maximize independent functioning despite the presence of brain disease.

Helping the person stay in a familiar environment, not taking over activities the person can do, and providing support and information to the family are all important elements of a treatment program for the organic patient (Zarit, 1980).

PERSONALITY AND ADJUSTMENT

Two decades ago researchers proposed two theories of successful aging. The disengagement theory of Cumming and Henry (1961) was developed from the Kansas City research findings of a shift from active to passive mastery, an increase in interiority, and a decrease in role activity from middle to old age. According to the disengagement theory, the individual and the society mutually withdraw their investments in each other, and this decreased role and emotional involvement is related to low morale in the aged. By contrast, the activity theory of successful aging postulates that continued activity and emotional and role involvements in old age are related to high life satisfaction. These theoretical formulations prompted a host of research studies, which suggest that there is no simple pathway to adjustment in old age. Among the many factors found to be related to satisfaction, morale, and adjustment in old age are financial resources, marital status, health, and personality (Britton & Britton, 1972; Thomae, 1975). Neugarten (1977) argues that personality type or personality organization is the key to understanding which individuals will age successfully. Further, she argues that the individual's personality helps him or her adapt to the biological and social changes that occur with advancing age and is instrumental in helping to create a style of existence that will result in the most life satisfaction.

Several studies suggest that personality is an important mediating factor in understanding the relationship between activity and life satisfaction. In one study, Neugarten, Havighurst, and Tobin (1968) examined the relationship among personality type, amount of role activity, and life satisfaction in a sample of aged men and women. They identified eight different patterns of aging: the Reorganizers, the Focused, the Disengaged, the Holding-on, the Constricted, the Succorance seeking, the Apathetic, and the Disorganized. The first four patterns were all high in life satisfaction, although they varied in the extent of social interaction and personality type. The researchers concluded that certain personality types were more likely to age successfully than others. A similar conclusion was reached by Reichard, Livson, and Peterson (1962), who studied patterns of adaptation in old age. They described three personality types that adapt well to aging: Mature, Rockingchair, and Armoured. They also identified two types that adapt poorly to old age: the Angry type and the Self-haters.

Lowenthal, Thurnber, and Chiraboga (1975), who studied men and women at four stages in the life course, suggest that freedom to disengage from activities that are no longer rewarding may be an important predictor of adjustment in later life. Lowenthal and her colleagues identified four major personality or lifestyle types, including the simplistic and the complex types. The simplistic type has few social activities and involvements, few resources, and few difficulties. By contrast, the complex type has many resources as well as many problems. Among young adults the investigators found that complex individuals were the most satisfied with their lives. Although they experienced difficulties and problems in coping, they had many resources and were involved in many activities. However, among the older subjects, the complex were the least happy, and the simplistic type was highest in life satisfaction. These researchers hypothesize that the low level of satisfaction in the older, complex individuals may be due to the fact that society offers reduced opportunities for participation and self-expression, which are essential to satisfaction for the complex individual. As our society becomes less age-conscious and provides more opportunities for older persons, complex personalities may more easily maintain their lifestyles and life satisfaction into old age (Neugarten & Hagestad, 1977).

Some research suggests that some personality styles that are not particularly adaptive earlier in adulthood may become more adaptive in later life. For example, Leiberman (1971, 1975) suggests that combativeness or grouchiness may be highly adaptive and contribute to longevity in old age. Similarly, Gutmann (1971) describes combativeness as a primary characteristic of long-lived men in preliterate societies. The implication is that different personality and coping styles may contribute to adaptation at different stages in adulthood.

In summary, no one pattern of aging appears to guarantee satisfaction in later life. Generally, adaptation, satisfaction, and morale in old age appear to be highly related to an individual's lifelong personality style and general way of handling stress and change. In many ways the past is prologue to the future. Although personality can change in response to life events, environmental and interpersonal stresses, aging, sociocultural influences, or therapeutic intervention, an individual's personality generally appears to remain fairly stable throughout the adult years into old age.

REFERENCES

Ahammer, J. M. Social learning theory as a framework for the study of adult personality development. In P. B. Baltes & K. W. Schaie (Eds.), *Life span developmental psychology: Personality and socialization.* New York: Academic Press, 1978.

Ahammer, J. M., & Baltes, P. B. Objective versus perceived age differences in personality: How do adolescents, adults, and older people view themselves and each other? *Journal of Gerontology,* 1972, *27,* 46–57.

Bakker, C. B. Psychological factors in angina pectoris. *Psychosomatics,* 1968, *8,* 43–49.

Beck, A. *Depression.* New York: Hoeber, 1967.

Berger, K. A., & Zarit, S. H. Late life paranoid states: Assessment and treatment. *American Journal of Orthopsychiatry,* 1978, *48,* 528–537.

Birren, J. E., Reedy, M. N., & Schroots, J. J. H. *Life review through guided autobiography.* Paper presented at the American Psychological Association Meeting, Montreal, Canada, 1980.

Birren, J. E., & Renner, V. J. *A brief history of mental health and aging.* Washington, D.C.: National Institute of Mental Health, 1979.

Botwinick, J. Cautiousness in advanced age. *Journal of Gerontology,* 1966, *21,* 347–358.

Botwinick, J. Disinclination to venture response versus cautiousness in responding: Age differences. *Journal of Genetic Psychology,* 1969, *115,* 55–83.

Botwinick, J. *Aging and behavior* (2nd ed.). New York: Springer, 1978.

Boureston, N. C., & Pastalan, L. *Death and survival: Relocation report no. 2.* Ann Arbor: University of Michigan, Institute of Gerontology, n.d.

Brim, O. G., Jr., & Wheeler, S. *Socialization after childhood: Two essays.* New York: John Wiley and Sons, 1966.

Britton, J. H., & Britton, J. O. *Personality changes in aging: A longitudinal study of community residents.* New York: Springer, 1972.

Brod, J. The influence of higher nervous processes induced by psychosocial environment on the development of essential hypertension. In L. Levi (Ed.), *Society, stress and disease.* London: Oxford University Press, 1971.

Brown, R. C., & Ritzman, L. Some factors associated with absence of coronary heart disease in persons aged 65 or older. *Journal of the American Geriatric Society,* 1967, *15,* 234–249.

Buhler, C. The curve of life as studied in biographies. *Journal of Applied Psychology,* 1935, *19,* 405–409.

Buhler, C., & Massarik, F. (Eds.), *The course of human life.* New York: Springer, 1968.

Busse, E. W. Psychoneurotic reactions and defense mechanisms in the aged. In P. H. Hock & J. Zubin (Eds.), *Psychopathology of aging.* New York: Grune & Stratton, 1961.

Busse, E. W., & Pfeiffer, E. Functional psychiatric disorders in old age. In E. W. Busse & E. Pfeiffer (Eds.), *Behavior and adaptation in late life* (2nd ed.). Boston: Little, Brown, 1977.

Butler, R. N. The life review: An interpretation of reminiscence in the aged. *Psychology,* 1963, *26,* 65–76.

Caffrey, B. Behavior patterns and personality characteristics related to prevalence rates of coronary heart disease in American monks. *Journal of Chronic Diseases,* 1969, *22,* 93–103.

Calden, G., & Hokanson, J. E. The influence of age on MMPI response. *Journal of Clinical Psychology,* 1959, *15,* 194–195.

Cattell, R. B. *Personality: A systematic, theoretical and factual study.* New York: McGraw-Hill, 1950.

Chown, S. M. Age and the rigidities. *Journal of Gerontology,* 1961, *16,* 353–362.

Chown, S. M. Personality and aging. In K. W. Schaie (Ed.), *Theory and method of research on aging.* Morgantown: West Virginia University Press, 1968.

Copeland, J. R. M., Kelleher, M. J., Kellett, I. M., Fountain-Gourlay, A. J., Cowan, D. W., Barron, G., & Degruchy, J. Diagnostic differences in psychogeriatric patients in New York and London. *Canadian Psychiatric Association Journal,* 1974, *19,* 267–271.

Cumming, E., & Henry, W. E. *Growing old.* New York: Basic Books, 1961.

Douglass, E. B., Cleveland, W. P., & Maddox, G. L. Political attitudes, age, and aging: A cohort analysis of archival data. *Journal of Gerontology,* 1974, *29,* 666–675.

Drachman, D. A. An approach to the neurology of aging. In J. E. Birren & R. B. Sloane (Eds.), *Handbook of mental health and aging.* Englewood Cliffs, N.J.: Prentice-Hall, 1980.

Eisdorfer, C., & Wilkie, F. Stress, disease, aging and behavior. In J. E. Birren & K. W. Schaie (Eds.), *Handbook of the psychology of aging.* New York: Van Nostrand Reinhold, 1977.

Erikson, E. H. Identity and the life cycle. *Psychological issues* (Vol. 1). New York: International Universities Press, 1959.

Erikson, E. H. *Childhood and society* (2nd ed.). New York: W. W. Norton, 1963.

Fozard, J. L. Predicting age in the adult years from psychological assessments of abilities and personality. *Aging and Human Development,* 1972, *3,* 175–182.

Friedman, M., & Rosenman, R. H. *Type A behavior and your heart.* New York: Alfred A. Knopf, 1974.

Gallup, G., & Hill, E. *The secrets of a long life.* New York: Bernard Geis Associates, 1960.

Gerber, I., Rusalem, R., Hannon, N., Battin, D., & Ankin, A. Anticipatory grief and aged widows and widowers. *Journal of Gerontology*, 1975, *30*, 225-229.

Gergen, K. J., & Back, K. W. Communication in the interview and the disengaged respondent. *Public Opinion Quarterly*, 1969, *33*, 17-33.

Gould, R. C. The phases of adult life: A study in developmental psychology. *American Journal of Psychiatry*, 1972, *129*, 521, 531.

Gurland, B. J. A broad clinical assessment of psychopathology in the aged. In C. Eisdorfer & M. P. Lawton (Eds.), *The psychology of adult development and aging*. Washington, D.C.: American Psychological Association, 1973.

Gurland, B. J. The comparative frequency of depression in various adult age groups. *Journal of Gerontology*, 1976, *31*, 283-292.

Gutman, G. M. A note on the MPI: Age and sex differences in extroversion and neuroticism in a Canadian sample. *British Journal of Social and Clinical Psychology*, 1966, *5*, 128-129.

Gutmann, D. L. An explanation of age configurations in middle and later life. In B. L. Neugarten, et al. (Eds.), *Personality in middle and late life*. New York: Atherton Press, 1964.

Gutmann, D. L. The country of old men: Cross-cultural studies in the psychology of later life. *Occasional papers in gerontology* (No. 5). Ann Arbor, Michigan: Institute of Gerontology, University of Michigan—Wayne State, 1969.

Gutmann, D. L. Dependency, illness and survival among Navajo men. In E. Palmore & F. C. Jeffers (Eds.), *Prediction of life span*. Lexington, Mass.: D. C. Heath, 1971.

Gutmann, D. L. Alternatives to disengagement: The old men of the Highland Druze. In R. A. LaVine (Ed.), *Culture and personality: Contemporary readings*. Chicago: Alpine, 1974.

Gutmann, D. L. Parenthood: Key to comparative study of the life cycle? In N. Datan & L. Ginsberg (Eds.), *Life-span developmental psychology: Normative life crises*. New York: Academic Press, 1975.

Havighurst, R. *Developmental tasks and education*. New York: David McKay, 1972.

Heron, A., & Chown, S. M. *Age and function*. London: Churchill, 1967.

Holmes, T. H., & Masuda, M. Life change and illness susceptibility. In J. P. Scott & E. C. Senay (Eds.), *Symposium on separation and depression*. Washington, D.C.: American Association for the Advancement of Science, 1973.

Holmes, T. H., & Rahe, R. H. The social readjustment rating scale. *Journal of Psychosomatic Research*, 1967, *11*, 213-218.

Jung, C. G. *Modern man in search of a soul*. New York: Harcourt, Brace, and World, 1933.

Kahn, R. L. The mental health system and the future aged. *Gerontologist*, 1975, *15*, 24-31.

Kenigsberg, D., Zyzanski, S. J., Jenkins, C. D., Wardwell, W. I., & Licciardello, A. T. The coronary-prone behavior patterns in hospitalized patients with and without coronary heart disease. *Psychosomatic Medicine*, 1974, *36*, 344-351.

Klein, R. Age, sex, and task difficulty as predictors of social conformity. *Journal of Gerontology*, 1972, *27*, 229-235.

Langer, E., & Rodin, J. The effects of choice and enhanced personal responsibility for the aged: A field experiment in an institutionalized setting. *Journal of Personality and Social Psychology*, 1977, *24*, 191-198.

Leiberman, M. A. Some issues in studying psychological predictors of survival. In E. Palmore & F. C. Jeffers (Eds.), *Prediction of life span*. Lexington, Mass.: D. C. Heath, 1971.

Leiberman, M. A. Adaptive processes in late life. In N. Datan & L. Ginsberg (Eds.), *Life-span developmental psychology: Normative life crises*. New York: Academic Press, 1975.

Levinson, D. J., Darrow, C. N., Klein, E. G., Levinson, M. H., & McKee, B. The psychosocial development of men in early adulthood and the mid-life transition. In D. F. Ricks, A. Thomas, & M. Roff (Eds.), *Life history research in psychopathology* (Vol. 3). Minneapolis: University of Minnesota Press, 1974.

Lewinsohn, P. M., Munoz, R. F., Youngren, M. A., & Zeiss, A. M. *Control your depression.* Englewood Cliffs, N. J.: Prentice-Hall, 1978.

Lopata, H. Z. *Widowhood in an American city.* Cambridge, Mass.: Schenkman, 1973.

Lowenthal, M. F., & Chiraboga, D. Social stress and adaptation: Toward a life course perspective. In C. Eisdorfer & M. P. Lawton (Eds.), *The psychology of adult development and aging.* Washington, D. C.: American Psychological Association, 1973.

Lowenthal, M. F., & Haven, C. Interaction and adaptation: Intimacy as a critical variable. *American Sociological Review,* 1968, *33,* 20–30.

Lowenthal, M. F., Thurnber, M., Chiraboga, D., Berkowitz, H., Crotty, W., Gruen, W., Gutmann, D., Lubin, M., Miller, D., Peck, R., Rosen, J., Shukin, A., Tobin, S., editorial assistant Falk, J., *Four states of life.* San Francisco: Jossey-Bass, 1975.

Neugarten, B. L. Adult personality: Toward a psychology of the life cycle. In B. L. Neugarten (Ed.), *Middle age and aging.* Chicago: University of Chicago Press, 1968.

Neugarten, B. L. The awareness of middle age. In B. L. Neugarten (Ed.), *Middle age and aging.* Chicago: University of Chicago Press, 1968.

Neugarten, B. L. Adaptation and the life cycle. *Journal of Geriatric Psychiatry,* 1970, *4,* 71–100.

Neugarten, B. L. Personality and aging. In J. E. Birren & K. W. Schaie (Eds.), *Handbook of the psychology of aging.* New York: Van Nostrand Reinhold, 1977.

Neugarten, B. L., et al. *Personality in middle and late life.* New York: Atherton Press, 1964.

Neugarten, B. L., & Gutmann, D. L. Age-sex roles and personality in middle age: A thematic apperception study. *Psychological Monographs: General and Applied,* 1958, *17,* whole no. 470.

Neugarten, B. L., & Hagestad, G. O. Age and the life course. In R. H. Binstock & E. Shanas (Eds.), *Handbook of aging and the social sciences.* New York: Van Nostrand Reinhold, 1977.

Neugarten, B. L., Havighurst, R. J., & Tobin, S. S. Personality and patterns of aging. In B. L. Neugarten (Ed.), *Middle age and aging.* Chicago: University of Chicago Press, 1968.

Nowlin, J. B., Williams, R., & Wilkie, F. Prospective study of physical and psychological factors in elderly men who subsequently suffer acute myocardial infarction (AMI). *Clinical Research,* 1973, *21,* 465.

Parkes, C. M., Benjamin, B., & Fitzgerald, R. G. Broken heart: A statistical study of increased mortality among widowers. *British Medical Journal,* 1969, *1,* 740–743.

Paykel, G. S. Recent life events and clinical depression. In E. K. E. Gunderson & R. H. Rahe (Eds.), *Life stress and illness.* Springfield, Ill.: Charles C Thomas, 1974.

Peck, R. Psychological developments in the second half of life. In B. L. Neugarten (Ed.), *Middle age and aging.* Chicago: University of Chicago Press, 1968.

Pfeiffer, E. Psychopathology and social pathology. In J. E. Birren & K. W. Schaie (Eds.), *Handbook of the psychology of aging.* New York: Van Nostrand Reinhold, 1977.

Reedy, M. N. Age and sex differences in personal needs and the nature of love: A study of happily married young, middle-aged and older couples. (Doctoral dissertation, University of Southern California, 1977). *Dissertation Abstracts International,* 38B, 3857.

Reichard, S., Livson, F., & Peterson, P. G. *Aging and personality.* New York: John Wiley and Sons, 1962.

Rosenman, R. H. The role of behavior patterns and neurogenic factors in the pathogenesis of coronary heart disease. In R. S. Eliot (Ed.), *Stress and the heart.* New York: Futura, 1974.

Ryff, C., & Baltes, P. B. Value transition and adult development in women: The instrumentality-terminality sequence hypothesis. *Developmental Psychology,* 1976, *12,* 567–568.

Sainsbury, P. Psychosomatic disorders and neurosis in outpatients attending a general hospital. *Journal of Psychosomatic Research,* 1960, *4,* 261–273.

Schaie, K. W., & Marquette, B. Personality in maturity and old age. In R. M. Dreger (Ed.), *Multivariate personality research: Contributions to the understanding of personality in honor of Raymond B. Cattell.* Baton Rouge, La.: Claitor's Publishing, 1972.

Schaie, K. W., & Parham, I. A. Stability of adult personality: Fact or fable? *Journal of Personality and Social Psychology,* 1976, *36,* 146–158.

Sealy, A. P., & Cattell, R. B. *Standard trends in personality development in men and women of 16 to 70 years, determined by 16 PF measurements.* Paper presented at British Psychological Society Conference, London, April 1965.

Slater, P. E., & Scarr, H. A. Personality in old age. *Genetic Psychological Monographs,* 1964, *70,* 229–269.

Sloane, R. B. Organic brain syndrome. In J. E. Birren & R. B. Sloane (Eds.), *Handbook of mental health and aging.* Englewood Cliffs, N. J.: Prentice-Hall, 1980.

Stevens-Long, J. *Adult life: Developmental processes.* Palo Alto, Calif.: Mayfield, 1979.

Theorell, T., & Rahe, R. H. Psychosocial characteristics of subjects with myocardial infarction in Stockholm. In E. K. E. Gunderson & R. H. Rahe (Eds.), *Life stress and illness.* Springfield, Ill.: Charles C Thomas, 1974.

Thomae, H. Theory of aging and cognitive theory of personality. *Human Development,* 1970, *13,* 1–16.

Thomae, H. (Ed.). *Patterns of aging: Findings from the Bonn longitudinal study of aging.* Basel, Switzerland: S. Karger, 1975.

Urberg, K. A., & Labovie-Vief, G. Conceptualizations of sex roles: A life-span developmental study. *Developmental Psychology,* 1976, *12,* 15–23.

U.S. Public Health Service. *Vital Statistics of the United States, 1970, Volume II, Mortality, Part A.* Rockville, Md.: U.S. Department of Health, Education and Welfare, Public Health Service, 1974.

Vaillant, G. E. *Adaptation to life.* Boston: Little, Brown, 1977.

Vaillant, G. E., & McArthur, C. C. Natural history of male psychological health: The adult life cycle from eighteen to fifty. *Seminars in Psychiatry,* 1972, *4,* 415–427.

Woodruff, D. S. *Can you live to be 100?* New York: Chatham Square Press, 1977.

Woodruff, D. S., & Birren, J. E. Age changes and cohort differences in personality. *Developmental Psychology,* 1972, *6,* 252–259.

Zarit, S. H. *Aging and mental disorders.* New York: Free Press, 1980.

CHAPTER 7

Age Changes in Adult Intelligence

K. Warner Schaie

The intelligence-quotient concept has been widely criticized in educational areas and other contexts. Nevertheless, the observations made by the student of behavior when he or she looks at the performance of young and old people on a variety of measures of intelligence may still be very useful, since many other socially significant behaviors can be predicted thereby. However, any discussion of intellectual functioning in adulthood requires attention, at least in passing, to some of the methodology issues involved in judging whether or not there is acceptable evidence on changes in intelligence from maturity to old age.

We often make the observation that older people tend to function systematically less well than younger people. One might, therefore, draw the conclusion that in the development of intelligence we reach our maximum peak as young adults; from then on we go downhill, slowly at first, more rapidly later. The life course of intelligence may be no different, then, than the life course of some other biological phenomena.

Even with this point of view, one might still ask whether developmental change in intelligence is a uniform phenomenon. Intelligence is not something tangible; it is a construct and as such is not different in its nature from other constructs. We make it more tangible by defining certain ways of measuring it through what we usually call an intelligence test. But a measure of intelligence, or IQ, is no more than a summary statistic; by summing over various dimensions that may be important for effective mental functioning, we can arrive at an index number by which we characterize the behavior of an individual. Thus, when we try to measure intelligence, we are measuring many different things. Although the life course of the summary index may indeed show growth and decline, it does not necessarily follow that such a life course would also be true for the components of intelligence.

We must keep in mind that there is not necessarily a direct isomorphic relationship between biological and psychological changes in the organism. Many aspects of

137

psychological developments depend very much on the interaction of the individual with the culture, and changes in an individual's behavior over his or her life course may be much more affected by changes in the culture than by bodily changes. Granted, there are some constraints. Only living organisms can answer questionnaires or take intelligence tests. One might reasonably assume, therefore, that intelligence will decline dramatically prior to death just as do other life functions. But there is no necessary reason why we have to accept the age decrement model for intelligence without first subjecting it to a number of serious questions. This chapter will examine two principal issues: (1) Is there any reason to suggest that the life courses of different intellectual functions are identical? (2) Is there any reason to accept inevitable decrement in the life course of intelligence?

STUDIES OF INTELLIGENCE IN ADULTHOOD

All of the early studies on intellectual development in adulthood have made use of what is known as the *cross-sectional method.* That is, in these studies the same intelligence test was given to a number of groups of people of different ages at the same point in time. For example, the Army-Alpha intelligence test was administered by Jones and Conrad in a New England community in the early 1930s. These investigators examined practically all persons in this small community from age 16 to 90, divided them up into subgroups by age, and were able to show that on many tests there was a peak in young adulthood and a drop thereafter. Similar findings were reported by Wechsler when he first reported age-related data with the Wechsler-Bellevue, an intelligence test whose revisions represent the standard measurement instrument used in clinical practice. Wechsler had to provide different norms for different age groups to adjust for these age differences (Matarazzo, 1972).

Let us now examine the methodological issues raised by such an approach. Whenever we consider the results of a cross-sectional study, we cannot assume a priori that differences between age groups have been caused by physiological age changes. People who differ by age frequently also differ by other characteristics. Most notably, they must belong to different generations; obviously there are no two individuals, say one aged 20 and one aged 30, who were born at the same time. Differences in age imply differences in life experience for which there cannot be overlap.

If we wish to understand the behavior of the aged, we must understand the particular kind of life experiences they have had. Different age groups must have had different life experiences, and it is frequently more plausible to argue that people of different ages differ on a given characteristic because they belong to a different generation, rather than because they differ in age. In fact, for many psychological variables it is much more plausible to argue that group differences are heavily affected by the particular circumstances of the environment that have changed. One of the major characteristics of our society is that it is in extremely rapid transition. In primitive agricultural societies change might not be an issue of concern, but it cannot be ignored in our case.

In order to solve the question of whether observed age differences are due to age or to generations, we would have to conduct some *longitudinal studies,* which follow the same individuals over their life course to find out if there are indeed age changes within the individual. Such studies are difficult to conduct, and few longitudinal studies may be found in the literature. Some of the more interesting longitudinal studies of intelligence include the Berkeley Guidance and Growth studies (Bayley, 1968); follow-up studies of Terman's *Study of Genius* in the late 1930s (Bayley & Oden, 1955); a study by Owens (1953), who retested men who were ROTC members at Iowa State University during World War I; Blum and Jarvik's study of aged twins (Blum, Jarvik, & Clark, 1970); and the Duke studies of normal aging (Eisdorfer & Wilkie, 1973).

Yet a problem also arises with the interpretation of data from longitudinal studies. We do not know to what extent observed changes in the behavior of individuals are due strictly to age and to what extent they were caused by some environmental event that occurred during the interval between our measurement points. Examples of such intervening events are transitory changes in nutritional levels due to war, depressions, and the like, and the dramatic changes in information transmission because of the introduction of TV. The latter event would affect one generation very much and another generation not at all, because they had either lived before the era of TV or within the era of TV. In other words, we need to differentiate between what change in function is due to age, and is thus characteristic of all members of a species, and what change is a transitory effect due to particular environmental events that occurred during the time period being examined. (For further elaboration of the distinction between age changes and age differences, see Schaie, 1967.)

Another issue is raised by the question of why we should expect that the course of different intellectual abilities should be the same. For example, Horn and Cattell (Horn, 1972) have proposed a model of intelligence that distinguishes between certain kinds of abilities that they call "crystallized" and others that they call "fluid." Crystalized abilities depend upon the acquisition of certain kinds of information and skills transmitted by the culture that are not available to the individual simply by virtue of his characteristics as a human being. Horn and Cattell argue that there is no reason to believe significant decrement should occur in such abilities, assuming that there is continued access to the content of our culture. But the second kind of ability, which they call "fluid ability," seems to be related to the physiological characteristics of the organism. If we accept the concept of a biological clock or of systematic age changes in the biological system, particularly with such variables as speed and reaction time, we would then reasonably expect that many abilities should indeed have a life course with an adult peak and some decrement thereafter. There could certainly be a significant difference in the life course of these two kinds of intelligence.

SOME RESEARCH EVIDENCE

Some research studies on the course of adult intelligence that my associates and I have conducted over the past twenty years or so shed light on these issues (see Schaie, 1979).

In our first study (Schaie, Rosenthal, & Perlman, 1953) we addressed the issue that there might be differences in intellectual functioning in the aged for different abilities. Instead of giving the traditional speeded intelligence test, I used a test measuring the "primary mental abilities," developed from the work of Thurstone (1941). This test consists of five different tasks, measuring separate mental abilities. The first is called *verbal meaning*. In this task the subject is given a stimulus word, say *old*. From a list of four other words—say, *new, young, bad, ancient*—the subject is then required to pick the one most similar to the stimulus word. This is a test of a person's passive recognition vocabulary. The second task, *space,* consists of geometric figures, some of which have been rotated clockwise and others counterclockwise. The subject must pick the ones that have been rotated clockwise. This test of spatial visualization may be predictive of real-life situations such as finding one's way across town from a map, or of visualizing how a piece of furniture bought in kit-form might look when assembled. The third task, *reasoning,* which involves the identification of rules in complex letter series, is a test of inductive thinking. Fourth is an arithmetic task, *number,* which involves the checking of simple addition problems. The fifth task, *word fluency,* requires the production of words starting with a given first letter. This is a test of a person's active vocabulary recall.

I had felt in talking to some older people that one of their problems seemed to be that they did not respond as quickly as they once had. The test (except for word fluency, which can be administered only as a speeded test) was therefore administered under standard as well as nonspeeded conditions in order to maximize differences between functions if they were present (see Figure 7-1). For numerical skills, with no speed limit, our subjects performed virtually at the top of the adolescent group. For verbal meaning they also performed at a very high level. But on other variables, such as spatial visualization and abstract reasoning, people in their 50s still did well, while in the high 60s or 70s there appeared to be a substantial drop. The peculiar upturn for the oldest group may simply reflect that my few very old people were probably highly selected and not representative of their age group. (But see Schaie & Strother, 1968b.) The results of this study suggest that if there was decrement in the several functions, it certainly was not a uniform phenomenon.

The same study was repeated later (Schaie, 1958) with a more carefully selected sample of 25 men and women in each five-year age interval from 21 to 70 years. As shown in Figure 7-2, we again find peaks in young adulthood and differential decrement gradients for the different abilities thereafter.

Both of the preceding studies are, of course, cross-sectional in nature and consequently have the validity problems outlined earlier in this chapter. I became seriously concerned about these problems when I reviewed data on some of the longitudinal studies on adult development. The latter studies, in contrast to my own findings and those by Jones and Conrad and by Wechsler, indicated the absence of age decrement in intelligence, especially in the verbal abilities.

In fact, Owens (1953) reported some increment over a 30-year period and showed that his subjects now in their 50s scored higher than they had in their 20s. Similarly, the follow-up of the Berkeley Growth study (Bayley, 1968) showed that in mid-life adults performed better than they had as adolescents. I then took another look at some cross-sectional studies and found that the so-called peak age seemed to be less than constant. When Terman standardized the original Stanford-Binet in 1916, he

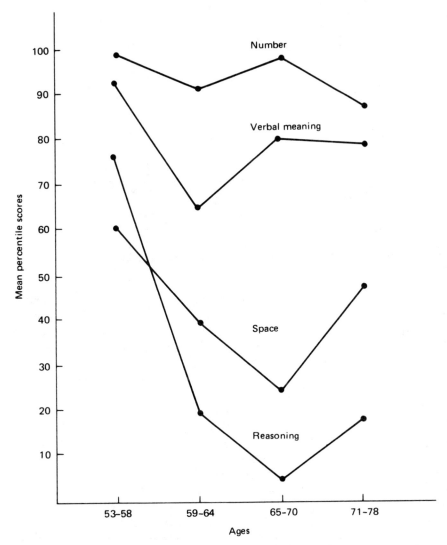

Figure 7-1. The primary mental abilities test administered as a power test to older persons. (*From Schaie, Rosenthal, & Perlman, 1953. Copyright by the Gerontological Society. Reproduced by permission.*)

assumed arbitrarily that adult intelligence peaks at age 16. In the 1930 study of Owens and Conrad the average peak occurs at about 20. When Wechsler standardized the Wechsler-Bellevue the first time around, his reference group was aged 20-24; when he restandardized for the newer WAIS version of his tests some 10 years later, the optimal level for some of them now was at ages 25-30. My own data collected in the mid-1950s suggested an average peak at ages 25-35. Curiously, the peak age of performance appeared to keep increasing (Schaie, 1970).

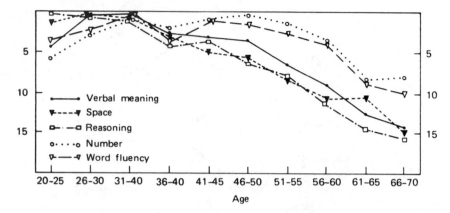

Figure 7-2. Performance differences on the primary mental abilities test from young adulthood to old age. (*From Schaie, 1958. Copyright by the American Psychological Association. Reproduced by permission.*)

Obviously, this discrepancy of findings requires explanation. We can approach the problem systematically by noting that different kinds of information are obtained in cross-sectional and longitudinal studies. Furthermore, if one compares results from different tests on different populations, one may be looking at some very special artifacts. It occurred to me, therefore, that one way in which one might solve the problem was to convert a cross-sectional study into a longitudinal one. In 1963 we conducted a follow-up study and retested about 60% of the sample I had first examined in 1956. This gave me a series of seven-year longitudinal studies (Schaie & Strother, 1968a). The advantage of this kind of design is that both cross-sectional and longitudinal data are obtained on the same subjects with the same measurement variables. Another concern is that in any study over time, peculiar test and retest effects may occur. Also, loss of subjects in longitudinal studies is not necessarily random. To handle this problem, we also obtained a new sample from the same population and age range seven years later, which we thought would be instructive with respect to the issue of shift in peak age of performance.

Our joint analysis of the cross-sectional and longitudinal data showed that scientists who from their cross-sectional studies argued that there was age decrement were right; but so were the other scientists who denied age decrement on the basis of longitudinal data. That is, in my studies we found that the cross-sectional data indeed showed apparent age decrement. But what we found was not really decrement; rather, we were talking about age differences. What I had shown was that different generations perform at different levels of ability. My longitudinal gradient within the generations looked quite level and showed only very mild decrement. Obviously, as it grows older, any given sample has a larger proportion of members who have some kind of pathology that interferes with their ability to respond; even for personal characteristics, such as inadequate visual correction, there would be a higher incidence in older people.

On the basis of our longitudinal studies we next contructed some composite age gradients. To demonstrate what happens when the appropriate cross-sectional and longitudinal data are compared, Figure 7-3 shows the age gradient for the verbal meaning test on the primary mental abilities test. If we examine the longitudinal data and compose the appropriate age gradient within generations, it turns out the peak is not at age 35, but at age 55. Even at age 70 the estimated performance is still of higher ability than it would have been at age 25.

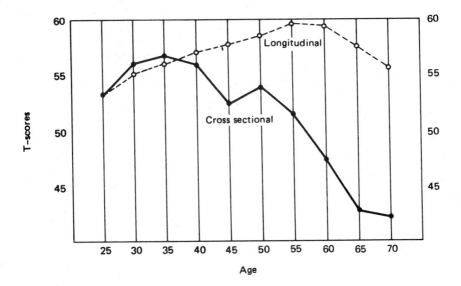

Figure 7-3. Comparable cross-sectional and longitudinal age gradients for the verbal meaning test. (*From Schaie & Strother, 1968a. Copyright 1968 by the American Psychological Association. Reproduced by permission.*)

Some of the results of our 1963 study were criticized because we had pieced together longitudinal gradients by considering data collected over a single 7-year period, which may have been an atypical period. In 1970 we were fortunate enough to be able to do another follow-up study of the same population (Schaie & Labouvie-Vief, 1974). We now have data for some people over a 14-year period, and data for many people for two distinct 7-year periods. We were now able to construct families of age gradients over a 14-year period. An example of our comparative cross-sectional and longitudinal data is shown in Figure 7-4. This figure shows data for the primary mental abilities variable of spatial visualization.

The left side of Figure 7-4 shows three cross-sectional gradients: the bottom one for data collected in 1956, the second one for 1963 data, and the third one for 1970 data. The shapes of these gradients are quite identical. But note the systematic displacement. That is, at each age, for consecutive seven-year periods, the later-born cohorts perform at a higher level than the earlier-born and, consequently, the peak

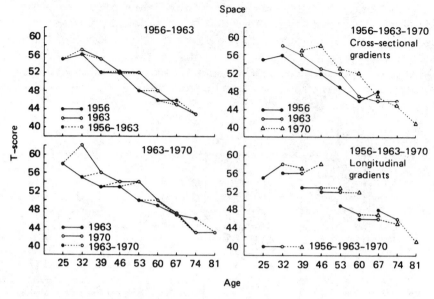

Figure 7-4. Cross-sectional and longitudinal age gradients for the space test from the primary mental abilities. The two graphs on the left depict changes over two different 7-year time periods for two different samples of subjects. The graphs on the right provide comparable cross-sectional and longitudinal gradients for a single sample followed over a 14-year period. (*From Schaie & Labouvie-Vief, 1974. Copyright 1974 by the American Psychological Association. Reproduced by permission.*)

ages keep increasing. This type of evidence can be accounted for only by generation differences; it confirms what some of us have suggested intuitively, namely, that we are smarter than our parents were, and that our children, in turn, are likely to be smarter than we are.

Now consider longitudinal data on the right of Figure 7-4. These are not estimates, but the actual data on the same people measured at three points in time, seven years apart. For the two youngest cohorts, ranging from the 20s to the 40s, spatial ability seemed to keep going up within these generations. For the next two cohorts, up to age 63, there is no change at all. The next gradient, which goes to about age 70, shows a minor decrement, and only for the very oldest cohort is there a significant drop. Even this drop must be viewed with caution because it could be characteristic of that particular generation. That is, it may be characteristic only for individuals who are now in this age range and who have had a history of infectious childhood diseases, which would be quite atypical for later cohorts.[1]

From these studies we can now conclude that on abilities where speed is not of primary importance there is very little change in intellectual function for an individual

---

[1] The findings reported here have been replicated in another data collection conducted in 1977 (see Schaie, 1979, 1982).

throughout adulthood. However, there are certainly marked differences between levels of function for successive generations. These differences are not just a matter of level but may also affect the rate of change. We may reasonably suggest that the present generation of old people, from age 70 on, experienced some intellectual decrement, although much less than we had previously suspected. But it is not at all clear whether such decrement will be found in future generations of old people. For one thing, many of the people whom we have looked at thus far have been individuals who are about to die. We probably happened to test them about three or four years before their death, and they may have already been in the stage before death, when a general decline of all functions is typically experienced (Riegel & Riegel, 1972). If we were able to examine persons who live until 90 or 95, we might observe no decrement at age 80. (For a more detailed popular discussion of these issues, see Baltes & Schaie, 1974.)

Although it is apparent from our studies that there is very little age decrement in intelligence in functions that do not require speeded response or are not affected by the slowing of reaction time within the individual, there are nevertheless marked differences in performance level between successive generations. Interestingly enough these findings hold equally for the so-called crystallized and fluid abilities; what differs among them seems primarily to be the extent of the generational differences. For practical purposes this means that, although many older people are functioning at least as well as they did when they were young, still the young of today function at a much higher level than those who were young 50 years ago. The implications of this conclusion for the practitioner, however, are dramatically different from those that would follow acceptance of the fact of intellectual decrement in the old (also see Schaie, 1980).

Our studies strongly suggest that in the areas of intellectual abilities and skills, old people, in general, if they are reasonably healthy, have not declined but rather have become obsolete. This conclusion might be viewed as a rather negative value judgment. That is not true at all, because obsolescence can be remedied by retraining, while deterioration would be irreversible. (For an example of a successful demonstration of cognitive training of older adults, see Plemmons, Willis, & Baltes, 1978).

If it can be shown that the real intellectual problem for older people is the fact that they are functioning at the level they attained in their younger days, but which is no longer appropriate for successful performance in contemporary society, it follows that we may be able to do something about this situation, rather than conclude that such individuals are simply deteriorated and bound to get worse. In such instances, the logical approach might be the development of compensatory education programs at about the time of retirement, perhaps comparable to the Operation Headstart programs attempted with culturally disadvantaged children (Schaie & Willis, 1978).

INDIVIDUAL DIFFERENCES IN CHANGES IN INTELLECTUAL FUNCTION WITH AGE

All the preceding material refers to findings on groups of people. What about the range of individual differences? Although it does not follow that all old people have declined intellectually, some indeed have—but so have some people at age 30. Our longitudinal studies of individuals show that we have some remarkable individuals who gained in level of performance into their 70s; others have declined by their 30s. What can account for these individual differences?

Two major classes of variables may be important. First, we suspect the role of cumulative health trauma, which may vary widely across individuals. In other words, individuals who have had significant and accumulative physical illness may be at a disadvantage. The effect of such adverse health conditions has been shown in the case of cardiovascular disease (Hertzog, Schaie, & Gribbin, 1978). Second, we know that young children function at the upper limits of their intellectual capability in terms of intelligence if they have been raised in a rich and complex environment. The maintenance and growth of intelligence of an adult may also have much to do with the complexity of his or her environment. We have conducted a series of field interviews in which we looked at the complexity of adult life in terms of such variables as the nature of activities, the kind of books and newspapers read, the characteristics of a person's friends, daily patterns of activities, extensiveness of travel, and so on. Results of these studies show that people who live in a varied environment are often the ones who show continued growth throughout life, while those who live in a static environment may be the ones who most likely show some decrement (Gribbin, Schaie, & Parham, 1980).

How important are the differences in intellectual performance between young and old? Scientists are often impressed by a difference that is *statistically significant*. But what does statistical significance of a difference mean? All that is implied by the term is that the difference is reliable; if the same experiment were done again, we would expect again to find the same difference or one of similar magnitude. It does not mean that the difference needs to be great. In fact, if one has large enough samples, practically any difference will be statistically significant. Some of the differences shown in the graphs in this chapter are so small as not to make much of a practical difference. If an individual at age 30 is able to produce 40 different words in a three-minute period but at age 70 can produce only 36 words, it is doubtful whether this "decrement" is going to make a lot of difference in his or her life. All it means is that it takes a little more time to come up with the required answers or that he or she may have to refresh his or her memory by taking more notes. Other differences are of a large enough magnitude to have some implications. For example, the generational differences in spatial visualization are of enough significance to cause the Federal Aviation Authority to change their age limits for pilots. This age limit has gone up successively because successive generations have been functioning at higher levels. Generational differences may be significant enough so that, by comparison with younger people, older people may indeed be at a disadvantage and compensatory procedures may be indicated. But often such data are simply used as rationalizations to deny the elderly societal roles they could well handle if they were allowed to do so (also see Schaie, 1973).

Another reason to question the practical significance of some of the previous findings on age changes in the elderly is related to the validity of using the same tasks to measure intelligence at all ages. For example, some of the subtests on the Wechsler-Bellevue intelligence test measure different aspects of intelligence in young adulthood than in old age, simply because the skills required to solve the particular problems on these tests tend to change with age.

Some investigators have in fact prepared tests on which older people do better by using materials that are more meaningful for the mature adult (cf. Gardner & Monge, 1977). Especially in the area of verbal behavior it can be shown that tests can be designed deliberately to favor different cohorts by maximizing item contents of terms that were fashionable when the particular cohort was at the young adult age level. Thus, the same arguments that have been used to claim discrimination when tests built for middle-class white children have been applied to minority group members can also be applied when tests built for young adults are applied to work with the aged.

A final matter of concern when viewing the significance of lower test performance by the aged is the tendency toward cautiousness found in the elderly (Botwinick, 1973). Consequently, many elderly are less willing to guess test items about which they are uncertain, unless tests are set up in such a way that it is clearly to the old person's advantage to guess (Birkhill & Schaie, 1975). Young people in most test situations tend to make many more errors of commission than omission, but the reverse is true for the elderly. Perhaps the old are more cautious because they have been discouraged often for doing the wrong thing. Cautiousness may often be adaptive, but in this instance it may make the elderly appear less able than they actually are.

REFERENCES

Baltes, P. B., & Schaie, K. W. Aging and IQ: The myth of the twilight years. *Psychology Today*, 1974, 7(10), 35–40.

Bayley, N. Cognition and aging. In K. W. Schaie (Ed.), *Theory and methods of research on aging*. Morgantown: West Virginia University, 1968.

Bayley, N., & Oden, M. M. The maintenance of intellectual ability in gifted adults. *Journal of Gerontology*, 1955, *10*, 91–107.

Birkhill, W. R., & Schaie, K. W. The effect of differential reinforcement of cautiousness in the intellectual performance of the elderly. *Journal of Gerontology*, 1975, *30*, 578–583.

Botwinick, J. *Aging and behavior*. New York: Springer, 1973.

Blum, J. E., Jarvik, L. F., & Clark, E. T. Rate of change on selective tests of intelligence: A twenty-year longitudinal study of aging. *Journal of Gerontology*, 1970, *25*, 171–176.

Eisdorfer, C., & Wilkie, F. Intellectual changes with advancing age. In L. F. Jarvik, C. Eisdorfer, & J. E. Blum (Eds.), *Intellectual functioning in adults*. New York: Springer, 1973.

Gardner, E. F., & Monge, R. H. Adult age differences in cognitive abilities and educational background. *Experimental Aging Research*, 1977, *3*, 337–383.

Gribbin, K., Schaie, K. W., & Parham, I. A. Complexity of life style and maintenance of intellectual abilities. *Journal of Social Issues*, 1980, *36*, 47–61.

Hertzog, C., Schaie, K. W., & Gribbin, K. Cardiovascular disease and changes in intellectual functioning from middle to old age. *Journal of Gerontology*, 1978, *33*, 872–883.

Horn, J. L. Intelligence: Why it grows, why it declines. In J. M. Hunt (Ed.), *Human intelligence*. New Brunswick, N. J.: Transaction Books, 1972.

Jones, H. E., & Conrad, H. S. The growth and decline of intelligence: A study of a homogenous group between the ages of ten and sixty. *Genetic Psychology Monographs*, 1933, *13*, 223–294.

Matarazzo, J. D. *Wechsler's measurement and appraisal of adult intelligence.* Baltimore: Williams & Wilkins, 1972.

Owens, W. A. Age and mental abilities: A longitudinal study. *Genetic Psychology Monographs,* 1953, *48,* 3–54.

Plemmons, J. K., Willis, S. L., & Baltes, P. B. Modifiability of fluid intelligence in aging: A short-term longitudinal training approach. *Journal of Gerontology,* 1978, *33,* 224–231.

Riegel, K. F., & Riegel, R. M. Development, drop and death. *Developmental Psychology,* 1972, *6,* 309–319.

Schaie, K. W. Rigidity-flexibility and intelligence: A cross-sectional study of the adult life span from 20–70. *Psychological Monographs,* 1958, *72,* 9.

Schaie, K. W. Age changes and age differences. *Gerontologist,* 1967, *7,* 128–132.

Schaie, K. W. A reinterpretation of age related changes in cognitive structure and functioning. In L. R. Goulet & P. B. Baltes (Eds.), *Life-span developmental psychology: Research and theory.* New York: Academic Press, 1970.

Schaie, K. W. Reflections on papers by Looft, Peterson and Sparks: Toward an ageless society. *Gerontologist,* 1973, *13,* 31–35.

Schaie, K. W. The primary mental abilities in adulthood: An exploration of psychometric intelligence. In P. B. Baltes & O. G. Brim, Jr. (Eds.), *Life-span development and behavior* (Vol. 2). New York: Academic Press, 1979.

Schaie, K. W. Intelligence and problem solving. In J. E. Birren & R. B. Sloane (Eds.), *Handbook of mental health and aging.* Englewood Cliffs, N. J.: Prentice-Hall, 1980.

Schaie, K. W., & Labouvie-Vief, G. Generational versus ontogenetic components of change in adult cognitive functioning: A fourteen-year cross-sequential study. *Developmental Psychology,* 1974, *10,* 305–320.

Schaie, K. W., Rosenthal, F., & Perlman, R. M. Differential mental deterioration of factorially "pure" functions in later maturity. *Journal of Gerontology,* 1953, *8,* 191–196.

Schaie, K. W., & Strother, C. R. A cross-sequential study of age changes in cognitive behavior. *Psychological Bulletin,* 1968, *70,* 671–680. (a)

Schaie, K. W., & Strother, C. R. Cognitive and personality variables in college graduates of advanced age. In G. A. Talland (Ed.), *Human aging and behavior: Recent advances in research and theory.* New York: Academic Press, 1968. (b)

Schaie, K. W., & Willis, S. L. Life-span development: Implications for education. *Review of Research in Education,* 1978, *6,* 120–154.

Schaie, K. W. The Seattle longitudinal study: A twenty-one year exploration of psychometric intelligence in adulthood. In K. W. Schaie (Ed.), *Longitudinal studies of adult psychological development.* New York: Guilford Press, 1982.

Thurstone, L. L. *Multiple factor analysis.* Chicago: University of Chicago Press, 1941.

CHAPTER **8**

Age Differences
in Learning and Memory

David A. Walsh

Three different theoretical views of learning and memory have guided research in gero-psychology. Research by theorists holding these separate views has frequently used different procedures and different materials and emphasized and ignored different problems. A direct comparison of research growing out of these different positions is impossible. Furthermore, selecting the "correct view" to present is no simple problem since one's theoretical bias will necessarily determine correctness. Choosing the correct view thus appears to be as straightforward as choosing the "correct religion"! The present chapter will characterize each of these theoretical views and review some of the research. Since space limitations prohibit an exhaustive cataloging of all research, I shall consider only the most relevant investigations that best characterize conceptual problems, approaches, and findings.

STIMULUS-RESPONSE ASSOCIATIONISM

Experimental investigations of higher mental processes were begun by Ebbinghaus in the 1870s. His theoretical and methodological decisions for investigating these phenomena have guided much of the subsequent research. Ebbinghaus's conception of learning and memory was taken directly from the British associationists. Memory, it was held, consists of associations between ideas or events. These associations are the product of experiences that are contiguous in time. To study learning, Ebbinghaus needed only to give a subject a series of experiences. If he counted how many times the subject had to be exposed to a series before he or she could recall it completely, he would have a measure of learning difficulty. The measurement of memory was more problematic. If you learn something to a given criterion of one correct recitation but the next day can recall none of it or only bits and pieces, how can the experimenter get a measure of memory? Ebbinghaus's insight was that he could require the subject to relearn the material on the next day and see how many rehearsals were required to reach the same criterion reached the day before. That is, he measured memory by calculating how much saving there had been in learning.

Another problem for Ebbinghaus was to find suitable material. Prose, poetry, and other meaningful material seemed too unequal in difficulty to use in studies that required careful measurement. Ebbinghaus's solution was to develop his own material: nonsense syllables. These syllables consisted of consonant/vowel/consonant combinations—such as SEB, WUC, LUP—which had the virtue of not meaning anything.

According to Ebbinghaus's procedure, his subject (himself) carefully read each syllable in the list to a ticking metronome. The reading was repeated until he felt he had completely learned the list. His procedure has been modified by contemporary psychologists to *serial anticipation learning*. Now material is exposed to a subject one item at a time on a fixed time schedule. The subject reads each item and tries to anticipate the next. The learning is complete when the subject successfully anticipates every item. A more popular method of studying verbal learning today is *paired-associate anticipation learning*. Here the subject is asked to learn pairs of words or nonsense syllables instead of a list. One member of the pair (the stimulus) is first presented alone. Then it is followed at some fixed interval (usually two seconds) by the other member of the pair (the response). The subject is required to anticipate the response before it appears. Between trials the order of the pairs, but not the items paired together, is usually changed. The subject is considered to have learned the list when he or she gives the correct response to each stimulus item as it appears before the response item is exposed.

Age differences in paired-associate and serial learning

These procedures have been used to generate a sizable body of research comparing aged persons to the young. Gilbert (1941) found a decline in performance with age on a variety of learning and memory tasks; the greatest decrement appeared in a paired-associate learning task. Many times since Gilbert's study, the paired-associate task has been found to be especially difficult for older persons to learn. Such findings were originally taken as evidence that the effectiveness of the associative machinery of learning declines with age. Arguments about the relationship between observable performance on paired-associate tasks and learning ability have suggested other explanations of these findings.

Botwinick (1973) draws a distinction between learning as an internal process and performance as an external act. The observer can see only the act, not the process; he or she must infer that learning ability is poor when little or no improvement in performance is observed after training. This conclusion may be wrong, however; the poor performance may result from factors other than the associative machinery such as poor motivation, lack of confidence, or unfavorable training conditions. When information about such noncognitive factors is available, more correct inferences about learning can be drawn.

Noncognitive factors are especially important to the stimulus-response (S-R) associationist when he or she tries to infer learning ability from changes in performance with age. What was regarded in the past as exclusively a deficiency in the associative machinery of learning is now seen by some researchers as a problem in the non-cognitive performance factors. In other words, older people may learn as well as young persons, but for noncognitive reasons they are unable or unwilling to demonstrate what they have learned. With the cognitive/noncognitive distinction in mind, we can proceed to consider those findings that suggest that some, but not all, of the performance deficits found in the aged are attributable to noncognitive factors.

Canestrari (1963) argued that most studies of paired-associate learning use a rapid rate of stimulus pacing that is not fair to older persons. Canestrari compared young and old (17–35 years and 60–69 years) persons across three pacing rates. The old persons showed the greatest deficit compared to the young with the fastest pacing (1.5 sec), less deficit with medium pacing (3.0 sec), and the least deficit with self-pacing. The self-pacing allowed subjects to take as much time as they wished to study the paired-associates and to respond. Canestrari reported that both old and young subjects utilized the time in making responses to stimulus words but did not increase the time spent studying the pairs. Since the old show the least deficit in the self-pacing condition, perhaps older people only need more time than is usually allowed to reproduce newly learned information.

The idea that older people perform poorly in quickly paced experimental tasks because of insufficient time to respond, rather than as a result of impaired learning ability, also receives some support from studies involving serial learning tasks. Eisdorfer (1965) varied both the exposure duration of the stimulus words (the time available to study the word) and the interval between the stimulus words (the time available to respond by anticipating the next word). Older subjects benefited from the longer inspection times and the longer response times. These findings show that although some of the performance deficits of older persons result from noncognitive factors, such as response speed, older adults have less of a deficit when they are allowed more time to study the stimulus materials. This suggests that the old may need more time to learn in the first place.

Thus, the performance deficits found for older persons in laboratory investigations of verbal learning are not explainable by either cognitive or noncognitive processes alone. When noncognitive factors, such as response time, are made more favorable to older persons, they show a definite improvement in performance. However, although older persons show even further improvement with longer study time, performance deficits are not entirely removed.

Other noncognitive causes of performance deficits

Although many of the performance deficits seen in older people may be the result of insufficient response time, researchers with associative theories have identified two other noncognitive factors that cause performance deficits: overarousal and meaningfulness.

Overarousal. Powell, Eisdorfer, and Bogdonoff (1964) used the level of free fatty acids (FFA) as an index of autonomic nervous system (ANS) arousal during a serial learning task and concluded that older persons were more aroused than young persons in this situation. Furthermore, FFA levels in the aged continued to rise even after the termination of the serial learning task. Powell and associates suggest that old people have a performance deficit in new learning situations because they are too aroused or too motivated. Performance deficits from overmotivation are not a new finding in psychology. In a classic study Yerkes and Dodson (1908) found that many learning situations have an optimal level of motivation which, when exceeded, impairs performance. Further investigation of the ANS overarousal hypothesis was undertaken by Eisdorfer, Nowlin, and Wilkie (1970), who administered to old people engaged in a serial learning task either a drug (propranolol), believed to suppress autonomic nervous system activity, or a placebo. Their hypothesis that excess autonomic arousal was the cause of performance decrements in the elderly was supported. In another experiment Eisdorfer (1968) considered the possibility that situational anxiety may also result in performance decrements. He reasoned that rapid-paced serial learning and the insertion of a needle when blood was sampled for FFA determination worked together to decrease performance through situational anxiety. He tested this hypothesis with a group of aged, who performed serial learning with both a four-second and a ten-second exposure duration, first without and then with the insertion of the needle. Results indicated that both the rapid rate of presentation and the anxiety caused by needle insertion resulted in a performance decrement.

A more recent attempt to replicate Eisdorfer's work on ANS overarousal and serial learning performance presents a different perspective. Comparing the effect of propranolol and a placebo drug on ANS arousal and performance in serial learning within the same subjects, Froehling (1974) was unable to replicate Eisdorfer et al. (1970). Old subjects in Froehling's study did not appear to be anxious in the learning situation, and their FFA levels and performance on the learning task did not show the deficits or improvements evident in the Eisdorfer work. Anxiety and overarousal may be transitory states occurring only in the older subjects' first few visits to the laboratory. Since Froehling trained her subjects and had them visit the laboratory and practice the serial learning task several times before actual testing, FFA level evaluation, and drug administration occurred, she may have prevented the occurrence of overarousal in the laboratory.

Meaningfulness. Task relevance is another factor affecting motivation and thus can be a noncognitive aspect of learning performance. Laboratory studies of learning have often been criticized for using tasks that are meaningless, trivial, and of little or no interest for older people. Shmavonian and Busse (1963) studied task involvement in young and old subjects. They found that when the young were presented with simple tones, they showed significantly greater amounts of responsiveness (as measured by galvanic skin response) than did the old people. However, when the stimuli were changed to meaningful spoken phrases, the differences between young and old subjects' responsivity diminished.

Although this study did not involve learning, it did suggest that older people were less involved in the laboratory task when it was less meaningful to them. A clearer example of the same effect in learning situations has been reported by Hulicka (1967). She tried to teach a paired-associate learning task in which response words such as *insane* were paired with stimulus letters such as *TL*. Hulicka reported an extremely high rate of attrition with elderly subjects (aged 65–80 years). Many of these older subjects refused to exert themselves to learn "such nonsense." When Hulicka changed the task and made it more meaningful (substituting occupation names and personal surnames for the letters and words respectively), the older subjects carried out the task willingly, although their performance was still inferior to that of a young comparison group.

Associational mediators

A number of procedures have been found to optimize learning of paired-associate and serial learning tasks, apparently because they increase the efficiency of the associative learning machinery. Canestrari (1968) surveyed the research literature involving these mediational techniques and found evidence suggesting that excellent performance in paired-associate learning occurs when subjects are told to form linkages between each word-pair associate. Such linkages or mediators may take the form of syntactical or verbal characteristics (sentences) or of visual imagery (mental pictures). Hulicka and Grossman (1967) believed that part of the learning deficit observed in old subjects might be due to failure to use mediational techniques spontaneously. This conclusion was drawn from an investigation in which they found that older persons did not use mediators spontaneously as did young people. However, older people showed a greater improvement than young people when both groups were specifically instructed to use mediators. Nonetheless, even with the greater improvement found for elderly subjects with mediator instructions, their performance was still poorer than that of the young.

A speculation by Hulicka and Grossman—that elderly persons use more verbal than visual image mediators as compared with the young and that verbal mediators are less beneficial—was investigated by Canestrari (1968). He provided subjects with both kinds of mediators and predicted that the visual mediators would help older subjects more than the verbal mediators. Contrary to his expectations, Canestrari did not find better learning with visual mediators than with verbal mediators for either young or old subjects. He did find, however, that both visual and verbal mediators resulted in a doubling of correct responses for the old subjects with no reliable change in the performance of the young. Despite this dramatic memory improvement for old subjects using mediators, absolute performance in the elderly was still poorer than that for young subjects.

INFORMATION-PROCESSING MODELS OF MEMORY

The development of modern computers required many engineering advances for the storage of information. For example, a computer must hold the first columns of information punched on an IBM card in a buffer register while successive columns are read. Once the information on a card has been read, the contents of the record buffer can be stored in the computer and the buffer itself cleared to hold the next card in sequence. The storage of the buffer's contents in the more permanent core memory of the computer usually involves an intermediate step. The buffer contents are loaded into a central processing unit register, which then assigns them to an address-specified location in core memory. Thus, three memory functions can be identified in modern computers: peripheral buffer memory, which holds items being read until appropriate size chunks have collected; working memory registers used to hold information actively being processed by the computer; and core memory, which holds large amounts of inactive but addressable information. The impressive performance of computers allowed by these storage functions has not gone unnoticed by psychologists. These concepts have been adapted as a theoretical framework in which to view human memory.

Murdock's (1967) modal model characterizes the work of theorists who developed computer analogy models (Atkinson & Shiffrin, 1968, 1971; Waugh & Norman, 1965). The model has three human storage capacities that parallel the storage functions of modern computers. Table 8-1 represents in outline these three components and their hypothesized characteristics (see Craik & Lockhart, 1972, for a more complete discussion). Sensory memory is further differentiated as to the sense modality of incoming information. It is called *iconic memory* when the sense modality is vision (Neisser, 1967) and *echoic memory* when auditory (Crowder & Morton, 1969).

TABLE 8-1. An outline of information-processing theories of memory

Features	Sensory memory	Short-term memory	Long-term memory
1. Entry of information	Preattentive	Requires attention	Rehearsal
2. Maintenance	Not possible	Continued attention (rehearsal)	Repetition/organization
3. Form of information	Literal copy of input	Phonemic	Semantic
4. Capacity	Large	Small (4–7 items)	Unlimited
5. Information loss	Decay	Displacement	Loss of accessibility
6. Trace duration	¼–2 sec	Up to 30 sec	Minutes to years
7. Retrieval	Readout	Items in consciousness	Retrieval cues

SOURCE: Adapted from Craik & Lockhart, 1972.

Investigations of iconic memory began in the early 1960s (Averbach & Coriell, 1961; Sperling, 1960) with tachistoscopic presentations that briefly exposed visual information. Averbach and Coriell presented subjects with 50-msec exposures of arrays of letters aligned in two rows of eight items. A marker pointing to one item in the array was presented simultaneously. Under these conditions subjects reported the marked letter with high accuracy. The marker was then delayed for various durations, and the accuracy of reporting the marked letter was observed. A high accuracy of partial report was maintained with delays of the marker as long as 250 msec. This performance contrasts sharply with the observation that subjects can report only four letters from the total 16-item array. Together these observations suggest that all of the visual information in tachistoscopic presentations is maintained in brief sensory memory that decays rapidly. The duration of visual sensory memory (iconic) has been found to be about 250 msec, but auditory sensory memory (echoic) appears to last for durations as long as 2 sec (Crowder & Morton, 1969; Haber & Standing, 1969, 1970).

As shown in Table 8-1, entry of information into sensory memory occurs in the absence of attention (preattentive). The contact of physical energy with the appropriate sensory system appears to be sufficient for the entrance of that information into sensory memory. No operations have been found for prolonging the duration of sensory memory. The format of information in sensory memory is a literal copy of the physical input and is assumed to contain all of the information presented. The presented information decays at a rapid rate, and this decay begins with the initiation of the stimulus (Haber & Standing, 1969, 1970). Information is retrieved from sensory memory by attending to it and thus bringing it under direct processing (consciousness).

Attention to the material in sensory memory is equivalent to reading it out and transferring it to short-term memory. Here verbal items are coded in some phonemic fashion (Schulman, 1971) or in auditory-verbal-linguistic terms (Atkinson & Shiffrin, 1968). Short-term memory is further distinguished from sensory memories by virtue of its limited capacity (Broadbent, 1958; Miller, 1956) and by the finding that information is lost principally by a process of displacement (Waugh & Norman, 1965). The rate of forgetting is much slower for short-term memory: estimates range from 5–20 sec, as compared with 250 msec–2 sec for sensory memories. The duration of short-term memory can be extended by an active process of rehearsal.

One of the major distinctions between short-term and long-term memory is storage capacity. Whereas short-term memory has limited capacity, long-term memory has no known limit. The coding characteristics of long-term memory serve as a second distinction: whereas verbal items are usually coded phonemically in short-term memory, they are coded in terms of their semantic content in long-term memory (Baddeley, 1966). Long-term memory also differs from short-term memory in rate of forgetting: loss from short-term memory is usually complete in 30 sec or less (following the termination of rehearsal), but forgetting from long-term memory may not occur or proceeds very slowly (Atkinson & Shiffrin, 1968). The three-stage model of memory is attractively easy to understand, but it has faced some criticism. Although detailed criticism will be considered later in this chapter, we might consider here the questions raised by Melton (1963). Melton has argued that the distinction between long-term and short-term memory is unnecessary: both show the same characteristics in that information is acquired gradually and forgetting results from interference by preceding and following items. These arguments have been questioned by Waugh and Norman (1965), who draw a distinction between the temporal duration of a retention period and the processes by which information is maintained. They introduce the terms *primary memory* and *secondary memory* to correspond to what is here called short-term and long-term memory. Primary memory, or short-term memory, involves the active process of information rehearsal, whereas secondary memory, or long-term memory, is a structured and organized store of semantic content. Waugh and Norman contend that the findings leading to Melton's criticism reflect storage and loss of information from secondary memory only. Waugh and Norman argue that Melton is confusing short and long retention periods with primary and secondary memory processes, respectively.

Keeping in mind this outline of information processing views of human memory, we can proceed to consider some of the research investigating age differences in these memory functions. The reader should realize the incompatibility of these views with those of S-R associationists. The questions to be investigated are not about the conditions required to form associations between stimuli and responses. Rather, the research assumes that the human organism has evolved in ways that maximize its capacity to process the information presented. Thus, the research focuses on how efficiently information presented once is maintained over time.

Sensory memory

The general discussion of sensory memory presented earlier distinguished between visual and auditory sensory memory systems. Since little research has investigated the development of auditory sensory memory during the adult years, we shall limit our discussion to the adult development of visual sensory memory. Investigations of visual sensory, or iconic, memory have used two different research paradigms: partial report and stimulus halves.

Partial report. The first investigations of age differences in iconic memory used the *partial report* paradigms developed by Sperling (1960) and Averbach and Coriell (1961) (cf. Abel, 1951; Walsh & Prasse, 1980). The partial report paradigm, shown in Figure 8-1, requires subjects to identify only part of a visual display composed of letters. The letters to be identified are designated by a visual marker pointing to the section of the display to be reported. The displays are shown for very brief periods—

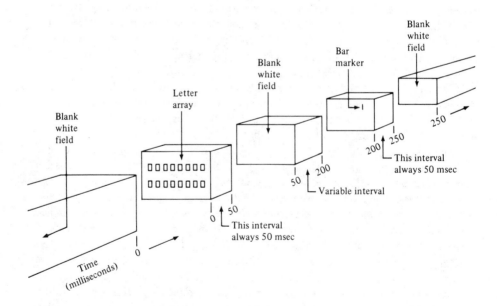

Figure 8-1. Stimulus sequence from a typical trial in the Averbach and Coriell (1961) investigations. (*Copyright 1961 by American Telephone and Telegraph Company. Reprinted by permission from the* Bell Systems Technical Journal.)

1/20th of a second (50 msec). Subjects cannot report more than four or five items from such brief displays when requested to report the "whole" display, but accuracy of "partial report" is much higher. Figure 8-2 shows the difference between whole and partial report performance and the decline in partial report performance associated with delays in presenting the marker.

Neisser (1967) proposed that the difference between subjects' partial report and whole report performance could be understood in terms of the cognitive processes required. He theorized that pattern recognition proceeds in sequential stages of pre-

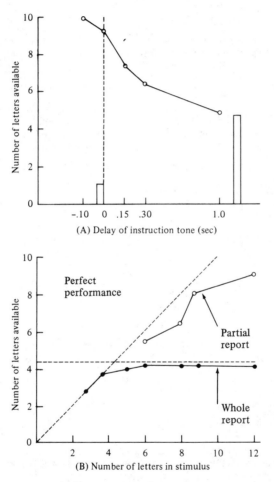

Figure 8-2. Large capacity and decay of information in iconic memory as shown by Sperling's (1960) partial report. The first graph (a) shows the decay of information with increasing delay of the partial report signal, and the second graph (b) shows the accuracy of whole report and partial report data as a function of the number of letters in the stimulus displays. (*Adapted from Sperling, 1960. Copyright 1960 by the American Psychological Association. Reprinted by permission.*)

attentive separation of clusters of visual features, followed by focal attention, and then pattern recognition of each cluster of features. Iconic memory is hypothesized to be a storage buffer for the preattentive step of separating clusters of visual features associated with each of the letters in a display. The limit of four items that can be reported from large letter arrays presented tachistoscopically is explained by the time requirements of shifts in focal attention and pattern recognition of separate letters: the time required to perform these processes on five letters equals or exceeds the duration of iconic memory for the separate clusters of features associated with each unidentified letter.

In a pilot study conducted by Walsh and Thompson (1978) an arrow was used to indicate one "to-be-reported" letter. Subjects are presented with 128 different arrays containing two rows of four letters each. Eight arrays and eight markers, sampling all letter positions, were presented in random order at each of 16 delay periods (0–700 msec). Before these experimental trials began, subjects were rehearsed until they could report at least 88% of the letters correctly when there was no delay between the array and the marker.

Nine young (18–31 years) and ten old (60–72 years) subjects participated in this experiment, and some of their data is presented in Figure 8-3. Figure 8-3 shows that the performance of both age groups declines gradually from about 95% at 0-msec delay of the marker to about 50% at 350-msec delay. The average curve for the young

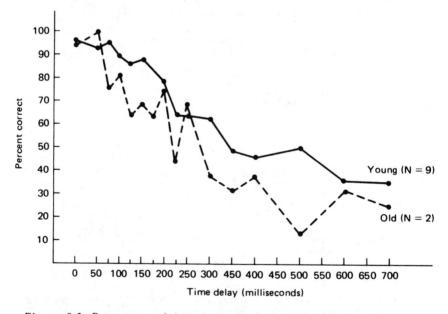

Figure 8-3. Percentage of letters reported correctly following tachistoscopic presentation as a function of the time-delay of a marker indicating which letter to report. The data of two exceptional old subjects, who did not find the task impossible, are compared to nine representative young subjects. (*Walsh & Thompson, 1978*)

subjects shows that they generally report more items correctly than the old at each delay of the marker. Figure 8-3 is based on nine young subjects but only two older subjects. Despite the small number of subjects completing this task, the performance of the two older subjects was found to be statistically different from the young. However, the results of this investigation should not be used to draw conclusions about age differences in iconic memory, because the partial report task presented a difficulty for eight of the ten older subjects tested. Young subjects typically were 100% correct when letters and marker occurred together, while eight of the older subjects were only 50% correct under these same conditions. We shall consider two possible explanations for the difficulty experienced by old subjects in this experiment. These explanations are suggested by Neisser's theoretical analysis of the partial report task presented earlier.

One possibility is that a large percentage of adults over 65 years of age has no iconic memory. They must have the stimulus continually present until successful pattern recognition has occurred. This possibility has been eliminated by other investigations using "direct measure" procedures, which will be discussed later.

A second possible explanation is related to age differences in the selective and focal attention requirements of the Averbach and Coriell (1961) procedure. Subjects are required to focus attention on a single cluster of features designated by the marker in the preattentively segregated iconic store. Thus, age-related differences in the rate of focusing attention could potentially explain the difficulty experienced by older subjects in this experiment. In fact, subsequent investigations in our laboratory have shown that older adults are at a disadvantage to the young in selectively attending to various locations in the visual field (cf. Walsh & Prasse, 1980). Thus, the partial report task involves some attentional and pattern recognition processes that require longer processing times for older adults. This extra time means that the partial report procedure will probably lead to underestimates of iconic memory capacity and duration for all older subjects. Furthermore, the inability of many older subjects to perform the partial report task means that it cannot be used to assess any aspect of their iconic memory performance.

The preceding conclusion is further strengthened by an investigation reported by Abel (1951). Abel found that it was necessary to use display exposures of 500 msec in order to have older subjects successfully perform a partial report task. These long exposure conditions provide older subjects with longer periods of available information so that they can successfully complete selective and focal attention and pattern recognition processes. However, the use of longer exposure durations is not a solution for making the partial report task more useful in studying age-related differences in iconic memory. These longer exposure durations operate to eliminate iconic memory (that is, poststimulus exposure information) and thus obviate any possible comparison of age differences in iconic memory capacity or duration.

Stimulus halves. Other researchers have tried to avoid the confounding influence of visual detection of a marker and readout time by using different tasks to assess iconic persistence. Eriksen and Collins (1967) used what they termed *stimulus halves*. As shown in Figure 8-4, each stimulus half (upper two panels) appears to be a random

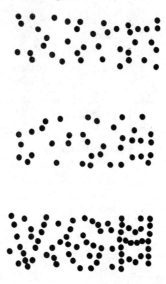

Figure 8-4. An example of *stimulus halves*. The upper two dot patterns, when superimposed, result in the bottom stimulus pattern in which the nonsense syllable *VOH* can be read. (*From Eriksen & Collins, 1967. Copyright 1967 by the American Psychological Association. Reprinted by permission.*)

collection of dots. When they are overlayed as in the lower panel, however, the halves combine to form the nonsense syllable *VOH*. Eriksen and Collins reasoned that if one stimulus half was followed by presentation of the second stimulus half after some delay, subjects would be able to identify the nonsense syllable only if that delay was shorter than the iconic duration of the first stimulus half. They found that the ability to identify the nonsense syllable decreased from about 90% at a delay interval of 0 msec to 30% at a delay of 300 msec. Further increases in the delay produced no further decrements in identification accuracy. The 300-msec value Eriksen and Collins obtained for the length of iconic storage agrees rather well with the estimate obtained by Averbach and Coriell (1961) and Sperling (1960).

Kline and his colleagues (Kline & Baffa, 1976; Kline & Orme-Rogers, 1978) have used the Eriksen and Collins procedure of stimulus halves to examine age differences in visual persistence. Kline and Baffa presented two age groups (average age of 55.6 years and 21.3 years) with two stimulus halves that together formed one of five three-letter words. The stimulus halves were separated by interstimulus intervals (ISI) ranging from 0 to 150 msec. Kline and Baffa found that the younger subjects were more accurate than older subjects across all ISIs in identifying the target word. Although this result indicates that iconic memory in the elderly is shorter in duration than in the young, Kline and Baffa argue that the stimuli used in their study may have disadvantaged the elderly subjects. Their stimulus halves were composed of black dots on a white background. Integrating these dots into a perceptual whole may have been more difficult for the older subjects than for the young; the poorer performance by the elderly may have been due to an inability to integrate the dots into a perceptual whole rather than as a result of shorter duration icons. This argument, like those presented earlier, emphasizes the difficulty of assessing age differences in iconic memory when task performance involves cognitive processes, such as pattern recognition and/or component integration.

Kline and Orme-Rogers (1978) replicated the Kline and Baffa (1976) experiment with one major exception: each stimulus half was constructed of straight-line segments that connected together to form the target words. The results of this study were opposite to those obtained by Kline and Baffa. Older subjects did much better than young subjects in identifying the target words when two halves were separated by ISIs of 60 and 120 msec. Kline and Orme-Rogers suggest these results support the idea that iconic memory persists longer in old than in young adults. This conclusion is based on the idea that the icon of the first stimulus half must persist until the second half is presented in order for successful identification to occur. Thus, the stimulus halves task is believed to involve the integration of two separate icons into a single whole.

The Eriksen and Collins stimulus halves method eliminates the subject's task of selecting among multiple elements, as is the case in partial report tasks, but it does not eliminate the need for subjects to read the stimulus word. Another task, reported by Haber and Standing (1969), was designed to provide a direct measure of iconic persistence. Figure 8-5 shows the logic behind this task. A circle is presented tachistoscopically at regular intervals, and its rate of presentation is under the control of the experimenter. Each presentation creates an icon that begins to decay. If the next presentation of the circle occurs before the icon from the first has faded, then subjects should perceive the illusion of a continually present form. However, if the second

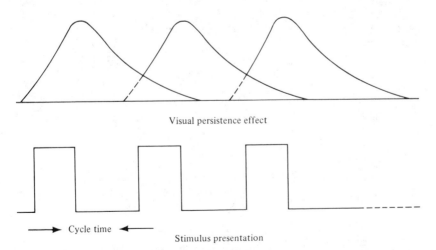

Visual persistence effect

Cycle time

Stimulus presentation

Figure 8-5. A hypothetical view of visual persistence as a result of a repeating stimulus. The subject's response of continuity or discontinuity is based upon whether he or she judges that the persistence from one flash reached zero before the next occurred. (*From Haber & Standing, 1969*)

presentation is delayed until the icon from the first has faded, then subjects will perceive the appearance, disappearance, and reappearance of the circle. By varying the interval between successive presentations of the circle and having subjects report if they perceive a continuous or discontinuous form, Haber and Standing were able to measure iconic persistence. These measures are direct in that the same form reappears in the same visual field location: subjects do not have to search for the form nor recognize it; rather, they need to judge if it disappears for some brief instant. Using this persistence of form task, Haber and Standing obtained measures indicating an average storage time of about 275 msec. Further investigations used the same persistence of form task but varied whether the circle was presented monoptically (to one eye) or dichoptically (to one eye, then the other). Subjects perceived the form as continuous whether it was presented every 270 msec to the same eye or alternated between eyes.

Walsh and Thompson (1978) used the direct measure procedure reported by Haber and Standing (1969) to examine age differences in iconic memory duration. The experimental conditions included three stimulus durations (10, 50, and 90 msec) and two viewing conditions (monoptic and dichoptic). In each condition subjects viewed two ascending and two descending sequences of trials. On the ascending trials the dark period between flashes was increased in 25-msec steps until the subjects could perceive the 0 disappear and reappear. In the descending series the dark period between flashes was decreased in 25-msec steps until subjects could no longer perceive the 0 disappear and reappear. Thus, the dependent variable recorded for each condition was an average of the longest intervals at which the subject saw the circle as continuous.

Table 8-2 presents the results of the Walsh and Thompson (1978) investigation. The only significant effect was the age of subjects: the iconic memory of the young

TABLE 8-2. The persistence of visual storage from stimulus offset to stimulus onset

		Monoptic conditions			Dichoptic conditions			
		Target duration (msec)						Marginal means
		10	50	90	10	50	90	
Young	Mean	284	306	295	269	290	288	289
	Standard deviation	31.5	38.6	44.7	30.5	27.4	64.5	
Old	Mean	255	254	230	244	255	246	248
	Standard deviation	57.0	66.2	86.0	68.8	83.9	61.0	
Marginal means		269	280	262	257	273	267	

persisted for 289 msec, as compared to 248 msec for the old sample. The data of Table 8-2 show that alternating the stimulus presentations between the two eyes (dichoptic condition) did not result in periods of perceived persistence different from repetitive stimulus presentations to the same eye (monoptic condition). This outcome supports the idea that the perceptual mechanism that creates the icon is a central mechanism mediating neural input from both eyes. Table 8-2 also shows that varying the duration of the stimulus flash across the range of 10–90 msec did not affect the perceived stimulus persistence for either age group.

This review of the research examining age differences in iconic memory does not produce any simple conclusion. It is clear, however, that adults over 60 years of age have a very difficult time in performing partial report tasks and that these tasks are probably not appropriate for studying age differences in iconic memory. The investigations of Kline and Baffa (1976) and Walsh and Thompson (1978) provide evidence for shorter iconic persistence in 60–75-year-olds than in 18–30-year-old adults. However, the Kline and Orme-Rogers (1978) results suggest the opposite—that is, iconic memory persists longer in older adults. In either case, any age-related differences in duration are small and unlikely to have any important effect for registration of information in later memory stages.

Short-term memory

Atkinson and Shiffrin (1971) conceptualize short-term memory as an important control system for all thinking and remembering. It is a holding system for the conscious processing of information. A number of different experimental paradigms produce data relevant to short-term memory functions. One source of data is the recency effect observed in free recall studies. The experimental procedure involves reading a list of items (usually English words) to subjects who know they will be required to remember them. Immediately after the list has been presented, subjects are allowed to recall the items in any order they wish. The classic findings are that subjects recall the last few items from the list first and that these items are more likely to be remembered than other items. These data are usually attributed to subjects still having the last few items in short-term memory, which is an active rehearsal memory. Using this experimental paradigm, Craik (1968b) and Raymond (1971), investigated age differences in short-term memory. Specifically, they compared the recency effect on young subjects to that of old. They found no difference as a function of age: older subjects were just as likely as young subjects to recall the last two or three items of a free recall list. These findings suggest that short-term memory functions remain stable and efficient with increasing age.

A second procedure used to assess age differences in short-term memory is the digit span test. Subjects are read strings of digits and are immediately asked to repeat them back to the experimenter. The number of digits that a subject can reliably repeat in correct sequence is taken as a measure of the storage capacity of his or her short-term memory. Investigations of age differences in short-term memory using the digit span test provide reasonable consensus in showing there is little (Botwinick & Storandt, 1974; Friedman, 1966; Gilbert, 1941) or no decline (Bromley, 1958; Craik, 1968a; Drachman & Leavitt, 1972) with age in short-term memory storage capacity.

A number of investigators have increased the difficulty of the digit span procedure by adding to the cognitive load placed on the subject. One modification requires the subject to repeat the digits in backward order. For example, the string 9, 3, 1, 6, 5 must be repeated as 5, 6, 1, 3, 9. The reorganization of the string requires active processing that involves further use of short-term memory to "hold" the original string. Thus, this task most likely reflects flexibility of processing and some component of long-term memory as well. It is, therefore, not inconsistent with other findings that backward span declines with age (Botwinick & Storandt, 1974; Bromley, 1958).

Although it seems clear that the storage capacity of short-term memory does not decline with age, an investigation by Anders, Fozard, and Lillyquist (1972) shows that the rate at which information can be retrieved from short-term memory does decline. Anders and associates used a procedure developed by Sternberg (1966). They presented subjects with lists of one, three, five, and seven digits and asked them (yes or no) if a single test digit appeared in the list. The time required to respond yes or no was measured. The rationale of this procedure assumes that subjects hold the list presented in short-term memory and retrieve it item by item to compare against the test digit. By increasing the number of items in the list, and observing increases in time to reach a decision, researchers can determine the rate of retrieving items from short-term memory. Figure 8-6 presents the findings of Anders and associates (1972) in their comparison of three age groups: 19–21 years, 33–43 years, and 58–85 years. The

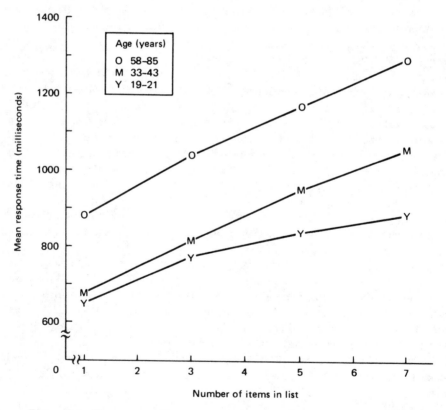

Figure 8-6. Mean recognition response time as a function of the number of digits in a list. (*From Botwinick, 1973, as adapted from Anders et al., 1972.*)

differences in response between age groups with one-item lists reflect overall response speed, including such factors as motor speed and encoding speed of the test digit. The differences in response speed between the longer and shorter lists reflect the rate at which items are retrieved from short-term memory. Figure 8-6 shows that the curves of the older groups were steeper in slope than those of the younger group; this may indicate that the older groups retrieve information at a slower rate from short-term memory.

Long-term memory

One of the clearest findings in the field of aging and memory research is that once the amount of material to be remembered exceeds the span of short-term memory, older individuals are unable to recall as much of the material as younger individuals. Consequently, the majority of recent research on aging and memory has concentrated on understanding the nature and causes of age-related deficits in long-term memory. Researchers have found it useful to differentiate between acquisition, storage, and retrieval operations (Melton, 1963) when formulating hypotheses about age differences in long-term memory. This distinction between separate stages of memory has guided several major lines of research. Since there has been little support for the notion that storage is impaired in older individuals (Craik, 1977; Smith, 1975), few researchers currently consider the storage stage of memory as a possible locus of age-related deficits. Instead, interest has been focused on acquisition and retrieval stages.

An important distinction between short-term and long-term memory, as shown in Table 8-1, is storage capacity. Watkins (1974) estimates the capacity of short-term memory to be 2.6–3.4 words. Baddeley (1970) and Murdock (1967) have made estimates that closely agree. Crannell and Parrish (1957), however, have reported that the capacity varies between 5 and 9 items depending on whether the items in question are words, letters, or digits. Whatever the precise values (if they exist), the previous section shows that little or no changes in capacity occur with age. Presumably, when the capacity of short-term memory is exceeded by incoming information, the information held must be transferred to long-term memory so that short-term memory is free to accept new inputs from sensory memory.

A number of researchers have investigated age differences in memory where the capacity of short-term memory is exceeded. Friedman (1966) presented two age groups with lists varying from 4 to 12 items and observed performance in serial recall. He found that the older group (60–81 years) performed more poorly than the young group (20–34 years). Craik (1968a) also investigated age differences in free recall when both the number of items presented and the size of the pool from which they were selected was varied. The number of items in the lists was varied from 5 to 20, and the size of the pool was manipulated by selecting the items from English county names, animal names, or unrelated words. Craik found that older subjects recalled fewer items than the young from longer lists and also that the older subjects recalled fewer items as the size of the pool of alternatives increased. Craik interprets these findings as evidence for a decline in long-term memory with age and argues that some part of the decline is attributable to inability to retrieve information, since the old show poorer performance when the pool of alternatives is large.

A retrieval explanation of age differences in long-term memory has received support from a number of investigations. Laurence (1967a) compared the free recall performance of young and old subjects on word lists chosen from a single conceptual category (animal names) and from multiple categories. She found that older subjects showed only minimal differences on single category lists but significant decrements with multiple category lists. A second investigation by Laurence (1967b) used a cued recall procedure designed to facilitate the retrieval of information from long-term memory. When the names of the conceptual categories composing the multiple category lists were used as cues, the age decrement in free recall was eliminated. This finding suggests that some of the observed age differences are attributable to the inability of older subjects to retrieve information stored in long-term memory. An investigation by Schonfield and Robertson (1966) provides further support for the hypothesis that older adults have difficulty retrieving information stored in long-term memory. These researchers presented old and young subjects with a list of 24 English words and required both age groups to recall the items and then recognize, out of sets of 4 items, which word was presented in the acquisition list. The recall task requires subjects to retrieve information stored in long-term memory, whereas the recognition test does not require retrieval. Schonfield and Robertson found a large age decrement on the free recall test but no age differences in recognition. Figure 8-7 presents these data, which suggest older adults are less able to retrieve information from long-term memory. This finding of no age differences in recognition has been replicated by Craik (1971), although other researchers have found a significant age difference in recognition memory (Botwinick & Storandt, 1974; Erber, 1974). These latter studies, however, also support the idea that a portion of the age differences seen in long-term memory results from retrieval difficulties; that is, they found the differences between old and young subjects to be considerably less in recognition than in free recall.

Whereas the preceding investigations looked at age differences in retrieval from long-term memory, other investigators have assessed age differences in the entry of information into long-term memory. A number of investigators have found no age differences in free recall of word lists from long-term memory when initial acquisition is equated (Hulicka & Weiss, 1965; Moenster, 1972; Wimer & Wigdor, 1958). Procedures equating initial acquisition usually require that all subjects reach a fixed criterion of 100% immediate recall. Age differences in recall from long-term memory are then assessed at a later point in time. The finding that old subjects require more trials to reach the fixed criterion but then remember as well as young subjects suggests that older adults are less efficient in entering information into long-term memory.

Mandler (1967) has equated the process of organization with entry of information into long-term memory. According to Mandler, to organize information is to store it in long-term memory. Mandler's experimental procedure requires subjects to sort a list of words into categories reliably. The words are printed on cards, and subjects are seated in front of sorting boxes. They sort the list repeatedly until they reach a criterion of two successive identical sorts. Then they are asked to remember the words. Mandler has found over a series of seven investigations that recall is a positive function of the number of categories used to sort the stimulus list (median correlation = .70) and that word recall is unrelated to the number of trials required by subjects to reach the criterion of two successive identical sorts.

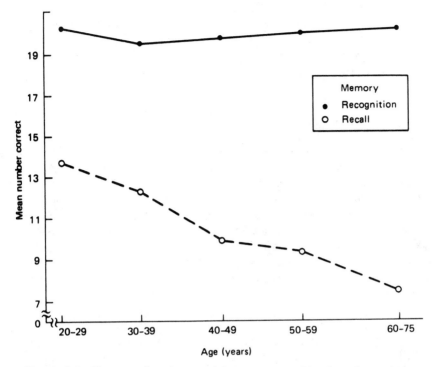

Figure. 8-7. Mean recall and recognition scores as a function of age. (*From Botwinick, as adapted from Schonfield & Robertson, 1966.*)

Hultsch (1969, 1971, 1974) has investigated the hypothesis that age differences in organizational efficiency explain the poor free-recall performance of older adults. Hultsch (1971) asked three age groups of adults to sort a set of stimulus words using Mandler's procedure. Three control groups were paired with experimental subjects of the same age and asked to inspect the word list, without sorting, for the same number of trials required by experimental subjects to reach the sorting criterion. Hultsch found that without sorting the two older groups of subjects (40-49 and 60-69 years) recalled fewer words than the younger subjects (20-29 years). The sorting task, however, had a positive effect on the recall of the older subjects. Both of the older groups showed an improvement in recall with the sorting task. However, the oldest group performing the sorting task was still poorer than the younger group without sorting. Although this finding does not show that all age decrements in recall from long-term memory result from poor organizational ability, it does show that some of these deficiencies result from organizational factors. Another investigation of the effect of age differences in organization on free recall supports this conclusion.

Hultsch (1969) presented three age groups of subjects with a free-recall task. Each age group was further divided into three subgroups that were given different organizing instructions. One group was given no specific instructions, a second group was told to "organize" the words, and a third group was told to "organize the words based on the alphabetical position of their first letter." Hultsch found that, for people of low verbal ability, the oldest age group and the middle-age group were poorer than the young with the first two types of instructions. However, with the third type of instructions—those most helpful in organizing the list—no age differences in free recall performance were found. These findings support the idea that older adults enter less information into long-term memory than the young because they are less likely to organize the information.

DEPTH OF PROCESSING

The attractiveness of separate storage components in information-processing theories is easy to understand. They provide a clear and simple analogy for conceptualizing human memory. However, as research motivated by these storage concepts has progressed, the independence and clarity of these separate storage functions has been lost (Craik & Lockhart, 1972). For example, estimates of the storage capacity of short-term memory now disagree. Researchers using words arrive at estimates of 20 items (Craik & Masani, 1969), as compared with estimates of 4 or 5 items when letters and digits serve as material. This finding suggests a flexible capacity that varies as a function of type of material used. Such a complication removes a defining characteristic of short-term memory.

Research by Shulman (1971) calls into question a second characteristic of short-term memory. He found evidence to support the idea that information in short-term memory can be coded semantically. Semantic coding has been an important criterion in information-processing theory for distinguishing long-term memory from short-term memory. The loss of the coding characteristics and storage capacity criteria upset the attractive simplicity of the three-store model. Also, in more recent formulations of information-processing theory (Atkinson & Shiffrin, 1971) control processes have been proposed. These executive functions are hypothesized to be responsible for moving items between short-term and long-term memory, and they add complexity to the once simple clarity of the model.

An alternative conceptualization of human memory has been outlined by Craik and Lockhart (1972). They suggest that information-processing theories that explain the duration of memory as a function of the particular memory store where the information is held can be replaced by one that focuses on perceptual processes. Craik and Lockhart conceptualize perceptual processes as involving at least three steps: the analysis of sensory features, the matching of constellations of features against stored abstractions collected from previous learning, and the elaboration and/or enrichment of the meaning of the items recognized. They believe the result of perceptual processing is a memory trace. The duration of a memory trace is believed to be a direct function of the "depth" at which it was processed. The deeper or more meaningful the perceptual processes carried out on information, the more persistent the memory trace. The coding characteristics of information are also determined by the level at which it was processed. Thus, items processed at the deepest (meaningful) level of perceptual analysis would be coded semantically, whereas items processed to less deep levels would be coded phonemically. These hypothesized operations lead to predictions compatible with existing findings: semantically coded items persist for longer durations, and phonemically coded items are more ephemeral.

The theoretical proposal of Craik and Lockhart distinguishes between two types of memory functions. Type I processes involve the processing of information to deeper and deeper levels. For example, a visual stimulus flashed for a short duration is first processed at a primitive level as contours, shadows, lines, and other simple features. A deeper level of processing interrelates these features to synthesize a global object, which, in turn, may be processed at a still deeper level of pattern recognition. This level of processing might categorize the stimulus as a picture of a cat. The recognized pattern may be processed at successively deeper levels, involving the verbal labeling of the object as a "cat" and relating it to other felines, shredded furniture, and veterinarian's bills. As each successively deeper level is arrived at, the coding characteristics of the stimulus change and the duration of the memory trace increases.

Type II processes involve "recirculation" at a given level of processing. For example, the verbal labeling of the visual stimulus might be repeated, producing what information-processing theories describe as *verbal or articulatory rehearsal*. Type II processing maintains a memory trace indefinitely as long as active recirculation continues; once it stops, the trace decays at a rate normal for information processed to that level. The ability to recirculate or reactivate the processes at a level varies directly with the depth of the processes. The shallowest levels are seen as incapable of being reactivated, providing an explanation compatible with the inability to maintain iconic memory.

The theoretical proposal of Craik and Lockhart was motivated by findings from an incidental learning paradigm adapted by Jenkins and his colleagues to the study of memory (Hyde & Jenkins, 1969, 1973; Johnston & Jenkins, 1971; Till & Jenkins, 1973; Walsh & Jenkins, 1973). The study by Walsh and Jenkins is representative of the procedures and findings of these investigations. They presented young subjects with a free-recall task in an incidental-learning situation. To disguise the memory requirements of the study and to direct the type of processes subjects would use, they assigned a number of different orienting tasks. One task, hypothesized to facilitate memory because it required the stimulus words to be processed as meaningful elements, involved the evaluation of each word's meaning as pleasant or unpleasant. A second task, hypothesized to be inefficient for memory because it required stimulus words to be processed as nonmeaningful collections of elements, involved the search for either the letter *E* or *G* in the spelling of each word. When undertaking these tasks, subjects were not informed that they should learn the words or that they would be asked to recall them. On the other hand, subjects in a control condition performed no orienting task but were told, as is typical in free-recall tasks, that they should remember the list of words. The hypothesis that meaningful processing would facilitate learning was supported. Subjects who processed words as meaningful elements recalled twice as many as subjects who processed the words as nonmeaningful elements. The control group that performed no orienting task but knew of the learning requirements recalled slightly fewer words than the meaningful processing group.

Thus, in the incidental learning paradigm, orienting tasks are used to control the cognitive processes of the subject. Tasks that involve the subject with phonemic or orthographic characteristics hold perceptual processing at shallow levels, while tasks that involve the meaning of words force processing to deeper levels. These experimental and theoretical paradigms offer new ways to conceptualize age-related changes in memory. One explanation of the finding of poorer free recall for older subjects is that they are deficient in their ability to carry out deep levels of analysis. A second possibility is that older adults are able to process at deeper levels but they fail to implement these strategies when presented with laboratory tasks. Typical laboratory studies of age differences in memory have made no effort to control the processes subjects use on materials. Thus, older adults may choose to process experimental materials at less deep levels than the young, and their poorer recall may reflect this shallow processing rather than any decline in memory processes per se. A test of these hypotheses is afforded by the orienting task methodology.

A study by Eysenck (1974) examined these hypotheses. Old and young subjects were tested in free recall after performing one of four orienting tasks. Two meaningful processing tasks required subjects to write meaningful adjectives and form an image of the words. Two nonmeaningful processing tasks required subjects to count the number of letters in the spelling and to write a word that rhymed. Eysenck found no difference in the recall of old and young in the nonmeaningful orienting task conditions. However, the old recalled significantly fewer words than the young when both groups had performed meaningful orienting tasks. Eysenck offers these findings as support for the hypothesis that older individuals are deficient in their ability to process information at deep levels. However, an investigation by White and Craik (as reported by Craik, 1977) suggests a different conclusion.

White and Craik asked old and young subjects to perform four tasks on 64 words—that is, each subject performed each of the four tasks on 16 words. Subjects tried to remember the word for later recall, or they determined whether the word was capitalized (the presentation was visual), whether it rhymed, or to what semantic category (animal, vegetable, or mineral) the word belonged. In free recall White and Craik found the same pattern of age differences reported by Eysenck (1974): under conditions of meaningful processing the old showed substantially poorer recall, as compared with the young.

White and Craik argue, however, that this finding may reflect retrieval deficits rather than processing deficits in the old. They reason that the old may have processed the words to as deep a level as the young producing a memory trace of equivalent duration. However, the old may be less able to retrieve the stored trace. They tested this hypothesis by measuring recognition memory following the orienting task and free recall procedures.

Their findings are presented in Figure 8-8. When the retrieval step was minimized with recognition procedures, the old subjects performed as well as the young in all but the learning condition. This latter condition does not control the processes used by subjects, and the finding of poorer recognition memory for the old is support for the idea that older adults do not, on their own, process laboratory tasks as deeply as the young. This pattern of recognition performance for young and old suggests two loci of explanation for age deficits in memory. First, the improved performance of old subjects using tasks requiring meaningful processing suggests that some of the memory deficit of older adults is attributable to how deeply they process. With intentions only to learn, older adults apparently process at less deep levels. Second, the differences between recall and recognition performance for the young and old

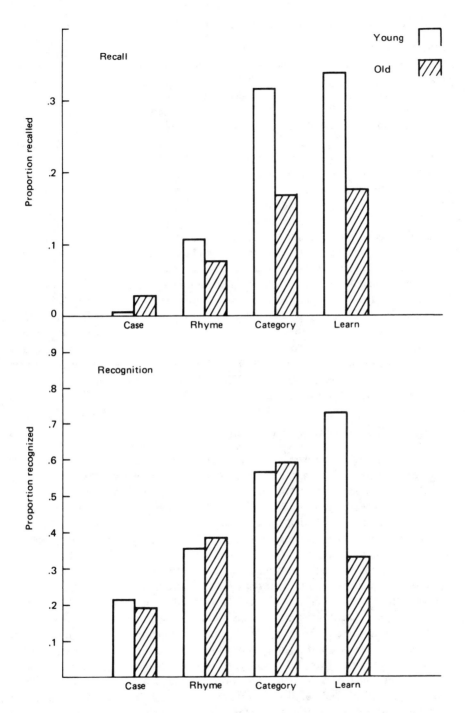

Figure 8-8. Proportion of words recalled and recognized following four different orienting task conditions. (*From White & Craik as reported by Craik, 1977.*)

on the meaningful category classifications task suggest that older adults are less able to retrieve memory traces even when durable traces have been built with deep levels of processing.

Additional support for this conclusion has been provided by other research (cf. Craik & Simon, 1980; Perlmutter, 1979). However, a study by Mason (1979) disagrees with these findings. Mason found that both recall and recognition were relatively more impaired in older adults when semantic processing was required by orienting tasks. Clearly, the source of the inconsistencies in this line of research requires further investigation. It will be important in the future to understand exactly how encoding and retrieval processes interact and how to guide encoding so that retrieval probability will be maximized in older individuals.

An attractive feature of the depth of processing approach to the study of aging and memory is that it suggests ways in which the "processing deficiencies" can be overcome by the use of "correct" strategies by older learners. However, the manipulation of processing strategies (for example, organizational factors, or depth of processing) has not generally resulted in a total elimination of age differences in performance. Further, a number of serious attempts have been made to employ memory improvement techniques in training studies with older individuals, and with few exceptions these programs, which stress the use of "effective" processing strategies, have not been successful in bringing older persons to the same level of performance as young persons (Poon, Walsh-Sweeney, & Fozard, 1980). Thus, although processing deficiency may account for some of the age-related differences in memory performance, it does not seem to account for all of the deficit.

RECENT DEVELOPMENTS AND NEW DIRECTIONS

The common characteristic of the work surveyed to this point, which represents the majority of research on age differences in learning and memory, is that it is concerned with memory for lists of words acquired in laboratory situations. As the evidence has revealed, age differences observed with these tasks are pervasive and substantial. An important issue that needs to be addressed concerns the extent to which we can reach general conclusions about age differences in memory on the basis of list-memory findings. Cognitive psychologists have often pointed out that word-list tasks typically call on kinds of learning that are not representative of the learning and remembering that people do in their daily lives. Consequently, there has been a developing trend to ask for "ecological validity" in research examining aging and memory.

A moment's reflection suggests there are large disparities between the learning and remembering demands of everyday life and the recent thrust of research in adult development of learning and memory. For example, much recent work examines the learning and memory of word lists and assesses performance by recall or recognition measures. Yet some thoughtful introspection suggests that, unlike memorizing lists of words, acquisition and recall of information presented in discourse are activities that most adults do on a daily basis. Information as diverse as dietary guidelines and spatial directions may be spoken or written in a discourse format. Measures other than direct recall or recognition may be used to assess performance. Evidence of remembering may be demonstrated by the individual's ability to carry out the dietary instructions or find his or her way in a given spatial environment. Although discourse comprehension is one of the most important sources for obtaining information, other modes of learning may be very important for specific types of information. For example, discovery, observation, and participation may be critical for learning procedures or skilled movements. In opening up new areas of investigation, however, researchers will have to take care to restrict their generalizations regarding patterns of adult development to the format in which the information was learned and to the method by which remembering was assessed. It is clear that at the present time we can make few generalizations about learning and memory differences between older and younger adults.

The issue of age differences in memory of information contained in discourse has received the attention of but a handful of researchers, and the results are not consistent. Using prose retention, Gordon and Clark (1974) demonstrated age differences between college students and elderly adults (65–81 years old). Recall was measured using an "intuitive" idea count. Age differences in number of ideas recalled were found at both immediate and one-week retention intervals, the magnitude of the difference between young and old adults being greater with delayed recall. Older adults also achieved lower recognition scores at both retention intervals; Gordon and Clark interpreted this result as evidence for a storage deficit in the elderly. Gordon and Clark concluded that the elderly have difficulty "in retaining information which is required in 'everyday' verbal experiences" (p. 71). Taub and Kline (1978) also found that memory for prose material was impaired in the elderly, but the age difference was not apparent until the third or fourth trial when learning short (60-word) passages. Neither of these investigations, however, employed propositional representation systems that would allow the locus of the recall deficit to be specified (whether gist or detail information). When assessing memory for prose material, one needs to determine the kinds of information most susceptible to loss and whether aspects of comprehension remain intact despite loss of certain kinds of specific information.

Zelinski, Gilewski, and Thompson (1980) investigated the relationship between metamemory and several laboratory memory tests, including prose recall. Subjects' recalls of a prose passage were scored using an adaptation of the Meyer (1975) system. There were no age differences in recall of propositions at the most superordinate level. This study represents one of the only published attempts at using an explicit semantic representation system to measure the amount and kind of information recalled from discourse by young and old adults.

Memory for information not explicitly stated in text material has been investigated by Walsh and Baldwin (1977); Walsh, Baldwin, and Finkle (1980); and Till and Walsh (1980). The first two investigations used the linguistic abstraction paradigm (Bransford & Franks, 1971) and found no age differences in the tendency for older and younger individuals to integrate a series of partial information statements into a holistic representation of the ideas contained across the parts. Till and Walsh (1980) asked subjects to listen to sentences from which an implication could be drawn. The sentences were heard under several conditions of encoding (deep or shallow). Free recall of the sentences did not differ as a function of age, but younger subjects were far superior to older subjects when recall was cued by an implication that could be derived from each sentence. However, this was not due to the inability of older adults to draw implications. When an implication was demanded at the time of original encoding and then recall was tested with an implicational cue, older individuals recalled as many sentences as younger individuals.

This brief review of recent work examining age-related differences in memory for high-level verbal materials underlines the need for further work in this area. Whereas large and pervasive age differences are typically found in word-list memory tasks, older adults have shown little disadvantage compared to the young in remembering sentences and discourse materials. Perhaps the next decade of research in aging and memory will result in a more reassuring picture of the fate of higher level learning and memory processes that are relevant to adult functioning in the natural environment.

REFERENCES

Abel, M. *The visual trace in relation to aging.* Unpublished doctoral dissertation. St. Louis, Mo.: Washington University, 1951.

Anders, T. R., Fozard, J. L., & Lillyquist, T. D. The effects of age upon retrieval from short-term memory. *Developmental Psychology,* 1972, *6,* 214–217.

Atkinson, R. C., & Schiffrin, R. M. Human memory: A proposed system and its control processes. In K. W. Spence & J. T. Spence (Eds.), *The Psychology of learning and motivation: Advances in research and theory.* New York: Academic Press, 1968.

Atkinson, R. C., & Shiffrin, R. M. The control of short-term memory. *Scientific American,* 1971, *224,* 82–89.

Averbach, E., & Coriell, A. S. Short-term memory in vision. *Bell Systems Technical Journal,* 1961, *40,* 309–328.

Baddeley, A. D. Short-term memory for word sequences as a function of acoustic, semantic, and formal similarity. *Quarterly Journal of Experimental Psychology,* 1966, *18,* 362–365.

Baddeley, A. D. Estimating the short-term component in free recall. *British Journal of Psychology,* 1970, *61,* 13–15.

Botwinick, J. *Aging and behavior.* New York: Springer, 1973.

Botwinick, J. & Storandt, M. *Memory related to age.* Springfield, Ill.: Charles C Thomas, 1974.

Bransford, J. D., & Franks, J. J. The abstraction of linguistic ideas. *Cognitive Psychology,* 1971, *2,* 331–350.

Broadbent, D. E. *Perception and communications.* New York: Pergamon Press, 1958.

Bromley, D. C. Some effects of age on short-term learning and remembering. *Journal of Gerontology,* 1958, *13,* 398–406.

Canestrari, R. E., Jr. Paced and self-paced learning in young and elderly adults. *Journal of Gerontology,* 1963, *18,* 165–168.

Canestrari, R. E., Jr. Age changes in acquisition. In G. A. Talland (Ed.), *Human aging and behavior.* New York: Academic Press, 1968.

Craik, F. I. M. Short-term memory and the aging process. In G. A. Talland (Ed.), *Human aging and behavior.* New York: Academic Press, 1968. (a)

Craik, F. I. M. Two components in free recall. *Journal of Verbal Learning and Verbal Behavior,* 1968, *7,* 996–1004. (b)

Craik, F. I. M. Age differences in recognition memory. *Quarterly Journal of Experimental Psychology,* 1971, *23,* 316–323.

Craik, F. I. M. Age differences in human memory. In J. E. Birren & K. W. Schaie (Eds.), *Handbook of the psychology of aging.* New York: Van Nostrand Reinhold, 1977.

Craik, F. I. M., & Lockhart, R. S. Levels of processing: A framework for memory research. *Journal of Verbal Learning and Verbal Behavior,* 1972, *11,* 671–684.

Craik, F. I. M., & Masani, P. A. Age and intelligence differences in coding and retrieval of word lists. *British Journal of Psychology,* 1969, *60,* 315–319.

Craik, F. I. M., & Simon, E. Age difference in memory: The roles of attention and depth of processing. In L. W. Poon, J. L. Fozard, L. S. Cermak, D. Arenberg, & L. W. Thompson (Eds.), *New directions in memory and aging: Proceedings of the George Talland memorial conference.* Hillsdale, N. J.: Lawrence Erlbaum Associates, 1980.

Crannell, C. W., & Parrish, J. M. A comparison of immediate memory span for digits, letters, and words. *Journal of Psychology,* 1957, *44,* 319–327.

Crowder, R. G., & Morton, J. Precategorical acoustic storage. *Perception and Psychophysics,* 1969, *5,* 365–373.

Drachman, D. A., & Leavitt, J. Memory impairment in the aged: Storage versus retrieval deficit. *Journal of Experimental Psychology,* 1972, *93,* 302–308.

Eisdorfer, C. Verbal learning and response time in the aged. *Journal of Genetic Psychology,* 1965, *107,* 15–22.

Eisdorfer, C. Arousal and performance: Experiment in verbal learning and a tentative theory. In G. A. Talland (Ed.), *Human aging and behavior.* New York: Academic Press, 1968.

Eisdorfer, C., Nowlin, J., & Wilkie, F. Improvement of learning in the aged by modification of autonomic nervous system activity. *Science,* 1970, *170,* 1327–1329.

Erber, J. T. Age differences in recognition memory. *Journal of Gerontology,* 1974, *29,* 177–181.

Eriksen, C. W., & Collins, J. F. Some temporal characteristics of visual pattern perception. *Journal of Experimental Psychology,* 1967, *74,* 476–484.

Eysenck, M. W. Age differences in incidental learning. *Developmental Psychology,* 1974, *10,* 936–941.

Friedman, H. Memory organization in the aged. *Journal of Genetic Psychology,* 1966, *109,* 3–8.

Froehling, S. *Effects of propranolol on behavioral and physiological measures of elderly males.* Unpublished doctoral dissertation. Duke University, 1974.

Gilbert, J. G. Memory loss in senescence. *Journal of Abnormal and Social Psychology,* 1941, *36,* 73–86.

Gordon, S. K., & Clark, W. C. Application of signal detection theory to prose recall and recognition in elderly and young adults. *Journal of Gerontology,* 1974, *29,* 64–72.

Haber, R. N., & Standing, L. Direct measures of short-term visual storage. *Quarterly Journal of Experimental Psychology,* 1969, *21,* 43–54.

Haber, R. N., & Standing, L. Direct estimates of apparent duration of a flash. *Canadian Journal of Psychology,* 1970, *24,* 216–229.

Hulicka, I. M. Age differences in retention as a function of interference. *Journal of Gerontology,* 1967, *22,* 180–184.

Hulicka, I. M., & Grossman, J. L. Age-group comparisons for the use of mediators in paired-associate learning. *Journal of Gerontology,* 1967, *22,* 46–51.

Hulicka, I. M., & Weiss, R. L. Age differences in retention as a function of learning. *Journal of Consulting Psychology,* 1965, *29,* 125–129.

Hultsch, D. Adult age differences in the organization of free recall. *Developmental Psychology,* 1969, *1,* 673–678.

Hultsch, D. Adult age differences in free classification and free recall. *Developmental Psychology,* 1971, *4,* 338–342.

Hultsch, D. F. Learning to learn in adulthood. *Journal of Gerontology*, 1974, *29*, 302–308.

Hyde, T. S., & Jenkins, J. J. The differential effects of incidental tasks on the organization of recall of a list of highly associated words. *Journal of Experimental Psychology*, 1969, *82*, 472–481.

Hyde, T. S., & Jenkins, J. J. Recall for words as a function of semantic, graphic, and syntactic orienting tasks. *Journal of Verbal Learning and Verbal Behavior*, 1973, *12*, 471–480.

Johnston, C. D., & Jenkins, J. J. Two more incidental tasks that differentially affect associative clustering in recall. *Journal of Experimental Psychology*, 1971, *89*, 92–95.

Kline, D. W., & Baffa, G. Differences in the sequential integration of form as a function of age and interstimulus interval. *Experimental Aging Research*, 1976, *2*, 333–343.

Kline, D. W., & Orme-Rogers, C. Examination of stimulus persistence as the basis for superior visual identification performance among older adults. *Journal of Gerontology*, 1978, *33*, 76–81.

Laurence, M. W. Memory loss with age: A test of two strategies for its retardation. *Psychonomic Science*, 1967, *9*, 209–210. (a)

Laurence, M. W. A developmental look at the usefulness of list categorization as an aid to free recall. *Canadian Journal of Psychology*, 1967, *21*, 153–165. (b)

Mandler, G. Organization and memory. In K. W. Spence & J. T. Spence (Eds.), *The psychology of learning and motivation. Advances in research and theory* (Vol. 1). New York: Academic Press, 1967.

Mason, S. E. The effects of orienting tasks on the recall and recognition performance of subjects differing in age. *Developmental Psychology*, 1979, *15*, 467–469.

Melton, A. W. Implications of short-term memory for a general theory of memory. *Journal of Verbal Learning and Verbal Behavior*, 1963, *2*, 1–21.

Meyer, B. J. F. *The organization of prose and its effects on memory.* Amsterdam: North Holland Publishing Co., 1975.

Miller, G. A. The magical number seven, plus or minus two: Some limits on our capacity for processing information. *Psychological Review*, 1956, *63*, 81–97.

Moenster, P. A. Learning and memory in relation to age. *Journal of Gerontology*, 1972, *27*, 361–363.

Murdock, B. B., Jr. Recent developments in short-term memory. *British Journal of Psychology*, 1967, *58*, 421–433.

Neisser, U. *Cognitive psychology.* New York: Appleton-Century-Crofts, 1967.

Perlmutter, M. Age differences in adult's free recall, cued recall, and recognition. *Journal of Gerontology*, 1979, *34*, 533–539.

Poon, L. W., Walsh-Sweeney, L., & Fozard, J. L. Memory skill training for the elderly: Salient issues on the use of imagery mnemonics. In L. W. Poon, J. L. Fozard, L. S. Cermak, D. Arenberg, & L. W. Thompson (Eds.), *New directions in memory and aging: Proceedings of the George Talland memorial conference.* Hillsdale, N. J.: Lawrence Erlbaum Associates, 1980.

Powell, A. H., Jr., Eisdorfer, C., & Bogdonoff, M. D. Physiologic response patterns observed in a learning task. *Archives of General Psychiatry*, 1964, *10*, 192–195.

Raymond, B. J. Free recall among the aged. *Psychological Reports*, 1971, *29*, 1179–1182.

Schonfield, D., & Robertson, E. H. Memory storage and aging. *Canadian Journal of Psychology*, 1966, *20*, 228–236.

Schulman, A. I. Recognition memory for targets from a scanned word list. *British Journal of Psychology*, 1971, *62*, 335–346.

Shiffrin, R. M., & Atkinson, R. C. Storage and retrieval processes in long-term memory. *Psychological Review*, 1967, *76*, 179–193.

Shmavonian, B. M., & Busse, E. W. The utilization of psychophysiological techniques in the study of the aged. In R. H. Williams, C. Tibbets, & Wilma Donohue (Eds.), *Process of aging–social and psychological perspectives.* New York: Atherton Press, 1963.

Shulman, H. G. Encoding and retention of semantic and phonemic information in short-term memory. *Journal of Verbal Learning and Verbal Behavior,* 1970, *9,* 499–508.

Smith, A. D. Aging and interference with memory. *Journal of Gerontology,* 1975, *30,* 319–325.

Sperling, G. The information available in brief visual presentations. *Psychological Monographs: General and Applied,* 1960, *74,* (II) 1–28.

Sternberg, S. High-speed scanning in human memory. *Science,* 1966, *153,* 652–654.

Taub, H. A., & Kline, G. E. Recall of prose as a function of age and input modality. *Journal of Gerontology,* 1978, *5,* 725–730.

Till, R. E., & Jenkins, J. J. The effects of cued orienting tasks on the free recall of words. *Journal of Verbal Learning and Verbal Behavior,* 1973, *12,* 489–498.

Till, R. E., & Walsh, D. A. Encoding and retrieval factors in adult memory for implicational sentences. *Journal of Verbal Learning and Verbal Behavior,* 1980, *19,* 1–16.

Turvey, M. T. On peripheral and central processes in vision: Inferences from an information-processing analysis of masking with patterned stimuli. *Psychological Review,* 1973, *80,* 1–52.

Walsh, D. A., & Baldwin, M. Age differences in integrated semantic memory. *Developmental Psychology,* 1977, *13,* 509–514.

Walsh, D. A., Baldwin, M., & Finkle, T. J. Age differences in integrated semantic memory for abstract sentences. *Experimental Aging Research,* 1980, *6,* 431–443.

Walsh, D. A., & Jenkins, J. J. Effects of orienting tasks on free recall in incidental learning: "Difficulty," "effort," and "process" explanations. *Journal of Verbal Learning and Verbal Behavior,* 1973, *12,* 481–488.

Walsh, D. A., & Prasse, M. J. Iconic memory and attentional processes in the aged. In L. W. Poon, J. L. Fozard, L. S. Cermak, D. Arenberg, & L. W. Thompson (Eds.), *New directions in memory and aging: Proceedings of the George Talland memorial conference.* Hillsdale, N. J.: Lawrence Erlbaum Associates, 1980.

Walsh, D. A., & Thompson, L. W. Age differences in visual sensory memory. *Journal of Gerontology,* 1978, *33,* 383–387.

Watkins, J. A review of short-term memory. *Psychological Bulletin,* 1974, *81,* 695–711.

Waugh, N. C., & Norman, D. A. Primary memory. *Psychological Review,* 1965, *72,* 89–104.

Wimer, R. E., & Wigdor, B. T. Age differences in retention of learning. *Journal of Gerontology,* 1958, *13,* 291–295.

Yerkes, R. M., & Dodson, J. D. The relation of strength of stimulus to rapidity of habit formation. *Journal of Comparative Neurological Psychology,* 1908, *18,* 459–482.

Zelinski, E. M., Gilewski, M. J., & Thompson, L. W. Do laboratory memory tests relate to everyday remembering and forgetting? In L. W. Poon, J. L. Fozard, L. S. Cermak, D. Arenberg, & L. W. Thompson (Eds.), *New directions in memory and aging: Proceedings of the George Talland memorial conference.* Hillsdale, N. J.: Lawrence Erlbaum Associates, 1980.

CHAPTER 9

Physiology and Behavior Relationships in Aging

Diana S. Woodruff

Identifying and explaining relationships between physiology and behavior is the goal of physiological psychology. Psychophysiologists concern themselves with examining how systems such as the cardiovascular, pulmonary, and nervous systems affect the way we act and, conversely, how our feelings and actions affect these physiological systems. The application of psychophysiological techniques is especially pertinent in the field of aging since physiological functions change with age. Indeed geropsychologists have tended to be so preoccupied with physiological age changes and how they affect behavior that they have often ignored behavioral influences on physiology.

Behavior has all too frequently been interpreted in terms of the biological decremental model of aging, which stipulates that aging is represented by decline in all physiological systems (Woodruff, 1973, 1980). This leaves psychologists in the unfortunate position of merely describing behavioral decrements, and, for the most part, this is the main perspective reflected in psychological studies of aging. If, on the other hand, geropsychologists more carefully viewed the interactive nature of physiology/behavior relationships, we would be in a better position to attempt to modify age changes in behavior and even age changes in physiology.

A major portion of this chapter will be devoted to the interactive perspective in the psychophysiology of aging and the implications of this research for the elderly. I shall also examine some of the new tools useful in the assessment of behavior, aging, and the nervous system, and some of the models used to explain behavioral aging. This information will then be used to guide us toward a realistic perspective of the behavioral capacities of the aged.

BEHAVIOR/PHYSIOLOGY INTERACTIONS

The gerontological literature abounds with references to behavior/physiology relationships. One striking example is the increased incidence of depression in old age. Indeed depression appears to be one of the major psychological problems of the aged (Busse, 1959; Butler, 1963; Lowenthal, 1964). At both a biochemical level and an environmental level the elderly may be predisposed toward depression. The environmental effects of significant losses—loss of income, loss of loved ones, loss of employment, and so forth—are tangible factors causing older individuals to feel depressed. Losses in physical capacity and energy level also undoubtedly play a role. Additionally, some evidence suggests that on a biochemical level production of certain neurotransmitters in the aging brain may be altered, which may also predispose old people to feel depressed. Thus, the aged may be in a state of double jeopardy. Whether biological changes are caused by these environmental stresses, whether the biological and physiological changes are completely independent, or whether they exacerbate one another has not clearly been determined. Perhaps we will find that biologically older organisms are more predisposed toward depression without any environmental stresses. This is all the more reason to alleviate the environmental stresses plaguing contemporary aged cohorts. Although we may not be able to eliminate losses due to deaths of friends and spouses, we can alter problems of inadequate income, housing, health care, and transportation. We can take a behavioral or environmental approach toward improving the lives of the elderly, which might affect the mood state of depression on a physiological or biochemical level.

In Chapter 7, Schaie points out the flaws in our thinking about intelligence and aging in terms of the biological decremental model. We assume that there is organic deterioration in the older brain when we note that the aged score lower on intelligence tests. In fact, the aged may score lower on intelligence tests as a result of educational obsolescence (Baltes & Schaie, 1974; Birren & Woodruff, 1973; Schaie, 1970) or as a result of other noncognitive factors (see Chapter 7). Several gerontologists have suggested the environmental intervention of education to reduce this obsolescence. Others have suggested a restructuring of the intelligence test so that it would not discriminate against the aged person.

Schaie also speculates that much of what we attribute to biological decline may be environmental influence and that the environment probably affects behavior in old age more than biology. This implies that while some of the biological changes in old age are irreversible, the environment is more salient than biology in behavior. The clear implication is that environmental interventions can successfully alleviate most of the behavioral deficits in old age. Although environmental influences and interventions are certainly critical in reversing decline in old age, we have not yet conclusively demonstrated that even the biological decline is inevitable or irreversible. Biological decline is being identified in descriptive studies of aging in animals and man, but few attempts have been made to manipulate biological variables to determine if decline can be reversed. When we do try to affect physiological functioning in the aged, we are surprising ourselves at how often we can observe beneficial results of the kind reported by deVries in Chapter 13.

deVries has found physiological reversals—that is, improvement in physiological functioning in the aged—as a result of moderate exercise. Age itself does not cause individuals to decline physiologically. Other factors, some of which it may be possible to alter, are associated with declining physiological capacity in the aged. DeVries demonstrated that one of the factors associated with physiological decline is disuse, the lack of exercise in contemporary sedentary lifestyles. Following a modified exercise program, even very old individuals can regain some of the physiological efficiency they had lost with advancing years.

If we are searching for new approaches and information in the psychology of aging and in gerontology generally, we must reexamine some of the changes thought to be irreversible. A number of biology and psychobiology laboratories are currently conducting this kind of research. For example, in Finch's laboratory at the University of Southern California investigations are being undertaken to examine how hormonal changes in aging rats might be reversed. Estrogen-replacement therapy has been one of the outcomes of this type of research, and progress in this area may lead to the maintenance of optimal hormonal levels in postmenopausal women. Such research has clear implications for sexual behavior in older women, who sometimes abstain from sex because of pain in the genital region, which has atrophied in the absence of normal hormone levels.

Why is it only now that we are beginning to take a new look in our studies of aging to see how much capacity is left? Why have we believed that only the brains and behavior of children and young animals are plastic? One of the major contributions to our thinking about brain plasticity comes from studies of accidents and language behavior. It has been demonstrated that if damage is caused to a specific area (located in the left cerebral cortex of right-handed individuals; for left-handed individuals it may be either in the right or left cortex) before a child reaches adolescence, the child will lose language function for a period of time and then be able to regain it. The same damage in an adult will render the adult mute for the rest of his or her life. The young brain appears to be plastic, able to compensate for damage in one area by relegating function to another area. Thus, on the basis of these accident studies we concluded that the youthful brain is malleable to a point, but after a certain age brain function ceases to be plastic. Investigators did not even include older animals in their brain plasticity studies because they thought it was useless even to test plasticity in older brains. Thus, when Dru and colleagues (Dru, Walker, & Walker, 1975) took the unorthodox step of including a group of old rats in their study of recovery of function in the visual cortical areas, their work represented a pioneering study demonstrating plasticity in older as well as younger brains.

Dru and associates (1975) trained rats to discriminate horizontal bars from vertical bars and required them to perform a discrimination avoidance task, choosing the appropriate stimulus in order to avoid shock. After the animals had learned the task to criterion, they received ablation lesions on one side of their visual cortices (Krieg's area) and were then placed in various environments: (1) total darkness for the interoperative period; (2) cages with diffuse light for four hours a day each day, and total darkness for the rest of the day; (3) a patterned visual environment containing horizontal bars, stripes, and triangles through which the animals were passively transported for four hours a day each day, with the rest of the day spent in darkness; and (4) access to the same patterned environment for four hours, but with no restrictions on the animals' ability to move around. These various environmental treatments were first used by Held and coworkers (Held & Hein, 1963), who demonstrated that normal visual development in young rats was dependent upon unrestricted movement through a visual field. Some kind of experience with visual-motor integration appeared to be crucial to normal perceptual development.

The results of Dru's work with the mature animals were consistent with the previous literature on young animals. All animals who had been placed in darkness, diffuse light cages, or passively transported through the patterned environment failed to relearn the task. Only those animals allowed free movement in the patterned environment recovered the avoidance task. Apparently, as in the normally developing brain, voluntary coordination between the visual system and the motor system are necessary for the neural reorganization needed to recover the behavioral function.

The crucial aspect of the experiment was the effect of the lesions on the aged animals. The older group performed almost identically to the mature group: older animals with free movement in the patterned environment recovered the task. They relearned the task significantly more slowly than the younger animals, yet they did recover the function. These results strongly suggest that the aged brain has not declined to the point where it cannot undergo functional reorganization following injury. Further, the age decrement noted in the speed of recovery may be a function of a greater amount of time in the deprived environment of standard laboratory housing before the experiment, rather than a function of aging itself. These results imply that a generalized decremental view of brain status with age is inaccurate.

CAN PHYSIOLOGICAL DECLINE BE REVERSED?

The most important point in this chapter is that physiological age functions may not be fixed and inevitable and that behavioral and biological intervention strategies may reverse some of the deleterious performance observed in old people.

EEG changes with age

The brain is composed of billions of nerve cells called neurons. The electrical activity of hundreds of thousands of neurons can be recorded by attaching electrodes to an individual's scalp and amplifying the tiny electrical signals roughly a million times. The characteristic oscillating pattern of electrical activity recorded in this manner is called the electroencephalogram (EEG). The EEG has been used as a clinical tool to identify abnormal brain activity and as an experimental tool to examine brain-behavior relationships. Since it is not feasible to invade the brain with recording techniques, the EEG is one of the few means available to measure human brain activity.

There are at least four identified rhythms in the EEG. The alpha rhythm is in the 8–13 cycle per second (cps) range and is the dominant or modal brain wave rhythm. Behaviorally, it is associated with a relaxed but alert state and is most prominent in the back parts of the head, especially when the eyes are closed. Beta activity is a faster rhythm, above 13 cps, and is associated with an alert, thinking state of consciousness.

Theta activity is in the 4–7 cps range and is associated with daydreaming and drowsiness. Activity in the 1–3 cps range is called delta and occurs during sleep. Thus, faster brain waves are associated with alertness and arousal, while slower rhythmic patterns are related to drowsiness and sleep. Clinical uses of the EEG include the identification of tumors and areas of pathology in the brain, which manifest themselves as areas of localized slowing of EEG activity. Thus, slowing is associated with drowsiness, sleep, and brain pathology.

The dominant brain wave rhythm of young adults is 10.2–10.5 cps (Brazier & Finesinger, 1944). One of the best-documented findings in the psychophysiological literature is that this dominant brain wave rhythm slows with age (see Obrist & Busse, 1965; Thompson & Marsh, 1973 for reviews). By the time an individual reaches the age of 60–65, his or her dominant brain wave rhythm is probably around 9 cps. Although some 80-year-olds have brain wave patterns similar to those of 20-year-olds, the normal pattern in even the healthiest of aging individuals is for EEG slowing to occur with age. Figure 9-1, taken from Obrist's work, illustrates slowing in the same individual over a ten-year period.

Obrist, Henry, and Justiss (1961) demonstrated that the slowing of the EEG alpha rhythm is a reliable phenomenon occurring in longitudinal as well as cross-sectional studies. In the ten-year period of Obrist's longitudinal study, two thirds of the subjects manifested slowing of the dominant rhythm. Since this slowing has been related to pathology, the subjects may have had some kind of disease, such as cerebral arteriosclerosis, which would cause a slower metabolic rate in the brain and lead to slower brain wave rhythms. It has been demonstrated that senile patients, patients with arteriosclerosis or severe brain atrophy, have very slow brain wave rhythms. One of the studies that convincingly demonstrates that alpha slowing occurs in even the healthiest of aged individuals was reported in a monograph by Birren, Butler, Greenhouse, Sokoloff, and Yarrow (1963). An extensive study was undertaken to examine biological and behavioral changes in 47 old men chosen because they were in optimal health. Obrist examined the EEGs of these men and found a slowing of the EEG alpha rhythm to 9 cps. Thus, alpha slowing is a phenomenon associated with normal aging and is not necessarily the result of disease.

The slowing of the dominant EEG rhythm is part of the legacy of descriptive studies of aging, and this finding is cited, along with numerous others, to support the biological decremental model of aging. Although at least 20 studies document deleterious age changes in the EEG, no attempts have been made until one quite recent study (Woodruff, 1975) to determine if these age changes in EEG are reversible.

Changes in reaction time with age

Another clear finding in the geropsychology research literature is the slowing of reaction time (RT) with age. Galton set up a health exposition in London in 1877 and collected RT data. In 1923 two investigators, Koga and Morant (1923), analyzed some of Galton's data and found that both visual and auditory reaction time was slower in the old than in the young subjects in this sample. This is one of the first studies in the literature on the psychology of aging, and hundreds of studies have substantiated it. Birren, Riegel, and Morrison (1962) undertook an interesting study in which they

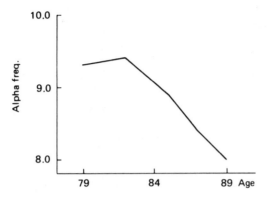

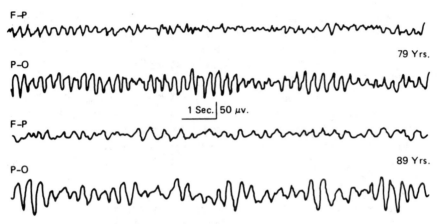

Figure 9-1. Alpha frequency plotted as a function of age for a mentally "normal" old man over a ten-year period. The top tracing was recorded at age 79, the bottom tracing at age 89. The latter EEG was associated with mild signs of intellectual impairment. F-P = Fronto-Parietal: P-O = Parieto-Occipital. (*From Obrist, Henry, & Justiss, 1961*)

factor-analyzed a large group of tasks in young and old subjects and found that one major factor in the old that was different in the young was speed. The speed factor could account for about three or four times as much of the variance in performance in old people as in the young. In a more recent study in which they factor-analyzed scores on tests of intellectual performance, Cunningham and Birren (1981) also found a factor involving speed of performance that was present in the data for the old subjects but that did not emerge from the data of the young subjects.

Reaction time slows in other species as well. Psychomotor slowing occurs in animals, and observing such data led Birren (1965) to state that slowing will occur in any individual who survives beyond young adulthood. This age change in RT, like the age change in EEG, is a normal aging phenomenon—that is, it occurs uniformly without regard to disease.

The healthy old men in the Birren et al. (1963) study cited previously had slowed RT. People who suffer from a chronic disease (and most old people have at least one chronic disease) have more psychomotor slowing. Such a wide range of studies has been done on slowing of behavior that Hicks and Birren (1970), who compared all the literature, found slowing ranging from 20% to 110%. Although the degree of slowing depends on the task, the investigator, and a number of variables, older people perform more slowly than the young.

Some investigators have used behavioral intervention strategies to determine if psychomotor slowing is reversible. Murrell (1970) and Hoyer, Labouvie, and Baltes (1973) used extensive practice and found that the aged could improve their speed and close some of the gap between their performance and the performance of young subjects. To alter motivation in old subjects, Botwinick (1959) has used the tactic of shocking subjects mildly when they responded more slowly than their normal responding time, and he found some improvement in performance under certain conditions. Although these strategies indicated that some of the behavioral slowing was reversible, the age differences could not be completely erased.

Brain waves and reaction time

Since scientists first began thinking about EEG, the EEG alpha rhythm has been associated with speed and timing in the nervous system. The possibility that the alpha rhythm reflects periodicity in the activity of the central nervous system was first considered by Bishop (1933, 1936) and Jasper (1936), who speculated that the alpha rhythm reflects cyclic fluctuations in brain excitability. Lindsley (1952) summarized a variety of psychological and neuropsychological research in support of this proposition and suggested that the waxing and waning in the alpha cycle may arise from synchronous and rhythmic metabolic or respiratory activities in large aggregates of neurons. Subsequent research (for example, Andersen & Andersson, 1968; Callaway, 1962; Dustman & Beck, 1965; Frost, 1968) has consistently supported the general notion that the alpha cycle reflects underlying modulations in brain responsiveness. Thus, a basic property of the nervous system may be that it is more excitable at some times than at other times. As regards the timing of behavior, if a signal is received at a time when the nervous system is most excitable, the system will respond more quickly than when the system is not excitable.

Surwillo attempted to determine if the slowing of RT with age could be accounted for by the slowing of the EEG alpha rhythm. In 1961 Surwillo reported a study in which he had simultaneously recorded RT and EEG in 13 subjects ranging in age from 18 to 72. In this study Surwillo found a rank-order correlation of .81 between the period of the alpha rhythm (inverse of alpha frequency) and simple RT to auditory stimuli. Surwillo (1963a) replicated these results with a sample of 100 subjects, and he also demonstrated (1963b, 1964a) that the alpha period was related to RT variability and to the latency of choice RTs (and hence presumably to central decision time). On the basis of these results Surwillo hypothesized that the alpha period represents a fundamental unit of time in the programming of events in the central nervous system.

Surwillo's hypothesis implies a causal relationship between alpha period and RT, but correlational evidence does not provide unequivocal support for this hypothesis. More convincing evidence for the hypothesis that alpha frequency determines RT could be derived from a demonstration that experimental alterations in alpha frequency lead to changes in RT. Surwillo (1964b) reported one such experiment in which he attempted to modify alpha frequency by flashing bright lights at subjects at rates of 6-15 flashes per second. This technique proved ineffective since only 5 of the 48 subjects showed evidence of alpha synchronization over more than a restrictively narrow range of photic frequencies. Consequently, the limited results of this study do not convincingly test Surwillo's hypothesis.

Until recently, alternative techniques for manipulating the alpha frequency, and hence for experimentally testing the relationship between alpha frequency and RT, were not available. The newly emergent biofeedback technique, however, provided another means by which alpha frequency could be manipulated. The work of Kamiya (1968) and others has demonstrated that subjects can increase and decrease the abundance of activity in the EEG band encompassing the alpha rhythm. Furthermore, it has been established that individuals can selectively increase the abundance of EEG activity in narrow frequency bandwidths (Green, Green, & Walters, 1970a, 1970b; Kamiya, 1969).

Biofeedback as an intervention

Biofeedback is a technique that provides individuals with information about the activity of bodily processes of which they are normally unaware. When a person becomes aware that he or she is producing a certain type of brain wave rhythm, that the heart is beating at a certain rate, or that blood pressure is at a certain level, he or she can learn to alter or maintain that physiological rate. Connecting an individual to an electronic system that amplifies physiological signals and then activates signals that provide information about internal states makes it possible for him or her to control those internal states.

In the case of the EEG alpha rhythm, a person typically is not aware that he or she is producing brain waves in the 8-13 cps (alpha) range. However, if one is placed in a situation in which brain waves are measured and the information is "fed back" in the form of a tone or light, which signals that alpha activity is or is not being produced, he or she can learn to increase or suppress that brain wave activity.

Biofeedback made it possible to determine if the slowing of the dominant brain wave frequency in older people could be reversed. That is, researchers could determine if old subjects could increase the time they spent producing alpha waves in the frequency bandwidths of young subjects. This biofeedback technique also made it possible to test Surwillo's hypothesis regarding the relationship between brain wave frequency and RT.

The author designed an experiment in which young and old subjects learned to increase the abundance of EEG alpha activity at the modal frequency and at frequencies 2 cps faster and slower than the mode. Old subjects were just as capable of manipulating brain wave frequency in this manner as were young subjects, suggesting that some of the alpha slowing may be reversible. Moreover, when the subjects produced fast brain wave frequencies, their RT was faster than when they produced slow brain wave frequencies. Thus, biofeedback provides a means to help older individuals to produce faster brain waves and possibly to speed their RT (Woodruff, 1975).

Research underway at the present time involves examination of concurrent and long-term effects of biofeedback on brain wave frequency and behavior (Woodruff, 1981). In the present research we are examining a number of cognitive and mood behaviors as well as reaction time as a function of long-term training at the biofeedback task. Biofeedback training consists of a sequence of ten one-hour training sessions after baseline performance on EEG and behavioral measures has been determined. Using very stringent criteria for success at the biofeedback task, we are finding that not all subjects can control their brain activity to the degree that we have specified. Of the subjects who have been able to demonstrate remarkable control of alpha activity, more have been old than young subjects. This result is interesting inasmuch as old subjects perform more poorly on most learning tasks.

Since there were such large between-subject performance differences in our data, we decided to attempt to identify characteristics that differentiated the good from the poor biofeedback learners. Although all of the analyses are not complete, we have identified one characteristic on which the two groups are different: habituation. Those who are successful in learning the biofeedback task are slower to habituate or do not habituate at all to an auditory signal presented 20 times over a seven-minute period. The measure of habituation is alpha blocking: subjects with successful biofeedback control present the alpha-blocking response to most trials, while most nonsuccessful learners do not. Thus, learners maintain attention and alertness, while the nonlearners may relax more and be less attentive to stimuli (Echenhofer & Woodruff, 1980).

Comparing EEG alpha reactivity to repetitive tone stimulation in our young and old subjects, we found patterns of response characteristic of young subjects to be different from the response patterns of the old. Young subjects were responsive at the beginning of the seven-minute period, but they became drowsy in the middle by the tenth stimulus. Then they became more reactive again and showed their initial level of reactivity by the end of the period. The old subjects show a consistent lessening of reactivity. They gradually became more drowsy throughout the seven-minute reactivity session, and they did not show the return to initial level of alpha blocking that the young subjects showed. Baseline alpha activity also dropped off in the old subjects; it dropped and then returned to initial session levels in the young subjects. The exception to the old pattern of reactivity was shown in two older women who showed great control of alpha activity. One of these women showed the young pattern of lowered reactivity in the middle of the session with a return to initial level; the other woman showed no decline in reactivity over the 20 stimulus trials. Thus, we may have a means to predict which subjects will do well on the biofeedback task (Echenhofer & Woodruff, 1980).

Biofeedback control of alpha activity turns out to be quite a difficult task, which requires the maintenance of effort for long periods. Although young subjects have shown evidence of learning control after ten or more hour-long biofeedback training sessions, none have shown the magnitude of control exhibited by several old subjects.

More women than men have demonstrated control of their EEG. Control subjects who hear tape-recorded feedback signals show no changes or decline in their alpha activity. Thus, we have identified a task that may be optimal for older women, and we are learning more about the unique skills of older women, which provide them with this capacity to control their brain electrical activity.

As a behavioral intervention to affect physiological decline in the elderly, biofeedback has great potential (Woodruff, 1971). With this technique we may be able to demonstrate that there is hitherto unknown residual capacity in the older organism.

NEW TOOLS IN THE ASSESSMENT OF BRAIN, BEHAVIOR, AND AGING RELATIONSHIPS

The advent of computers has led to the development of new brain measures that identify the brain's electrical responses in one case and topography in the other case. *Event-related potentials (ERPs)* are computer-averaged EEG responses to experimentally controlled stimuli. *Computerized axial tomography (CAT)* involves computer analysis of X-ray density scans of the brain and provides a picture of internal brain structures. Both brain measures, which are useful at all phases of the life cycle, have been used by gerontologists to gain insight into brain changes with aging.

Event-related potentials

Brain electrical responses to specific stimuli are usually not apparent in recordings of ongoing EEG; however, if one takes a number of epochs in which the same stimulus event has occurred and sums or averages across these epochs, the activity related to the stimulus becomes apparent. The assumption is that random activity not associated with the stimulus cancels to a flat voltage pattern, while activity time-locked to the stimulus cumulates and emerges from the random background "noise" of the ongoing EEG. A number of different bioelectric signals exhibit stable temporal relationships to a definable external event, and these can be elicited in most of the sensory modalities. Most research involves auditory, visual, or somatosensory stimulation. The general term for these signals is event-related potentials, and a number of categories of ERPs exist.

Long latency potentials related to complex psychological variables. The P3 wave of the ERP is prominent only when the stimulus that has elicited the ERP has some meaning or significance to the subject. A number of studies have indicated that the amplitude of the P3 component, regardless of the stimulus modality, is inversely related to the degree that the subject expects the stimulus to occur (for example, Duncan-Johnson & Donchin, 1977). The factor that appears to determine the latency of the P3 component is decision time—more specifically, the time required for the subject to perceive and categorize the stimulus according to a set of rules (for example, Kutas, McCarthy, & Donchin, 1977). When task difficulty is increased, young subjects have prolonged processing times and longer P3 latencies.

Comparisons of the P3 in young and old subjects have led gerontologists such as Thompson and Marsh (1973; Marsh & Thompson, 1977) to suggest that the ERPs of the two age groups are more similar during active processing than during passive stimulation. The amplitude and shape of the P3 component have been similar in many of the age comparative experiments. However, the fact that the latency of P3 is delayed in older subjects has been consistent since the first report of P3 research in aging (Marsh & Thompson, 1972). Thus, the P3 research offers direct confirmation of the aging phenomenon to which behavioral studies have been pointing for decades. Processing time is slower in the aged central nervous system.

Using a task in which the subject is asked to count the number of occurrences of an infrequent tone, Goodin, Squires, Henderson, and Starr (1978) tested 40 healthy subjects between the ages of 15 and 76 years. Data from six of these subjects, ranging in age from 15 to 71 years, are presented in Figure 9-2. The primary result of this study was that the latency of the P3 component systematically increased with age. Regression analysis indicated that P3 component latency increased at a rate of 1.64 msec/year. This results in almost a 100 msec increase in the P3 component in the decades between the 20th and 80th year. Some of the other components increased in latency with age, but the magnitude of these latency increases was not more than half of the magnitude of the P3 latency. Goodin et al. (1978) demonstrated that these age changes were not a function of auditory sensitivity by noting that behavioral performance (detection of higher frequency tones) was equal in young and old; that all subjects reported they could hear the tones clearly; and that the N1 component, which is dramatically affected by tone intensity, was different by only 6 msec between the young and old subjects. Thus, ERPs provide differential information about the effects of aging and auditory acuity.

Steady potential shifts. Most investigations of steady potential shifts have focused on the *contingent negative variation (CNV)*. The term *CNV* denotes a class of negative slow potential shifts lasting in the order of seconds (as compared to milliseconds of duration of most other ERPs); these occur in conjunction with certain sensory, motor, and cognitive activities. Donchin, Ritter, and McCallum (1978) describe the CNV as a cortical change that occurs when an individual's behavior is directed toward a planned action in response to a sequence of two or more events. The action can be an overt motor response, the inhibition of a motor response, or a decision. The optimal situation for the production of the CNV, first demonstrated by Walter and colleagues (1964), is a simple reaction-time task in which the first stimulus (S1) serves as a ready signal for a second stimulus (S2) to which an operant motor response is made. Walter (1968) suggested that a massive deplorization of the dentrites in the frontal cortex was likely to be involved in the generation of the CNV. This waveform has been of interest to gerontologists because it has been conceived as a measure of attention and arousal (Tecce, 1972).

Initial studies of the CNV in aging yielded no age differences in CNV amplitude in scalp locations over central motor areas (Marsh & Thompson, 1972; Thompson & Nowlin, 1973). However, Loveless and Sanford (1974) found age differences in the shape of the CNV in long S1–S2 intervals, and they suggested that the aged failed to modulate arousal as efficiently as the young. Recent CNV studies involving a wider array of electrode recording sites and more complex tasks have found significant age differences.

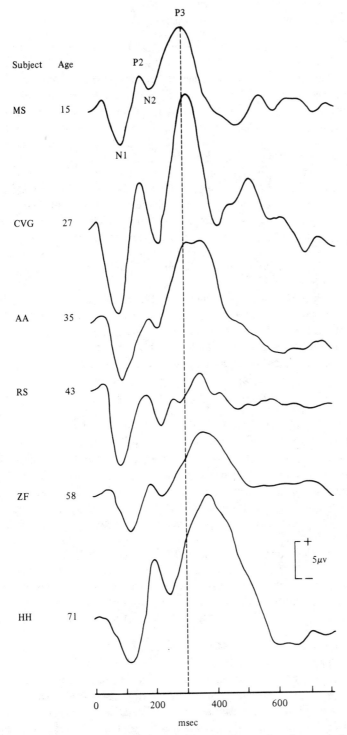

Figure 9-2. Rare-tone evoked-potential waveforms for six normal subjects shown in order of increasing age (top to bottom). The dashed line represents 300-msec poststimulus onset. (*From Squires, Goodin, & Starr, 1979*)

Tecce (1979a) identified a CNV rebound effect occurring when a short-term memory task, demanded of subjects on half of the CNV trials, was absent. A normal CNV developed in a control condition when the typical S1–S2 reaction time paradigm was used; however, when three letters, which the subject later had to remember, were presented between the S1 and S2, CNV amplitude was diminished. On half of the trials in the short-term memory condition, the letters were not present. This is when the CNV rebound effect occurred. CNV amplitude was greater than in the control condition or when letters were present. Reaction time to S2 was also faster when the letters were not present. Young subjects verbalized a strategy of recognizing that after a certain time interval past S1 the letters would not appear. Then they concentrated solely on responding to S2. The supranormal increase in CNV amplitude was interpreted as reflecting a switching of attention from the divided attention set intrinsic to letters trials to an undivided attention set in no-letters trials. Tecce (1979b) tried this task in older subjects and found that the CNV rebound effect was diminished in fronto-central brain areas. None of the older subjects verbalized the strategy of realizing that no letters were coming and hence preparing only for S2, and their CNV indicated that they did not use this strategy. The older subjects also made significantly more perseverative responses than young subjects on the Wisconsin card sorting test, a finding associated with frontal lobe patients (Milner, 1963). Tecce concluded that the diminution of CNV rebound in the older group appeared to indicate a perseverative attention set that was mediated significantly by fronto-central brain areas and that interfered with the switching of attention. Figure 9-3 depicts the lower amplitude CNV in fronto-central areas in the old subjects, which was found in Tecce's laboratory.

Using a task similar to the task employed by Tecce (1979b), Michalewski, Thompson, Smith, Patterson, Bowman, Litzelman, and Brent (1980) independently produced the same result. In this study the subjects heard letters in every trial; on one block of trials they had to remember the letters, while they were not required to remember the letters on another block of trials. There was also a block of trials using the classical S1–S2 CNV paradigm with no letters. Frontal CNVs for the older individuals were reduced in every condition compared to the young group. Changes in midline activity were the same for both age groups. Michalewski et al. (1980) pointed out that this overall reduction in frontal CNV activity in the aged suggests a process of selective aging in the frontal lobes. Albert and Kaplan (1980) reviewed the neuropsychological evidence that suggests that many behavioral deficiencies apparent in the elderly resemble behavioral deficits in patients with frontal lobe lesions. Scheibel and Scheibel (1975) identified losses of dendritic masses in prefrontal and temporal areas of aging brains in histological studies. Thus, the reduced CNV in frontal areas may reflect a cellular change.

Pfefferbaum, Ford, Roth, Hopkins, and Kopell (1979) appear to have replicated the results of Tecce (1979b) and Michalewski et al. (1980). In a group of extraordinarily healthy and active old women they noted a marked reduction in frontal recording sites in a wave they called the *late sustained potential* (SP). This wave occurs as a negative wave 300-450 msec after a stimulus. The SP is maximal at frontal recording sites and is similar in form to the CNV. Thus, the brain generators of the two waveforms may be the same. Pfefferbaum et al. (1979) suggested that the diminished SP might result from a loss in dendritic mass in frontal areas in the elderly.

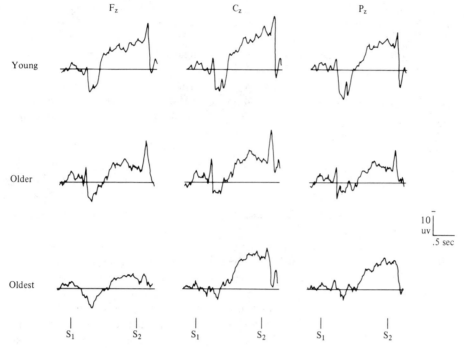

Figure 9-3. Examples of CNV traces for frontal (Fz), central (Cz), and parietal (Pz) recording sites of young and older subjects. Averaged CNVs are based on 22 trials for the young subject and 14 and 18 trials for the older and oldest subjects, respectively. Relative negativity at Fz, Cz, and Pz (referred to linked earlobes) is depicted upward. (*From Tecce, 1979b*)

Three independent laboratories have reported diminished electrophysiological activity at frontal recording sites in brains of normal elderly subjects. The generators of these CNV and SP waveforms are thought to be dendritic layers in the frontal lobes. In two of the laboratories the diminished frontal activity occurred as a correlate of diminished capacity to switch attention. These data, coupled with behavioral and histological evidence, begin to point rather compellingly to a selective aging of the frontal lobes, which impairs the capacity of the elderly to modulate attention.

Computerized axial tomography

Another brain measure, which has primarily clinical applications, is computerized axial tomography, better known as the CAT scan. Until quite recently the assessment of patients with behavioral disorders required indirect measures of nervous system function or dangerous invasive techniques that involved risks and potential complications to patients (for example, angiography, pneumoencephalography). Computerized axial tomography is a safe and painless procedure that provides a picture of the living brain. It is a method of visualizing cerebral structures including the ventricular system and cortical sulci. The value of this technique in neurological assessment of patients of all ages is so great and has been recognized so rapidly that many hospitals throughout the country have already installed the relatively expensive apparatus, even though it has been commercially available only since the mid-1970s. Thus, the CAT scan can be used in most large cities in the United States to assess geriatric patients showing symptoms of cerebral impairment, and it can be undertaken upon referral by the attending physician.

The CAT scan uses a rotating X-ray source, which takes over 28,000 readings in approximately five minutes. This procedure usually consists of a scan that has viewed two contiguous slices of brain tissue in a transaxial plane at the selected level of the brain. The entire procedure takes less than half an hour. Readings are processed by a computer, which calculates 6400 absorption values for each brain slice. The computer calculates the density of tissue scanned by the X-ray beam, and different densities of tissue are translated into lighter or darker areas on a cathode-ray tube display. A Polaroid photograph is then taken of the display so that a permanent record can be assessed by a neuroradiologist or neurologist. The data are also stored on magnetic tape.

The photograph is essentially a picture of a transaxial slice of the brain. Dense bone and calcified areas look white in the computerized tomograms; gray matter of the brain looks gray; and the least dense areas, the ventricles, look almost black.

Huckman, Fox, and Topel (1975) have devised and validated specific quantitative criteria for evaluation of cerebral atrophy and senile dementia. They have indicated that both enlarged ventricles and enlarged sulci are necessary for a reliable diagnosis of senile dementia, and they have provided numerical standards for the width of the ventricles at two points and for the width of the four largest sulci that can be considered atrophied (Huckman et al., 1975). These criteria applied to tomograms yielded results as reliable as assessments based on pneumoencephalographic examination and pathologic examination at autopsy.

CAT scans have been used to diagnose senile dementia and to identify geriatric patients with treatable brain pathology (Huckman et al., 1975). This technique has also been used in conjunction with behavioral assessment to determine the relationship between behavioral capacity and brain structure. Kaszniak (1977) assessed the memory of 50 patients for whom a CAT scan was available, and he demonstrated that CAT scans predict behavioral changes. However, his correlations were moderate, and more recent evidence indicates that the severity of dementia cannot be predicted by CAT scan data (Fox, Kaszniak, & Huckman, 1979; Kaszniak, Garron, Fox, Bergen, & Huckman, 1979). In 78 hospital patients aged 50 years or older with suspected changes in mentation in the absence of focal or other organic brain disease, EEG slowing was the strongest and most general pathologic influence on cognition (Kaszniak et al., 1979). Physiological functioning of the brain rather than neuroanatomical structure was the best correlate of cognitive function. Thus, although the CAT scan is a powerful tool for evaluating patients with dementia and can be used to rule out potentially treatable disorders, it is not terribly useful for demonstrating the severity of dementia or the ultimate prognosis.

Ford and Pfefferbaum (1981) reported preliminary results of their attempt to correlate ERP changes with structural changes in the brain as assessed by the CAT scan. They derived measures of the proportion of fluid to tissue in the frontal and parietal cortex and a measure of ventricular volume from CAT scans of 14 patients who had participated in their ERP experiments. Among their findings was a high correlation (r = .77) between the increase in the ratio of fluid compared to brain tissue (meaning less brain tissue) and longer latency P3 waves. This result linking decreases in brain tissue with longer latency P3 waves is in accordance with other data indicating that P3 latency increases dramatically in dementia patients. Ford and Pfefferbaum also found a high correlation (r = .81) between more negative slow waves recorded over the frontal area and less brain tissue. This result supports the suggestion that behavioral, neuroanatomical, and ERP data are converging to suggest a deficit with age in the frontal lobes.

The main application of CAT scan data may be clinical, and this tool has great significance in the diagnosis of senile dementia. However, CAT scans are beginning to be used in conjunction with ERP and behavioral measures to provide greater precision of information about brain and behavior relationships in aging.

MODELS IN THE PSYCHOPHYSIOLOGY OF AGING

What are some of the psychological models of aging? What has the descriptive research told us? What are some of the hypotheses in the psychophysiology of aging? Since researchers have been carrying out psychophysiological studies in psychology for about 30-40 years, we can now draw on a relatively large body of descriptive literature to derive more general principles about behavior and aging. These models are useful because they organize and draw together a number of divergent studies and lead us to devise research to test the models.

Discontinuity hypothesis

From his extensive work with old individuals, Birren (1963) developed the discontinuity hypothesis, which states that only when a physiological function becomes abnormal does the physiological variable affect behavioral variables. When a physiological variable goes into an abnormal range, then and only then may it affect behavior. In other words, physiological variables that do not affect behavior when they are in a normal range in young subjects may affect behavior in old subjects when the physiological function reaches an abnormal level.

A few examples may help to illustrate the discontinuity hypothesis. In the study of 47 healthy old men mentioned previously (Birren et al., 1963), the investigators used a sophisticated battery of clinical tests. This testing procedure was more intensive than a normal physical examination, and although the investigators had selected a group of what they thought were 47 extremely healthy men, they found that even among these healthiest of aged individuals, about half had a subclinical form of disease, that is, disease that would not be detected by a physician in a routine examination. In the healthiest group there were only five statistically significant correlations between all of the physiological variables and all of the behavioral variables. In the less healthy, subclinical pathology group, 26 of the physiology/behavior relationships were statistically significant. This suggests that only when we start getting into poor health or start shading in the range of poorer health does physiology affect behavior.

Another study supporting the discontinuity hypothesis was undertaken at Duke University. In a longitudinal study relating blood pressure to behavioral variables such as memory and intelligence, Wilkie and Eisdorfer (1971) found that only when blood pressure was elevated did it relate to or affect the behavioral variables. Blood pressure in the normal range does not appear to be related to behavior. So again, only when there was pathology was there a behavior/physiology relationship.

What implications does this have in daily life? For one thing, it stresses the incredible adaptability of old people and the hope that, although some physiological functions decline, the lifestyles of the elderly may not have to change dramatically.

Old people are extremely adaptable. Birren tells a story about an experience he had while doing research on visual perception. To be in contact with elderly subjects, he set up his experiment at a local nursing home, and a part of the experiment involved giving the subjects a visual acuity test. One of the volunteers for the project was an 85-year-old man who was active in the home and a leader in its activities. He had the leading role in the home's production of a play. He was well known and well liked by most of the residents. When Birren tested him for visual acuity, he found that the old man was functionally blind. Birren went to the nursing home administrator and asked if the administrator knew that Mr. X was blind. The administrator could not believe Birren. Observing the old man's behavior very carefully, Birren found that the man was always accompanied by his wife, and she very subtly guided him and gave him cues so that, although this man was functionally blind, not even the nursing home staff were aware of it. This remarkable example stresses the adaptibility of old people.

Arousal level

Another model in the psychophysiology of aging involves the concept of arousal. Psychologists have been exploring the relationship between level of arousal and efficiency of performance for years. In its simplest form the arousal hypothesis states that there is a U-shaped relationship between level of arousal and efficiency of performance. On a conceptual level this means that if you are underaroused—tired or drowsy, for example—you will not be at your most efficient level for performance. As you become more alert and aroused, you perform more efficiently until you reach an optimal level of performance. If you exceed that optimal level by becoming anxious, this interferes with performance. Investigators who have speculated about the arousal level of older individuals have interpreted some evidence to suggest that old people are underaroused and other evidence to suggest that the aged are overaroused. Still other investigators have attempted to integrate and explain these seemingly contradictory results. Here we shall examine the evidence for both positions and try to find some resolution to the controversy.

Support for the notion that older individuals are underaroused comes from a number of psychophysiological studies where EEG measures of central nervous system (CNS) activity have been used. (The CNS includes the brain and the spinal cord. The EEG measures CNS activity inasmuch as EEG recordings reflect electrical activity generated in the brain.) Slower brain wave frequencies, which occur in older people, have been related to underarousal in young subjects, and more complex EEG measures, such as the event-related potential (ERP), have suggested underarousal in the aged

(Schenkenberg, 1970). Other evidence for underarousal comes from tasks such as critical flicker fusion (CFF). If you flash a strobe light at around 40 cycles per second, people are unable to perceive that there are individual flashes. The threshold for critical flicker fusion is higher in old age than it is in young. In other words, the old will perceive a continuous signal at fewer flashes per second than the young. This is related to arousal because Fuster (1958) found that if you stimulate in the brain stem in the reticular formation, which seems to be the brain site that is related to activation and arousal, you get lower CFF thresholds. Since the aged have higher CFF thresholds, this is a sign that perhaps older people are less aroused.

Of course, the reaction time data also indicate that the old are less aroused. People who are less alert and less aroused also perform more slowly on reaction time tests. It is also true, however, that people who are overaroused perform more slowly on reaction time tests.

Data from Eisdorfer's laboratory, which used autonomic nervous system (ANS) measures, suggest that on serial learning performance tests old people are actually more aroused than young subjects (Eisdorfer, 1968). The autonomic nervous system is the part of the nervous system that innervates the glands and the viscera—that is, all of the organs over which an individual supposedly has no conscious control. (Biofeedback research has demonstrated that this is probably inaccurate. The term *autonomic* was used as if some functions were autonomous—neither consciously controlled nor subject to conscious control. Using biofeedback, one can bring ANS functions under conscious control.) Using biochemical measures of autonomic nervous system function, researchers have suggested that older people are overaroused (Powell, Eisdorfer, & Bogdonoff, 1964). This means that during certain stresses, such as performing a serial learning task, older subjects had a higher level of ANS activity than younger subjects.

How do we integrate these data? Thompson and Marsh (1973) have suggested that perhaps both notions of underarousal and overarousal are true—old people are both overaroused and underaroused, depending on what aspect of the nervous system is measured. In the case of central nervous system measures (measures of brain function such as EEG and evoked potentials), the older organism may be underaroused. But, on the other hand, some parts of the autonomic nervous system may not be integrated as well in the functioning of the central nervous system in old people as in young. Thus, by these autonomic measures, the old may be overaroused. What Thompson and Marsh have suggested is a desynchronization hypothesis. As one ages, the total integration of the nervous system—that is, the integration between central nervous system and autonomic nervous system functioning—may deteriorate.

What does this mean in terms of practical applications? If old people are underaroused, then they should be stimulated. Levels of illumination should be increased, old people should be spoken to more loudly, and input to all of their sensory systems should be increased. On the other hand, if old people seem to be overaroused, they should be relaxed.

One of the characteristics of the studies in which overarousal has been demonstrated has been that the subjects are threatened. They are forced to learn a list of word pairs in a limited time. Such a task may be especially threatening to old people.

Froehling (1974) demonstrated, however, that once older people are exposed to this task several times, they no longer respond in terms of biochemical overarousal. For educators the practical lesson from this research is to familiarize older learners with the classroom and allow them to learn at their own pace in a relaxed atmosphere so that they will not suffer from anxiety and hence biochemical overarousal.

Sensory deprivation

Compared with the young, the old have been considered to be in a state of sensory deprivation. Researchers have determined—again, from the biological, decremental perspective—that sensory acuity declines due to deficits in the peripheral sensory systems (Corso, 1971). In the visual system at a peripheral level the lens thickens, the pupil aperture narrows, and the muscles in the eye function less well so that accommodation is not as efficient. Generally, it takes more light energy to have the same effect on the older eye as on the younger eye. Some studies have indicated that there is no way that you can compensate for the difference between the old and the young eye. Physical changes in the eye make it less responsive to light. The hearing apparatus also changes. Ability to hear high tones declines with age. Again, less auditory information is available to the older ear. In terms of the skin, receptors for touch and pain are lost. The skin loses its elasticity, and, generally, touch declines in old age. About two thirds of the taste buds in the mouth die by the time an individual is 70. (Taste, however, is also clearly a learned ability to some extent. Most gourmets are old. This means that there is compensation that takes place even though taste buds are lost.) The sense of smell also declines. A large percentage of the sensory receptors in the nose die with age. Generally, then, less sensory information goes to the older brain.

Studies on sensory deprivation have indicated that when an individual is deprived of sensory information, he or she experiences some difficulty. The brain appears to need a certain level of stimulation or a certain amount of sensory input to function optimally. The old may be in a state of sensory deprivation, and for this reason, they may function less efficiently. Kemp (1971) tried to get at this issue by putting both young and old subjects in a sensory deprivation chamber to see if the old were selectively more affected than the young by this procedure. There were no age differences, so the hypothesis that the old are in a state of sensory deprivation is at this point relatively unproven.

The sensory deprivation model again suggests that old people need stimulation. Stroke patients who receive additional stimulation seem to recover faster. At the hospital where Kemp carried out his research, a very interesting thing happened as a result of sensory deprivation studies. While sensory deprivation research was underway, the researchers talked to some of the therapists and explained theoretical issues in the area of sensory deprivation. One of the therapists got the notion that if sensory deprivation does affect people in a negative way, then patients in comas who are unstimulated are perhaps being mistreated. Hospital staff decided to institute a program in which they started talking to patients in comas, even though the patients could not respond. As a result of this treatment there seemed to be some improvement in recovery time.

TOWARD A REALISTIC PERSPECTIVE OF AGING

A major premise of this chapter has been that we need to undertake more intervention research to examine the true potential of the aged. It is possible that we are overreacting to the negative stereotype of old age and are, therefore, adopting an overly positive approach. Gerontologists writing in this volume have stated that future cohorts of old people will be better off than earlier cohorts. For example, fewer of them will be foreign born, thus leaving the majority more adapted to American society. They will be economically less disadvantaged, and they are going to live longer. They will be healthier and better educated. In Chapter 7 Schaie states that most of the declines in intelligence with age are really a myth. Until people are ready to die, they appear to perform intellectually as well as when they are young. It has been suggested that even some of the biological decrements described in Chapters 11, 12, and 13 may be reversible.

Is this optimism appropriate? Those working daily with old people are aware that age differences are not entirely a myth. Although gerontologists speak about normal aging as if there were not disease, most old people suffer from one chronic disease, and many are affected with three or four chronic diseases. Why do gerontologists present such a positive perspective? One reason is to dispel the negative myths about aging, which have arisen in a youth-oriented culture.

Although we must look at old age positively, we must also be realistic. Scientists and laymen must come together and agree on a realistic perspective of aging that will help us to aid old people and to improve the quality of life in old age. Such a perspective will help us all to be able to age with dignity rather than with despair.

REFERENCES

Albert, M. S., & Kaplan, E. F. Organic implications of neuropsychological deficits in the elderly. In L. W. Poon, J. Fozard, L. Cermak, D. Arenberg, & L. W. Thompson (Eds.), *New directions in memory and aging: Proceedings of the George A. Talland memorial conference.* Hillsdale, N. J.: Lawrence Erlbaum Associates, 1980.

Andersen, P., & Andersson, A. *Physiological basis of the alpha rhythm.* New York: Appleton-Century-Crofts, 1968.

Baltes, P. B., & Schaie, K. W. Aging and IQ: The myth of the twilight years. *Psychology Today,* 1974, *7*, 35–40.

Birren, J. E. Psychophysiological relations. In J. E. Birren, R. N. Butler, S. W. Greenhouse, L. Sokoloff, & M. R. Yarrow (Eds.), *Human aging: A biological and behavioral study.* Washington, D.C.: U.S. Government Printing Office, 1963.

Birren, J. E. Age changes in speed of behavior: Its central nature and physiological correlates. In A. T. Welford & J. E. Birren (Eds.), *Behavior, aging and the nervous system.* Springfield, Ill.: Charles C Thomas, 1965.

Birren, J. E., Butler, R. N., Greenhouse, S. W., Sokoloff, L., & Yarrow, M. (Eds.), *Human aging: A biological and behavioral study.* Washington, D.C.: U.S. Government Printing Office, 1963.

Birren, J. E., Riegel, K. F., & Morrison, D. F. Age differences in response speed as a function of controlled variations of stimulus conditions: Evidence for a general speed factor. *Gerontologia,* 1962, *6*, 1–18.

Birren, J. E., & Woodruff, D. S. Human development over the life span through education. In P. B. Baltes & K. W. Schaie (Eds.), *Life-span developmental psychology: Personality and socialization.* New York: Academic Press, 1973.

Bishop, G. H. Cyclic changes in excitability of the optic pathway of the rabbit. *American Journal of Physiology*, 1933, *103*, 213–224.

Bishop, G. H. The interpretation of cortical potentials. *Cold Spring Harbor Symposium on Quantitative Biology*, 1936, *4*, 305–319.

Botwinick, J. Drives, expectancies and emotions. In J. E. Birren (Ed.), *Handbook of aging and the individual: Psychological and biological aspects.* Chicago: University of Chicago Press, 1959.

Brazier, M. A. B., & Finesinger, J. E. Characteristics of the normal electro-encephalogram. I. A study of the occipital-cortical potentials in 500 normal adults. *Journal of Clinical Investigation*, 1944, *23*, 303–311.

Busse, E. L. Psychopathology. In J. E. Birren (Ed.), *Handbook of aging and the individual.* Chicago: University of Chicago Press, 1959.

Butler, R. N. The facade of chronological age: An interpretive summary. *American Journal of Psychiatry*, 1963, *119*, 721–728.

Callaway, E. Factors influencing the relationship between alpha activity and visual reaction time. *Electroencephalography and Clinical Neurophysiology*, 1962, *14*, 674–682.

Corso, J. F. Sensory processes and age effects in normal adults. *Journal of Gerontology*, 1971, *26*, 90–105.

Cunningham, W. R., & Birren, J. E. Age changes in the factor structure of intellectual abilities in adulthood and old age. Manuscript submitted for publication, 1981.

Donchin, E., Ritter, W., & McCallum, W. C. Cognitive psychophysiology: The endogenous components of the ERP. In E. Callaway, P. Tueting, & S. H. Koslow (Eds.), *Event-related brain potentials in man.* New York: Academic Press, 1978.

Dru, D., Walker, J. P., & Walker, J. B. Self-produced locomotion restores visual capacity after striate lesions. *Science*, 1975, *187*, 265–266.

Duncan-Johnson, C., & Donchin, E. On quantifying surprise: The variation of event-related potentials with subjective probability. *Psychophysiology*, 1977, *14*, 456–467.

Dustman, R. E., & Beck, E. C. Phase of alpha brain waves, reaction time, and visually evoked potentials. *Electroencephalography and Clinical Neurophysiology*, 1965, *18*, 433–440.

Echenhofer, F. G., & Woodruff, D. S. *The effects of repetitive stimulation upon EEG reactivity and arousal in young and old adults.* Paper presented at the 33rd annual scientific meeting of the Gerontological Society, San Diego, 1980.

Eisdorfer, C. Arousal and performance: Experiments in verbal learning and a tentative theory. In G. A. Talland (Ed.), *Human aging and behavior.* New York: Academic Press, 1968.

Ford, J. M., & Pfefferbaum, A. The utility of brain potentials in determining age-related changes in central nervous system and cognitive functions. In L. W. Poon (Ed.), *Aging in the 1980s: Psychological issues.* Washington, D.C.: American Psychological Association, 1981.

Fox, J. H., Kaszniak, A. W., & Huckman, M. Computerized tomographic scanning not very helpful in dementia—nor in craniopharyngioma. (Letter) *New England Journal of Medicine*, 1979, *300*, 437.

Froehling, S. *Effects of propranolol on behavioral and physiological measures of elderly males.* Unpublished doctoral dissertation, Duke University, 1974.

Frost, J. D. EEG-intracellular potential relationships in isolated cerebral cortex. *Electroencephalography and Clinical Neurophysiology*, 1968, *24*, 434–443.

Fuster, J. M. Effects of stimulation of brain stem on tachistoscopic perception. *Science*, 1958, *127*, 150.

Goodin, D., Squires, K., Henderson, B., & Starr, A. Age-related variations in evoked potentials to auditory stimuli in normal human subjects. *Electroencephalography and Clinical Neurophysiology*, 1978, *44*, 447–458.

Green, E. E., Green, A. M., & Walters, E. D. Self-regulation of internal states. In J. Rose (Ed.), *Progress of cybernetics: Proceedings of the International Congress of Cybernetics, London, 1969.* London: Gordon & Breach, 1970. (a)

Green, E. E., Green, A. M., & Walters, E. D. Voluntary control of internal states: Psychological and physiological. *Transpersonal Psychology,* 1970, *2,* 1–26. (b)

Held, R., & Hein, A. Movement produced stimulation in the development of visually guided behavior. *Journal of Comparative and Physiological Psychology,* 1963, *56,* 872–876.

Hicks, L. H., & Birren, J. E. Aging, brain damage, and psychomotor slowing. *Psychological Bulletin,* 1970, *74,* 377–396.

Hoyer, W. J., Labouvie, G. V., & Baltes, P. B. Modification of response speed and intellectual performance in the elderly. *Human Development,* 1973, *16,* 233–242.

Huckman, M. S., Fox, J., & Topel, J. The validity of criteria for the evaluation of cerebral atrophy by computed tomography. *Radiology,* 1975, *116,* 85–92.

Jasper, H. H. Cortical excitatory state and synchronism in the control of bioelectric autonomous rhythms. *Cold Spring Harbor Symposium on Quantitative Biology,* 1936, *4,* 320–338.

Kamiya, J. Conscious control of brain waves. *Psychology Today,* 1968, *1,* 56–60.

Kamiya, J. Operant control of EEG alpha rhythm and some of its reported effects on consciousness. In C. T. Tart (Ed.), *Altered states of consciousness.* New York: John Wiley and Sons, 1969.

Kaszniak, A. W. Effects of age and cerebral atrophy upon span of immediate recall and paired associate learning in older adults. *Dissertation Abstracts International,* 1977, *37* (7-B), 3613–3614.

Kaszniak, A. W., Garron, D. C., Fox, J. H., Bergen, D., & Huckman, M. Cerebral atrophy, EEG slowing, age, education, and cognitive functioning in suspended dementia. *Neurology,* 1979, *29,* 1273–1279.

Kemp, B. J. *Simple auditory reaction time of young adult and elderly subjects in relation to perceptual deprivation and signal-on versus signal-off conditions.* Unpublished doctoral dissertation, University of Southern California, 1971.

Koga, Y., Morant, G. M. On the degree of association between reaction times in the case of different senses. *Biometrika,* 1923, *15,* 346–371.

Kutas, M., McCarthy, G., & Donchin, E. Augmenting mental chronometry: The P300 as a measure of stimulus evaluation. *Science,* 1977, *197,* 792–795.

Lindsley, D. B. Psychological phenomena and the electroencephalogram. *Electroencephalography and Clinical Neurophysiology,* 1952, *4,* 443–456.

Loveless, N. E., & Sanford, A. J. Effects of age on the contingent negative variation and preparatory set in a reaction-time task. *Journal of Gerontology,* 1974, *29,* 52–63.

Lowenthal, M. F. Social isolation and mental illness in old age. *American Sociological Review,* 1964, *29,* 54–70.

Marsh, G., & Thompson, L. W. Age differences in evoked potentials during an auditory discrimination task. *Gerontologist,* 1972, *12,* 44.

Marsh, G., & Thompson, L. W. Psychophysiology of aging. In J. E. Birren & K. W. Schaie (Eds.), *Handbook of the psychology of aging.* New York: Van Nostrand Reinhold, 1977.

Michalewski, H. J., Thompson, L. W., Smith, D. B. D., Patterson, J. V., Bowman, T. E., Litzelman, D., & Brent, G. Age differences in the contingent negative variation (CNV): Reduced frontal activity in the elderly. *Journal of Gerontology,* 1980, *35,* 542–549.

Milner, B. Effects of different brain lesions on card sorting. *Archives of Neurology,* 1963, *9,* 90–100.

Murrell, F. H. The effect of extensive practice on age differences in reaction time. *Journal of Gerontology,* 1970, *25,* 268–274.

Obrist, W. D., & Busse, E. W. The electroencephalogram in old age. In W. P. Wilson (Ed.), *Applications of electroencephalography to psychiatry: A symposium.* Durham, N. C.: Duke University Press, 1965.

Obrist, W. D., Henry, C. E., & Justiss, W. A. Longitudinal study of EEG in old age. *Excerpta Medical International Congress,* 1961, Serial no. 37, 180–181.

Pfefferbaum, A., Ford, J. M., Roth, W. T., Hopkins, W. F., & Kopell, B. S. Event-related potential changes in healthy aged females. *Electroencephalography and Clinical Neurophysiology,* 1979, *46,* 81–86.

Powell, A. H., Eisdorfer, C., & Bogdonoff, M. D. Physiologic response patterns observed in a learning task. *Archives of General Psychiatry,* 1964, *10,* 192–195.

Schaie, K. W. A reinterpretation of age related changes in cognitive structure and functioning. In L. R. Goulet and P. B. Baltes (Eds.), *Life-span developmental psychology: Research and theory.* New York: Academic Press, 1970.

Scheibel, M. E., & Scheibel, A. B. Structural changes in the aging brain. In H. Brody, D. Harmon, & J. M. Ordy (Eds.), *Aging, Volume I.* New York: Raven Press, 1975.

Schenkenberg, T. *Visual, auditory, and somatosensory evoked responses of normal subjects from childhood to senescence.* Unpublished doctoral dissertation. University of Utah, 1970.

Squires, K., Goodin, D., & Starr, A. Event related potentials in development aging, and dementia. In D. Lehman & E. Callaway (Eds.), *Human evoked potentials.* New York: Plenum Press, 1979.

Surwillo, W. W. The relation of simple response time to brain wave frequency and the effects of age. *Electroencephalography and Clinical Neurophysiology,* 1963, *15,* 105–114. (a)

Surwillo, W. W. The relation of response time variability to age and the influence of brain wave frequency. *Electroencephalography and Clinical Neurophysiology,* 1963, *15,* 1029–1032. (b)

Surwillo, W. W. The relation of decision time to brain wave frequency and to age. *Electroencephalography and Clinical Neurophysiology,* 1964, *16,* 510–514. (a)

Surwillo, W. W. Some observations on the relation of response speed to frequency of photic stimulation under conditions of EEG synchronization. *Electroencephalography and Clinical Neurophysiology,* 1964, *17,* 194–198. (b)

Tecce, J. J. Contingent negative variation (CNV) and psychological processes in man. *Psychological Bulletin,* 1972, *77,* 73–108.

Tecce, J. J. A CNV rebound effect. *Electroencephalography and Clinical Neurophysiology,* 1979, *46,* 546–551. (a)

Tecce, J. J. Diminished CNV rebound and perseverative attention set in older subjects. In D. Lehmann & E. Callaway (Ed.), *Human evoked potentials: Applications and problems.* New York: Plenum Press, 1979. (b)

Thompson, L. W., & Marsh, G. R. Psychophysiological studies of aging. In C. Eisdorfer and M. P. Lawton (Eds.), *The psychology of adult development and aging.* Washington, D.C.: American Psychological Association Press, 1973.

Thompson, L. W., & Nowlin, J. B. Relation of increased attention to central and autonomic nervous system states. In L. R. Jarvik, C. Eisdorfer, & J. E. Blum (Eds.), *Intellectual functioning in adults: Psychological and biological influences.* New York: Springer, 1973.

Walter, W. G. The contingent negative variation: An electro-cortical sign of sensori-motor reflex association in man. In E. A. Asratyan (Ed.), *Progress in brain research, Volume 22, Brain reflexes.* Amsterdam: Elsevier, 1968.

Walter, W. G., Cooper, R., Aldridge, V. J., McCallum, W. C., & Winter, A. L. Contingent negative variation: An electric sign of sensori-motor association and expectancy in the human brain. *Nature (London),* 1964, *203,* 380–384.

Wilkie, F., & Eisdorfer, C. Intelligence and blood pressure in the aged. *Science,* 1972, *172,* 959–962.

Woodruff, D. S. Biofeedback—implications for gerontology. In D. S. Woodruff (Chair), *Design strategies and hypotheses of psychobiological research in aging.* Mini-symposium presented at the 24th annual meeting of the Gerontological Society, Houston, October 1971.

Woodruff, D. S. The usefulness of the life-span approach for the psychophysiology of aging. *Gerontologist,* 1973, *13,* 467–472.

Woodruff, D. S. Relationships between EEG alpha frequency, reaction time, and age: A biofeedback study. *Psychophysiology,* 1975, *12,* 673–681.

Woodruff, D. S. Intervention in the psychophysiology of aging: Pitfalls, progress, and potential. In R. Turner & H. W. Reese (Eds.), *Life-span developmental psychology: Intervention.* New York: Academic Press, 1980.

Woodruff, D. S. *Successful biofeedback conditioning in young and old and its predictors.* Paper presented at the 12th International Congress of Gerontology, Hamburg, Germany, 1981.

CHAPTER **10**

Human Sexuality and Aging

Robert E. Solnick and Nan Corby

INTRODUCTION

A major theme of aging to which the gerontologist returns with disconcerting regularity is the theme of loss. Old age is most often characterized by what it is *not*; those things comprising the list of what it *is* typically have been laden with negative connotations. Because a number of very real losses do occur in old age (in addition to those that are merely losses from the viewpoint of the young), and because some of the concomitants of aging are unpleasant for many people (for example, a decrease in energy, health, or income), it is not surprising that one of the facets of human life most closely associated with youth or young adulthood is presumed to be absent in old age. This is especially understandable when one realizes that between generations people do not talk about sex openly or personally. In addition, our closest ties with the "older generation" are usually with our own parents, with whom we are especially reluctant to discuss personal sexuality, as they are with us.

Such generalizations also hold true for researchers, who, with few exceptions, have been equally reticent to investigate sexuality among old people. Hence, we lack real information about what old people do or think about sexually, about what sexual changes occur with age, and about what is "normal" or "not normal" in old age. Because little has been known about sexuality in the elderly, the typical assumption has been that there is little to know. The arrogance of this assumption—that sexlessness is the normal state in old age because we are ignorant of sexiness in old age—has led those older people who do feel sexy to question their own normalcy. It has also led to the shock, dismay, and disgust of others who become aware of the sexual interests or behavior of a specific older person: a parent or a patient, for example. The direct effects of those negative attitudes on the older person himself or herself can only be imagined, but they are not likely to enhance self-esteem or pleasure.

This chapter, which presents an overview of sexuality in old age, aims to provide sufficient information so that the reader will be able to revise those beliefs that describe all older people as either sexless or pathological. First, we shall discuss the sexual activities of people in later life and explore the ways in which these differ from those of younger people. We shall then examine the normal physiological changes that might have an effect on sexuality. Following this, we shall look at broader areas influencing sexual behavior—from the sociocultural influences to the effects of disease. We shall also describe the types of sexual dysfunction most often found among the elderly and the current therapies for those dysfunctions. In the final section we shall look at three specific subpopulations—the elderly homosexual, the institutionalized elderly person, and the no-longer-married older woman—and try to evaluate the special issues each must face and resolve with regard to his or her own sexuality.

SEXUAL ACTIVITIES

What are we talking about when we talk about sex? What kinds of things comprise human sexuality? Do we mean sexual intercourse alone? Or, do we also include sexual thoughts and daydreams? When does affectionate caressing turn into foreplay? If it does not end in orgasm, is it still sex? These are just some of the questions that complicate any description of sexuality.

Accurate descriptions are usually enhanced by research, and research requires specific definitions and measurements of things that can be measured, described, and replicated by other scientists in other places at other times. Because of these requirements, and because scientists have not yet agreed on how to measure certain things (such as orgasms in women), or describe others (such as love), some of these areas remain unresearched to any great degree. Indeed some of the topics we shall be discussing here are nebulous, since the technologies of measurement and description are still in the process of development in sex research and because their precision has not been verified to the degree that we might prefer.

Nonetheless, selected components of sexuality have been measured (even if not with perfect consensus and replication) and described (though not always with exactness and objectivity). Among them are factors that have been objectively observed and those that consist of the subjective descriptions of the people who have experienced them. Sex researchers generally report their findings in terms of frequencies (how often a target behavior occurred), incidences (what proportion of the people did it), or magnitudes or levels (the strength or intensity of something, often compared to a standard). Although these sorts of data obviously do not comprise the sum total of all that is important about sexuality, they provide a place to begin an examination of what sex is like in later life.

Male

As males age, proportionately fewer of them are sexually active, whether the index of sexual activity is sexual intercourse, masturbation, morning erections, number of ejaculations, or reports of sexual interest (Hegeler, 1976; Kinsey, Pomeroy, & Martin, 1948; Martin, 1975; Pfeiffer, Verwoerdt, & Davis, 1972). Not only are fewer males sexually active, but those older men who are active are less active than younger men (DeNigola & Peruzza, 1974; Finkle, Moyers, Tobenkin, & Karg, 1959; Kinsey et al., 1948; Pfeiffer et al., 1972; Pfeiffer, Verwoerdt, & Wang, 1968, 1969). The reported rates of these decreases in sexual incidence and frequency in later life vary from study to study and by specific activity examined, but the apparent fact of the decrease remains largely unchallenged.

Some interesting patterns become apparent as we look at the data in greater detail. First, although a wide variation is evident in the ages at which men report themselves first experiencing a decline in sexual interest or frequency, a noticeably larger proportion report that age to be around 50 (Pfeiffer, Verwoerdt, & Davis, 1972). A second noticeable drop, this one in incidence or numbers of men sexually active, has been reported to occur in the 70s (Hegeler, 1976; Pfeiffer et al., 1968; Verwoerdt, Pfeiffer, & Wang, 1969a); one report, however, has this second drop occurring somewhat earlier, in the late 60s (Martin, 1975).

A longitudinal study that collected data three to four years apart found specific and differing patterns of changes in sexual activity. Some of the men surveyed (27%) were not sexually active at either interview. Others (31%) were not sexually active at the second interview, although they had been at the first. Continuing unchanged sexual activity was reported by 22%. Increased sexual activity was reported by 20% (Verwoerdt, Pfeiffer, & Wang, 1969b). One apparently misses important individual differences in sexuality in later life by only looking at grouped cross-sectional data.

Female

A much different picture of sexuality in later life has been found among women. Certainly age-associated declines occur in both the numbers of women who are sexually active and in the frequency of their activities. The Kinsey study of women, however, concluded that there is "no evidence that the female ages in her sexual capacities" (Kinsey, Pomeroy, Martin, & Gebhard, 1953). This conclusion was matched by Masters and Johnson's (1966) report that "there is no time limit drawn by the advancing years to female sexuality."

Orgasmic response, although occurring in fewer women and less often with age, has been reported by research to occur among women in their 70s "and older" (Kleegman, 1959). The authors of this chapter have clinically noted reports of orgasmic response from women in their 80s.

Although a woman's capacity for sexual activity and enjoyment may remain throughout her life, far fewer older women than older men are sexually active. The reported figures range from 20 to 40% of married female subjects over age 60 versus 53–60% of the married males over age 60 (Newman & Nichols, 1960; Verwoerdt et al., 1969a). A follow-up study seven to nine years later indicated that the figures had dropped by about a quarter among each group (Verwoerdt et al., 1969a).

According to the Kinsey report (Kinsey et al., 1953), this decrease in activity among women is "controlled by the male's desires, and it is primarily his aging rather than the female's loss of interest or capacity which is reflected in the decline." The dependence of an older woman's sexual activity on that of her husband has been confirmed by data collected in two of the Duke studies of sexuality in old age. The lack of a partner was cited as the reason for ending intercourse by 48% of the women in each of these studies, and by 10% and none of the men in the two studies. Spousal illness or lack of sexual interest or ability was given as the reason by 48% and 42% of the women and by 30% and 29% of the men. One's own illness or lack of interest or ability was given by 14% and 10% of the women and by 58% and 71% of the men (Pfeiffer et al., 1968; Pfeiffer et al., 1972). A third Duke study found six out of eight couples agreeing that they stopped intercourse for reasons having to do with the husband; one couple attributed cessation to the wife, and in the last couple, each assumed responsibility for cessation (Pfeiffer et al., 1969).

As we have seen so far, sexuality is most often studied by examining data having to do with those sexual activities resulting, or intending to result, in orgasm. Most often they have to do with coitus. Occasionally the activities surveyed are more or less solitary ones such as masturbation, nocturnal orgasms, or morning erections. Almost never are oral or anal sexual activities the topic of research. Indeed, even the non-genital touching and caressing, which many people find a very enjoyable and sexual part of lovemaking—whether or not they lead to coitus—are almost as ignored in the literature, though they form an increasingly important component of one's sexual pleasure as one ages (Weinberg, 1969).

Sexual interest, which is another measure of sexuality, has been ascertained by direct questioning of subjects and inferred from reports of sexual thoughts, dreams, and fantasies. As with sexual activity, sexual interest of various sorts appears to diminish with age. It should be noted, however, that sexual interest remains higher than sexual activity, especially among men. The increasing gap between the two forms of sexuality in men may be due to male reticence to admit a disinterest in sex (Botwinick, 1973). Males are under more pressure than females to report sexual interest. Adolescent males receive a great deal of peer support for reports of sexual prowess (Simon & Gagnon, 1969), and older males are more often the object of jeering condescension about their presumed lack of sexual capacity. Although the data on women's sexual interest also show a decline with age and a gap between interest and activity, the decline is not as steep and the gap is not as wide as for men; however, sexual interest among older women remains, like sexual activity, below that for men.

PHYSIOLOGICAL CHANGES

We can broadly categorize physiological changes into those changes directly related to sexual functioning, those indirectly related to sexual functioning, and those not related to sexual functioning in any important way. We shall be dealing only with the first two categories, of course. For example, hormonal changes and changes related to the breasts and genitals belong in the first category, whereas changes related to general body image belong in the second category. The reader should bear in mind that even though physiological changes do occur with age, the degree to which these changes affect sexual behavior and pleasure is difficult to determine since physiological and psychological influences are difficult to separate.

Hormonal changes

A great deal of controversy still surrounds the consequences of hormonal changes on sexual behavior. Persky, Lief, Strauss, Miller, and O'Brien (1978) point out that in spite of the research findings to date, "the general role of the endocrine system in human sexual behavior is not well understood."

Male. The concentration of plasma testosterone in the male declines after the age of 50, although it is highly variable within each age category. The testosterone level in some older men may be as high as that in younger men. The effect of a reduction in testosterone continues to be a matter of debate. Most researchers have tended to reject the idea of a male climacteric tied to hormone levels, but recently more evidence seems to confuse the relationship between testosterone levels and climacteric symptoms such as depression, headache, fatigue, and insomnia in men (Greenblatt, Nezhat, Roesel, & Natrajan, 1979). Also, there appears to be a departure from the previously held view (Raboch, Mellan, & Starka, 1975) that almost all impotence is due to psychological factors and that testosterone levels, per se, play a minor role in this problem. Some researchers have found that testosterone therapy is effective in treating both climacteric symptoms (Greenblatt et al., 1979) and impotence (Spark, White, & Connolly, 1980).

Female. The most significant hormonal changes for the female occur during the climacteric, which extends over several years and includes the cessation of menses —that is, the menopause. One may think of the climacteric as the counterpart of puberty, and menopause as the counterpart of menarche (Timiras & Meisami, 1972). Following menopause, the production of estrogen and progesterone by the ovary diminishes to insignificant levels, but some production of estrogen continues as a result of the peripheral conversion of androgens to estrogen (Monroe & Menon, 1977; Vermeulen, 1976). Androgens continue to be secreted in significant amounts by the postmenopausal ovary and by the adrenal cortex; in addition, the conversion of androgens to estrogens seems to increase with age (Vermeulen, 1976).

There is substantial disagreement as to the role that reduced estrogen production plays in the development of menopausal symptoms such as headaches, backaches, nervousness, hot flashes, coldness, and other uncomfortable responses. Until recently most researchers seemed to feel that the only confirmed physiological changes related to decrease in estrogen were symptoms of vasomotor instability, such as hot flashes and sweats, and of genital atrophy, such as pain during intercourse (Eisdorfer & Raskind, 1975). Recently, however, one source has reported (Research Resources Reporter, 1979) that hot flashes appear to originate in the hypothalamus area of the brain rather than in the peripheral parts of the body as some researchers had previously proposed. In addition, new information seems to indicate that apparently psychological manifestations such as anxiety, depression, and headaches may be hormone-related (Greenblatt et al., 1979) and not entirely due to psychogenic factors. It also appears that the percentage of women who experience such symptoms has been exaggerated (Weg, 1978).

Other changes directly related to sexual functioning

Male. As in the case of the female, the male also experiences a general decline in sexual responsiveness as he passes into his 50s. Solnick and Birren (1977) reported that the time rate of increase of penile diameter was about six times faster for a group of males in their 20s as it was in a group in their 50s, when exposed to the same erotic stimulus. Often full erection is not attained for the older male until ejaculation is imminent. The ejaculation usually is not as intense, and the time required for the older male to be aroused again following ejaculation increases. A full 24 hours may be required before erectile capacity returns. Detumescence in the younger male almost always occurs in two stages, whereas it often appears as one stage for the man past 50. Full testicular elevation, which is a highly consistent occurrence prior to ejaculation in the male under 50, is no longer the case for the older male. On the positive side, the older male finds it easier to maintain an erection for longer periods of time before he feels the urge to ejaculate. This tends to come closer to matching the needs of the female, since many women require more time than males to become aroused.

Female. The major source of data regarding the physiological changes that take place in the female and male sexual systems as they age is an important study conducted by Masters and Johnson (1966). The information in the following paragraphs briefly synopsizes their findings with regard to aging. Other data are cited where appropriate.

A general decline occurs in the sexual responsiveness of the female as she passes into her 50s. For example, increase in breast size during sexual stimulation is markedly reduced; muscle tension elevation declines; rectal sphincter contractions, so common in younger women, rarely occur; preorgasmic color change of the labia, which was present in all of the women under 50 in the study, was reduced to 27% in the group aged 61–80. Probably the most important changes were in the vagina. Approximately five years after the cessation of menses, the steroid-starved vagina appeared to become much thinner, and vaginal lubrication was reduced in both rate and amount.

Nipple erection and the response of the clitoris to stimulation, however, remained intact with increasing age. This is particularly important when one considers the critical role that the clitoris plays for the female during the process of reaching orgasm. For this and many other reasons, sexual activity can continue to be a highly pleasurable and important aspect of the older woman's life, in spite of the other psysiological changes she may experience.

One must conclude that, although many physiological sexual responses change or decline with age, few of these changes have a significant impact on the basic ability to enjoy sex. Much physiological potential for sexual pleasure remains in both the male and female. When the sexes are compared, the female is less likely to suffer functional loss since the source of her orgasm, the clitoris, remains responsive throughout her life.

Changes indirectly related to sexual functioning

Many physiological changes that take place in people as they age and that do not directly involve the sexual system may have an effect on sexual functioning. For example, changes in the firmness of the body may affect partner perception of physical and sexual attractiveness. This effect is certainly exacerbated by the continuing stress on youth and on the association of youth with beauty in our culture.

Obesity is a problem that is by no means limited to older persons, but maintaining one's weight becomes increasingly difficult as a person moves into the middle and later years. The ratio of fat to muscle tissue tends to increase with age, making even the person who is able to maintain the same weight throughout his or her life appear less youthful.

Men often lose their hair, and both men and women turn gray. One need only attend to advertising pertaining to products for changing hair color, removing wrinkles, replacing hair or losing weight to be aware of the importance of these factors in sexual attractiveness. Cosmetic surgery for other than reconstructive purposes has also become increasingly common.

All these things indicate the role that a youthful body image plays in our sexuality. Body image has been shown to be related to self-image and self-concept, which often have an effect on sexual behavior. Changes in the body are thought to have an especially negative effect on women. Many men may be considered sexually attractive throughout their lives; few women are.

A decline occurs in overall energy levels for most people as they age, and this affects the amount of energy they have available for sexual activities. If one may speak of a "psychic energy," the finding that a larger portion of this psychic energy is turned inward as persons move into their 50s (Neugarten, Wood, Kraines, & Loomis, 1968) may influence sexual expression.

INFLUENCES ON SEXUAL BEHAVIOR

The three major factors affecting sexual behavior in later life are gender, age, and past sexual experience. More men are more sexually active than women. More younger people are more sexually active than older people. The "use-it-or-lose-it" dictum is supported by the finding that people who have been more sexually active early in life tend to remain more sexually active later in life (Pfeiffer & Davis, 1972). Insofar as sexual activity has been quantified, this much appears to be true. However, exceptions and enormous variations also exist: many older people are more sexually active than some younger people, and many women are more active than men. In addition, there is a group of "late-blooming" women, whose sexuality does not come into full flower, as it were, until their 30s and who remain sexually active later and more than might be predicted (Christenson & Johnson, 1973). Nonetheless, the trend is for the younger and the male to be more active, and for the more active at younger ages to remain more active in later life.

When one separates the data by gender to investigate further the factors influencing sexual activity, some interesting differences appear. Among older men, frequency of intercourse is predicted by past sexual enjoyment, interest, and frequency; by age (negatively correlated); and by expectations of future life satisfaction. Among women, frequency of intercourse is predicted by past enjoyment and past frequency (but not by past sexual interest), by marital status and future life satisfaction (positively correlated), and by age and being postmenopausal (negatively correlated) (Pfeiffer & Davis, 1972). We shall look at some of these issues in more detail.

Past sexual experience

Among men, past sexual enjoyment, interest, and frequency are highly correlated with present sexual interest and activity (Pfeiffer & Davis, 1972). Correlations between early- and late-life sexual frequency and sexual daydreams have also been established among men (Giambra & Martin, 1977). The importance of regularity of sexual expression in maintaining sexual function throughout life has been emphasized by many (Masters & Johnson, 1966; Pfeiffer, 1969). Among women, past sexual enjoyment (but not past frequency of intercourse or past sexual interest) appears to be highly predictive of current sexual interest and frequency of intercourse (Pfeiffer & Davis, 1972).

The "quality-of-sex" issues deserve more research attention than they have yet received. One of the few studies examining this found that current sexual enjoyment among older people, like activity, was predicted most strongly by past enjoyment, by gender (maleness was positively correlated), and by age (older age was negatively correlated). Also positively correlated among men were present health, social class, present life satisfaction, and early health status; age, antihypertensive or sleeping medication, and excessive concern over physical condition were all negatively correlated. Among women, past enjoyment and marital status (positively correlated) and age (negatively correlated) were most highly predictive of current sexual enjoyment; education plays a smaller but still significant role (Pfeiffer & Davis, 1972). Another study found the capacity to experience coital orgasm fairly regularly to be a strong predictor of sexual enjoyment in later life among women (Christenson & Gagnon, 1965).

The larger question of what constitutes "current sexual enjoyment" in later life (or earlier) has not yet been satisfactorily answered. Is it duration of the sexual experience, number or intensity of orgasms, preorgasmic emotional excitement or physiological arousal, postorgasmic relaxation or satisfaction, intensity of a sense of closeness with or love for another, maximization of sensual immersion in a sensory/sexual encounter, increased self-esteem, or a sense of well-being? Moreover, we do not yet know if these things change with age.

Another set of questions might be asked about the role of sexuality in one's life, and how this might (or might not) change over one's lifetime. Obviously procreation is not the purpose of sexual activity for postmenopausal women. We suspect, however, that were one to compare the number of pregnancies to the frequency of coitus among premenopausal women, one would find that procreation is not the major purpose of sexual activity among that group either. Although the direct components of sexual enjoyment may well be some of the experiences listed previously, the larger role of sexuality for some may have as much to do with establishing or maintaining a relationship, being close to another, pleasing one's partner (either to give pleasure or to avoid that partner's displeasure), or habit ("It's Saturday morning again"). Among some older couples, sexuality may also have come to mean affordable entertainment with no risk of pregnancy and with positive benefits that include, in addition to sensual and orgasmic pleasure, feelings of intimacy and release from physical tension.

Marital status

Marital status is an important predictor of sexual activity among women but not among men. The heterosexual activity of women in later life has been shown to be highly dependent on the presence of a socially acceptable, sexually active partner (Kinsey et al., 1953; Newman & Nichols, 1960; Pfeiffer & Davis, 1972). For women the availability of those partners diminishes increasingly with age. Although at birth male infants outnumber female infants, by middle age (45–64 years of age) there are 92 men to every 100 women in the United States. That figure drops to 69 men per 100 women at ages 65 and over (U.S. Bureau of the Census, 1977). Further reducing socially acceptable heterosexual opportunity for older women is the difference in marital status between older men and women. Whereas 63% of all women over 65 are unmarried, only 27% of all men over 65 are also unmarried, resulting in roughly 30 single men to every 100 single women over 65.

The tendency of women to marry men an average of four years older than they (Newman & Nichols, 1960) has two additional effects on heterosexual opportunity for older women. First is the social effect. If a woman's potential partners are limited to men older than she, and fewer of them are around, then her heterosexual opportunities contract. Obviously the older man's opportunities expand (theoretically, at least), since the pool of women younger than he expands as he ages. The second effect of the one-way age discrepancy has to do with health. Ill health increases with age. If men are older, they are likely to be less healthy and, therefore, less sexually active. The fact that men die an average of seven years younger than women also mitigates against female heterosexual opportunity in old age.

Health

Among women, health factors appear to play very little of a role in sexual functioning. Among men, an objective health rating (by physicians) was correlated to frequency of intercourse. Sexual interest and enjoyment, however, appear to be more dependent on a man's subjective assessment of his own health (Pfeiffer & Davis, 1972). The effects of specific disease processes and disabilities will be discussed in the next section of this chapter.

EFFECTS OF DISEASE

Approximately 85% of people over age 65 have chronic health problems. Many of these problems are not serious disease states, yet they may certainly influence sexual behavior in some ways. For example, Glover (1977), reports that some elderly couples suffering from arthritis and osteoporosis are able to change their negative attitudes toward oral and anal stimulation because they are more practical ways for them to achieve sexual satisfaction. Many other chronic conditions such as bursitis, general muscular atrophy, back and joint problems, and obesity could influence the frequency and type of sex in which older people engage.

Although some diseases do affect sexual functioning more or less directly (Glover, 1977; Rossman, 1978), the degree to which a person is affected is highly variable (Zilbergeld, 1978, p. 297). Different people with the same diseases and the same physiological effects on their bodies will vary tremendously in their adaptation to their condition and in their sexual expression. Given sufficient motivation, only the most severe diseases could completely block sexual pleasure.

Heart and circulatory disease

Even though a great deal has been written about the minimal effect heart disease should have on sexual functioning, research indicates that many cardiovascular patients continue to function at levels below their sexual potential (Bloch, Maeder, & Haissly, 1975). The factors that seem to be important in this finding are fear of relapse, latent depression, and fear of sudden death. Actually less stress is put on the heart during intercourse than during standard laboratory tests given to many patients (Kavanaugh & Sheppard, 1977). The death rate during treadmill testing is 1 per 100,000 tests. Documented instances of death during intercourse are even more rare (Glover, 1977). Generally a person who can comfortably climb one or more flights of stairs following a heart attack is ready to resume sexual activity.

In cases of severe circulatory problems, a person may require aorto-iliac surgery, which may involve nerve damage and subsequent changes in sexual functioning. These changes can be minimized if the surgeon is familiar with the nerves affecting sexual response and considers the preservation of the patient's sexuality a worthwhile objective along with other surgical objectives.

Diabetes

Approximately 50% of men with diabetes mellitus will suffer from some degree of impairment of their erectile responsiveness. Ejaculatory response is not usually affected by this disease. In addition, the incidence of diabetes-caused impotence increases after the age of 60 (Kent, 1975). Undoubtedly peripheral neuropathy is associated with diabetes (Braddom, Hollis, & Castell, 1977; Ellenberg, 1971), which could explain the impotency, but there have been no studies indicating a clear relationship between the severity of the neuropathy and impotency. One study does, however, show a correlation between duration of the disease and impotency. In this case the average duration of the disease was 6.1 years in the potent subjects and 10.4 years in the impotent subjects (Braddom et al., 1977). At one time it was thought that impotence in diabetics reflected an endocrinologic problem, but now it appears that is not the case (Ellenberg, 1973; Kolodny, Kahn, Goldstein, & Barnett, 1974).

In at least one study of female diabetics the findings seem to indicate little or no effect on sexual response when the research data are evaluated in terms of libido and orgasm (Ellenberg, 1977). Orgasmic response and an interest in sex were present in 81.5% of the subjects with neuropathy and 79% of those without, and these percentages were not significantly different from those found in a nondiabetic group. There are at least two possible explanations for the different findings for the male and female. One is that the decline in erectile response is a clear indicator of a problem for the male but no easily measured similar response exists in the female. The female may be affected in ways that have not been detected as yet. Ellenberg (1977) prefers to offer a second explanation, which relates to the difference in sexual socialization for the sexes. He takes the position that the male sex drive is primarily physical, whereas the female functions at a "higher" psychosocial and emotional level as a result of her enculturation. The final explanation of this difference will have to await the outcome of more thorough arousal-measurement studies of the female suffering from diabetes.

Prostatectomy

The probability that a male may require a prostatectomy has increased as male life expectancy has increased. Various studies show that 5%–40% of patients subjected to a transurethral prostatectomy will experience a decrease or loss of potency (Madorsky, Ashamalla, Schussler, Lyons, & Miller, 1976; Zohar, Meirag, Maoz, & Durst, 1976). In the transurethral prostatectomy, surgery is performed on the prostate gland via the urethral canal. In approximately 80%–90% of these cases, the patient experiences retrograde ejaculation as a result—that is, the ejaculate flows into the bladder and is excreted later. In more serious cases, such as those involving cancer of the prostate, the surgery may involve the perineal or abdominal approach, in which case the probability of impotency will be higher. For the transurethral patient, Zohar et al., (1976), found that providing a sympathetic explanation and a willingness to answer questions regarding the operation were decisive factors in determining postoperative sexual prognosis. Five of eight patients receiving no explanation became impotent, whereas none of the seven patients who received explanations became impotent.

Colectomy and ileostomy

As in the case in prostatectomy, the probability of a person needing to undergo a colectomy or ileostomy increases with age. Fortunately not all persons who undergo this type of surgery are affected sexually. The crucial factors in determining the effect of these surgical procedures are the amount of rectum remaining and age. Burnham, Lennard-Jones, and Brooke (1977) found that none of the 42 men with an intact rectum experienced any change in sexual functioning. The 118 men who had a portion of the rectum removed experienced sexual impairment as follows: (1) 15% of those under the age of 35, (2) 44% of those between 35 and 45, and (3) 53% of those over 45. However, only 17% of the men over 45 developed complete erectile impotence. As in the case of diabetes, the effect of this type of surgery appears to be less for the female than for the male. There is a psychological effect for both sexes. Approximately 50% of the patients reported feeling less sexually attractive, although only 10% of their partners agreed with them.

Mastectomy

Although breast cancer tends to occur most frequently during the middle years, the disease may have long-lasting effects on a woman's sexual relationships and may come at a time when she is facing other adjustment problems in her life—for example, menopause. It is the leading cause of death in American women between 40 and 50 years of age. Approximately 7% of the women in America will eventually develop the disease (Polivy, 1977). Radical mastectomy—the removal of the breast, underlying tissue, and axillary lymph nodes—has been the treatment of choice in the past, but surgeons are beginning to be more conservative in the extent of surgery undertaken today.

Psychological issues play a very important role for both the woman and her partner in her adjustment to the loss of one or both breasts (Ervin, 1973; Jamison, Wellisch, & Pasnau, 1978; Polivy, 1977; Witkin, 1978). A mastectomy is psychologically more traumatic than other surgery since it involves an important, visible symbol of femininity (Polivy, 1977). Mastectomy patients often engage in denial, which accounts for the finding that decline in body image and self-image often does not occur until months after surgery.

Suicidal ideation is quite common among women who undergo a radical mastectomy, and concern over sexual adjustment appears to be an important predictor of suicidal thought. Emotional suffering seems to outweigh by far the physical pain that a woman may experience as the result of a mastectomy. Younger women (under 45) tend to rate their postoperative adjustment as significantly poorer than older women (over 45). Perhaps the older woman has already dealt with some of the emotional problems associated with loss of body image and self-image as part of the aging process (Jamison, Wellisch, & Pasnau, 1977).

A key factor in postmastectomy adjustment appears to be the mate's evaluation of the marital relationship. Specifically, there seems to be a significant correlation between the effect of mastectomy on the sexual relationship and evaluation of the general relationship (Wellisch, Jamison, & Pasnau, 1978).

Three major preventative actions may be taken to maximize postmastectomy adjustment: (1) presurgical counseling of both the husband and wife, including involving the husband in her recuperation through intimate contact such as changing her surgical dressings; (2) participation of the woman in open-ended groups of other mastectomy patients to assist her in dealing with grief and other emotional adjustments, and (3) sensitivity and responsiveness of the surgeon to evidences of depression in the patient.

Hysterectomy and oophorectomy

Hysterectomies (removal of all or part of the uterus) and oophorectomies (removal of one or both ovaries) are surgical procedures that occur most frequently in the middle years. Research indicates incidences of diminished sexual functioning of from 10% to 38% among patients following surgery. The extent to which sexual functioning is affected is, in large part, related to the woman's expectation regarding her postoperative sexual desire and enjoyment (Dennerstein, Wood, & Burrows, 1977). When both ovaries are removed, estrogen administration may be necessary to prevent pain during intercourse (dyspareunia) due to thinning of the vaginal wall and poor lubrication. Estrogen administration, however, does not appear to have any primary effect on sexual desire or enjoyment.

Urinary infections

Vaginitis is probably the most common infection of elderly women seeking gynecologic help (Ledger, 1977). Women who are sexually active are particularly susceptible to urological problems because of the changes taking place in their genitals as a result of aging. The resulting dyspareunia can discourage sexual activity. Reduced sexual activity may present emotional problems for the woman and her partner as well as tend to further reduce the body's production of estrogen (Masters & Johnson, 1966). Since estrogen levels are related to the aging effect on the external and internal genitalia, reduced sexual activity would have the effect of exacerbating the problem.

The solution, then, is not for the woman to reduce sexual activity, but to take precautions with medical help to minimize the effects of the aging process on the genitals.

Alcoholism

There are clearly long-term effects on erectile responsiveness for the male who has used excessive amounts of alcohol for many years. In a study of 17,000 alcohol-abuse patients (Lemere & Smith, 1973), 8% of the patients complained of impotency. In half of these cases the impotency continued after years of sobriety. The cause of impotency appears to be related to neurological damage (as in the case of diabetes) and liver damage, which may cause a reduction in testosterone levels in the body (Lemere, 1976). Few, if any, women alcoholics complain of sexual dysfunctions, which tends to confirm the findings discussed previously relative to the absence of any effect of diabetes on women.

Alcohol may have a short-term as well as a long-term effect on a male's potency. Overindulgence in alcohol may lead to an episode of impotency, particularly for the older male who is more vulnerable to the effects of alcohol than is his young counterpart (Masters & Johnson, 1966). An incident such as this is reversible if the male does not become overly concerned about it. If he does become anxious about this occasional alcohol- or fatigue-induced episode of impotency, the anxiety may cause him to embark on a downward spiral, which will lead to psychogenic impotency.

SEXUAL DYSFUNCTIONS

The most common sexual dysfunctions for women in the middle and later years are dyspareunia (pain during intercourse) and situational orgasmic dysfunction. A woman suffering from situational orgasmic dysfunction is unable to reach orgasm consistently enough to satisfy herself and/or her partner, although she has reached orgasm by some means at least once during her lifetime. Often a woman who has been orgasmic fairly consistently early in her life loses this capacity later in life, although with treatment this can be remedied.

The most common sexual dysfunction among men in the middle and later years is secondary impotency, the inability to achieve and/or maintain an erection of sufficient quality to accomplish coital connection 75% of the time (Masters & Johnson, 1970). Approximately 50% of the general population experiences some degree of sexual dysfunction.

Diagnosis

With the exception of impotency for the male, diagnosis of a sexual disorder is usually straightforward. It is not difficult, of course, to detect the male's reduced erectile capacity, but it is difficult to determine if the problem is due to psychological or physiological factors. This differentiation is important to the course of treatment. One of the simplest methods of making this determination involves the use of a penile plethysmograph to measure the male's erectile pattern during sleep. Based on extensive research, it has been found that all normally functioning males, regardless of their age, experience two or three erections during an eight-hour period of sleep (Karacan,

Williams, Thornby, & Salis, 1975). An experienced therapist can determine with a high degree of accuracy whether the impotence is psychogenic or biogenic by examining the recording of a male whose erectile pattern has been monitored during three or more nights' sleep (Karacan, Scott, Salis, Attia, & Ware, 1977).

It is not surprising to find that many physicians are untrained and uncomfortable in the area of sexual function and dysfunction when one considers that the first course in human sexuality taught in an American medical school was not offered until 1960. Urologists often are the first specialists to see a male with'sex problems, and many of them have little or no training in counseling patients with sexual problems (Finkle & Finkle, 1977). In one study almost twice as many sexual problems were uncovered by physicians asking about this subject during history-taking than by physicians who waited for the patients to raise the issue. Only 7% of the 60 physicians who participated in this particular study had received training in medical school in managing sexual problems. This situation has improved in recent years with the addition of courses in human sexuality to many medical school curricula, but many physicians still remain somewhat uncomfortable discussing sex with their patients.

Types of dysfunction

Dyspareunia and orgasmic dysfunction. Dyspareunia is common among older women because of reduced levels of lubrication, thinning of the vaginal walls, changes in vaginal tissue tone, and shortening of both vagina length and width. The causes of situational orgasmic dysfunction are complex and may involve physiological, psychological, and sociological factors. For example, dyspareunia could be a contributing physiological factor. The asexual stereotype of the older woman, so common even in today's society, is an example of a sociological influence.

Impotence. The male becomes increasingly vulnerable to impotency as he ages. Several studies (Kinsey et al., 1948; Pearlman, 1972; Pfeiffer et al., 1969) have shown the incidence of impotence in various age categories to be as follows: 5% by the age of 40, 11% in the 50s, 25%-35% in the 60s, 50%-60% in the 70s, and 75%-85% after the age of 80.

Influence of medication on sexual dysfunction. Hypertension, depression, anxiety, arteriosclerosis, heart disease, and psychoses are common among many older persons, and their treatment often involves the use of medications. Many of these medications may affect sexual functioning. Studies conducted to evaluate the effects of these drugs on males have found substantial evidence that many of them cause erectile and/or ejaculatory problems (Segraves, 1977). Fewer studies have been reported on females. This may be due to a lack of interest on the part of male researchers or to an actual infrequent disturbance of female sexual responsivity by pharmacological agents.

Intervention

Treatment. Most of the several different models of sex therapy lean very heavily on the model developed by Masters and Johnson (1970). Their model combines behavioral, learning, experiential, and psychodynamic approaches. The key elements in their treatment regimen are as follows: (1) removal of performance anxiety by prohibiting intercourse for a period of time; (2) use of a male/female cotherapy team; (3) dealing with the problem as a couple's problem, not as a problem of one member of the pair. Failure rates of this method have been reported in some detail, and there is some indication that the age of the patient is a factor. The average failure rate for older women was approximately 41% compared with 19% for the entire research sample. For males over 50, the failure rate was approximately 25%, compared with 17% for the total male sample.

Most other therapy models see the patient once a week instead of daily, as is the case in the two-week intensive Masters and Johnson schedule (Annon, 1974, 1975; Kaplan, 1974). Additionally, Kaplan (1974) does not insist on seeing both partners and does not use a male/female therapy team. Either the individual patient or the couple may be seen by a male or a female individual counselor in Kaplan's clinic. She reports that her results are similar to those of Masters and Johnson.

Another model of therapy involves a hierarchical approach of the relatively fixed program followed by Masters and Johnson. Annon (1974, 1975) believes that persons suffering from sexual problems experience their difficulties at various levels of complexity. In his approach the levels of treatment, starting with the least complex, involve permission, limited information, specific suggestions, and intensive therapy.

Hormone therapy. Estrogen and testosterone have been used extensively in the treatment of sexual problems. During the past few years, however, concern has grown over the use of these hormones. The use of estrogen has been questioned because of its possible role in the development of endometrial cancer and circulatory problems in women. Physicians have suggested the use of topical creams to resolve the lubricating problem, and minimal doses of estrogen or a combination of estrogen and progesterone to resolve other problems (Greenblatt et al., 1979).

The use of testosterone in the male has been questioned because of its possible role in the development of prostatic cancer (Fellman, Hastings, Kupperman, & Miller, 1975; Finkle & Finkle, 1977). Since only very recently has it been proposed that testosterone may be more effective in treating impotence than was previously supposed (Spark et al., 1980), urologists have been conservative in its use.

Prosthetic devices. Two types of penile prostheses have been developed in recent years for use in cases where it has been determined that the male's impotency is due to organic causes. One type uses inflatable silastic cylinders placed inside each corpus cavernosum and connected by tubing to a pumping mechanism implanted in the scrotal pouch (Scott, Bradley, & Timm, 1973). The other type consists of two partially foam-filled silicone rods, which are inserted in the corpus cavernosa (Loeffler & Iverson, 1976). Good results have been obtained using both types (Furlow, 1976; Gottesman, Kosters, Das, & Kaufmann, 1977).

Need for therapy. There is an increasing interest among older persons in enhancing their sexual functioning (Sviland, 1975, 1978). However, many of them find it difficult to seek help for dealing with their sex problems because of the personal nature of the problem and society's view of sex and the older person. Somehow the message has been generated that the resolution of sex problems is a worthwhile pursuit for the young but not for the old. This is unfortunate, since it is the opinion of the authors that essentially all older persons have the potential to reach higher levels of sexual pleasure, even though they may not attain a specific functional goal that they have too rigidly set for themselves.

SPECIAL POPULATIONS

Elderly homosexuals

As there are sterotypes about age and heterosexuality, there are stereotypes about age and homosexuality, especially with regard to male homosexuality. Homosexual males are stereotyped as being even more youth-oriented than heterosexual males. Because of this supposed orientation to youth, they are stereotypically thought to have more negative views of aging and be more likely to label themselves old earlier than heterosexual males. Data supporting this view have, however, usually been gathered from subjects frequenting gay bars, where interactions emphasize casual sexual contact and where, therefore, youth and physical attractiveness are more important than those characteristics that might lead to an ongoing relationship (Harry & DeVall, 1978; Humphreys, 1970).

Oft-repeated stereotypes about homosexual males state that aging is especially stressful on them (Weinberg, 1970) and that they are lonely, isolated, and despairing (Allen, 1961). Adjustment to homosexuality, however, implies learning to cope with loneliness and alienation. The kind of social network they are likely to develop helps insulate them from a certain amount of the stress associated with aging. The male homosexual social role contains elements comparable to those found in the female heterosexual social role. When not satisfactorily resolved, these will, of course, contribute to poor adjustment in old age. The coping skills that must be developed in the resolution allow for greater flexibility in dealing with certain crises of aging (Francher & Henkin, 1973).

The limited data about aging among homosexual women are of the case study sort, and they indicate a sexual aging pattern similar to other never-married women—that is, an early discontinuance of sexual activity (Christenson & Johnson, 1973). No coherent single pattern of partner gender selection was found in interviews with bisexual women (Blumstein & Schwartz, 1976).

Institutionalized elderly

One cannot discuss sex and the institutionalized elderly without also introducing the topic of attitudes about sex. The institutionalized are probably more dependent than any group on the attitudes of others for freedom to be sexual, and the elderly are probably the most likely to face negative sexual attitudes from those in control.

Attitudes do not tell the entire story, however. A discrepancy often occurs between stated attitudes and actual behavior. This was evidenced in one report of positive responses by a nursing home staff to freedom of sexual expression among the elderly nursing home residents, but little actual support for such activities in their own facility (Wasow & Loeb, 1977).

Many of the elderly living in some sort of congregate living circumstance accept the negative stereotype themselves. In one nursing home, 49% of the residents agreed that "sex over 65 is ridiculous." That response has been attributed to an internalization of society's negative evaluation of sex in old age (Kahana, 1976). Indeed one does not have to be in a nursing home to accept that view of sex in old age. Many elderly people accept their waning sex lives as part of the normal process of aging (Lieberman, 1971; Riley & Foner, 1968). Although some will argue (no doubt correctly to some degree) that this is the result of a self-fulfilling prophecy arising from social attitudes, it may also come from the realities of illness for a number of physically ill elderly people.

A specific logistic issue also influencing the practicality of sex for the nursing home resident (besides that of illness and whether the acutely uncomfortable patient is even interested in sex) has to do with privacy. Not only do institutions rarely have places where their married residents can have sex privately (Burnside, 1975; Schlessinger & Miller, 1973), they often ignore or deny the sexual interests of their non-married residents. This is effectively done by isolating the sexes or by ridiculing or labeling as pathological any sexual expression by a patient. When the isolation of male and female patients from each other was ended in one nursing home, the results were better social adjustments, a richer social life for the residents, improved grooming, and a reduction in profanity. There were also one sexual relationship and other overt sexual contacts reported (Silverstone & Wynter, 1975).

Sexual opportunity among nursing home residents can certainly be pleasurable. It can reduce the amount of inappropriate sexual expression and provide relief from anxiety (Wasow, 1977). Unfortunately it can also cause an increase in anxiety among families of some older people (Dean, 1966). Some solutions have been proposed to problems of sexual privacy, sexual rights of the institutionalized, staff education, and the medico-legal issues that administrators and physicians may face (Miller, 1978; Wasow, 1977). Still more solutions are needed, and effective steps for their implementation must be developed.

Number of women

Two factors—the tendency of women to marry men an average of four years older than themselves (Newman & Nichols, 1960) and the tendency of men to die younger than women by an average of seven years (Brotman, 1971)—results in a population of women over 65 that is 53% widowed. Widowhood, besides its definitional status of the loss of a spouse by death, also usually means the loss of an intimate confiding relationship (Miller & Ingham, 1976). It involves an involuntary shift from a familiar and probably comfortable way of living to an unfamiliar reliance on a group of similarly unattached women (Cumming & Henry, 1961). At best, this represents a loss of morale; at worst, it results in suicide (Bernardo, 1968, 1970).

In between these two extremes are the types of physical and mental disturbances most often believed to be associated with spousal bereavement. Evidence suggests that the physical and mental health of a surviving spouse is seriously at risk in the year following the bereavement, and that the degree of morbidity actually experienced is significantly related to the support received from family and friends. When these relationships are not there, problems increase (Henderson, 1977; Miller & Ingham, 1976).

Remarriage occurs less often among widows than among widowers (Treas & Van Hilst, 1976) for mostly demographic and economic reasons, but also because many older women do not want to give up their new freedom in order to become a nurse for an ill older man or to deal with problems associated with adult stepchildren, who may view with suspicion their father's new wife. Demographically, we have seen that there are also few older men from which the older woman can select a husband. Frequently income may be reduced from sources that pay widows so long as they do not remarry (Jacobs & Vinick, 1977).

In addition to the 53% of the over-65 women who are widows, another 10% are separated, divorced, or never married. This results in what has been called an "unexpected community" of women in old age (Hochschild, 1973; Jacobs, 1969). This kind of community can allow easy access to the development of relationships that provide the emotional support necessary to good physical and mental functioning (Henderson, 1977; Miller & Ingham, 1976). Whether or not that happens depends on more than the fact of single women living in proximity to one another. Contrary evidence, for instance, comes from a group of single women living among a larger group of single men in a slum hotel. The relationships among those women were characterized by hostility, jealousy, and competition. Relationships among the men who surrounded them were quite cohesive (Stephens, 1974). The women's common ages, singleness, economic circumstances, and desires to maintain independence were apparently not enough to bring them together into close-knit supportive relationships. Whether this was caused by the characteristics that led them to life in a slum hotel in the first place, by their minority status among a large group of men, or by some other factor is not known.

As might be expected, married older women have a higher incidence of sexual activity than unmarried women (Christenson & Gagnon, 1965; Kinsey et al., 1953; Pfeiffer & Davis, 1972). Among older women not currently married, the divorced have higher incidences of sexual activity than the widowed (Gebhard, 1971), and together the formerly married have a higher incidence of sexual activity than the never-married (Christenson & Johnson, 1973).

SUMMARY

Although much more research is needed, certain patterns emerge as one considers the information that is currently available. Sexual interest remains high throughout a male's life, but sexual activity declines. Among women, sexual interest and activity remain relatively stable, but the level is consistently lower than for men. For both sexes, those persons who are more active early in life tend to be more active later in life, given that they have a partner. The psychosocial issue having the greatest influence on female sexuality in later life is partner availability. Only a small percentage of women stop having sex for any other reason than the lack of a healthy, acceptable partner.

Both sexes undergo physiological changes as they age, some of which may affect their sexual functioning. The aging male will need more stimulation and require more time to become erect. The postmenopausal woman will not lubricate as rapidly or profusely in response to sexual arousal as she did earlier in her life. In general, however, men and women retain their physiological capacity to have and enjoy sex throughout their lives.

The effect of the changes in male and female hormones with age is not completely clear, although it does appear that these changes may contribute to mid-life symptoms for both the male and female to a greater extent than realized heretofore. As always, these effects must be evaluated in the light of psychological issues as well as physiological ones.

The effect of most diseases on sexual functioning is very much related to the psychological adjustment of the individual and to his or her motivation to minimize its effect on sexual pleasure. For the male, one disease that does appear to have definite organic effects on erectile capacity is diabetes, but even in this case, motivation and an understanding and cooperative partner can reduce the sexual consequences.

The most common sexual dysfunctions for older women are dyspareunia and situation orgasmic dysfunction; for the male, secondary impotency is the most common dysfunction. At age 65, approximately 25% of the males are impotent, whereas at age 80, approximately 75% are impotent. The use of drugs to treat chronic diseases common among older persons may exacerbate the impotency problem. If one views sexuality as being much more inclusive than merely intercourse, however, the prospects of sexual pleasure at any age become much brighter. There is little doubt that almost all older people can enjoy a full sexual expression throughout their lives, once they broaden their concept of sexuality and refuse to see themselves in the asexual role that our society attempts to assign to them.

REFERENCES

Allen, C. The aging homosexual. In I. Rubin (Ed.), *The third sex.* New York: New Book Co., 1961.

Annon, J. S. *The behavioral treatment of sexual problems. Volume I: Brief therapy.* Honolulu: Enabling Systems, 1974.

Annon, J. S. *The behavioral treatment of sexual problems. Volume II: Intensive therapy.* Honolulu: Enabling Systems, 1975.

Bernardo, F. M. Widowhood status in the United States: Perspective on a neglected aspect of the family life-cycle. *Family Coordinator,* 1968, *17,* 191–203.

Bernardo, F. Survivorship and social isolation: The case of the aged widower. *Family Coordinator,* 1970, *19,* 11–15.

Bloch, A., Maeder, J., & Haissly, J. Sexual problems after myocardial infarction. *American Heart Journal,* 1975, *90,* 536–537.

Blumstein, P. W., & Schwartz, P. Bisexuality in women. *Archives of Sexual Behavior,* 1976, *5,* 171–181.

Botwinick, J. *Aging and behavior: A comprehensive integration of research findings.* New York: Springer, 1973.

Braddom, R. L., Hollis, J. B., & Castell, D. O. Diabetic peripheral neuropathy: A correlation of nerve conduction studies and clinical findings. *Archives of Physical Medicine and Rehabilitation,* 1977, *58,* 308–313.

Brotman, H. B. *Facts and figures on older Americans, number 2. The older population revisited: First results of the 1970 census.* Washington, D.C.: Administration on Aging, U.S. Department of Health, Education and Welfare, 1971.

Burnham, W. R., Lennard-Jones, J. E., & Brooke, B. N. Sexual problems among married ileostomists. *Gut,* 1977, *18,* 673–677.

Burnside, I. M. Sexuality and the older adult: Implications for nursing. In I. M. Burnside (Ed.), *Sexuality and aging.* Los Angeles: University of Southern California Press, 1975.

Christenson, C., & Gagnon, J. Sexual behavior in a group of older women. *Journal of Gerontology,* 1965, *20,* 351–356.

Christenson, C. V., & Johnson, A. B. Sexual patterns in a group of older never-married women. *Journal of Geriatric Psychiatry,* 1973, *6,* 80–98.

Cumming, E., & Henry, W. H. *Growing old: The process of disengagement.* New York: Basic Books, 1961.

Dean, S. R. Sin and senior citizens. *Journal of the American Geriatrics Society,* 1966, *14,* 935–938.

DeNigola, P., & Peruzza, M. Sex in the aged. *Journal of the American Geriatrics Society,* 1974, *22,* 380–382.

Dennerstein, L., Wood, C., & Burrows, G. D. Sexual response following hysterectomy and oophorectomy. *Obstetrics and Gynecology,* 1977, *49,* 92–96.

Eisdorfer, C., & Raskind, M. Aging, hormones, and human behavior. In B. E. Eleftheriou & R. L. Sprott (Eds.), *Hormonal correlates of behavior.* New York: Plenum Press, 1975.

Ellenberg, M. Impotence in diabetes: The neurologic factor. *Annals of Internal Medicine,* 1971, *75,* 213–219.

Ellenberg, M. Impotence in diabetes: A neurologic rather than an endocrinologic problem. *Medical Aspects of Human Sexuality,* 1973, *7,* 12–18.

Ellenberg, M. Sexual aspects of the female diabetic. *Mount Sinai Journal of Medicine,* 1977, *44,* 495–500.

Ervin, C. V. Psychologic adjustment to mastectomy. *Medical Aspects of Human Sexuality,* 1973, *7,* 42–65.

Fellman, S. L., Hastings, D. W., Kupperman, H., & Miller, W. W. Should androgens be used to treat impotence in men over 50? *Medical Aspects of Human Sexuality,* 1975, *9*(7), 32–43.

Finkle, A. L., & Finkle, P. S. How counseling may solve sexual problems of aging men. *Geriatrics,* 1977, *32,* 34–89.

Finkle, A. L., Moyers, T. G., Tobenkin, M. I., & Karg, S. J. Sexual potency in aging males: I. Frequency of coitus among clinic patients. *Journal of the American Medical Association,* 1959, *170,* 1391–1393.

Francher, J. S., & Henkin, J. The menopausal queen: Adjustment to aging and the male homosexual. *American Journal of Orthopsychiatry,* 1973, *43,* 670–674.

Furlow, W. L. Surgical management of impotence using the inflatable penile prosthesis. *Mayo Clinic Proceedings,* 1976, *51,* 325–328.

Gebhart, P. Postmarital coitus among widows and divorcees. In P. Bohannan (Ed.), *Divorce and after.* Garden City, N.Y.: Doubleday, 1971.

Giambra, L. M., & Martin, C. E. Sexual daydreams and quantitative aspects of sexual activity: Some relations for males across adulthood. *Archives of Sexual Behavior,* 1977, *6,* 497–505.

Glover, G. H. Sex counseling of the elderly. *Hospital Practice,* 1977, *12*(6), 101–113.

Gottesman, J. E., Kosters, S., Das, S., & Kaufman, J. J. The small-carrion prosthesis for male impotency. *Journal of Urology,* 1977, *117,* 289–290.

Greenblatt, R. B., Nezhat, C., Roesel, P. A., & Natrajan, P. K. Update on the male and female climacteric. *American Geriatrics Society,* 1979, *27,* 481–490.

Harry, J., & DeVall, W. Age and sexual culture among homosexually oriented males. *Archives of Sexual Behavior,* 1978, *7,* 199–209.

Hegeler, S. *Sexual behavior in elderly Danish males.* Paper presented at the International Symposium on Sex Education and Therapy, Stockholm, Sweden, 1976.

Henderson, S. The social network, support and neurosis: The function of attachment in adult life. *British Journal of Psychiatry,* 1977, *131,* 185–191.

Hochschild, A. R. *The unexpected community.* Englewood Cliffs, N. J.: Prentice-Hall, 1973.

Humphreys, L. *Tearoom trade.* Chicago: Aldine, 1970.

Jacobs, R. H. The friendship club: A case study of the segregated aged. *Gerontologist,* 1969, *9,* 276–280.

Jacobs, R., & Vinick, B. *Reengagement in later life.* Greylock Publishers, 1977.

Jamison, K. R., Wellisch, D. K., & Pasnau, R. O. Psychosocial aspects of mastectomy: I. The woman's perspective. *American Journal of Psychiatry,* 1978, *135,* 432–436.

Kahana, B. Social and psychological aspects of sexual behavior among the aged. In E. S. E. Hafez (Ed.), *Aging and reproductive physiology* (Vol. 2). Ann Arbor, Mich.: Ann Arbor Science, 1976.

Kaplan, H. S. *The new sex therapy.* New York: Brunner/Mazel, 1974.

Karacan, I., Scott, F. G., Salis, P. J., Attia, S. L., & Ware, J. C. Nocturnal erections, differential diagnosis of impotence, and diabetes. *Biological Psychiatry,* 1977, *12,* 373–380.

Karacan, I., Williams, R. L., Thornby, J. I., & Salis, P. J. Sleep-related tumescence as a function of age. *American Journal of Psychiatry,* 1975, *132,* 932.

Kavanaugh, T., & Sheppard, R. J. Sexual activity after myocardial infarction. *Canadian Medical Association Journal,* 1977, *116,* 1250–1253.

Kent, S. Impotence as a consequence of organic disease. *Geriatrics,* 1975, *30,* 155–157.

Kinsey, A. C., Pomeroy, W. B., & Martin, C. R. *Sexual behavior in the human male.* Philadelphia: W. B. Saunders, 1948.

Kinsey, A. C., Pomeroy, W. B., Martin, C. E., & Gebhard, P. H. *Sexual behavior in the human female.* Philadelphia: W. B. Saunders, 1953.

Kleegman, S. Frigidity in women. *Quarterly Review of Surgery, Obstetrics, and Gynecology,* 1959, *16,* 243–248.

Kolodny, R. C., Kahn, C. B., Goldstein, H. H., & Barnett, D. M. Sexual dysfunction in diabetic men. *Diabetes,* 1974, *23,* 306–309.

Ledger, W. J. Infections in elderly women. *Clinical Obstetrics and Gynecology,* 1977, *20,* 145–153.

Lemere, F. Sexual impairment in recovered alcoholics. *Medical Aspects of Human Sexuality,* 1976, *10,* 69–70.

Lemere, F., & Smith, J. D. Alcohol-induced sexual impotence. *American Journal of Psychiatry,* 1973, *130,* 212–213.

Lieberman, B. *Human sexual behavior: A book of readings.* New York: John Wiley and Sons, 1971.

Loeffler, R. A., & Iverson, R. E. Surgical treatment of impotence in the male. *Plastic and Reconstructive Surgery,* 1976, *58,* 292–297.

Lowenthal, M. F. Social isolation and mental illness in old age. In B. L. Neugarten (Ed.), *Middle age and aging.* Chicago: University of Chicago Press, 1968, pp. 220–234.

Madorsky, M. L., Ashamalla, M. G., Schussler, I., Lyons, H. R., & Miller, G. H. Post-prostatectomy impotence. *Journal of Urology,* 1976, *115,* 401–403.

Martin, C. E. Marital and sexual factors in relation to age, disease, and longevity. In R. D. Wirt, G. Winokur, & M. Roff (Eds.), *Life history research in psychopathology* (Vol. 4). Minneapolis: University of Minnesota Press, 1975.

Masters, W. H., & Johnson, V. E. *Human sexual response.* Boston: Little, Brown, 1966.

Masters, W. H., & Johnson, V. E. *Human sexual inadequacy.* Boston, Little, Brown, 1970.

Miller, D. G. Sexual practices and administrative policies in long-term-care institutions. In R. L. Solnick (Ed.), *Sexuality and aging.* Los Angeles: University of Southern California Press, 1978.

Miller, P. M., & Ingham, J. G. Friends, confidants, and symptoms. *Social Psychiatry,* 1976, *11,* 51–58.

Monroe, S. E., & Menon, K. M. J. Changes in reproductive hormone secretion during the climacteric and postmenopausal periods. *Clinical Obstetrics and Gynecology,* 1977, *20,* 113–122.

Neugarten, B. L., Wood, V., Kraines, R. J., & Loomis, B. Women's attitudes toward the menopause. In B. L. Neugarten (Ed.), *Middle age and aging.* Chicago: University of Chicago Press, 1968.

Newman, G., & Nichols, C. R. Sexual activities and attitudes in older persons. *Journal of the American Medical Association,* 1960, *173,* 33–35.

Pearlman, C. K. Frequency of intercourse in males at different ages. *Medical Aspects of Human Sexuality,* 1972, *6,* 92.

Persky, H., Lief, H. I., Strauss, D., Miller, W. R., & O'Brien, C. P. Plasma testosterone level and sexual behavior of couples. *Archives of Sexual Behavior,* 1978, *7,* 157–173.

Pfeiffer, E. Sexual behavior in old age. In E. W. Busse & E. Pfeiffer (Eds.), *Behavior and adaptation in late life.* Boston: Little, Brown, 1969.

Pfeiffer, E., & Davis, G. C. Determinants of sexual behavior in middle and old age. *Journal of the American Geriatrics Society,* 1972, *20,* 151–158.

Pfeiffer, E., Verwoerdt, A., & Davis, G. C. Sexual behavior in middle life. *American Journal of Psychiatry,* 1972, *128,* 1262–1267.

Pfeiffer, E., Verwoerdt, A., & Wang, H. S. Sexual behavior in aged men and women. I. Observations on 254 community volunteers. *Archives of General Psychiatry,* 1968, *19,* 753–758.

Pfeiffer, E., Verwoerdt, A., & Wang, H. S. The natural history of sexual behavior in a biologically advantaged group of aged individuals. *Journal of Gerontology,* 1969, *24,* 193–198.

Polivy, J. Psychological effects of mastectomy on a woman's feminine self-concept. *Journal of Nervous and Mental Diseases,* 1977, *164,* 77–87.

Raboch, J., Mellan, J., & Starka, L. Plasma testosterone in male patients with sexual dysfunctions. *Archives of Sexual Behavior,* 1975, *4,* 541–545.

Research Resources Reporter. Hot flashes in the brain. *Research Resources Reporter,* 1979, *3,* 10–11.

Riley, M. W., & Foner, A. E. *Aging and society, Vol. 1: An inventory of research findings.* New York: Russell Sage Foundation, 1968.

Rosow, I. Housing and local ties of the aged. In B. L. Neugarten (Ed.), *Middle age and aging.* Chicago: University of Chicago Press, 1968.

Rossman, I. Sexuality and aging: An internist's perspective. In R. L. Solnick (Ed.), *Sexuality and aging.* Los Angeles: University of Southern California Press, 1978.

Schlessinger, B., & Miller, G. A. Sexuality and the aged. *Medical Aspects of Human Sexuality,* 1973, *3,* 46–52.

Scott, F. G., Bradley, W. E., & Timm, G. W. Management of erectile impotence: Use of implantable inflatable protheses. *Urology,* 1973, *2,* 80–82.

Segraves, R. T. Pharmacological agents causing sexual dysfunctions. *Journal of Sex and Marital Therapy,* 1977, *3,* 157–176.

Silverstone, G., & Wynter, L. The effects of introducing a heterosexual living space. *Gerontologist,* 1975, *15,* 83–87.

Simon, W., & Gagnon, J. H. On psychosexual development. In D. A. Goslin (Ed.), *Handbook of socialization theory and research.* Chicago: Rand McNally, 1969.

Solnick, R. L., & Birren, J. E. Age and male erectile responsiveness. *Archives of Sexual Behavior,* 1977, *6,* 1–9.

Spark, R. F., White, R. A., & Connolly, P. B. Impotence is not always psychogenic. *Journal of the American Medical Association,* 1980, *243,* 750–755.

Stephens, J. Romance in the SRO. *Gerontologist,* 1974, *14,* 279–282.

Sviland, M. A. P. Helping elderly couples become sexually liberated: Psycho-social issues. *Counseling Psychologist,* 1975, *1*(5), 67–72.

Sviland, M. A. P. A program of sexual liberation and growth in the elderly. In R. L. Solnick (Ed.), *Sexuality and aging.* Los Angeles: University of Southern California Press, 1978.

Timiras, P. S., & Meisami, E. Changes in gonadal function. In P. S. Timiras (Ed.), *Developmental physiology and aging.* New York: Macmillan, 1972.

Treas, J., & Van Hilst, A. Marriage and remarriage rates among older Americans. *Gerontologist,* 1976, *16,* 132–136.

U.S. Bureau of the Census. *Statistical abstract of the United States: 1977* (98th ed.). Washington, D.C.: U.S. Government Printing Office, 1977.

Vermeulen, A. The hormonal activities of the postmenopausal ovary. *Journal of Clinical Endocrinology and Metabolism,* 1976, *42,* 247–253.

Verwoerdt, A., Pfeiffer, E., & Wang, H. S. Sexual behavior in senescence. Changes in sexual activity and interest of aging men and women. *Journal of Geriatric Psychiatry,* 1969, *2,* 163–180. (a)

Verwoerdt, A., Pfeiffer, E., & Wang, H. S. Sexual behavior in senescence. II. Patterns of sexual activity and interest. *Geriatrics,* 1969, *24,* 137–154. (b)

Wasow, M. Sexuality in homes for the aged. *Concern in the Care of the Aging,* 1977, *3*(6), 20–21.

Wasow, M., & Loeb, M. B. Sexuality in nursing homes. In R. L. Solnick (Ed.), *Sexuality and aging.* Los Angeles: University of Southern California Press, 1978.

Weg, R. B. The physiology of sexuality in aging. In R. L. Solnick (Ed.), *Sexuality and aging.* Los Angeles: University of Southern California Press, 1978.

Weinberg, J. Sexual expression in late life. *American Journal of Psychiatry,* 1969, *126,* 713–716.

Weinberg, M. The male homosexual: Age-related variation in social and psychological characteristics. *Social Problems,* 1970, *17,* 527–537.

Wellisch, D. K., Jamison, K. R., & Pasnau, R. O. Psychosocial aspects of mastectomy: II. The man's perspective. *American Journal of Psychiatry,* 1978, *135,* 543–546.

Witkin, M. H. Psychosexual counseling of the mastectomy patient. *Journal of Sex and Marital Therapy,* 1978, *4,* 20–28.

Zilbergeld, B. *Male sexuality: A guide to sexual fulfillment.* Boston: Little, Brown, 1978.

Zohar, J., Meirag, D., Maoz, B., and Durst, N. Factors influencing sexual activity after prostatectomy: A prospective study. *Journal of Urology,* 1976, *116,* 332–334.

PART III

BIOLOGICAL PERSPECTIVES

CHAPTER 11

The Biological Basis of Aging

Paul Denny

A central theorem of biology is that cells are the fundamental units of structure and function of all living creatures. Although many important parts of the organism are essentially noncellular, such as bone and connective tissue, their formation and functions are dependent upon cell-mediated processes. Furthermore, the complex functions of the organism such as sensory perception, movement, and communication are the results of organized efforts of individual cells or groups of cells. The coordinators of these high-level functions, such as hormones or nerve impulses, are themselves of cellular origin or manufacture. In short, the function and well-being of the organism are intimately dependent upon cellular activities.

The first part of this chapter presents a brief overview of relevant principles of cell biology. Following this, we shall survey the nature and extent of cellular changes associated with aging. Then, based primarily upon experimental manipulations, we shall discuss the degree to which cellular aging is due to intrinsic or extrinsic factors. In the fourth section we shall describe the two systems that are mainly responsible for extrinsic control and look at some important age-related changes. Finally, we shall evaluate some basic explanations for the aging phenomenon.

PRINCIPLES OF CELL BIOLOGY

As we look at what constitutes a cell, the reader should bear in mind that this review is by no means comprehensive but emphasizes those cellular activities that can be associated with or implicated in the aging process. The three main divisions of the cell are the plasma membrane, the cytoplasm, and the nucleus (see Figure 11-1). The plasma membrane serves as the interface between the living cell and its surrounding environment. This membrane is composed of proteins and lipids (fats), which have

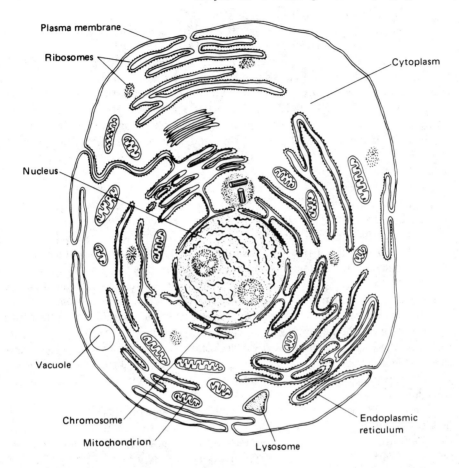

Figure 11-1. The cell and its organelles.

both polar and nonpolar (water soluble and nonsoluble) portions arranged in such a way that the cell's integrity is maintained while the membrane allows selected nutrients to pass in and waste products to go out.

Though cells are complete living units, they are responsive to their environment. One of the key ways this occurs is by receptor proteins attached to the surface of the plasma membrane or circulating freely in the cytoplasm. There are specific receptor types for each environmental cue. Cell function is often regulated through this mechanism by hormones and chemical transmitters of neural impulses. Different cell types may have different sets of receptors and thus respond to a different set of environmental stimuli.

The nucleus plays one of the most central roles in the cell since it contains within the chromosomes the genetic material—DNA. The cellular DNA has the blueprint for the organization and development of the entire organism and is the source for most of the information, in the form of RNA, required for the everyday maintenance of cellular integrity and function. Thus, if the DNA becomes defective, if the environmental cues to DNA are interrupted, or if the flow of information from RNA to the rest of the cell is impaired, cellular function will be affected.

The cytoplasm is a highly ordered mixture of organelles (literally, the organs of the cell) and compounds that accomplish many different functions. One of these functions, performed in this case by the mitochondria, is respiration, which provides the energy-rich compound ATP. The mitochondria are self-contained and show a highly characteristic pattern of membrane organization (Figure 11-1). Since ATP is required for many other cellular functions and syntheses, the efficiency of mitochondria in converting nutrients to ATP is a major factor in determining the efficiency of cellular activities.

Another process occurring in the cytoplasm is protein synthesis. This requires not only ATP but also three different types of RNA—ribosomal, messenger, and transfer—which are derived from the DNA of the nucleus. Protein synthesis supplies the cell with many of its structural components and with the enzymes necessary to catalyze crucial reactions. Without these enzymes the synthesis of other important compounds including carbohydrates, lipids, DNA, and RNA would not be possible. It also provides, either directly or indirectly, such compounds as hormones, antibodies, and digestive enzymes, which operate outside of cells to benefit the entire organism.

The cytoplasm also contains organelles, which are responsible for intracellular digestion as might be required when a white blood cell ingests a pathogen or when a cell dies. These membrane-enclosed vesicles, called lysosomes, are smaller than mitochondria and contain, among other elements, enzymes for breaking down DNA, RNA, proteins, and lipids. As we shall discuss later, these structures have been implicated in the aging process.

From this brief survey of cellular components and processes one can imagine how defects in, or abnormal outputs of, any of the cell's component parts could impair the functional capacity of the entire cell, which might, in turn, lead to organism-wide secondary effects. Because of the interrelated nature of cellular processes, we cannot easily identify the primary or first cause of reduced cellular activity. This is one of the major problems faced by investigators of aging phenomena.

DO CELLS AGE IN VIVO?

Lipofuscin formation

Having seen the critical role of the cell within the organism, we can now consider the fundamental question "Do cells age?" Based upon many different examples, there is no doubt that cells do show age-related changes, but as will become apparent, the direct relationships of these changes to aging and death are not yet clear.

The most striking change observed in cells with increasing age is the appearance of "age pigment" called lipofuscin. The pigment is contained in granules, which are round to oblong, have a diameter between 1 and 3 microns, and have a color range of yellow to brown. They do not accumulate in all tissues but are found most commonly in neural, muscle, liver, spleen, adrenal, pancreas, thymus, epididymus, and seminal vesical cells. Deposition of lipofuscin in some of these cells begins relatively early and increases in a linear fashion during the life span (Figure 11-2).

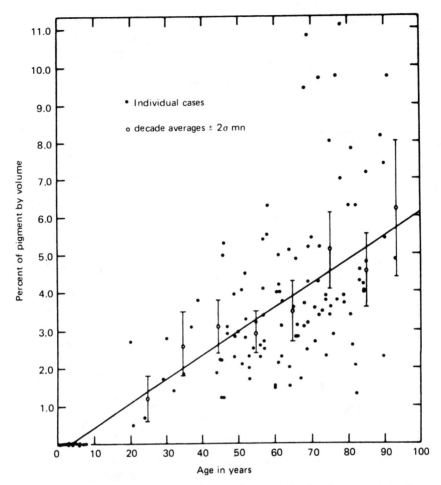

Figure 11-2. The relationship between age and lipofuscin content in the human myocardium. (*Strehler et al., 1959. Used by permission.*)

The granules are found in organisms throughout the animal kingdom, from protozoa to mammals, and their appearance is clearly a function of the animal's "age" relative to its life span rather than to the passage of time. For instance, nematodes (a kind of simple worm) show the same pattern and extent of lipofuscin accumulation over their 28-day life span as do mice over a period of 3 years and humans over a period of 100 years.

Though the etiology of the granules is not yet conclusive, the chemical reaction (peroxidation) of a lipid-protein complex appears to be involved. A variety of observations (see Sanadi, 1977) also suggest that lysosomes are the source of the granules and that the inability of lysosomal enzymes to metabolize efficiently certain lipid byproducts is responsible.

One of the major questions remaining about the "age pigment" is how it might contribute to age-related impairment of function. So far, there has been no demonstration of a positive correlation between lipofuscin accumulation and reductions in heart tissue capabilities in humans, rats, or mice. On the other hand, observations of exceptionally large accumulations in neurons have been associated with degenerative changes, but even here no evidence has been found for a causal relationship (Timiras, 1972a). Thus, though the possible sources of lipofuscin formation have been indicated, there is as yet no evidence of the effects of lipofuscin accumulation on the whole organism.

Response to stress

Measurements of a wide variety of cellular functions have not singled out any key age-related changes in nondiseased cells. However, it has been noted that the mitochondria of kidney, liver, and cardiac muscle cells tend to become swollen, and the endoplasmic reticulum, instead of maintaining its usual thin bilayer configuration, becomes more vesicular (Timiras, 1972b). Both of these changes are probably due to a decline in the membrane function that controls osmotic balance in these organelles. Whether this decline is due to reductions in the availability of ATP or to intrinsic membrane changes is not known. However, what is seen as only a tendency under nonstressful conditions becomes pronounced with stress, often with fatal consequences. For instance, under conditions of low-oxygen tension (stress) mitochondria in cardiac muscle and autonomic nerve cells from old rats swelled and became fragmented, whereas in young rats under similar conditions no changes were observed (see Figures 11-3 and 11-4) (Sulkin & Sulkin, 1967).

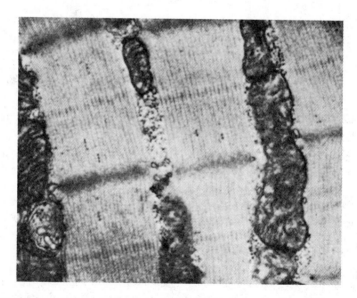

Figure 11-3. Cardiac muscle from 118-day-old rat in the anoxic chamber for 28 days at final oxygen level of 5.5%. Muscle appears normal. X32,600. (*Sulkin & Sulkin, 1967. Used by permission.*)

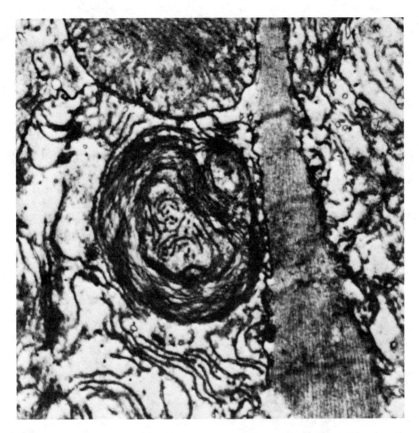

Figure 11-4. Cardiac muscle from 1032-day-old rat in anoxic chamber for 28 days at final oxygen level of 5.5%. Mitochondria markedly swollen with severe alterations of the cristate. Myofibrils show alterations in striation. X32,600. (*Sulkin & Sulkin, 1967. Used by permission.*)

Age-related impairment of cellular responses to stress is a widely observed phenomenon. An example of this at the biochemical level is shown in the classic experiments of Finch, Foster, and Mirsky (1969). Young, adult, and senescent mice were subjected to an environmental temperature of 9° C for two hours (chill stress) and then returned to room temperature (24° C). Upon encountering the stress, the response of the young and adult groups of mice was to increase immediately their rate of synthesis of the liver cell enzyme tyrosine aminotransferase. By contrast, the increase in enzyme synthesis was delayed in the old animals by nearly two hours. Further analysis of the delay indicated that the fault was apparently not that of the liver cells but a delay in production by adrenal gland cells of a hormone that regulates the liver cells. Does the age-related defect then lie with the adrenal gland? Maybe not. Suppose the cells of the pituitary, which make the hormone that regulates the adrenal cells, do not respond immediately or the cells of the hypothalamus that regulate pituitary gland cells are insensitive. Thus, although the cellular stress response clearly becomes less effective with age, the origins of the impairment are obscured by the complexities of the regulatory systems. Some of the broader aspects of aging and cellular regulation will be discussed later.

Cell renewal

The process of cell replacement is central to the maintenance of many functions in the organism and on theoretical grounds could be a key to longevity. On examination we see that cell renewal occurs in most tissues but at different rates (Cameron, 1971). Two notable exceptions are all neurons and cardiac muscle cells. Tissues undergoing some degree of renewal may be classified in three main groups: (1) those showing a complete cellular turnover in less than 30 days, (2) those taking more than 30 days but still within the life span of the animal, and (3) those showing some cell division activity but probably not renewing all of the cells within the life span. These groupings are used primarily for reference to the steady state condition of the mature adult and not to the expanding cell populations observed during development.

The first class is composed of those cell types whose life span is necessarily limited for reasons of mechanical wear and/or specialized function. Examples are cells of the lining of the gastrointestinal tract, skin (epidermis), and red (hemopoietic) and white (lymphopoietic) blood cells. The second category includes cell populations in the lining of the respiratory tract (epithelium), certain glandular cells (pancreas, salivary, and adrenal cortex), liver cells (hepatocytes) and connective tissue of the skin (dermis). The group demonstrating the lowest index of cell division includes smooth muscle cells, bone cells (osteocytes), glial cells of the brain, and tubule cells of the kidney. Most of these observations have been made on animal rather than human tissues, and a yet unresolved question is whether the cell division time intervals remain the same or get longer with the longer life span.

In most of the tissues that have been examined, the percentage of cells in division at any given time decreases with age (Buetow, 1971). In the case of the stem cells responsible for maintaining the lining of the small intestine, a thorough analysis of the phenomenon in mice (Thrasher & Gruelich, 1965) indicated that a decline occurred in the number of cells exhibiting DNA synthesis (DNA synthetic index). This was interpreted as an increase in the length of time between division (generation cycle) (Table 11-1). These data clearly suggest that, on the basis of the increase in the cell generation-cycle time, the rate of cell renewal declines with age. Assuming that the amount of wear and tear on tissues remains the same, or at least does not decrease with age of the individual, one can understand why certain tissues show an age-related decrease in the total cell number.

EVIDENCE OF INTRINSIC LIMITATIONS

Cell replicative potentials in vivo

Having established that there is a cellular aging phenomenon, we now approach causal analysis with the most elementary of questions. What are the relative roles of intrinsic and extrinsic factors in producing age-associated cellular change? We also

TABLE 11-1. Influences of age on mouse duodenal crypt cell division

Age groups	DNA synthetic index	Generation cycle (hours)
Infant (10 days)	63.3	11.4
Young adult (30–70 days)	57.9	12.4
Adult (380–399 days)	53.4	14.0
Senescent (579–638 days)	50.2	15.0

SOURCE: Adapted from Thrasher and Gruelich, 1965.

must move from the realm of description to experimentation and turn to the so-called animal model systems. This refers to the practice of selecting a cell population or tissue whose characteristics lend themselves to answering a particular question. One always hopes that the conclusions drawn from such a study will have broad application.

The use of animals other than humans has many advantages, not the least of which is working with short life spans. Another very important advantage of using nonhuman animal systems is that experiments can be performed under relatively defined conditions and proper controls can be maintained. A development that has been invaluable to the study of aging mechanisms has been the production of syngenetic mice. Through repeated sibling matings and stringent selection criteria, mouse strains have been developed in which intrastrain tissue transplants can be made without eliciting the usual immunological tissue rejection reactions. With these animals cellular aging can be examined under continuing conditions that are optimal for growth and development, and the relative effects of intrinsic and extrinsic factors can be evaluated.

An extensive analysis has been provided by experiments of C. W. Daniel and his coworkers (1968) with mouse mammary gland cells. Normally the mammary gland begins as an invagination of cells from the abdominal skin layer shortly after birth. These cells form tubules and, through the process of cell division, make a highly branched network, infiltrating the abdominal fat pad. The available space within the pad is usually occupied by six to eight weeks, and growth by cell proliferation ceases. If the initial bud of invaginating cells is surgically removed, glandular tissue does not form, indicating that neither the fat pad nor the overlying skin layers have the ability to regenerate the gland. On the other hand, if mammary gland cells from another mouse of the same syngenetic strain are implanted at this site, normal growth and development begins and goes to completion in the usual length of time. Therefore, by serial transplantations, one can ask whether mammary gland cells can repeat this cell proliferation cycle indefinitely or whether a limited growth potential exists. In order to discount the effects of host aging, the cells may be retransplanted into young female mice each time. When the mammary gland cells were serially transplanted at regular intervals, the amount of proliferation declined steadily as measured by the percentage of available fat pad filled by the transplant. Growth eventually ceased, and the maximum number of passages seen in any of these experiments has been eight. Furthermore, several different syngenetic mouse strains have been tested, and all have given similar results, suggesting that this is a general phenomenon. Surprisingly, however, when the growth potential of young (3 weeks) and old (26 months) mouse mammary gland tissues were compared side by side on 3-week-old hosts, no significant difference was evident.

These results suggested that some factor other than the passage of time was limiting the proliferative response. To test this, Daniel and Young (1971) compared colonies of mammary gland cells that were serially transplanted at 3- or 12-month intervals. Under these experimental conditions the transplants made at 3-month intervals displayed a continuous growth phase, whereas the 12-month intervals allowed for long periods of nongrowth due to space limitations once the fat pad was filled. The results of these experiments are quite clear: cells transplanted on the short-interval schedule had a greatly reduced temporal life span. Even cells that were begun on the long-interval schedule and were then shifted to the short, showed an immediate decline in proliferative capacity, indicating that there was nothing inherently different in the long-term colony cells. The most likely interpretation of these findings is that the potential for cellular proliferation is indeed limited, but the experiment did not rule out the possibility that the trauma of transplantation might be additive.

A second series of experiments (Daniel and Young, 1971) explored this further by attempting to rule out any variation introduced by the difference in number of times the cells were transplanted on the 3- and 12-month schedules. Based on the observation that growth and branching within the developing gland take place primarily at the tips of the ducts, it follows that cells at the periphery of the gland undergo almost continuous proliferation while those at the center divide only during the early growth phase. Therefore, separate colonies were started from cells of the central and peripheral mammary gland regions of young mice and serially transplanted at similar time intervals. The pattern of donor cell selection in each subsequent transplant was consistent with the original donor site, so that the distinction between continuous and intermittent proliferation was maintained throughout. As with the other series of experiments, the continuously proliferating cells showed a more rapid decline in capacity. Thus, mammary gland cells have a self-contained limit on the number of times they can divide. Studies with other model systems in animals strongly support the concept of a limited proliferative potential for mammalian cells. However, it is not known if this applies to all cell types. Furthermore, the number of potential replications varies from cell type to cell type and appears to be as unique to a particular cell type as its specialized structures and functions.

Cell replicative potentials in vitro

An intrinsic limitation on replicative potentials has also been demonstrated in cultures of human fetal cells in vitro. These experiments employ tissue culture techniques and were initially performed by L. Hayflick and P. Moorhead (1961). In these experiments cell suspensions derived from human fetal tissues by mild trypsin treatment were added to bottles containing a synthetic growth medium and incubated at 37° C. The cells first settle and attach on the bottom where they undergo divisions until all the available surface area is covered by a single layer (confluency). When confluency is reached, cell division ceases. The next step is to subculture the cells by loosening them from the vessel, again by mild trypsin treatment. Then, before they are reintroduced into fresh culture bottles, they are diluted to an extent that on settling the bottom density will be one-half confluency. Therefore, each time confluency is reached it represents a population doubling. A plot of the proliferative ability of a culture of cells derived from human fetal lung tissue is shown in Figure 11-5. This plot is based upon the doubling times and cell counts. The so-called phase II represents a period of constant doubling times, which lasts for about 50 population doublings, and phase III is a period during which the cell doubling time slows down exponentially until all division ceases.

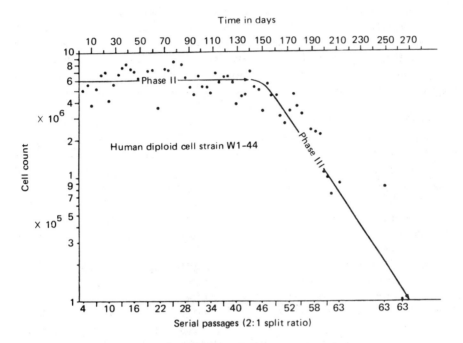

Figure. 11-5. Cell counts determined at each passage of strain WI 44. The figure results in a curve suggestive of multiple-hit or multiple-target inactivation phenomena as an explanation for the mechanism of the occurrence of phase III. The initial plateau during phase II, with no apparent loss of biological function as measured by constant doubling time, is followed by phase III, where doubling time increases exponentially. (*Hayflick, 1965*)

The question that arises is whether the decrease in cell division rate is determined by intracellular or environmental factors such as accumulated toxins or microorganisms in the medium. To test this, researchers (Hayflick and Moorhead, 1961) mixed male human fetal cells, which had already experienced 49 doublings (old), with female human cells at passage 13 (young). Seventeen doublings later the cells were examined by chromosome analysis and found to consist entirely of cells of female origin. Since the young cells continued to proliferate while the old cells died, the findings indicated that the environmental conditions for growth had not been altered and further that neither population of cells had any effect on the other.

The number of cell doublings achieved has a high degree of consistency, even when the temporal sequence is interrupted by storage at -190° C in liquid nitrogen. Regardless of whether the cells of a single strain are cultured continuously or are cultured, stored frozen for up to 15 months, and recultured, the population doublings in every case fall within the same range (50 ± 10). This has been taken as evidence for excluding the passage of calendar time as a factor in determining the onset of phase III (Hayflick, 1965). Because it is not clear how storage at -190° C might affect time-related changes, this conclusion does not necessarily follow. However, by using a nutritional block to interrupt divisions, cells have shown as much as a four-month increase in life span prior to phase III without any significant increase in number of accumulated population doublings (Dell'Orco, Mertins, & Kruse, 1974). Since the cells remained metabolically active throughout the period of nondivision, these findings give strong support to the concept of an intrinsically limited proliferative capacity in normal cells derived from mammalian tissues rather than a chronological effect.

Implications of a limited replicative potential

A number of studies demonstrate a rough correlation between species' longevity and cellular replicative potentials. The replicative potential remaining in a particular tissue also appears to decrease with the age of the individual (see Hayflick, 1980). However, from the serial transplant experiments, researchers have generally observed that full realization of the replicative potential can extend the temporal life span of the transplanted tissue several times longer than that of the original donor. Thus, it is not likely that death results from the disappearance of a particular cell type because it exhausted its allotment of divisions.

The limit on replicative potential does appear to play a major role in the aging process by a different mechanism. As noted previously, the rate of growth of the mammary gland transplants decreased gradually as they approached the limits of their replicative potential. This gradual decrease in growth is consistent with our earlier observation that the rate of cell renewal declines with age. This phenomenon could result in the reduction of a vital cell population to a level that is no longer sufficient to maintain a critical body function at maximum, even though the potential proliferative capacity far exceeds the requirements for a "normal" life span.

The experimental demonstration of this effect is seen when spleen tissue from young and old mice is used to "rescue" young hosts that had been lethally irradiated. When tested for the ability to restore immunological activity the old spleens revealed that certain cellular functions were reduced (Price & Makinodan, 1972a, b). The most striking effect was an 80% decline in the number of cells capable of mounting a localized immunological assault on foreign cells. Since the transplants were made into young hosts, the conclusion may be made that the age-related change was intrinsic within the spleen cells themselves. The experiment did not stop there. What happens when young and old spleens are transplanted into irradiated old mice? In each case, the cell-based immunological response was one-half what it had been in young hosts; that is, young spleens into old mice was 50% of young into young, and old spleens into old mice was 10% of young into young. These observations indicated not only an intrinsic aging mechanism but also an extrinsic or systemic effect on the cellular proliferative capacity. The combined result is an immune system with a substantially reduced level of effectiveness. This is likely to be a contributing factor in the age-related increase in susceptibility to disease.

EXTRINSIC FACTORS IN CELLULAR AGING

Endocrine and autonomic nervous systems

As we have seen, close examination of the cellular aging phenomenon often indicates that the source of the impairment is extracellular. The two systems intimately involved with regulating and coordinating cellular function in the body are the endocrine and autonomic nervous systems. The endocrine system comprises several glands such as thyroid, adrenal, and pituitary, which release a variety of hormones into the general circulation. The hormones are carried to all locations of the body, but only those cells possessing the specific receptors for a given hormone will respond. The coordinating role of hormones is demonstrated by the observation that different kinds of cells, regardless of location in the body, can be stimulated by the same hormone. In this fashion a number of different cellular responses may be called forth simultaneously to provide the types of complex reactions that are often elicited by stressful situations.

The autonomic nervous system acts similarly to integrate and coordinate internal body functions. The key difference between the two systems is that the signal travels most of the way to the target organ as a nerve impulse rather than as a hormone. The final submicroscopic distance from the end of the nerve cell to the target cell is, however, transversed by a neurotransmitter hormone. In general, the time from the stimulus to the response is much quicker by the neural transmission route than by the endocrine route. The two systems interact and are themselves coordinated by the hypothalamic region of the brain. This coordination depends in part on a cascade of interactions that may involve several endocrine glands in tandem. Some of the same glands may also be innervated directly, thus bypassing the first steps of the endocrine cascade. In addition, some target tissues are directly innervated by the autonomic nerves, thus providing the ability to elicit individual responses.

The adaptive potential of this system of controls is illustrated by the observation that the same neurotransmitter hormone, norepinephrine, which is involved in many of the individual responses of neural origin, can be released into the bloodstream from the adrenal medulla. This results in a coordinated response involving all target tissues, which are individually innervated. Thus, the system can select any one of a number of responses or elicit them all together. The sensitivity of the control system is based to a large extent upon so-called feedback loops. The hypothalamus cells, or those of one of the intermediary glands, have receptors that can detect and judge the levels of an end-product produced by the stimulation. In this way the stimulus can be modulated to produce just the right levels of product.

Changes in the control system

There does not appear to be any significant age-related decline in the rate of neural transmission. Thus, changes in autonomic control probably are associated with the neurotransmitter hormones. We shall discuss these later.

Numerous changes have been noted in the endocrine system, but the primary cause of the aging phenomenon remains obscure. Some hormones show consistent reductions in circulating levels, others show no change, and a few may increase (Gregerman & Bierman, 1974). Some of these changes have consequences that are generally considered to be age-associated. Such is the case of the estrogen decline in females (see Finch, 1976).

The circulating levels of estrogen are reduced approximately 90% in females following menopause, and they no longer show cyclic changes. As a result, target tissue in the uterus and vagina atrophy. Since estrogen replacement therapy reverses this effect, the target cell changes are clearly based upon the extrinsic estrogen loss.

Estrogen synthesis and release by the ovaries are greatly reduced in postmenopausal females. Is it because of an age-related change intrinsic to the ovary or to some extrinsic factor? The experiments performed to address this question transplanted ovaries from old rats into young rats and also transplanted ovaries from young rats into old hosts (Peng & Huang, 1972). In over 80% of the old-into-young transplants the ovaries resumed cycling, whereas over 80% of the young-into-old transplants lost function. By contrast the control transplants of young ovaries into young hosts were 85% successful. These results suggest that ovarian cycling and maintenance of premenopausal levels of estrogen are lost because of changes extrinsic to the ovary.

Failure to cycle is the main cause of reduction in estrogen production by the ovary following menopause. Is this due to a lack of production of hormones that stimulate the ovary? In fact, the pituitary gonadotropins, FSH and LH, are five to ten times higher in postmenopausal females than in females with cycling ovaries. However, these hormones do not show any cyclic changes either. Moving further up on the endocrine regulatory cascade, we see that the hypothalamic factors, the gonadotropin releasing hormones (GnRH), which regulate the supply of FSH and LH are also present in high quantities but show no cyclic changes. Although the basic mechanisms for control appear to be intact, the stimulus for cycling is missing.

We must shift our attention to the estrogen feedback loop to complete the regulatory scheme. Not all of the steps in this regulatory pathway have been identified. We know that an underlying mechanism in the ovarian cycling phenomenon is the ability of estrogen to modulate the levels of GnRH produced by the hypothalamus. Experiments in which radioactive estrogen is injected into female rats show that the estrogen enters cells of the hypothalamus (via cytoplasmic receptors) and is concentrated in the nuclei (McEwen, 1976). The presence of estrogen in the nucleus indicates that the hormone is involved in regulating the synthesis of cellular products by regulating the genetic activity of DNA. Other evidence (see McEwen, 1976) suggests GnRH is not synthesized in these cells and that estrogen is regulating the release of brain neurotransmitter hormones such as dopamine, norepinephrine, and seratonin. The levels of these substances classed as catecholamines appear to control the release of GnRH by other cells in the hypothalamus. It is known that as the catecholamine levels of the hypothalamus are increased, the level of GnRH also increases (Kamberi, Mical & Porter, 1969; Schneider & McCann, 1969). Two observations suggest that it is in this segment of the control loop that a defect leads to the loss of ovarian cycling. First, injections of L-DOPA (the precursor to all catecholamines) into postreproductive rats restores ovarian cycling (Huang & Meites, 1975). Second, injections of inhibitors of catecholamine metabolism into cycling rats terminate it (Kalra & McCann, 1973).

Measurements of catecholamine levels in the brain show no changes with age. The metabolism of these neurohormones is, however, significantly altered. The rate at which the hypothalamus can dispose of these once they have been released decreases nearly 50% (Finch, 1976). The long-term effect of this impairment is probably to dull progressively the sensitivity of the system to changes in catecholamine levels. Eventually, normal physiological differences may no longer be adequate to trigger the cycling phenomenon, and menopause results.

Use of female menopause as a model system for the study of extrinsic influences in the aging process illustrates the far-ranging consequences of modifications in the control systems. Other endocrine organs and their control loops are also known to be altered in older individuals, often with equally far-ranging consequences, especially when pushed to their limits in stress responses (Andres & Tobin, 1977).

MOLECULAR MECHANISMS IN AGING

Mechanistic analysis of the broad aspects of control, regardless of the system, eventually leads back to impaired cell function. The best available evidence suggests that the loss of ovarian cycling is from a decline in the ability of the hypothalamus cells to bind and remove catecholamines from the surrounding environment (Finch, 1976). This is likely to be a result of reduced cell membrane receptor activity.

The thyroxine feedback loop to the pituitary shows a similar change with age. The binding of glucocorticosteroid hormones to control regions of the brain is reduced by 30% in old rats (Roth, 1974). Maturity-onset diabetes is in part a disease of reduced cell membrane receptors for the hormone insulin (Notkins, 1979). These examples suggest that an underlying cause of the aging phenomenon is the change in the ability of cells to recognize environmental cues.

While searching for what goes wrong with the membrane receptor system with age, investigators discovered another phenomenon that indicates that we are still some distance from getting at the basis of biological aging. In obese patients with maturity-onset diabetes, the number of insulin-binding receptors on target cells is greatly reduced (Notkins, 1979). The number of receptors returns to normal, however, when the patients are placed on weight-reducing diets. Thus, the dietary habits that led to obesity also resulted in near-constant bathing of the target cells with insulin. The cellular reaction to this level of stimulation was to reduce the number of receptors so that insulin was less effective. This ultimately gives rise to higher glucose levels in the blood, and the symptoms of diabetes appear. From this and other observations, it is now clear that cells can adjust their number of receptors to a specific hormone in response to environmental conditions. Thus, we do not know if age-associated receptor changes originate as a part of intrinsic cellular aging or again from the environment. If from the environment, then what and where was the initial perturbation?

Several other molecular phenomena might contribute to the aging process. Cells are known to accumulate defective proteins in the course of aging (Gershon & Gershon, 1973). Since plasma membrane receptors are protein and the DNA regulatory factors are protein, one can easily visualize the possible application of this phenomenon to age-related reductions in cellular function and responsiveness. We do not know if cells synthesize more defective proteins with age or simply become less able to discriminate between normal and defective proteins, thereby allowing more and more defective ones to remain (Bradley, Hayflick, & Schimke, 1976).

The problem of the decline in cell divisions with age obviously has dual components. The extrinsically induced effect probably results from reduced concentrations of hormones or other stimulatory factors. The nature of the intrinsic change is unknown, but experiments cited by Hayflick (1980) suggest that the nucleus may be the location within the cell where the change has occurred. In these experiments nuclei were exchanged between "young" and "old" cells. The age of the nucleus appeared to determine the number of potential divisions remaining to the cell, regardless of the age of the cytoplasm. The possibility arises from these experiments that changes in the proteins that regulate DNA function may also underlie the age-dependent decline in cell divisions.

OVERVIEW

Regardless of what level of the organism (neuroendocrine system, cellular, or molecular) we pursue concerning the problem of aging, the first cause still eludes us. In fact, there may be no first cause to the aging process; perhaps it is the combination of many factors, each by itself not being determinative. A further consideration is that regulatory cascades, as illustrated by the endocrine system, are also known to exist within cells. These cascades amplify and diversify signals from control centers. This may have its negative aspects when subtle changes, which occur at the beginning of the cascade, are amplified. In combination with feedback loops, regulatory cascades become circular; once change has begun, it might be self-promoting. In reality, complex functions decline more rapidly with age than individual functions (Shock, 1977). This general observation has led many to the view that the control systems are the key to understanding the aging phenomenon.

REFERENCES

Andres, R., & Tobin, J. D. Endocrine systems. In C. E. Finch & L. Hayflick (Eds.), *Handbook of the biology of aging.* New York: Van Nostrand Reinhold, 1977.

Bradley, M. O., Hayflick, L., & Schimke, R. T. Protein degradation in human fibroblasts (WI-38). *Journal of Biological Chemistry,* 1976, *251,* 3521-3529.

Buetow, D. E. Cellular content and cellular proliferation changes in the tissues and organs of the aging mammals. In I. L. Cameron & J. D. Thrasher (Eds.), *Cellular and molecular renewal in the mammalian body.* New York: Academic Press, 1971.

Cameron, I. L. Cell proliferation and renewal in the mammalian body. In I. L. Cameron & J. D. Thrasher (Eds.), *Cellular and molecular renewal in the mammalian body.* New York: Academic Press, 1971.

Daniel, C. W., & Young, L. J. T. Life span of mouse mammary epithelium during serial propagation *in vivo*: Influence of cell division on an aging process. *Experimental Cell Research,* 1971, *65,* 27-32.

Daniel, C., DeOme, K., Young, J., Blair, P., & Faulkin, L. The *in vivo* life span of normal and preneoplastic mouse mammary glands: A serial transplantation study. *Proceedings of the National Academy of Sciences, U.S.A.,* 1968, *61,* 53-60.

Dell'Orco, R., Mertins, J., & Kruse, P., Jr. Doubling potential, calendar time, and donor age of human diploid cells in culture. *Experimental Cell Research*, 1974, *84*, 363–366.

Finch, C. E. The regulation of physiological changes during mammalian aging. *Quarterly Review of Biology*, 1976, *51*, 49–83.

Finch, C., Foster, J., & Mirsky, A. Ageing and the regulation of cell activities during exposure to cold. *Journal of General Physiology*, 1969, *54*, 690–712.

Gershon, H., & Gershon, D. Inactive enzyme molecules in aging mice: Liver aldolase. *Proceedings of the National Academy of Sciences, U.S.A.*, 1973, *70*, 909–913.

Gregerman, R. I., & Bierman, E. L. Aging and hormones. In R. H. Williams (Ed.), *Textbook of endocrinology*. Philadelphia: W. B. Saunders, 1974.

Hayflick, L. The cell biology of human aging. *Scientific American*, 1980, *242*, 58–65.

Hayflick, L. The limited *in vitro* lifetime of human diploid cell strains. *Experimental Cell Research*, 1965, *37*, 614–636.

Hayflick, L., & Moorhead, P. The serial cultivation of human diploid cell strains. *Experimental Cell Research*, 1961, *25*, 585–621.

Huang, H. H., & Meites, J. Reproduction capacity of aging female rats. *Neuroendocrinology*, 1975, *17*, 289–295.

Kalra, S. P., & McCann, S. M. Effect of drugs modifying catecholamine synthesis on LH release induced by preoptic stimulation in the rat. *Endocrinology*, 1973, *93*, 356–362.

Kamberi, I. A., Mical, R. S., & Porter, J. C. Luteinizing hormone-releasing activity in hypophysial stalk blood and elevation of dopamine. *Science*, 1969, *166*, 388–390.

McEwen, B. S. Interactions between hormones and nerve tissue. *Scientific American*, 1976, *235*, 48–58.

Notkins, A. L. The causes of diabetes. *Scientific American*, 1979, *241*, 62–73.

Peng, M. T., & Huang, H. H. Aging of hypothalamic-pituitary-ovarian function in the rat. *Fertility and Sterility*, 1972, *23*, 535–542.

Price, G. B., & Makinodan, T. Immunologic deficiencies in senescence. I. Characterization of intrinsic deficiencies. *Journal of Immunology*, 1972, *108*, 403–412. (a)

Price, G. B., & Makinodan, T. Immunologic deficiencies in senescence. II. Characterization of extrinsic deficiencies. *Journal of Immunology*, 1972, *108*, 413–417. (b)

Roth, G. S. Age-related changes in specific glucocorticoid binding by steroid-responsive tissues of rats. *Endocrinology*, 1974, *94*, 82–90.

Sanadi, D. R. Metabolic changes and their significance in aging. In C. E. Finch and L. Hayflick (Eds.), *Handbook of the biology of aging*. New York: Van Nostrand Reinhold, 1977.

Schneider, H. P. G., & McCann, S. M. Possible role of dopamine as transmitter to promote discharge of LH-releasing factor. *Endocrinology*, 1969, *85*, 121–132.

Shock, N. W. Systems integration. In C. E. Finch & L. Hayflick (Eds.), *Handbook of the biology of aging*. New York: Van Nostrand Reinhold, 1977.

Strehler, B. L., Mark, D., Mildvan, A. S., & Gee, M. Rate and magnitude of age pigment accumulation in the human myocardium. *Journal of Gerontology*, 1959, *14*, 430–439.

Sulkin, V. M., & Sulkin, D. F. Age differences in response to chronic hypoxia on the fine structure of cardiac muscle and autonomic ganglion cells. *Journal of Gerontology*, 1967, *22*, 485–501.

Thrasher, J., & Gruelich, R. The duodenal progenitor population. II: Age related changes in size and distribution. *Journal of Experimental Zoology*, 1965, *159*, 385–396.

Timiras, P. S. Structural, biochemical and functional aging of the nervous system, *Developmental physiology and aging*. New York: Macmillan, 1972. (a)

Timiras, P. S. Degenerative changes in cells and cell death, *Developmental physiology and aging*. New York: Macmillan, 1972. (b)

CHAPTER **12**

Changing Physiology of Aging: Normal and Pathological

Ruth B. Weg

SEARCH FOR IMMORTALITY AND EVERLASTING YOUTH

> "A drug company may one day
> just come out with an antiaging pill,
> without any advance notice."
>
> Joel Kurtzman, 1978

Historical patterns

The search for youth and immortality is in part a history of magic and sorcery: potions, alchemists' elixirs, animal and plant tissues, and folk remedies. Poets, pharmacists, priests, scientists, and charlatans have written prescriptions and recipes to hold off the "ravages of time." Human fear of aging and death, which appears in the earliest written records, seems to motivate, often dominate, human behavior from prehistory through the present.

Prolonged youth, fear of death. Probably the earliest epic of the human family, the Epic of Gilgamesh, had its origin in the Sumerian culture approximately 5000 years ago. This poignant tale describes the fruitless human yearning for immortality. The hero, who is "obsessed with fear of death," becomes free of his depression "only through a resolve to escape the fate of mankind and gain immortal life" (Segerberg, 1974, p. 16). Gilgamesh fails several trials in his attempts to qualify for immortality and, finally, accepting the loss of perpetual life, he finds joy in work with his hands.

Genital rites. The extension of life and youth by means of certain sexual rituals was a frequent theme in ancient times. One of these, gerocomy, held that a man

242

absorbs youth from close contact with a young female virgin. King David (I Kings 1:1-4), when he was old and ill, was treated in this way. Such a maiden "cherished the king, and ministered to him: but the king knew her not." Australian aborigines usually give a semen "potion" to the feeble or dying (Trimmer, 1970, p. 45).

The Taoists of China developed a cohesive folk religion between 350 and 250 B.C. In their search for immortality they tried to exist on air and saliva with small quantities of roots, berries, and other fruits. Celibacy was not encouraged, but the practice of preservation of *ching*, or life essence, was strongly advised. *Ching* was perceived as the semen of the male and the menstrual fluid of the female, both presumed diminished in illness and totally absent in the elderly (Segerberg, 1974). Taoism recommended that the male bring the partner to orgasm and stop just prior to his own climax.

> He who is able to have coitus tens of times in a single day and night without allowing his essence to escape will be cured of all maladies and will have his longevity extended. If he changes his woman several times, the advantage is greater; if in one night he changes his partner ten times, that is supremely excellent. [Maspero quote in Segerberg, 1974, pp. 75, 76]

Ancient Babylonian cuneiform tablets and Chinese pharmacopoeias described aphrodisiacs and preparations with tigers' testes for achieving sexual vitality and thus youth and longevity (Trimmer, 1970).

Roger Bacon, a philosopher/alchemist/Franciscan monk of the 13th century, also believed in the capacity for rejuvenation in the breath of a young virgin, but without any licentiousness. His logic posed the question, "If disease is contagious, why not vitality?" (Segerberg, 1974).

The significance to the human family of prolonged youth is referred to many times in the literature of the world. Goethe's *Dr. Faustus,* Swift's *Gulliver's Travels,* and Wilde's *The Picture of Dorian Gray* are examples of the tragedy of the choice of youth above all else.

Fountain of youth. The so-called fountain of youth has taken many forms throughout human history. This varied search for everlasting youth represents more evidence of the continuing pursuit of immortality. The second chapter of Genesis mentions a river flowing out of Eden; Psalm 36 refers to a "fountain of life." Ponce de Leon, a 16th-century explorer, had heard Indian tales of a fountain on the island of Bimini in the Bahamas, whose waters "refreshed the weary and rejuvenated the aged" (Segerberg, 1974). In his search he found Florida, where elders still go today to recapture earlier vitality and vigor.

The following two examples are representative of the numerous allusions to renewal and perpetual life in Greek mythology. Hera, Zeus' wife, renewed her "maidenhood" each year by bathing in a special spring. Goddess Aurora was not so successful: Her mortal lover and husband, Tithonus, was granted immortality by Zeus at Aurora's request. However, as Tithonus grew old and disabled, he prayed for the freedom of death. Aurora realized she had failed to ask for eternal youth for his immortal life (Guillerme, 1963).

In the 11th century, Ibn-Sina (known to Europeans as Aicenna) the physician of the Arab world, envisioned an elixir for medical purposes and with universal application. This was the origin of a panacea, a cure-all, or an elixir of eternal youth (Segerberg, 1974).

Roger Bacon, who accepted the principles of alchemy (transmutation of base elements to gold or silver), believed that the life span of his day (usually not more than 45 years) could be tripled by alchemy (Segerberg, 1974).

Longevity goal. Luigi Cornaro, a 16th-century Italian philosopher and architect, did not seek youth or immortality but rather desired the long and happy life. Longevity, he advised, is based in part on the enjoyment of life and old age and on a positive attitude. His emphasis was on moderation and temperance, particularly in diet, as keys to health and long life. Whether his own design for the good life was the cause or not, Cornaro lived to be 96 years old in relatively good health for most of them (Gruman, 1966; Guillerme, 1963; Segerberg, 1974).

René Descartes, a French mathematician and philosopher of the 16th and 17th centuries and one of the scientists of the Age of Reason, looked to science for the realization of life prolongation. In his *Discourse on the Method* (1637) he predicted: "We could free ourselves from an infinity of maladies of body as well as of mind, and perhaps, also even from the debility of age, if we had sufficiently ample knowledge of their causes, and of all the remedies provided for us by nature" (Gruman, 1966; Segerberg, 1974).

Sir Francis Bacon (1561-1626) was among the first modern philosopher/scientists to call for knowledge to be more than "talk"; it must be applied to improve the human condition. He suggested that if this approach were practiced for a few centuries, science would perform marvelously for humanity (Segerberg, 1974).

Benjamin Franklin, 18th-century statesman and philosopher, also looked to the future optimistically and wrote to Joseph Priestley that the time would come when "all diseases may by sure means be prevented or cured, not excepting that of old age, and our lives lengthened at pleasure even beyond the antediluvian standard" (Dubos, 1965, p. 344).

Inevitable aging versus immortality. Since its earliest beginnings, the human family has lived with the conflict and apparent contradiction between two concepts: the acceptance of old age as the inevitable, debilitated end of life and the powerful drive for longevity and immortality.

Aristotle (384-322 B.C.), one of the world's earliest observers and classifiers of all living systems, wrote that, "aging is not disease, because it is not contrary to nature" (Guillerme, 1963).

Cicero (106-43 B.C.) in his essay "On Old Age" also accepted the notion of aging as natural and inevitable, arguing "that it is not old age that is at fault, but rather our attitude toward it." In response to the fact that some old men become invalids, he said, "But a disability of this degree is not peculiar to old age; it is rather the usual concomitant of ill health" (trans. 1967, p. 21).

Galen, a renowned Greek physician of the second century, built his philosophy and practice on the early Greco-Roman medical thought and described aging as "beginning at the very moment of conception" (Guillerme, 1963).

Contemporary efforts

Youth-seeking goes on still: the promise is no longer immortality but the delay or reversal of aging. Today's efforts range from wishful thinking and blind faith to science.

Gerovital-H$_3$.   A now famous drug, Gerovital-H$_3$, in use since 1953, has been the object of claims of reversal and delay of aging. Dr. Ana Aslan of Bucharest, now about 85 years old, developed the "KH$_3$" injections in the early 1950s to treat elderly patients of the hospital in which she had a major post. This "procaine and vitamin" therapy was also alleged to alleviate or cure a variety of pathologies and disorders that plague the later years: cardiovascular disease, Parkinson's disease, depression, decline in memory, arthritis, loss of energy, sexual dysfunction, graying of hair, baldness, and wrinkled skin (Aslan, 1972, 1974).

Because controlled studies in Great Britain and the United States failed to support the claims made by Aslan, most physicians and scientists were soon convinced that Gerovital is useless. Nevertheless, thousands of people believe in its value and buy it where they can—in England, Mexico, Jamaica, and other islands of the Caribbean.

Many people choose to be treated at the Geriatric Institute in Bucharest, where Aslan is still the active director. This geriatric center also provides Aslavital, a new product that contains procaine and two other factors that are "efficient in the prophylaxis and cure of . . . the process of aging of the central nervous system and the cardiovascular apparatus." The patient stays in the Romanian clinic for at least two weeks and upon leaving is given a one-year supply of Gerovital and Aslavital (Kent, 1980, p. 231). A recent investigation has demonstrated some unexpected effects with Gerovital: mice had a 33% increased survival rate, and cell membranes showed a tendency for stabilization of structure and function (Samorajski, Sun, & Rolstein, 1976).

Nevada is the only state that has approved the clinical use of Gerovital. The U.S. Food and Drug Administration has supported research with Gerovital but is testing only its antidepressant value (Olsen, Bank, & Jarvik, 1978; Zung, Gianturco, Pfeiffer, Wang, Whanger, Bridge, & Potkin, 1974). No reliable data have proved that Gerovital is antiaging, but sufficient evidence suggests its therapeutic efficacy as a mild antidepressant and an obtundent agent in arthritis.

Cell therapy.   Another therapy that has gathered increasing adherence is "embryonic lamb cell therapy," which began 51 years ago in Switzerland. Dr. Paul Niehans, who died in 1971 at the age of 89, initiated this work in the belief that the treatment could rejuvenate or revitalize the body. His approach was born out of an episode that used legitimate replacement therapy as a recommended regimen for hormone dysfunction. In 1931 Neihans was called to help a female patient in distress after a thyroidectomy. The patient's parathyroids had also been accidentally removed. He injected the patient with fragments of parathyroid of a freshly killed calf, and she recovered.

Neihans moved from that successful incident to the working theory that specific embryonic cells could be used effectively to combat specific disease. Further, he suggested, these injections could maintain health and vigor—that is, youth; diseases could be delayed or prevented. The cell therapy technique and derivatives thereof, such as frozen and lyophilized cells and cell extracts, are now used in many "youth clinics" in England, Switzerland, Germany, and the Bahamas. Many apparently satisfied recipients can be found among the world's notables in the clergy, the arts, and politics. Since in this instance, as with Gerovital, experimental controls are difficult if not impossible, the alleged success or failure of the technique has been based largely on the claims of the clinics that use it and the patients who would not be denied its use (Kent, 1980; Prehoda, 1968).

On the face of it, the efficacy of cell therapy would be doubted due to the body's immunological defenses that could be expected to react defensively to any foreign protein. Perhaps, if the embryonic cells migrated to the damaged organs and were modified by macrophagy and combination with antibodies, the broken-down cell constituents might be useful as a source of metabolites and energy. Otherwise cell therapy conjures up the notion of "sympathetic magic," such as Achilles eating bone marrow to give him strength, and concurs with Paracelsus' 16th-century concept of "like cures like." Its use and popularity are not related to any valid data.

Placental tissue therapy. In use at the Filatov Institute in the Soviet Union since 1965, this treatment is considered useful in the prevention and treatment of premature aging. The director of the institute makes no claim for this as a "youth elixir." A ten-year study of 130 geriatric patients reported fewer complaints of symptoms generally identified as inevitable with aging: general weakness, fatigue, limited mobility, memory weakness, vision weakness, reduction or loss of sexual potency, and heart and joint pains (Kent, 1980).

Ginseng. This aromatic root used by the Chinese and Koreans for thousands of years has achieved its notoriety primarily as an aphrodisiac and rejuvenator. A study reported at the 11th International Congress of Gerontology (Tokyo, 1978) that a ginseng mixture had lowered blood pressure in hypertensives, improved pancreatic function in diabetics, and enhanced mental activities in a majority of 540 treated patients. These investigations, carried out by the Swiss manufacturer of the ginseng product, have not been validated and lack the support of American or English scientists (Bittles, Fulder, Grant, & Nicholls, 1979).

Nucleic acid therapy. Frank (1979) considers dietary ribonucleic acid (RNA) in association with other nutrients such as amino acids, sugars, vitamin B complex, and minerals able to effect a significant increase in cell energy. This, he states, enables the organism to fight disease, reduce stress, and reverse aging symptomology. His most recent work uses a diet rich in nucleic acid and vegetable juice, vitamin B complex, vitamins C and E, and superoxide dismutase (an enzyme that appears to minimize the possible toxic consequences of oxygen metabolism). He found that 18 persons (aged 40–87 years) of both sexes demonstrated more energy and vitality, increased strength, tightened skin and reduced wrinkling, less gray hair, and improved vision. However, without scientific validation and without affiliation with an educational or scientific institution, his work and theory remain in question (Rosenfeld, 1976).

Beyond the generalized, salutary effect of RNA proposed by Frank, RNA administration has been said to result in measurable improvement and raised memory scores in older patients with memory deficits (Solyom, Enesco, & Beaulieu, 1967). However, Nordgren, Woodruff, and Bick (1970) demonstrated that RNA does not even get past the blood/brain barrier.

Antioxidants. For almost a quarter of a century, megadoses of various antioxidants have been reported to extend the mean life span of mice but to leave the maximum life span unaffected (Harman, 1968). However, other studies suggest that dietary antioxidants cannot be considered to be effective antiaging substances since failure to extend life span and modest extension of life span have both been reported. The fact that the most significant positive results have been in specially bred mice, who develop cancer and die before old age (Kent, 1977; Kohn, 1971), also minimizes the applicability of the results.

Bionics, cryonics, cloning, young blood infusion, lowering body temperature, decreased dietary intake. These rejuvenation techniques are just a few of the growing number of procedures and theories in various stages of proof, discard, and/or application. Overview examinations of these and others can be found elsewhere (Kent, 1980; Rosenfeld, 1976; Segerberg, 1974).

Whenever possible, current therapies to correct dysfunction of particular organ systems will be presented with each of the systemic changes noted; specifically, the measurable diminution of or increase in cell debris, metabolites or organelles (for example, acetylcholine and brain neurons; thymosin and the immune system).

In spite of the apparent failure to halt, slow, or reverse aging, the quest continues, hoping for success, with the promise of imminent victory (Comfort, 1979; Segerberg, 1974; Strehler, 1977) and some cautious optimism (Fries, 1980; Makinodan, 1977).

PHYSIOLOGY OF AGING

The mechanism(s) of aging (more appropriately, of aging processes) still elude the scientific community, although suggestions and theories multiply. Physiological aging can be considered to include all time-dependent changes in structure and function of the organism that eventually contribute to diminished efficiency and increased vulnerability to disease and death. Aging processes are characteristically decremental, but aging is clearly not disease.

Data collection

Information about organ system changes has come from two major method-ologies: the earlier cross-sectional and the more recent longitudinal studies.

Until the middle 1950s the only available data about functional changes with age came from biased comparison between healthy, young college adults and ill, institu-tionalized elderly. Predictably, older persons were found to possess only marginal percentages of the capacities of youth.

A more accurate and ongoing evaluation of changes in physiology with age has been derived from longitudinal studies. In 1958 Shock of the Gerontology Research Center (GRC), the intramural research arm of the National Institute on Aging, began a study of age changes in 600 healthy males between 20 and 96 years of age living in the community (Shock, 1962; Shock, 1968). This work continues under the guidance of the current medical director, Dr. Reubin Andres, and others. Moreover, the addition in 1978 of women as part of the subject population provides necessary, heretofore missing, information (Higbie, 1978).

Another study at the National Institute of Health (Birren, Butler, Greenhouse, Sokoloff, & Yarrow, 1963, 1971) of healthy, elderly men began at about the same time. A third important longitudinal study was undertaken at the Duke Center for the Study of Aging in 1955 with persons 60-90 years of age and was completed in 1973. The Duke Center carried out final examinations in 1973 in still another longitudinal study begun in 1968 with persons 46-70 years of age (Palmore, 1970, 1971).

The rate and substance of individual aging is not understandable from only cross-sectional comparisons. Longitudinal data have made it possible to conclude that not all decremental changes with age are due to time-dependent processes; some result from disuse/misuse, and others are pathological (Butler, 1975; deVries, 1970, 1974).

Such an observation holds positive implications for intervention and suggests that recognized "health habits" may not only support health maintenance and prevent or delay disease (Belloc, 1973; Belloc & Breslow, 1973), but may retard or eliminate time-related changes assumed to be inevitable with aging. The longitudinal studies continue to build a more balanced, accurate composite of individual aging.

Physiological age changes: general characteristics

Individual differences. The older population is heterogeneous. There is no "the aged." Older people are less alike than ever before, fulfilling a unique heredity within a particular lifestyle. Individuals age at different rates from one another; within the same individual, each organ system ages both differently and in coordination with other systems under the integrative control of the neuroendocrine system. Therefore, although it is useful to calculate and compare the average decline of a function(s), it is equally important to keep in mind that any one person may not fit that specific picture.

Differences within the group aged 65-90 are frequently greater than the differ-ences that exist between the middle-aged group, 40-64 years old, and the older group. For example, they differ in regard to mobility, energy level, work activity, health, and whether housebound or in the community.

Gradual decline. The rate of decrement in a number of systems may be no greater from 60 to 70 years old than from 30 to 40 years old. In the absence of overt pathology, a slow decline in function occurs during the greater part of adult life. However, many functional capacities remain at a satisfactory level for most lifestyles. The observable, gradual rate of decline is explainable, at least in part, by the enormous reserve and redundancy in tissue and organ system capacity.

Complex functions. Decrements are greater in the performance of coordinated activities involving a number of connections between nerve and nerve, nerve and muscle, and nerve and gland. Important differences between young and old are at the level of interacting systems. For example, the decline in velocity of nerve conduction is less than the decrease in maximum breathing capacity. A single physiological system is involved with the former, the latter relates to the coordination of numerous nerve and muscle activities.

Systemic reserve and redundancy. Although a reduction in reserve does take place with the years, homeostasis is maintained moderately well, albeit at another level. Without pathology or stress, persons may be unaware of the slow erosion of function. An individual can survive (under particular conditions) with less than 49% of the liver, fractions of stomach and intestines, one lung, and one kidney. However, if emotional and physiological crises arise, functional demands can no longer be met, homeostasis is severely diminished, and pathology may result (Shock, 1974).

Homeostasis. Perhaps the single most critical and salient difference with age involves the diminishing ability to respond to stress (physical and/or emotional) and return to the prestress level in a reasonable time period—that is, a decrease in homeostatic capacity (Selye, 1970; Shock, 1974). This relates most to the changes in neuroendocrine interaction as well as to other systemic alterations in responsivity to the nervous and endocrine systems separately. Various physiological parameters such as blood pH and volume, blood glucose, and proteins appear relatively constant over the years. In a number of older individuals, blood pressure and heart rate may be comparable to the values of younger persons, but only "at rest."

Stress reveals the declining capacity to mount the extent and intensity of response equivalent to the younger years. Characteristically, increased time is needed to return to prestress levels. Demands can no longer be adequately met, the reduction in reserve capacity is finally missed, and pathology may develop. In response to stressors, whether physical, as in exercise, or emotional, as in excitement or fear, the magnitude of displacement may be greater, and the rate of recovery is slower with increasing age.

Quantification of certain hormones in the urine makes possible the identification of the changing capacity for stress response. One of the first measurable hormonal responses to stressors is the increase of the trophic hormone of the anterior pituitary, adrenocorticotropin (ACTH). This, in turn, stimulates the adrenal cortex to secrete corticoids, which elicit, among other biochemical changes, an increase in glucose from the liver, the major metabolite used in evolution of energy. An initial increase also occurs in the urine concentration of adrenaline and noradrenaline secreted from the adrenal medulla. These hormones stimulate related activities in the circulatory, digestive, and nervous systems.

Further evidence of a breakdown in homeostatic efficiency is demonstrable in adjustment to environmental temperature change. Exposure of young and old subjects to 5°-15° C for 45-120 minutes resulted in a fall of 0.5°-1° C among the old but insignificant rectal temperature changes among the young. Other experiments have demonstrated that adaptation to heat is also more difficult for older persons. Measurement of heat loss from the hand, in calories/unit volume, under standard conditions was approximately 33% lower at age 70 than at 24 (Pickering, 1936). Water loss from fingertips and toes also measured significantly less in older subjects. Decreased heat and water loss both contribute to the reduction of heat loss from evaporation, an important body cooling mechanism (Burch, Cohn, & Neuman, 1942). In a statistical overview the death rate from heat stroke rose sharply after the age of 60: 8/100,000 deaths for ages 70-79 compared with 80/100,000 deaths for ages 90-100 years (Shattuck & Hilferty, 1932).

As one grows older, a prolonged exposure to even a moderate reduction in environmental temperature can cause an abnormally low body temperature—that is, accidental hypothermia. This drop in deep body temperature, a disorder only recently acknowledged, is potentially fatal for the older person and may be recognizable by nodding, withdrawn behavior and an absence of shivering. Observers often inappropriately assign these symptoms to "aging" itself rather than to diminished or absent homeostatic reflex reactions to conserve body heat. In some instances, prescribed drugs, such as phenothiazine tranquilizers, exacerbate the effects of impaired temperature regulatory mechanisms.

Another indication of reduced homeostasis accompanying aging can be found in glucose metabolism. A measurable age-associated reduction in glucose tolerance takes place, so that a glucose load is disposed of more slowly. Individual cells receive less glucose, and more remains in the blood. The rate of return to the preglucose load level (a range between 80 and 90 mg/100 ml of blood) is slowed, and blood glucose may remain at a higher level.

In some older persons, aged 55-70, the decrease in glucose tolerance may be so significant as to cause a physician to diagnose maturity-onset diabetes. However, the small changes in tolerance after a glucose load, which are absent in the fasting state, are considered by some as a part of "normal aging" (Davis, 1978b).

Two possible mechanisms have been suggested as primary age deficits to explain the rise in blood glucose levels: a reduction in pancreatic beta cell sensitivity to blood sugar, and/or the diminished sensitivity of the target organ to insulin, specifically a reduction in the number and function of its membrane receptors. Andres (1971) and Andres and associates (1969) have noted that no age difference in peripheral utilization of glucose has been found. However, older persons do demonstrate a reduced insulin release after a glucose load. Not only is the insulin secretion delayed, but the volume is also reduced in "apparently normal subjects" (Davis, 1978b). Moreover, notes Davis, more inactive insulin (prolinsulin) is released by older persons.

The question remains "Are the alterations in glucose tolerance maturity-onset diabetes—that is, a pathological state—or a normal physiological decrement of homeostatic capacity in the later years?"

This question may remain unanswered until sufficient normative data concerning older persons can be accumulated. Only such data can make possible the development of nomograms for glucose tolerance and other physiological parameters enabling a reasonable reference standard for persons over 55 (Andres & Tobin, 1977; Reichel, 1978, Figure 1). Standards for glucose tolerance based only on values of young persons inappropriately label a large number of elders diabetic.

Vulnerability to disease. Morbidity and mortality increase with age. Older persons are generally more vulnerable to disease than younger persons, and they are twice as likely to be physically disabled and to require hospitalization. Cardiovascular disease, cancer, and cerebrovascular accidents, the nation's three major chronic diseases and killers, have their greatest incidence among older persons. The illnesses and diseases associated with old age have their etiology in the young adult years, but they are frequently diagnosed in the late-middle and older years. Yet each successive cohort has more elderly who are healthier and longer lived (Brotman, 1980; Weg, 1979). Diseases accompany aging, but aging is not a "curable disease."

Looking old. The years leave recognizable marks: a slow but manifest series of changes. Societal adoration of youth has placed a premium on looking young. Although the old appearance has no direct impact on vigor, function, and good health, millions of middle-aged and older women (and some older men) suffer damaged egos, diminished self-images, and indirect effects on health status. The cosmetic industry and cosmetic surgeons have prospered in the atmosphere of "young is better."

The negative images of aging are familiar: the skin grows thinner, wrinkled, and dotted with "liver spots"; hair thins out, grays, and loses its luster; the frame settles and becomes shorter; bones are more brittle and less flexible; the knees are slightly bent and the shoulders drawn forward; eyes appear grayer and dull with cataracts; and the gait and general movement are slow. These are the visible results of change on organ and system levels, as well as the underlying molecular changes.

Not everyone experiences all of these observable changes; not all people show these changes at the same time. Some elders show so few of these signs that society gratuitously categorizes them as young.

The young, unlined, and gently curvaceous body of the woman and the lithe but macho and powerful body of the man cannot be preserved forever. The mythology of age and the realities of societal attitudes toward aging and the aged have helped to create the fearsome image of old age that can be likened to a punishment.

An examination of physical, systemic aging does not support the frequent labeling of elders as roleless, invalid, and relegated to mindless senility and death. Although systemic decrement, loss of reserve, and a decrease in homeostatic control occur, they do not necessarily also cause inevitable disengagement, incompetence, and invalidism. For the majority of older persons more than enough systemic capacities are available to meet the demands of contemporary lifestyles. Each individual also has the opportunity and responsibility to nurture and extend the remaining capacities.

Tissue, systemic, and functional changes with time

Gerontologists agree that a steady, slow decline occurs in functional capacities of most organ systems (Shock, 1962, 1974). Some of these changes are shown in Figure 12-1. However, continuing research demonstrates that not all functional changes in older persons are due to aging: some are pathological, others are due to misuse or disuse (Butler, 1975; deVries, 1970, 1974; Fries, 1980).

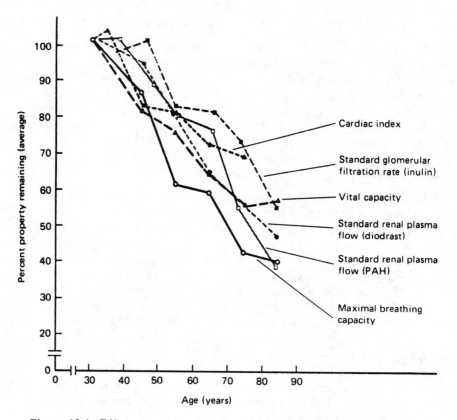

Figure 12-1. Efficiency of human physiological mechanisms as a function of age. Level at three years is assigned a value of 100%. (*Modified from Shock, 1962*)

Musculoskeletal. The older locomotor system and decreasing work capacity are associated with muscle, bone, and nervous tissue changes (Birren, 1971; Shock, 1962, 1974; Smith, Bierman, & Robinson, 1978).

Lean muscle mass appears to decrease with the years, and fat tissue increases. However, more recent longitudinal studies suggest that this age-related decline of lean body mass may be more apparent than real. People with smaller, lean body mass may live longer (Winick, 1976). Others suggest that, in part, the loss of lean body mass may be secondary to the decrease in activity and the age-dependent changes in connective and circulatory tissues so intimately connected with muscle.

Older muscle tissue evidences a slow decline in strength, tone, speed, and flexibility (see Figure 12-2). Appropriate exercise regimens, however, can restore a percentage of flexibility, muscle tone, and strength at any age. Speed and endurance also show improvement (deVries, 1970, 1975).

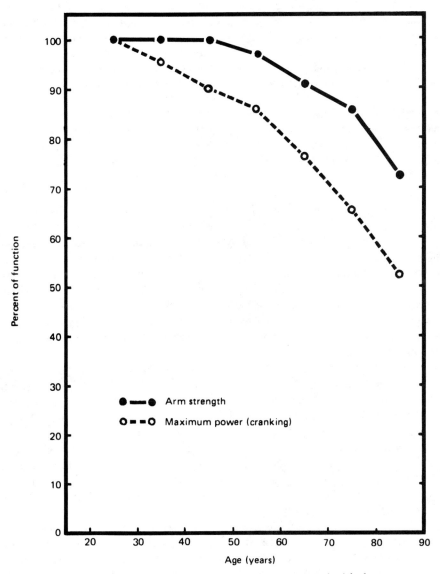

Figure 12-2. Age decrements in muscle strength compared with decrements in maximum powers developed in a coordinated movement (cranking) utilizing the same muscle groups. (*Adapted from Shock & Norris, 1970*)

The skeletal frame experiences an obvious "settling" and brings the expected decrease in height. This occurs as a function of altered posture, dehydration, and thinning of the intervertebral cartilaginous discs.

Some loss of compact bone takes place in most older persons. Frequently this creates additional stress to the weight-bearing areas, which consequently are more susceptible to fracture.

Joints do undergo a number of alterations. In most persons over 50 years of age, a degree of deterioration is measurable. Calcification within cartilage and ligaments occurs (Hazzard & Bierman, 1978). As cartilage is eroded, pain and crepitation (noise due to bone touching bone) occur. Some persons may experience a loss of elasticity in particular joints and preosteoarthritic degeneration in the joint cartilage. Therapeutic exercises and dietary intake may minimize these effects (Jowsey, 1976).

Neuronal. Anatomical, chemical, and functional changes take place in the nervous system. There are changes in the number, ultrastructure, and connectivity of nerve and glial cells; a decrease occurs in brain size and volume. Due to the central role of the central nervous system (CNS) in homeostatic control and in integration and coordination of other body systems, the significance of these changes exists for more than the nervous tissue itself.

Simple reflex time is relatively constant during adulthood (Hügin, Norris, & Shock, 1960). This response, primarily by way of the spinal cord, represents the transmission of nerve impulses through few synapses. On the other hand, reaction time shows significant decline over the years and involves a complex of factors in the CNS as well as a number of synapses and systems. A low level loss (10-15%) in the speed of impulse conduction is amplified by the complexity of daily living requirements— for example, walking, bathing, and cooking (Shock, 1974) (see Figure 12-3). Electrical activity (brain waves) also changes with age. Although the dominant adult brain waves slow down with age, they alter CNS function little unless pathology exists (Woodruff, 1975).

Basis for the decline in function of the nervous system has generally been assumed from earlier studies to be the apparent loss of the postmitotic neurons. The alleged decrease in memory and learning capacity and the inevitable confusion were supposedly due to the accelerated loss of neurons in the later years (Brody & Vijayashankar, 1977). These conclusions may have been related to autopsies on brain tissue with pathologies that were missed or poorly characterized. Additional investigations have suggested that the major loss of cells occurs before maturity and that decreased connectivity among neurons is notable in older brains. The loss of neurons appears to be selective, rather than widespread and random (Brody & Vijayashankar, 1977, Scheibel & Scheibel, 1975).

The loss of neurons in the hypothalamus (sensitive to osmolality) may contribute to the decreased awareness of thirst and dehydration among elders. Dehydration can have other troublesome consequences such as confusion and constipation.

Diminishing neuronal capacity may also be secondary to a dysfunction of the vascular system (arteriosclerosis, atherosclerosis) and resulting decreased blood flow,

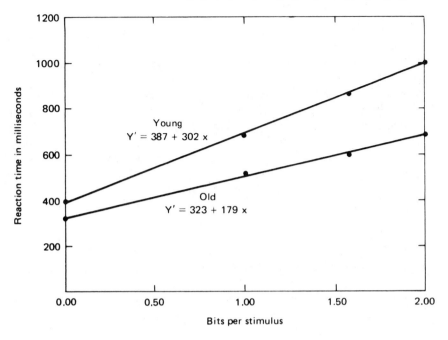

Figure 12-3. Reaction time as a function of stimulus information and age.
(*From Suci, Davidoff, & Surwillo, 1960*)

changes in tissue permeability and alterations of the connective tissue, changes in responsivity of receptor organs, and decreased concentration of brain neurotransmitters.

Inquiry into changes in the nervous system with aging is currently focused on the activity and concentration of brain neurotransmitters. In animal studies, Finch (1973, 1977) has found hypothalamic catecholamines are reduced in aging male mice; Huang and Meites (1975) "reinitiated ovarian cycles in a majority of old rats" with the administration of L-dopa, epinephrine, and eproniozide. Rather than gonadal aging or a lack of viable eggs, the loss of estrous cycling may be a catecholamine deficiency in the hypothalamus.

A more recent development in the investigation of neurotransmitters relates to the decreased syntheses and activities of acetylcholine, serotonin, and dopamine in the brain (Wurtman & Growdon, 1978). Preliminary therapeutic trials are encouraging: the regimens include the use of dietary choline and/or choline containing lecithin in the treatment of depression, mania, memory loss, pain sensitivity, and peripheral disorders—for example, myasthenia gravis (Wurtman, 1980).

Decremental changes described in the nervous system have suggested that intellectual capacity may also be inevitably diminished among elders. Studies thus far indicate the contrary: intellectual capacity is fairly stable until the early 60s. Through the mid-70s there may be a decrease of "some but not all abilities, for some, but not all individuals." But beyond 80, decrement is the rule for most individuals (Schaie, 1980).

However, some of the noted decline may be less than suggested since the data have been derived from investigations that used techniques and tests designed for children and young adults. Intellectual decrement may be a function of body pathology, especially severe cardiovascular disease, and/or a socially and emotionally deprived environment.

Sensory function is also less efficient with time. Diminution in smell and taste affect appetite and finally nutritional status. Proprioception is also impaired (Smith, Bierman, & Robinson, 1978) and can be perceived in the difficulties with balance and coordination among some elders. The gradual loss of visual acuity frequently necessitates the use of glasses for the first time in many middle-aged and older persons. Loss in audition, which typically begins in the 30s, appears to peak between 40 and 50 years and is largely characteristic of the higher frequencies.

The decline in touch sensitivity and therefore response does not appear to be as critical to well-being and behavior as other major systemic decrements. Nevertheless, the sensation of touch is part of the individual's capacity for adaptation to the environment (Kenshalo, 1977). Other changes include the decrease in perception of vibration and temperature and an increased pain threshold; each makes a contribution to the decrease in response capacity.

In general, then, the capacity for awareness and internalization of environmental stimuli declines and causes a concomitant decrease in responsivity and adaptation.

Pulmonary. A measurable reduction occurs in the efficiency of the breathing mechanism, characterized by decreases in maximum breathing capacity, residual lung volume, total capacity, and basal oxygen consumption; these bring about a diminished metabolic rate. A decrease in functional alveoli and thickening membranes are barriers to O_2 and CO_2 exchange. Weakened external and internal costal muscles and altered bronchiolar elastic fibers contribute to the decreased flexibility and elasticity of the lungs (Rockstein & Sussman, 1979).

The building blocks (amino acids, glucose, fatty acids) and energy, which are required for syntheses and all intermediary metabolic reactions, are derived from the combination of oxygen with food in the processes of digestion, cell respiration, and assimilation. Since less oxygen may be available for metabolism, and nutrition falls off as well, there may be a decrease in the reserves for all body functions. Health maintenance is dependent upon protective and repair mechanisms, which, in turn, require sources of metabolites for syntheses and energy.

Digestive. Adequate function in the digestive system is essential to an appropriate nutritional status so necessary to the health and activities of other organ systems. The capacity to digest, absorb, and assimilate food is not seriously impaired with age, but many elders experience an "irritable bowel." Constipation, hiatus hernia, gallbladder dysfunction, viral hepatitis, diverticulosis, polyps, gastric ulcer, ulcerative colitis, and cancer are the most common of gastrointestinal disorders.

A number of apparent digestive problems relate to other organ system dysfunctions and health-risk behavior. For example, depression (nervous system) diminishes appetite and activity, the usual bases for eating; drug abuse often causes hypovita-minoses and can interfere with trace mineral absorption.

Normal age changes affecting digestive processes include the following:

- decline in sensitivity to sweet, sour, salt, and bitter
- diminished fluid intake
- decrease in volume of digestive juices
- diminished ability of stomach parietal cells to secrete hydrochloric acid (HCL is responsible for the optimum pH in protein digestion)
- altered mobility of esophagus
- decreased rate of peristalsis
- absorption relatively unaffected except for calcium (Ca absorption can be seriously modified by drugs.)

The widely prescribed drugs for the elderly (for example, laxatives, salicylates, and strong sedatives) often reduce the efficiency of digestion and/or absorption with consequent nutrient deficiencies.

Attention to diet, drugs, and exercise can minimize at least some of the functional disorders (constipation, hiatus hernia, diverticulosis) (Weg, 1979, 1981).

Cardiovascular. Reduced effectiveness without pathology in this system relates, in part, to the lowered efficiency of the various control mechanisms. Cardiac output, stroke index, stroke volume, and vasomotor tone decrease; the heart "pump" works harder to accomplish less. In many older persons blood vessels have narrowed with atherosclerosis and/or arteriosclerosis, increasing peripheral resistance, circulation time, and diastolic and systolic pressure. Arrythmia becomes more frequent; recovery of contractility and irritability is slowed; heart rate response to stressors is decreased (Harris, 1975; Kohn, 1977).

Studies suggest that ample regular exercise contributes positively to cardiovascular health, for it lowers the resting heart rate; increases the efficiency of the heart, lungs, and blood vessels; lowers hypertension; reduces blood cholesterol and increases serum high density lipoproteins (HDL); lowers serum glucose and triglycerides and stored fat (Cantwell, 1978; Monkerud, 1978; Paffenbarger, Hale, Brand, & Hyde, 1977; Harris, 1975). No satisfactory evidence has proved that exercise will prevent a heart attack, but prescribed physical activity may ensure recovery and delay death. However, a recent report from Boston University Medical Center describes a study in which monkeys on a regular treadmill exercise regimen withstood the ravages of a diet designed to produce a coronary artery disease (Johnson, 1982).

Excretory. The kidney loses nephrons (kidney tubule, the functional unit), so that in an average life span, about one half of the birth number remain. With this degree of reduced reserve, stress can more easily precipitate kidney failure in the older person. Although the kidneys still participate in homeostasis, more time is required (Epstein, 1979).

Renal blood flow, glomerular filtration, and tubular rates decrease (Shock, 1970, 1974). Sclerotic and fibrotic changes are common in renal arteries. Shock (1970, 1974) estimates a 55% fall in blood plasma flow between the ages of 30 and 80 years. Part of this reduction is due to the decreased volume of blood being pumped by the heart.

Changes with age in urination patterns can also be traced to changes in the elasticity and responsivity of the bladder: an increase in frequency of urination, and a larger residual urine volume after voiding (Lindeman, 1975).

Immunity. Immune capacity appears to be less responsive and efficient with the years. The thymus—its hormones and lymphocytes ("T" and "B" cells)—do most of the important work of the immune system. As the body ages, the thymus gland involutes but continues to secrete decreased amounts of the hormone thymosin. Changes in the number and proliferative capacity of "T" (thymus dependent for maturity) and "B" (bone marrow dependent lymphocytes) take place (Adler, Jones, & Brock, 1978; Makinodan, 1977).

Immune surveillance (searching out and elimination of cancerous or other aberrant cells) decreases. Autoimmune responses increase and are considered to be implicated in diseases that include among other effects destruction of body tissues (for example, rheumatoid arthritis, hemolytic anemia, and multiple sclerosis) (Walford, 1967). Consequences follow from the slowly "failing" immune function. Elders demonstrate a higher mortality rate from pneumonia (six to seven times the rate of young adults) and greater incidence of cancer and tuberculosis.

Recent work in "rejuvenating" the immune system holds promise for elders and health maintenance. Goldstein, Guhe, Zatz, Hardy, and White (1972) suggest that an increase in blood thymosin may retard or even prevent a number of age-associated diseases. The infusion of stem cells and implantation of thymic epithelial cells of young donors into old mice were immunologically rejuvenated (Hirokawa & Makinodan, 1975). Makinodan (1977) perceives the immune system as "perhaps the most attractive" of all systems being studied in the search for techniques that can slow down the rate of aging and that may delay, moderate, and/or prevent some of the pathology that accompanies the later years.

Endocrine. Few generalizations or unifying theories are appropriate to the complexities of the hormonal system. The activities (responsivity, apparent synthesis, secretion, and disposal rate) of some glands remain relatively constant with age; other hormones are present but at lower serum levels possibly due to decreased synthesis and/or increased degradation and disposal rates (Gregerman & Bierman, 1974).

There is some consensus that decreased effectiveness of the hormonal system develops with age, but there is less agreement concerning mechanism(s). Several fairly recent studies focus on the decrease in number and/or binding capacity of hormone receptors on the cell membrane for surface active hormones, and intracellular receptor sites for gene active hormones. The suggestion is that a decrease in receptor/hormone binding may be due to dysfunctional or reduced receptors. Specific explanation for their dysfunction or loss remains to be clarified (Roth, 1978).

Some definitive decreases in hormonal effectiveness are unequivocal: activities and concentrations of the sex hormones, insulin synthesis, and response to stressful stimuli. The slower clearing and utilization of a glucose load described earlier have been identified as consequences of reduced target organ sensitivity to insulin (Marx, 1979).

It may be that the most important changes occur, not in the altered activity or concentration of any single hormone, but in the integration and coordination at the neuroendocrine level. In this regard, the findings of scientists that there is a reduction of hypothalamic neurotransmitters (Finch, 1977) is a case in point. Physiological changes affecting human sexuality discussed in Chapter 10 will not be discussed here.

HEALTH MAINTENANCE

As we have maintained thus far, functional decline is measurable in a number of physiological capacities among older persons. This may suggest to the reader that the stereotypes of aging are close to the facts. However, what is significant is not that these gradual diminutions do occur, but that the majority of older persons accommodate well to these changes, and that approximately 87% of persons over 65 remain in their communities with no limitations on their mobility (Brotman, 1980; Weg, 1981). They demonstrate more than adequate coping behavior in meeting the challenge of everyday living. Nonetheless, the lowered efficiency of a number of organ systems does lead to increased susceptibility to disease.

What factors determine whether or not an individual will succumb to illness? Do primarily intrinsic characteristics or environmental variables play critical roles?

Life events and illness

Persuasive arguments by some researchers emphasize the "social environment as initiator" of stimuli and neuroendocrine responses. Repeated and/or prolonged, these interactions can lead to illness and disease (Cassel, 1974; Henry & Stephens, 1977; Holmes & Rahe, 1967; Rahe, 1974). Other determinants also play a part. The "perception of the social environment" (Henry & Stephens, 1977) and "the meaning of situations to them" (Cassel, 1974), rather than the direct action of the social stimuli on the individual, determine the nature and length of the particular illness or response. Other factors are involved since perception is molded by the individual's background, life experiences, familial ties, roles, status, relationships, and emotional and physical states.

The early work on the impact of the social environment on life-change events and illness (Holmes & Rahe, 1967) found a 75% correlation on a "Social Readjustment Rating Scale" between the number of life-change units and the severity of illness that followed within a six-month or one-year period (see Table 12-1). This correlation has been validated among pregnant women, leukemia patient families, and retirees. A highly significant correlation has also been identified between life-change scores and chronic disease as well as other disorders: leukemia, cancer, heart attack, schizophrenia, menstrual difficulties, and warts. Death of a spouse, marriage, retirement, divorce, residential move, job change, financial stress—enough of these events (both positive and negative) in one year could lead to illness.

TABLE 12-1. Holmes-Rahe life-change events for Seattle adults

	Life-change unit values
Family	
Death of spouse	100
Divorce	73
Marital separation	65
Death of close family member	63
Marriage	50
Marital reconciliation	45
Major change in health of family	44
Pregnancy	40
Addition of new family member	39
Major change in arguments with wife	35
Son or daughter leaving home	29
In-law troubles	29
Wife starting or ending work	26
Major change in family get-togethers	15
Personal	
Detention in jail	63
Major personal injury or illness	53
Sexual difficulties	39
Death of a close friend	37
Outstanding personal achievement	28
Start or end of formal schooling	26
Major change in living conditions	25
Major revision of personal habits	24
Changing to a new school	20
Change in residence	20
Major change in recreation	19
Major change in church activities	19
Major change in sleeping habits	16
Major change in eating habits	15
Vacation	13
Christmas	12
Minor violations of the law	11
Work	
Being fired from work	47
Retirement from work	45
Major business adjustment	39
Changing to different line of work	36
Major change in work responsibilities	29
Trouble with boss	23
Major change in working conditions	20
Financial	
Major change in financial state	38
Mortgage or loan over $10,000	31
Mortgage foreclosure	30
Mortgage or loan less than $10,000	17

SOURCE: Rahe, 1972.

NOTE: A reference value of 50 units was arbitrarily assigned to marriage, and each subject was then asked to assign proportional values to others.

A review of life changes and illness studies (Rahe & Arthur, 1978) identifies the essentially positive data that have accumulated from very diverse samples. They note that earlier studies (Holmes & Rahe, 1967; Rahe, Meyer, Smith, Kjaer, & Holmes, 1964) were simplistic and that, with growing supportive data for the general concept, it has become essential to "think in terms of the complexity of the social, psychological, and physiological variables involved" (Rahe & Arthur, 1978). These researchers recognize that this is a fertile field for interdisciplinary cooperation in the pursuit of the roles of the variables discussed earlier.

The variability among groups was identified in the analysis of data from 19 studies and was found "not only in their perceptions of the impact of life events, but also in the frequency of occurrence of these events" (Masuda & Holmes, 1978, p. 258). Differences were highlighted as they compared groups regarding "age, marital status, sex, socioeconomic status, ethnicity, education, culture and experiencing of event" (Masuda & Holmes, 1978, p. 258).

Studies and data concerning life changes and health appear particularly applicable to elders. The aged in contemporary society experience a great many changes, perhaps more than other groups: change in living arrangements, loss of job, decrease in income, loss of friends and relatives, a diminished self-image, and, in some, a significant decline of former physical capacities. These multiple changes represent mounting stressors that finally tax homeostasis and declining physiological and psychological capacities to the limit. The consequent breakdown of adaptability leads to illness, disease, and death (Kagan & Levi, 1974; Moss, 1973).

Wellness, wholism (holism), and health

Health has had many meanings, but the meaning closest to the growing strategy today is that which the World Health Organization (WHO) developed some time ago. Health is a "state of complete physical, mental and social well being, not merely the absence of disease or infirmity" (WHO, 1947). The emphasis on the whole person rather than any particular disease, keeps that definition contemporary. A multidimensional unity fits with the "emerging ecologic system model of man's nature and behavior" (Hoyman, 1975).

An important flaw in this WHO ideal concept of health is the suggested perfection, which is rarely attainable. Moreover, there are degrees of health. There are also different perceptions of "healthy," even in the face of one or two chronic diseases. Health is a positive quality of life, not a measure of the number of diseases. Health is a state involving the interaction and integration among body, mind, and spirit. The whole person—that is, the genome, lifestyle, all of life's experiences, and the public environment—takes part in health. However, the WHO ideal does serve as a goal, and the objectives in achieving good health serve as a framework for living.

Wellness is a state of becoming, and high-level wellness "means taking good care of your physical self, using your mind constructively, expressing your emotions effectively, being creatively involved with those around you, being concerned about your physical and psychological environment" (Leonard, 1977). The lack of illness does not necessarily indicate wellness. Even without physical symptoms, depression, tension, anxiety, and boredom can often contribute to biochemical and physical change and to the increased use of so-called stress relievers such as smoking, drinking, and overeating.

Holism cannot be looked upon as a new procedure or technique such as relaxation, herbal medicine, and so on, but rather as a distinct departure from the traditional way of practicing medicine and perceiving the patient. Perhaps the most difficult adjustment for some allied health professionals is the rejection of the "medical model." In this traditional, medical mold people first must become ill, then be diagnosed, and finally must let themselves be cured before a healthy status can be reached.

Holistic medicine, which is more than drugs and surgery, includes "prevention, life style modification, psychological counseling and supporting the patient as a responsible individual" (Pelletier, 1979, p. 38). Holistic health care engages the person as a partner with the doctor in the preservation of health and prevention of disease. The practice of self-care and acceptance of responsibility are essential ingredients. According to this philosophy, preventive medical care is the only effective, efficient care (Dychtwald, 1980).

PATHOLOGY

Aging—that is, physiological (and anatomical), psychological, and sociological changes with time—is not disease. However, at this period of expertise in aging, morbidity and mortality do go up with age (see Figures 12-4 and 12-5). It may not always be so. In this country today geriatrics is moving to a position of legitimacy as an area of inquiry, research, and practice. More talent, funds, and commitment will probably be applied to reduce further the morbidity and premature mortality now associated with age.

One of the major characteristic changes in relation to pathology with age is the shift from acute to chronic disease. "Eighty percent of the years of life lost to non-traumatic, premature deaths have been eliminated and most premature deaths are now due to the chronic diseases of the later years" (Fries, 1980). The greater number of cases of total disability in the later years is also due to the chronic diseases of the later years (Fries, 1980).

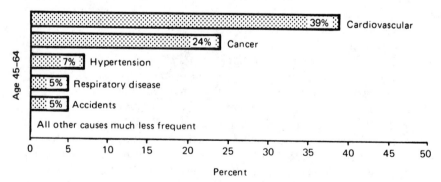

Figure 12-4. Common causes of death in middle age, as percent of total deaths between ages 45 and 64. (*From Smith & Bierman, 1973*)

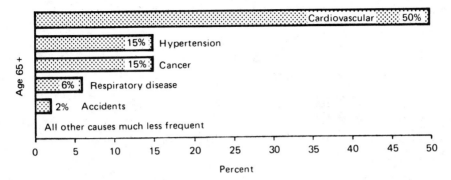

Figure 12-5. Common causes of death in old age (above age 65) as percent of the total. (*From Smith & Bierman, 1973*)

Since most chronic disorders actually begin development in the early years, clinically evident disease with its characteristic symptomology is likely to increase with age (see Figure 12-6). Fries (1980) and others discuss the logical possibility that chronic disease is preventable and that the most effective strategy is postponement, not cure (Weg, 1980). If the postponement is for a long time and through the natural life span of the individual, the disease is clinically prevented and eliminated (Fries, 1980). Increasingly, chronic illness can be postponed or eliminated by changes in lifestyle in such areas as nutrition, exercise, stress management, drug abuse, purposeful activities, social support systems, and so on (Fries, 1980; Richmond, 1979).

Additional research is sorely needed to establish norms for levels of systemic function in middle-aged and older persons. For example, many older persons experience an apparently normal increase in diastolic and systolic blood pressure. Some develop the pathological entity: hypertension. Similarly, the decrease in glucose tolerance, found in a number of older persons, may not necessarily be a prelude to diabetes. Continued study of the changing physiology enables identification of subtle clues in early nonpathological alterations, which could determine those persons who are at risk and likely to develop hypertension or diabetes. This screening effort makes possible a course of preventive intervention for a particular disease or illness. A brief overview of the more common diseases and/or serious dysfunctions will help to describe the population under consideration.

Obesity

Nutritional and metabolic dysfunctions frequently become apparent in the middle years and are carried over into old age: obesity, gallbladder disease, and anemia. These disturbances are important to correct, not only to alleviate the particular symptoms of discomfort and decreased efficiency, but also because of their interaction and possible antecedent roles in other dysfunctions such as diabetes mellitus, atherosclerosis, varicose veins, hernia, osteoarthritis, cardiovascular disease, peptic ulcer, and hypertension.

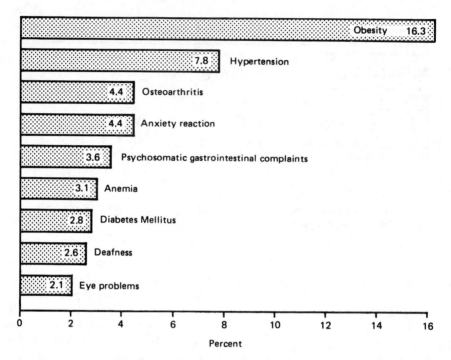

Figure 12-6. Disorders of middle age. (*From Sharpe & Keen, 1968*)

A sex difference exists in the lifelong pattern of weight and weight gain. Females generally arrive at a maximum average weight between ages 55 and 64 and males between 35 and 54 (Stoudt, Damon, McFarland, & Roberts, 1965). The number of persons who are 20% or more above "best" weight increases with age up to a point and then drops close to the sixth decade (Goodhart & Shils, 1973). Overweight individuals experience increased mortality risk when obesity and hypertension coexist. Dr. Ralph Nelson, head of clinical nutrition at Mayo Clinic, blames overnutrition for reducing the life span (Dosti, 1974). An obese population appears to have an unusual concentration of afflictions (Weg, 1979). Nearly one half of 541 overweight subjects had one or more of a wide range of disorders and diseases, any one of which increases mortality risk. Overweight patients are also high risks for surgery as a result of respiratory difficulties, heightened frequency of thromboembolism, infection, and wound breakdown (Smith & Bierman, 1978).

Fadry, Fodor, Hejl, Braun, and Zcolanhona (1964) in Czechoslovakia showed that with an increase in meal frequency overweight, hypercholesterol, and diminished glucose tolerance tend to improve. A later study also found that the percentage of subjects with diagnosed ischemic heart disease decreased markedly with increased meal frequency (Fabry, Fodor, Hejl, Geizeronva, & Balcarova, 1968).

A current, relatively successful approach to the treatment of obesity and permanent weight reduction is behavior modification (Weg, 1979, pp. 34, 35). Although weight control in the past has had a strong identification with cosmetic need, it now 1979).

Clinical and research observations have recently put some emphasis on the potential consequences of undernutrition and low body weight among elders. The malnutrition of inadequate dietary intake has been implicated in a number of pathological states (Weg, 1980a). The elderly are frequently more at risk, not from obesity, but from the dangerously low margin of body weight available during a period of surgical or medical stress (Weg, 1980b). Very lean persons in the Framingham studies showed equal mortality with the obese (Sorlie, Gordon, & Kannel, 1980). In his research at the Gerontology Research Center, Andres has found that the degree of fat is not significant at all levels: the correlation with mortality and length of life is critical in instances of less than 10% body fat or more than 35%, whereas the values in between appear irrelevant (Andres, 1980).

Stress-induced and stress-related disease

The significant killers in American society—hypertension, cardiovascular disease, and cancer—appear to correlate strongly with stressful lifestyles and particular stressors. These diseases and others will be examined individually for their incidence, nature, and impact among older persons. However, a more general discussion of the role of environmental stress in disease and its biochemical and physiological consequences may help in exploring probable mechanism(s) involved.

Stress is not easily defined. Early in the 20th century Cannon's description of the "fight or flight" response put stress clearly in the capacity category of an organism. In 1946 Selye continued this approach and made famous the meaning of stress as an adaptive capacity (Harvard Medical School Letter, 1979a). The often predictable cluster of body responses includes shallow, rapid breathing; muscle tension; dramatic rise in blood pressure; and an accelerated heart rate. Recently, the term *stress* has been used to describe the gamut of social or psychological stimuli that could call out such body responses.

Common acute illnesses such as a tension/migraine headache or a digestive upset are rather easily perceived as related to stress-filled situations. It is more difficult to accept the connection between stress and the major chronic diseases such as cardiovascular disease and cancer. The cause and effect relationship continues to elude the clinician, researcher, and patient in such disorders as asthma, allergies, ulcers, colitis, and migraine.

The earlier discussion of life changes and health is one dimension of the stress/disease interaction. Another dimension involves the neuronal and hormonal body responses and the accompanying, often resultant biochemical and electrical alterations. The stressor—whether emotional (tragedy, excitement, or fear) or physical (tactile, painful, odiferous, pressure, or biochemical)—initiates a sequence of events. Recognition of stress in the brain is quickly transformed for transmission to the endocrine system, which responds with measurable hormonal changes in pituitary adrenocorticotrophic hormone (ACTH), adrenal corticoids, adrenal medullary norepinephrine (noradrenalin), and epinephrine (adrenalin). As the concentration of these hormones reaches a threshold level for various target organs, the changing bio-chemistry can be monitored by measuring the mobilization of additional glucose, cholesterol, and fatty acids from the liver into the blood.

Daily, ordinary happenings—for example, a conversation about a troublesome event or an accountant hard at work with tax returns—can effect an increase in serum cholesterol (Tanner, 1976). Smoking, specifically nicotine, acts as a stimulant to the central nervous system (CNS), which releases increased norepinephrine, triggering higher serum cholesterol and increased blood pressure.

Elimination of all stress in postindustrial societies is not possible, necessary, or desirable. When stress is intermittent and positively resolved, it can function to in-crease appropriate raw materials and energy necessary to cope with the requirements of the situation. The greatest hazard exists in the persistence of unrelenting, unresolved stressful situations. In managing the stressful response to change progress can be made to minimize any negative consequences.

Hypertension

Blood pressure is labile—that is, responsive to body and environmental needs. Therefore, the term *hypertension* should be used primarily when there is a consistent pattern of elevated blood pressure. High blood pressure is a major risk factor in cardio-vascular disease. Excessive weight and high salt intake appear to contribute signifi-cantly to the risk of hypertension. About three quarters of the congestive heart failure patients appear to have uncontrolled hypertension (Castelli, 1978). The Framingham study (Kannel & Sorlie, 1975) found that systolic pressure is as "predictive as diastolic of coronary heart disease," and the risk increases with age (Castelli, 1978, p. 48). If such "at risk" individuals are identified early and treated, the number of congestive heart failure patients can be reduced. Changes in dietary intake, reduction in salt intake, loss of weight, and/or the use of drugs are among those steps that have been helpful. A blood pressure goal of 140/90 can be a guideline in hypertension manage-ment. Hypertension, diabetes, and abnormalities in serum lipids are correlated with an increased risk of cerebrovascular disease. Stroke appears earlier in hypertensive patients (Robbins, 1978).

A preventive approach in the middle and older years might take its cue from the recent decline in death rates from coronary heart disease and cerebrovascular disease (Page & Friend, 1978; Walker, 1977). Some experts attribute this drop to change in lifestyle and therapeutic techniques such as relaxation, meditation, and biofeedback (Harvard Medical School Newsletter, 1979b).

Coronary heart disease (CHD)

The Framingham study, which was begun in 1949, has emphasized that a number of the major risk factors are at work in the older population. This suggests that early preventive approach or appropriate management factors could result in a postpone-ment, or at least the minimization of the symptomology of CHD. The study identified the following as important risk factors subject to intervention: hypertension, ele-vated blood lipids (including cholesterol), cigarette smoking, diabetes mellitus, left ventricular hypertrophy, and hyperuricemia (Gordon, Castelli, & Hjortland, 1977a; Kannel, 1976; Tall & Small, 1978). Not all lipoproteins are harmful; high density lipoprotein (HDL), as contrasted with low density lipoprotein (LDL), shows a strong negative correlation with coronary heart disease incidence in both sexes (Gordon, Castelli, & Hjortland, 1977a).

Elders at risk are as responsive as younger persons to attention in the preservation of normal blood pressure, heart function, and cholesterol levels. Modifications in diet, exercise, and stress management can alter the symptoms and prognosis (Castelli, 1978).

Cancer

Cancer is generally described as a disease of older people, and the cancer incidence rate rises with increasing age (Holmes & Hearne, 1981). Incidence provides a more satisfactory measure of cancer in the later years than mortality rate, since the death of many elders is often reported as due to various other diseases (cardiovascular, respiratory, and so on). This is particularly true if the malignancy is asymptomatic (Lew, 1978). The probability that a person will experience cancer during the next five years is 1 in 700 for the 25-year-old, and 1 in 14 for the 65-year-old (Pitot, 1977). Age does appear to be a risk factor.

A number of mechanisms have been suggested to explain the increased incidence with age:

1. Effects of a slowly acting carcinogen take time.
2. Prolonged "development time" is necessary for growth to be observable.
3. Prolonged preexposure time is required.
4. Failing immune surveillance capacity is characteristic of increased age.

In general, elders are affected by the same carcinogens as other age groups: ionizing and solar radiation, chemicals, viruses, and sex hormones. All are either enhanced or minimized by nutrition, immune state, and detoxification mechanisms (Shimkin, 1976). Different cancers demonstrate varied time periods between initiation and recognition of the malignancy. Some require only a single dose of carcinogen (for example, lung tumors in mice after a single dose of urethane); others require several or continuous doses. The "incubation" period between can be shortened by cocarcinogens, promotors, inhibition of the immune response, and/or an excessive, opulent diet (Shimkin, 1976).

A diet rich in excess fats, particularly unsaturated fats, increases the incidence of tumors (mammary carcinoma). Vitamin A deficiency may contribute to an increased risk of cancer in cigarette smokers (Wynder, 1977). Epidemiologic evidence suggests that nutrition and diet, both in excess and/or deficiency, are importantly involved in the pathogenesis of some cancers (Wynder, 1976). Male sex hormone appears to support the development of hepatomas in younger animals; additional female hormone estrogen (estrogen replacement therapy) has been implicated in uterine cancer and possibly breast cancer. However, an examination of former studies has found "no association between exogenous estrogens and endometrial cancer" (Horowitz & Feinstein, 1977).

Malignancy in old age (the 65 and older group) now ranks third as a cause of death. Carcinoma of lung, colon, rectum, prostate, stomach, and breast represents almost two thirds of total cancer mortality. Cancer often presents itself differently in the old and may be obscured by other chronic diseases. For example, cancer may present as anorexia, anemia, weight loss, weakness, general malaise, and/or fatigue—that is, symptoms frequently assigned to "aging." A loss of competence, a decrease in mobility, and the general loss of drive and interest, which are also possible cancer symptoms, may be assigned to depression, early dementia, or aging. Such inappropriate diagnoses highlight the need for geriatric training among health professionals.

An important and unique investigation conducted by the American Cancer Society is recording the "mortality experiences of a cohort of 13,500 persons," who in 1975 would have reached 88 years or older for the male and 90 years or older for the female. The data (from July 1, 1960 to June 20, 1972) include family history, personal history of disease, physical complaints, occupational experiences, personal habits, diets, and so on. Individuals who survived to advanced age without contracting cancer will be characterized to provide a valuable profile for use in prevention behavior (Lew, 1978).

Immunity dysfunction and disorder

Salient features of the older immune system are the decreased efficiency of the antigen/antibody response, the diminished serum concentration of thymic hormones and particular lymphocytes, and the increase in the "reaction against or rejection of body constituents" (that is, autoimmunity).

Some researchers (Bylinsky, 1976; Makinodan, Perkins, & Chen, 1971; Walford, 1967) suggest that with the declining immune capacity, cancerous cells, earlier eliminated by an effective immune system (immune surveillance) are able to "take hold" in the later years when the lymphocytes may fail to recognize the cancerous cells as nonself.

Autoimmune diseases such as pernicious anemia, Addison's disease, and chronic thyroiditis show increased incidence. An increase in the circulating immunoglobins (IgC and IgA) may be related to a decline in cognitive abilities (Roseman & Buckley, 1975). Blumenthal (1976) reports on his own and his colleagues' studies, which found an accumulation of brain reactive antibodies with age—and binding of these antibodies to neurons in a sample of human subjects of various ages. He found a significant increase in antineuron antibodies and neuron binding with age, which damaged and finally inactivated these neurons. Another interesting suggestion is that a "break in the blood-brain barrier is an essential antecedent to the expression of an immune response in the CNS" (Blumenthal, 1976, p. 328). Possibly, the disruption of this barrier injured some of the neurons near the break, causing a release of intracellular proteins which stimulated the immune response. The autoantibodies then formed bound to additional neurons.

The changes in the older immune system, like the neuronal changes, are a threat to the integrity and health maintenance activities of the whole organism.

Arthritis

Eighty percent of recently retired persons have "some rheumatic complaint," and four out of every ten elders need treatment (Kolodny & Klipper, 1978). One of the many earmarks of increased individual differences with age is that arthritis among elders is not a single disease entity. Included in the group of related diseases are rheumatoid arthritis (inflammatory), osteoarthritis (degenerative joint disease), gout, connective tissue diseases, polymyalgia, osteoporosis, and others (Kolodny & Klipper, 1978). Clinicians are of the opinion that "all patients over 60 have roentgenographic or physical evidence of arthritis," but only 25% of the females and 15% of the males are symptomatic (Rodman, McEwen, & Wallace, 1973).

Although etiology of rheumatic disorders is still unclear, therapeutic progress has been made concerning pain control and joint mobility (Howell, Sapolsky, Pita, & Woessner, 1976; Smythe, 1975). Countless anti-inflammatory drugs, including gold suspension, aspirin and exogenous cortisone derivatives are used to minimize the inflammation and pain. Mild exercise, heat and cold are variously employed to maintain joint mobility and strength. Further progress is needed, both in the identification of pathogenesis and the development of therapy to postpone or effectively eliminate this major cause of limited activity among older persons.

Osteoporosis and periodontal disease

Age-related bone loss, as found in osteoporosis, is most probably not a function of any single pathological or aging process, but rather the result of a number of interacting changes with time (Garn, 1975). Neuronal, hormonal, digestive, renal, and nutritional activities, which are related to bone synthesis and breakdown and which all impact on the individual genetic base, are subject to preventive intervention in the early years and rehabilitation in the later years (Weg, 1979).

Age of onset appears to be decreasing, and evidence is mounting for the gradual beginning of osteoporosis at approximately 25 years of age, rather than the sudden development in middle or old age (Rose, 1970). There is no simple definition of this disease, and diagnosis is problematic, as evidenced by the lack of symptomology in the so-called normal person who may have bone loss comparable to a person with diagnosed osteoporosis (Jowsey, 1976).

This painful disease, a loss in total bone mass, frequently results in later middle and old age in diminished height, instability in maintenance of normal posture, and susceptibility to fracture. Osteoporosis may be found in as many as 30% of people aged 65 and over and is four times more common in women than in men.

The etiology of osteoporosis is unclear, and the results of studies are not definitive. Although at one time it was thought to be estrogen dependent (with increasing incidence in the postmenopausal woman), some estrogen-treated women and men are stabilized while others are not (Bartter, 1973). Some research suggests that lifelong dietary habits may be more important than estrogen in maintenance of bone structure (Lutwak, 1976). Good results have been reported with increased dietary calcium, which promotes protein retention and activation of osteoblasts. A genetic factor may determine the porosity of the bone, since females tend to be born with light, more porous bones. Those with more porous bones may be more susceptible to any estrogen-primed alteration in calcium metabolism.

The therapy of choice at this time involves increased dietary calcium, vitamin D metabolites, fluoride, and, occasionally, estrogen (Jowsey, 1976; Weg, 1981b). More recently, vitamin K has been added to the therapy. Inactivity and stress appear to enhance bone resorption, whereas exercise generally benefits retention of calcium and osteoblastic activity.

Periodontal disease leads to the loss of teeth in about 35 million people, most of whom are older persons (Baird & Kelly, 1970). Edentulous persons tend to be mal-nourished and often behave similarly to those with poorly fitting dentures. Earlier eating patterns may be altered and more soft, high carbohydrate food consumed (Lutwak, 1976). Periodontitis may be an early or concomitant expression of osteo-porosis. Confirmation of the relationship between periodontitis and osteoporosis was found in retrospective observations of patients with periodontal disease—that is, vertebral osteoporosis existed (Krook, Lutwak, Whalen, Henrickson, Lesser, & Uris, 1972). Interestingly, most patients who were diagnosed with severe axial osteoporosis also were endentulous. Studies continue to test the hypothesis that human periodontal disease could be a form of nutritional osteoporosis. Lutwak (1976) suggests that the bone demineralization is consequent to "chronic dietary deficiency of calcium and chronic dietary excess of phosphorus."

Pulmonary disease

Chronic bronchitis, fibrosis, and emphysema are manifestations of chronic obstructive pulmonary disease, which increases with age and may lead to disability and death in old age. Four times as many men as women have succumbed to these diseases, probably because of a combination of age changes in the lung connective tissue and the continued assaults from cigarette smoking and air pollution in the community and at work. Should these pathological tissue changes continue unchecked, death may come with the additional insult from infections, right ventricular heart failure, and severe hypoxia (Smith, Bierman, & Robinson, 1978).

Allergic responses appear to increase with age, and hypersensitivity to bacterial products and pollutants often begins during the middle years and may become a cause of disability. Asthma, if persistent, may contribute to pulmonary emphysema and respiratory insufficiency. Drug allergies in particular show greater incidence with age. These may be, in part, a function of the decrements in physiological capacities, but they are no doubt also related to the growing use and frequent abuse of multiple drug agents, especially sedatives, tranquilizers, antidepressants, and antibiotics.

The realization that there is an interaction between drug action and declining physiological capacities, together with the rise in allergic reactions, has stimulated increased research and informed awareness related to the prescription and administra-tion of drugs to older persons (Roe, 1976; Weg, 1978).

Drugs and changing physiology

Out of a per capita health cost for fiscal year 1977 of $1745 for those aged 65 and over, 7%, or $121, was spent for drugs (Brotman, 1980). Serious abuse of drug use in the older population unfortunately is often a result of physician prescription, ignorance, and neglect. Faulty drug administration is well documented, especially as a result of nursing home investigations.

A 1970 General Accounting Office (GAO) audit entitled "Continuing Problems in Providing Nursing Home Care and Prescribed Drugs under the Medicaid Program in

California" provided frightening details about faulty drug administration practices; these are further explained in *Old Age: The Last Segregation* (Townsend, 1971). Records of 106 MediCal patients at 14 nursing homes for one month revealed "311 doses were administered in quantities in excess of those prescribed; 1,210 prescribed doses were not administered." Unfortunately, GAO auditors in 1966 reported similar abuses related to nursing home care for California welfare recipients. Too often the doctors come in once a month, sign without reading the daily reports, and fail to evaluate the total therapeutic regimen for a particular person.

The already lowered capacity for homeostatic control increases the possibility of undesirable side effects. A hypotensive drug, frequently important in the treatment of hypertension, may result in a pressure too low to deliver adequate blood to all parts of the body, especially the brain, and may lead to confusion, forgetfulness, and fainting. Generally speaking, most drugs, even at reduced dosage levels, may be more active in older people. In view of the overall decrease of functional capacities, the greater individual differences, and the drug interaction with particular organ systems, the choice of drugs is complex and at best must be made with regard for making the most of whatever potential and capacities do remain.

The frequently marginal nutritional status of older persons is at further risk in face of the widespread polypharmacy (Weg, 1978). Drugs can displace nutrients from their usual binding sites, combine with the particular nutrient, or both (Roe, 1976). This contributes to an increased potential for malnutrition. Other drugs can cause an altered sense of taste, anorexia, changes in metabolic rate of absorbed nutrients, in the rate of transport, storage, and elimination (Hartshorn, 1977). All the drug-induced changes effectively contribute to malnutrition and trigger observable symptoms such as confusion, fatigue, and arrythmia, which are usually labeled aging.

Drug-related hypovitaminoses (B complex, ascorbic acid, and vitamins A, D, and K) and altered availability, excretion, and possibly absorption of minerals are measurable. Drugs are both a benefit and a hazard in human health and disease. Therefore, prudent use of drugs based on current knowledge of drugs and aging is essential to minimize iatrogenesis—the drug-induced illness—possible invalidism, and premature death (Lamy & Vestal, 1978; Weg, 1978; Weg, 1979).

NORMAL AGING

The promise that greater numbers of persons will grow old with little or no pathology is suggested by the presence of active, moderately healthy older persons in this society, and by the existence of even small pockets of relatively long-lived working peoples of the world. With the victory over infectious diseases and infant mortality in the past century, the elimination of the chronic diseases associated with old age would appear to be the next major task for biomedical research in the private and governmental sectors. Even now, at the birth of geriatrics in this country and without formal recognition of the uniqueness of the older patient, each cohort of elderly is healthier and longer living (Brotman, 1980; Weg, 1981).

Life expectancy at birth has increased significantly since 1900—when 47 years was the average as compared with 74.3 years today (for males 70.5 and females 78.1).

But life expectancy at age 65 (maximum life span) has risen only 4.4 years—16.3 years today as compared with 11.9 years at the turn of the century. Approximately 14,000 centenarians live in America, according to a "sample study" of persons covered by Medicare (Brotman, 1980).

If efforts to modify lifestyles and the rate of aging are successful and if current aging research makes modest progress, the chronic illnesses discussed in the preceding pages will be postponed, the average age of observable and meaningful disability and/or infirmity will be raised, and the morbidity and mortality curves will become even more rectangular (Fries, 1980). In the future increasing numbers of elders may die of "old age" (Fries, 1980; Weg, 1975).

Longevity predictors and long-lived peoples

The common predictors for increased longevity (and they would appear related as well to the improved quality of life) were summarized by two independent researchers, Chebotarev in the USSR and Palmore in the United States (Chebotarev, 1971; Palmore & Jeffers, 1971; Sachuk, 1970). These predictors were not related to heredity (as in the choice of long-lived parents and grandparents) nor in a major way dependent on absence of disease. The four predictors were as follows: (1) maintain a role in the society, (2) hold a positive view of life and positive self-concept, (3) have moderately good physical function, (4) and be a nonsmoker. Although the results of these studies have been questioned, the concept remains attractive and becomes even more so with the recent emphasis on patient involvement in health maintenance and coping strategies.

These predictors fit in well with the information that has been gathered and examined concerning the long-lived populations in Abkhasia of the Georgian Soviet Republic (Benet, 1976; Leaf, 1973a, 1973b), in the land of the Hunza of the Karkoram Range in Kashmir (Leaf, 1973a, 1973b), and in the Andean village of Vilcabamba in Ecuador (Davies, 1973).

The lifestyle of these peoples is predictable. Each person has a task and is expected to work at something during his or her life span, although hours are reduced as age advances. There is no rocking-chair philosophy in Abkhasia. Work is rigorous and outdoors in the mountainous terrain.

The low-calorie diet is generally simple, low in saturated animal fat and meat, and high in fruit and vegetables. Alcoholic beverages and nicotine are absent or used in only small amounts. Little pathology has been recorded. When it does exist, disease has seldom been incapacitating or necessitated hospitalization. Other characteristics, which appear logically related to the active life, include high energy, motivation for living, physical activity, sexual expression, and minimal environmental stress.

Many American and Soviet scientists have correctly suggested that an absence of long-term record keeping, inaccurate birth records, and some age exaggeration in claims should lead to caution in the evaluation of these reports. Leaf (1978) revisited Vilcabamba several years ago and found confirmation of age exaggeration. Two other scientists also visited Vilcabamba and reviewed the baptismal, marriage, and death records to provide necessary data for a study of bone calcium loss in old age. The records documented the oldest Vilcabamban to be 96, not 140 or 150, and that the addition of 10–20 years to actual age began in the 7th decade (Mazess & Forman, 1979).

Even with the errors and exaggerations, these peoples are visibly old yet relatively free of the chronic diseases of the developed, industrialized countries. Perhaps they are 100 years old, rather than 128, or 96, rather than 148 years. Even so, they may provide useful information about aging and health maintenance applicable to health needs generally.

What can be done

A careful examination of functional capacities emphasizes the continuum of life. The level of capacity available at 70 and 80 is a consequence of all that has gone before: heredity in interaction with human and physical environments, nutrition, exercise, coping with stress, and intellectual and affective pursuits.

Manipulation of the environment. It would seem possible and desirable to alter those factors in the environment that appear to contribute to the kind and degree of functional changes and diseases that have been discussed. In a number of the organ systems a percentage of the loss appears to be due to disuse or misuse, and thus susceptible to control or at least retardation.

Recent studies on aging and the aged suggest the association, if not causal relationships, between particular aspects of the environment and physiological dysfunction, psychology, and frank pathology (see Table 12-2). These relationships include many factors already mentioned and attest to the interdependent nature of the quality of life.

Available information related to these environmental variables suggests a number of possibilities for change.

Exercise. Ubiquitous joggers, so-called health spas, and ads for exercise mats and machines attest to the shift from a recent inactive middle-aged/aging existence to a more active life with regular exercise as an integral part of living.

Studies have documented the fact that continued use and exercise of many physiological capacities prolong retention of those capacities (Bierman & Hazzard, 1973; deVries, 1970, 1974; Freeman, 1965; Monkerud, 1978; Cantwell, 1978; Paffenbarger, Hale, Brand & Hyde, 1977). As with other environmental factors, exercise does affect various organ systems: size and strength of muscles, flexibility and pain of joints, efficiency and health of heart and limbs, blood circulation, rate of nutrient metabolism, and amount of body fat. The measurable improvement in aerobic ventilation and usable O_2 and the improvement in cardiovascular efficiency maximize the limited capacities of individuals who are already at risk with coronary disease. The suggestion that atheromatous plaque formation is slowed by exercise identifies another controllable risk factor for coronary artery disease that can be reduced significantly (Stamler & Epstein, 1972). Exercise decreases serum cholesterol and blood pressure and slows the blood clotting rate. This is measurable evidence of the impact of exercise on stress.

The absence of exercise or minimal exercise, which is common in illness or continual bed rest, can stimulate or exacerbate a number of destructive age-related

TABLE 12-2. Physiological dysfunction and lifestyle

Disorders/disease	*Lifestyle factors*
Arteriosclerosis, atherosclerosis, coronary disease, and hypertension	High fat, highly refined carbohydrate diet, high salt; obesity; sedentary lifestyle; cigarette smoking; heavy drinking, alcoholism; unresolved, continual stress; personality type
Cerebrovascular accidents	Sedentary lifestyle; low fiber, high fat or high salt diet; heavy drinking, alcoholism (which contribute to atherosclerosis, arteriosclerosis and hypertension, risk factors for cerebrovascular accidents)
Osteoporosis and periodontitis	Malnutrition—inadequate calcium, protein, vitamin K, fluoride, magnesium and vitamin D metabolite; lack of exercise; immobility; for women, sex steroid starvation
Chronic pulmonary disease	Cigarette smoking; air pollution; stress; sedentary habits
Obesity	Low caloric output (sedentary), high caloric intake; high stress levels; heavy drinking, alcoholism; low self-esteem
Cancer	Possible correlation with personality type; stress; exposure to environmental carcinogens over a long period of time; nutritional deficiencies and excesses; radiation; sex steroid hormones; food additives; cigarette smoking; occupational carcinogens (for example, asbestos); occult viruses; diminution of immune response (immune surveillance)
Dementia and pseudo-dementia	Malnutrition; long illness and bed rest; drug abuse (polypharmacy, iatrogenesis); anemia; other organ system disease; bereavement; social isolation
Sexual dysfunction	Ignorance (the older individual and society at large); societal stereotypic attitudes; early socialization; inappropriate or no partner; drug effects (for example, antihypertensive drugs); psychogenic origin; long periods of abstinence; serious systemic disease

processes. These processes are recognizable as those physiological changes with age discussed earlier: a lower cardiac output, a decrease in blood volume returned to heart, a drop in blood cell formation, loss of calcium from long bones, accumulation of fluid in tissues, and a sluggish gastrointestinal tract.

deVries has demonstrated that an exercise regimen of 6-8 weeks regains some of the muscle strength and tone among older men aged 60-90 years, provides more energy, diminishes fatigue and tension, heightens libido and increases sexual activity, and generally increases the feeling of well-being (Adams & deVries, 1973; deVries, 1975).

Diet and nutrition. Normal, healthy growth and development of infants and children require an adequate, and at times, an optimal nutritional status. Increasing age may require more careful assessment and food choices as the decreasing systemic efficiency makes nutrient balance and wellness more difficult to maintain (Weg, 1979; Weg, 1980a; Young, 1978).

Stressful situations common among older persons (for example, illness, bereavement, depression, loss of work status and familiar living quarters, and so on) tend to build on any existing mild nutrient deficiency. Thus, requirements for particular nutrients may increase even further.

Correlations between health status and the westernized diet are supported by biomedical and behavioral investigations. The current American inadequate dietary intake, whether in excess or undernutrition, is correlated with the major chronic diseases (morbidity and mortality) that so frequently accompany the late middle and older years. The implication of this diet in the diseases of civilization—atherosclerosis, coronary heart disease, hypertension, diabetes, and cancer—is particularly significant since all of the foregoing occur with increasing morbidity and mortality in the middle and later years (Almy, 1976; Berg, 1976; Bierman, 1976; Gresham, 1976; Watkin, 1979; Weg, 1980; Weg, 1980a).

The typical American diet remains low in fiber and whole grains; high in fats and refined carbohydrates; and deficient in fresh fruits, vegetables, and proteins with high concentration of the essential amino acids. This kind of diet is inadequate in vitamins, minerals, essential amino acids, roughage, and energy.

Few controlled studies have tested causal relationships. However, epidemiological data indicate that countries with the so-called westernized diet experience a high incidence of these diseases (for example, the United States, Sweden, and Japan). On the other hand, those countries and areas in which diets are high in fiber, whole grains, fresh fruits, and vegetables and relatively low in refined sugars and fats have a low incidence of these diseases (for example, Africa, Ecuador, and Abkhasia).

During the period from 1910 to 1976 the American diet underwent significant change—from complex carbohydrates and fresh fruits and vegetables to fast foods, creamy foods, highly refined flour and sugar, richly marbled meats, sugared cereals, and fewer fresh fruits and vegetables. Total fat consumption increased to 45% of total calories; complex carbohydrates dropped from 37% to 21% of daily caloric intake, and there was a rise of 50% in refined sweeteners (mostly sugar) from 12% to 18% of total calories (Center for Science in the Public Interest, 1978).

Researchers who reviewed American governmental and nongovernmental agency nutritional reports found the most frequent deficiencies and borderline low levels among older persons included the following: minerals, calcium, iron, magnesium, and vitamins A, C, B complex (thiamin, niacin, and folic acid), as well as serum proteins. From these data, it is probable that large numbers of older persons are nutritionally at risk (Beauchene & Davis, 1979; Weg, 1979).

Acute confusional states, learning difficulties and depression among elders have been identified as nutrition dependent in a number of studies (Andrews, 1968; Whanger, 1973; Wurtman & Growdon, 1978; Weg, 1980b). Dietary intake as intervention takes on special importance in the areas of cognition, emotional stability, and dementia.

A recent report suggests that the American diet may be undergoing another, more positive, alteration. Since 1964, there has been a decrease in the use of tobacco, in the per capita consumption of animal fat and oils, butter, liquid milk, cream, eggs and an increase in the consumption of vegetable fats and oils (Walker, 1977). The American consuming public may have responded seriously, albeit slowly, to the Surgeon General's 1963 warning about tobacco use and to the 1964 dietary recommendations of the American Heart Association to reduce the intake of saturated fats and cholesterol. Data on age-specific cerebrovascular and coronary decline in mortality rates for the period between 1963 and 1975 appear to support the idea of a public receptive to health advice and information.

In view of the many related factors impacting on nutritional status—reduced income, living alone, depression, other illness—and long-standing suboptimal eating patterns, many older persons are likely to develop marginal, subclinical malnutrition (Exton-Smith, 1973; McGovern, 1970; Mayer, 1974; Weg, 1979). The observable effects of a prolongation of this state include general malaise, listlessness, fatigue, headache, insomnia, irritability, loss of body weight and appetite, confusion, failing memory, and anxiety (Bender, 1971; Clements, 1975; Weg, 1979; Weg, in press). Such symptoms have long been considered an inevitable part of aging and have therefore gone undiagnosed and untreated.

Other issues concerning age and nutrition, which also affect various organ systems, are under discussion in the literature and in the field. These topics cover such concerns as recommended daily dietary allowances, low caloric dietary intake, protein requirements, deficiencies of regulatory substances (vitamins, minerals), food and drug interactions, and diet and brain function. Discussions are presented in greater detail in a number of articles and chapters (Brin & Bauernfeind, 1978; Fernstrom, 1979; Scrimshaw & Young, 1976; Weg, 1979, 1980; Weg, 1981b; Young, 1978).

Food is not the elixir of youth nor the singular road to longevity and health. But adequate, appropriate nutrition remains a primary agent largely in the control of each individual for enhancement of health and quality of life.

Cigarette smoking. There is now documented excess morbidity and mortality related to smoking in oral and lung cancer, other pulmonary disease, and cardiovascular disease. There appears to be a positive correlation between smoking and another disorder related directly to the effect of nicotine on peripheral blood vessels. Cessation or reduction in smoking have both been demonstrated to decrease excess morbidity and premature death (Smith, Bierman, & Robinson, 1978).

Stress. The development of coping strategies and stress management remains difficult in the competitive American work-oriented society. Lifestyle alterations suggested earlier often compete unsuccessfully with the compulsive achievement and deadline psychology of the workplace and the home.

The serious dysfunctional consequences of stress for cardiovascular and affective health and for freedom from malignancy and cognitive decline are marked by an increase in stress-related hormones—adreno-corticoids, catecholamines, and sex hormones. These increases are recognizable in generalized metabolic effects and specific toxic effects on the heart muscle and blood vessels.

Absence of the stress of industrialized societies among the long-lived peoples and the absence or minimal level of organic disorders among them are persuasive clues in the continuing evaluation of the relationship between diseases and stress.

CONCLUSION

"Normal aging" remains an ideal or a goal that is not yet integrated into societal attitudes or the scientist's framework. Admittedly, decrements in physiological function do occur with time, but these changes are generally gradual and compatible with an active lifestyle. Longitudinal studies continue to clarify the image of the aged. Recent studies in lifestyle modifications (diet, exercise, and so on) have demonstrated that a portion of diminution in capacities with age is due to disuse and misuse rather than time. Data suggest that to the degree that people use, nourish, and extend remaining capacities, so will the body, mind, and spirit prosper. The emerging commitment of the allied health professions to geriatrics will help create positive attitudes and atmosphere essential to preventive whole person care.

The negative image of the old as invalid is a legacy born out of mythology and history. With altars built to youth and fear of age reinforced daily, there is no clear vision of the individuality and heterogeneity of human aging. Indeed, there have been and still are the ill, dependent, almost lifeless elderly who may fit part or all of the defeating imagery. However, there are increasingly larger numbers of older persons who live longer, enjoy better health and education, and are more vocal and determined to remain in the mainstream of society.

Human aging is comprehensible, but not if we study physiology, the psyche, the affect, the spirit, or social forces alone. The processes and people in aging are most knowable in the examination of the interaction of all these aspects in the men and women of later years.

No one theory, intervention, or incantation has proven to be the "magic bullet" to slow or eradicate aging. The reasonable direction would seem to be to continue disciplinary and multidisciplinary research into mechanism, to work toward a maintenance and promotion of optimum function that is possible into the later years, and to apply the growing knowledge of gerontology and geriatrics to all of the life span. Perhaps then it will be more possible to realize the words of Albert Sabin, aged 73, who described his hopes for the future as follows: man should not die "from cardiovascular disturbances, from malignancies, from senile psychosis and depression. My hope is that in the future we may die, ultimately, in good health" (Parrott, 1980).

REFERENCES

Adams, G. M., & deVries, H. A. Physiological effects of an exercise training regimen upon women aged 52–79. *Journal of Gerontology*, 1973, *28*(1), 50–55.

Adler, W. H., Jones, K. H., & Brock, M. A. Aging and immune function. In J. A. Behnke, C. E. Finch, & G. B. Moment (Eds.), *The biology of aging*. New York: Plenum Press, 1978.

Almy, T. B. The role of fiber in the diet. In M. Winick (Ed.), *Nutrition and aging*. New York: John Wiley and Sons, 1976.

Andres, R. Aging and Diabetes. *Medical Clinics of North America*, 1971, *55*(4), 835–846.

Andres, R. Personal communication, June 1980.

Andres, R., Swerdloff, R., & Tobin, J. D. Effect of age on plasma insulin response to hyperglycemia studies in man with a servo-control technique. *Proceedings of Eighth International Congress of Gerontology*, 1969, *1*: 36–39.

Andres, R., & Tobin, J. D. Endocrine systems. In C. E. Finch & L. Hayflick (Eds.), *Handbook of the biology of aging*. New York: Van Nostrand Reinhold, 1977.

Andrews, J. Aspects of malnutrition in the elderly. *Proceedings of the Nutrition Society*, 1968, *27*(1), 196–201.

Aslan, A. Principles of drug therapy. *Proceedings of the Ninth International Congress of Gerontology Symposia Reports*, 1972, *2*, 115–118.

Aslan, A. Theoretical and practical aspects of chemo-therapeutic techniques in the retardation of the aging process. In M. Rockstein, M. Sussman, & J. Chesky (Eds.), *Theoretical aspects of aging*. New York: Academic Press, 1974.

Baird, J. T. Jr., & Kelley, J. E. Need for dental care among adults, United States, 1960–1962. *National Center for Health Statistics, Series II*, 1970, *36*, 1–9. Washington, D.C.: Public Health Service, U.S. Government Printing Office.

Bartter, F. C. Bone as a target organ: Toward a better definition of osteoporosis. *Perspectives in Biology and Medicine*, 1973, *16*(2), 215–231.

Beauchene, R. E., & Davis, T. A. The nutritional status of aged in the U.S.A. *Age*, 1979, *2*(1), 23–28.

Belloc, N. B. Relationship of health practices and mortality. *Preventive Medicine*, 1973, *2*(1), 67–81.

Belloc, N. B., & Breslow, L. Relationship of physical health status and health practices. *Preventive Medicine*, 1972, *1*(3), 409–421.

Bender, A. E. Nutrition of the elderly. *Royal Society of Health Journal (England)*, 1971, *91*(3), 115–121.

Benet, S. *How to live to be 100: The life style of the people of the Caucasus*. New York: Dial, 1976.

Berg, J. W. Nutrition and cancer. *Seminars in Oncology*, 1976, *2*(1), 189–195.

Bierman, E. L. Obesity, carbohydrate and lipid interactions in the elderly. In M. Winick (Ed.), *Nutrition and aging*. New York: John Wiley and Sons, 1976.

Bierman, E. L., & Hazzard, W. R. Old age, including death and dying. In D. W. Smith & E. L. Bierman (Eds.), *The biologic ages of man*. Philadelphia, Pa.: W. B. Saunders, 1973.

Birren, J. E., Butler, R. N. Greenhouse, S. W., Sokoloff, L., & Yarrow, M. R. *Human aging: A biological and behavioral study*. Washington, D.C.: U.S. Government Printing Office, 1963 (1971).

Bittles, A. H., Fulder, S. J., Grant, E. C., & Nicholls, M. R. The effect of ginseng on lifespan and stress responses in mice. *Gerontology*, 1979, *25*(3), 125–131.

Blumenthal, H. T. Immunological aspects of the aging brain. In R. D. Terry & S. Gershon (Eds.), *Aging: Neurobiology of aging* (Vol. 3). New York: Raven Press, 1976.

Brin, M., & Bauernfeind, J. C. Vitamin needs of the elderly. *Postgraduate Medicine*, 1978, *63*(3), 155–159, 162–163.

Brody, H. & Vijayashankar, N. Anatomical changes in the nervous system. In C. E. Finch & L. Hayflick (Eds.), *The handbook of the biology of aging*. New York: Van Nostrand Reinhold, 1977.

Brotman, H. *Every ninth American.* Prepared for Developments in Aging, Special Committee on Aging, United States Senate, 1980.

Burch, G. E., Cohn, A. E., & Neumann, C. A study of the rate of water loss from the surface of the fingertips and toe tips of normal and senile subjects and patients with arterial hypertension. *American Heart Journal, 1942, 23,* 185–196.

Butler, R. N. *Why survive? Being old in America.* New York: Harper and Row, 1975.

Bylinsky, G. Science is on the trail of the fountain of youth. *Fortune, 1976, 94*(1), 134–140.

Cantwell, J. D. Running. *Journal of American Medical Association, 1978, 239,* 357–359.

Cassel, J. Psychosocial processes and stress: Theoretical formulation. *International Journal of Health Services, 1974, 4*(3), 471–482.

Castelli, W. P. CHD risk factors. In W. Reichel (Ed.), *The geriatric patient.* New York: H. P. Publishing Co., 1978.

Center for Science in the Public Interest. The changing American diet (1910–1976). *New York Times,* 9 July 1978.

Chebotarev, D. Fight against old age. *Gerontologist, 1971, 11*(4), 359–361.

Cicero, Marcus Tullus. *De Senectute (On old age)* (F. Copley, trans.). Ann Arbor: University of Michigan, 1967.

Clements, F. W. Nutrition 7: Vitamin and mineral supplementation. *Medical Journal of Australia, 1975, 1*(19), 595–599.

Comfort, A. *The biology of senescence* (3rd ed.). New York: Elsevier, 1979.

Davidson, J. Reported in J. L. Marx, Hormones and their effects in aging body. *Science, 1979, 206* (4420), 805–806.

Davies, D. A shangri-la in Ecuador. *New Scientist,* 1 February 1973, 236–238.

deVries, H. A. Physiological effects of an exercise training regimen upon men aged 52–88. *Journal of Gerontology, 1970, 25*(4), 325–336.

deVries, H. A. *Vigor regained.* Englewood Cliffs, N.J.: Prentice-Hall, 1974.

deVries, H. A. Physiology of exercise and aging. In D. S. Woodruff & J. E. Birren (Eds.), *Aging: Scientific perspectives and social issues.* New York: Van Nostrand Reinhold, 1975.

Dosti, R. Overnutrition blamed for shortening of the lifespan. *Los Angeles Times,* 25 April 1974, *P.* VI, pp.1, 8.

Dubos, R. *Man adapting.* New Haven: Yale University Press, 1965.

Dychtwald, K. From remarks on health care at the Western Gerontological meeting, San Diego, March 1980.

Epstein, M. Effects of aging on the kidney. *Federation Proceedings, 1979, 38*(2), 168–172.

Exton-Smith, A. N. Nutritional deficiencies in the elderly. In A. N. Howard & I. McLean (Eds.), *Nutritional deficiencies in modern society.* London: Baird Newman, 1973.

Fabry, P., Fodor, J., Hejl, Z., Braun, T., & Zcolanhona, K. The frequency of meals: Its relationship to overweight, hyper cholesterolemia and decreased glucose-tolerance. *Lancet, 1964, 2*(7360), 614–615.

Fabry, P., Fodor, J., Hejl, Z., Geizeronva, H., & Balcarova, O. Meal frequency and ischemic heart disease. *Lancet, 1968, 2*(7561), 190–191.

Fernstrom, J. A. Food and brain function. *Professional Nutritionist, 1979, 11*(3), 5–8.

Finch, C. E. Monomine metabolism in the aging male mouse. In M. Rockstein & M. Sussman (Eds.), *Development and aging of the nervous system.* New York: Academic Press, 1973.

Finch, C. E. Neuroendocrine and autonomic aspects of aging. In C. E. Finch & L. Hayflick (Eds.), *The handbook of biology of aging.* New York: Van Nostrand Reinhold, 1977.

Frank, B. S. *Nucleic acid and antioxidant therapy of aging.* New York: Royal Health Books, 1979.

Freeman, J. T. *Clinical features of the older patient.* Springfield, Ill.: Charles C Thomas, 1965.

Fries, J. F. Aging, natural death and the compression of morbidity. *New England Journal of Medicine,* 1980, *303*(3), 130–136.

Garn, S. M. Bone loss and aging. In R. Goldman & M. Rockstein (Eds.), *The physiology and pathology of human aging.* New York: Academic Press, 1975.

Goldstein, A., Guhe, A., Zatz, M. M., Hardy, M. & White, A. Purification and biological activity of thymosene, a hormone of the thymus gland. *Proceedings of the National Academy of Science,* 1972, *69*(7), 1800–1803.

Goodhart, R. S., & Shils, M. E. *Modern nutrition in health and disease* (5th ed.). Philadelphia, Pa.: Lea and Febiger, 1973.

Gordon, T., Castelli, W. P., & Hjortland, M. C. High density lipoprotein as a protective factor against coronary heart disease: The Framingham study. *American Journal of Medicine,* 1977, *62*(5), 707–713. (a)

Gordon, T., Castelli, W. P., & Hjortland, M. C. Predicting coronary disease in middle-aged and older persons: The Framingham study. *Journal of American Medical Association,* 1977, *238*(6), 497–499. (b)

Gregerman, R. I., & Bierman, E. L. Aging and hormones. In R. H. Williams (Ed.), *Textbook of endocrinology* (5th ed.). Philadelphia, Pa.: W. B. Saunders, 1974.

Gresham, G. A. Atherosclerosis: Its causes and potential reversibility. *Triangle,* 1976, *15*(2, 3), 39–43.

Gruman, G. A history of ideas about the prolongation of life. *Transactions, American Philosophical Society,* 1966, *56* (P. 9), 1–102.

Guillerme, J. *Longevity.* New York: Walker and Co., 1963.

Harman, D. Free radical theory of aging: Effect of free radical inhibitors on the life span of male LAF mice—second experiment. *Journal of Gerontology,* 1968, *23* (4), 476–482.

Harris, R. Cardiac changes with age. In R. Goldman & M. Rockstein (Eds.), *The physiology and pathology of human aging.* New York: Academic Press, 1975.

Hartshorn, E. A. Food and drug interactions. *Journal of the American Dietetics Association,* 1977, *70,* 15.

Harvard Medical School. A leisurely look at stress. *Harvard Medical School Health Letter,* 1979, *4*(12), 1–5. (a)

Harvard Medical School. A look at high blood pressure, Part II. *Harvard Medical School Health Letter,* 1979, *4*(9), 1–2, 5. (b)

Hazzard, W. R., & Bierman, E. L. Old age. In D. W. Smith, E. L. Bierman, & N. M. Robinson (Eds.), *The biologic ages of man.* Philadelphia, Pa.: W. B. Saunders, 1978.

Henry, J. P., & Stephens, P. M. *Stress, health and the social environment.* New York: Springer-Verlag, 1977.

Higbie, L. *To understand the aging process: The Baltimore longitudinal study of the NIA.* Washington, D.C.: Public Health Service, 1978, 78–134.

Hirokawa, K., & Makinodan, T. Thymic involution: Effect on T cell differentiation. *Journal of Immunology,* 1975, *114*(6), 1659–1664.

Holmes, F. F., & Hearne, E. Cancer state to age relationship: Implications for cancer screening in the elderly. *Journal of the American Geriatrics Society,* 1981, (2), 55–57.

Holmes, T. H., & Rahe, R. H. The social readjustment rating scale. *Journal of Psychosomatic Research,* 1967, *11*(2), 213–218.

Horowitz, R. I., & Feinstein, A. R. New methods of samplings and analysis to remove bias in case control research. *Clinical Research,* 1977, *25*(3), 459.

Howell, D. S., Sapolsky, A. S., Pita, J. C., & Woessner, J. F. The pathogenesis of osteo-arthritis. *Seminars in Arthritis and Rheumatism,* 1976, *5*(4), 365–383.

Hoyman, H. S. Rethinking an ecologic system model of man's health, disease, aging, death. *Journal of School Health,* 1975, *45*(9), 509–518.

Huang, H. H., & Meites, J. Reproductive capacity of aging female rats. *Neuroendo-crinology,* 1975, *17*(4), 289–295.

Hügin, F., Norris, A., & Shock, N. Skin reflex and voluntary reaction time in young and old males. *Journal of Gerontology,* 1960, *15*(3), 388–391.

Johnson, G. T. (Ed.) An update on exercise–in monkeys. *Harvard Medical School Newsletter,* 1982, (5)5.

Jowsey, J. Prevention and treatment of osteoporosis. In M. Winick (Ed.), *Nutrition and aging.* New York: John Wiley and Sons, 1976.

Kagen, A. R., & Levi, L. Health and environment–psychosocial stimuli: A review. *Social Science Medicine,* 1974, *8*(5), 225–295.

Kannel, W. B. Some lessons in cardiovascular epidemiology from Framingham. *American Journal of Cardiology,* 1976, *37*(2), 269–282.

Kannel, W. B., & Sorlie, P. Hypertension in Framingham. In O. Paul (Ed.), *Epidemiology and control of hypertension.* Miami, Fla.: Symposia Specialists, 1975.

Kenshalo, D. R. Age changes in touch, vibration, temperature, kinesthesis and pain sensitivity. In J. E. Birren & K. W. Schaie (Eds.), *Handbook of the psychology of aging.* New York: Van Nostrand Reinhold, 1977.

Kent, S. Do free radicals and dietary antioxidants wage intracellular war? *Geriatrics,* 1977, *32*(1), 127–129, 132–133, 136.

Kent, S. *The life-extension revolution.* New York: William, 1980.

Kohn, R. R. Effect of antioxidants on life span of C57BL mice. *Journal of Gerontology,* 1971, *26*(3), 378–280.

Kohn, R. R. Heart and the cardiovascular system. In C. E. Finch & L. Hayflick (Eds.), *Handbook of the biology of aging.* New York: Van Nostrand Reinhold, 1977.

Kolodny, A. L., & Klipper, A. Bone and joint diseases. In W. Reichel (Ed.), *The geriatric patient.* New York: H. P. Publishing Co., 1978.

Krook, L., Lutwak, L., Whalen, J. P., Henrikson, P. A., Lesser, G. V., & Uris, R. Human periodontal disease morphology and response to calcium therapy. *Cornell Veterinarian,* 1972, *62*(1), 32–53.

Kurtzman, J. Quoted by Fowles, J. The impending society of immortals. *The Futurist,* 1978, *12*(3), 175–181.

Lamy, P. L., & Vestal, R. E. Drug prescribing for the elderly. In W. Reichel (Ed.), *The geriatric patient.* New York: H. P. Publishing Co., 1978.

Leaf, A. Every day is a gift when you are over 100. *National Geographic,* 1973, *143*(1), 93–118. (a)

Leaf, A. Growing old. *Scientific American,* 1973, *229*(3), 44–53. (b)

Leaf, A. Paradise lost. *Nutrition Today,* 1978, *13*(3), 6–9.

Leonard, G. The holistic health revolution. *Journal of Holistic Health,* 1977, *2,* 80–86.

Lew, E. A. Cancer in old age. *CA-A Cancer Journal for Clinicians,* 1978, *28*(1), 2–6.

Lindeman, R. D. Age changes in renal function. In R. Goldman, M. Rockstein, & M. Sussman (Eds.), *The physiology and pathology of human aging.* New York: Academic Press, 1975.

Lutwak, L. Periodontal disease. In M. Winick (Ed.), *Nutrition and aging.* New York: John Wiley and Sons, 1976.

Makinodan, T. Science is on the trail of the fountain of youth, G. Bylinsky. *Fortune,* 1976, *94*(1), 134–140.

Makinodan, T. Immunity and aging. In C. E. Finch & L. Hayflick (Eds.), *Handbook of the biology of aging.* New York: Van Nostrand Reinhold, 1977.

Makinodan, T., Perkins, E. H., & Chen, M. G. Immunologic activity of the aged. *Advances in Gerontological Research,* 1971, *3,* 171–198.

Marx, J. L. Hormones and their effects in the aging body. *Science,* 1979, *206*(4420), 805–806.

Maspero, H. Tao Tsang. *Journal Asiatique,* 1937, *229,* 384–385.

Masuda, M., & Holmes, J. H. Life events: Perceptions and frequencies. *Psychosomatic Medicine,* 1978, *40*(3), 236–261.

Mayer, J. Aging and nutrition. *Geriatrics,* 1974, *29*(5), 57–59.

McGovern, G. Invisibility of aged may mask scope of malnutrition problem. *Geriatrics,* 1970, *25*(1), 40–44.

Monkerud, D. Running into consciousness: Caution—running may be good for your health. *New Realities,* 1978, *11*(3), 48–53.

Moss, G. E. *Illness, immunity and social interaction: The dynamics of biosocial resonation.* New York: John Wiley and Sons, 1973.

Nordgren, R. A., Woodruff, D. S., & Bick, M. D. The effect of exogenous RNA on the retention of discriminative learning in the rat. *Physiology and Behavior,* 1970, *5,* 1109–1171.

Olsen, E. J., Bank, L., & Jarvik, L. F. Gerovital-H$_3$: A clinical trial as an antidepressant. *Journal of Gerontology,* 1978, *33*(4), 514–521.

Paffenbarger, R. S., Jr., Hale, W. E., Brand, R. J., & Hyde, R. T. Work energy level, personal characteristics, and fatal heart attack. *American Journal of Epidemiology,* 1977, *105,* 200–213.

Page, L., & Friend, B. The changing United States diet. *BioScience,* 1978, *28*(3), 192–198.

Palmore, E. (Ed.). *Normal aging: Report from the Duke longitudinal study, 1955–1969.* Durham, N.C.: Duke University Press, 1970.

Palmore, E., & Jeffers, F. C. *Prediction of life span recent findings.* Lexington, Mass.: D. C. Heath, 1971.

Parrott, J. Newsmakers. *Los Angeles Times,* 23 September 1980, P. 1, p. 2.

Pelletier, K. R. *Holistic medicine: From stress to optimum health.* New York: Delacorte Press/Seymour Lawrence, 1979.

Pickering, G. W. The peripheral resistance in persistent arterial hypertension. *Clinical Science,* 1936, *2,* 209–235.

Pitot, H. C. Carcinogenesis and aging—two related phenomena. *American Journal of Pathology,* 1977, *87*(2), 444–472.

Posner, B. M. *Nutrition and the elderly: Policy development, program planning, and evaluation.* Lexington, Mass.: Lexington Book, D. C. Heath, 1979.

Prehoda, R. W. *Extended youth.* New York: G. P. Putnam and Sons, 1968.

Rahe, R. H. Subjects' recent life changes and their near future illness reports. *Annals of Clinical Research,* 1972, *4,* 250–265.

Rahe, R. H. The pathway between subjects' recent life changes and their near-future illness reports: Representative results and methodological issues. In B. S. Dohrenwend & B. P. Dohrenwend (Eds.), *Stressful life events: Their nature and effects.* New York: John Wiley and Sons, 1974.

Rahe, R. H., & Arthur, R. T. Life changes and illness studies. *Journal of Human Stress,* 1978, *4*(11), 3–15.

Rahe, R. H., Meyer, M., Smith, M., Kjaer, G., & Holmes, J. H. Social stress and illness onset. *Journal of Psychosomatic Research,* 1964, *8,* 35–44.

Reichel, W. (Ed.). *The geriatric patient.* New York: H. P. Publishing Co., 1978.

Richmond, J. B. Healthy people: The Surgeon General's report on health promotion and disease prevention, 1979. Washington, D.C.: DHEW (PHS) Publication No. 79–55071.

Robbins, S. Stroke in the geriatric patient. In W. Reichel (Ed.), *The geriatric patient.* New York: H. P. Publishing Co., 1978.

Rockstein, M., & Sussman, M. *Biology of aging.* Belmont, Calif.: Wadsworth, 1979.

Rodman, G. P., McEwen, C., & Wallace, S. L. (Eds.), *Primer on the rheumatic diseases* (7th ed.). Atlanta: Arthritis Foundation, 1973.

Roe, D. A. *Drug-induced nutritional deficiencies.* Westport, Conn.: Avi, 1976.

Rose, G. A. Clinical aspects of calcium metabolism bone disease. *Transactions of the Medical Society of London,* 1970, *86,* 62.

Roseman, J. M., & Buckley, C. E. Inverse relationship between serum IgG concentrations and measures of intelligence in elderly persons. *Nature,* 1975, *254*(5495), 55–56.

Rosenfeld, A. *Prolongevity.* New York: Alfred A. Knopf, 1976.

Roth, G. Hormone receptor changes during aging. In J. A. Behnke, C. E. Finch, & G. B. Moment (Eds.), *The biology of aging.* New York: Plenum Press, 1978.

Sachuk, N. Population longevity study: Sources and indices. *Journal of Gerontology,* 1970, *25*(3), 262–264.

Samorajski, T., Sun., & Rolstein, C. Effects of chronic dosage with chlorpromazine and gerovital-H$_3$ in the aging brain. In K. Nandy & J. Sherwin (Eds.), *Aging brain and senile dementia.* New York: Plenum Press, 1976.

Schaie, K. W. Intelligence and problem solving. In J. E. Birren & R. B. Sloane (Eds.), *Handbook of mental health and aging.* Englewood Cliffs, N. J.: Prentice-Hall, 1980.

Scheibel, M. E., & Scheibel, A. B. Structural changes in the aging brain. In H. Brody, D. Harmon, J. M. Ordy (Eds.), *Aging, clinical, morphologic and neurochemical aspects in the aging central nervous system* (Vol. 1). New York: Raven Press, 1975.

Scrimshaw, N. S., & Young, V. R. The requirements of human nutrition. *Scientific American,* 1976, *235*(3), 51–64.

Segerberg, O., Jr. *The immortality factor.* New York: E. P. Dutton, 1974.

Selye, H. A. Stress and aging. *Journal of the American Geriatrics Society,* 1970, *18*(9), 669–690.

Sharpe, C., & Keen, H. *Presymptomatic detection and early diagnosis.* London: Pitman, 1968.

Shattuck, G. C., & Hilferty, M. M. Sunstroke and allied conditions in the United States of America. *American Journal of Tropical Medicine,* 1932, *12*(3), 223–245.

Shimkin, M. B. *Neoplasia advances in American medicine: Essays at the bicentennial.* New York: Macy Foundation, 1976.

Shock, N. W. The physiology of aging. *Scientific American,* 1962, *206*(1), 100–110.

Shock, N. W. Physiological aspects of aging. *Journal of the American Dietetic Association,* 1970, *56*(6), 491–496.

Shock, N. W. Physiological theories of aging. In M. Rockstein, M. L. Sussman, & J. Chesky (Eds.), *Theoretical aspects of aging.* New York: Academic Press, 1974.

Shock, N. W., & Andres, R. In D. F. Chebotarev (Ed.), *Adaptive capacities of an aging organism.* Kiev, USSR: Academic Science, 1968.

Shock, N. W., & Norris, A. H. Neuromuscular coordinating as a factor in age changes in muscular exercise. In D. Brunner & E. Jokl (Eds.), *Medicine and sport, Vol. 4: Physical inactivity and aging.* 1970.

Smith, D. W., & Bierman, E. L. (Eds.), *The biologic ages of man.* Philadelphia, Pa.: W. B. Saunders, 1973.

Smith, D. W., Bierman, E. L., & Robinson, N. M. (Eds.), *The biologic ages of man.* Philadelphia, Pa.: W. B. Saunders, 1978.

Smythe, H. Nonsteroidal therapy in inflammatory joint disease. *Hospital Practice,* 1975, *10*(9), 51–56.

Solyom, L., Enesco, H. E., & Beaulieu, C. The effect of RNA on learning and activity in old and young rats. *Journal of Gerontology,* 1967, *22*(1), 3–7.

Sorlie, P., Gordon, T., & Kannel, W. Body build and mortality—the Framingham study. *Journal of the American Medical Association,* 1980, *243,* 1828–1831.

Stamler, J., & Epstein, F. M. Coronary heart disease: Risk factors as guides to preventive action. *Preventive Medicine,* 1972, *1,* 27–28.

Stoudt, H. W., Damon, A., McFarland, R., & Roberts, J. Weight, height, and selected body dimensions of adults, United States 1960-1962. *National Center for Health Statistics, Series II* (8), June, 1965.

Strehler, B. L. *Time, cells and aging.* New York: Academic Press, 1977.

Suci, G. J., Davidoff, M. D., & Surwillo, W. W. Reaction time as a function of stimulus information and age. *Journal of Experimental Psychology,* 1960, *60,* 242-244.

Tall, A., & Small, D. Plasma high-density lipoproteins. *New England Journal of Medicine,* 1978, *299,* 1232-1236.

Townsend, C. *Old age: The last segregation.* New York: Grossman, 1971.

Trimmer, E. J. *Rejuvenation.* New York: A. S. Barnes, 1970.

Walford, R. L. Autoimmune phenomena in the aging process. *Symposia of the Society for Experimental Biology,* 1967, *21,* 351-373.

Walker, W. J. Changing United States life styles and declining vascular mortality: Cause or coincidence? *New England Journal of Medicine,* 1977, *297*(3), 163-165.

Watkin, D. M. Nutrition for the aging and the aged. In R. S. Goodheart & M. E. Shills (Eds.), *Modern nutrition in health and disease* (6th ed.). Philadelphia, Pa.: Lea and Febiger, 1979.

Weg, R. B. Changing physiology of aging: Normal and pathological. In D. S. Woodruff & J. E. Birren (Eds.), *Aging: Scientific perspectives and social issues.* New York: D. Van Nostrand Company, 1975.

Weg, R. B. Drug interaction with the changing physiology of the aged: Practice and potential. In R. C. Kayne (Ed.), *Drugs and the elderly.* Los Angeles: University of Southern California Press, 1978.

Weg, R. B. *Nutrition and the later years.* Los Angeles: Andrus Gerontology Center, University of Southern California Press, 1979.

Weg, R. B. Prolonged mild nutritional deficiencies: Significance for health maintenance. *Journal of Nutrition for the Elderly,* 1980a, *1*(1), 3-22.

Weg, R. B. *The aged: Who, where, how well.* Los Angeles: University of Southern California, Davis School of Gerontology, 1981.

Weg, R. B. Changing physiology and nutrition in aging. A symposium: New horizons in nutrition for the health professions. In H. Slavkin (Ed.), *U. S. C. Journal of Continuing Dental Education,* 1980a, *1*(2), 38-70.

Whanger, A. Vitamins and vigor at 65 plus. *Postgraduate Medicine,* 1973, *53*(2), 167-172.

WHO. Constitution of the World Health Organization. *Chronicle of WHO,* 1947, *1,* 1-2.

Winick, M. Nutrition and aging. *Journal of Medical Society of New Jersey,* 1979, *76*(3), 216-217.

Woodruff, D. S. A physiological perspective of the psychology of aging. In D. W. Woodruff & J. E. Birren (Eds.), *Aging: Scientific perspectives and social issues.* New York: Van Nostrand Reinhold, 1975.

Wurtman, R. J., & Growdon, J. H. Dietary enhancement of CNS neurotransmitters. *Hospital Practice,* 1978, *13*(3), 71-77.

Wurtman, T. *New approaches to senile dementia.* Paper presented at Perspectives on aging: A tribute to longevity, Andrus Gerontology Center, University of Southern California, 25 March 1980.

Wynder, E. L. Nutrition and cancer. *Federation Proceedings,* 1976, *35*(6), 1309-1315.

Wynder, E. L. Dietary environment and cancer. *Journal of American Dietetic Association,* 1977, *71*(4), 385-392.

Young, V. R. Diet and nutrient needs in old age. In J. A. Behnke, C. E. Finch, & G. B. Moment (Eds.), *The biology of aging.* New York: Plenum Press, 1978.

Zung, W. W. K., Gianturco, D., Pfeiffer, E., Wang, H. S., Whanger, A., Bridge, T. P., & Potkin, S. G. Pharmacology of depression in the aged: Evaluation of gerovital-H_3 as an antidepressant drug. *Psychosomatics,* 1974, *15*(3), 127-131.

CHAPTER 13

Physiology of Exercise and Aging

Herbert A. deVries

As we grow older, losses in functional capacity appear to occur at the cellular, tissue, organ, and system levels of organization. However, as pointed out by Shock, decrements in physiological functions are most readily apparent in the responses of the whole organism to stress (Shock, 1961a). As an exercise physiologist my raison d'être lies in the measurement of the human organism's responses to the most physiological of stressors—that is, physical activity or exercise—or the stress of increased energy demands from whatever source. I am most concerned with the various functional capacities of the human individual: how they may be lost through aging or other processes; how they may be improved through such modalities as physical conditioning, improved nutrition, and better relaxation.

Since functional losses are greatest when the whole organism is under stress, exercise physiology is the vernier on the scale of general physiology. The methods of exercise physiology provide us with a rather sensitive tool for evaluation of physiological decline in aging. Thus, for example, if some of the metabolic capacity is lost at the cellular level, this would not be easily observed or measured under resting conditions, but the measurement of maximal oxygen consumption in the exercise laboratory would display losses in metabolic capacity dramatically. A man of 75 has on the average only about 50% of his oxygen consumption value at age 20, while his resting oxygen intake has only declined by 20%-25% over the same period of time (Robinson, 1938). In recent years cardiologists have realized that in some cases early ischemic heart disease, which shows no electrocardiogram (EKG) changes at rest, may be successfully diagnosed if the individual's EKG is observed during the stress of a treadmill run or bicycle ergometer ride, such as is used daily in the exercise physiology laboratory.

Thus, as we look at the physiological changes accompanying the aging process, our rather circumscribed vantage point is that of the exercise physiologist who is interested, not in disease processes, but primarily in the gross losses of functional capacity that the aging individual experiences as a creeping loss in "vigor." This is not to deny the interest of the exercise physiologist in the entire spectrum of physiological changes, but only to suggest a focus upon those systems that in the "normal" older individual are most likely to be limiting with respect to physical working capacity (PWC) and that are most likely to be amenable to improvement by physical conditioning. Excellent reviews are available for the reader desiring a more comprehensive treatment of physiological age changes (Robinson, 1938; Shock, 1961b; Chapter 12, this volume.)

PHYSIOLOGICAL CHANGES INVOLVED IN THE AGE-RELATED LOSS OF VIGOR

When evaluating the effects of the aging process on human performance, we face several problems. First, it is difficult to separate the effects of aging per se from those of concomitant disease processes (particularly cardiovascular and respiratory problems) that become more prevalent with age. Second, the sedentary nature of adult life in the United States makes it very difficult to find "old" populations to compare with "young" populations at equal activity levels. Lastly, very few longitudinal studies of the same population over a period of time have been conducted. Conclusions drawn from cross-sectional studies in which various age groups of different people are compared must be accepted with reservations because the "weaker biological specimens" are not likely to be represented in as great numbers in the older populations tested as in the younger, due to a higher mortality rate. Thus we must be careful to realize that the age changes described are at best only representative of the average losses and that even these mean values may be derived in some cases from very small samplings.

Just as various individuals within the human species age at different rates, so various physiological functions within the individual seem to have their own rates of decline with increasing age. Indeed, some functions do not seem to degenerate with age (Shock, 1961a). For example, under resting conditions no changes in blood sugar level, blood pH, or total blood volume are apparent. In general, the functions involving the coordinated activity of more than one organ system, such as aerobic capacity and physical work capacity (PWC), decline most with age. Changes due to the aging process are most readily observed when the organism is stressed. Homeostatic readjustment is considerably slower with increasing age (see Chapter 12 for a discussion of aging and homeostasis).

Cardiovascular system

Assuming appropriate levels of muscle strength and endurance, oxygen transport has been widely accepted as one of the two major factors determining the limits of physical working capacity (PWC), if the activity lasts more than a minute or two. (The other is the capacity for O_2 utilization by muscle tissue.) Oxygen transport as defined by the Fick equation (Oxygen consumption in milliliters/minute = cardiac output in liters/minute $\times$ arteriovenous difference in milliliters/liter blood) depends upon cardiac output and the arteriovenous difference in oxygen. Cardiac output is, in turn, determined by heart rate and the volume of blood per beat (stroke volume).

Studies of age differences in cardiac output are scarce, but enough work has been done to provide suggestive evidence. With respect to cardiac output at rest, data are available from the work of Brandfonbrener, Landowne, and Shock (1955) on 67 healthy males ranging in age from 19 to 86. They found a significant age-related decrease of about 1% per year. Their measurements of cardiac output are supported by the ballistocardiographic data of Starr (1964), who estimated a loss in strength of the myocardium (the heart muscle) at about 0.85% per year after the age of 20. This constitutes fairly close agreement from two very different methodological approaches as to the changes in function of the heart at rest.

Of the several studies available regarding age changes in cardiac output at submaximal exercise, only two were found in which cardiac output was measured during exercise and in which the subjects and exercise loads were sufficiently similar to allow any meaningful comparisons. Becklake, Frank, Dagenais, Ostiguy, and Guzman (1965) found cardiac output to increase by small amounts with increasing age; Granath, Jensson, and Strandell (1964) found a small but constant difference in the other direction. Since even in these two studies the methods differed and physical fitness levels were not ruled out among the different age levels, age changes in cardiac output during submaximal exercise must still be considered an open research question.

Most important to our discussion here, however, is the question of what happens to the functional capacity of the heart in terms of cardiac output. This means measurement (or estimation) of maximal cardiac output. The data from Julius, Amery, Whitlock, and Conway (1967), the only study found, appear to allow valid age group comparisons and cautious conclusions. They used the indicator-dilution technique to measure cardiac output in 54 subjects in three age groups: I (18–34), II (35–49), and III (50–69). The three groups appear to have been roughly equated in body surface area and physical activity levels. The cardiac outputs at maximum tolerated exercise on a bicycle ergometer were found to be 16.19, 14.96, and 11.98 liters/minute for groups I, II, and III respectively. The age data probably represent a reasonable estimate of the loss in maximum cardiac output with age in a relatively sedentary population. Thus, from the third decade to the sixth and seventh decades, we may postulate a loss of 26%. Taking an assumed mean age of 26 for group I and 59 for group III (individual age data were not provided) results in an approximation of the yearly loss at about 0.80% per year, a figure roughly similar to the loss rates found for resting cardiac output and myocardial strength.

In 1938 Robinson's classic study showed that maximum heart rate goes down with age. Evidence also suggests that stroke volume declines with age (Strandell, 1964), so that on these bases we might expect maximum cardiac output to decline at a greater rate than maximum heart rate, which declines almost linearly from 190–195 beats/minute at age 20 to about 160 at age 70 (Robinson, 1938). Assuming a resting rate of 70, this would then result in a lowered capacity for heart-rate response of approximately 0.56% per year, over the age range of 20–70. Thus, the loss of 0.80% per year in maximum cardiac output found by Julius et al. (1967) is in the range of what might have been predicted.

These losses in the pumping function of the heart are best explained by decrements in cardiac dynamics such as the decreased rate of pressure development and ejection of blood, which have been reported from experiments on intact humans

(Eddleman, 1969; Harrison, Dixon, Russell, Bidwai, & Coleman, 1964; Landowne, Brandfonbrener, & Shock, 1955). These age-related losses in power of the human myocardium as a whole can now be accounted for on the basis of alterations in contractile properties at the muscle fiber level, and these, in turn, seem to be related to changes in the enzymatic properties of the protein filaments making up the muscle fibers (Heller & Whitehorn, 1972; Urthaler, Walker, & James, 1978).

With respect to age-related changes in the vasculature, we have known since the early work of Hallock in 1934 that both the large central arteries and the smaller peripheral arteries tend to grow stiffer with age. More recent work corroborates the early findings (Gozna, Marble, Shaw, & Holland, 1974; Mozersky, Sumner, Hokanson, & Strandness, 1973). Such increased stiffness in the vascular bed contributes to an increased total peripheral resistance, which the weakening myocardium must overcome. Thus, age-related decrements in cardiac output are the expected result.

Respiratory system

Maximal ventilation attained during exhausting work shows a gradual decline of about 60% from the late teens to the eighth decade (Robinson, 1938). Vital capacity (the volume of air that can be expelled by the strongest possible expiration after the deepest possible inspiration) also declines with age (Norris, Shock, Landowne, & Falzone, 1956; Norris, Shock, & Falzone, 1962; Pemberton & Flanagan, 1956). There appears to be no very good evidence for any change in total lung capacity. Therefore, since vital capacity and residual volume (the volume of air remaining in the lungs after the strongest possible expiration) are reciprocally related, residual lung volume increases with age (Norris et al., 1956; Norris et al., 1962). Aging therefore increases the ratio of residual volume to total lung capacity, and anatomic dead space also increases with age (Comroe, Forster, Dubois, Briscoe, & Carlsen, 1962).

The available evidence suggests that lung compliance increases with age (Turner, Mead, & Wohl, 1968), resulting in less elastic recoil to aid in the expiratory process; but even more importantly, thoracic wall compliance decreases. Since the elastic stretch and recoil is reduced (Mittman, Edelman, Norris, & Shock, 1965, Rizzato & Marazzini, 1970; Turner et al., 1968). Thus, the older individual may do as much as 20% more elastic work at a given level of ventilation than the young, and most of the additional work will be performed in moving the chest wall (Turner et al., 1968).

Recent work corroborates these findings (Gelb & Zamel, 1975; Knudson, Clark, Kennedy, & Knudson, 1977). On the basis of these age-related changes in the work of breathing it is not surprising that, compared with the young, the elderly must bring about greater levels of lung ventilation per unit work done and also per unit of O_2 consumption, even when age-relative physical fitness is equated (deVries & Adams, 1972a).

Age changes in muscle function

Strength decreases very slowly during maturity. After the 5th decade, strength decreases at a greater rate, but even at age 60 the loss does not usually exceed 10%–20% of the maximum; women's losses are somewhat greater than those of men (Montoye & Lamphiear, 1977; Petrofsky & Lind, 1975). When maximal grip strength was investigated in 100 men who all did similar work in a machine shop, no change in either grip strength or endurance was found from age 22 to 62 (Petrofsky & Lind, 1975). These data suggest that in this age bracket the more typical finding of small losses with age may be largely due to disuse rather than to age. However, in old age sizable decrements in strength do occur.

Changes at the cellular level. Animal studies have shown that important age changes occur at the cellular level. First, there is a loss of contractile elements, which accounts for the decrement in strength. Although this loss could be the result of losses in motor nerve fibers, this has been ruled out in studies on rats. These studies have shown that muscle fiber numbers may be down by about 25% in old rats but that no change occurs in nerve fibers (Gutman, Hanzlikova, & Jakoubek, 1968). The second important change at the cell level is a reduction in respiratory capacity, which accounts for losses in muscle endurance and capacity for recovery (Ermini, 1976).

It has also been shown that the loss in human muscle tissue with age can entirely account for the downward trend in basal metabolism, which has been an accepted fact in metabolic studies for nearly a century (Tzankoff & Norris, 1977).

Age and capacity for hypertrophy. Goldspink and Howells (1974) taught hamsters to lift weights in order to evaluate cellular hypertrophy. After weight training for 5 weeks the mean fiber area of the biceps in the young animals increased very significantly by 35.6%. The old animals increased by 17.7%, which was of marginal significance. All signs of hypertrophy were lost in 15 weeks.

With respect to human strength gain, Moritani and deVries (1980) investigated the time course of strength gain through weight training in old and young men in order to define the contribution of hypertrophy and such neural factors as "disinhibition" to the total change in strength over a period of eight weeks (Moritani & deVries, 1980). Young and old men showed similar and significant percentage increases in strength, although the young made greater absolute gains. However, the physiological adaptations were quite different. Whereas young subjects showed highly significant hypertrophy, the strength gained by the old men was almost entirely due to "learning" to achieve higher activation levels as measured by EMG (electromyographic) methods.

Force-velocity and other aspects of strength. Damon (1971) has shown that age decrements in strength exist whether measured in isometric, concentric, or eccentric muscle contraction and also whether measured as maximal instantaneous force achieved, or as a mean value over a finite time period. However, his work showed isotonic strength to be affected to a greater extent than isometric. The maximum velocity produced against any given mass is less for the old than the young, although the shape of the force velocity curve is similar. Thus, loss of strength with age consists of two components: (1) a decrease in ability to maintain maximum force statically, and (2) a decrease in ability to accelerate mass.

Muscle endurance. With respect to muscular endurance, or fatigue rate, Evans (1971) has shown, with the EMG fatigue curve technique, that fatigue rate is significantly greater in the old than the young when holding isometric contractions of 20%, 25%, 30%, 35%, 40%, or 45% of MVC (maximal voluntary contraction).

Physical working capacity (PWC)

The best single measure of physical working capacity (PWC) is the maximal oxygen consumption, sometimes referred to as aerobic capacity. Two excellent studies have related this variable to age in men (Robinson, 1938) and women (Astrand, 1960). After a maximum value in early adulthood, there is a gradual decline for both sexes. For men, the maximal values were found at mean age of 17.4 years, and they declined to less than half those values at mean age 75. For women, the maximal values were found in the age group 20-29, and they fell off by 29% in the age group 50-65, the oldest tested.

These data are cross-sectional and reflect only what happens to a statistical average value. Kasch and Wallace (1976), who followed 16 men (aged 32-56 at the start) over a 10-year training regimen, concluded that the usual 9%-15% decline in PWC or VO_2 max from age 45 to 55 years can be forestalled by a regular endurance exercise. Drinkwater, Horvath, & Wells (1975) came to a similar conclusion with respect to women—that is, habitual levels of activity rather than age per se determines PWC for women in the 20-49 age group.

Body composition

It is typical (though not desirable) for humans to increase their weight with age. Brozek (1952) has provided interesting data on the composition of the human body as it ages. These data clearly show that the weight gain in the sample represented a mean increase of 27 pounds of fat from age 20 to age 55, while the fat-free body weight had actually decreased.

Shock, Watkin, Yiengst, Norris, Gaffney, Gregerman, and Falzone (1963), used estimates of intracellular water as an index of the amount of metabolizing tissue. They found losses of active protoplasm (which is protein tissue mass, not fat tissue) to average about 0.44% per year after age 25. Measurements using total body potassium (Allen, Anderson, & Langham, 1960) are in relatively good agreement.

Thus, even if we maintained body weight at our young adult value, we would nevertheless be getting fatter since we are losing active protoplasm at approximately 3%-5% per decade after age 20-25.

AGING PROCESSES VERSUS HYPOKINETIC DISEASE

It is easy to see how the age-related losses in function described earlier can individually and in concert result in the relatively large losses in PWC, which accompany the aging process and which are interpreted by the aging individual as a loss in vigor. However, we must be cautious with respect to attributing all of this functional decline to the aging process per se. Indeed, the entire body of knowledge regarding the loss of function with increasing age must be viewed with caution, since the effect of habitual physical activity has been controlled or ruled out in very few cases. Wessel and Van Huss (1969) have shown that physical activity decreases significantly with increasing age. This is not surprising news, but it does provide scientific validation of the need for consideration of this variable in all investigations directed toward aging changes in performance. To support this contention further, Wessel and Van Huss showed that age-related losses in physiological variables important to human performance were related more highly to the decreased habitual activity level than to age itself.

It would seem that "hypokinetic disease," a term coined by Kraus and Raab (1961) to describe the whole spectrum of somatic and mental derangements induced by inactivity, may be of considerable importance as one factor involved in bringing about an age-related decrement in functional capacities.

For example, most of the age-related changes described in previous sections can also be brought about in young, well-conditioned men in as little as three weeks by the simple expedient of enforced bed rest. One of the outstanding studies in this area found that in three weeks of bed rest the maximal cardiac output decreased by 26%, the maximal ventilatory capacity by 30%, oxygen consumption by 30%, and even the amount of active tissue declined by 1.5% (Saltin, Blomquist, Mitchell, Johnson, Wildenthal, & Chapman, 1968). Thus, inactivity can produce losses in function similar to those brought about more slowly in the average individual when he or she grows more sedentary with age (Wessel & Van Huss, 1969). These observations lead us to question how much of the observed losses in function as people grow older are functions of aging and how much may be brought about by the long-term deconditioning of the increasingly sedentary life we usually lead as we grow older. Clearly the physiological changes accompanying the aging process may not be the result of aging alone. Indeed, at least one other process could conceivably account for some of the changes observed. Incipient disease processes, undiagnosable and unrecognized in their early states, could also contribute to the losses in function. For example, the coronary arteries, whose occlusion by fatty deposits ultimately results in a heart attack, may show early changes even in the teenager. Autopsies on 200 battle casualties of the Korean War (mean age 22.1 years) indicated that 77.3% of the hearts showed some gross evidence of coronary arteriosclerosis. Some of these casualties were in their teens (Enos, Holmes, & Beyer, 1953).

Thus, we may hypothesize that the functional losses that have been observed and identified in the medical and physiological literature as age changes must be considered as resulting from at least three factors, only one of which is truly an aging phenomenon. Of the other two factors, unrecognized incipient disease processes may or may not be causally related to aging. The third factor, disuse or hypokinetic disease, is the only one of the three factors that can easily be reversed. The remainder of this chapter is directed toward the physiological and methodological considerations involved in achieving and maintaining physical fitness in middle and old age.

TRAINABILITY OF THE OLDER ORGANISM

Only a few years ago, the trainability of older people was still in question. In Germany, researchers had concluded that commencement of physical training in a person unaccustomed to sport causes only slight effects of adaptation after the age of 40 and that after 60 there is practically no observable effect (Hollman, 1964; Nöcker, 1965). An article from Japan also stated that marked improvement of physical ability by training could not be expected in older people (Katsuki & Masuda, 1969).

On the other hand, Czechoslovakian physiologists had reported better physical performance and functional capacities in a sample of physically active older men than in a comparable sample of sedentary older men (Fischer, Pariskova, & Roth, 1965). Two other investigations had shown significant improvement in physical working capacity and cardiac function by conditioning older people, although the sample size was very small in both—8 in one (Barry, Daly, Pruett, Steinmetz, Page, Birkhead, & Rodahl, 1966) and 13 in the other (Benestad, 1965). An excellent series of investigations from Stockholm clearly demonstrated the trainability of men in the 34-50 age bracket (Hartley, Grimby, Kilbom, Nilsson, Astrand, Bjure, Ekblom, & Saltin, 1969; Kilbom, Hartley, Saltin, Bjure, Grimby, & Astrand, 1969; Saltin, Hartley, Kilbom, & Astrand, 1969). This work demonstrated a 14% improvement in aerobic capacity, a 13% increase in cardiac output, and some suggestion of decreased numbers of EKG abnormalities. However, it is difficult to consider even the upper end of this age bracket as old, although the investigators did refer to their subjects as "middle-aged and older" men.

We have entered into a series of experiments regarding the trainability and training methodology for older men and women. This work was done at the Laguna Hills retirement community under sponsorship of the Administration on Aging (HEW).

In the first experiment (deVries, 1970) 112 older Caucasian males aged 52-87 (mean = 69.5) volunteered for participation in a vigorous exercise training regimen. They exercised at calisthenics, jogging, and either stretching exercises or aquatics at each workout for approximately one hour, three times per week under supervision. All subjects were pretested, and 66 were retested at 6 weeks, 26 at 18 weeks, and 8 at 42 weeks on the following parameters: (1) blood pressure, (2) percentage of body fat, (3) resting neuromuscular activation (relaxation) by electromyogram (EMG), (4) arm muscle strength and girth, (5) maximal oxygen consumption, (6) oxygen pulse at heart rate = 145, (7) pulmonary function, and (8) physical work capacity on the bicycle ergometer. A subgroup of 35 was also tested before and after 6 weeks of training for (1) cardiac output, (2) stroke volume, (3) total peripheral resistance, and (4) work of the heart, at a workload of 75 watts on the bicycle.

The most significant findings were related to oxygen transport capacity. Oxygen pulse and minute ventilation at heart rate 145 improved by 29.4% and 35.2%, respectively. Vital capacity improved by 19.6%.

Significant improvement was also found in percentage of body fat, physical work capacity, and both systolic and diastolic blood pressure for the large six-week group (N = 66). In the smaller group, which exercised for 42 weeks (N = 8), statistical significance was not achieved, although the same trends were observed. Controls did not improve upon any of the above measures. No significant changes were seen in any of the hemodynamic variables tested.

A group of seven men was placed in a modified exercise program because of various cardiovascular problems. This group exercised in the same manner except that they substituted a progressive walking program for the jogging and were restricted to a maximum heart rate of 120. This group was exercised for six weeks, at which time their improvement showed a similar pattern to that of the harder working normal subjects at six weeks.

Life history of physical activity was evaluated in a subgroup of 53. Neither the mean of high and low years of activity nor the peak level of activity engaged in for a period of six weeks or more correlated positively with physiological improvement found.

It was concluded that the trainability of older men with respect to physical work capacity is probably considerably greater than had been suspected and does not depend upon having trained vigorously in youth.

Since no untoward incident occurred during the 18-month tenure of our exercise program, and in view of the improvements in function demonstrated, we concluded that the exercise regimen as developed was both safe and effective for a normal population of older men in the presence of medical and physiological monitoring.

In a subsequent study, 17 older women (aged 52–79) from the same community participated in a vigorous three-month exercise program. Again physical fitness was significantly improved, although the women did not show the large improvement in the respiratory system shown by the men (Adams & deVries, 1973).

On the basis of these studies, we conclude that the older organism is definitely trainable. Indeed the percentage of improvement is entirely similar to that of the young. Recent work by other investigators has corroborated our findings (Niinimaa & Shephard, 1978; Pollock, Dawson, Miller, Ward, Cooper, Headley, Linnerud, & Nomeier, 1976; Sidney & Shephard, 1977a; Sidney & Shephard, 1978).

IMPROVEMENT OF HEALTH FACTORS

Since we had earlier found in our electromyographic investigations that vigorous exercise has a well-defined tranquilizer effect (both immediate and long term) upon young and middle-aged men (deVries, 1968), we decided to evaluate this effect of exercise in our older population. Toward this end, the tranquilizer effect of single doses of exercise and meprobamate (a commonly used tranquilizer pill supplied on prescription as either Miltown or Equanil) were compared with respect to reduction of muscle action potentials in ten elderly, anxious subjects (deVries & Adams, 1972). Thirty-six observations were made of each subject before and after (immediately, 30 minutes, and 1 hour after) each of the five following treatment conditions: (1) meprobamate, 400 mg, (2) placebo, 400 mg lactose, (3) 15 minutes of walking-type exercise at a heart rate of 100, (4) 15 minutes of walking-type exercise at heart rate of 120, and (5) resting control. Conditions 1 and 2 were administered double blind (the investigators did not know which subjects received the drug or placebo). It was found that exercise at a heart rate of 100 lowered electrical activity in the musculature by 20%, 23%, and 20% at the first, second, and third posttests, respectively. These changes were significantly different from controls at the 1% confidence level. Neither meprobamate nor placebo treatment was significantly different from control. Exercise at the higher heart rate was only slightly less effective, but the data were more variable and approached, but did not achieve, significance.

Our data suggest that the exercise modality should not be overlooked when a tranquilizer effect is desired, since in single doses, at least, exercise has a significantly greater effect, without any undesirable side effects, than does meprobamate, at the time one of the most frequently prescribed tranquilizers. This is especially important for the older individual in that this approach can avoid the further impairment of motor coordination, reaction time, and driving performance, which may occur with any of the tranquilizer drugs. A 15-minute walk at a moderate rate (sufficient to raise heart rate to 100 beats per minute) is a sufficient stimulus to bring about the desired effect, which persists for at least one hour afterward.

Many investigators have found decreases in arterial blood pressure resulting from the physical conditioning process. One of the best-controlled studies is that of Boyer and Kasch (1970), who found highly significant decreases of 12 mm Hg in diastolic and 13 mm Hg in systolic pressures in 23 hypertensive subjects who exercised for six months. The subjects with normal blood pressure showed only small and nonsignificant decreases as expected. It seems likely that this normalization of hypertension may be related to the tranquilizer effect discussed earlier.

Two different groups of investigators have reported a regression of abnormalities in the electrocardiogram as the result of physical conditioning (Barry et al., 1966; Sidney & Shepard, 1977). In male albino rats, exercise training resulted in significant improvement in the ratio of capillary to muscle fiber in the heart muscle (Tomanek, 1970). The animal data provide a physiological rationale for the regression of ECG abnormalities, but much further investigation is needed.

Other important health benefits from exercise have been observed with respect to improved joint mobility (Chapman, deVries, & Swezey, 1972; Frekany & Leslie, 1975) and with respect to bone accretion in elderly women for whom osteoporosis is a very serious problem (Smith & Reddan, 1977).

With respect to body composition, Greene (1939), who studied 350 cases of obesity, found that inactivity was associated with the onset of obesity in 67.5% of the cases and that a history of increased food intake was present in only 3.2%. Pariskova (1964), who analyzed the body composition of 1460 individuals of all ages, concluded, "One of the most important factors influencing body composition is the intensity of physical activity, and this is true in youth, adulthood, and old age." Many other investigations, too numerous to cite, provide indirect support for the belief that lack of physical activity is the most common cause of obesity. Thus, a clear-cut case can be made for the importance of habitual, lifelong, vigorous physical activity as a preventive measure against obesity.

Apparently, vigorous physical conditioning of the healthy older organism can bring about significant improvements in (1) the cardiovascular system, (2) the respiratory system (at least in the male), (3) the musculature, and (4) body composition. In general the result is a more vigorous individual who can also relax better. Other health benefits are likely to include a lower blood pressure and lower percent body fat with the concomitant lessening of "risk factors" for development of coronary heart disease. The individual will have a lesser tendency to develop osteoporosis and will experience better joint mobility.

PRESCRIPTION OF EXERCISE: DOSE-RESPONSE DATA

Precautions

Because the older organism has lost much of its capacity to respond to homeo-static displacements and also because degenerative diseases of the cardiovascular and pulmonary systems progress with age, we must base the use of vigorous exercise for the older individual upon experimentally derived "dose-response" data.

Indeed our experience over the last six years with older men and women in a series of exercise physiology investigations leads us to believe that the physician/ patient relationship should be a close one. This is necessary to maximize benefit and minimize hazard. For at least three "normal" subjects in our experiments, our standard exercise program was found at six-week retest to have overloaded them. It would seem that "prescription" of exercise is almost as necessary as the prescription of drugs.

Leadership by professionally trained physical educators with a strong back-ground in physiology of exercise and physical fitness work is needed to produce the maximum in benefits with a minimum of hazard for the older age group—if the exer-cise program is to be vigorous. I will define the term *vigorous* as any activity that raises the heart rate more than 40% of the way from resting to maximal. Any exercise of less intensity is unlikely to bring about benefits to the cardiorespiratory systems (deVries, 1971a). Although it is possible that some significant physiological benefits to muscles and joints may occur at lower intensity exercise, these are not as yet defined by scientific research.

"How much is enough?"

In order to provide objective levels of stress for our subjects to govern their workouts, we furnish each subject with three reference heart rates for guiding his or her personal progress: (1) minimum rate for cardiorespiratory improvement; (2) target rate for optimal improvement; and (3) maximum, or "do not exceed," heart rate. These values are calculated from % Heart Rate Range (HRR) as follows:

$$\% \, HRR = \frac{EHR - RHR}{MHR - RHR} \times 100,$$

where   EHR = exercise heart rate

RHR = resting heart rate in standing position

MHR = maximum heart rate predicted from age by use of Table 13-1.

Minimum heart rate is set at 40% HRR, target heart rate at 60% HRR, and maximum "do not exceed" heart rate is set at 75% HRR.

Thus, for example, an individual aged 73 with a resting heart rate of 70 beats/ minute would be given the following values:

HRR = MHR − RHR
   = 153 − 70 = 83 beats/min

Minimum   HR = RHR + 40% HRR
                = 70 + (0.40 × 83) = 70 + 33 = 103 beats/min

Target   HR = RHR + 60% HRR
                = 70 + (0.60% × 83) = 120 beats/min

Maximum   HR = RHR + 75% HRR
                = 70 + (0.75 × 83) = 132 beats/min

TABLE 13-1. Maximal heart rates in older men

Age	Heart rate	Age	Heart rate	Age	Heart rate	Age	Heart rate
50	174	60	166	70	156	80	147
51	173	61	165	71	155	81	146
52	172	62	164	72	154	82	145
53	172	63	163	73	153	83	145
54	171	64	162	74	152	84	144
55	170	65	161	75	152	85	143
56	169	66	160	76	151	86	143
57	168	67	159	77	150	87	142
58	168	68	158	78	149	88	141
59	167	69	157	79	148	89	141

SOURCE: Robinson, 1938.

   This approach is based on one of our studies in which 52 asymptomatic male volunteers from the Laguna Hills retirement community participated in a six-week jogging program, which constituted a varying level of stress for the participants, depending upon their physical fitness level. They were tested before and after the exercise regimen with the Astrand bicycle ergometer test (Astrand & Ryhming, 1954) for prediction of their maximal oxygen consumption. During the six-week exercise regimen, they kept daily records of the heart rate elicited by each of the five to ten run phases, and the daily peak heart rate was used in calculating the mean exercise heart rate for the six-week period. This mean peak heart rate was then used in calculating the percentage of heart-rate range at which each subject worked.

   The findings were as follows:

   1. Improvement in cardiovascular-respiratory function (aerobic capacity) varied directly with the percentage of heart-rate range at which the subject worked.

   2. Improvement in aerobic capacity varied inversely with the physical fitness level (Astrand score) at the start of the program.

   3. The exercise-intensity threshold for older men appears to be about 40% of heart-rate range compared with about 60% found by others for young men.

   4. Normalizing the percent heart-rate range (% HRR) for physical fitness level furnishes the best estimate of the exercise-intensity threshold. On this basis, men in this age bracket need to raise their heart rate slightly above that % HRR represented by their aerobic capacity in milliliters per kilogram per minute to achieve the intensity threshold necessary for a training effect.

   5. On the basis of the data, men in their 60s and 70s of average physical fitness need only raise their heart rates above 98 and 95, respectively, to provide a training

stimulus to the cardiovascular system. Even well-conditioned men in these age brackets need only exceed 106 and 103, respectively (when heart rate is taken immediately *after* exercise).

6. For all but highly conditioned older men, vigorous walking, which raises heart rate to 100–120 beats per minute for 30–60 minutes daily, constitutes a sufficient stimulus to bring about some, though possibly not optimal, improvement in cardio-vascular-respiratory function.

Table 13-1 provides the data on maximal exercise heart rates for men based on the data of Robinson (1938). Similar data for women are as yet not available, but our experience in the laboratory suggests that these data may also be used for the older women, until more specific data are developed.

Figure 13-1 shows the relationship of the improvement from training (Δ Astrand score = estimated maximum oxygen consumption) to the intensity of the training stimulus (percentage of HRR normalized for pretraining fitness level).

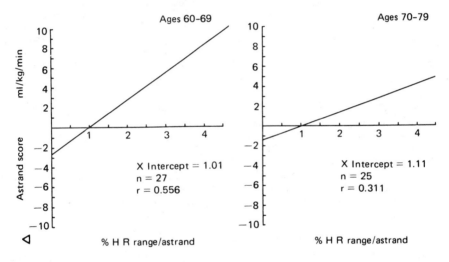

Figure 13-1. Change in Astrand Test score after six weeks of training as a function of percentage of HR range/pre-Astrand. (*From deVries, 1971a. Used by permission.*)

Figure 13-2 provides a nomogram developed from telemetered heart rates of healthy men aged 60–79 during various combinations of run/walk (deVries, 1971b). The broken line illustrates its application in the prescription of a jogging program for a man with an aerobic capacity of 30 ml/kg/min. Going upward on the 30 ml ordinate to its intersection with the 50 run/50 walk line shows its intersection to lie at a heart-rate value of 118, which is the predicted response for this individual based on our data. The standard error of prediction is 8–10 beats per minute for all of the 5 regression lines. We may, therefore, predict that approximately five sixths of the men in this age bracket with an aerobic capacity of 30 ml/kg/min would not exceed

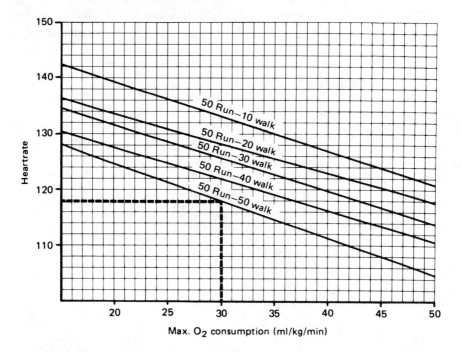

Figure 13-2. Nomogram for the estimation of heart-rate response to a given "dose" of jog/walk for men aged 60–79. Example: for a man in this age bracket with a measured (or estimated from Astrand test) maximal O_2 consumption of 30 ml/kg/min, go vertically from 30 on the horizontal axis to the intersection with the 50 run/50 walk regression line. Now go horizontally to the heart-rate axis to read 118, which represents the mean response to this dose. The standard error for the 5 regression lines is 8 to 10 beats/min. (*From deVries, 1971b. Used by permission.*)

a heart rate of 118 ± 10 or 128 beats per minute in performance of 5 sets of 50 steps run/50 steps walk.

IMPORTANCE OF TYPE OF EXERCISE

So far we have talked about exercise in very general terms, and what has been said applies only to rhythmic exercise of large body segments such as found in walking, jogging, running, or swimming.

For any given workload that the body as a whole is subjected to, the work of the heart is greater under conditions of (1) static (isometric) muscular contraction or (2) high activation levels of small muscle masses (Astrand, Guharay, & Wahren, 1968; Lind & McNicol, 1968). This is so because the blood pressure response to exercise loading is set, not by the total body work accomplished, but by the arterial blood pressure required to perfuse that muscle that requires the greatest perfusion pressure. Thus, even a small muscle working at 90–100% of its maximum strength occludes muscle blood flow and can raise the systemic blood pressure very significantly (Lind & McNicol, 1967a, 1967b). Isometric exercise would be undesirable, because not only are high levels of muscle contraction attained, but they are maintained without the relaxation pauses provided by rhythmic activity during which blood flow is unrestricted. Thus, we may conclude that exercise programs for older people should maximize the rhythmic activity of large muscle masses and minimize (1) high activation levels of small muscle masses and (2) static (or isometric) contractions. The natural activities of walking, jogging, running, and swimming seem to be best suited to this purpose. If properly designed to conform to these principles, calisthenics can also be very beneficial.

SUMMARY

With respect to the age-related losses in functional capacity of the human organism, it is important to recognize that the observed and reported decrements do not represent the true aging process alone, but may also reflect the functional decline resulting from losses in physical fitness (the "hypokinetic disease" described by Kraus and Raab, 1961) and incipient, undiagnosed degenerative disease processes as well.

The loss in vigor experienced by older people is undoubtedly the result of the well-documented losses in aerobic capacity, which are reflected in lessened physical working capacity. The losses in aerobic capacity are to be expected on the basis of the reported decrements in function in the cardiovascular system, the respiratory system, the skeletal musculature, and changes in body composition. The extent to which changes in each of these factors contribute requires further elucidation.

The importance of the hypokinetic disease factor in contributing to the loss in aerobic capacity and to the systemic physiological decrements, which may act as determinants, is suggested by the results of many bed rest studies, which have produced physiological changes in a matter of weeks in young, well-conditioned individuals. Such changes approximate the long-term aging effects. Indeed, evidence has been presented that apparent age-related losses in physiologic variables important to human performance were more related to decreased habitual activity than to age itself.

Evidence suggests that both middle-aged and older healthy men and women are as relatively trainable as young people. Their percentage improvement from the conditioning process is roughly equivalent to that of the young, although they start from lower achievement levels. The author has found no reason to believe that this trainability depends in any way upon a previous history of physical conditioning.

It has been shown that training effects in the middle-aged and older individual are demonstrable in the cardiovascular and respiratory systems and in the musculature and that important health benefits such as decreased percentage of body fat, lowered blood pressure, and a better ability to achieve neuromuscular relaxation may result as well.

Since the older organism has lost much of its capacity for response to homeostatic displacements and also because degenerative diseases of the cardiovascular and respiratory systems progress with age, certain precautions are necessary in the use of vigorous physical conditioning for the elderly. A preliminary medical examination is required, and for group exercise, well-trained professional leadership is highly desirable.

Rudimentary dose-response data have been presented to allow the beginnings of a "prescription" approach to the vigorous activity of jogging (alternate jog/walk). In general, improvement from training varies directly with the intensity of the exercise (within limits) and inversely with the pretraining aerobic capacity. The author's data suggest that a minimum exercise intensity (intensity threshold) of 40% of the individual's heart-rate range (HRR) is required for a training effect in the 60-79 age bracket when workouts are taken three times per week. Sixty percent of HRR is used as the "target heart rate," and 75% is the "maximum (do not exceed) heart rate." Every participant in a vigorous exercise program (defined as requiring more than a 40% HRR response) should be carefully instructed in taking his or her own pulse rate, after which he or she is provided with the minimum, target, and "do not exceed" heart rate values on the basis of observed resting heart rate and age-predicted maximum.

For a poorly conditioned elderly male (age 60-79), brisk walking constitutes a sufficient stimulus to bring about some training effect, though this may not provide the optimal effect. A nomogram is provided to allow estimation of heart-rate response to varying levels of training stimulus in the jog/walk regimen.

The type of exercise is almost equally as important as the intensity level. Exercise programs for older people should maximize the rhythmic activity of large muscle masses and minimize: (1) high activation levels of small muscle masses, and (2) static (or isometric) contractions. The natural activities of walking, jogging, running, and swimming are best suited to this purpose.

REFERENCES

Adams, G. M., & deVries, H. A. Physiological effects of an exercise training regimen upon women aged 52-79. *Journal of Gerontology*, 1973, *28*, 50-55.

Allen, T. H., Anderson, E. C., & Langham, W. H. Total body potassium and gross body composition in relation to age. *Journal of Gerontology*, 1960, *15*, 348-357.

Astrand, I. Aerobic work capacity in men and women with special reference to age. *Acta Physiologica Scandinavica*, 1960, *49*, suppl. 169.

Astrand, I., Guharay, A., & Wahren, J. Circulatory responses to arm exercise with different arm positions. *Journal of Applied Physiology*, 1968, *25*, 528-532.

Astrand, P. O., & Ryhming, I. A nomogram for calculation of aerobic capacity (physical fitness) from pulse rate during submaximal work. *Journal of Applied Physiology*, 1954, *7*, 218-221.

Barry, A. J., Daly, J. W., Pruett, E. D. R., Steinmetz, J. R., Page, H. F., Birkhead, N. C., & Rodahl, K. The effects of physical conditioning on older individuals. *Journal of Gerontology*, 1966, *21*, 182-191.

Becklake, M. R., Frank, H., Dagenais, G. R., Ostiguy, G. L., & Guzman, C. A. Influence of age and sex on exercise cardiac output. *Journal of Applied Physiology*, 1965, *20*, 938-947.

Benestad, A. M. Trainability of old men. *Acta Medica Scandinavica*, 1965, *178*, 321-327.

Boyer, J. L., & Kasch, F. W. Exercise therapy in hypertensive men. *Journal of American Medical Association*, 1970, *211*, 1668-1671.

Brandfonbrener, M., Landowne, M., & Shock, N. W. Changes in cardiac output with age. *Circulation*, 1955, *12*, 557-566.

Brozek, J. Changes of body composition in man during maturity and their nutritional implications. *Federation Proceedings*, 1952, *11*, 784–793.

Chapman, E. A., deVries, H. A., & Swezey, R. Joint stiffness: Effects of exercise on old and young men. *Journal of Gerontology*, 1972, *27*, 218–221.

Comroe, J. H., Forster, R. E., Dubois, A. G., Briscoe, W. A., & Carlsen, E. *The lung.* Chicago: Ill.: Yearbook Publishers, 1962.

Damon, E. L. *An experimental investigation of the relationship of age to various parameters of muscle strength.* Doctoral dissertation. University of Southern California, 1971.

deVries, H. A. Immediate and long-term effects of exercise upon resting muscle action potential level. *Journal of Sports Medicine and Physical Fitness*, 1968, *8*, 1–11.

deVries, H. A. Physiological effects of an exercise training regimen upon men age 52–88. *Journal of Gerontology*, 1970, *25*, 325–336.

deVries, H. A. Exercise intensity threshold for improvement of cardiovascular-respiratory function in older men. *Geriatrics*, 1971, *26*, 94–101. (a)

deVries, H. A. Prescription of exercise for older men from telemetered exercise heart rate data. *Geriatrics*, 1971, *26*, 102–111. (b)

deVries, H. A., & Adams, G. M. Comparison of exercise responses in old and young men: 11 ventilatory mechanics. *Journal of Gerontology*, 1972, *27*, 349–352. (a)

deVries, H. A., & Adams, G. M. Electromyographic comparison of single doses of exercise and meprobamate as to effects on muscular relaxation. *American Journal of Physical Medicine*, 1972, *51*, 130–141. (b)

Drinkwater, B. L., Horvath, S. M. & Wells, C. L. Aerobic power of females, age 10–68. *Journal of Gerontology*, 1975, *30*, 385–394.

Eddleman, E. E. The effect of age on the normal kinetocardiogram. *Alabama Journal of Medical Science*, 1969, *6*, 22–26.

Enos, W. F., Holmes, R. H., & Beyer, J. Coronary disease among United States soldiers killed in action in Korea. *Journal of American Medical Association*, 1953, *152*, 1090–1093.

Ermini, M. Ageing changes in mammalian skeletal muscle. *Gerontology* (Basel), 1976, *22*, 301–316.

Evans, S. J. *An electromyographic analysis of skeletal neuromuscular fatigue with special reference to age.* Unpublished doctoral dissertation. University of Southern California, 1971.

Fischer, A., Pariskova, J., & Roth, Z. The effect of systematic physical activity on maximal performance and functional capacity in senescent men. *Internationale Zeitschrift Fuer Angewandte Physiologie Einschliesslich Arbeitsphysiologie*, 1965, *21*, 269–304.

Frekany, G. A., & Leslie, D. K. Effects of an exercise program on selected flexibility measurements of senior citizens. *Gerontologist*, 1975, *15*, 182–183.

Gelb, A. F., & Zamel, N. Effect of aging on lung mechanics in healthy nonsmokers. *Chest*, 1975, *68*, 538–541.

Goldspink, G., & Howells, K. F. Work induced hypertrophy in exercised normal muscles of different ages and the reversibility of hypertrophy after cessation of exercise. *Journal of Physiology*, 1974, *239*, 179–193.

Gozna, E. R., Marble, A. E., Shaw, A., & Holland, J. G. Age-related changes in the mechanics of the aorta and pulmonary artery of man. *Journal of Applied Physiology*, 1974, *36*, 407–411.

Granath, A., Jensson, B., & Standell, T. Circulation in healthy, old men, studied by right heart catherization at rest and during exercise in supine and sitting position. *Acta Medica Scandinavica*, 1964, *176*, 425–446.

Greene, J. A. Clinical study of the etiology of obesity. *Annals of Internal Medicine*, 1939, *12*, 1797–1803.

Gutman, E., Hanzlikova, V., & Jakoubek, B. Changes in the neuromuscular system during old age. *Expl. Geront.*, 1968, *3*, 141–146.

Hallock, P. Arterial elasticity in man in relation to age as evaluated by the pulse wave velocity method. *Arch. Int. Med.,* 1934, *54,* 770–798.

Harrison, T. R., Dixon, K., Russell, P. O., Bidwai, P. S., & Coleman, H. N. The relation of age to the duration of contraction, ejection and relaxation of the normal human heart. *American Heart Journal,* 1964, *67,* 189–199.

Hartley, L. H., Grimby, G., Kilbom, A., Nilsson, N. J., Astrand, I., Bjure, J., Ekblom, B., & Saltin, B. Physical training in sedentary middle-aged and older men: III. Cardiac output and gas exchange at submaximal and maximal exercise. *Scandinavian Journal of Clinical and Laboratory Investigation,* 1969, *24,* 335–344.

Heller, L. J., & Whitehorn, W. V. Age associated alterations in myocardial contractile properties. *American Journal of Physiology,* 1972, *222,* 1613–1619.

Hollman, W. Changes in the capacity for maximal and continuous effort in relation to age. In E. Jokl & E. Simon (Eds.), *International research in sport and physical education.* Springfield, Ill.: Charles C Thomas, 1964.

Julius, S., Amery, A., Whitlock, L. S., & Conway, J. Influence of age on the hemodynamic response to exercise. *Circulation,* 1967, *36,* 222–230.

Kasch, F. W., & Wallace, J. P. Physiological variables during 10 years of endurance exercise. *Medical and Scientific Supplements,* 1976, *8,* 5–8.

Katsuki, S., & Masuda, M. Physical exercise for persons of middle and elder age in relation to their physical ability. *Journal of Sports Medicine,* 1969, *9,* 193–199.

Kilbom, A., Hartley, L. H., Saltin, B., Bjure, J., Grimby, G., & Astrand, I. Physical training in sedentary middle-aged and older men: I. Medical evaluation. *Scandinavian Journal of Clinical and Laboratory Investigation,* 1969, *24,* 315–322.

Knudson, R. J., Clark, D. F., Kennedy, T. C., & Knudson, D. E. Effect of aging alone on mechanical properties of the normal adult human lung. *Journal of Applied Physiology,* 1977, *43,* 1054–1062.

Kraus, H., & Raab, W. *Hypokinetic disease.* Springfield, Ill.: Charles C Thomas, 1961.

Landowne, M., Brandfonbrener, M., & Shock, N. W. The relation of age to certain measures of performance of the heart and circulation. *Circulation,* 1955, *12,* 567–576.

Lind, A. R., & McNicol, G. W. Circulatory responses to sustained hand-grip contractions performed during other exercise, both rhythmic and static. *Journal of Physiology,* 1967, *192,* 595–607. (a)

Lind, A. R., & McNicol, G. W. Muscular factors which determine the cardiovascular responses to sustained rhythmic exercise. *Canadian Medical Association Journal,* 1967, *96,* 706–713. (b)

Lind, A. R., & McNicol, G. W. Cardiovascular responses to holding and carrying weights by hand and by shoulder harness. *Journal of Applied Physiology,* 1968, *25,* 261–267.

Mittman, C., Edelman, N. H., Norris, A. H., & Shock, N. W. Relationship between chest wall and pulmonary compliance and age. *Journal of Applied Physiology,* 1965, *20,* 1211–1216.

Montoye, H. J., & Lamphiear, D. E. Grip and arm strength in males and females, age 10 to 69. *Research Quarterly,* 1977, *48,* 109–120.

Moritani, T., & deVries, H. A. Neural factors versus hypertrophy in the time course of muscle strength gain in young and old men. *Journal of Gerontology,* 1980, *35,* 672–682.

Mozersky, D. J., Sumner, D. S., Hokanson, D. E., & Strandness, D. E. Transcutaneous measurement of arterial wall properties as a potential method of estimating aging. *Journal of American Geriatrics Society,* 1973, *21,* 18–20.

Niinimaa, V., & Shephard, R. J. Training and oxygen conductance in the elderly: II. The cardiovascular system. *Journal of Gerontology,* 1978, *33,* 362–367.

Nöcker, J. Die bedeutung des sportes den alten menschen (Importance of sport for the elderly). In A. Hittmair, R. Nissen, & F. H. Schultz (Eds.), *Handbuch der praktischen geriatrie*. Stuttgart: F. Enke, 1965.

Norris, A. H., Shock, N. W., & Falzone, J. A., Jr. Relation of lung volumes and maximal breathing capacity to age and socio-economic status. In H. T. Blumenthal (Ed.), *Medical and clinical aspects of aging*. New York: Columbia University Press, 1962.

Norris, A. H., Shock, N. W., Landowne, M., & Falzone, J. A., Jr. Pulmonary function studies: Age differences in lung volume and bellows function. *Journal of Gerontology*, 1956, *11*, 379–387.

Pariskova, J. Impact of age, diet and exercise on man's body composition. In E. Jokl & E. Simon (Eds.), *International research in sport and physical education*. Springfield, Ill.: Charles C Thomas, 1964.

Pemberton, J., & Flanagan, F. G. Vital capacity and timed vital capacity in normal men over forty. *Journal of Applied Physiology*, 1956, *9*, 291–296.

Petrofsky, J. S., & Lind, A. R. Aging, isometric strength and endurance, and cardiovascular responses to static effort. *Journal of Applied Physiology*, 1975, *38*, 91–95.

Pollock, M. L., Dawson, G. A., Miller, H. S., Ward, A., Cooper, D., Headley, W., Linnrud, A. C., & Nomeier, M. M. Physiologic responses of men 49–65 years of age to endurance training. *Journal of American Geriatrics Society*, 1976, *24*, 97–104.

Rizzato, G., & Marazzini, L. Thoracoabdominal mechanics in elderly men. *Journal of Applied Physiology*, 1970, *28*, 457–460.

Robinson, S. Experimental studies of physical fitness in relation to age. *Arbeitsphysiologie*, 1938, *10*, 251–323.

Saltin, B., Blomquist, G., Mitchell, J. H., Johnson, R. L., Wildenthal, K., & Chapman, C. B. Response to exercise after bed rest and after training. *American Heart Association Monograph, no. 23*. New York: American Heart Association, 1968.

Saltin, B., Hartley, L. H., Kilbom, A., & Astrand, I. Physical training in sedentary middle-aged and older men: II. Oxygen uptake, heart rate, and blood lactate concentration at submaximal and maximal exercise. *Scandinavian Journal of Clinical and Laboratory Investigation*, 1969, *24*, 323–334.

Shock, N. W. Current concepts of the aging process. *Journal of American Medical Association*, 1961, *175*, 654–656. (a)

Shock, N. W. Physiological aspects of aging in man. *Annual Review of Physiology*, 1961, *23*, 97–122. (b)

Shock, N. W., Watkin, D. M., Yiengst, M. J., Norris, A. H., Gaffney, G. W., Gregerman, R. I., & Falzone, J. A., Jr. Age differences in the water content of the body as related to basal oxygen consumption in males. *Journal of Gerontology*, 1963, *18*, 1–8.

Sidney, K. H., & Shephard, R. J. Activity patterns of elderly men and women. *Journal of Gerontology*, 1977, *32*, 25–32. (a)

Sidney, K. H., & Shephard, R. J. Training and electrocardiographic abnormalities in the elderly. *British Heart Journal*, 1977, *39*, 1114–1120. (b)

Sidney, K. H., & Shephard, R. J. Frequency and intensity of exercise training for elderly subjects. *Medical and Scientific Supplements*, 1978, *10*, 125–131.

Smith, E. L., & Reddan, W. Physical activity—a modality for bone accretion in the aged. *American Journal Roentgen Radium Therapy and Nuclear Medicine*, 1977, *126*, 1297.

Starr, I. An essay on the strength of the heart and on the effect of aging upon it. *American Journal of Cardiology*, 1964, *14*, 771–783.

Strandell, T. Circulatory studies of healthy old men. *Acta Medica Scandinavica Supplementum,* 1964, 414.

Tomanek, R. J. Effects of age and exercise on the extent of the myocardial capillary bed. *Anatomical Record,* 1970, *167,* 55–62.

Turner, J. M., Mead, J., & Wohl, M. E. Elasticity of human lungs in relation to age. *Journal of Applied Physiology,* 1968, *25,* 664–671.

Tzankoff, S. P., & Norris, A. H. Effect of muscle mass decrease on age-related BMR changes. *Journal of Applied Physiology,* 1977, *43,* 1001–1006.

Urthaler, F., Walker, A. A., & James, T. N. The effect of aging on ventricular contractile performance. *American Heart Journal,* 1978, *96,* 481–485.

Wessel, J. A., & Van Huss, W. D. The influence of physical activity and age on exercise adaptation of women aged 20–69 years. *Journal of Sports Medicine,* 1969, *9,* 173–180.

PART **IV**

SOCIAL ISSUES

CHAPTER 14

Health Care: Physical and Mental

Bruce Sloane

CARE OF PHYSICAL ILLNESS

The World Health Organization (WHO) reported in 1972 that the number-one priority of the future should be care of the aging. The intervening years have seen the United States reluctantly beginning to grasp this thistle.

Aging is a time of multiple illnesses: arthritis, rheumatism, and vascular lesions of the central nervous system including stroke, heart conditions, and high blood pressure. Depression and dementia often compound these problems.

The health hazards of the elderly are highlighted by the startling fact that the death rate from accidents among persons over the age of 65 (at 116 per 100,000) is more than twice that of all other ages. In the age group 65–74, accidents were the fifth most common cause of death and greater than those for pneumonia. Nearly half of these fatalities occurred in the victims' own homes. The factors contributing to this accident liability illustrate the gamut of problems the older patient faces (Rodstein, 1978).

Psychological changes, which deny physical limitations and which may be associated with depression and minor degrees of intellectual impairment, accentuate the hazards. Among the common problems are the following:

1. Visual defects, especially decrease in night vision with reduced glare tolerance and recovery time.
2. Diminished hearing and balance.
3. Liability to orthostatic hypotension.
4. Dizziness that may be often precipitated by movement of the head.
5. Impaired gait due to joint disease.
6. Instability of the long muscle groups.

7. Parkinsonism or muscle weakness combined with diminution of proprioceptive reflexes, which tell the person where his or her limbs are in space.
8. Osteoporosis, especially in females, which precipitates fractures. Fractures of the femur are five times as common at age 70–79 as at 50–59, and in females the incidence of such fractures doubles every five years in old age.
9. Attacks of acute coronary insufficiency and cardiac arrhythmias undoubtedly contribute to the occurrence of automobile accidents among aged drivers.
10. Vertebral and carotid artery atherosclerosis lead to reduction of blood supply to the brain when the vessels are compressed by the extension backwards and upwards of the head. This results in dizziness, faintness, and falling and explains the frequency of the falls among aged individuals when putting in light bulbs, adjusting drapes, and getting things off high shelves.
11. Finally, the multiple drugs that the aged may be receiving for their multiple disabilities, together with their predilection for over-the-counter medication, provides further danger of obtundity.

Most old people present for medical care because of mental confusion, falling, immobility, or incontinence. These symptoms subsume a variety of diagnoses, and their general care lies within the province of medicine and its allied professions.

There is increased interest in the so-called channeling of older patients out of institutions, such as skilled nursing facilities, by providing alternate services. Great Britain and other European nations have long put an emphasis on home care. A visiting nurse, social worker, recreational and occupational therapist, meals-on-wheels program, and home chore service can keep many people much longer or permanently out of an institution. Also, for a few weeks old folks may be admitted to "respite beds" to allow their relatives to have vacations or relieve them of the chores of care for a short while. The day-care center and day hospital also allow many marginal people to stay in the community.

Although there is considerable scepticism in this country of the cost effectiveness of such measures, Rossman (1978) has shown that the day hospital program at Montefiore Hospital costs approximately half that of a modern skilled nursing facility and somewhat less than a health-related facility delivering custodial care to a group of oldsters who are able to walk to a dining room. The British believe that home and a familiar environment have many advantages, not the least of which is the humanistic one. Certainly, specialized housing with supportive services, home and aftercare programs, and day care are all desirable alternatives to institutionalization.

Public housing may be at any level. The British have pioneered those involving an official warden who facilitates provision of other health and social services. These are aided by the National Health Service and regionalization of both it and social services. The general practitioners work with a team of such persons as a visiting nurse and social worker who greatly aid the care of the elderly. Both geriatricians and psychogeriatricians make home visits before deciding on hospitalization.

In this country congregate housing facilities provide a residential environment, which includes services such as meals, housekeeping, health, personal hygiene, and transportation. These assist impaired but not ill elderly tenants to maintain or return to a semi-independent lifestyle and avoid institutionalization as they grow older. Some may have clinics and health programs.

Retirement villages come in a variety of forms. Even when purposefully built, the majority seem to lack ease of peripatetic activities on the part of their inmates. Despite sociological studies showing their success, segregation by age would seem an implausible way of dealing with life epochs.

In addition, resident clubs and hotels provide a variety of services and meals and sometimes health care. Perhaps the most interesting development is the multi-type or campus-type facility that includes different kinds of living arrangements (housekeeping or nonhousekeeping), and nursing home facilities under the same roof. Options here may range from completely independent living to residence club or hotel facilities with central dining rooms, where residents may partake of meals. At the other extreme is a nursing home facility that provides skilled medical, nursing, and rehabilitating services and, occasionally, a complete acute hospital unit. Sometimes the last is provided by having the facility juxtaposed to an acute general hospital with a geriatric service.

CARE OF MENTAL ILLNESS

Although mental illness has been arbitrarily separated from physical illness, the two are inseparably intertwined. Inevitably the mental problems of aging reflect the physical ones.

Delirium

Acute confusional or delirious states are one of the commonest causes of admission of the elderly to institutions. Many derangements, whether they are physical, mental, or even social, present in this way. The prognosis depends greatly on their accurate diagnosis and careful management, and outcomes extend from full recovery to death or established dementia. Close cooperation of physicians, psychiatrists, and other health professionals is needed, both for diagnosis and treatment.

Such acute brain disorders are contrasted to the chronic brain disorders of dementia. In both, the primary symptoms are intellectual impairment; the most important varieties are as follows:

1. Impairment of all intellectual functions including comprehension, calculation, knowledge, learning, and others. Ideation tends to be impoverished and associated with stereotyped repetition (perseveration) and compensative fabrications (confabulation).
2. Impairment of orientation—most marked for time, less for place and person.
3. Impairment of memory—most marked for recent events, less so for those of the remote past.
4. Impairment of judgment, conscience, and ability to plan for the future.
5. Shallowness or lability of affect and emotional response (Gregory, 1968).

Delirium causes the temporary, reversible change of brain cell function, whereas dementia causes permanent, irreversible damage. Such irreversibility is, of course, not always the case. Myxedema (reduced function of the thyroid) is potentially irreversible, though it is usually classified as a dementia. Delirium and dementia are often intertwined. Nevertheless, most persons react to acute brain damage with a clinical syndrome of delirium or stupor and to chronic brain damage with a clinical syndrome of dementia. Delirium is usually characterized by a clouded sensorium and imaginary experiences that are more illusional than delusional or hallucinatory. Distractibility and increased or decreased pyschomotor activity may also occur. Dementia, by contrast, usually evidences an obtundity or slowing of mental grasp, which does not have delirium's characteristic perplexity and its associated disorders of perception.

The Diagnostic Criteria from the DSM-III of the American Psychiatric Association (1980a) describe delirium as follows:

1. Clouding of consciousness (reduced clarity of awareness of environment), with reduced capacity to shift focus and sustain attention to environmental stimuli.
2. At least two of the following:
   a. perceptual disturbance: misinterpretations, illusions, or hallucinations
   b. speech that is at times incoherent
   c. disturbance of sleep-wakefulness cycle with insomnia or daytime drowsiness.
   d. increased or decreased psychomotor activity.
3. Disorientation and memory impairment (if testable).
4. Clinical features that develop over a short period of time (usually hours to days) and tend to fluctuate over the course of a day.
5. Evidence from the history, physical examination, or laboratory tests of a specific organic factor judged to be etiologically related to the disturbance.

Etiology. Acute, potentially reversible mental changes have been termed by Libow as "pseudosenility" (Libow, 1973); depression is a common example. Causes include medications, metabolic imbalance, malnutritional states, intracranial tumors, cirrhosis of the liver or hepatitis, cardiovascular disease, cerebrovascular accidents, any fever, pulmonary disease, and acute alcohol intoxication.

Rarely is there a single cause for delirium in the aged. Usually there are multiple defects, some of which produce the delirium. A common example is the elderly patient with mild congestive heart failure, anemia, and hypoxia who is given diuretics and sedative drugs for agitation, thus causing electrolyte imbalance. In patients whose symptoms are of relatively short duration or where there is a minor head injury involved, a subdural hematoma should always be considered.

Postoperative delirium is not infrequent in the aged. Metabolic imbalance, fever, anoxia, postanesthetic effects, and disorientation from unfamiliar surroundings all contribute to its genesis. To all this may be added the specific defects of deafness or loss of sight, such as the familiar postcataract confusional state.

Medications. The forgetfulness of the elderly lends itself unkindly to self-administration of the multiple medications that are often prescribed. The older person may not remember whether he or she took the heart pills, the chest pills, and, perhaps most dangerous of all, the tranquilizing pills in the right dose in the right order. A repeat overdosage frequently results. In this respect calendar packs, such as those now used for contraceptive pills, would be useful. In the meantime, the physician might try the paper bag test, whereby the elderly patient or a relative is invited to bring all medications to the office. Sometimes the paper bag is quite a large sack. All drugs that act on the central nervous system, especially sedatives, are likely to cause delirium, especially in the presence of marginal cerebral oxygenation.

Metabolic imbalance. Inadequate fluid intake in severely ill or mentally impaired patients leads quickly to electrolyte disturbances. Renal impairment may be accompanied by delirium and, frequently, urinary infection, which may or may not be associated with an underlying chronic pyelonephritis. Among elderly males, obstruction to urine flow, secondary to benign prostatic enlargement, is very common. Endocrine disturbances, hyper- or hypoglycemia, and hyper- or hypothyroidism may present as dementias, and patients with hyperthyroidism may appear apathetic. Malnutrition occurs in at least 10% of older people in the United States, and anemia may contribute to cerebral or cardiac ischemic events.

Intracranial space-occupying lesions. Such lesions contribute to the dementias, and metastases from malignant tumors of the lung and breast account for almost one half of all brain tumors seen in a general hospital. Subdural hematoma in aged patients is frequently insidious in onset and reveals few physical signs.

Measures for management. The first conditions to consider are reduction of oxygen (hypoxia), reduction of blood sugar (hypoglycemia), and metabolic acidosis. Such acidosis is due to addition of acid or loss of alkalies from the body fluids more rapidly than the kidney can excrete them, impairment of the kidney, or commonly both. Posner suggests certain general therapeutic measures applicable to all delirious patients: ensure oxygenation, maintain circulation, give glucose, restore acid base balance, treat infection, control body temperature, and stop seizures (Posner, 1975).

An adequate airway and oxygenation must be ensured, and extra oxygen should be given to mildly hypoxic patients. Transfusions should be given to those with significant anemia. An intake and output chart of both food and fluid is essential. Parenteral fluid and glucose may be necessary. Vital signs and states of consciousness must be checked frequently and charted.

A quiet, single room away from the unfamiliar noises and activity of a general ward is helpful. A single sitter, who may be a relative or a friend, helps the delirious patient regain orientation. Physicians and nurses can reassure the patient by introducing themselves, telling the time, and explaining where he or she is. Rooms should be well lighted and a light kept burning at night because darkness accentuates disorientation and hallucinations.

Dementia

Dementia is a symptom arising from cerebral disease and is often progressive. It is characterized by a decline of intellect and personality and reflects a disturbance of memory, orientation, and capacity for conceptual thought and affect (Pearce & Miller, 1973). More explicitly, it is the loss of intellectual ability, memory impairment, and at least one of the following:

1. Impairment of abstract thinking, as manifested by concrete interpretation of proverbs; inability to find similarities and differences between related words; difficulty in defining words and concepts; and other similar tasks.
2. Impaired judgment.
3. Other disturbances of higher cortical function, such as aphasia (disorder of language due to brain dysfunction), apraxia (inability to carry out motor activities despite intact comprehension and motor attention), agnosia (failure to recognize or identify objects despite intact sensory function), "constructional difficulty" (for example, inability to copy three-dimensional figures, assemble blocks, or arrange sticks in specific designs).
4. Personality change.

The state of consciousness is not clouded—that is, it is not a delirium. Physical examination, laboratory tests, or a history reveal evidence of a specific organic factor etiologically related to the disturbance; or, in the absence of such evidence, such an organic factor may be presumed if conditions other than organic mental disorders have been reasonably excluded (American Psychiatric Association, 1980a).

Many cases of presenile and senile dementia are ushered in by an acute delirium, but any suggestion that the illness is of recent origin makes it extremely unlikely that it is a dementia. The various causes of a delirium, however, need to be excluded as they may also lead to dementia.

Dementia is also difficult to differentiate from depression. At times the diagnosis may be so difficult that it is necessary to treat the patient for depression before assessing whether or not there is an underlying dementia. Snowdon (1972) has suggested that all demented patients be treated with antidepressants because 25% of patients with dementia suffer an associated depression responding to a therapeutic trial.

The commonest cause is Alzheimer's disease, which is arbitrarily divided into presenile and senile, dependent on its occurrence before or after the age of 65. Katzman (1976) argues that both Alzheimer's disease and senile dementia are progressive dementias that evidence similar changes in the mental and neurological signs and that are indistinguishable by careful clinical analyses. The pathological findings are identical: atrophy of the brain, minor loss of neurons, neurofibrillary tangles, granulovacuolar changes, and neuritic (senile) plaques. Ultrastructural studies have established the identity of the neurofibrillary tangle with its twisted tubule, and senile plaque in its amyloid core and degenerating neurites, in the brains of patients with Alzheimer's disease (under the age of 65) and senile dementia (over the age of 65).

Symptoms and course of the disease. Both presenile and senile dementia follow the general signs of dementia, leading eventually to global disintegration of personality. This is characterized by impairment of memory, followed by deterioration of intellect and change of personality with or without focal neurological symptoms and associated affective disorder. There may be early increase of muscle tone or rigidity of the extrapyramidal type. Sometimes this is described as cogwheel and sometimes as a combination of cogwheel and clasp-knife. The gait may become slow, unsteady, and clumsy (T. Sjogren, H. Sjogren, & Lindgren, 1952). Later in the disease the gait may take on the character of "marche à petits pas."

Apraxias and agnosias, especially of dressing, are not infrequent. Loss of urinary control may occur early and is later followed by fecal incontinence. It is quite common to deny such events, and Wells (1977) underlies the necessity of such defenses to the patient whose mind is disintegrating. Notable early are the easy fatigue and tiring of the patient, lack of attention span, and dysphasias affecting both expression and comprehension and leading to a rapid disruption of speech. There is difficulty in naming, and sentences are left incomplete with jumbled words and phrases. This may lead to an incoherent aphasic jargon.

Etiology of the dementias. Although there are many potential causes of dementia, most of them are quite rare. However, it is important to exclude treatable causes, which have been found in 15%-30% of cases in patients admitted with a presumptive diagnosis of dementia (Freemon, 1976; Marsden & Harrison, 1972). Depression has been found most commonly, followed by drug toxicity, intracranial mass lesions, arterial disease, and alcoholism. Less frequent are normal pressure hydrocephalus and miscellaneous illnesses such as syphilis of the central nervous system or hypothyroidism, and occasional subdural hematomas.

Alzheimer's disease, the commonest cause, is followed next most frequently by vascular disease, which probably occurs in somewhat less than 10% of patients (Wells, 1978).

Alzheimer's disease

Etiology. The etiology of Alzheimer's disease is presently unknown. Among the hypotheses being investigated are the following:

1. *Genetic.* There is a strong suggestion of a hereditary factor and Larsson, Sjogren, and Jacobson (1963) showed that siblings, parents, and children of subjects with senile dementia showed a morbid risk for this condition 4.3 times greater than any corresponding segment of the general population. Kay, Beamish, and Roth (1964) found advanced age to be the main etiological factor in senile dementia. Patients with Down's syndrome appear to have a high incidence of Alzheimer's disease, especially if they survive beyond 40. Usually Alzheimer's is regarded as multifactorially inherited.

Heston and Mastri (1977) found that the relatives of probands with histologically confirmed Alzheimer's disease not only had excessive morbidity from Alzheimer's disease itself but also from Down's syndrome and hematological malignancy. This has been reported previously, and the histopathological changes of the two syndromes are indistinguishable. There is also a 20-fold increase of the incidence of leukemia in Down's syndrome. Heston suggests a unitary genetic etiology, possibly expressed through disorganization of the microtubules. Stam (Op Den Velde & Stam, 1973) points to the significantly increased HP 1 gene frequency in patients with Alzheimer's disease and senile dementia. Persons of the HP 1 genotype also have a greater incidence of leukemia and a poorer immune response than persons of the HP 2 genotype (Nevo & Sutton, 1968), and the incidence of trisomy 21 (Down's syndrome) is excessive among relatives of patients with Alzheimer's disease. Such findings, Stam suggests, point to a multifactorial genesis of Alzheimer's disease with the HP 1 gene considered as a facilitative factor in the etiology of the disease.

2. *Infective.* The possibility that Alzheimer's disease is a slow infection in which a conventional virus plays a major role is an attractive but unlikely theory. Traub, Gajdusek, and Gibbs (1977) reviewed the relationship of transmissible virus dementia and spongiform encephalopathy to Creutzfeldt-Jakob disease (CJD) and Alzheimer's disease. Sixteen of the 126 patients who suffered with CJD had senile amyloid-containing plaques. Six of these were patients who had transmissible virus disease, and 10 were those whose disease had still not been transmitted. Their opinion was that the CJD agent might perhaps affect a brain already damaged by Alzheimer's. Others continue to question whether Alzheimer's disease is, in fact, transmissible. A cluster of CJD and presenile dementia has been reported by Mayer, Orolin, and Mitrova (1977) in southeast Slovakia. So-called familial Alzheimer's disease has twice been transmitted in lower animals (Gajdusek & Gibbs, Jr., 1975). This may be a variant of either Alzheimer's disease or Creutzfeldt-Jakob disease, which may be familial.

CJD is rare, causing a rapidly progressive dementia, myoclonus, and a characteristic EEG with diffuse slowing and periodic sharp wave complexes (Burger, Rowan, & Goldenson, 1972). There are a variety of neurological changes involving pyramidal, extrapyramidal, cerebellum and lower motor neuron lesions. The virus of CJD disease is transmissible to humans and lower animals, and the virus bears close resemblances to that of the disease occurring in sheep and scrapie, and to that of kuru, which causes a dementing and neurologically disordered disease in cannibalistic New Guinea natives.

In order to produce a slow infection, a conventional virus must possess mechanisms that enable it to evade normal host defenses and persist in relationship with tissue cells, thereby provoking minimal but cumulative tissue damage. To date, in Alzheimer's disease antibody levels for a range of classical viruses have shown no abnormality (Whalley et al., 1980).

3. *Metals.* Zinc (Constantinidis, 1979) and aluminum (Yates, 1979) have both been indicted as possible causes of Alzheimer's. The role of aluminum remains controversial, but increased concentrations of aluminum in the brain have been reported in three clinical conditions: a worker in an aluminum mill (McLaughlin et al., 1962); dialysis encephalopathy (Alfrey, LeGendre, & Kaehny, 1976; McDermott et al., 1978); and Alzheimer-type dementia (Crapper, Krishnan, & Quittkat, 1976). However, aluminum may be merely age correlated, not dementia correlated (McDermott et al., 1977).

4. *Cholinergic defect.* A variety of investigators (Bowen et al., 1976a, 1976b, 1979; Davies & Maloney, 1976; Perry et al., 1977; Reisine et al., 1978; White et al., 1977) have demonstrated that choline acetyltransferase (CAT) and acetylcholinesterase (AChE) activity is reduced in both biopsy and autopsy specimens in Alzheimer's disease. This marker of cholinergic neurons appears to be relatively unaffected by the terminal state. Bowen and colleagues (1979) have shown that by using biochemical methods on the temporal lobe there is no significant loss of neocortical neurons in histologically normal brains from nondemented elderly people. However, CAT activities per lobe and per gram of cortex are independent of age of control but nevertheless markedly decreased in Alzheimer's disease. Muscarinic cholinegic beta adrenergic and opiate receptors are not depleted. However, CAT may not be the rate-limiting factor in acetylcholine (ACH) synthesis (Tucek, 1978). Thus ACH content may not be reduced in Alzheimer's disease (Bowen, 1978). Furthermore, CAT activity may depend

upon neuronal activity, which itself may be reduced in dementia patients (Bowen et al., 1979). Receptor-binding data indicate that GABA (gamma-aminobutyric acid) as well as serotonin pathways may deteriorate, suggesting that there are changes in several transmitter systems (Reisine et al., 1978).

5. *Immunological factors.* Immunological dysfunction may be associated with the development of Alzheimer's. Amyloid is deposited in the tissues under conditions of altered immunity. This incidence of amyloidosis also increases progressively in old age and is accompanied by a loss of T cell functions, which are the thymus-derived portions of the immune system. Patients with Alzheimer's disease show impaired T cell effects. There is an association with a histocompatibility antigen HLA-A2 (Wilcox, Caspary, & Behan, 1980). Such an overrepresentation of one HLA antigen suggests the possibility that immune response genes play a role in etiology. Harman, Heidrick, and Eddy (1977), postulate that endogenous free radical reactions that are impaired in aging may contribute to this poorer immune response.

Treatment. There is a ferment of interest in possible etiological factors and their treatment application. The cholinergic defect in Alzheimer's disease has spawned a number of encouraging clinical studies of the effect of precursor supplements of acetylcholine but as yet not a double-blind control (Boyd et al., 1977; Christie et al., 1978; Corser et al., 1979; Etienne et al., 1978; Signoret et al., 1978; Smith, Swash, et al., 1978). The problems spring from the diversity and severity of some of the types of Alzheimer's disease that are being treated and the substance used as an acetylcholine precursor. Choline chloride can be prepared fairly readily with a comparable control but has a short bench life. As yet, there is insufficient evidence of its efficacy, and lecithin may be a preferable compound. However, the commercially available preparations of lecithin, especially in the United States, are low in lecithin, and it is not known whether the free choline, the phosphatidyl choline, or the essential fatty acid is the active component. Compounds with known percentages of components are commercially available in Europe but are likely to require extensive testing before being approved by the FDA in this country.

Other pharmacological approaches, whether directed to the cholinergic defect or the putative hypoxic or metabolic impairment defect, have had a checkered career. Piracetam (1-acetamide-2-pyrrolidone) has been shown in a double-blind trial by Dencker and Lindberg (1977) to have no effect in patients with dementia and by Gustafson and his colleagues (1978) in a double-blind crossover to have no significant effect either on mental function or on cerebral blood flow.

Deanol (2-dimethyl-aminoethanol) was shown by Ferris et al. (1977) to have no effect on memory or other cognitive function. Hydergine, which is a mixture of ergot alkaloids, is probably the most frequently prescribed drug for cognitive impairment secondary to both cerebrovascular insufficiency and senile dementia. It was marketed initially as a vasodilator, but it may provide stimulation of nerve cell metabolism (Emmeneger & Meier-Ruge, 1968) and interference with norepinephrine uptake (Pacha & Salzman, 1970). Of the 18 efficacy studies that were carefully controlled, 14 showed that it was superior to placebo (Hicks et al., 1980). Moreover, the longer the study, the greater the improvement. It may well be that it needs to be used in a higher maximum daily dose of up to 6 mg rather than the usual 3 mg that have been used. Thus, its effects may be due to its antidepressant quality. Shader and Goldsmith (1979), who compared Hydergine and imipramine to placebo, found that both of the active drugs were superior to the placebo but only after 9 weeks of therapy, which would be in keeping with an antidepressant effect.

Procaine hydrochloride (Gerovital-H$_3$) probably owes its unsubstantiated reputation as a panacea in old age (Jarvik & Milne, 1975; Ostfeld, Smith, & Stotsky, 1977) to its possible mild antidepressant properties (Zung et al., 1974). Olsen, Bank and Jarvik (1978) failed to confirm even this antidepressant action.

Hyperbaric oxygen has been shown by a number of investigators to have no significant change in cognitive functioning when carefully controlled (Goldfarb et al., 1972; Thompson et al., 1976).

At present cholinergic stimulation seems to be the most fruitful path. Sitaram, Weingartner, and Gillin (1978) showed that both arecholine and choline significantly enhanced serial learning in normal human subjects. Physostigmine has also produced improvement of intermediate and long-term memory in man (Davis et al., 1978), and Smith and her colleagues (Smith, Swash, & Exton-Smith, 1979) and Mohs and Davis (1979) report some promising results. However, acute experiments are probably not best suited to demonstrate its efficacy in dementia, and a trial of considerable length would be necessary to have measurable cognitive effects.

There are also some intriguing possibilities. If some forms of Alzheimer's disease are related to Creutzfeldt-Jakob disease, which is probably due to a transmissible slow virus similar to that of kuru and scrapie, oral transmission from sheep infected by scrapie becomes a possible though improbable cause.

For both Alzheimer's and multiinfarct dementia, antipsychotic drugs may be necessary at times for the acute disturbed states or even the extreme restlessness and rambunctiousness seen in the aged. Thiothixene (Navane) and haloperidol (Haldol) in very small divided doses of 1-5 mg are probably the safest and most effective ones to use. Both give rise to extrapyramidal symptoms for which anticholinergic agents should be used with caution because they are apt to produce urinary retention, constipation, glaucoma, and confusion. Thioridazine (Mellaril) is frequently used in doses of 25 mg three or even four times a day and sometimes given in a nocturnal loading dose of up to 100 mg at night. However, it may produce a fall in blood pressure and cardiac arrhythmias. In the presence of physical illness it is best to avoid it, although long usage has shown it to be a safe drug.

Repeated or multiinfarct dementia

The severity of this disorder appears related to repeated infarcts of the brain rather than to the extent of cerebral artereosclerosis. Usually more than 50 cc of brain tissue are lost to produce symptoms of general intellectual impairment as well as focal neurological signs (Hachinski, Lasson & Marshall, 1974). Often the patient is hypertensive, and there is a high correlation between the presence of hypertension and stroke. In patients with a primary degenerative dementia there is no impairment of cerebral blood flow, but an inverse relationship exists in patients with multiinfarct dementia. The condition as a major contributor to dementia is found in some 8% of cases (Wells, 1978) and associated with Alzheimer's disease in another 6% (Tomlinson, Blessed, & Roth, 1970).

Clinical features. The incidence in males is about double that of females. The presence of cerebrovascular lesions of markedly remittent or fluctuating course, the preservation of the personality, a large measure of insight until a relatively late stage, explosiveness or incontinence of emotional expression, and epileptiform attacks make it distinguishable from senile and other dementias.

The illness usually begins in the 60s or 70s but sometimes as early as the middle 40s. The syndrome may be ushered in by a delirium with clouding of consciousness. The condition may often clear in a few weeks, and only careful testing will show residual intellectual disability. Underlying the acute episodes is often a steady personality deterioration with a gradual caricature of personality traits taking place. The general changes of intellectual deterioration occur, so that memory concentration and comprehension are affected, leading eventually to loss of drive and initiative.

Treatment. A patient with hypertension should be given hypertensive medication and investigated for the possibility of a primary disease. Anticoagulants are usually not indicated and may increase morbidity (Hill, Marshall, & Shaw, 1960). Where angiography reveals the presence of arterial blockage, a thromboendarectomy may help (Paulson, Kapp, & Cook, 1966; Williams & McGee, 1964). Antipsychotic drugs may be necessary for acutely disturbed states; thiothixene or haloperidol in divided doses of 2–8 mg a day is probably the safest.

Depression

Symptoms. Depression is not only a common cause of "pseudodementia" but in its various forms has been found to be a major health problem for the elderly. Probably the single most common illness in the aged, its prevalence is over 25% in those over the age of 65 (Balier, 1968; Kay, Beamish, & Roth, 1964; Watts, 1966). It is not clear whether this prevalence increases with age (Schwab, Holzer, & Warheit, 1973; Stenback, Kumpulainen, & Vauhkonen, 1979; Warheit, Holzer, & Schwab, 1973). More important yet are the increase of suicide with age, especially of white males, and a high ratio of successfully completed suicides (Grueneberg, 1977; Kreitman, 1972; Parkin & Stengel, 1965; Shneidman & Farberow, 1961).

Much diagnosis in psychiatric illness is self-diagnosis. A feeling of unhappiness may be ratified by a mental health professional as depression and therefore becomes an illness. Clearly, the aged have much to be unhappy about; nevertheless, to constitute a major depressive affective disorder, the following diagnostic criteria need to be satisfied (American Psychiatric Association, 1980a):

1. Dysphoric mood (depressed, sad, blue, hopeless, low, down in the dumps, irritable) or loss of interest or pleasure in all or almost all usual activities and pastimes.

2. At least four of the following symptoms:
   a. poor appetite or significant weight loss (when not dieting) or increased appetite or significant weight gain
   b. insomnia or hypersomnia
   c. psychomotor agitation or retardation
   d. loss of interest or pleasure in usual activities, or decrease in sexual drive
   e. loss of energy; fatigue
   f. feelings of worthlessness, self-reproach, or excessive or inappropriate guilt (either may be delusional)
   g. complaints or evidence of diminished ability to think or concentrate
   h. recurrent thoughts of death, suicidal ideation, wishes to be dead, or suicide attempt

A major depressive episode may be part of a bipolar disorder in which the patient has had one or more manic episodes characterized by elevated, expansive, or irritable mood; overactivity; inflated self-esteem; decreased need for sleep; and poor judgment. Manic episodes as part of a bipolar or unipolar illness (that is, where the patient has only suffered manic or hypomanic attacks) are rare in old age.

Much of the depression in the aged is colored by physical symptoms and hypochondriasis. Agitation is more common than retardation. Usually, depression is more sudden in onset than dementia, which has a clear history of recent deterioration. Many patients with depression complain of impairment of memory, which is an extremely rare complaint in dementia. Often memory can be demonstrated to be unimpaired, but if depression is severe, retardation mimics memory loss (Zarit, Miller, & Kahn, 1978). Biological features of a depression such as loss of appetite, loss of weight, poor sleep, early morning awakening, constipation, and dry mouth are more pronounced in a depression than a dementia. Also, the mood disturbance tends to be more marked but may be masked by the patient's preoccupation with the physical aspects of his or her illness.

Etiology. There are many concomitants of late-life depressions such as the presence of physical illness, personal losses, and reoccurrence of lifelong anxieties. Post (1972) found that depressive illness in persons over 60 was often preceded by a major stress such as death of a spouse, illness, or disorientation following a move, which are common at any age. In addition, there is undoubtedly a biochemical basis in which there is an increase of monoamine oxidase with resultant depletion of amines and instability of brain catecholamine levels (Finch, 1976).

Treatment. After more than two decades of dominance of the tricyclic antidepressants in the treatment of depression of old age, their efficacy has been challenged by some new psychotherapies. The comparative efficacy of psychotherapy of various modalities alone or in combination with an antidepressant versus an antidepressant alone has been investigated in the younger age groups. These studies were extensively reviewed by Hollon and Beck (1978), who concluded that overall no evidence supports the efficacy of traditional psychotherapies in depression. Some evidence suggests the potential efficacy of behavioral or cognitive interventions in depression. Very little is known of their effect in depressions of the aged. Beck, Rush, Shaw, and Emery (1979) reviewed all published reports of control studies of the psychotherapy of depression to date and concluded that cognitive or behavioral or combined cognitive-behavioral treatments show a significant superiority over a control or comparison group.

In contrast to the somewhat debatable issue of psychotherapy efficacy, tricyclic antidepressants have been widely accepted as the treatment of choice in depression, although most of the studies have also been done on age groups below 60 (Klein & Davis, 1969; Morris & Beck, 1974). Interestingly enough, patients over the age of 40 responded better to imipramine in Raskin, Schullerbrandt, Reatig, and McKeon's study (1970). It is probable that the tricyclics are more effective the more closely the condition approximates an endogenous depression.

Almost all the studies of the efficacy of tricyclics in the depressions of older people have involved small numbers or uncontrolled or poorly controlled conditions (Cameron, 1959; Delachaun & Schwed, 1962; Grauer & Kral, 1960; Nans, Cornil, & Alzenberg, 1962). Not much evidence exists of the relative efficacy of one tricyclic against another, although Hodern, Holt, Burt, and Gordon (1963) showed that amitriptyline was superior to imipramine in depressed women, especially those over the age of 50. Haider (1968) compared desipramine and nortriptyline in a depressed group containing some older patients and found no significant differences between the two. Chesrow and colleagues (1964) found in a group of 47 old patients, most of whom had a variety of serious illnesses, that nortriptyline was not only effective but very safe and without complications, even when given for several months.

Friedel and Raskind (1975) found that eight older patients showed moderate to marked improvement on a mean daily dose of 157 mg of doxepin with a mean plasma level of 111 ng per cc, in contrast to seven patients who did not improve on a mean daily dose of 104 mg achieving a mean plasma level of 50 ng per cc.

In the aged, physiological changes in the body affect pharmacokinetics (Triggs & Nation, 1975). They decrease cardiac and renal output; lower hepatic enzyme activity and the concentration of albumen relative to globulin; lessen absorption of sugar, fats, and vitamins; and alter drug distribution as fat replaces lean mass in the aging process. These changes lead to prolongation of the drug elimination half-life, reduction in total drug clearance, inconsistent changes in the volume of distribution, decreased clearance by the kidney, and occasional increases in the unbound drug concentration due to the lower serum albumin. More important even than this is the drug interaction of antidepressants with those medications that may be required for concomitant physical illness. Thus, studies of Rivera-Calimlim (1976) and her group suggest that the co-administration of agents with strong anticholinergic effects may impair the absorption of many drugs. Impairment of L-dopa absorption by imipramine has been demonstrated, and tricyclic antidepressants probably also delay gastric emptying, impairing the absorption of other drugs given by mouth.

Imipramine, desipramine, and amitriptyline have elevated steady-state serum levels, which are correlated with age. Nortriptyline may be the drug of choice, despite its slightly greater anticholinergic effect. In contrast to desipramine, which has a half-life almost twice that in younger subjects, nortriptyline's half-life is unchanged in the aged (Nies et al., 1978). Among the more serious side effects of tricyclics are cardiotoxicity, ranging from sinus tachycardia to quinidinelike effects to arrhythmias (Bigger et al., 1978; Rodstein & Som Oei, 1979). Moreover, since many of the depressions in the aged are agitated, the greater sedative effect of nortriptyline is additionally helpful, compared with the stimulating properties of protriptyline, desipramine, and imipramine. The claim that doxepin is less cardiotoxic than other tricyclics may be valid, but this has to be contrasted with the clinical feeling that it may not be as potent as the other tertiary amines. The further advantage of nortriptyline is that there is considerable evidence that it acts within a therapeutic level of 50-150 ng per cc (Asberg et al., 1971; Kragh Sorenson, Asberg, & Eggert-Hansen, 1973). In dealing with the aged, blood levels, which are now routinely available, are a great help.

Nortriptyline can be safely started with a night dose of 10 mg, increasing to 20 mg or more in the first week. Thereafter, the dose may be adjusted to produce a plasma level of 50-150 ng per cc. In view of the non-age-correlated plasma levels, a nocturnal loading dose of the drug may be given after the first week. Of a total daily dose of 30 mg, 20 mg may be given at night and proportionately with increased dosage, which provides an additional benefit of night sedation. If a hypnotic is needed, chloral hydrate (500 mg) is a safe and effective drug. If a benzodiazepine is used, oxazepam (10-20 mg), which is shorter acting than fluorazepam, is preferable due to its much shorter half-life. It is important to remember that all bedtime medication should be given about two hours before retirement due to the slower absorption in the elderly.

When hypomanic or manic episodes occur, lithium probably still remains the best mood modulator and prophylactic. The dosage is usually started at 300 mg, two or three times a day, to raise the blood level to the therapeutic range, around 1.1 mEq. Because the half-life of lithium varies from 18 to 30 hours in younger patients to as long as 36 hours in the elderly (Schou, 1968), as much as a 50% decrease in dose may be necessary to compensate for the decline in lithium clearance. Moreover, it should be remembered that lithium has been found to be a nephrotoxic irrespective of age (Jefferson & Greist, 1979). As in younger patients, a neuroleptic drug such as haloperidol is also necessary. The dose should be started low and titrated with the degree of mania.

To such a pharmacological approach undoubtedly should be added a psychotherapeutic one. The work of Weissman (1979) has suggested that in younger persons, although the antidepressant drugs help somatic symptoms, the disturbances of interpersonal relationships respond well to interpersonal therapy. Thus, either interpersonal therapy based on a social work model of reality orientation dealing with the conflicts within the environment and with other meaningful persons or the cognitive behavioral therapeutic approach of Beck (1979) are probably helpful. Whether they are more helpful than other psychotherapies remains to be proven. Beck and Greenberg (1979) have used cognitive therapy in which they suggest that emotions follow from meanings attributed to events and emotional disturbance results when events are given distorted meanings. Such distorted meanings may result from "automatic thoughts," which were at the fringes of consciousness. Patients may conclude that something is wrong simply on the basis of how they feel. They are trained to recognize this by being asked how much it is overgeneralized, how arbitrarily they have made the judgment, and how selectively they have listened to their own thoughts. They are also encouraged to consider whether the thought processes correspond to a factual reality and to analyze the practical consequences for holding a belief. With practice the patient begins to observe patterns in the kinds of events that are distressing and to note that he or she has a stereotyped cognitive response to these events, namely a bias in interpretation. The patient may also recognize that his or her beliefs lead to behavior that, in turn, reinforces the beliefs. Such an approach may be aided by practical demonstrations of homework—simple tasks that the person can perform and report back on—or even some home instruction in their performance. The ability of the therapist to encourage and persuade the patient to perform tasks within his or her capacity encourages the belief that he or she is of greater worth than the depressive mood seemed to indicate. At the same time the completion of the task provides self-encouragement and further approval of the therapist. All this helps to break the vicious circle of "I am hopeless, I can do nothing."

Schizophrenic-like illness

Schizophrenic-like illnesses lead to more florid and bizarre symptomatology. These are not just delusions of thefts but beliefs of interference. Food is poisoned; electricity is tampered with; gases are pumped into rooms; false, provocative, and sexually insulting remarks come from strangers; and the plot thickens. Paranoid schizophrenic-like states, the most florid, are very similar to schizophrenia at any age. Nevertheless, formal schizophrenic thought disorder is rare.

Affective symptoms are often common in paraphrenic illnesses. Among 93 patients with confirmed persistent persecutory disorders, 57% did display some affective symptoms, and these were well marked in 23% (Post, 1980).

In addition, there may at times be a persistent organic paranoid psychosis in which paranoid symptoms occur in the late-life dementias. Senile recluses occasionally hoard possessions and have been reported as living in dirt and poverty, despite the fact that many of them were wealthy and considerable sums of money were found hidden away after their death (Granick & Zeman, 1960).

The sexual allusions and hallucinations are obviously frequently undisguisedly genital ones and may be easily understandable by the isolation of the person's life. Post's experience of 71 patients treated with phenothiazines was that all but 6 responded and over half became symptom free.

Tardive dyskinesia

Tardive dyskinesia may occur spontaneously, especially in the aged, or secondarily to psychotropic medication. This condition is manifested by a wide variety of involuntary movements including orolingual (mouth and tongue) dyskinesia, chorea, athetosis, dystonia, tics, and facial grimacing but excluding rhythmic tremor. The severity and extent of dyskinesias range from isolated orolingual dyskinesia to widespread and sometimes disabling dystonia. Age may influence the topographic distribution of involuntary movements; for example, oral-lingual movements are especially common in the elderly (American Psychiatric Association, 1980b). The prevalence is at least 10%-20% of the patients at risk and higher among the elderly. Various studies have shown a prevalence of .05%-56%, the latter probably due to minimal mild non-progressive symptoms (Ananth, 1979). Forty patients among 170 elderly residents of a state mental hospital were reported by Mallya (1979) to be suffering from tardive dyskinesia. No significant correlation was found between treatment with any particular agent and the development of tardive dyskinesia, nor were there statistically significant differences between patients with and without tardive dyskinesia as regards the total amount of neuroleptic used, the average total duration, or the average age at which antipsychotic drugs were first administered. However, those with tardive dyskinesia had received greater amounts of the anticholinergic drugs such as trihexyphenidyl (Artane), or benztropine (Cogentin) for a longer period of time. However, it is probable that older patients and women may be at a higher risk and may have a poorer prognosis for eventual remission (Smith, Kucharski, et al., 1979; Smith, Oswald, et al., 1978). Also, the aged brain may have an increased likelihood of neuroleptic-related tardive dyskinesia, especially of the oral region. Moreover, even in the elderly, studies show that the prevalence of spontaneous buccolingual-masticatory movement abnormalities was close to that found in neuroleptic medicated geriatric patients (Delwaide & Desseilles, 1977; Greenblatt et al., 1968).

At present, it is impossible to say whether patients showing slight hyperactivity of the tongue and slight choreic movements of the fingers have tardive dyskinesia. The etiology is not established at present. However, as the APA Task Force says, "an important and relatively selective action of the antipsychotic-neuroleptic drugs is to block the actions of dopamine as a neurotransmitter in various regions of the central nervous system." Blocking action may lead to functional overactivity of extrapyramidal mechanisms mediated by dopamine. The so-called "dopamine supersensitivity" of the basal ganglia, the compensating mechanism, actually tends to increase the effectiveness of dopamine as a neurotransmitter. Maintenance treatment with neuroleptics is supported by scientifically sound data only for schizophrenia, as the Task Force points out. The lesson for geriatric care is clear. Neuroleptics should only be used in small doses in intermittent episodic treatment. There is no place for prolonged maintenance therapy, except in the presence of schizophrenia.

Assessment techniques

In Britain, where home visits are still the fashion, Arie (1973) suggests seeing the relative prior to the patient and emphasizes that the state of the household is a good indicator of the capacity for self-care. The functional capacity can be elicited by finding out what the patient can do for himself or herself and whether he or she wanders or is aggressive or incontinent.

Some attempt at an estimate of memory is always helpful. The ability to remember the examiner's name and to state the name of the place where the examiner and patient are talking is helpful, or one might give the patient a short name and address to be remembered later in the interview. Also, the ability of patients to dress or undress themselves and make simple change can be tested. The face-hand laterality test (FHT) is very sensitive (Green & Bender, 1952). In this test the right and left cheeks and the backs of the right and left hands are touched in a variety of single and double, ipsilateral and contralateral trials with the patient's eyes closed. If the patient makes no errors in identifying the locations of the touches, he or she is unlikely to have significant cerebral damage. The short portable mental status questionnaire (SPMSQ) described by Pfeiffer (1975) consists of ten items: date, day of the week, name of this place, telephone number or street address of the patient, age, birth date, president of the United States, previous president, patient's mother's maiden name and the subtraction of 3 from 20 and subtracting 3 for each new number all the way down. The scoring is standardized, and adjustment can be made for both education and race. Over four errors suggests moderate to severe intellectual impairment.

Haglund and Schuckit (1976) concluded that a combination of the SPMSQ and the FHT was the most empirically useful test. Inglis's paired-associate learning test (Inglis, 1966) is one of the best-known of the verbal learning tasks that tap the deficit in short-term memory. They have been widely used in "organic-functional diagnosis" and have been reported by Kuriansky and Gurland (1976) to be highly correlated with independent measures of the patient's self-care capacity, duration of hospitalization, and the psychiatric diagnosis. When testing disturbances of new learning, one must teach to a criterion (namely, until the patient learns or clearly never will do so, when the test can be abandoned) and give the patient both the time and the unstressed situation in which to learn.

Spatial and constructional ability can be tested by asking the patient to execute simple drawings and copy simple designs such as a circle, cross, and triangle and line drawings of greater complexity such as a three-dimensional cube.

To the normal mental status examination should be added the following essentials:

1. A complete medical and neurological examination. The former should cover especially the systems liable to lead to secondary dementia. The latter should pay special attention to the cranial nerves, which should include fields of vision, and the motor system.

Diffuse brain dysfunction may be revealed by the presence of abnormal reflexes such as the sucking or snout reflex. Focal signs may provide localizing value.

2. The state of consciousness with precise recording of the orientation: name, place, and person. If the person is disoriented in place, do they understand the quality of where they are? Often the precise calendar date is not of great significance to elderly people. However, do they understand the time of the year or season or have some approximate orientation? Personal identity is lost only in advanced disease, but marital names of women may often be forgotten.

3. The state of language and motor functions (aphasias and apraxias). The following questions should be answered: Is there a disturbance of articulation, namely dysarthria (problems with the muscles of articulation) or dysphasia indicated by wrong words or words that do not exist or that are nearly but not exactly correct? Can the patient write, read, repeat speech, and comprehend speech? Can he or she name common objects? Is he or she able to follow simple and complex purposeful movements involving laterality? Has he or she got visual, spatial, and constructual ability, being

able to imitate patterns of matches or constructional drawings? Can he or she use numbers and make change involving carryover?

4. In addition to the clinical tests, Wells urges the smallest possible battery as basic routine diagnostic tests in patients thought to have organic brain disease: urinalysis, chest roentgenogram, blood studies (complete blood count, serological test for syphilis, standard metabolic screening battery, serum thyroxin by column [CT4], and vitamin B_{12} and folate levels), and CT scan of the head. With these tests, the reversible causes of dementia are almost certain to be picked up (Wells, 1978). It is probable that such a battery, especially the CT scan, would usually be reserved for patients below the age of 75 years.

Neuroses, living problems and personality disorders

There are many emotional vicissitudes in the aged, sometimes flare-ups of earlier problems, sometimes apparently new. Bergmann (1975) has described late onset neurotic disorders as compatible with a relatively undisturbed earlier life and more often associated with physical ill health, especially cardiovascular disorder. There is less suffering, even when symptoms are florid, than in the young, and the picture is often a mixture of depression and anxiety, sometimes with associated phobic features. Finally, the illness is relatively silent, leading mainly to isolation and reduced enjoyment of life. By and large, preexisting neurotic and depressive symptomatologies tend to improve during senescence (Ciompi, 1969), but they may be replaced by anxious depressive states. Neurotic symptoms occurring for the first time may mask the onset of an early dementia. Hypochondriasis is common in later life but may portend a more serious depressive illness. Although much emotional illness at this time is combined with ill health, such physical illness itself is not a necessary and sufficient cause for the neurotic illness. Moreover, a good proportion of older people whose ill health continues do, in fact, recover from their neurotic disorders (Bergmann & Eastham, 1974).

Alcoholic and drug abuse in the elderly

Simon, Epstein, and Reynolds (1968) found that of 534 patients aged 60 and older admitted to a psychiatric screening unit 28% had serious drinking problems. This has been confirmed in a number of other studies. Zimberg (1974), for instance, found that many patients aged 65 and older in a community mental health center had abused alcohol.

Prescription drugs such as the benzodiazepines and in particular diazepam (Valium) are likely to be abused. Such medication should be avoided in the elderly because of its prolonged duration in the body. When prescribed, it should be prescribed episodically rather than on a continuous basis. Good advice is "This is a powerful drug. I only want you to take a very small dose when your symptoms are really bad." The small dose of Valium might be 2 mg repeated not more than once or twice a day and for not longer than for two or three days at a time. The patient should not be given larger supplies than this.

Psychotherapeutic approaches

Many psychiatrists and psychotherapists have avoided the older patient, possibly out of fear of intimacy and identification with an older person who has already passed through life situations that the therapist has not yet experienced. Old persons are embarrassed to seek help from younger ones and often need to know that they are liked and approved of in this relationship. This helps raise their self-esteem and also their belief that they may be able to use their ability to manipulate life and authority in other ways. It is probable that whatever the therapist does is less important than the ability to empathize with the feelings and realistic problems of the older people, as well as with their fantasies. It is often more difficult to be as humanistic and fore-bearing with the old as with the young, if only because we have experienced the one and not the other. The therapist as a model of the benevolent, understanding parent, who is willing to solve many problems but who also expects some measure of inde-pendence from his children, remains as good for the old as for any other age. Probably the therapist needs to be more active than with younger people (Pfeiffer, 1971). He or she may need to go over the specific determinants of the problems and try realis-tically to see how the losses of the elderly person, whether of job, friends, spouse, or prestige, can be replaced.

Little controlled study of psychotherapy has been made in the aged, but the fol-lowing approaches have been used:

1. *Psychodynamic.* Grotjahn (1951) suggested that the old person try to inte-grate past life experiences as they *were* rather than as they *might* have been. Goldfarb and Turner (1953) tried to use the increased dependency of the older person as a ther-apeutic tool, whereby the patient could take on the parental role and the therapist the filial one. He felt he produced an illusion in patients that they were powerful parental figures, which provided gratification and fulfilled needs for respect and protection.

2. *Group approaches.* Researchers who have used younger persons as catalysts in groups of elderly people have reported encouraging results. Only one experimental evaluation of group therapy with the elderly psychiatric patient has shown convincing evidence of efficacy (Wolk & Goldfarb, 1967).

3. *Family therapy.* This is usually somewhat of a melange, with the old as with the young. One approach has encouraged the families of patients at a geriatric center to have an awareness of their own feelings as well as a clear understanding of aging (Manaster, 1967). Control studies do not seem to have been carried out.

4. *Reminiscence therapy.* Butler (1975) believed that the life review was a fruitful form of psychotherapy. Often during reminiscence older persons may feel powerless because their fate depends on so many elements over which they have little or no control. However, during this process of thinking and talking of the past, many people may discover times when in fact they did exert control. This may tend to balance the feeling of hopelessness that they are presently experiencing in the depres-sive aspects of old age.

5. *Behavioral approaches.* These have been well reviewed by Gotestam (1980). They may take the form of environmental stimulation such as introduction of live plants, family pictures and other mementos, daily calendars and clocks, musical

presentations, or religious services and bedside visiting (Loew & Silverstone, 1971). Sommer and Ross (1958) showed that they could greatly increase social interaction in a geriatric ward of senile demented patients by arranging the chairs in small groups rather than having them placed along the walls. Gotestam and Melin (1979) showed in a well-controlled study that senile demented patients showed considerable improvement in communication, table manners and eating behavior, and activity by improving reality orientation. Socialization has been shown to be improved by the introduction of modest amounts of alcohol (Black, 1969; Carroll, 1978), milieu sessions (Quilitch, 1974), and token economy systems (Libb & Clements, 1969). Where token economies have been used in incontinence, often the approach seems to have been somewhat naive. It is more likely that simple charting of the incontinence patterns throughout the 24 hours and conducting the patient to the bathroom an hour before the typical incontinence time would have far better results, as has been shown in Britain (Brocklehurst, 1980).

Gotestam (1980) concluded from the body of research he reviewed that the most promising approaches were directed to the physical and psychological environment and reminiscent memories. Learning new material and training in new skills did not seem to be effective. He suggested tender loving care, a stimulating environment, problem-oriented therapy, and ambulatory treatment. He also pleaded for more specific research. The general problem of all psychotherapy is that little attention has been given to the specific form and technique of psychotherapy, the proper amount, and the type of patient for each treatment. Gotestam also raised the interesting possibility that motor memory reminiscences such as those evoked by singing, dancing, and playing games might be more easily recalled and fruitful for psychotherapeutic approaches.

In conclusion, the psychotherapeutic approaches to the elderly perhaps only mirror the nihilism that has existed in the approach to all treatment in this group. Psychotherapy of all ages has applied few research-oriented studies until the last decade. Perhaps we may look forward optimistically to the next decade and its progress in this area with the elderly and in all therapeutic modalities.

REFERENCES

Alfrey, A. C., LeGendre, G. R., & Kaehny, W. D. The dialysis encephalopathy syndrome. *New England Journal of Medicine*, 1976, *294*, 184–188.

American Psychiatric Association. *Diagnostic and statistical manual of mental disorders (DSM-III)*. Washington, D.C.: American Psychiatric Association, 1980. (a)

American Psychiatric Association. Tardive Dyskinesia: Summary of a task force report of the American Psychiatric Association. *American Journal of Psychiatry*, 1980, *137*, 1163–1172. (b)

Ananth, J. Drug induced dyskinesia: A critical review. *International Pharmacopsychiatry*, 1979, *14*, 21–33.

Arie, T. Dementia in the elderly: Diagnosis and assessment. *British Medical Journal*, 1973, *4*, 540–543.

Asberg, M., Cronholm, B., Sjoqvist, F., & Tuck, D. Relationship between plasma level and therapeutic effect of nortriptyline. *British Medical Journal*, 1971, *3*, 331–334.

Balier, C. Les etats nevrotiques chez les personnes agees. *Gazette Medicale de France,* 1968, *75,* 3415–3420.

Beck, A. T., & Greenberg, R. L. Brief cognitive therapies. In R. B. Sloane & F. R. Staples (Eds.), *Brief psychotherapy* in the series *Psychiatric clinics of North America.* Philadelphia, Pa.: W. B. Saunders, 1979.

Beck, A. T., Rush, A. J., Shaw, B. F., & Emery, G. *Cognitive therapy of depression.* New York: Guilford Press, 1979.

Bergmann, K. Nosology. In J. G. Howells (Ed.), *Modern perspectives in the psychiatry of old age.* New York: Brunner/Mazel, 1975.

Bergmann, K., & Eastham, E. J. Psychogeriatric ascertainment and assessment for treatment in an acute medical ward setting. *Age and Ageing,* 1974, *3,* 174–188.

Bigger, J. T., Kantor, S. J., Glassman, A. H., & Perel, J. M. Cardiovascular effects of tricyclic drugs. In M. A. Lipton, A. DiMascio, & K. F. Killam (Eds.), *Psychopharmacology: A generation of progress.* New York: Raven Press, 1978.

Black, A. L. Altering behavior of geriatric patients with beer. *Northwest Medicine,* 1969, *68,* 453–456.

Bowen, D. M. Vulnerability of cholinergic neurones in Alzheimer's disease. *British Journal of Clinical Practice,* 1978, *32* (Suppl. 2), 19–21.

Bowen, D. M., Goodhardt, M. J., Strong, A. J., Smith, C. B., White, P., Branston, N. M., Symon, L., & Davison, A. N. Biochemical indices of brain structure, function and "hypoxia" in cortex from baboons with middle cerebral artery occlusion. *Brain Research,* 1976, *117,* 503–507. (a)

Bowen, D. M., Smith, C. B., White, P., & Davison, A. N. Neurotransmitter-related enzymes and indices of hypoxia in senile dementia and other abiotrophies. *Brain,* 1976, *99,* 459–496. (b)

Bowen, D. M., White, P., Spillane, J. A., Goodhardt, M. J., Curzon, G., Iwangoff, P., Meier-Ruge, W., & Davison, A. N. Accelerated ageing or selective neuronal loss as an important cause of dementia? *Lancet,* 1979, *1,* 11.

Boyd, W. D., Graham-White, J., Blackwood, G., Glen, J., & McQueen, J. Clinical effects of choline in Alzheimer senile dementia. *Lancet,* 1977, *2,* 711.

Brocklehurst, C. J. Personal communication, 1980.

Burger, L. F., Rowan, A. J., & Goldenson, E. S. Creutzfeldt-Jakob disease: An electroencephalographic study. *Archives of Neurology,* 1972, *26,* 428–433.

Butler, R. N. *Why survive? Being old in America.* New York: Harper & Row, 1975.

Cameron, D. E. The use of Tofranil in the aged. *Canadian Psychiatric Association Journal,* 1959 (Suppl.) *4,* 160–165.

Carroll, P. J. The social hour for geropsychiatric patients. *Journal of the American Geriatrics Society,* 1978, *26,* 32–35.

Chesrow, E. J., Kaplitz, S. E., Breme, J. T., Sabatini, R., Vetra, H., & Marquardt, G. Nortriptyline for the treatment of anxiety and depression in chronically ill and geriatric patients. *Journal of the American Geriatrics Society,* 1964, *12,* 271–277.

Christie, J. E., Blackburn, I. M., Glen, A. I. M., Zeisel, S., Shering, A., & Yates, C. M. Effects of choline and lecithin on CSF choline levels and on cognitive function in patients with presenile dementia of the Alzheimer type. In A. Barbeau, J. H. Growdon, & R. J. Wurtman (Eds.), *Nutrition and the Brain, 5,* New York: Raven Press, 1979.

Ciompi, L. Follow-up studies on the evolution of former neurotic and depressive states in old age. *Journal of Geriatric Psychiatry,* 1969, *3,* 90–106.

Constantinidis, J. Zinc metabolism in presenile dementias. In A. I. M. Glen & L. J. Whalley (Eds.), *Alzheimer's disease: Early recognition of potentially reversible deficits.* Edinburgh: Churchill Livingstone, 1979.

Corser, C. M., Baikie, E., & Brown, E. Effect of lecithin in senile dementia: A report of four cases. In A. I. M. Glen & L. J. Whalley (Eds.), *Alzheimer's disease: Early recognition of potentially reversible deficits.* Edinburgh: Churchill Livingstone, 1979.

Crapper, D. R., Krishnan, S. S., & Quittkat, S. Aluminium, neurofibrillary degeneration and Alzheimer's disease. *Brain,* 1976, *99,* 67–80.

Davies, P. & Maloney, A. J. F. Selective loss of central cholinergic neurones in Alzheimer's disease. *Lancet,* 1976, *2,* 1403.

Davis, K. L., Mohs, R. C., Tinklenberg, J. R., Hollister, L. E., Pfeifferbaum, A., & Kopell, B. S. Physostigmine: Enhancement of long-term memory functions in normal subjects. *Science,* 1978, *201,* 274–276.

Delachaun, A., & Schwed, S. On the use of Tofranil in a geriatric rehabilitation clinic. *Praxis,* 1962, *23,* 597–600.

Delwaide, P. J., & Desseilles, M. Spontaneous bucco-lingual-facial dyskinesia in the elderly. *Acta Neurologica Scandinavica,* 1977, *56,* 256–262.

Dencker, S. J., & Lindberg, D. A controlled double-blind study of piracetam in the treatment of senile dementia. *Nord Psykiatr Tidskreft,* 1977, *31,* 48–52.

Emmeneger, H., & Meier-Ruge, W. Actions of Hydergine on the brain. *Pharmacology,* 1968, *1,* 65–78.

Etienne, P., Gauthier, S., Johnson, G., Collier, B., Mendis, T., Dastoor, D., Cole, M., & Muller, H. F. Clinical effects of choline in Alzheimer's disease. *Lancet,* 1978, *1,* 508–509.

Ferris, S. H., Sathananthan, G., Gershon, S., & Clark, C. Senile dementia: Treatment with deanol. *Journal of the American Geriatrics Society,* 1977, *25*(6), 241–244.

Finch, C. E. The regulation of physical changes during mammalian aging. *Quarterly Review of Biology,* 1976, *51,* 49–83.

Freemon, F. R. Evaluation of patients with progressive intellectual deterioration. *Archives of Neurology,* 1976, *33,* 658–659.

Friedel, R. O., & Raskind, M. A. Relationship of blood levels of Sinequan to clinical effects in the treatment of depression in aged patients. In J. Mendels (Ed.), *Sinequan: A monograph of recent clinical studies.* Princeton: Excerpta Medica, 1975.

Gajdusek, D. C., & Gibbs, C. J., Jr. Slow virus infections of the nervous system and the laboratories of slow, latent, and temperate virus infections. In D. B. Tower (Ed.), *The nervous system* (Vol. 2). New York: Raven Press, 1975.

Goldfarb, A. I., Hochstadt, N., Jacobson, J. H., & Weinstein, E. A. Hyperbaric oxygen treatment of organic mental syndrome in aged persons. *Journal of Gerontology,* 1972, *27,* 212–217.

Goldfarb, A. I. & Turner, H. Psychotherapy of aged persons. *American Journal of Psychiatry,* 1953, *109,* 116–121.

Gotestam, K. G. Behavioral and dynamic psychotherapy with the elderly. In J. E. Birren & R. B. Sloane (Eds.), *Handbook of mental health and aging.* Englewood Cliffs, N. J.: Prentice-Hall, 1980.

Gotestam, K. G., & Melin, L. Improving well-being for patients with senile dementia by minor changes in the ward environment. In L. Levi (Ed.), *Society stress and disease: Aging and old age.* London: Oxford University Press, 1979.

Granick, R., & Zeman, F. D. The aged recluse—An exploratory study with special reference to community responsibility. *Journal of Chronic Disease,* 1960, *12,* 639–642.

Grauer, H., & Kral, V. A. The use of imipramine (Tofranil) in psychiatric patients of a geriatric outpatient clinic. *Canadian Medical Association Journal,* 1960, *83,* 1423–1426.

Green, M. A., & Bender, M. B. The face-hand test as a diagnostic sign of organic mental syndrome. *Neurology,* 1952, *2,* 46–58.

Greenblatt, D. L., Dominick, J. R., Stotsky, B. A. & DiMascio, A. A phenothiazine-induced dyskinesia in nursing home patients. *Journal of the American Geriatrics Society,* 1968, *16,* 27–34.

Gregory, I. *Psychiatry: Biological and social.* Philadelphia, Pa.: W. B. Saunders, 1968.

Grotjahn, M. Some analytic observations about the process of growing old. *Psycho-analysis and Social Sciences,* 1951, *3,* 301–312.

Grueneberg, F. Zuizidalitat bei patienten einer geriatrischen abteilung. *Aktuelle Gerontologie,* 1977, *7,* 91–100.

Gustafson, L., Risberg, J., Johanson, M., Fransson, M., & Maximilian, V. A. Effects of piracetam on regional cerebral blood flow and mental functions in patients with organic dementia. *Psychopharmacology,* 1978, *56,* 115–117.

Hachinski, V. C., Lassen, N. A., & Marshall, J. Multi-infarct dementia: A cause of mental deterioration in the elderly. *Lancet,* 1974, *874*(2), 207–210.

Haglund, R. M., & Schuckit, M. A. A clinical comparison of tests of organicity in elderly patients. *Journal of Gerontology,* 1976, *31*(6), 654–659.

Haider, I. A comparative investigation of desipramine and nortriptyline in the treatment of depression. *British Journal of Psychiatry,* 1968, *114,* 1293–1294.

Harman, D., Heidrick, M. L., & Eddy, D. E. Free radical theory of aging: Effect of free-radical-reaction inhibitors on the immune response. *Journal of the American Geriatrics Society,* 1977, *25*(9), 400–407.

Heston, L. L., & Mastri, A. R. The genetics of Alzheimer's disease: Associations with hematological malignancy and Down's syndrome. *Archives of General Psychiatry,* 1977, *34*(8), 976–981.

Hicks, R., Funkenstein, H. H., Dysken, M. W., & Davis, J. M. Geriatric psychopharmacology. In J. E. Birren & R. B. Sloane (Eds.), *Handbook of mental health and aging.* Englewood Cliffs, N. J.: Prentice-Hall, 1980.

Hill, A. B., Marshall, J., & Shaw, D. A. A controlled clinical trial of long-term anti-coagulant therapy in cerebrovascular disease. *Quarterly Journal of Medicine,* 1960, *29,* 597–609.

Hodern, A., Holt, N. F., Burt, C. G., & Gordon, W. F. Amitriptyline in depressive states: Phenomenology and prognostic considerations. *British Journal of Psychiatry,* 1963, *109,* 815–825.

Hollon, S. D., & Beck, A. T. Psychotherapy and drug therapy: Comparison and combinations. In S. L. Garfield & A. E. Bergin (Eds.), *Handbook of psychotherapy and behavior change: An empirical analysis.* New York: John Wiley and Sons, 1978.

Inglis, J. *The scientific study of abnormal behavior.* Chicago: Aldine, 1966.

Jarvik, L. F., & Milne, J. F. Gerovital-H$_3$: A review of the literature. In S. Gershon & A. Raskin (Eds.), *Aging* (Vol. 2). New York: Raven Press, 1975.

Jefferson, J. W., & Greist, J. H. Lithium and the kidney. In J. M. Davis & D. J. Greenblatt (Eds.), *Psychopharmacology update: New and neglected areas.* New York: Grune & Stratton, 1979.

Katzman, R. The prevalence and malignancy of Alzheimer's disease. *Archives of Neurology,* 1976, *33,* 217–218.

Kay, D. W. K., Beamish, P., & Roth, M. Old age mental disorders in Newcastle-upon-Tyne, Part I: A study of prevalence. *British Journal of Psychiatry,* 1964, *110,* 146–158.

Klein, D. F., & Davis, J. M. *Diagnosis and drug treatment of psychiatric disorders.* Baltimore: Williams and Wilkins, 1969.

Kragh Sorenson, P., Asberg, M., & Eggert-Hansen, C. Plasma nortriptyline levels in endogenous depression. *Lancet,* 1973, *1,* 113–115.

Kreitman, N. Aspects of the epidemiology of suicide and "attempted suicide" (parasuicide). In J. Waldestrom, T. Larsson, & N. Ljungstedt (Eds.), *Suicide and attempted suicide.* Stockholm: Nordiska Bokhandelns Forlag, 1972.

Kuriansky, J., & Gurland, B. The performance test of activities of daily living. *International Journal of Aging and Human Development,* 1976, *7,* 343–352.

Larsson, T., Sjogren, T., & Jacobson, G. Senile dementia. *Acta Psychiatrica Scaninavica,* 1963, *39* (Suppl. 167), 3–259.

Libb, J. W., & Clements, C. B. Token reinforcement in an exercise program for hospitalized geriatric patients. *Perceptual and Motor Skills*, 1969, *28*, 957–958.

Libow, L. S. Pseudosenility: Acute and reversible organic brain syndrome. *Journal of the American Geriatrics Society*, 1973, *21*, 112–120.

Loew, C. A., & Silverstone, B. M. A program of intensified stimulation and response facilitation for the senile aged. *Gerontologist*, 1971, *11*, 341–347.

Mallya, A., Jose, C., Baig, M., Williams, R., Cho, D., Mehta, D., & Volavka, J. Antiparkinsonics, neuroleptics and tardive dyskinesia. *Biological Psychiatry*, 1979, *14*, 645–649.

Manaster, A. The family group therapy program at Park View Home for the Aged. *Journal of the American Geriatrics Society*, 1967, *15*, 302–306.

Marsden, C. D., & Harrison, M. J. G. Outcome of investigation of patients with presenile dementia. *British Medical Journal*, 1972, *2*, 249–252.

Mayer, V., Orolin, D., & Mitrova, E. Cluster of Creutzfeldt-Jakob disease and presenile dementia. *Lancet*, 1977, *2*, 256.

McDermott, J. R., Smith, A. I., Iqbal, K., & Wisniewski, H. M. Aluminium and Alzheimer's disease. *Lancet*, 1977, *2*, 710–711.

McDermott, J. R., Ward, M. K., Smith, A. I., Parkinson, I. S., & Kerr, D. N. S. Brain-aluminium concentration in dialysis encephalopathy. *Lancet*, 1978, *1*, 901–903.

McLaughlin, A. I. G., Kazantis, G., King, E., Teare, D., Porter, R. J., & Owen, R. Pulmonary fibrosis and encephalopathy associated with the inhalation of aluminium dust. *British Journal of Industrial Medicine*, 1962, *9*, 253–263.

Mohs, R. C., & Davis, K. L. Cholinomimetic drug effects on memory in young and elderly adults. In A. I. M. Glen & L. J. Whalley (Eds.), *Alzheimer's disease: Early recognition of potentially reversible deficits*. Edinburgh: Churchill Livingstone, 1979.

Morris, J. B., & Beck, A. T. The efficacy of antidepressant drugs: A review of research 1958 to 1972. *Archives of General Psychiatry*, 1974, *30*, 667–674.

Nans, J., Cornil, J., & Alzenberg, D. Therapeutic trials with G22-355 (imipramine) in older patients in a psychiatric clinic. *Annals of Medical Psychology*, 1962, *120*, 57–70.

Nevo, S. S., & Sutton, H. E. Association between response to typhoid vaccination and known genetic markers. *American Journal of Human Genetics*, 1968, *20*, 461–469.

Nies, A., Robinson, D. S., Friedman, M. J., Green, R., Cooper, T. B., Ravaris, C. L., & Ives, J. O. Relationship between age and tricyclic antidepressant plasma levels. *American Journal of Psychiatry*, 1978, *134*, 790–793.

Olsen, E. J., Bank, L., & Jarvik, L. F. Gerovital-H$_3$: A clinical trial as an antidepressant. *Journal of Gerontology*, 1978, *33*(4), 514–520.

Op Den Velde, W., & Stam, F. C. Haptoglobin types in Alzheimer's disease and senile dementia. *British Journal of Psychiatry*, 1973, *122*, 331–336.

Ostfeld, A., Smith, C. M., & Stotsky, B. A. The systemic use of procaine in the treatment of the elderly: A review. *Journal of American Geriatrics Society*, 1977, *25*, 1–19.

Pacha, W., & Salzman, R. Inhibition of the re-uptake of neuronally-liberated noradrenaline and receptor blocking action of some ergot alkaloids. *British Journal of Pharmacology*, 1970, *38*, 439–440.

Parkin, D., & Stengel, E. Incidence of suicide attempts in an urban community. *British Medical Journal*, 1965, *2*, 133–138.

Paulson, G. W., Kapp, J., & Cook, W. Dementia associated with bilateral carotid artery disease. *Geriatrics*, 1966, *21*, 159–166.

Pearce, J., & Miller, E. *Clinical aspects of dementia*. London: Bailliere Tindall, 1973.

Perry, E. K., Perry, R. H., Blessed, G., & Tomlinson, B. E. Necropsy evidence of central cholinergic deficits in senile dementia. *Lancet*, 1977, *1*, 189.

Pfeiffer, E. Psychotherapy with elderly patients. *Postgraduate Medicine*, 1971, *50*, 254–258.

Pfeiffer, E. A short portable mental status questionnaire for the assessment of organic brain deficit in elderly patients. *Journal of the American Geriatrics Society*, 1975, *23*(10), 433–441.

Posner, J. B. Delirium and exogenous metabolic brain disease. In P. B. Beeson & W. McDermott (Eds.), *Textbook of medicine* (Vol. 1). Philadelphia, Pa.: W. B. Saunders, 1975.

Post, F. The management and nature of depressive illnesses in late life. *British Journal of Psychiatry*, 1972, *121*, 393–409.

Post, F. Paranoia, schizophrenia-like, and schizophrenic states in the aged. In J. E. Birren and R. B. Sloane (Eds.), *Handbook of mental health and aging.* Englewood Cliffs, N. J.: Prentice-Hall, 1980.

Quilitch, H. R. Purposeful activity increased in a geriatric ward through programmed recreation. *Journal of the American Geriatrics Society*, 1974, *22*, 226–229.

Raskin, A., Schullerbrandt, J. G., Reatig, N., & McKeon, J. J. Differential response to chlorpromazine, imipramine and placebo: A study of sub-groups of hospitalized depressed patients. *Archives of General Psychiatry*, 1970, *23*, 164–173.

Reisine, T. D., Bird, E. D., Spokes, E., Enna, S. J., & Yamamura, A. I. Pre and postsynaptic neurochemical alterations in Alzheimer's disease. *Transactions of American Society of Neurochemistry*, 1978, *9*, 203.

Rivera-Calimlim, L. Impaired absorption of chlorpromazine in rats given trihexyphenidyl. *British Journal of Pharmacology*, 1976, *56*, 301–305.

Rodstein, M. Accidents among the aged. In W. Reichel (Ed.), *Clinical aspects of aging.* Baltimore: Williams and Wilkins, 1978.

Rodstein, M., & Som Oei, L. Cardiovascular side effects of long term therapy with tricyclic antidepressants in the aged. *Journal of the American Geriatrics Society*, 1979, *27*, 231–234.

Rossman, I. Newer options for the elderly patient other than institutionalization. In W. Reichel (Ed.), *Clinical aspects of aging.* Baltimore: Williams and Wilkins, 1978.

Schou, M. Lithium in psychiatric therapy and prophylaxis. *Journal of Psychiatric Research*, 1968, *6*, 69–95.

Schwab, J. J., Holzer, C. E., & Warheit, G. J. Depressive symptomatology and age. *Psychosomatics*, 1973, *14*, 135–141.

Shader, R. I. & Goldsmith, G. N. Dihydrogerated ergot alkaloids and papaverine: A status report on their effects in senile mental deterioration. In D. F. Klein & R. Gittelman-Klein (Eds.), *Progress in psychiatric drug treatment* (Vol. 2). New York: Brunner/Mazel, 1979.

Shneidman, E. S., & Farberow, N. L. Statistical comparisons between attempted and committed suicides. In N. L. Farberow and E. S. Shneidman (Eds.), *The cry for help.* New York: McGraw-Hill, 1961.

Signoret, J. L., Whiteley, A., & Lhermitte, F. Influence of choline on amnesia in early Alzheimer's disease. *Lancet*, 1978, *2*, 837.

Simon, A., Epstein, L. J., & Reynolds, L. Alcoholism in the geriatric mentally ill. *Geriatrics*, 1968, *23*, 125–131.

Sitaram, N., Weingartner, H., & Gillin, J. C. Choline. Selective enhancement of serial learning and encoding of low imagery words in man. *Life Sciences*, 1978, *22*, 1555–1560.

Sjogren, T., Sjogren, H., & Lindgren, A. G. H. Morbus Alzheimer and morbus Pick: Genetic, clinical and patho-anatomical study. *Acta Psychiatrica et Neurologica Scandinavica*, 1952, *82* (Suppl.), 1–52.

Smith, C. M., Swash, M., & Exton-Smith, A. N. Effects of cholinergic drugs on memory in Alzheimer's disease. In A. I. M. Glen & L. J. Whalley (Eds.), *Alzheimer's disease: Early recognition of potentially reversible deficits.* Edinburgh: Churchill Livingstone, 1979.

Smith, C. M., Swash, M., Exton-Smith, A. N., Phillips, M. J., Overstall, P. W., Piper, M. E., & Bailey, M. R. Choline in Alzheimer's disease. *Lancet*, 1978, *2*, 318.

Smith, J. M., Kucharski, L. T., Eblen, C., Kautsen, E., & Linn, C. An assessment of tardive dyskinesia in schizophrenic outpatients. *Psychopharmacology*, 1979, *64*, 99–104.

Smith, J. M., Oswald, W. T., Kucharski, L. T., & Waterman, L. J. Tardive dyskinesia: Age and sex differences in hospitalized schizophrenics. *Psychopharmacology*, 1978, *58*, 207–211.

Snowdon, J. When is dementia presenile? *British Medical Journal*, 1972, *2*, 465.

Sommer, R., & Ross, H. Social interaction on a geriatric ward. *International Journal of Social Psychiatry*, 1958, *4*, 128–133.

Stenback, A., Kumpulainen, M., & Vauhkonen, J-L. Depression in septuagenerians. *Aktuelle Gerontologie*, 1979, *9*, 112–121.

Thompson, L. W., Glenn, C. D., Obrist, W. D., & Heymann, A. Effects of hyperbaric oxygen on behavioural and physiological measures in elderly demented patients. *Journal of Gerontology*, 1976, *31*, 23–28.

Tomlinson, B. E., Blessed, G., & Roth, M. Observations on the brains of demented old people. *Journal of the Neurological Sciences*, 1970, *11*, 205–242.

Traub, R. D., Gajdusek, D. C., & Gibbs, C. J., Jr. Transmissible virus dementias. The relation of transmissible spongiform encephalopathy to Creutzfeldt-Jakob disease. In L. Smith & M. Kinsbourne (Eds.), *Aging and dementia*. New York: Spectrum, 1977.

Triggs, E. J., & Nation, R. L. Pharmacokinetics in the aged: A review. *Journal of Pharmacokinetics and Biopharmaceutics*, 1975, *3*, 387–418.

Tucek, S. *Acetylcholine synthesis in neurons*. London: Chapman and Hall, 1978.

Warheit, G. J., Holzer, C. E., & Schwab, J. J. An analysis of social class and racial differences in depressive symptomatology: A community study. *Journal of Health and Social Behavior*, 1973, *14*, 291–299.

Watts, C. A. H. *Depressive disorders in the community*. Bristol, England: John Wright and Sons, 1966.

Weissman, M., Prusoff, B., DiMascio, A., Neu, C., Goklaney, M., & Klerman, G. L. The efficacy of drugs and psychotherapy in the treatment of acute depressive episodes. *American Journal of Psychiatry*, 1979, *136*, 555–558.

Wells, C. E. *Dementia* (2nd ed.). Philadelphia, Pa.: F. A. Davis, 1977.

Wells, C. E. Chronic brain disease: An overview. *American Journal of Psychiatry*, 1978, *135*(1), 1–12.

Whalley, L. J., Urbaniak, S. J., Darg, C., Peutherer, J. F., & Christie, J. E. Histocompatibility antigens and antibodies to viral and other antigens in Alzheimer's presenile dementia. *Acta Psychiatrica Scandinavica*, 1980, *61*(1), 1–7.

White, P., Goodhardt, M. J., Keet, J. P., Hiley, C. R., Carrasco, L. H., Williams, I. E. I., & Bowen, D. M. Neocortical cholinergic neurones in elderly people. *Lancet*, 1977, *1*, 668–670.

Wilcox, C. B., Caspary, E. A., & Behan, P. O. Histocompatibility antigens associated with Alzheimer's disease. *European Neurology*, 1980, *19*(4), 262–265.

Williams, M., & McGee, T. E. Psychological study of carotid occlusion and endarterectomy. *Archives of Neurology*, 1964, *10*, 293–297.

Williamson, J., Stokoe, I. H., & Gray, S. Old people at home: Their unreported needs. *Lancet*, 1964, *1*, 1117–1120.

Wolk, R. L., & Goldfarb, A. I. The response to group psychotherapy of aged recent admissions compared with long-term mental hospital patients. *American Journal of Psychiatry*, 1967, *123*, 1251–1257.

Yates, C. M. Aluminium and Alzheimer's disease. In A. I. M. Glen & L. J. Whalley (Eds.), *Alzheimer's disease: Early recognition of potentially reversible deficits*. Edinburgh: Churchill Livingstone, 1979.

Zarit, S. H., Miller, N. E., & Kahn, R. L. Brain function, intellectual impairment and education in the aged. *Journal of American Geriatrics Society*, 1978, *21*(2), 58–67.

Zimberg, S. The elderly alcoholic. *Gerontologist,* 1974, *14,* 222–224.

Zung, W. W. K., Gianturco, D., Pfeiffer, E., Wang, H. S., Whanger, A., Bridge, T. P., & Potkin, S. G. Pharmacology of depression in the aged: Evaluation of Gerovital-H_3 as an antidepressant drug. *Psychosomatics,* 1974, *15,* 127–131.

CHAPTER **15**

Retirement and Employment

Stephen R. McConnell

Employment and retirement are among the most important issues in the study of aging. Employment sets the stage for growing old by contributing to a sense of identity for most men and an increasing number of women, and by affecting health and income—two important determinants of positive or negative experiences in old age. Likewise, retirement is significant as a symbol of the transition into old age. The retirement event, whether viewed as a crisis or as a normal part of aging, makes a profound statement to the individual and to society that a major role shift has occurred.

Today retirement and aging are often viewed as synonymous, but this was not always the case, and it is not likely to be the case in the future. Retirement is a 20th-century institution made available by industrialization, surplus labor, and a rising standard of living. It is an institution that is under attack, however, as systems designed to sustain it sag under the weight of continued inflation, declining birth rates, and diminishing economic growth. To be old and retired is a luxury that society may decide it can no longer afford. As a result, work, which has been increasingly confined to the middle years, may become an expected part of old age.

This chapter examines employment and retirement policies, trends, and experiences. The first section looks at retirement in its historical context, contemporary retirement trends, the influences upon individual decisions to retire, the retirement experience, and, as a lead into the second section, the economic crisis in retirement.

Employment is the focus of the second section. It is explored both as a solution to the retirement crisis and as an important institution in its own right. The section begins with a summary of several policy issues pertaining to employment and aging. This is followed by a discussion of demographic trends in employment, attitudes of older workers toward work, and stereotypes about older workers.

RETIREMENT

For many, retirement equals old age: retired people are old, and old people are retired. This notion arises from the widespread use of age 65 as both the "normal" retirement age and the age at which a person is legally defined as old. Although retirement is one of the most significant events in a person's life and contributes in an important way to the meaning of old age in modern society, it does not equal old age. First, many people retire well before their 65th birthday, while others work well into their 8th decade. Second, some people have never worked and therefore never retire. This, of course, does not mean they are eternally young. Last, some people retire and return to work numerous times throughout their lives.

This section examines the history and meaning of retirement in American society. For this discussion we must have a reasonably complete definition of retirement. Avoiding unnecessary complexity, and at the risk of oversimplification, we define retirement as the point at which a person (1) withdraws fully or partially from the labor force and (2) begins collecting a pension, Social Security benefits, or other retirement income. Notice that both conditions must be met. Thus, the definition excludes those who retire from one job with a pension but go to work full-time at another job, as well as those who simply reduce their work hours but do not begin drawing retirement income.

History of retirement

Retirement is a 20th-century phenomenon. Prior to industrialization in the mid-19th century, workers were tied to their jobs both because their labor was needed and because they could not afford to retire. Retirement was available only to the rich nobility.

As industrialization proceeded, several forces acted at once to create an atmosphere conducive to the emergence of retirement as an institution. These forces were as follows: (1) decline in the demand for labor—a trend beginning in the 1870s and reaching its peak in America with 30% unemployment in the Depression of the 1930s; (2) technological transformations of the economy, which led to "accelerated obsolescence of the knowledge and skills of older workers" (Ward, 1979, p. 184); (3) growth of large-scale bureaucracies with impersonal rules and regulations governing, among other things, the retirement decision, and (4) growth of private pensions and Social Security, which provided the economic base to support retirement.

The emergence of retirement as an officially sanctioned event is traced back to German Chancellor Otto von Bismarck, who in 1891 legislated the Old Age and Survivors Pension Act, which established age 70 retirement (Meier & Dittmar, 1979). Retirement came of age in America with the development of economic programs to support the aged outside the work force. The early 1920s marked the beginning of the drive for old-age economic security in the United States as aging-based organizations sought a government-sponsored national pension system (Pratt, 1976). The Great Depression, however, forced the country to take notice of the economic plight of the aged. The result was the Social Security Act in 1935, which not only provided a degree of economic security to many persons aged 65 and over but also set into motion a trend toward labor-force exit at or before age 65.

Retirement trends

Retirement rates increased dramatically during the early 1950s as Social Security coverage and benefit levels were expanded and as private pensions began to emerge. At the turn of the century, more than 60% of men aged 65 and over were in the labor force; by 1950 this had dropped to only 39%, and today only 19% are employed (see Figure 15-1). In contrast, the labor-force participation rate for women over age 65 has remained relatively stable since 1950.

In 1956, women were enabled to retire "early" (age 62) with reduced Social Security benefits, and in 1961 this early retirement option was extended to men. As a result of this and the expansion of other benefits (disability, private pensions), labor-force participation has decreased among those under age 65. For men aged 55–64, the labor-force participation rates declined by 17% between 1950 and 1980. Similarly, the labor-force participation rate among men aged 45–54 has declined by 5% during this same period. As will be discussed later, this dramatic increase in retirement rates among middle-aged and older men is the direct result of improvements in retirement income systems.

The employment picture for older women is very different from that of men, but retirement patterns are similar. Unlike older men, women between the ages of 45 and 64 are entering (or reentering) the work force at a staggering rate. Since 1950, female labor-force participation increased by more than 50% among this age group. Despite this dramatic trend, most women still retire by age 65. In 1980, for example, only 8.1% of all women continued working beyond age 65.

What contributes to these retirement trends? Why are so few people in the work force after age 65? We can best address these questions by examining factors influencing individual retirement decisions.

Decision to retire

One of the most important questions in industrial gerontology is "Why do people retire?" Employers seek answers to this question so they can maintain control over the makeup of their labor forces by providing either incentives or disincentives for retirement. Congress, the Social Security Administration, the Department of Labor and other branches of the federal government need to know the causes of retirement for developing more rational employment and retirement policies such as those directed toward eliminating age discrimination in employment, reducing unemployment, and financing Social Security. Even individual workers want to know why people retire so they can better make plans for their own retirement.

Older workers decide to retire for many reasons. Some are bored or dissatisfied with their jobs; others are in poor health and do not feel they are physically able to continue working. Mandatory retirement rules force some workers off the job, just as the promise of lucrative pension benefits is an incentive for others to retire. Some plan for many years for their retirement and eagerly await a life of leisure. Others retire unexpectedly and unwillingly due to a sudden change in health, family relationships, or company policies.

When examining why people retire, one must first understand that not everyone retires at the same age. Retirement ages vary greatly but can be grouped into four distinct categories (see Table 15-1). Each category is associated with a unique set of retirement "causes." These include retirement income, health, attitudes about retirement, job satisfaction, and occupation. The following sections briefly describe the types of people who fall within each category.

Percentage of men aged 65 and over in work force

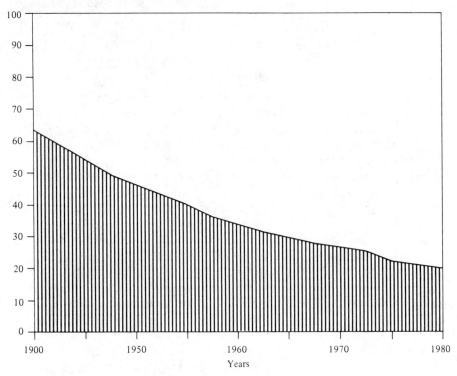

SOURCE—Bureau of Labor Statistics, U.S. Department of Labor.

Figure 15-1. Percentage of men aged 65 and over in work force. (*Bureau of Labor Statistics, U.S. Department of Labor.*)

TABLE 15-1. The four categories of retirement ages

Retirement category	Age
Very early	61 or earlier
Early	62–64
Normal	65
Late	66 or later

Very early retirement. Very early retirement, which occurs prior to age 62, represents one of the most interesting and complex phenomena in the study of retirement. Those who retire very early do so for widely different reasons. A longitudinal study of retirement patterns conducted by the University of Michigan found that very early retirees were either in high income brackets and reasonably good health or in poor health with low incomes (Morgan, 1980). Thus, some retired voluntarily because they could afford to, while others were forced into very early retirement due to poor health or chronic unemployment. The vast majority of very early retirees, however, reported poor health and low incomes, and a substantial portion died within a few years of retirement (Kingson, 1979).

For so-called hazardous occupations, very early retirement is often mandatory. These occupations, which include fire fighters, police officers, airline pilots, and bus drivers, have been interpreted by the courts to fall within an exempted category of the Age Discrimination in Employment Act (ADEA). Although the ADEA protects most private sector workers between the ages of 40 and 70, it does allow an exemption when age is considered to be a "bona fide occupational qualification." To qualify for the exemption, an occupation must be shown to require abilities for which members of specific age groups are unqualified because of their age. Retirement ages for these exempted occupations are often very low. For example, in 1977 the average retirement age for police officers in Los Angeles was 48; in New York State it was 49 (Meier & Dittmar, 1979).

Early retirement. Most workers, in fact, retire between the ages of 62 and 64. In 1979, more than two thirds of all workers covered by Social Security accepted reduced benefits for early retirement, usually at age 62 (Social Security Administration, 1980). As with very early retirement, the determinants of early retirement are varied.

In a now classic study of early retirement conducted by Barfield and Morgan (1975) at the University of Michigan, the researchers found that finances, health, retirement attitudes, and job-related attitudes were the most important predictors of early retirement. Barfield and Morgan surveyed a national sample of 3647 families and 4974 older workers in the auto industry. They found that finances was the most important factor in early retirement decisions: the higher the expected retirement income, the more likely were plans for early retirement. Corroborating this finding in a follow-up survey conducted 13 years later, Morgan (1980) found that inadequate or unstable income acts as a deterrent to early retirement.

The importance of an adequate and stable retirement income has led many observers of retirement trends to speculate that continued high inflation will cause workers to postpone their retirement date. As noted earlier, however, national trends still show a steady decline in retirement ages, despite high inflation rates. To the extent workers are postponing retirement at all due to fears about inflation, they apparently are doing so by only six months or less.

Health also influences early retirement. In a study of 145 British male factory workers, eight out of ten of those who reported "poor" health wanted to retire, whereas seven out of ten reporting "good" health wanted to continue working beyond the pensionable age (Jacobsen, 1972). Data from the U. S. Public Health Service indicate that nearly two thirds of older males who were not in the labor force reported some type of chronic health limitation (Bowen & Finegan, 1969). Similarly, the U.S. Department of Labor's National Longitudinal Survey disclosed that workers who reported health limitations in 1966 were more likely to be absent from the labor force in 1973 (Sheppard, 1977).

Attitudes are important in retirement decisions but are less important than either income or health. Those who had positive attitudes about retirement and negative attitudes toward their jobs are more likely to retire early. Among the British factory workers just cited, a preference for working beyond the pensionable age was, in part, the result of fears that retirement would be detrimental to their health (Jacobsen, 1972). The demands of the job also influenced these factory workers' retirement preferences. Those who worked in physically demanding and stressful jobs were more likely to prefer early retirement. Negative attitudes toward work, however, do not necessarily coincide with positive attitudes toward retirement, or vice versa. A study of nonacademic employees at a university medical center concluded that "only when the job is of prime importance as the central organizing factor of a person's life should it affect his retirement attitude. It reaches such a level of importance for only a few people, typically for self-employed and upper-echelon businessmen, for self-employed professionals and for academics" (Fillenbaum, 1971, pp. 244–248).

In sum, early retirement occurs when retirement income is expected to be adequate, health is perceived to be poor, or attitudes toward retirement are very positive. Job dissatisfaction, on the other hand, affects the decision to retire early only if the job is of central importance to the individual.

Normal and late retirement. With the availability of Social Security early retirement benefits and increasing private pension coverage, fewer workers are remaining in the work force until the "normal" retirement age of 65. Thus, so-called normal retirement is becoming increasingly abnormal.

Despite the early retirement trend, however, normal retirement age retains its significance in public and private sector policies. For example, Social Security still pays full-retirement benefits at age 65. The Employee Retirement Income Security Act of 1974 (ERISA), which governs private pension plans, retained age 65 as the normal age at which pension plan benefits reach maturity. Similarly, the ADEA allows employers to discontinue contributions to an employee's pension at age 65, even though the same law prohibits other forms of age discrimination before age 70. The net result of this last policy is a subtle pressure on workers over 65 to retire, since discontinued pension contributions are equivalent to a cut in pay.

Normal and late retirees exhibit similar characteristics. They are often self-employed (Morgan, 1980), which means they are personally very committed to their work and free of external policies that would "encourage" them to leave the work force early. An example of the commitment to work and desire to remain employed as long as possible was expressed very strongly in a study of older members of the Writers Guild of America (McConnell & Fiske, 1980, p. 33). This study of television, motion picture, and radio writers over the age of 60 discovered that one third of those interviewed planned to retire as late as possible. In response to a question about the meaning of retirement, these self-employed professionals revealed their heartfelt commitment to continue to work: "Retirement is dull living—rusting out; it means waking up bonkers one day and not knowing which way is up; turning into a zucchini" (McConnell & Fiske, 1980, p. 33).

Thus, the decision to retire is influenced by many factors. Economics plays a central role, both for its direct impact on perceptions about the feasibility of retirement and indirectly as a contributor to worker health and job satisfaction. Health is the second most important influence on retirement decisions. Poor health, when it is combined with an adequate retirement income, results in early or very early retirement. In contrast, poor health and an inadequate income tends to delay retirement out of necessity. Attitudes about retirement and work enter into the decision process but often only indirectly. For example, those who work at physically demanding or stressful jobs tend to retire early because they are less satisfied with their jobs, whereas those who are self-employed retire late, largely due to higher levels of job satisfaction. Mandatory retirement provisions affect only a minority of workers, but retirement income policies are often discriminatory and discourage most workers from continuing beyond age 65.

Retirement experience

There is a widespread belief among Americans that retirement, and especially mandatory retirement, is bad for one's health. A report by the American Medical Association's (AMA) Committee on Aging is often quoted in support of this belief:

> Compulsory retirement on the basis of age will impair the health of many individuals whose job represents a major source of status, creative satisfaction, social relationships, or self-respect. It will be equally disastrous for the individual who works only because he has to, and who has a minimum of meaningful goals or interests in life, job-related or otherwise. Job separation may well deprive such a person of his only source of identification and leave him floundering in a motivational vacuum with no frame of reference whatsoever [American Medical Association, 1968, p. 2].

This AMA report gained wide publicity and is often quoted, not only because it comes from a "credible" source, but because it supports the pervasive American ethic that work defines our very existence and without work life has little meaning.

There is no question that the loss of the work role causes trauma among some people. An example of such trauma is the situation of Mr. Winter, a valued employee who, upon forced retirement, became catatonic and bedridden. Retirement had effectively turned Mr. Winter into a "vegetable." When his company was forced to call him back to work because no one could be found to perform his job, Mr. Winter arose from his bed, and "within a few days, this 'vegetable' was operating at full steam, interacting with people as he had years before" (U.S. Department of Health, Education and Welfare, 1973, p. 79).

In contrast to the AMA report and Mr. Winter's situation, a large body of research indicates that many older people are quite satisfied and well-adjusted in retirement (Atchley, 1976; Back, 1966; Cottrell, 1969; George, 1980; Kimmel, Price, & Walker, 1978; Streib, 1971). These studies show that retirees do not miss their jobs; they do not suffer a loss of identity; they remain at least as optimistic as they were before retirement; they continue to feel useful; and they do not suffer an increase in loneliness, anxiety, or depression upon retirement. In short, retirement, according to these studies, is not a major cause of depression, decline, or death among the elderly.

How do we reconcile these conflicting views of retirement? We must look at the background of retirees and at what they bring into retirement in order to understand how the experience affects them. It is not strictly an individual issue, though personality factors do play a role. Rather, one finds common patterns of responses to retirement; such responses vary according to occupational status, income level, health status, the nature of one's job, the state of the economy, marital status, sex, ethnicity, and so on. Depending on a person's status in society, retirement is good for some people, indifferent to some, and bad for others. The causes of differing responses to retirement are discussed in greater detail in the following section.

On balance, more people express positive feelings in retirement. A positive retirement experience is more likely if: (1) retirement is voluntary rather than forced; (2) one's income and health are good enough to live comfortably in retirement; (3) work is not the most important thing in one's life; and (4) some preparation and planning for retirement have occurred.

Voluntary retirement is viewed more positively than forced retirement. Mandatory retirement can create stress in retirement, especially if work was very important (Thompson, Streib, & Kosa, 1960). It is a maxim of American life that compulsory activities are viewed more negatively than those that are voluntary. National surveys have confirmed this: compulsory retirement rules are viewed negatively by most Americans, and most feel that mandatory retirement should be eliminated altogether (Harris, 1975). Mandatory retirement rules have not automatically created a negative retirement experience, however, because most people have been willing to retire before or upon reaching mandatory retirement age. This is partly due to the fact that mandatory retirement rules are often accompanied by a pension system, which makes retirement more desirable. Also, most older workers have developed expectations that they will retire by age 65. Thus, retirement can be relatively positive, even under mandatory retirement rules, as long as the person is willing to retire at the mandatory age. According to one study—which was conducted before the 1978 Amendments to the Age Discrimination in Employment Act that raised the permissible mandatory retirement age to 70—only 7% of the work force was faced with mandatory retirement rules and was both unwilling to retire and physically capable of continuing to work (Schultz, 1974). Although the number of employees facing mandatory retirement has declined since this study, the number wishing to stay in the work force has increased dramatically, largely because of inflation.

Income and health are the most important factors in successful retirement. Those living on high incomes retire early and generally enjoy retirement; those with low incomes are forced to retire later and are less happy in retirement. Furthermore, all but the highest status retirees suffer declines in satisfaction over time, largely due to losses in income.

Health also is a primary determinant of satisfaction with retirement. Those in poor health retire early and resent retirement; those in good health retire at various ages and are happier in retirement. Contrary to popular belief, health does not decline dramatically upon retirement; in some cases health improves (Haynes, 1978). Most of those who die shortly after retirement were in poor health prior to retiring (George & Maddox, 1975; Stokes & Maddox, 1968).

When work is a central force in life, as it is with many professionals and high status workers, retirement is more difficult—at least initially. Higher status workers derive greater intrinsic rewards from their jobs. Thus, they tend to resist retirement and retire as late as possible. Despite their greater work orientation and reluctance to retire, high status persons show increases over time in satisfaction with retirement (Rowe, 1972; Streib & Schneider, 1971). Low status workers, on the other hand, are more willing to retire, but over time they show decreasing satisfaction with retirement, largely due to income problems.

Few retirees have had any formal retirement preparation, but those who have had preparation tend to feel more positive about retirement (Davidson & Kunze, 1965). Middle-class workers spend the most time reviewing information about retirement, usually through reading or discussing it with coworkers (Simpson, Back, & McKinney, 1966). Upper and lower status persons are least likely to prepare for retirement.

Retirement is satisfying for most people—if they have a decent income, enjoy good health, were not forced to retire, and were not wedded to their jobs. Some people are unhappy in retirement, but this occurs more because of income and health problems than because of loss of the work role. Work is important, though, in determining income and may be essential for survival in the face of high inflation. Although the loss of the work role is not an important cause of dissatisfaction in retirement, it is one of the few resources available to many older persons for improving their overall well-being.

Growing economic crisis in retirement

Inflation and unemployment pose serious problems for retirees by threatening the purchasing power of private pensions and the financial stability of Social Security. The cost of living has increased an average of 7.4% annually over the past decade, thereby reducing the purchasing power of private pensions by more than 50% (unless periodic benefit increases have been provided by the company). A sustained inflation rate of 12%, not uncommon in recent years, would reduce a fixed pension by two thirds in 10 years and by 90% in 20 years. To offset inflation Congress tied Social Security benefit increases to the Consumer Price Index (CPI) beginning in 1974, but most private pension plans provide no such protection. As a result, poverty among those aged 65 and older showed a significant increase in 1979 (from 13.9% in 1978 to 15.7% in 1980).

Retirement income policy in the United States is supposed to rest on a three-legged stool consisting of Social Security, savings, and private pensions. Unfortunately, most retirees do not enjoy benefits from all three legs. In 1980, more than one quarter (28%) of all retirees were forced to subsist on Social Security alone. Personal savings have declined dramatically over the past five years—from 7% of disposable income in 1974 to 4.5% in 1979 (Joint Economic Committee, 1980). Moreover, private pensions are paying benefits to only 25% of retirees. Thus, the majority of retirees must rely on the Social Security system for survival.

The heavy reliance on Social Security as a sole source of income has created a crisis in Social Security financing. Despite a more than six-fold increase in the tax rate since the program began, the Social Security system is expected to face a short-term financing crunch by late 1983 and a more serious long-term shortfall beginning in 2020, unless Congress acts to increase revenues or reduce outlays. The problem stems, in part, from high inflation—a 1% increase in the CPI results in a $1 billion increase in Social Security expenditures—and high unemployment—for every one million workers laid off for one month in 1980, the Social Security funds lost approximately $100 million in revenues (Joint Economic Committee, 1980).

The crisis in retirement income systems is also fueled by two conflicting trends. One is the trend toward earlier retirement, which has already been discussed. The other is that life expectancy is on the rise. As pointed out in Chapter 2, life expectancy at birth has increased from 49 years in 1900 to 73 years today. If a person survives to the age of 65, he or she has an average of 8 more years to live. Longer life expectancy and earlier retirement, then, result in prolonged dependence on Social Security and other retirement funds. If both trends continue, the result spells economic disaster for all retirement income systems.

A partial solution to this pending disaster would be to fit the retirement income stool with a fourth leg consisting of income from employment. The next section examines the issue of employment for older persons—a topic that is receiving increasing attention as the economic crisis worsens.

EMPLOYMENT

Employment is one means of enhancing the economic well-being of older persons. It also is a means of salvaging the financially pressed Social Security and private pension systems. Without an increase in the average retirement age, the retiree-to-worker ratio (the *dependency ratio*) will decline over the next 30 years from three workers for each retiree to only two workers per retiree. Since Social Security is a pay-as-you-go system—that is, contributions made by workers are immediately transferred to retirees—the projected change in the dependency ratio creates a dilemma. To preserve the Social Security system, we must increase the burden on workers through higher taxes, reduce benefits for retirees, or both. Employment is one solution to this apparent dilemma.

Policies affecting employment

The financial woes of the Social Security system have caused many public and private sector policymakers to rethink employment and retirement policies. For example, in 1978 Congress amended the Age Discrimination in Employment Act

(ADEA) to raise the permissible mandatory retirement age from 65 to 70 and expand protections for workers aged 40–70. This was done in the hopes of eliminating some of the obstacles to prolonged employment and a later retirement age. Similarly, some employers abolished their mandatory retirement practices altogether, and others initiated hiring programs for older workers.

Despite these policy changes, the average retirement age continues to decline as increasing numbers of middle-aged and older workers opt for early retirement. One reason for this lies in the absence of a coherent and consistent national policy toward employment and retirement. The inconsistencies in existing policies are briefly discussed in the following sections.

ADEA. The 1978 Admendments to the ADEA represent a significant step toward protecting the employment rights of older Americans. Serious loopholes in the law, however, belie an ambivalence among policymakers about the goal of retaining older workers in the labor force. For example, while federal employees have no mandatory retirement age, private sector employees can still be forcibly retired at age 70 or earlier. A special provision in the law allows mandatory retirement at age 65 for "high policymaking executives" who would receive $27,000 in pension benefits and, until July 1982, for tenured college teachers. Employers are allowed to discourage continued employment among older workers by "freezing" all contributions and accrual of pension benefits at age 65. Finally, forced early retirement under the "bona fide occupational qualification" provision discussed earlier is being permitted by the courts, not only for so-called hazardous occupations such as front-line police officers and fire fighters, but also for nonhazardous positions such as police chiefs.

Social Security. Social Security discourages older employees from delaying retirement beyond age 65 by allowing a meager 3% increase in benefits for each additional year worked. To be actuarially fair this post-65 adjustment should be as high as 7–9% per year. In actuality, then, the delayed retirement credit acts as a disincentive, or at least a nonincentive, to continued employment beyond age 65.

Social Security also discourages employment after retirement through the application of the "retirement test." The retirement test specifies that Social Security benefits are to be reduced by $1 for every $2 of wages earned above a specified annual limit. (The limit is $6,000 in 1982, which will rise each year after that in proportion to the increase in average earnings taxed for Social Security.) In testimony before the House Select Committee on Aging, Anthony Pallechio, an economist with the National Bureau of Economic Research, concluded, "It is clear that the retirement test makes workers subject to it hold their earnings below the exempt amount in order to receive full benefit payments" (Pallechio, 1980, p. 7). If the retirement test were liberalized, older persons would increase their work effort accordingly.

Private pensions. Private pensions encourage older workers to leave the labor force by offering lucrative early retirement benefits. According to the 1980 Corporate Pension Plan Study by Bankers Trust Company, nine out of ten plans provided early retirement benefits that are not actuarially reduced (Bankers Trust Company, 1980). In other words, benefit reductions are not made at a level that would fully compensate for the longer period over which benefits must be paid. In purely economic terms, then, employees are wise to take early retirement.

Another way private pensions discourage continued work is by designating a "normal retirement age"—usually 65—and not accruing additional benefits after that. This acts as a powerful disincentive to work beyond age 65. The net effect of these pension inducements is a wholesale exodus from the work force at ever earlier ages.

Employment programs. The public sector jobs programs designed to assist older persons through training, placement, and the creation of jobs are inadequately funded. The Senior Community Service Employment Program (SCSEP), funded under Title V of the Older Americans Act, provides part-time, minimum-wage jobs for approximately 54,200 low income persons over the age of 55. This may appear to be a large program, but there are 8 million persons aged 55 and over who meet the low income requirements to qualify for these jobs. Thus, the program, which received $277.1 million in 1982, provides fewer than 1% of the needed jobs for older workers.

Similarly, the Comprehensive Employment and Training Act (CETA) offers only minimal employment assistance to older workers. The CETA program is biased toward younger workers despite congressional efforts to direct an appropriate share of resources toward older workers. A study of the CETA program by the U. S. Commission on Civil Rights concluded that "persons in each of the age groups over 44 are enrolled at less than half their proportion of the unemployed population" (U. S. Commission on Civil Rights, 1979, p. 134). In 1979 only 7% of all CETA positions were allocated to persons aged 45 and older, despite their representing one third of the poor and unemployed in the United States. The inadequate funding levels for CETA and SCSEP are indications of an apparent lack of commitment toward employment opportunities for older persons.

Thus, older workers are confronted with mixed messages. The ADEA protects their right to continue working until age 70 in most jobs (and indefinitely in federal jobs), but Social Security and private pensions provide strong incentives to leave the labor force early. Moreover, those who retire and find they cannot make ends meet financially are confronted with age discrimination, inadequately funded jobs programs, and, via the Social Security retirement test, economic disincentives to work after retirement. A consistent set of policies guiding work and retirement decisions is needed. If an early retirement age is desirable, then retirement income systems should provide an adequate and inflation-proof income for all retirees. If, on the other hand, later retirement is desirable, incentives should be developed to delay retirement, and all obstacles to continued work should be eliminated.

Employment trends

Given the numerous disincentives to work in old age, it is not surprising that fewer and fewer older persons choose to remain in the labor force. As described in the retirement section earlier, labor-force participation among those aged 65 and over has declined dramatically since 1950. This section examines in greater detail the characteristics of those who are employed.

Table 15-2 illustrates two interesting employment trends. First, the total labor-force participation rate for those aged 65 and over has declined by 50% since 1950. Nearly all of this decline, however, is accounted for by men leaving the labor force; the rate for women has remained relatively constant. Second, although the percentage of working men aged 55–64 has declined by 16%, the employment rate for this age group as a whole has remained almost constant. The reason for this is that women aged 55–64 have increased their participation in the labor force by more than 50%. (The same pattern holds for women aged 45–54.)

TABLE 15-2. Labor-force participation rates by sex and age for 1950, 1960, 1970, and 1980

	Year			
	1950 %	*1960* %	*1970* %	*1980* %
Age 65 and over				
Total	26.7	20.8	17.0	12.6
Men	45.8	33.1	26.8	19.1
Women	9.7	10.8	9.7	8.1
Age 55–64				
Total	56.7	60.9	61.8	56.0
Men	86.9	86.8	83.0	72.3
Women	27.0	37.2	43.0	41.5
Age 45–54				
Total	66.4	72.1	73.5	75.0
Men	95.8	95.7	94.2	91.2
Women	37.9	49.8	54.4	59.9

SOURCE: U.S. Department of Labor, Employment and training report to the president, Washington, D.C.: U.S. Government Printing Office, 1981.

This dramatic rise in the number of middle-aged and older women who are working can be accounted for by several social and economic trends. These include the following: (1) changing social values regarding acceptable roles for women, (2) declines in home responsibilities due to decreased family size, (3) increase in the number of families living in urban areas, which typically offer greater employment prospects, (4) rise in expectations for a higher standard of living, which has resulted in the need for two earners per family, (5) rise in divorce rates, and (6) expansion of jobs typically available to women such as finance, education, service, medicine, and retail (Nussbaum, 1980; Sheppard, 1976).

Older workers can be found in jobs that initially require considerable education and long training periods or those that have flexible retirement policies (Morse, 1979). They also are less likely to be in physically demanding jobs, low-level or entry level jobs, and those jobs in which new technologies have only recently been perfected (for example, computers). Males aged 65 and over tend to be concentrated among self-employed professionals, physicians, managers and administrators, bookkeepers, and farmers and farm managers. Many of these occupations allow individual discretion over the retirement decision, thus permitting workers to extend their work lives into old age.

Older workers also tend to be found in part-time jobs. In 1978, nearly half of all workers over age 65 (39% of men and 54% of women) were working part-time (Deuterman & Brown, 1978). Despite overall declines in labor-force participation among this age group, part-time jobs have become increasingly popular. Older persons would probably be more likely to work if part-time jobs were more widely available. It should be noted, however, that part-time jobs tend to pay considerably less than full-time jobs. In May 1977, the average wage for part-time was $2.87 per hour, compared with $5.04 per hour for full-time workers (Owen, 1978). Thus, part-time work is a mixed blessing.

Availability of retirees for work

There is considerable interest in the number of retirees who would prefer to be working. There is good reason for this: older persons who work are better off financially than those who do not work. The median household income for those aged 65 and over who were employed in 1976 was 82% higher than those not employed (Grad & Foster, 1979). Furthermore, those who were not working were four times as likely to fall below the poverty line.

The declining labor-force participation rates discussed earlier are not an accurate reflection of the desire to work among individuals. Many older workers retire, and then regret their decision. Others are forced off their jobs by age discrimination, poor health, or declines in the availability of jobs. Many would prefer to be working but are prevented from doing so by a shortage of jobs, pension policies, age-discriminatory personnel policies, and ill health.

Several national surveys indicate a widespread interest in working among present retirees. For example, a 1979 Harris survey found that nearly half of all retirees would prefer to be working and more than half would have preferred to continue working rather than retire (Harris & Associates, 1979). These findings have been corroborated by other national and local surveys (Harris & Associates, 1975; McConnell, Fleisher, Usher, & Kaplan, 1980).

Not all studies are consistent on the subject of preferences for work, however. Data from the 1979 Current Population Survey conducted by the U.S. Department of Labor indicate that fewer than 3% of retirees would prefer to be working (Rones, 1980). How do we reconcile these discrepant findings?

One explanation suggested by a Bureau of Labor Statistics economist is that many older people who would like to work are not able to do so because they are in ill health or cannot find suitable jobs (Rones, 1980). An analysis of data from the Social Security Retirement History Study offers support for this notion (Motley, 1978). The findings show that 30% of retirees were not healthy enough to work (by self reports); 20% could work only part-time because of health limitations; and 14% were healthy but not interested in working. This left 36% who were potentially available for work, and only 12% were readily available—they were healthy, interested in working, and needed to work for financial reasons. Thus, the desire to work may not be matched by the physical ability or the appropriate job.

What kinds of jobs would allow older persons to reenter the labor force in large numbers? Research conducted at the University of Southern California's Andrus Gerontology Center sheds some light on that question. A study of 281 older employees in two distinct work settings found that one half of them would continue working beyond their planned retirement date *if* work options were available (McConnell et al., 1980). The most popular work option among these older workers was part-time; others preferred flexible scheduling, modified jobs, or transfers to lighter jobs. These findings indicate that if flexible work options were available, older persons would choose to continue working longer and many older retirees would return to work. This study also found that few would want to postpone retirement for a part-time job unless they were also able to draw at least a portion of their pension.

Older worker stereotypes

Aside from health and a shortage of suitable jobs, negative stereotypes about older workers also inhibit their ability to find and retain jobs. These stereotypes were evident in a study of 1570 subscribers to the *Harvard Business Review*. Respondents were asked to assume an administrative role in a fictitious organization and then make judgments about a series of incidents in which the key worker was either "older" or young. Half of the respondents received only the older descriptions, the other half received only the young. When the responses of the two groups were compared the researchers found a bias against the older workers. The older workers were viewed as more resistant to change; less motivated to keep up with new technology; less creative; and less capable of handling stressful situations. The conclusion: "When managers expect a decline in motivation they might make discriminatory decisions that have the effect of lowering motivation and performance among older workers" (Rosen, 1978; p. 34).

As other chapters in this book clearly illustrate, older persons are capable of coping with change, new technology, and stress. They are capable of learning and have been shown to be as productive as younger persons in many jobs. Nonetheless, the stereotypes persist, which may, in part, account for the large number of age discrimination charges filed with the Equal Employment Opportunity Commission (Select Committee on Aging, 1980).

CONCLUSION

America's population is graying, but the work force is not. Mortality and birth rate declines are contributing to an older age structure in the general population, while the trend toward early retirement is contributing to a younger age structure in the work force. As a result, a crisis is brewing in the nation's retirement income systems. Greater numbers of retirees are relying on Social Security and private pensions for longer periods of time, but fewer workers are available to make the necessary contributions to ensure the financial stability of these systems.

Since the enactment of Social Security in 1935, employment has diminished in importance as an income source for older Americans. The average retirement age has declined to the point that few workers remain employed beyond age 62. Most workers choose to retire early for economic reasons or are forced to retire because of poor health. If one's income is adequate and health is good, retirement is generally a positive experience. Unfortunately, increasing numbers of retirees are suffering from the effects of inflation, and although many would like to return to work, major obstacles stand in their way.

The biggest obstacle to continued employment among older persons is the patchwork of inconsistent and contradictory retirement policies, which, on the one hand, claim to protect the employment rights of the elderly, while at the same time provide strong disincentives to continued work. There is growing awareness of the need for a more coherent national policy that recognizes the interconnections between retirement income policies and employment. Small advances are being made by a handful of employers who have found the older worker to be a valuable asset. Solutions will not be forthcoming, however, until federal and state policies governing delayed retirement credits under Social Security, mandatory pension contributions for those who work beyond age 65, actuarially reduced early retirement benefits, and adequate enforcement of anti-age discrimination laws are strengthened and made consistent with individual and national needs.

REFERENCES

American Medical Association, Committee on Aging. *Retirement: A medical philosophy and approach.* Chicago: AMA, 1968.

Atchley, R. *The sociology of retirement.* Cambridge, Mass.: Schenkman, 1976.

Back, K., & Guptill, C. Retirement and self-ratings. In I. H. Simpson & J. C. McKinney (Eds.), *Social aspects of aging.* Durham, N. C.: Duke University Press, 1966.

Bankers Trust Company. *Corporate pension plan study: A guide for the 1980s.* New York: Bankers Trust, 1980.

Barfield, R. E., & Morgan, J. N. *Early retirement: The decision and the experience and a second look.* Ann Arbor, Mich.: University of Michigan Press, 1975.

Bowen, W. G., & Finegan, T. A. *The economics of labor force participation.* Princeton, N. J.: Princeton University Press, 1969.

Cottrell, F., & Atchley, R. *Women in retirement: A preliminary report.* Oxford, Ohio: Scripps Foundation, 1969.

Davidson, W., & Kunze, K. Psychological, social, and economic meanings of work in modern societies: Their effects on the worker facing retirement. *Gerontologist,* 1965, *5,* 129-133.

Deuterman, W., & Brown, S. Voluntary part-time workers: A growing part of the labor force. *Monthly Labor Review,* 1978, *101*(6), 3-10.

Fillenbaum, G. On the relation between attitude to work and attitude to retirement. *Journal of Gerontology,* 1971, *26,* 244-248.

George, L. *Role transitions in later life.* Monterey, Calif.: Brooks/Cole, 1980.

George, L., & Maddox, G. Subjective adaptation to loss of the work role: A longitudinal study. *Journal of Gerontology,* 1975, *30,* 225-229.

Grad, S., & Foster, K. Income of the population aged 55 and older, 1976. *Social Security Bulletin,* 1979, *42*(7), 16-32.

Harris, L., & associates. *The myth and reality of aging in America.* Washington, D.C.: National Council on the Aging, 1975.

Harris, L., & associates. *1979 study of American attitudes toward pensions and retirement.* New York: Johnson and Higgins.

Haynes, S., McMichael, A., & Tyroler, H. Survival after early and normal retirement. *Journal of Gerontology,* 1978, *33,* 269-278.

Jacobsen, D. Willingness to retire in relation to job strain and type of work. *Journal of Industrial Gerontology,* 1972, *2,* 65–74.

Joint Economic Committee. *Social security and pensions: Programs of equity and security.* A staff study by the Joint Economic Committee of the U.S. Congress. Washington, D.C.: U.S. Government Printing Office, 1980.

Kimmel, D., Price, K., & Walker, J. Retirement choice and retirement satisfaction. *Journal of Gerontology,* 1978, *33,* 575–585.

Kingson, E. *Men who leave work before age 62: A study of advantaged and disadvantaged very early labor force withdrawal.* Unpublished dissertation, Heller School, Brandeis University, Waltham, Mass., 1979.

McConnell, S. R., & Fiske, S. J. *The survey of older writers.* Unpublished report, Andrus Gerontology Center, University of Southern California, Los Angeles, Calif., 1980.

McConnell, S., Fleisher, D., Usher, C., & Kaplan, B. *Alternative work options for older workers: A feasibility study.* Los Angeles, Calif.: Andrus Gerontology Center, University of Southern California, 1980.

McConnell, S., Newquist, D., Kahn, K., Castillo, G., Berger, M., Martinez, C., & Burton, L. *No gold watch: The retirement experiences of older blacks and Mexican Americans.* Los Angeles, Calif.: Andrus Gerontology Center, University of Southern California, 1980.

Meier, E., & Dittmar, C. *Varieties of retirement ages.* Staff working paper of the President's Commission on Pension Policy, Washington, D.C., 1979.

Morgan, J. *Economic realities of aging.* Paper presented at the Convocation on Work and Retirement, University of Southern California, Los Angeles, Calif., 1980.

Morse, D. *The utilization of older workers.* Special Report no. 33, National Commission for Manpower Policy, Washington, D.C., 1979.

Motley, D. Availability of retired persons for work: Findings from the retirement history study. *Social Security Bulletin,* 1978, *41*(4), 18–35.

Nussbaum, K. *Working women, vanished dreams: Age discrimination and the older women workers.* Cleveland, Ohio: National Association of Office Workers, 1980.

Owen, J. Why part-time workers tend to be in low wage jobs. *Monthly Labor Review,* 1978, *101*(6), 11–14.

Pallechio, A. *The effect of the social security retirement test on the earnings of retirement aged workers.* Testimony before the House Select Committee on Aging, Subcommittee on Retirement Income and Employment, Washington, D.C., 1980.

Pratt, H. *The gray lobby.* Chicago: University of Chicago Press, 1976.

Rones, P. The retirement decision: A question of opportunity. *Monthly Labor Review,* 1980, *103,* 14–17.

Rosen, B. Management perceptions of older employees. *Monthly Labor Review,* 1978, *101,* 33–35.

Rowe, A. The retirement of academic scientists. *Journal of Gerontology,* 1972, *27,* 113–118.

Schultz, J. The economics of mandatory retirement. *Industrial Gerontology,* 1974, Winter, 1–10.

Select Committee on Aging. *EEOC enforcement of the age discrimination in employment act.* Hearing before the House Select Committee on Aging. Washington, D.C.: U.S. Government Printing Office, 1980.

Sheppard, H. L. Factors associated with early withdrawal from the labor force. In S. Wolfbein (Ed.), *Men in the pre-retirement years.* Philadelphia, Pa.: School of Business Administration, Temple University, 1977.

Sheppard, H. L. Work and retirement. In R. H. Binstock & E. Shanas (Eds.), *Handbook of aging and the social sciences.* New York: Van Nostrand Reinhold, 1976.

Simpson, I., Back, K., & McKinney, J. Exposure to information on, preparation for, and self-evaluation in retirement. In I. H. Simpson & J. C. McKinney (Eds.), *Social aspects of aging.* Durham, N. C.: Duke University Press, 1966.

Social Security Administration. OASDI cash benefits—Table Q-6. *Social Security Bulletin,* USDHEW, 1980, *43*(6), 75.

Stokes, R., & Maddox, G. Some social factors in retirement adaptation. *Journal of Gerontology,* 1968, *22,* 329–333.

Streib, G., & Schneider, G. *Retirement in American society.* Ithaca, N. Y.: Cornell University Press, 1971.

Thompson, W., Streib, G., & Kosa, J. The effect of retirement on personal adjustment: A panel analysis. *Journal of Gerontology,* 1960, *15,* 165–169.

U.S. Commission on Civil Rights. *The age discrimination study: Part II.* Washington, D.C.: U.S. Government Printing Office, 1979.

U.S. Department of Health, Education, and Welfare. *Work in America.* Washington, D.C.: U.S. Government Printing Office, 1973.

Ward, R. A. *The aging experience: An introduction to social gerontology.* New York: J. B. Lippincott, 1979.

CHAPTER **16**

Housing and Environment

Victor Regnier

The problems associated with housing and environments for older people have long been considered important public policy concerns. These concerns have resulted in the development of numerous programs and legislative efforts that have attempted to redress inequities. The special problems older people have encountered in securing decent, safe, and sanitary housing arrangements were recognized 20 years before the more recent development of comprehensive social and health service programs for the aged. Although solutions to the housing problems of older Americans were tested during the late 1950s, this early start has neither simplified the problem nor brought about significant gains in its resolution. The critical elements of cost, production efficiency, and choice continue to plague policymakers, producers, and consumers.

Production efficiency and cost are the two major problems limiting supply. However, the quality of newly constructed housing and the evaluation of its impact on the older housing recipient have undergone extensive scrutiny during the past decade. Data collected by social science researchers documenting the impact of housing on the older person and criticizing the unsatisfactory attributes of poorly designed housing have contributed to a state-of-the-art knowledge base far superior to that existing 15 years ago.

This chapter will, therefore, concentrate on social and psychological impacts of housing and environments rather than policy and production concerns. It will clarify and underscore some of the consistent findings of researchers in this field. Housing will be treated along with the critical and more comprehensive issue of neighborhood quality.

Research conducted within the past ten years has provided convincing evidence of how skillfully planned housing can improve morale, life span, social interaction, life satisfaction, and health. Furthermore, we have been sensitized to the symbolic and functional impacts on the older resident of poorly located or awkwardly designed housing. The problems of housing design and planning have become more a matter of how to direct alternatives than what those alternatives should be. During its eight years of activity the Housing and Environments Project of the Gerontological Society found the major impediment to quality design products to be the exchange of information with design decision-makers, rather than a lack of applicable quality research.

HOUSING

As a society we are in need of greater quantities of housing located in areas of cities that support the present and future lifestyles of our elderly population. Housing needs to be of better quality and must be offered to older people at an affordable cost. During the past 20 years numerous housing projects for the elderly have been designed and constructed. In contrast with low-income family housing, elderly projects have not met strong community resistance, and the quality has generally increased. It is common to find newly completed housing projects with waiting lists three to four times the capacity of the project. Not only have elderly projects met less initial resistance from surrounding neighbors than family projects, but they have generally been stable, successful, and attractive community additions that have provided local politicians with visible proof of what they are doing for the elderly and the poor in their communities. The less expensive and more flexible Section 8 housing supplement program was initially created as a response to vandalism and stigma problems primarily encountered in family housing. However, older consumers have also responded favorably to the program. Researchers and planners have criticized it for reasons of production and quality. Because Section 8 units do not directly stimulate new construction, this program may actually reduce the number of units available to older people who must search for low-cost rental housing in the conventional housing market. Past additions to low cost stock through federal and state programs were generally insulated from existing housing demand. Additionally, conventional housing, which meets minimum Section 8 requirements, can be of lower quality, may be located in less convenient neighborhoods, and may be less sensitively designed for the special social and physical needs of the aged recipient.

Management factors

Research in specially-built housing for the elderly has documented how influential management and staff can be in either reducing or creating new problems for tenants. Lawton (1974) writes in detail about the counseling duties implicit in the role of the elderly housing manager, underscoring how failure to deal sensitively with the special psychosocial problems of elderly tenants can impact their satisfaction. Housing managers exercise tremendous control over the programming and administration of a housing facility, and thus their policies greatly affect the use of the housing facility. The more dependent the housing type, such as homes for the aged and nursing homes, the greater the impact of managerial policy. In dependent types of housing administrative policies or rule structures can control and limit the choice of residents (Bennett & Nahemow, 1965). Lipman and Slater (1977) have hypothesized that the presence of staff can undermine independence as well as the functional capability of residents in group homes. Their suggestion is to design facilities that separate staff in such a way so as to place them under the control of the residents, rather than the converse. Dudley and Hillery (1977), who viewed a similar dependent group of elderly in group housing, concluded that the level of alienation experienced by residents is partly a result of the social restrictions that limit the ability of residents to make choices. These findings are reinforced by studies of age-integrated public housing such as that conducted by Francescato, Weidemann, Anderson, and Chenoweth (1979), which concludes that "satisfaction with management was found to be among the strongest predictors of overall (housing) satisfaction." Comprehensive management training materials developed through the National Center for Housing Management (1974) have clearly outlined major duties and suggested effective strategies for housing managers to follow in response to problems.

Housing and services: A continuum

Researchers have documented the cumulative losses associated with retirement: death of friends, relatives, and spouse; role loss; and income reductions. The loss continuum displayed in Table 16-1 illustrates the typical problems these losses often create as an individual enters retirement.

TABLE 16-1. Personal losses prompted by change in age

50–64	65–74	75–84	85 and over
Children leave household, begin to prepare for retirement.	Loss of job, spouse, friends, income, some body image loss.	Increased loss of sensory activity, health, strength, and independence.	Serious loss of health and independence.

SOURCE: Adapted from Pastalan & Carlson, 1970, p. 98.

In order to counter these losses, the elderly must have an environment that provides augmenting medical, social, and psychological supports. Lawton and Nahemow's (1973) "Environmental Docility Hypothesis" suggests that an individual of high competence (mental, physical, and social) is relatively free from the pressures of the environment, whereas an individual of low competence is often affected adversely by a difficult environmental context. As a counteractive measure for older people who have suffered losses in overall competence, the environment must provide added support.

Support can be provided in the form of social, physical, or psychological boosts. For example, the installation of grab-bars, handrails, and other prosthetic devices in corridors and bathrooms provide physical supports that help to compensate for loss of balance control and strength in the lower limbs. Social programs such as friendly visitors, meals on wheels, telephone reassurance, and various crime control services provide physical and psychological supports. In other words, as the older person becomes less able to cope with the environment, his or her dependence on added supports, whether from prosthetic devices or social services, increases.

The continuum of supportive housing arrangements can range from and include independent, age-segregated residential units; slightly more supportive congregate housing with provided meals and transportation; the more traditional home for the aging with mandatory meals, maid service, perhaps a nurse on call, and transportation;

the intermediate care facility with all of the preceding, including a full-time nursing staff; and finally, at the opposite end, the skilled nursing facility with the capability of providing long-term convalescent care.

The two ends of this continuum (public housing and nursing homes) have received nominal financial support through public expenditures. Traditional homes for the aged and congregate care facilities have generally been sponsored by nonprofit, primarily nonpublic funding. Although greater numbers of housing units are needed to meet the pressing demand for independent housing, and although some evidence suggests that inadequate reimbursement amounts are responsible for the generally minimum care provided to Medicaid recipients, the middle area of housing with services has been almost completely overlooked.

Several publications have demonstrated the need and demand for cost effectiveness and the role of congregate care facilities in providing adequate housing to older community residents (Heumann, 1976; Urban Systems Research and Engineering, 1976). Interestingly enough, support for congregate care has developed both from a realization of the increasing housing needs of older, frail community residents and from the gradual aging of current residents in independent, age-segregated housing. The City Housing Authority of Chicago, for example, has developed congregate housing that is expected to be filled by recruiting older, frail residents from existing Chicago Housing Authority projects. Lawton, Greenbaum, and Liebowitz (1980) have written about the continual increase in the average age of York House residents at the Philadelphia Geriatric Center since its opening in the 1960s. Their suggestion is that either adaptable facilities be planned to accommodate changes in resident competency or that these individuals be moved to a new, more supportive setting as their needs for services increase. To ignore this phenomenon of facility aging seems foolish and financially hazardous.

Age-segregated versus age-integrated housing

This controversial issue will never be fully resolved because both choices provide benefits and costs to the housing recipient. Lawton has conducted the most precise inquiry in this area. Examining the results of a national survey of elderly public housing tenants in both age-related and age-segregated settings, Teaff, Lawton, Nahemow, and Carlson (1978) concluded that people in age-segregated environments participate more in organized activities within the housing environment and have higher morale, higher housing satisfaction and greater mobility in their neighborhood. A portion of the sample, however, was from age-integrated public housing, which in general has had a well-documented history of conflicts between older and younger residents (Newman, 1972). This research also does not resolve the question of how detrimental policies of age segregation may eventually be to society as a whole. However, the evidence in favor of age segregation is mounting, while citations extolling the virtues of age integration come either from organizations such as the Gray Panthers or from the general arguments of architects or urbanists (Grant, 1970). The stimulation, novelty, and personal experience associated with social exchanges between members of different age groups can be a source of profound enlightenment and delight, just as exchanges between racial or ethnic groups can be. However, the need for this exchange to occur in a setting where both actors maintain some amount of control over the interaction is extremely important. To this end, a more detailed examination of successful age-integrated environments is necessary in order to isolate the attributes of the setting that contribute to success.

Housing satisfaction and well-being

Examinations into satisfaction and preference have primarily been undertaken with special housing types and often with a control group of respondents who did not benefit from the move to new housing. The best-known study is perhaps Carp's longitudinal analysis of Victoria Plaza in San Antonio, Texas. Carp developed a battery of instruments that were given to 352 individuals who had applied for admission to a new housing project. Of that total, 204 were eventually accepted as residents of the facility. Carp interviewed 190 tenants and 105 community members at the end of the first year of Victoria Plaza's operation and 127 tenants and 62 community respondents at the end of the eighth year. The results, which have been compiled in a book (Carp, 1966), and numerous articles (Carp, 1975a; Carp, 1975c; Carp, 1976; Carp, 1977) uncover significant differences between residents and community controls. Although some changes did occur between the move and the first-year follow-up that could be attributed to a "honeymoon" period of new adjustment, at the end of the first year and the eighth year none of the indicators of life satisfaction or morale showed non-residents being happier or better satisfied with life than the tenants of Victoria Plaza. In a follow-up article controlling for medical condition, Carp found statistically significant evidence that older residents of Victoria Plaza actually lived longer and more healthful lives than the matched community sample. This is extremely strong evidence in favor of the beneficial effects of age-segregated planned housing for the elderly. One major criticism of the study is that the income-enhancing benefit associated with low-cost housing alone could account for some of the discrepancy between community residents and housing recipients. A better study design would provide the community sample with a Section 8 rent supplement to free a portion of their fixed income for other expenditures such as food, transportation, and medical care. This design would allow the measurement of positive impacts attributed to residence in an age-segregated facility versus comparable housing in the community.

Lawton and Cohen (1974) performed a similar analysis with residents of five new housing sites (n = 574) and a control group of subjects drawn from similar neighborhoods (n = 324). The result of the first year follow-up interview is consistent with Carp's findings at Victoria Plaza. The rehoused were significantly better off than the community residents on five factor-derived indices including morale, perceived change for the better, housing satisfaction, external involvement, and satisfaction with the status quo. However, the rehoused were rated poorer in functional health and maintained similar scores on the indices of loner status, orientation to children, and activity breadth.

Other preference research (Blonsky, 1975) conducted in a neighborhood surrounding a new elderly high-rise apartment building in St. Louis has shown that the total amount of living space and the arrangement of that space are important determinants in the decision to move to new housing. In this study, nearly three-quarters of the neighborhood sample felt their existing unit was better than newly constructed, purpose-built housing, even though, in most cases, the new units were more modern and secure, as well as less expensive than comparable housing in the neighborhood. Unfortunately, this study was conducted in one neighborhood and may represent a situation where newly constructed smaller size units cannot compete with existing housing stock. Neighborhood market conditions and crime patterns are external factors greatly influencing the perceived benefit of newly constructed housing.

Community housing options

In the middle to late 1970s, emphasis was centered on the inventory and examination of independent community housing such as single-family housing, communal/ shared housing, and conventional apartment-type rental housing. This interest in community housing was brought about by several factors including (1) the Department of Housing and Urban Development's increased use of community housing through its Section 8 program; (2) the impact of elderly owner-occupied single-family housing on the success of newly implemented neighborhood improvement strategies; and (3) increases in the cost of new construction, which forced the examination of less expensive alternatives. The 1973 Annual Housing Survey (AHS) provided much of the empirical data for assessments of the overall housing situation of older Americans. Using this data base, Struyk (1977b) documented that "30% of all elderly-headed (rural) households live in substantially lower quality dwellings than their urban (elderly) counterparts" and that "the urban elderly, while generally inhabiting dwellings of reasonable quality, often live in neighborhoods which they perceive to have serious problems." Later, Struyk (1977a) used the 1974 AHS to examine the expense-to-income ratio of elderly households and clearly demonstrated the disadvantageous position of older renters and low-income households in competing for reasonable cost shelter. He found that nearly 50% of renters spend 30% or more of their income on housing and that two out of every three elderly households with incomes under $2000 spend 30% of income on housing. These figures are in marked contrast to the 29% of total elderly households who spend over 30% of income on housing. Struyk and Soldo (1980) in more recent work discuss the dilemma of housing older Americans in changing neighborhood settings.

Shared housing has more recently become a popular area for study. Among the factors stimulating exploration of the concept are the economics of shared arrangements, the communal ethic inherent in this type of living, and the logical exchange between homeowners with large houses and financially overburdened renters. McConnell and Usher (1980) systematically explored various programs established to facilitate shared arrangements in the United States. Their results show that the two principal types of organizations involved in house sharing are agencies matching owners of larger homes with renters and community organizations developing experimental housing prototypes.

Probably the best-researched example of the latter is the Philadelphia Geriatric Center (PGC) Intermediate Housing Program. This program was originally devised to create a housing prototype halfway between independent living and congregate care. Brody, Kleban, and Liebowitz (1975) describe in detail remodeling changes made to walk-up row house apartments adjacent to the Philadelphia Geriatric Center. The research matched the satisfaction and well-being of in-movers to the project with Control Group I, community members who moved to other arrangements; and members of Control Group II, non-movers who had stayed in their original accommodations and had not moved by the six-month follow-up period. At the end of six months the intermediate housing program residents and Control Group I were more satisfied with the neighborhood than Control Group II. In-movers to the PGC program were the most satisfied with their overall living arrangement and were least likely to express an urge to move. In an excellent review article, Liebowitz (1978) develops a thorough discussion of the administrative and coordination problems inherent in community housing and reviews other programs developing throughout the country.

Shared arrangements hold promise as one potential long-term solution to community housing problems. By itself, the concept has limited utility, but as one element of a larger comprehensive program it can provide another important option and choice for housing consumers.

ENVIRONMENTS

Neighborhood environment

When the subject of environments for the elderly is discussed, the image that normally comes to mind is that of special housing types. As thus far demonstrated, housing and living arrangements have been the subject of extensive research seeking ways to improve the environment for older people. In much of the literature, housing and environment have become synonymous, because most research that is focused on environments for the elderly has been conducted within the specific contexts of public housing, homes for the aged, or nursing homes. Housing, however, should be viewed as one component of a larger environmental system, which not only provides opportunities, supports, and diversions but also confronts the older person with potentially dangerous or anxiety-producing situations. Older retired people spend a great deal of time inside their housing units because they no longer travel to work or perform shopping duties for a large family. However, the interface with the larger scale environment remains an important source of stimulation.

The notion that control over the manipulation of space varies with age has been expressed by other researchers (Pastalan & Carson, 1970). Throughout our lives our interaction with the environment is controlled by social, economic, and societal policies manifested by the built environment. An individual's ability to control and manipulate the environment as he or she progresses through life might plausibly be plotted as a simple curve such as that illustrated in Figure 16-1. The shape of the curve suggests that life space (that is, the environment over which one has control) decreases at both ends of the life span. Some researchers have categorized this process as an inevitable by-product of a larger, more comprehensive loss continuum (Pastalan, 1970). Table 16-2 describes how the losses associated with aging affect housing consumption as a middle-aged person enters retirement. This loss continuum affects every person's options and choices for housing and environments.

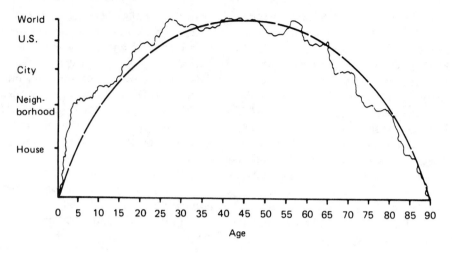

Figure 16-1. Life space change with age. (*Regnier, 1975c*)

TABLE 16-2. Age-related environmental changes and personal losses

50–64	65–74	75–84	85+
Loss of relationship to younger friends and acquaintances of children. Loss of neighborhood role to schools and youth. Home is too large, but mortgage payments are low and equity high.	Loss in relation to work environment, loss of mobility due to lessened income. Dissolving of professional work associations and friendships. Move to apartment, smaller home, or struggle with increased maintenance costs of larger home.	Loss of ability to drive independently. Must rely on bus or relatives and friends. Connections with community, church associations slowly severed. Move to more supportive housing, such as apartments with meals and maid service. Maintenance costs for single-family house unmanageable.	Losses of ability to navigate in the environment. Loss of strong connection with outside neighborhood. Dependence on supportive services. Move to supportive environment necessary, such as nursing home, home for the aged or siblings' home.

SOURCE: Adapted from National Center for Housing Management, 1974.

As the individual ages, his or her dependence on the local environment is increased. In particular, the age cohorts between 65 and 85 have a special relationship with the neighborhood. Children and the elderly are more dependent and rely more on the collection of local resources that we normally think of as a neighborhood. For this reason the environmental needs of older persons must be considered in the design and structure of an optimum neighborhood.

Urban design and planning guidelines for neighborhoods have always considered the lessened mobility and spatial dependence of children. The garden city plans of Ebenezer Howard as well as the advanced city planning concepts and theories developed for experimental new towns, such as Columbia, Maryland, have considered lessened spatial mobility by placing grade schools and convenience stores within walking distance of residential locations. Most of this thinking ignores the needs of older people. The formats of postwar European new towns go as far as to suggest centralized locations for homes for the aged. Recently, the United States new towns of Reston, Virginia, and Irvine, California have planned or located housing projects for older people near their respective town centers (Wylie, 1976). However, there is a total lack of planning and urban design theory to guide improvements for the elderly in existing neighborhoods and in newly designed neighborhoods.

Neighborhood and public policy

The individual's ability to exercise control inside a dwelling unit is much greater than the control available to that person in the neighborhood. The most sterile living spaces can be augmented and decorated to suit one's tastes and preferences. On the other hand, decisions regarding the allocation and provision of neighborhood public services and the location of public transit lines, senior citizen centers, retail stores, social services, and low-cost housing are largely reserved for the public policy arena. Older persons have not been successful in affecting policy because group cohesiveness and age consciousness are necessary prerequisites to impact the political process and because few avenues of influence are open to the elderly. Advocacy and activist groups, such as the Gray Panthers, provide an institutional structure through which participation in the decision-making process can occur, but the influence of these groups has not been great. If conflicts with the neighborhood are extremely disturbing, the older person may consider moving to a location that is less dissonant and more congruent with his or her needs. However, the option of relocation has limited applicability because older people are not as likely to possess the mental, physical, and financial strength to make a radical change in their environment.

When older people do relocate, they may find it difficult to adapt or adjust to a new setting. Involuntary relocation, in particular, can have a deleterious effect on mental and physical well-being (Markus, Blenkner, Bloom, & Downs, 1971; Niebanck & Pope, 1965; Pastalan, 1975).

Because the older person lacks the power to effect positive change and suffers from lessened mobility, he or she is often left behind in deteriorated neighborhoods that are not supportive of his or her needs. The inability of older people to exercise adequate influence on social and environmental policies that affect the surrounding neighborhood means that planners and decision makers must take a more active role as advocates. This is particularly important when changes are contemplated that affect the interest and well-being of the older person. Changes in the level of service of transit lines, the location of social and health services, and zoning restrictions limiting retail goods and services should be noted to clarify the positive and negative impacts of these changes on older community members (Glenn, Alley, & Shirasawa, 1979).

Importance of the neighborhood

Improvements in neighborhoods can provide a setting for increased social interaction as well as a convenient location for supportive goods and services. The importance of the neighborhood has been demonstrated in case study research and national survey data.

Crime is an extremely important concern of older people. Safe and convenient neighborhood settings are often mentioned in research findings as important pre-requisites to a satisfying and comfortable lifestyle. The Harris poll (Harris, 1974) commissioned by the National Council on the Aging in 1975 documents fear of crime as the highest rated "very serious" problem of older people. Although criminal vic-timization cannot be considered solely a neighborhood problem, street assault (purse snatch) is a common crime perpetrated against older people.

Research comparing housing with neighborhood concerns often shows neighbor-hood issues to be a more critical consideration than housing satisfactions. Using national survey data from the Annual Housing Survey, Struyk (1977b) found that urban elderly inhabit "dwellings of reasonable quality," but they often live in neigh-borhoods "which they perceive to have serious problems." A study conducted in seven different neighborhoods in the city of Chicago (Bild & Havighurst, 1976), found that "despite wide differences in housing conditions, an overwhelming majority of the respondents were satisfied with their homes or apartments." In this study only one group expressed higher than 20% dissatisfaction with their housing; however, between one-fifth and two-thirds of the seven groups were dissatisfied with their neighbor-hoods. Reviewing follow-up satisfaction data from the Victoria Plaza study, Carp (1976) mentioned that 98% of the residents rated the apartment building "very good," whereas a majority (54%) found the location "disadvantageous." Most of the complaints about the neighborhood centered on "lack of stores, churches, and eating places in the area" or fear regarding the potential for victimization.

Reviewing findings from a neighborhood study of older Jews living in an urban, low-income, high crime area, Lawton, Kleban, and Carlson (1973) suggest the neigh-borhood has inadvertently trapped many residents. The familiarity of the environment, supportive social relationships, and nostalgic attachment to place has unduly influ-enced the choice to remain in an unsafe, combative environment.

The unquantifiable, ephemeral, emotional, and symbolic influences of the neigh-borhood have received little attention, although it is common knowledge that older community residents who have lived in a neighborhood for many years often express strong attachments to these settings. Characterizing the many different types of neighborhood domains that are attractive to the older community dweller, Lawton (1977) identifies four separate "resource" environments: physical, functional, per-ceived, and salient. The salient resource environment consists of neighborhood re-sources that are valued highly by the individual, sometimes for supportive attachment. Rowles (1977), a social geographer, describes this type of attachment to place when referring to the opportunities of the environment for stimulating fantasy, which, in turn, promotes comfort and happiness. Using the results of extensive case-study inter-views with a small number of older residents, Rowles suggests that reminiscing and fantasizing about the environment complement and accompany progressive spatial constriction and increased attachment to a local area.

The local neighborhood can also take on special importance as a location for the delivery of social services. One must understand the structure of these settings in order to bring about positive change. To accomplish this, a viable strategy must be established for identifying neighborhoods and assessing their major strengths and weaknesses. Although the definition of *neighborhood* is vague and may vary from one individual to another, certain characteristics are identifiable, such as heavily patronized local stores and services, informal meeting places (parks, bars, seating areas, etc.), and formal institutions for social exchange (senior centers, churches, etc.).

The most pervasive question regarding neighborhood improvement is where and how a neighborhood should be altered to best provide older residents with a supportive yet stimulating environment. Viewed from the perspective of the urban design planner, the improvement process could include questions regarding improvements that need to be made in the neighborhood and the location of those improvements. Improvements could include the addition of physical structures, transit lines, or police patrols, as well as the alleviation of environmental hazards.

Needs analyses can be helpful in outlining specific neighborhood problems (Cantor, 1975; Gelwicks, Feldman, & Newcomer, 1971), but they have not been successful in specifying strategies for meeting these needs.

In addition to descriptive data, researchers have sought to understand more about how older persons use neighborhood resources and how they navigate within the larger city-scale environment (Cantilli & Smeltzer, 1970).

Travel patterns and use of goods and services

A great deal of research has explored the relationship between older people and the surrounding resources available to them in the environment. Transportation researchers have reported that (1) the number and percentage of vehicle-assisted trips designated for shopping or personal business increase with age (Ashford & Holloway, 1972; Golant, 1972; Markowitz, 1971; Wachs, 1979); (2) reduction in the number of trips for older people are greater for the lower income versus the upper income (Golant, 1972; Wachs, 1979); and (3) vehicle-assisted trips vary inversely with population density (that is, the higher the total population density, the lower the number of vehicle-assisted trips) (Markowitz, 1971).

A major gap in the transportation literature is the lack of information regarding walking trips. The limited research suggests that walking trips are more commonly made by urban city-center residents, nondrivers, and residents of neighborhoods with high nonwhite populations (Carp, 1971).

As pedestrianism increases in importance, so do the locations of convenient services. Perhaps the best review of important "critical" services has been developed by Lawton (1977). He has used the research of Nahemow and Kogan (1971), Newcomer (1973), Lawton and Nahemow (1973), Regnier (1974), Carp (1973, 1975b), Cantor (1975), and Bourg (1975) to develop Table 16-3, which specifies distances and use patterns of important neighborhood resources. More recent in-depth research, which was conducted by Regnier, Gordon, and Murakami (1981), and which utilized consistent instrumentality with 400 respondents in four Los Angeles communities, verifies the general selection and ordering of resources. This latter study outlines a more complete list of important retail destinations.

Because the percentage of respondents that report using a service is often a rather poor indicator of the strength of attachment to a neighborhood resource, two criteria were used to establish a list of valued neighborhood goods and services.

TABLE 16-3. Modal use, time, and distance to resources from several studies

	Median % using	Modal freq. of use (users)	Modal freq. of use (all)	Modal travel time (users)	Modal use distance-NYC[a]	Modal nearest distance-PH[b]
Grocery	87	2/week	1 or 2/week	7 min	1–3 blocks	1–3 blocks
Physician	86	"several"/year	several/year	15 min	> 20 blocks	4–10 blocks
Visit one or more children	98	1/week	1/week–never	20 min	< 10? blocks	
Other shopping	70	1 or 2/month	never			
Church	67	1/week	1/week	12 min	4–6 blocks	4–10 blocks
Bank	64	1/month			4–6 blocks	
Visit friends	61	2 or 3/week	never	7 min	4–6 blocks	
Visit other relatives	57	several/year	never	35 min		
Beauty/barber shop	40					1–3 blocks
Restaurant	31	several/year			> 20 blocks	1–3 blocks
Park	30				1–3 blocks	
Clubs, meetings	29	1/month	never	15 min	> 20 blocks	
Entertainment	19	1/month	never	20 min	> 20 blocks	> 11 blocks
Library	18					> 11 blocks

SOURCE: Lawton, 1977.

[a] Cantor (1975), New York City poverty-area residents.

[b] Newcomer (1973), public housing tenants.

Services were rank-ordered first by the number of monthly trips made to that generic destination as well as the percentage of the sample that claimed to use that service. Thus, destinations such as a doctor's office, which would be visited infrequently but would be used by a high percentage of respondents, would meet only one criterion and be dropped. When the top 15 rank-ordered services from both tables were compared, the following nine destinations were common to both: supermarket, bank, post office, department store, pharmacy, restaurant, beauty/barber, variety, and church. Department store and church are of particular interest in this list of nine important services. These two destinations were located an average of more than nine blocks from the respondent's home. Their appearance in the top nine is a testimony to their attractiveness to older community residents. These nine services are indeed a minimum neighborhood package and should not be construed as the optimum collection. Other important services include an out-patient clinic (medical) and senior citizen center (social). These destinations however, are often visited less than once per month and are often located further than walking distance. Accessible transportation should also be available to link the site with other areas of the city, particularly the downtown. In cities where inexpensive public transportation is not available, this list of critical services should be expanded to include hospital, library, senior club/senior center, and dry cleaners. Distances to important services should be kept within three to six blocks. Six blocks should be considered the longest reasonable walking distance. When applying this average distance, one must note that the surrounding environmental context can vary substantially. For example, a six-block distance up a steep hill, across several busy streets, or into a high crime area is much more difficult to navigate than the same six blocks on the flat or with several intervening benches on the route. Perceived distance is a subjective concept and may not mirror the actual cartographic distance. Although a hypothetical six-block distance can be measured, understood, and applied, the actual six blocks under consideration can be modified or distorted by a diverse set of social and physical delimiters and incentives (Regnier, 1974a).

Some of these factors are easy to identify and have universally positive or negative effects on the older person, whereas other factors may be perceived as hazardous or helpful only to different individuals. A few examples of these incentives and delimiters include topography, street crime, land-use, percentage of elderly, bus routes/public transportation, ethnic identification, traffic patterns, district designations, and visual quality.

Each of these characteristics could exert a positive or negative impact on the use of neighborhood resources. Census data or previously collected environmental planning data, often available from the local city planning department, can be used to evaluate the quality of a site location. Combined with distance criteria, this data can provide an accurate impression of the overall quality of a chosen location.

STRATEGIES FOR NEIGHBORHOOD INTERVENTION

Beyond the identification of important neighborhood resources our major concern is the issue of improvement strategies. How should the attempt to improve the service base of the neighborhood take place? Two basic intervention approaches are available.

Reinforcement by redefinition

This approach assumes that any concentration of elderly residents within the city possesses both an obvious and underlying social and physical structure. City ecologists have documented the process by which concentrations of elderly residents within cities often result from the aging of the population in place (Golant, 1975). In the western third of the United States, current elderly concentrations have resulted from development that took place early in the 20th century. Both the housing stock and the home owners have aged. Areas that normally have a large aged population also have attracted retail stores and city services that meet their needs. Because of their geographical proximity to central business districts, these neighborhoods are often in need of protection from institutional or commercial business expansion. Furthermore, their crime rates, traffic problems, and fire safety needs are generally much greater because of the condition of the housing stock. One approach that has been successful in many planning ventures (Jacobs, 1978) is to define precisely and clearly the neighborhoods affected by various problems. Likewise, areas considered to be positive, familiar neighborhood spaces are as important to define as the territories considered dangerous by community residents.

Cognitive mapping procedures developed by Regnier (1974b) and Eribes (1973) have been used successfully to isolate key geographic areas within large city boundaries that older individuals regard as important. These mapping methodologies can be useful for determining the geographical context within which services and improvements can be made.

In the studies just cited, respondents were asked to outline the portion of a large-scale city map they considered as "their neighborhood" and the area they considered "dangerous and unsafe." Each individual response was coded, and a synagraphic computer process created an overall consensus map that outlined the neighborhood territory and dangerous areas selected by the greatest number of respondents.

Figures 16-2 and 16-3 were created by combining the dangerous area perceptions and neighborhood perceptions of 100 randomly distributed older residents of an older Los Angeles neighborhood. This neighborhood, known as the Westlake district of the city, contains the highest concentration of elderly residents within the city of Los Angeles and is an example of an inner-city, low-income neighborhood that has attracted and maintained a high concentration of elderly residents because of low rent and accessible services.

These maps provide the community planner with a sense of the territories that are valued as part of a collective image of neighborhoods, as well as an idea of which areas are feared or considered dangerous and undesirable. Such an analysis can help planners to pinpoint geographic areas within which systematic improvements, such as rerouting bus lines, or incremental improvements, such as selecting a good location for a senior center, can be implemented.

Reinforcement by selective intervention

The second approach addresses the most common condition: an unstable neighborhood that has continued to lose elderly residents from attrition and relocation. In such areas of the city, because the social and physical fabric is less contiguous, the

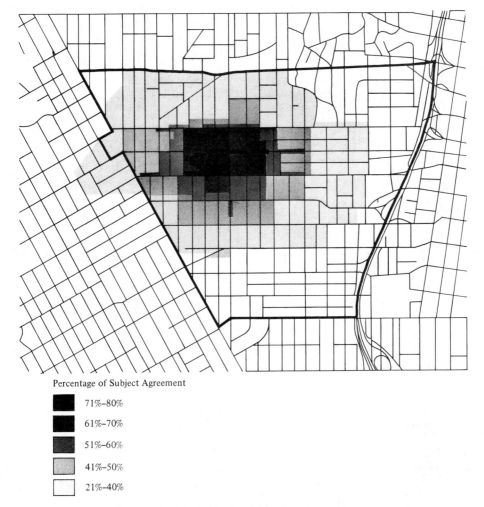

Percentage of Subject Agreement

■ 71%–80%

■ 61%–70%

■ 51%–60%

▨ 41%–50%

☐ 21%–40%

Figure 16-2. Consensus of individual neighborhood cognitive maps.

elderly are isolated and divorced from the companionship of peers and the support of conveniently located retail stores. This condition is typical in many cities where a radical change in the social fabric of the community has resulted from an influx of low-income family residents or the initiation of a publicly sponsored urban-renewal project. Often these older neighborhoods have recycled into commercial or high-income residential use.

The strategy in this situation places improvements, such as housing projects or social services for the elderly, near the greatest concentration of older residents to provide a central core for the neighborhood. By selective additions, elderly concentrations can be established in the most conducive neighborhood environment. In such neighborhoods relocation from dispersed neighborhood housing to safe, easy-to-

Percentage of Subject Agreement[a]

■ 43.4%–64.4%

■ 26.8%–43.3%

■ 21.2%–26.7%

▨ 15.7%–21.1%

☐ 10.1%–15.6%

☐   0%–10.0%

[a] N = 90, Dangerous-Area maps

Figure 16-3. Consensus of individual dangerous-area maps.

maintain, conveniently located, low-cost apartments has positive advantages. This strategy allows older persons to live within a familiar neighborhood.

CONCLUSIONS

The housing and environmental problems that affect older people are complex, multidimensional, and difficult to resolve. The state-of-the-art knowledge base relating to social and psychological dimensions of the environment has advanced significantly during the past 15 years.

Safe, secure and convenient housing may extend life expectancy and improve life satisfaction significantly. However, the production of new planned housing has been meager in comparison to demand. Nevertheless, many cities, towns, and rural areas have new projects that benefit older people, who for many years have been ignored and forgotten.

The major challenge of the 1980s will be to improve neighborhoods, thus improving the larger physical setting within which most older people and the general population must live. Planners and environmental decision-makers are beginning to understand the special needs of the elderly. As the slow communication process continues to build momentum, the actions and interventions of the next decade will be more effective and beneficial to an ever-growing aging population.

REFERENCES

Ashford, N., & Holloway, F. Transportation patterns of older people in six urban centers. *Gerontologist,* 1972, *12*(1).

Bennett, R., & Nahemow, L. Institutional totality and criteria of social adjustment in residences for the aged. *Journal of Social Issues,* 1965, *21.*

Bild, B., & Havighurst, R. Senior citizens in great cities: The case of Chicago. *Gerontologist,* 1976, *16*(1, Pt. 2).

Blonsky, L. The desire of elderly nonresidents to live in a senior citizens apartment building. *Gerontologist,* 1975, *15,*(1).

Bourg, C. Elderly in southern metropolitan areas. *Gerontologist,* 1975, *15*(1).

Brody, E., Kleban, M., & Liebowitz, B. Intermediate housing for the elderly: Satisfaction of those who moved in and those who did not. *Gerontologist,* 1975, *15*(4).

Cantilli, E., & Smeltzer, J. *Transportation and aging: Selected issues.* Washington, D.C.: U.S. Government Printing Office, 1970.

Cantor, M. Life space and the social support system of the inner-city elderly of New York. *Gerontologist,* 1975, *15*(1).

Carp, F. *A future for the aged: The residents of Victoria Plaza.* Austin: University of Texas Press, 1966.

Carp, F. Walking as a means of transportation for retired people. *Gerontologist,* 1971, *2*(2, Pt. 1).

Carp, F. Life style and location within San Antonio. Mimeo report. Berkeley, Calif.: Wright Institute, 1973.

Carp, F. Impact of improved housing on morale and life satisfaction. *Gerontologist,* 1975, *15*(6). (a)

Carp, F. Life style and location within the city. *Gerontologist,* 1975, *15*(1). (b)

Carp, F. Long range satisfaction with housing. *Gerontologist,* 1975, *15*(1). (c)

Carp, F. Users evaluation of housing for the elderly. *Gerontologist,* 1976, *16*(2).

Carp, F. Impact of improved living environment on health and life expectancy. *Gerontologist,* 1977, *17*(3).

Dudley, C., & Hillery, G. Freedom and alienation in homes for the aged. *Gerontologist,* 1977, *17*(2).

Eribes, R. *The spatio-temporal aspects of service delivery: A case study.* Unpublished masters thesis, University of Southern California, 1973.

Francescato, G., Weidemann, S., Anderson, J., & Chenoweth, R. *Residents' satisfaction in HUD-assisted housing: Design and management factors.* Washington, D.C.: U.S. Department of Housing and Urban Development, 1979.

Gelwicks, L., Feldman, A., & Newcomer, R. *Report on older population: Needs, resources and services.* Los Angeles: Andrus Gerontology Center, 1971.

Glenn, J., Alley, S., & Shirasawa, K. Physical form and land-use analysis techniques. In V. Regnier (Ed.), *Planning for the elderly: Alternative community analysis techniques*. Los Angeles: University of Southern California Press, 1979.

Golant, S. The residential location and spatial behavior of the elderly (Research paper no. 143). Chicago: Department of Geography, University of Chicago, 1972.

Golant, S. Residential concentrations of the future elderly. *Gerontologist,* 1975, *15*(1).

Grant, D. An architect discovers the aged. *Gerontologist,* 1970, *10*(4).

Harris, L., & associates. *Myth and reality of aging.* Washington, D.C.: National Council on Aging, 1974.

Heuman, L. Estimating the local need for elderly congregate housing. *Gerontologist,* 1976, *19*(5).

Jacobs, A. *Making city planning work.* Chicago: American Society of Planning Officials, 1978.

Lawton, M. P. *Planning and managing housing for the elderly.* New York: Interscience, 1974.

Lawton, M. P. The impact of the environment on aging and behavior. In J. Birren & K. W. Schaie (Eds.), *Handbook of the psychology of aging.* New York: Van Nostrand Reinhold, 1977.

Lawton, M. P., & Cohen, J. The generality of housing impact on the well-being of older people. *Journal of Gerontology,* 1974, *29*(2).

Lawton, M. P., Greenbaum, M., & Liebowitz, B. The lifespan of housing environments for the aging. *Gerontologist,* 1980, *20*(1).

Lawton, M. P., Kleban, M., & Carlson, D. The inner-city resident: To move or not to move. *Gerontologist,* 1973, *13*, Winter.

Lawton, M. P., & Nahemow, L. Toward an ecological theory of adaptation and aging. In W. Preiser (Ed.), *Environmental design and research* (Vol. 1). Stroudsburg, Pa.: Dowden, Hutchinson and Ross, 1973.

Liebowitz, B. Implications of community housing for planning and policy. *Gerontologist,* 1978, *18*(2).

Lipman, A., & Slater, R. Homes for old people: Toward a positive environment. *Gerontologist,* 1977, *17*(2).

Markowitz, J. Transportation needs of the elderly. *Traffic Quarterly,* 1971, *25*(2).

Markus, E., Blenkner, M., Bloom, M., & Downs, T. The impact of relocation upon mortality rates of institutionalized aged persons. *Journal of Gerontology,* 1971, *26*.

McConnell, S., & Usher, C. *Intergenerational house-sharing: A research report and resource manual.* Los Angeles: University of Southern California Press, 1980.

Nahemow, L., & Kogan, L. *Reduced fare for the elderly.* New York: City University of New York, Center for Social Research, 1971.

National Center for Housing Management. *The on-site housing manager's resource book: Housing for the elderly.* Washington, D.C.: National Center for Housing Management, 1974.

Newcomer, R. *Housing services and neighborhood activities.* Paper presented at the 26th Annual Meeting of the Gerontological Society, Miami, 1973.

Newman, O. *Defensible space.* New York: Macmillan, 1972.

Niebanck, P. L., & Pope, J. *The elderly in older urban areas.* Philadelphia: University of Pennsylvania, 1965.

Pastalan, L. Privacy as an expression of human territoriality. In L. Pastalan & D. Carlson (Eds.), *Spatial behavior of older people.* Ann Arbor: University of Michigan Press, 1970.

Pastalan, L. Research in environment and aging: An alternative to theory. In P. G. Windley, T. O. Byerts, & F. G. Ernst (Eds.), *Theory development in environment and aging.* Washington, D.C.: Gerontological Society, 1975.

Pastalan, L., & Carlson, D. *Spatial behavior of older people.* Ann Arbor: University of Michigan Press, 1970.

Regnier, V. *The effects of environmental incentives and delimiters on the use and cognition of neighborhood areas.* Paper presented at the 27th Annual Meeting of the Gerontological Society, Portland, Oregon, 1974. (a)

Regnier, V. Matching older persons' cognition with their use of neighborhood areas. In D. Carson (Ed.), *Man-environment interactions: Evaluations and applications.* Milwaukee: Environmental Design Research Association, 1974. (b)

Regnier, V. Neighborhood planning for the urban elderly. In D. Woodruff & J. Birren (Eds.), *Aging: Scientific perspectives and social issues* (1st ed.). New York: D. Van Nostrand, 1975. (c)

Regnier, V., Gordon, S., & Murakami, E. How neighborhood characteristics affect travel patterns. In U.S. Department of Transportation (Ed.), *Transportation for the elderly and handicapped: Programs and problems II.* Washington, D.C.: U.S. Government Printing Office, 1981.

Regnier, V., & Hamburger, J. *Comparison of perceived and objective crime against the elderly in an urban neighborhood.* Paper presented at the 30th Annual Meeting of the Gerontological Society, Dallas, Texas, 1978.

Regnier, V., & Murakami, E. *The relationship of goods and services retrieval trips to the perceived neighborhood context of four Los Angeles communities.* Paper presented at the Seventh National Transportation Conference for Elderly and Handicapped, Orlando, Florida, 1979.

Rowles, G. *Prisoner of space?: Exploring the geographic experience of older people.* Boulder, Colo.: Westview Press, 1977.

Struyk, R. The housing expense burden of households headed by the elderly. *Gerontologist,* 1977, *17*(5). (a)

Struyk, R. The housing situation of elderly Americans. *Gerontologist,* 1977, *17*(2). (b)

Struyk, R., & Soldo, B. *Improving the elderly's housing.* Cambridge, Mass.: Ballinger, 1980.

Teaff, J., Lawton, M. P., Nahemow, L., & Carlson, D. Impact of age integration on the well-being of elderly tenants in public housing. *Journal of Gerontology,* 1978, *33*(1).

Urban Systems Research and Engineering. *Evaluation of effectiveness of congregate housing for the elderly: Final report.* Washington, D.C.: U.S. Government Printing Office, 1976.

Wachs, M. *Transportation for the elderly: Changing lifestyles, changing needs.* Berkeley: University of California Press, 1979.

Wylie, M. New communities. In M. P. Lawton, R. J. Newcomer, & T. O. Byerts (Eds.), *Community planning for an aging society.* Stroudsburg, Pa.: Dowden, Hutchinson, and Ross, 1976.

CHAPTER **17**

Economics of Aging

Robin Jane Walther

The increasing proportion of older persons in the U.S. population has stimulated renewed interest in the economics of aging. Attention has been focused on the economic position and economic activities of the older population, as well as on the macroeconomic influences of the aging population.

This chapter examines the economic position of the older population and some of the work-related activities of this population. It also looks at the relationship between the older population and the economy, including a review of the impact the economy has on the older population and the impact the older population has on the economy. Although the chapter does consider the contribution of Social Security and other retirement benefits to the economic status of the older population and the influence of these programs on work activities and savings, a detailed discussion of the economics of Social Security and private pensions is beyond the scope of this presentation. Those readers interested in pursuing these topics in greater depth should consult the monograph entitled *Economics of Aging* by Schulz (1980), the survey article by Clark, Kreps, and Spengler (1978) and the articles listed in the reference section at the end of the chapter.

ECONOMIC STATUS OF THE OLDER POPULATION

The economic position of the older population has improved substantially over the past ten years, and many expect these improvements to continue on into the future (U.S. Senate, Special Committee on Aging, 1980). Evidence of these improvements may be found in increases in the median incomes of older units and in the declines in the proportion of persons aged 65 and older classified as poor by the U.S. Bureau of the Census. The statistics on poverty rates reported in Table 17-1 are of particular interest since they indicate that these improvements have not been steady nor have all groups participated in these improvements to the same extent. The only years during which substantial declines occurred in these poverty rates were

370

TABLE 17-1. Percentage below poverty of persons aged 65 and older by sex and race

	1968	*1970*	*1972*	*1974*[a]	*1976*	*1978*
Percentage below poverty						
Males	20.3	19.0	13.1	10.8	10.8	10.0
White	18.2	17.0	11.3	9.3	9.1	8.3
Black	47.7	48.0	39.9	34.3	34.8	33.9
Females	28.5	28.5	22.4	17.3	17.9	16.7
White	26.8	26.5	20.6	15.3	16.0	14.7
Black	45.2	41.3	34.4	25.9	28.0	26.7

SOURCE: U.S. Bureau of the Census, *Current population reports*, Series P-60, no. 124. Characteristics of the population below the poverty level: 1978, U.S. Government Printing Office, Washington, D.C., 1980, Table 3, pp. 22–23.

[a] The figures reported are based on revised methodology.

the early 1970s, a period in which Social Security and public assistance payments were increased substantially. The gaps existing between older men and older women and between whites and blacks at the beginning of the period also did not diminish to any great extent.

This section examines variations in incomes both within and between demographic subgroups in the population aged 55 and older and the sources of these incomes within the given subgroups. It also discusses alternative indicators of economic status that recognize other resources available to the older person and measures of adequacy.

Incomes of older persons

A closer examination of the economic status of the older population reveals the heterogeneous character of the older population. Significant proportions of older persons do have incomes substantially above the poverty cutoff points, allowing them to live with some economic security. Likewise, substantial proportions of the older population have incomes that place them below the official poverty line or only slightly above this somewhat arbitrary landmark. In contrast to their more fortunate peers, these latter older persons still live in a world in which they are barely able to satisfy their most basic needs. The probability of having barely enough income to satisfy one's basic needs is higher for the unmarried, women, blacks, and those in the older age brackets. The economic hardships that these groups face reflect a lifetime of discrimination and economic hardship, as well as recent events such as retirement, loss of a spouse, and declining health. In all cases, the chances are very low that a person aged 65 and older will somehow manage to move from the economically deprived to the more fortunate economically secure group (Morgan, K. Dickinson, J. Dickinson, Benus, and Duncan, 1974).

To illustrate these points, Tables 17-2 and 17-3 present data on the economic position in 1976 of aged units distinguished by age, sex, marital status, and race. These data are taken from a paper by Grad and Foster (1979), which provides more detail on the incomes of older persons. Following the practice of the Social Security Administration, the unit of analysis is the aged unit—that is, either a married couple living together with at least one member aged 55 and above or a nonmarried person

TABLE 17-2. Total money income of aged units by age, marital status, and sex, 1976

	Total number (in thousands)	Median income[a]	Percentage with income Below $5,000	Percentage with income Above $15,000
All units				
55–61	9,763	$12,100	22	40
62–64	3,751	8,830	31	28
65 and older	17,321	4,700	53	8
Married couples				
55–61	6,241	16,490	9	57
62–64	2,138	12,750	12	41
65 and over	6,799	7,890	22	19
Unmarried men				
55–61	1,182	7,730	38	19
62–64	447	5,910	43	15
65 and older	2,354	3,870	65	4
Unmarried women				
55–61	2,340	4,540	55	7
62–64	1,166	3,990	59	6
65 and older	8,168	3,230	75	3

SOURCE: S. Grad & K. Foster, Income of the population aged 55 and older, 1976, *Social Security Bulletin,* 1979, *42*(7), 16–32.

[a] Rounded to nearest $10.

TABLE 17-3. Money income of aged units 65 and above by race and marital status

	Total number (in thousands)	Median income[a]	Percentage with income Below $5,000	Percentage with income Above $15,000
All units				
White	15,572	$4,940	51	10
Black	1,552	2,990	75	3
Married couples				
White	6,285	8,150	21	19
Black	439	5,460	44	9
Unmarried men				
White	1,974	4,090	62	4
Black	337	2,930	80	b
Unmarried women				
White	7,313	3,370	73	3
Black	776	2,480	92	b

SOURCE: S. Grad & K. Foster, Income of the population aged 55 and older, 1976, *Social Security Bulletin,* 1979, *42*(7), 16–32.

[a] Rounded to nearest $10.

[b] Due to the small number of persons receiving incomes, the percentages could not be calculated from published tables.

aged 55 and older. This practice differs from that of the U.S. Bureau of the Census, which uses the family or person as the unit of analysis. The use of the aged unit is based on the assumption that the economic resources of older persons should be distinguished from the economic situation of other family members. This assumption ignores both the income support received from other family members and the income support provided to other family members by the older person. The comparisons of economic status of aged units in Tables 17-2 and 17-3 included comparisons of median incomes. (Note: the median income is the income that divides the group into two equal parts—that is, those with incomes below the median and those with incomes above the median.) They also include comparisons of the percentage of persons with incomes below $5,000 and with incomes above $15,000.

Table 17-2 distinguishes the economic status of aged units aged 55 and older by age, marital status, and sex. Incomes of older units are considerably lower than the incomes of the comparatively younger units. The median income for all aged units declines from $12,100 for units aged 55–61 to $4,700 for units aged 65 and older. Consistent with the decline in median income associated with age is the corresponding decline in the percentage of units with incomes greater than $15,000 and the increase in the percentage of units with incomes below $5,000. These same declines in economic status associated with age are also observed within the three marital status groups: married couples, unmarried males, and unmarried females. Comparisons across the three marital status groups also provide evidence of the substantially better position of married couples as compared with unmarried persons and of the substantially better position of unmarried males as compared with unmarried females. For example, in the 65 and over age group, only 22% of the married couples had incomes below $5,000; 65% and 75% of the unmarried men and unmarried women had incomes below $5,000.

Table 17-3 continues our comparisons of aged units, 65 years and above, and focuses on racial differences within the older population. In all marital status groups, black incomes are substantially below those of white units. Distinctions among marital status groups noted for all races persist for blacks, and unmarried black females are the most deprived of the demographic groups considered.

Although much more detail on the incomes of older persons could be presented, these tables illustrate many of the basic facts. Incomes of older persons are related to age, marital status, and race. Unmarried females 65 and older, particularly unmarried black females in this group, are the most deprived of all the subgroups considered. The variations within even the most economically secure also are noticeable, as illustrated by the percentage of units in both the under-$5,000 and over-$15,000 categories.

Sources of income

The variations in the economic position of older persons are attributable to a number of factors including a lifetime of individual decisions, a wide range of public policies, and luck. An examination of sources of income suggests how these experiences and activities—some within the control of the individual and others not—have been translated into the economic differences just reported.

The major sources of income for the aged units are earnings, Social Security benefits, other retirement benefits including public and private pensions, annuities, and income from assets including interest, rents, and dividends (U.S. Department of Health, Education and Welfare, 1980). Tables 17-4 and 17-5 report by age, marital status, and race the percentage of aged units receiving income from these four sources and from public assistance. The reader should note that these data report only on sources from which income is received and not on the proportion of income received from these sources.

TABLE 17-4. Percentage of aged units with money income from specified sources by marital status and age [a]

	All units	Married couples	Unmarried persons Men	Women
Units aged 55–61				
Total number (in thousands)	9,763	6,241	1,181	2,340
Percentage with				
Earnings	83	92	74	62
Social Security [b]	13	12	10	21
Other retirement benefits	12	13	10	9
Assets	55	64	33	44
Public assistance	5	2	7	14
Units aged 62–64				
Total number (in thousands)	3,751	2,138	447	1,166
Percentage with				
Earnings	67	80	61	46
Social Security	49	43	49	59
Other retirement benefits	22	26	18	16
Assets	58	67	45	47
Public assistance	7	3	7	14
Units aged 65 and above				
Total number (in thousands)	17,321	6,799	2,353	8,168
Percentage with				
Earnings	25	41	21	14
Social Security	89	90	87	88
Other retirement benefits	31	42	32	22
Assets	56	66	44	51
Public assistance	11	6	15	15

SOURCE: S. Grad & K. Foster, Income of the population aged 55 and older, 1976, *Social Security Bulletin*, 1979, *42*(7), 16–32.

[a] Income from source is ascertained from yes/no question with imputation.

[b] Social Security income includes all types of benefits.

Table 17-4 presents information on income sources by age, marital status, and sex. Comparisons across age groups indicate that aged units, regardless of their marital status, are much less likely to receive any portion of their incomes from earnings and much more likely to be relying on incomes from Social Security and other retirement

TABLE 17-5. Percentage of aged units 65 and over with money income from specified sources by race [a]

| | Married couples | | Unmarried persons | |
	White	Black	White	Black
Total number (in thousands)	6,285	439	9,287	1,113
Percentage with				
Earnings	40	49	15	16
Social Security [b]	90	90	89	80
Other retirement benefits	43	23	25	13
Assets	70	20	54	13
Public assistance	4	22	12	39

SOURCE: S. Grad & K. Foster, Income of the population aged 55 and older, 1976, *Social Security Bulletin*, 1979, *42*(7), 16–32.

[a] Income from source is ascertained from yes/no question with imputation.

[b] Social Security income includes all types of benefits.

benefits as they move from the 55–61 age group to the 65 and over age group. The proportion of aged units receiving income from assets does not appear to be associated with age. In contrast, the proportion receiving income from public assistance does increase with age; 11% of aged units 65 and over receive income from this source, compared with 5% of the 55–61 age group.

The distinctions among the marital status groups with regard to income sources are possibly of greater interest, reflecting a wide range of individual experiences. In all age ranges, married couples are more likely than either unmarried men or women to be receiving income from earnings. Married couples are also more likely to be receiving income from other retirement benefits and assets. This most likely reflects the higher status and better paying jobs held by married men at earlier points in time. Both unmarried men and women are also more likely than married couples to be receiving income from public assistance; this reflects the current low incomes of these groups noted previously.

Table 17-5 shows the sources of income for white and black aged units aged 65 and older. Among married units, 90% of both the black and white units report receiving income from Social Security. However, black couples are more likely to have some earnings and much less likely to have income from assets and from other retirement benefits. These racial differences may be explained by limited employment opportunities in areas offering security of retirement incomes and the adequate salaries necessary to allow for some savings. Comparisons of unmarried persons also provide evidence of the earlier hardships experienced by older blacks. Whereas 89% of the white unmarried units receive income from Social Security, only 80% of black unmarried units are receiving income from this source. The low incomes of older black units reported in Table 17-3 are also reflected in the much greater likelihood that they receive some income from public assistance in comparison to white units.

This brief examination of sources of income provides some intermediate suggestions for the variations in income within the older population. The groups with higher incomes are more likely than those groups with low incomes to be receiving income from other private or public pensions and from assets. In addition, work as evidenced by the receipt of earnings is also more likely among the higher income groups.

Alternatives to money income

The preceding discussion has adopted money income as defined by the U.S. Bureau of the Census as the sole indicator of economic resources. This indicator includes most regular sources of money income such as wage and salary income, property income (that is, interest, rents, dividends), Social Security and other government transfers, and public and private pension income. Although the measure does succeed in including most regular sources of money income, it has been widely criticized for being an imperfect measure of potential consumption. Government transfers received in the form of money are counted, but neither tax liabilities nor benefits received in kind are considered. Benefits from asset ownership are restricted to benefits received in the form of money; nonmonetary benefits received from asset ownership, specifically from homeownership, are excluded. The utility or disutility obtained from leisure activities and household productivity also is ignored.

Although there is widespread agreement on the limitations of money income as an indicator of economic resources, there is only limited agreement regarding appropriate procedures for adjusting money income. Moreover, the data required to make these adjustments—such as the value of assets and, particularly, home equity and the eligibility and receipt of in-kind transfers—are frequently lacking. In this chapter, comparisons of older persons according to their financial assets are restricted to comparisons of unmarried older women, unmarried older men, and married couples in 1967 and 1969. With regard to the use of expanded measures of economic well-being, which incorporate the benefits of programs such as Medicare and Food Stamps as well as financial assets, most research efforts have not focused on the older population (Garfinkel & Haveman, 1977; Moon & Smolensky, 1977; Morgan et al., 1974; Smeeding, 1977; Taussig, 1973). In cases where the older population has been the focus of attention (Moon, 1977; Walther, 1979), the emphasis has been on comparing alternative measures of economic well-being. The results indicate that the choice of a measure of economic well-being is important in characterizing the economic position of older persons. However, the assumptions required to create such a measure are complex and controversial. If used, these assumptions should be carefully reviewed. This task is beyond the scope of this chapter.

Insight into the impact of adopting expanded measures of economic resources may be obtained from comparisons of the level of financial assets among older persons. Selected comparisons are made for two samples of older persons: one is a sample of units aged 65 and above, and the second is a sample of units aged 58 to 63. In both cases the data were collected more than a decade ago, and reporting on financial assets was incomplete. Slightly more than 75% of the weighted populations reported on financial assets in both samples (Tables 17-6 and 17-7). For both samples unmarried women report lower levels of financial assets than either married couples or unmarried men. In addition, the financial assets of homeowners are consistently higher than the financial assets of nonhomeowners, as measured by the median amount.

TABLE 17-6. Median amount of financial assets for aged units by sex, marital status, and homeownership, aged 65 and over, 1967

	All units	Married couples	Unmarried Men	Unmarried Women
Total (in thousands)	15,779	5,989	2,356	7,434
Reporting on financial assets (in thousands)	12,040	4,397	1,961	5,682
Percentage reporting on financial assets	76.3	73.4	83.2	76.4
Median amount				
All reporting units	$ 550	$1,800	$ 300	$ 223
Units with financial assets	3,000	4,000	3,000	2,000
Homeowners (noninstitutionalized) (in thousands)	8,234	4,598	821	2,814
Reporting on financial assets (in thousands)	6,060	3,356	672	2,032
Percentage reporting on financial assets	73.6	73.0	81.9	72.2
Median amount				
All reporting units	$ 1,800	$2,100	$2,000	$ 875
Units with financial assets	3,800	4,400	4,375	2,600

SOURCE: Bixby, Finegan, Grad, Kolodrubetz, Lauriat, and Murray, 1975. *Demographic and economic characteristics of the aged: 1968 Social Security survey.* Washington, D.C.: U.S. Government Printing Office, 1975, pp. 115–116.

Table 17-6 compares the median amount of financial assets for all units reporting on financial assets and all units reporting owning financial assets for three groups of units aged 65 years and over—married couples, unmarried men, and unmarried women. According to these data, older unmarried women, and particularly older unmarried women who are homeowners, have fewer financial assets than either their male counterparts or married couples. Undoubtedly, there are some women with extensive financial holdings in this sample of older persons, but, according to these measures of central tendency, they are the exception.

A comparison of the financial assets of a slightly younger sample of persons is consistent with the findings for the older sample. As noted in Table 17-7, the financial asset holdings for homeowners are consistently higher than those reported for non-homeowners. In addition, when classified by homeownership, older women have more limited asset holdings than either their male counterparts or married couples. Probably the most important point to be made following these comparisons is that the financial asset holdings of a majority of the older population were limited in the late 1960s, and undoubtedly continued to be limited in the late 1970s.

Alternative measures of economic status that incorporate the benefits received from financial assets and from other sources of assets indicate that for some individuals

TABLE 17-7. Financial assets for persons aged 58-63 by sex, marital status, and homeownership, 1969

		Amount of financial assets			
	Total *(in thousands)*	Reporting on amount of financial assets	Quartile values for units with financial assets		
			First	Median	Third
Total reporting on homeownership	6043	4953	$ 751	$3237	$11978
Married men					
Homeowners	2899	2290	984	4135	13834
Nonhomeowners	738	635	500	2500	10560
Unmarried men					
Homeowners	247	212	1107	4000	13846
Nonhomeowners	350	316	473	1688	9812
Unmarried women					
Homeowners	857	684	694	2784	10706
Nonhomeowners	949	816	405	1653	6672

SOURCE: Sherman, Assets on the threshold of retirement, *Social Security Bulletin,* August 1973, pp. 2-16.

these benefits are significant. However, as noted previously, the procedures used to impute the benefits of asset ownership are controversial. For example, the benefits of homeownership may be incorporated as the rental value net of taxes and maintenance costs or as the annuitized value of the house, a procedure that recognizes differences in average life expectancy. Similar questions occur in efforts to incorporate the benefits of Food Stamps and of Medicare. Thus, income is an incomplete measure of economic status, and alternative measures of economic status may be preferred in specific situations.

Standards of adequacy

In the introduction to this section we indicated that there have been substantial improvements in the economic position of the older population. The basis for this statement was evidence that the percentage of older persons with incomes below the poverty line had decreased between 1968 and 1978. At this point, a more detailed discussion of the methods available for assessing income adequacy is warranted.

The data on poverty incidence provided by the U.S. Bureau of the Census and reported in Table 17-1 were derived by first establishing poverty cutoff points for families (not aged units) and then determining the number of persons with specific characteristics residing in families with incomes below the poverty cutoff points. The poverty cutoff points and the use of the family as the unit of analysis are the result of carefully considered but basically arbitrary decisions (Poverty Studies Task Force, 1976; Schulz, 1980). Using information on the consumption patterns and nutritional requirements of individuals, analysts develop separate poverty cutoff points that incorporate differences in the age and sex of family members and the size and location of the unit. Each year the poverty cutoff points are adjusted for changes in the cost of living.

What is the impact of adopting alternative criteria for determining poverty or the distribution of poverty within the older population? The alternative criteria, which have been examined by Mollie Orshansky (1978), incorporate changes in the unit of analysis and changes in the income level used to define *poverty*. More specifically, the family unit is replaced by the aged unit—that is, the married couple or the unmarried individual. This results in neither the resources nor the needs of other persons in the household being considered in determining poverty populations. Three adjustments of the specified incomes, or poverty cutoff points, required for an adequate standard of living also are considered. The use of criteria for married couples and unrelated individuals as opposed to the family unit is based on the assumption that older persons "should have enough income to maintain themselves alone (or with a spouse) without relying on added income support from other relatives" (Orshansky, 1978, p. 202).

There is little question that adopting alternative poverty lines and units over which resources are assumed to be shared will alter the reported incidence of poverty. The extent to which these changes will alter the proportions of older males and older females in the poverty population is the question being considered. Since a higher proportion of older women live with other family members, one may expect the adoption of the aged unit in place of the family unit to have a greater impact on the incidence of poverty among older women as compared to the incidence of poverty among older men. However, the result depends on the incomes attributable to older men and women as compared with other family members. The issue may be resolved by examining data regarding the proportions of older men and older women classified as poor.

The distributions of the total population aged 65 years or older and of populations from the same age range classified as poor, using alternative criteria, are reported in Table 17-8. These distributions are based on the reported numbers of persons classified as poor according to the various criteria. An examination of these data indicate that over 60% of all persons aged 65 or older and classified as poor are unmarried women. The adoption of the aged unit as opposed to the family unit increases the proportion of unmarried women in the poverty population and concurrently decreases the proportion of older men classified as poor. However, the adoption of more liberal definitions of poverty (that is, definitions increasing the number of persons classified as poor) also decrease the proportion of older women classified as poor. Thus, the impact of adopting definitions of poverty depends on the specific change that is made. Some changes increase the proportions of older women classified as poor, whereas others increase the proportion of older men classified as poor.

Additional criticisms of the measures of income adequacy are somewhat more basic in nature. Some of the criticisms of this index have concentrated on the absolute nature of the measure; other criticisms have concentrated on the imperfect relationship between reported income and resources available for consumption.

As part of the first set of criticisms, the argument has been made that the concept of *adequacy* is a relative concept and that a set of fixed subsistence incomes cannot be

TABLE 17-8. Poverty among the older population using alternative criteria, 1976

| Sex and marital status | Total all income | Income below specified standards of adequacy | | | | |
| | | Current poverty line and living arrangements | Current poverty line | Potential for independent living | | |
				Current near-poor line	Orshansky update of poverty line	BLS lower budget
Numbers (in millions)						
Total 65 or older	22.1	3.3	4.7	7.4	8.7	5.5
Women 65 or older	13.0	2.3	3.5	5.3	6.2	3.6
Married, spouse present	4.8	0.3	0.4	0.7	1.0	0.9
Other	8.2	2.0	3.1	4.6	5.2	2.7
Men 65 or older	9.1	1.0	1.2	2.1	2.5	1.9
Married, spouse present	6.8	0.5	0.6	1.1	1.3	1.3
Other	2.3	0.5	0.6	1.0	1.2	0.6
Percentages						
Total 65 or older	100.0	100.0	100.0	100.0	100.0	100.0
Women 65 or older	58.8	69.7	74.5	71.6	71.3	65.5
Married, spouse present	21.7	9.1	8.5	9.5	11.5	16.4
Other	37.1	60.6	66.0	62.2	59.8	49.1
Men 65 or older	41.2	30.3	25.5	28.4	28.7	34.5
Married, spouse present	30.8	15.2	12.8	14.4	14.9	23.6
Other	10.4	15.2	12.8	13.5	13.8	10.9

SOURCE: Orshansky, Prepared statement before the House Select Committee on Aging, in *Poverty among America's aged.* Hearing before the Select Committee on Aging, U.S. House of Representatives, Washington, D.C.: U.S. Government Printing Office, 1978.

used to approximate the concept. More specifically, the argument is that the need of a family or individual is related to the gap between their income and that of other individuals in the society. Based on this view, one economist has suggested that the low-income level should be defined as a fixed percentage of the median income of persons in the society (Fuchs, 1969). Others have argued that the low-income level should be related to both the monetary and psychological needs of the family. Thus, the adequacy of pension income should be related to previous income while working (Schulz, 1980). This position regarding the definition of *adequacy* could result in higher low-income levels being specified for retired engineers than for retired laborers (Bok, 1967). Some consider this a ridiculous suggestion, but there is some precedent for such a notion.

The second set of criticisms of the low-income index is based on the view that, in assessing the welfare and needs of the population, policymakers are not interested in how many dollars a family has relative to a subsistence income level but instead in the extent to which the needs of the family are satisfied. This suggests that the adequacy standard should be based on the concept of potential consumption, not current income. As a consequence, a low-income index that relies solely on a comparison of current income to a subsistence income measure is generally considered inferior to measures that approximate potential consumption (Morgan, 1965).

The preceding discussion of the economic status of the older population has been far from complete. However, we have considered questions regarding the adequacy of money income as an indicator of economic resources and the arbitrary nature of poverty cutoff points. In addition, we have noted some of the basic patterns in the distribution of income and sources of income within the older population. Both current and previous work activities appear to be closely related to the economic status of older persons, which leads us to the following discussion on work and the older person.

WORK, RETIREMENT, AND THE OLDER PERSON

Current and previous work experiences of the older population are major determinants of the economic position of this population. Social Security eligibility and benefit levels are directly related to previous earnings histories. The receipt of other public pension and private pension benefits are dependent on previous contributions to a pension program. Moreover, earnings are dependent on one's current work status as well as previous work experiences. The actual benefits from Social Security, other pensions, and earnings are influenced by public policies and overall economic conditions, but the role of work in determining the economic position of the older individual is well established.

Although there are many facets to the work experiences of older persons, this chapter focuses on the participation of older workers in the labor force. We review some basic trends and patterns in the labor-force participation of older workers, and we consider some explanations for these trends and patterns. Questions related to the productivity and employment problems of older workers and to the employment histories of these workers are beyond the scope of this chapter. The interested reader may consult a number of discussions of these issues (Clark, Kreps, & Spengler, 1978; Schultz, 1980; Sheppard, 1976; U.S. Senate, Special Committee on Aging, 1980).

Trends and patterns in age at retirement

The following description of the work experiences of older workers is restricted largely to a discussion of changes in the work status of older persons. More specifically, we shall examine patterns and trends over the past 30 years in the labor-force participation rates for various groups of older persons. The labor-force participation rate is the proportion of persons in a specified population who are defined as working, temporarily absent from work, or having actively looked for a job in the past four weeks and having been available for work (U.S. Department of Labor, 1979). Several alternative definitions of retirement, including reductions in work effort, departure from a "life-time" occupation, and receipt of Social Security or other retirement benefits could be used as indicators of work status. However, labor-force participation rates, which are a fairly unambiguous measure of withdrawal from the paid labor market, are available for a relatively long historical period (1947 to the present) and, as a result, permit an examination of trends as well as patterns in unemployment experiences for the past 30 years.

The period 1947-1977 has witnessed both the increased withdrawal of older men and the increased participation of older women. As noted in Table 17-9, the labor-force participation rates for males aged 65 and over have declined fairly steadily over the 30-year period, although there are suggestions that these rates are now stabilizing. For the 55-64 group, the declines in labor-force participation rates are first

TABLE 17-9. Civilian labor-force participation rates for persons aged 55 years and over by sex and age, 1947-1977

Year	Males		Females	
	55-64	*65 and over*	*55-64*	*65 and over*
1947	89.6	47.8	24.3	8.1
1952	87.5	42.6	28.7	9.1
1957	87.5	37.5	34.5	10.5
1962	86.2	30.3	38.7	9.9
1967	84.4	27.1	42.0	9.6
1972	80.5	24.4	42.1	9.3
1977	74.0	20.1	41.0	8.1

SOURCE: U.S. Department of Labor, *Handbook of Labor Statistics 1975—Reference Edition,* U.S. Government Printing Office, Washington, D.C., 1975, p. 35; U.S. Department of Labor, *Handbook of Labor Statistics 1978,* U.S. Government Printing Office, Washington, D.C., 1979, pp. 33-34.

observable in the late 1950s with the rate of decline having accelerated during the period 1967 to 1977. A more detailed examination of these trends by age (Rosenfeld & Brown, 1979) indicates that the declines in participation during the last decade for the ages 62-64 dominate. The experiences of women during this period are clearly different. The labor-force participation rates for females aged 65 and above have always been relatively stable and low; the labor-force participation rates for females aged 55–64 increased dramatically between 1947 and 1967 and leveled off in the 1970s. These patterns have frequently been attributed to the sexual revolution, but the timing of the trends suggests that other factors, such as rising divorce rates and improved work opportunities, may have been of greater importance.

The trends in retirement, or more accurately withdrawal from the labor force, have been associated with a number of characteristics including age, marital status, occupation, and education. Table 17-10, which shows labor-force participation rates for persons aged 65 and over by marital status, illustrates some basic patterns. Among

TABLE 17-10. Civilian labor-force participation rates for persons aged 65 years and over by marital status and sex, 1957–1977.

	1957	*1962*	*1967*	*1972*	*1977*
Males					
Married, spouse present	42.3	33.8	30.1	26.4	21.8
Single	31.0	28.4	22.1	23.5	19.6
Other	25.0	20.2	18.3	16.9	13.1
Females					
Married, spouse present	6.6	6.3	6.9	7.4	7.1
Single	23.7	18.5	19.4	17.2	14.4
Other	11.2	11.2	10.1	9.7	8.2

SOURCE: U.S. Department of Labor, *Handbook of Labor Statistics 1978,* U.S. Government Printing Office, Washington, D.C., 1979, pp. 38–39.

males aged 65 and over, labor-force participation rates for married men have been consistently higher than the labor-force participation rates for either single or other unmarried men. However, over the past 20 years, the differences in these labor-force participation rates have diminished with the more rapid withdrawal of married men from the labor force. Among women aged 65 and above, labor-force participation rates for married women have been consistently below the rates for either single or other unmarried women. Between 1957 and 1977 the rates for both single and other un-married women declined, whereas the rates for married women increased, if ever so slightly. Thus, labor-force participation rates for older workers, as well as trends in labor-force participation rates, have varied by sex and marital status.

Variations in the labor-force participation rates of older workers by education and occupation may also be observed (Rones, 1978). Based on the Retirement History Survey of men and unmarried women aged 58–63 in 1969, Schwab (1974) noted that men were more likely to be working if their occupation was relatively high status. Approximately 25% of the farm and nonfarm laborers were out of the labor force, whereas only 10% of the professional workers and 13% of the managers were out of the labor force (Table 17-11). When corresponding patterns by education level were also reported, the more educated were more likely to be still working. Comparing rates for 1962 and 1977, Rosenfeld and Brown (1979) noted that the declines in labor-force participation rates for males aged 55 and above were generally greater for the less educated. The reverse pattern was observed for females: participation rates for females

TABLE 17-11. Percentage out of labor force by occupation of longest job and by education, men aged 58–63: 1969

	Percentage out of labor force
Occupation of longest job	
Professional	10
Farmer	12
Manager	13
Clerical	17
Sales	11
Craftsman	16
Operative	21
Service	21
Farm laborer	24
Nonfarm laborer	27
Years of school	
0–8	21
9–11	17
12	11
13 or more	12

SOURCE: Schwab, 1974, p. 10.

aged 55–64 with four or more years of college decreased from 64.8% in 1962 to 52.2% in 1978. This decrease in participation of educated women occurred as participation rates for all women aged 55–64 were increasing on average. Treas (1980) has suggested that the sex difference in these participation rates is due to the concentration of older college-educated women in teaching and nursing positions—that is, positions that lack the flexibility of many male professional positions. In addition to the occupational and educational differences just discussed, patterns and trends associated with race, health, receipt of pension benefits, and labor-force status of spouse could be considered in a more detailed discussion (Bixby, 1976).

Reasons for retirement

All the differences noted here suggest a number of explanations (Clark, Kreps, & Spengler, 1978; U.S. Senate, Special Committee on Aging, 1980). The majority of research efforts have recognized that individuals have different reasons for withdrawing from the labor force, including desire for leisure, physical strain of work, availability of monthly Social Security and other retirement income, absence of dependents requiring support, and difficulties of finding satisfactory employment due to aggregate economic factors. The income-related reasons, specifically the availability of Social Security and other retirement benefits, and the health-related reasons have received the most attention (Bixby, 1976; Campbell & Campbell, 1976). The consensus appears to be that Social Security benefits and other income-related benefits as well as health status do contribute to the patterns and trends in labor-force participation rates. However, no consensus on the significance of the various factors is available.

Several problems must be faced when determining the significance of the various factors contributing to the basic patterns and trends in the labor-force withdrawal of older workers. First, the definitions of withdrawal from the labor force have varied, thus decreasing the comparability of the various studies (Clark, Kreps, & Spengler, 1978). Second, the theoretical framework of most studies views an individual as choosing between working and not working. However, the choice is not usually that simple, and information on the two or more alternatives is not free to the individual nor generally available to the researcher. This has resulted in efforts to estimate the earnings of persons not in the labor force (Quinn, 1977) and to estimate the present value of retirement benefits of persons currently employed (Burkhauser, 1979). A third problem is associated with the measurements of health. On surveys of individuals that include information on work status, health information is generally self-reported. Biases may result since persons who are not working may report themselves as in poor health, despite their actual health status, due to the social stigma attached to not working prior to the usual age of retirement. The influence of poor health on retirement also depends on the specific characteristics of a job; this information is difficult to obtain for large and heterogeneous samples. For all of these reasons—the measurement of labor-force withdrawal, the characterization of alternatives, and the determination of health—one should question any precise estimates regarding the influence of increases in Social Security benefits or any other change on retirement.

To summarize, the past 30 years have witnessed major declines in the labor-force participation rates of older workers. These patterns, which have a direct influence on the economic status of the older population, have varied by various demographic characteristics including age, marital status, sex, race, and health status. Studies of these trends such as the paper by Parsons (1980) have frequently emphasized the role of Social Security benefit increases and the increased availability of income. However, others have focused on broader social changes involving the increased urbanization and industrialization of job opportunities (Rones, 1978; Sheppard, 1976). Patterns observed have emphasized both the role of income and health and the interaction between these factors. The many complex explanations of patterns and trends in labor-force participation rates as well as related employment experiences reflect the heterogeneous nature of the older population.

THE ECONOMY AND THE OLDER POPULATION

The economic status and work experiences of the older population are the result of a multitude of actions taking place within a complex economy. This section looks at the interaction between the economy and the older population. First, we consider the impact of the economy on the older population. This topic relates back most directly to the two previous sections on the economic status and work experiences of the older population. Next we examine the impact of the older population on the economy. This section is of particular importance today since the proportion of persons in the older population is projected to increase. However, the treatment of this subject is relatively brief, and the reader is urged to read more (Clark, Kreps, & Spengler, 1978; Espenshade & Serow, 1978; Kreps, 1976; Russell, 1979; U.S. Senate, Special Committee on Aging, 1980).

Impact of the economy on the older person

Both the work experiences and economic position of the older population are directly related to economic conditions. The level of prosperity and the availability of employment when workers first enter the labor market have lifetime influences on the work experience. Similarly, the size of one's cohort has been argued to depress the earnings and to increase the likelihood of unemployment (Russell, 1979; U.S. Senate, Special Committee on Aging, 1980). One should not ignore the influence of economic conditions on the current economic position of the older population. Unemployment, which does not in itself particularly cause large groups of older persons to be listed as unemployed, increases competition for part-time jobs held by older workers and encourages premature withdrawals from the labor force. The influence of inflation on the elderly has been altered with the indexing of Social Security, the primary source of income, and Supplementary Security Income. At present, older retired persons are likely to fare better than their working counterparts since real wages—that is, wages adjusted for inflation—have not increased as rapidly as the inflation-indexed Social Security Income benefits of older persons. Among the older population, those most dependent on income that is indexed have been least affected (Kreps, 1976; Schulz, 1980). However, by focusing on real income changes, these studies tend to deemphasize the hardships that individuals experience when fixed payments, such as rents, are increased by relatively large discrete amounts.

Overall economic growth also influences the economic condition of the older population. However, the extent or direction of the impact of economic growth on the older population depends on how the elderly are supported and how the benefits of the growth are allocated between the productive and dependent populations. Initially, economic growth benefits workers and the owners of capital, and the influence on the economic position of the older population depends on how the older population is supported. In the United States older persons who have savings and investments are likely to benefit directly, whereas others who rely more on pension benefits will benefit from growth to the extent that benefit levels are increased. Despite the lack of direct relationships, economic growth is not likely to hurt the economic position of older people in absolute terms, although their relative position may deteriorate.

Impact of the older population on the economy

Although it is the subject of much speculation, the impact of the older population on the operation of the economy is not well established. The avenues through which the older population may influence the economy include their influence on employment, both as consumers and as workers. To the extent that the consumption patterns of older persons differ from those of younger persons, increases in the proportion of older persons are likely to alter the demand for specific types of workers. As workers, increasing proportions of older persons may decrease reported unemployment rates, alter productivity, and discourage occupational mobility. Despite much speculation, the direction or extent of these influences is far from established.

With respect to consumption, one can expect obvious changes in the demand for age-specific occupations: decreases in the demand for primary grade teachers and increases in the demand for nursing home administrators. One may get additional insights into the potential influence of an increasing number of older persons from studies of the consumption patterns of persons characterized by age. A study by Park and Barten (1973) of consumption patterns in 14 developed countries found that older persons spend less of their income on housing and durables and more on food, clothing, and other goods (an aggregate good including medical care) than younger persons with the same income. A more recent study of families in the United States found that families with heads of household aged 65 and above spend the same proportion of income on energy (approximately 10% of pretax income) as families with heads under age 65 with the same income. However, the older families spent a larger proportion on home energy and a smaller proportion on gasoline (Siler, 1980). This only serves to indicate that changes in consumption patterns associated with age and the impacts of these changes on employment opportunities are complex subjects.

There has been considerably more speculation and possibly less consensus regarding the influence of the older population on worker productivity, individual mobility, and unemployment. To the extent that an aging population is associated with slower population growth, increases in the amount of capital in the form of machines that each worker has to work with can be increased more rapidly, since less capital is required to maintain the ratio of capital to labor. The more machines the workers have to work with, the greater will be their productivity; thus, an aging population at the macro level contributes to productivity (Phelps, 1972).

Evidence of the impact of age on productivity at the micro level is generally flawed, and no consensus on the impact of age on productivity is available (U.S. Senate, Special Committee on Aging, 1980). With regard to occupational mobility, Spengler (1972) and others have argued that decreasing population growth discourages mobility and, thus, discourages innovation and growth. There is little question that decreasing population growth increases the proportion of older workers, and evidence also suggests that membership in a relatively larger cohort decreases earnings. However, the influence of the age structure on individual occupational mobility is not well established since changes in the age structure may alter the occupational structure. As discussed by Russell (1979), the influence of demographic change on unemployment in the 1960s has been examined by Wachter (1976) and more recently by Gordon (1978). The evidence suggests that an aging population will reduce unemployment rates, but these results do not mean that manpower will be used more effectively. Some portion of unemployment among young workers is investment in job searching, an activity that has less promise for return for older workers. To conclude, the potential impact of an aging population on employment has received considerable attention, but the attention has not yet led to a general consensus regarding the direction or significance of economic growth on employment.

The final topic to be covered is the influence of an older popoulation on savings and consumption. The issues concern the influence of an aging population both on aggregate savings and on the form of consumption. The first topic is of particular interest since savings is associated with investment and investment determines the extent to which output will increase in the future. The form of consumption is also of importance since changing consumption patterns associated with changes in the age structure influence the demand for labor.

The major issue related to aggregate savings and an aging population has revolved around the influence of Social Security on savings (Esposito, 1978; Munnell, 1977). From an individual standpoint the Social Security benefit is likely to be a substitute for private savings or a private pension. However, from a macroeconomic perspective the Social Security and private pensions are quite distinct, because Social Security operates as a pay-as-you-go system, whereas private pensions are at least designed to be fully funded. As the expected level of benefits increases, private savings and contributions to private pensions should decrease. This is the basis for the concern that the pay-as-you-go Social Security system, when substituted for individual savings or private pensions, decreases investment and growth.

Recent investigations of this relationship have recognized that increases in Social Security benefits alter retirement plans and specifically encourage early retirement, resulting in an increase in savings (Esposito, 1978; Feldstein, 1974; Munnell, 1977). Research efforts using aggregate time series data have indicated an association between increases in Social Security benefits and declines in private savings. However, the magnitude of the relationship is sensitive to the specification of the relationship, thus calling into question any claims that Social Security has reduced private savings by any fixed percentage. Another set of studies has found a relationship between individual savings levels and Social Security (Feldstein & Pellechio, 1979). Some have used these results to argue for major reforms of the financing of Social Security designed to make Social Security resemble private pension programs more closely. Others view these proposals both as unnecessary and unacceptable politically. The consensus is that an inverse relationship exists between Social Security and savings, but the significance of the relationship is uncertain. The desired response to this relationship is an area of little agreement among economists.

CONCLUSION

The economics of aging is a complex subject involving both the study of the economic status and economic activities of older persons and the study of the influences of the older population on the economy. This chapter has focused on three areas: (1) economic status of the older population; (2) work status of the older population; (3) relationship between the economy and the aging population. Throughout the chapter we have stressed the heterogeneity of the older population and the tentative nature of many research findings. There is still more speculation than consensus in this subject area, and the need for more research is sometimes painfully obvious.

REFERENCES

Bixby, E. Retirement patterns in the United States: Research and policy interaction. *Social Security Bulletin,* 1976, *33*(4), 3–34.
Bok, D. C. Emerging issues in social legislation: Social Security. *Harvard Law Review,* 1967, *80*(4), 717–764.
Burkhauser, R. V. The pension acceptance of older workers. *Journal of Human Resources,* 1979, *14*(1), 63–75.

Campbell, C. D., & Campbell, R. G. Conflicting views on the effect of old-age and survivors insurance on retirement. *Economic Inquiry*, 1976, *14*, 369–388.

Clark, R., Kreps, J., & Spengler, J. Economics of aging: A survey. *Journal of Economic Literature*, 1978, *16*(3), 919–962.

Espenshade, T. J., & Serow, W. J. (Eds.). *The economic consequences of slowing population growth*. New York: Academic Press, 1978.

Esposito, L. Effect of Social Security on saving: Review of studies using U.S. time-series data. *Social Security Bulletin*, 1978, *41*, 9–17.

Feldstein, M. Social Security, induced retirement and aggregate capital accumulation. *Journal of Political Economy*, 1974, *82*(5), 905–926.

Feldstein, M., & Pellechio, A. Social Security and household wealth accumulation: New microeconomic evidence. *Review of Economics and Statistics*, 1979, *61*(3), 361–368.

Fuchs, V. R. Comment. In L. Soltow (Ed.), *Six papers on the size distribution of wealth and income. Studies in income and wealth* 33. New York: National Bureau of Economic Research, 1969.

Garfinkel, I., & Haveman, R. H. *Earnings capacity, poverty and inequality*. New York: Academic Press, 1977.

Gordon, R. A. *The need to disaggregate the full employment goal*, Special report no. 17. Washington, D.C.: National Commission for Manpower Policy, 1978.

Grad, S., & Foster, K. Income of the population aged 55 and older, 1976. *Social Security Bulletin*, 1979, *42*(7), 16–32.

Kreps, J. The economy and the aged. In R. H. Binstock & E. Shanas (Eds.), *Handbook of aging and the social sciences*. New York: Van Nostrand Reinhold, 1976.

Moon, M. *The measurement of economic welfare—Its application to the aged poor*. New York: Academic Press, 1977.

Moon, M., & Smolensky, E. (Eds.). *Improving measures of economic well-being*. New York: Academic Press, 1977.

Morgan, J. N. Measuring the economic status of the aged. *International Economic Review*, 1965, *6*(1), 1–17.

Morgan, J. N., Dickinson, K., Dickinson, J., Benus, J., and Duncan, G. *Five thousand American families: Patterns of economic progress* (Vol. 1). Ann Arbor: Institute for Social Research, University of Michigan, 1974.

Munnell, A. *The future of Social Security*. Washington, D.C.: Brookings Institution, 1977.

Orshansky, M. Prepared statement before the House Select Committee on Aging. In *Poverty among America's aged*. Hearing before the Select Committee on Aging. Washington, D.C.: U.S. Government Printing Office, 1978.

Park, R. W., & Barten, A. P. A cross-country comparison of the effect of prices, income, and population composition on consumption patterns. *Economic Journal*, 1973, *83*, 834–852.

Parsons, D. O. The decline in male labor force participation. *Journal of Political Economy*, 1980, *88*(11), 117–134.

Phelps, E. S. Some macroeconomics of population levelling. In E. R. Morss & R. H. Reed (Eds.), *Economic aspects of population change. Commission on population growth and the American future* (Vol. 2). Washington, D.C.: U.S. Government Printing Office, 1972.

Poverty Studies Task Force. *The measure of poverty*. Washington, D.C.: U.S. Department of Health, Education and Welfare, 1976.

Quinn, J. F. Microeconomic determinants of early retirement: A cross sectional view of white married men. *Journal of Human Resources*, 1977, *12*(3), 329–346.

Rones, P. L. Older men—the choice between work and retirement. *Monthly Labor Review*, 1978, *101*(11), 3–10.

Rosenfeld, C., & Brown, S. C. The labor force status of older workers. *Monthly Labor Review,* 1979, *101*(11), 12–18.

Russell, L. B. The macroeconomic effects of changes in the age structure of the population. In M. B. Ballabon (Ed.), *Economic perspectives: An annual survey of economics* (Vol. 1). Amsterdam: Harwood Academic Publishers, 1979.

Schulz, J. H. *The economics of aging* (2nd ed.). Belmont, Calif.: Wadsworth, 1980.

Schwab, K. Early labor-force withdrawal of men: Participants and nonparticipants aged 58–63. *Social Security Bulletin,* 1974, *37*(8), 24–38.

Sheppard, H. Work and retirement. In R. H. Binstock & E. Shanas (Eds.), *Handbook of aging and the social sciences.* New York: Van Nostrand Reinhold, 1976.

Siler, A. *A comparison of energy expenditures by elderly and nonelderly households —1975 and 1985.* Analysis Report, Office of Energy Use Analysis. Washington, D.C.: U.S. Department of Energy, 1980.

Smeeding, T. M. The economic well-being of low-income households: Implications for income inequality and poverty. In M. Moon & E. Smolensky (Eds.), *Improving measures of economic well-being.* New York: Academic Press, 1977.

Spengler, J. J. Declining population growth: Economic effects. In E. R. Morss & R. H. Reed (Eds.), *Economic aspects of population change. Commission on population growth and the American future* (Vol. 2). Washington, D.C.: U.S. Government Printing Office, 1972.

Taussig, M. K. *Alternative measures of the distribution of economic welfare.* Princeton, N. J.: Princeton University Press, 1973.

Treas, J. Women's employment and its implications for the economic status of the elderly of the future. In J. March, S. Keisler, V. Oppenheimer, & J. N. Morgan (Eds.), *The elderly of the future.* New York: Academic Press, 1980.

U.S. Department of Health, Education and Welfare. *Income and resources of the aged.* Social Security Administration, Office of Policy. Washington, D.C.: U.S. Government Printing Office, 1980.

U.S. Department of Labor. *Handbook of labor statistics 1978.* Washington, D.C.: U.S. Government Printing Office, 1979.

U.S. Senate Special Committee on Aging. *Emerging options for work and retirement policy.* Washington, D.C.: U.S. Government Printing Office, 1980.

Wachter, M. L. The changing cyclical responsiveness of wage inflation. *Brookings Papers on Economic Activity,* 1976, *1,* 115–159.

Walther, R. J. *Target efficiency, economic well-being, and the older population.* Los Angeles, Calif.: Social Policy Laboratory, Andrus Gerontology Center, 1979.

CHAPTER **18**

Public Policy and Aging

Paul A. Kerschner and Ira S. Hirschfield

This chapter looks at the premises upon which legislation involving America's elderly is based and analyzes the relationship of this framework to delivery systems and public policy outcomes. We shall posit that policy outcomes, whether positive or negative, are a direct result of four prevailing approaches to the legislative process.

Traditionally, when public policy failures occur, Americans rely on the restructuring of internal organizational processes as a means of improving public service programs. When problems arise in the operation or delivery of public programs, we typically look to their organizational context for relief. Wilcox (1969) documents this pattern and states that the alteration of agency structure has become the vehicle for change in the minds of many authorities in the field of organizational theory and analysis.

This major approach to and philosophy of changing public policy stems from a "sickness model," which assumes that any pathology lies at the end of the policy train—in the operationalizing agency—rather than at the beginning within the offices of the legislator and his or her policy development staff. Although little evidence supports the notion that reorganization of public agencies brings about public policy effectiveness, many organizational models still recommend the "curative" approach. Major surgery or administrative transplants in the form of systems reorganization and structural gerrymandering remain the typical suggestions.

We are now learning the hard way that if legislation is written with insufficient data concerning the nature of the problem or, even worse, with inaccurate data, no amount of structural manipulation will result in clear and accurate policy outcomes. In contrast to the structural manipulation approach is the strategy presented in this chapter. We shall begin by examining the genesis of the problem—namely, the basis upon which policymakers enact legislation in the field of aging.

Legislation is generally formulated from four model dichotomies: *categorical versus generic; holistic versus segmented; crisis versus rational;* and *political context versus future planning.* After explaining these model dichotomies, we shall examine each of them in juxtaposition to the major legislative enactments for older Americans: health care, housing, and income maintenance. In addition to the information provided from this legislative analysis, we shall present alternative approaches to public policy investigation.

The traditional methods of exploring public policy have focused on the bureaucratic process, organizational structure, or service delivery system. This chapter's perspective should be more useful for those wishing to influence legislative procedure.

MODEL PUBLIC POLICY DICHOTOMIES

Categorical versus generic

Legislation in aging has suffered from a lack of understanding of the clientele it intends to assist. The proverbial question is whether the aged should be singled out categorically for purposive and specific age-oriented action, or whether they should be only one segment of a larger generic grouping and thus forced to compete for attention, programs, and funds. Any discussion of service programs for the elderly in the United States inevitably turns to the issue of categorical versus noncategorical programs. How do we best serve the elderly: by improving services for all groups, including the elderly, or by singling out the pressing and sometimes unique problems of the elderly for intensive action in hopes that some day such individual programs can become part of a more comprehensive system? The debate between these two groups continues to rage within legislative, as well as gerontological, circles, indicating the need for a clear philosophy from which to design public policy.

The same discussion also occurs within federal agencies. Here it centers on the placement of resources within an autonomous bureau controlling its own network of delivery systems. The prevailing situation, however, is the proliferation of resources and responsibilities in and among a variety of agencies and departments, each of whom has a minimum of responsibility or autonomy. The issue of nutrition and aging exemplifies this proliferation of resources and responsibilities. The U.S. Departments of Agriculture and Labor and the Administration of Aging each handle varying components of the nutrition issue. Since no single agency coordinates these efforts, the consequences are inefficiency, repetition, and competition. Compelling evidence suggests that a *categorical* stance is vitally needed.

This conflict in "strategy" strikes at the heart of the policy initiation process. Accepting the *generic* approach, whereby the aged are one among many groups to be affected by legislation, public policymakers can use a more general data base than would be necessary if they were solely applying a categorical approach. For example, when developing a mass transit system serving a total (*generic*) population, policymakers need to know the specific preferences of the aged (routes, times, costs, accessibility). Given the limitations in available resources, however, these preferences may be disregarded in an effort to serve the larger population.

If, on the other hand, one utilizes the *categorical* approach, whereby legislation and programs are tailored exclusively to the requisites of older adults, then the data base must be absolutely accurate as well as focused, or it may well be destructive to the well-being of the user population. For example, a mass feeding program designed for the elderly should be structured around a detailed knowledge of age-related issues such as diet, eating periods, and group versus individual preferences.

Legislation affecting the aged has been neither wholly categorical nor wholly generic in approach. What has occurred is a continual shifting between the two approaches, resulting in chaos within the public policy process. The dilemma is like that of an individual who is constantly having to shift between cooking for one person and cooking for a family of ten. He or she would be dealing with two distinct types of data bases with varying needs for specificity and accuracy. The Social Security Administration, like the alternating chef, once served primarily the aged, but now has expanded its scope to also include the blind, poor, disabled, and dependent survivors. Like many organizations, it has had to reorient itself to serving a more comprehensive population. Such a reorientation often results in greater inefficiency and inadequate delivery of services to its recipients.

Summarizing the categorical versus generic approach, one might quote from the British experience:

> Services for the elderly, whether medical services or social services, may be integrated with services for other age groups or developed separately. Proponents of integrated services argue that unless special provisions are made for the elderly, the low status of this group among professional workers and the general public will result in their being ignored in program planning and resource allocation [U.S. Senate, 1971, p.5].

Holistic versus segmented

In addition to the categorical issue, those initiating policy in the aging field appear to have had difficulty addressing the older adult in anything but a segmented manner. For too many years we have divided the aged individual into segments separated in much the same manner that a butcher sorts out cuts of beef. Essentially, we have categorized the aged into selective needs and then passed legislation and designed programs to address those specific needs. Thus, perusing the national and state aging scene, we discover a landscape dotted with specialized divisions: institutional care, home health care, Supplemental Security Income, nutrition, and recreation.

The result of this segmentation has been a twofold dilemma. First, legislative formulation, already suffering from the categorical versus generic difficulty, has not reflected the integration of data resulting from other aged programs and legislation, but rather has been contrived within a vacuum of isolated and unrelated information. Second, the older adults who have attempted to utilize those segmented services have been required to visit a number of agencies, most often geographically distant from one another. They not only have been forced to assemble their own constellation of services, but also have had to struggle with the difficult task of securing access to them.

The structure of social service agencies in this country has contributed greatly to the segmentation of services approach. Few departments of social services have created a protective services unit for older adults. The lack of such units is all the more puzzling given the success of protective services for children. Indeed, it could be argued that since children have many surrogate parents available to them (such as courts, adoption agencies, foster parents, big brothers) existing resources should be spent on the aged, who are largely without protectors.

Taking a holistic approach has been one of the most difficult tasks for policy-makers; our natural inclination is to "home in" on those problems that are most visible and amenable to solution. Thus, the segmented, divide-and-conquer approach appears to be both humane and productive, although it could be argued that it further divides and dehumanizes the older adult.

Political context versus future planning

Social legislation reflects society's values at the time of its enactment. In other words, public policy is a reflection of what the times, or better yet, the market will bear. Legislation consistently is based on prevailing social standards and conditions of the present, and rarely on the anticipated needs of the future. Public policy, there-fore, is usually reactive and seldom proactive (initiatory).

The political context approach requires the ability to sense society's readiness to accept certain new policies or legislation. One example is the passage of the Workmen's Compensation Act. Political folklore presents Franklin Roosevelt as being prepared in the 1930s to introduce a form of national health insurance to Congress and the nation. His secretary of labor, Frances Perkins, convinced him that Congress would accept this idea at any time and advised him to defer its introduction in order to devote full attention to passing the then controversial issue of workmen's compensation. We will never be able to determine if the American society would have accepted national health insurance at that time, but the example of Perkins's assessment of Congress, based on its "buying" mood, is a classic example of operating within a political con-text rather than future planning (Lansdale, 1972).

Similarly, given the bitter climate that evolved around the Medicare issue, Lyndon Johnson's Congress could not have written a bill focusing on outpatient and preventive medicine, rather than on curative and institutional care. Even in 1965, a year of sky-rocketing health costs, society was far too distant from the concept of national health insurance even to consider it. Instead, it opted for the more conservative approach of Medicare.

The tragic elements of this approach, from a public policy perspective, are that most legislation in aging evolves not from a group of policy scientists drafting pro-grams for the future, but rather from some pragmatic assumptions about what will be tolerated by the dominant forces in the society.

Crisis versus rational approach

It has long been known that a vast percentage of public policy has been derived from the onset of a crisis. The Social Security Act, for example, did not grow out of a long-planned move to insert the federal government into the economy on a massive scale. Rather, the Social Security Act was a direct outgrowth of the crisis of the Depression. Once the initial shock hit and people began to lose their jobs, it became apparent that older workers were being deprived of occupations, incomes, and savings.

The three major health programs serving the elderly, as well as other age groups, also resulted from the onset of a crisis. The Medical Assistance for the Aged Program,

Title XIX of the Social Security Act (Medicaid—for the medically indigent), and Title XVIII of the Social Security Act (Medicare—for those 65 and over) grew from the health care cost crisis sweeping the nation in the 1960s. An additional example is the Supplemental Security Income Program (Title XVI of the Social Security Act), which provides federal control of the state-operated payment programs for the aged, blind, and disabled. The supplemental program was hastily enacted in part to calm the dismay resulting from the failure to enact the far broader Family Assistance Proposal (HRI).

This demonstration of the "crisis reaction" process contradicts the administrative purists who deny the crisis theme and yet continue to rail against the poor conceptual framework of public policy. They are convinced that public policy emerges out of a rational examination of the available facts and pertinent data. This is far from the truth, however, since experts cannot even agree on what is considered to be a sound conceptual framework. If we were to analyze a series of issues such as the economy, the antiballistic system, and age-related topics, we could immediately line up experts on each side of the debates who claim to have the best approach to rational planning. Scientific data are useful but not the magic wand for opening the door to rational policymaking. We can listen to economic experts such as Schultz, Samuelson, Friedman, and Galbraith. We can examine pages of statistical facts verifying the overwhelming numbers of older Americans suffering from malnutrition, and we can read about the mortality rates in the Sudan. Yet the hard core facts are not simply the statistics or the deaths. Facts can reveal crisis situations daily, but change cannot occur unless this information gets into the right hands and is subsequently communicated to and accepted by the general public.

We are suggesting here that—given the stalemates of the dilemmas created by categorical versus generic approaches, holistic versus segmented programming, current political context versus future planning designs, and crisis versus rational planning—aging legislation has been caught in a morass of conflicting and competing interests and issues. The result of these fragmented approaches is that in most cases involving major aging legislation, policymakers have abdicated moral responsibility by passing laws based on flimsy and often inaccurate data. At the same time, researchers in the field of gerontology have all but ceased to provide any current data useful for drafting legislation. They have often despaired over being able to influence the policy process.

To illustrate the problems of these four approaches to political decision-making, let us examine the recent major pieces of legislation for the aged. It will become apparent that our public policymakers have primarily opted for the categorical, segmented, politically acceptable, and crisis-oriented approach to political decision-making.

HEALTH CARE (MEDICARE AND MEDICAID)

The basic goal of Title XVIII of the Social Security Act (Medicare) has been to provide America's older adults with financial protection against the heavy costs associated with hospital, nursing home, and physician care. The president's and Congress's choice of the aged as the population category to be served was based not so much on an overwhelming concern for the older person, but rather on a compromise hammered out with the medical profession, which had vehemently opposed most public policy in the medical care field.

Once the political decision had been made and the program designed categorically, an immediate search should have begun to uncover and validate the specific health problems of the aging. The development of a health program based on the needs of older adults requires accurate research data in the areas of utilization patterns of older persons, types and incidence of disease prevalent in older adults, percentage of illnesses resulting in restricted mobility, and health-spending patterns of older persons including funds spent on preventive care. What occurred, however, was an initial policy decision to "go categorical" with a subsequent legislative and administrative move to ignore the data needed to create a categorical program.

The decision on a categorical emphasis with little knowledge or use of a sophisticated data base has had long-term and tragic implications for the older person. The discussion in recent years of the need for alternatives to institutionalization, and the demand that we get those 25% of all inappropriately placed nursing home residents back into their homes (Kerschner, 1973) is a result of that ill-planned categorical decision. Little investigation was undertaken of the use older persons would make of services such as day hospitals or outpatient clinics. As it became clear that there were few reimbursable outpatient services available, older adults had no choice but to go into institutions, thus increasing the total Medicare bill and adding to the notion that what was needed were more institutional services (namely, beds). Although many citizens have become aware of the vicious circle being created, public policy has yet to alter significantly its original direction or scope.

As the legislative process in 1965 moved to develop and clarify the Medicare Act, many in the health care field realized that not only was the categoric system being subjected to generic-like manipulation, but also that Congress was opting for a fragmented rather than a comprehensive approach. The legislators had an opportunity to devise legislation and put into operation a program that would have addressed the total health needs of the total person. They lost the opportunity to provide coverage for varying types and levels of care, which would have ensured that only a minimum of health care needs went unaddressed and unfinanced.

Research conducted at Brandeis University, the University of Southern California, and by the Senate Special Committee on Aging indicates the overwhelming need for preventive and home-based medical care for older adults. Even with these numerous studies indicating that older adults require services beyond those offered within health care institutions, the Medicare Act concentrates almost exclusively upon inpatient care.

The passage of Medicare represented a major departure in the financing of health care in this nation; it did not, however, represent a radical shift in health care quality, quantity, or mode of delivery. Partly as a result of the segmented and categorical approach discussed earlier, health care for the aged, poor, and disabled has gone in the direction of less coverage and higher costs. In 1977, the average person aged 65 and over paid $313 more out-of-pocket expenses for his or her medical care than in 1966, one year after the passage of the Medicare Act. This represents an annual average increase of 6.6%. In 1977, 29% of the elderly's health bill was an out-of-pocket expense.

Even with staggering inflation, a plan that is touted as being low cost, categorical, and comprehensive should more than "hold-the-line" in its coverage of personal expenditures.

This continual increase in personal cost is due, in large part, to the acceptance of a basic myth put forth at the time of the act's passage and reinforced by later segmental decisions. Because factual data was overlooked or disregarded, the assumption was that the elderly primarily would utilize inpatient care, the coverage of which was relatively extensive under Medicare. What transpired, however, was that the aged increasingly required, or desired, preventive outpatient services, the costs of which were usually personally borne. Glasser's Senate testimony is instructive in this regard: in 1973, Medicare covered less than 50% of the personal health costs of the individuals in the aged and poor and disabled class. Almost 50% of the aged in 1973 did not have supplemental insurance coverage in addition to Medicare, leaving a substantial portion unable to meet their share of the medical bills (Glasser, 1974). A more damaging figure is one quoted by former Health, Education and Welfare Secretary, Wilbur J. Cohen. He revealed that in 1967 only about 10% of persons aged 60 years and over visited private physicians for general medical examinations. If, as Cohen continues, "no fewer than 86% of all persons 65 years and over have one or more abnormalities" (Cohen, 1968, p. 14), then surely the basic tenets of the Medicare Act contain some rather glaring deficiencies.

Obviously, the inconsistencies are great. Only 10% of the elderly visited private physicians, yet at least 86% have one or more chronic illnesses. People are spending more time utilizing outpatient care, and yet money continues to be poured into inpatient services. Medicare has not satisfactorily addressed the needs of the older person, and a major share of the blame lies with its original philosophy. Those early decisions, which were categorically and segmentally based, forced the scope and direction of the program toward a bias of institutionalization (inpatient care).

A recitation of the financial figures supports the belief that the decision to make Medicare basically an inpatient service was not based on any "real" data as to older patient utilization and that it has resulted in a movement over the years that has reinforced and increased rather than evened out the institutional bias. Table 18-1

TABLE 18-1. Medicare reimbursements

Period	Recipient	Reimbursement in thousands
Jan.–Nov. 1979	Inpatient hospital	$14,273,908
Jan.–Nov. 1979	Skilled nursing facility	274,233
Jan.–Nov. 1979	Home health	306,582
Jan.–Dec. 1979	Outpatient hospital	781,702
Jan.–Dec. 1979	Physicians	5,791,830

SOURCE: *Health care financing review,* Spring 1980, pp. 95–96.

indicates dollar amounts reimbursed by Medicare for periods shown. The discrepancy among the figures clearly shows that either outpatient and physician care is not required or desired by older adults, or that the system forces inpatient utilization. We suggest that the latter is the predominant case. Bed disability days of the over-65 population come to 14.5 days of bed disability per person per year (1978). In 1977, 0.7% of all discharges, aged 65 and over, were hospitalized 61 days or more. These figures suggest a need for an immediate reordering of health care services to older adults. A study under the auspices of the state of Maryland found that many older adults indicated that a major unmet need was that of easily accessible and reimbursable outpatient services. In an open-ended discussion with the same group, a majority indicated that they would allow themselves to be placed in a hospital or nursing home for reasons of payment rather than for the facility's ability to meet their specific health requirements (Kerschner, 1973).

In the area of health care, policymakers at the federal level have evidently responded to pragmatic political realities instead of to clear indications of the type of services desired and required by the older adult. (The recent proposals of national health insurance appear to acknowledge this past flaw; the majority of them reflect a movement toward the preventive side of the health delivery system). Although there should have been extensive inquiry into and use of age-related data, we know that due to the political pressures in the environment, the program did not reflect the critical needs of the elderly. Instead, Medicare reflected what the politicians could safely legislate at the time.

Many significant activities were occurring in 1965. Bills for health care were requiring astronomical sums, and the Older American Act and the War on Poverty were beginning their legislative lives. It was obvious that the poor, disadvantaged, and elderly would require a specific and comprehensive focus. Some form of health insurance would have to be passed if we were to protect the health of our older citizens. The prevailing political atmosphere appears to have been the critical factor in deciding the final form of legislation. In view of John Kennedy's death, Lyndon Johnson's legislative power, the vast sums of money being channeled into the battle by the American Medical Association, and the conservatives' fear of socialized medicine, legislators apparently considered the prevailing political climate and built a system they hoped would be open to incremental changes during subsequent years.

The final Medicare bill, as well as the regulations that preceded it, did not reflect the accumulated data available regarding the health needs of older adults. Rather, it was based on the prevailing environmental constraints, opposing political pressures, and a growing crisis atmosphere. Thus, the realities of constructing public policy in 1965 precluded the possibility of a revolutionary piece of health care legislation.

We have stated that in order to devise a health plan for older Americans, we first must become knowledgeable about their health needs. Then a system must be developed to utilize this data in a comprehensive delivery scheme. Medicare was a major breakthrough in the battle to ensure older adults access to health care. Yet, it has been built upon a shaky philosophical foundation unbuttressed by solid data.

Now it is up to the researchers and public policymakers to cooperate to ensure that the next phase is constructed upon a more solid foundation. We must move to a point where health care legislation has a knowledge, rather than a political-mood, base. The solution appears readily accessible, yet in reality its application is exceedingly difficult. In order to succeed, statistically sound scientific data will have to take precedence over the fierce lobbying powers and intense political pressures that bear down upon our legislators.

HOUSING

Congressional acts

Another area in which legislation for the elderly currently exists is housing. There is a close association between the need for legislation on housing for the elderly and the need for legislation on medical care. Both involve the need for alternatives to institutionalization. Health officials have difficulty deciding to discharge elderly patients from mental hospitals and nursing homes if sufficient and appropriate housing suitable for these displaced individuals does not exist.

In an attempt to ameliorate the housing problem substantial national legislation has provided for the planning, development, and construction of housing specifically designed for occupancy by elderly persons. We shall present the most significant of these housing acts followed by commentary linking this legislation to the four models previously discussed. (Also see the Annual Reports of the U.S. Senate Special Committee on Aging, U.S. Senate, published annually by the Committee since its inception in 1959.)

The Housing Act of 1937 is the basic piece of legislation for low-rent public housing for the poor and elderly. According to Moon (1977), only 1.28% of elderly families benefit from this $1.8 billion (1978) program.

The 1956 Amendments to the National Housing Act. These amendments authorized mortgage-insurance financing of cooperative housing and nonprofit housing for the aged. In addition, they required local public housing authorities to give first priority to the aged in their admission policies and removed the legal prohibition to housing of single elderly widows and widowers in federally subsidized housing projects.

Prior to the 1956 amendments, the categorical versus generic issue had been a critical one. Because no specific quota of elderly was specified, they were forced to compete for public housing with the general population, many of whom could argue greater need because of their dependent children. This same rationale based on dependent children was used to disallow single elderly access to public housing. It was argued that providing housing for the single elderly was poor use of limited housing resources.

The 1959 Amendments to the National Housing Act. These amendments also authorized housing programs for the aging. Section 202 provided a direct, long-term, low-cost loan program designed for those with moderate incomes. Section 231 was a mortgage insurance program designed for those with above-average incomes as well as for strengthening and expanding low-rent public housing for the elderly.

The enactment of these amendments is representative of the holistic versus segmented issue as well as of the political context versus future planning approach. Policymakers assumed that through the provision of low-cost monies the needs of older citizens could be met. What was ignored, however, is that the mere provision of a roof and walls addresses only one of the many needs of older adults. Missing, for example, were the needed provisions for both health and social services. Yet once again, as in the case of Title XVIII (Medicare), policymakers believed that legislation with an incremental approach, the expansion and alteration of which could take place over time, stood the best chance for passage and implementation.

The regulations for Section 202 now mandate that the projects "provide the necessary services for the occupants, which may include among others, health, continuing education, welfare, informational, recreational, homemaker, counseling, and referral to facilitate access to these activities" (*CFR*, Part IV, Subpart A, S. 885.1 (a), March 1, 1978). According to a HUD survey, however, few services are actually being provided (see Table 18-2).

TABLE 18-2. Facilities and services provided by Section 202 of the 1959 Amendments to the National Housing Act

	Percentage of 202 projects
Space	
Laundry facilities	91
Community rooms	94
Dining rooms	22
Infirmaries	3
Recreational facilities	86
Services	
Air conditioning	54
Meals	7
Physical therapy	3
Medical care	4
Nursing care	4
Maid and linen service	4

SOURCE: U.S. Congress, Senate Special Committee on Aging, *Developments in Aging: 1979*. U.S. Government Printing Office, Washington, D.C., 1980, p. 143.

The Amendments to the Housing Act of 1964, P. L. 88-560. These amendments further expanded the low-rent public housing program and included specific provisions for relocation assistance, relocation rental assistance, and rehabilitation loans. In addition, they extended the rural mortgage insurance program of housing for the elderly.

The 1964 amendments expanded the incremental improvements begun earlier, but remained anchored within a segmented base, using monetary reimbursement as the panacea for improving the general standard of living. The assumption appears to have been that money would or could be translated into services by the recipient, a thesis unsupported by both past and present data.

The Housing and Urban Development Act of 1965. This act extended the existing federally assisted housing programs for the elderly and authorized grants for home rehabilitation and neighborhood facilities in addition to rental supplements. This was the first time that the Housing Act included provisions for neighborhood facilities, thus appearing to reflect a change to a slightly more holistic philosophy. However, there was little if any integration of the housing and service components except on a very isolated, demonstration-project basis.

The Housing and Urban Development Act of 1968. This act called for a further extension of a number of existing federal housing programs including rent supplements and Model City Programs. Section 236 of this act provided interest subsidies for moderate-income housing programs sponsored by nonprofit organizations.

Section 236 finally began to move the federal government from the posture of reactor to that of a proactive catalyst. It was hoped that the growth of Section 236 would attract segments of the private building market in numbers sufficient enough to make a dent in the documented need for moderate income elderly housing. The exciting aspect of this housing act was that nonprofit organizations were tuned in to the categorical as well as holistic approach.

The 1969 National Housing Act. This act included such provisions as increased authorization for the Section 202 direct loan program, and limited rents fixed by public housing agencies to no more than 25% of a tenant's income. It mandated that in instances of urban renewal, for every housing unit razed, a new, low-income unit would have to be built in the city or county involved.

In the housing arena, this act reflected little deviation from the existing philosophy of the federal government. HUD was still operating from a segmented base and with an apparently limited perception of the existing social climate.

The Housing and Community Development Amendments of 1979 reauthorized loan authority of Section 202 housing for three years, 1980–1982. An effort was made during the writing of this legislation to mandate HUD to establish an assistant secretary for elderly housing. The secretary regarded this amendment as interference by Congress into an executive agency, but he agreed to set up a special assistant for elderly housing, who would report to the assistant secretary for housing.

In any discussion of a framework underlying housing programs for the aged, one must relate the reason for the framework to the larger social trends existing in the country at the time. Although it is true that during the late 1950s and the 1960s the Department of Housing and Urban Development moved to fund and develop large-scale, high-rise facilities for the aged poor, the emphasis was upon high-rise dwellings for low-income persons in general. This emphasis upon the generic approach ensured that assumptions that proved invalid for the poor were equally inaccurate for the aged. The final results of the large high-rise developments were generally increased crime, greater social disorganization, and the breakup of family and community ties.

We have previously mentioned that much of this housing was not built solely for older people. However, a few thoughts on the ramification of these high-rise dwellings for the elderly are in order. Studies, beginning with those in Boston (Fried, 1963), have indicated that when the elderly are subjected to relocation, they suffer subsequent moving traumas and isolation. Regardless of the improvement in their environments or conditions, their death rates rise precipitously. Once living in these high-rise apartments, many older people found themselves far removed from their families and friends. The large buildings, long corridors, numerous elevators, and masses of people added to their isolation. The friendliness, familiarity, and closeness of their past dwelling experience had been completely removed from them. Instead of the familiar, albeit unclean, horizontally located ghettos, the elderly found themselves in lonely, unadaptable vertical ghettos.

In addition, private developers and builders have not aided the impoverished elderly in any significant manner. For many years the construction of new housing for low-income and elderly persons has been by and large an unprofitable venture. Section 236 started to attract a lot of private developers, but since it has ended, very little private money has been freed for "low cost" housing.

Major issues

Perhaps the assumption most difficult to destroy is that public housing could make a dramatic impact upon the general housing situation. Public housing may be a drop in the bucket, its major attribute being that of allowing the general public to state collectively, "See, we are doing something." Obviously, when 50% of single-family households over 65 are living below the poverty level, a massive and comprehensive assistance program is needed. We would need billions of dollars to help people find or afford decent housing.

Rather than dwell on a point that should now be clear—namely, that housing for the elderly was derived from some rather questionable assumptions, we can sum up the housing program by providing a discussion of some major issues in need of attention by those designing future housing programs:

1. Immediate attention must be given to the rising incidence of crimes committed against the elderly living in deteriorated neighborhoods and public housing projects. The deterioration of the housing projects may very well be a direct result of the segmented approach, wherein housing has been seen as a self-standing, nonintegrated solution separate from social and health needs.
2. Despite legislation that is trying to address increased rates, the elderly homeowner faces the continuing problem and burden of rising property taxes. The flurry of activity on this issue around election time is a good example of the crisis versus rational approach to planning for the elderly.

Existing housing programs are not meeting the need for specially designed housing for low and moderate income older people. Although existing laws require all buildings funded with federal money to be barrier free (by eliminating such physical barriers as stoops), the provisions are either not sharply drawn or no one is willing to enforce the regulations. This is a good ecample of the importance of implementing existing legislation. If federal funds were cut off on projects not including barrier-free access, the projects would probably be designed to include features such as ramps, lower curbs, wider doors, and accessible bath facilities.

INCOME MAINTENANCE

The majority of the elderly in this country are dependent upon some type of retirement income to pay for their basic needs. Their standard of living is determined largely by the adequacy of civilian and military pensions, Social Security, and, for the poorest of the poor, public assistance. Thus, the elderly are primarily dependent on the efforts and paternalism of others. Herman Brotman, formerly with the Administration on Aging, has very aptly described the posture of the aged in this regard:

> When someone retires, he does not have a basement stuffed with goods and services he will need for the rest of his life. For him, as for everyone else, practically everything consumed comes out of the current production of goods and services. The owners, the managers and the members of the labor force exercise first claim. The non-producers, including the aged, get a share based mostly on the producers' willingness to share. The size of the aged's share is determined by how much purchasing power is transferred to them. Methods of financing and the like are important, but incidental. It comes down to the younger group's willingness to share—in other words, on the ordering of our national priorities [Brotman, 1973].

In short, there is no program of adequate, standardized care for our aged. Social Security and Old Age Assistance (now SSI) do not provide incomes that meet even officially-defined poverty levels. In fact, 14% of the elderly in our country live below this income line. This percentage translates into well over three million old people who live a poverty-stricken existence. Income is only one aspect of the problem. It is closely related, for example, to the issue of long-term care, when a person is in need of continued medical and personal care assistance. Without adequate finances, however, it is impossible to pay for that care, let alone receive the nutrition necessary to maintain an adequate diet.

The natural inclination has been to focus on the need for increased funds. This emphasis, however, is a good example of the segmented approach as it relates to program design for income maintenance. Even though 75% of the elderly are living above the government's poverty income level, and even though there is an emphasis on upgrading those below the poverty line, our approach still is a segmented one, focusing solely on the economic aspects and thus refusing to concentrate on the total human being. To provide only enough money to pay for basic essentials while ignoring accompanying life support requirements is to ignore the overall needs of the person, in favor of placing bandaids on a few of his or her critical wounds. If one analyzes the major financial programs provided for older adults, one realizes that each is representative of one of the policy models or approaches presented throughout this chapter.

Private retirement plans

Today private retirement plans are an important economic mechanism for providing income for old age. These plans have shown significant growth since 1950, when pension plans first became accepted as a proper issue for collective bargaining. This was a result of the Supreme Court's decision in the 1949 Inland Steel case. As retirement coverage has grown, so have the number of beneficiaries—450,000 in 1950, 1.8 million in 1960 and 7.1 million at present. Benefit payments likewise have increased over the years, rising from $370 million in 1950 to $1.8 billion in 1960 and up to more than $23.1 billion in 1975.

These statistics convey the impression that private retirement plans have gained considerable ground in terms of their support for the aged. Data Resources Inc. analyzed income sources for persons 55 and over in 1977. They assessed that of all income sources, only 7.74% came from pensions. For persons with incomes under $5,000, 3.35% came from pensions.

The Employee Retirement Income Security Act of 1974 (ERISA) provides major protection of a worker's pension and welfare benefits. It regulates participation provisions, vesting, funding and fiduciary standards, disclosure, and reporting, and it provides insurance in cases of plan termination. According to the General Accounting Office, 16,500 plans terminated in the first three years of ERISA regulation, citing ERISA compliance as the sole cause in one-third of the terminations. The U.S. Department of Labor reported that very few workers were affected by these plans, having an average of seven workers per plan.

Another piece of major pension legislation is now pending in Congress. It would provide insurance for multi-employer plans (as in the case of unions), but it may cause a reduction in the worker's benefit of up to 25%.

A number of factors have contributed to this discrepancy. First, when companies go out of business, the pension plan is dissolved, leaving the workers with little or none of the retirement investment they had earned. Another circumstance may be the failure of the retirement plan itself through financial mismanagement or even corruption and misuse of assets. The long absence of vesting provisions is another explanation for the proportionately small number of pension plan beneficiaries. Vesting is the right of a participant in a pension plan to receive accrued benefits if he or she discontinues employment. Plans to provide vesting have been on the increase in recent years, but it is estimated that currently about a quarter of the private pension plans have no vesting provision. Closely related to vesting is the portability of pension investment. If, as is now generally conceded, the employer's contribution to an employee's pension fund is part of his or her remuneration and is a charge of ongoing business, the employee clearly has a right to accrued pension credits when he or she leaves the employment, whether voluntarily or involuntarily. Although both vesting and portability have been receiving increased attention in the Congress, constructive measures to protect the rights and financial investments of workers in private employment are essential.

Although recent reform legislation has significantly tightened the pension system, we question the basic approach. The reforms do not reflect concerted long-term planning. Rather they are indicative of those incremental changes acceptable to both the Congress and the general public.

Retirement benefits under Social Security

These benefits are the single most important source of income for the retired aged. As of June 1978, 899 persons of every 1000 persons aged 65 and older were receiving cash benefits. The Social Security Administration reports that, as of 1979, 95% of the population 65 and over were eligible for Social Security retirement benefits and 4% were eligible to draw benefits if they or their spouses retired. By the year 2000, it is expected to reach 96–98%.

The average monthly cash benefit paid by Social Security for the month of April 1980 and the average cash benefit awarded in that month can be seen in Table 18-3. It should be obvious that Social Security payments are not sufficient to match an individual's preretirement standard of living.

TABLE 18-3. Average monthly cash benefits from Social Security, April 1980

	Average benefit	*Average award*	*Monthly benefits (in thousands)*
Retired workers 62+	$295.51	$315.00	$5,638,885
Wives and husbands	148.86	149.09	444,025
Special age, 72 benefits	N/A	N/A	9,518

SOURCE: U.S. Social Security Administration, *Monthly Benefits Statistics,* 15 June 1980, no. 5.

Table 18-4 shows the total number of retirement insurance beneficiaries aged 62 and over, the number by sex, and the average monthly payment for June 1980.

TABLE 18-4. Retirement insurance beneficiaries 62+, June 1980

	Number	*Average monthly benefits*
Male	10,278,490	$376.51
Female	8,889,141	294.41
Total	19,167,631	338.43

SOURCE: U.S. Social Security Administration. Office of Research and Statistics. Unpublished data.

It is difficult to attack an institution as venerated as the Social Security Administration. Yet, as perhaps the single most visible age-related program, we must seek to purge it of any misconceptions originally included in its legislation or inherently acquired over the years.

Social Security was, and is, intended to be a postretirement income *supplement.* As such, it assumes that:

1. The individual is able to save for retirement.
2. Pensions provide for *decent primary* retirement income.
3. Older people require less and thus can afford to live on less.

We think that these statistics and the annual congressional scramble to raise Social Security payments indicate the inadequacy of this program as an income supplement. Attempts by the Ford administration to hold down Social Security payments as an inflation-fighting device indicate that public policy tools can be a two-edged sword. Although we might argue in favor of the categorical approach as an advocacy device ensuring further aid for the aged, it can also be used to select the aged out of support programs necessary for retaining a decent standard of living.

Supplemental Security Income program

Under the Social Security Amendments of 1972, the combined federal-state programs of Old Age Assistance, Aid to the Blind, and Aid to the Totally Disabled were repealed. A new federal program known as Supplemental Security Income (SSI), administered by the Social Security Administration, became operative on January 1, 1973. Individuals or couples are eligible for assistance if their monthly income is less than the standard payment (for basic living costs) of $238 a month per person and $357.00 for an individual with an eligible spouse (as of July 1980).

This program provides funds for those elderly in abject poverty or who are blind or disabled. Althouth SSI is a major first step toward a comprehensive program to provide an income floor for older adults, its philosophy, rules, and regulations perpetuate many of the inadequacies contained in the former state-operated welfare programs. First, it assumes that federally based, means-tested (recipient must prove poverty) programs are less acceptable to the elderly than to the poor in general. This is true, it is argued, due in large part to their relatively recent entry into the poverty category. Second, the SSI program appears to legitimize the invalid assumption that lump sum payments are sufficient tools for raising one's standard of living. Professionals in the field continue to be concerned about the deterioration in services required over and above the availability of cash.

The SSI program has exacerbated rather than ameliorated the trend toward service denigration and elimination. In this regard, the following comments in an administrative memorandum by Robert Ball, the former Commissioner of Social Security, are significant:

> Social Security has always resisted becoming a center for the provision of social services, but it has willingly accepted the responsibility for knowing about community resources, for participating in their development, and for the operation of a referral service. This function has now been assigned to SSA by the President. A considerable upgrading of the service has already taken place, but it will not be possible to fully implement an advertised, in-depth service until after the implementation of the recent social security amendments (H.R. 1); the new legislation puts just too many additional demands on SSA offices to make this feasible [Ball, 1973].

Not only is the Social Security Administration unwilling to provide its own service, but also it has made it extremely difficult for the aged individual to link up with services provided by outside agencies. This provision of income without service reflects the classic segmented model. Once again, we reiterate that programs providing only money cannot help to solve the multifaceted needs and problems of the elderly. Even if the Social Security Administration successfully survived the onerous burdens thrust upon it beginning in 1965, the problems it has in administering the SSI program are greater than Medicare and the other post-1965 changes.

SSI is a revolutionary way of dealing with old problems. It has shifted older people from established institutions (state welfare agencies) to a vast and untried operation within an agency already carrying a heavy load of related (Title II and Disability) but dissimilar activities. At some point we may come upon a crisis of such magnitude that it might destroy the Social Security operation. Although it would be a costly way of forcing change, this might lead to an appraisal of the federal government's role in providing financial support to poor, elderly, and disabled adults.

Reappraisal of the federal role

Some $9.1 billion in monthly cash benefits are being made from federal funds for retirement or disability benefits. The Supplemental Security Income program added another $149 million in payments in December 1979. Moreover, planners anticipate a substantial rise in military retirement payments and in veterans compensation and pensions over the next few years.

Currently there is no high-level public policy body with sufficient clout to reevaluate the federal role of providing financial aid to retired and disabled adults. No continuing examination is made of the financing of these programs. In addition, no critical analysis has been made of overlapping payments to individuals.

With the welfare of millions of elderly at stake, and in full recognition of the responsibility borne by younger workers, we need to analyze and appraise current federal programs for retired and disabled adults, as well as the retirement plans of private industry. We must develop policy recommendations to correct present inequities and to provide creative and responsible direction for future action.

Current statistics have revealed the need for a complete examination of possible new avenues of revenue for the Social Security Administration. According to present figures, Social Security payments are greatly exceeding the intake of taxed income. A presidential commission might examine the whole area of the economics of aging in the United States in an effort to reform and perhaps reconstitute the system.

The relief for the problems described here may come about only from an overwhelmingly negative, crisis-oriented response. As the aged poor enter into critical situations in the areas of health, counseling, transportation and nutrition, our policymakers will have to realize that money is not a substitute for services, but rather a supplement. The services crisis may then result in new legislation seeking to integrate these two vital needs. Should a holistic approach be utilized, we then can move away from the notion of income floors *or* social services to a posture wherein the two are combined in a systematic manner.

CONCLUSION

Policymaking is at best a complex and at worst an irrational and idiosyncratic process. It is a difficult procedure to explain, it is even more difficult to comprehend, and it is most difficult to undertake.

We have attempted to describe specific aspects of the policy process and their relationship to the design and operation of programs for the aged. It is appropriate that we provide the reader with some thoughts about the types of improvements and new directions that would be both possible and desirable.

Pluralism in this nation is a viable system when all parties have an equal ability to enter the process. Given the plethora of interest groups dotting the landscape, successful competition requires that a group gather considerable power. Until the aged caucus and organize themselves into a competitive power base capable of participating in pluralistic competition, the larger society will address their needs and problems in a categoric rather than generic manner. Once the aged have gained the necessary clout (through the efforts of groups such as the Gray Panthers or the American Association of Retired Persons and the National Retired Teachers Association), we can reintroduce them into the policy "pot" and allow the fight for limited resources to continue. One example representing a categorical commitment to aging research is the newly formed National Institute on Aging.

There is yet another issue to face once policymakers have made the decision to deal with the aged as a specialized enclave. Through chronological tyranny the older person is subject to segmented deprivation. Year by year he or she loses individuality, income, housing, health, friends, and a general sense of self esteem. The least the policy formulators can do is to design ameliorative programs in as holistic a manner as possible.

In a nation that appears bored during periods of noncrisis, the plea for rational planning may fall upon deaf ears. Those working in the field of service delivery must continually point out that the aged, as a group constantly "at risk," cannot afford to be subject to the whims and variations of crisis-based programs. Indeed, it might be better to consider launching fewer programs than to begin consistently from a crisis position that usually fails to retain its level of energy and commitment.

There is an optimistic note in relation to policymaking and the prevailing political atmosphere. The unanticipated consequences of our ill-planned policy of the past decade has given new life to the "art" of long-range planning. We may now move beyond the enactment of legislation that antagonizes the fewest people toward a futuristic stance designed to anticipate the needs of an ever-increasing population of aging and aged peoples.

REFERENCES

Ball, R. Administrative memorandum to Social Security employees. 8 February 1973.

Brotman, H. B. The aging: Who and where. *Perspectives on aging,* 1973, *2,* 1.

Cohen, W. J. *HEW feasibility study on preventive services and health education for medicare recipients.* A report to the Congress. December 1968.

Data Resources Inc. *Inflation and the elderly: Summary report.* Washington, D.C.: National Retired Teachers Association/American Association of Retired Persons, 1980.

Fried, M. Grieving for a lost home. In L. J. Duhl (Ed.), *The urban condition.* New York: Basic Books, 1963.

Glasser, M. A. Testimony regarding effects of administration comprehensive health insurance proposals on the elderly. United States Senate Special Committee on Aging, Sub-committee on Health of the Elderly, 1974.

Kerschner, P. A. (Ed.). Report of the Governor's commission on nursing homes. State of Maryland, 1973.

Lansdale, R. T. From a private interview with P. A. Kerschner, 1972.

Moon, M. *The measurement of economic welfare: Its application to the aged poor.* New York: Academic Press, 1977.

U.S. Senate Special Committee on Aging. Developments in aging, 1979 and 1980.

U.S. Senate Special Committee on Aging. Making services for the elderly work: Some lessons from the British experience, 1971a.

U.S. Senate Special Committee on Aging. Some health services in the U.S.: A working paper on current status, 1971b.

Wilcox, H. G. Hierarchy, human nature, and the participative panacea. *Public Administration Review,* 1969, *7,* 46–53.

CHAPTER **19**

Age and Political Behavior

Neal E. Cutler

Political scientists who are interested in the relationship between age and political behavior seek answers to a variety of questions. For example, since they are generally interested in explanations of why people vote, why they participate in other kinds of political actions, and why they hold certain patterns of political attitudes, they often analyze the political orientations of various groups within society. Groups of people categorized on the basis of age are an important element of this kind of search for explanations of political behavior. Since social gerontologists have learned that many different psychological and sociological orientations are affected by the age of a person, it follows that explanations of political attitudes and behavior will also be enhanced by analyses concerning age (Cutler, 1977b).

At a more global level political scientists are interested in the stability and change of political systems over time. Questions concerning people's attitudes toward the political system in general as well as their attitudes toward specific issues are important in understanding how political institutions manage simultaneously to remain relatively stable and to change and respond to the flow of historical events. The political system at any point in time contains individuals of different ages, and the interaction among age groups produces patterns of both continuity and change. Younger persons are new members of the system and may make certain political demands stimulated by the events of the day or the era. Older members of the system have more years of political experience and skill, and thus might be in a position to make better political decisions. Or, since older members of the political system were reared and obtained their experience in an earlier era, they might be out of date with contemporary politics and thus make poorer political decisions than younger people. Of course, there is no simple answer to this kind of question, but it does serve to indicate the importance of age in the study of politics.

And at a quite practical level of analysis, students of politics may be interested to know if political issues are likely to become centered on questions of age. Furthermore, if age issues become a substantial element of politics, is it likely that all old people will stick together in their attitudes and voting patterns? Will politics become young versus old, or will the question of age become merged with the long-standing bases of political conflict, such as ethnic and socioeconomic status?

The subject of political attitudes and behavior has only recently emerged as a substantial concern of gerontologists. Consequently, the available evidence is fragmentary and incomplete on two levels. First, many topics of concern to political analysts have not been subjected to any formal age analysis. Second, even for those subjects for which some evidence is available, the research is only in preliminary stages, and new evidence and/or improvements in conceptual and methodological strategies may alter the generalizations. Nonetheless, a fair amount of attention has been paid to the relationship between age and political behavior, and this will form the substance of this discussion.

AGE, POLITICAL PARTICIPATION, AND POLITICAL ATTITUDES

Voter participation and age

Several political analysts have studied trends in voting participation over the life cycle. A generalized sequence has been identified in which new voters at the youngest end of the life cycle have a relatively low rate of voter participation; participation gradually increases and reaches a peak in the 40s and 50s, and then drops off in the 60s and beyond. Milbrath and Goel (1977) make this generalization on the basis of their review of nine separate voting studies.

Milbrath and Goel cite three factors that "intervene" between chronological age and voting behavior in accounting for this pattern: (1) integration with the community—younger persons are typically not as integrated into their communities as are older adults who have families, own homes, have children in the local school system, and pay local as well as federal taxes; (2) the availability of blocks of free time—as children grow up and eventually leave home, parents have more available time to be involved in politics; (3) good health—toward the end of the life cycle a deterioration in mental and physical health may yield a lower rate of participation (sometimes referred to as "disengagement" as discussed in Chapter 4) in many forms of social behavior, including politics.

Factors other than age affect a person's voting participation. It can be argued that sex and education, viewed across the whole society, are more important predictors of participation than age. If we take the 1976 presidential election as an example, Table 19-1 demonstrates the combined effects of age, education, and sex.

The "total" column on the right-hand side of this table does conform to the general pattern just described. In the youngest age group—both male and female—less than half of those eligible actually voted. The proportion increases through the early 60s and then drops off. Yet when we examine the various columns of the table, each representing a different level of education, we see within each of the age rows larger educational differences in voting participation than between the age groups. Thus, for example, only 8% of the youngest females with just an elementary education voted, whereas 75% of this group with four years of college or more voted. At the oldest end of the life cycle these educational differences are also found. In fact,

TABLE 19-1. Voter participation by age, sex, and education, November 1976 (% voting)

| | Years of education | | | | | | |
| | Elementary | | High school | | College | | |
	0-7	8	1-3	4	1-3	4 or more	Total
Total 18+ population	37	51	47	59	68	80	59
Females							
18–24	8	12	20	39	60	75	43
25–34	19	20	33	54	66	79	56
35–44	23	39	45	70	77	84	64
45–54	34	47	59	74	80	85	68
55–64	43	56	64	75	80	83	68
65+	36	52	61	70	77	81	58
Total 18+	33	47	47	61	70	81	59
Males							
18–24	6	13	20	37	56	70	41
25–34	12	30	31	48	62	75	55
35–44	30	42	46	62	73	81	63
45–54	37	56	59	72	81	85	68
55–64	49	64	70	77	82	86	72
65+	53	66	75	78	80	84	68
Total 18+	42	56	48	57	67	79	60

SOURCE: Adapted from U.S. Bureau of the Census, *Current population reports,* Series P-20, no. 322, Voting and Registration in the Election of November 1976. Washington, D.C.: U.S. Government Printing Office, 1978, Table 10, pp. 57–60.

within every age group, and for both males and females, *without exception,* the higher the level of formal education (that is, across each row), the higher the voter turnout of the group in question. As will be discussed here, this pervasive pattern is critical to keep in mind whenever the political attitudes and behavior of younger and older persons are compared.

Furthermore, a comparison of the top and bottom sections of Table 19-1 indicates quite noticeable sex differences in patterns of participation: in general, males participate more than females, and the old-age drop-off is somewhat greater for females than for males. But even the pattern of sex differences interacts with educational differences. For example, among the oldest voters, males vote with greater frequency than females at every level of education. Within the youngest age group, females with four years of high school or more actually out-vote their male counterparts. This latter pattern is seen even more clearly when the 35–44 age group males and females are compared. For the three educational levels with less than a full four years of high school, males out-vote females, but in the three highest educational levels there is a clear reversal: females vote at a noticeably higher frequency than males.

What causes interactions of voter participation with age, sex, and education? Although there are no simple answers, one strong possibility is that of generational differences. This is an issue to which we shall turn in greater detail in the next section of this chapter, but a word or two is appropriate in connection with these voter participation data. People who are older are also people who were born and raised in a historically different social and political context than younger people. Since mass public education is a relatively recent phenomenon, older people of 1976 represent a generation with less formal education, on the average, than younger people of 1976. Consequently, one of the first axioms of the analysis of age differences (especially in social and political terms) is that the comparison of young and old is, simultaneously, the comparison of the more educated with the less educated. The incautious observer could all too easily mistake education differences for age differences simply because old and young have different average levels of education.

Table 19-1 demonstrates another generational element: the political role of women in American society. Women now in their 60s and 70s were raised in a society in which females were not generally involved in politics; many of these older women did not receive the right to vote until they were already in their 30s or 40s. Thus, even among the highly educated older segments of Table 19-1, males out-vote females. But, as was noted earlier, such is not the case in the younger generation; better educated females out-vote the better educated males. Therefore, the generational distinctions in sex differences and voting mirror the generational distinctions in educational differences and voting. That is, when we compare old and young, we are comparing different generations.

The importance of generational differences in political participation in gender terms, however, is not simply of historical interest. As Chapter 2 discussed, because of sex differences in mortality (women live longer than men), an older age group has more females in it than a younger age group. Thus, another basic axiom of the analysis of age differences is that the comparison of old and young is, simultaneously, the comparison of a more female group with a less female group. Since we know that in generational terms females historically participated less in politics than is the case in contemporary society, the incautious observer could all too easily mistake age differences in social and political behavior for sex differences—simply because old and young have different percentage composition of males and females. A careful inspection of Table 19-1 yields substantial evidence of these generational distinctions.

Another perspective on the voter participation of older persons is illustrated when we compare voter turnout in a presidential election year with voter turnout in an "off-year" congressional election. Table 19-2 compares data for the presidential election of 1976 (these data are simply taken from Table 19-1) with data for the congressional election of 1978—in both cases the most recent data available as of this writing. Two initial observations can be made about the 1978 off-year election voter turnout, which are quite similar to what we have seen for the 1976 election: first, there is a slight drop-off in voter participation among the older age groups, and second, males in 1978 tend to out-vote females except for the younger age groups. The more dramatic difference between 1978 and 1976, however, is that for all age and sex groupings, voter participation in the congressional election is substantially lower than in the presidential election. Such is the nature of off-year elections. The fact that the basic pattern of age-sex distinctions appears in this rather different kind of electoral

TABLE 19-2. Voter participation by age and sex, November 1976 versus November 1978 (percentage voting)

Age	Voted 1976		Voted 1978		Ratio, 1978/1976	
	Males	*Females*	*Males*	*Females*	*Males*	*Females*
Total 18+ by sex	60	59	47	45	.78	.76
18–24	41	43	23	24	.56	.56
25–34	55	56	37	39	.67	.70
35–44	63	64	50	50	.79	.78
45–54	68	68	57	56	.84	.82
55–64	72	68	63	59	.89	.87
65+	68	58	63	51	.93	.88
Total 18+ population	59		46		.78	

SOURCE: For 1976 data see Table 19-1. For 1978 data: U.S. Bureau of the Census, *Current population reports,* Series P-20, no. 344, Voting and registration in the election of November 1978. Washington, D.C.: U.S. Government Printing Office, 1979, Table 2, p. 11.

campaign context serves to reinforce the validity of the comments made with respect to Table 19-1.

A very different kind of interpretation, however, can be made when the voter participation data in Table 19-2 are interpreted in terms of the potential political influence of older people in American society. The last two columns of this table present the ratio of the 1978 off-year turnout to the 1976 presidential election turnout. These ratios may be seen as the proportion (of any group) of 1976 voters who voted in 1978. For example, for the total adult (aged 18 and older) population, .78 of the number who voted in the 1976 presidential election voted in the 1978 off-year election. From the perspective of political gerontology, however, the point of Table 19-2 is that the ratio of 1978 to 1976 voters increases with age. Even among the 65 and older age group, in which there is a slight percentage decrease from 55–64, the ratio of off-year to presidential-year voters increases. Furthermore, the data show that this pattern is similarly valid for both male and female voters.

The importance of this observation is simply that the voting influence of older persons may be greater in precisely those election situations where the interest of the rest of the electorate is less. A congressional off-year election is one of several types of elections that may be called "low stimulus" or low interest elections. In a congressional election, for example, the issues and candidates are typically local, the coverage by the mass media is typically less than in a presidential election, and the psychological identification of an individual with the act of voting may be less intense. Other types of low interest elections include primary elections, special referendum elections, local city elections, and local "special authority" elections (such as school boards or water districts). If older people turn out to vote in greater numbers in these kinds of elections—as Table 19-2 demonstrates for congressional voting—then the potential for the mobilization and political influence of the older population is enhanced. This is not to say that voting is the only kind of political participation (as will be discussed in the concluding pages of this chapter), but this analysis suggests that older people do have potential voting strength.

Thus, voter participation is modestly associated with age. Younger people appear to vote less, and there is a slight drop in voter turnout toward the end of the life cycle. This latter observation, however, must be interpreted very cautiously, given the fact that sex and education differences in voter turnout are even more pervasive than age differences. Furthermore, since older age groups tend to be, in the aggregate, less educated and more female than younger age groups, even the slight drop-off in old age voter turnout may be more a function of sex and education factors than age itself. Finally, not only do older persons exhibit high levels of voter turnout, but in certain kinds of elections, which may be called low interest or low stimulus elections, evidence suggests that older persons have an even higher relative level of participation.

Political attitudes and age

When we turn to the subject of political attitudes, we find a number of conflicting hypotheses concerning the impact of age. The range of attitudes studied by political scientists is certainly great; an inventory of them would be well beyond the purpose of this chapter (for general reviews see Flanigan, 1972; Key, 1963; McClosky, 1967). Any discussion of political attitudes could focus on broad ideologies, such as liberalism and conservatism, or on citizens' evaluations of a specific policy-relevant issue, such as the issue of the government provision of medical aid. Similarly, students of political behavior have looked at general orientations toward participation, such as political alienation and cynicism, and at attitudes that are more immediately relevant to voting, such as a person's partisan affiliation. Any and all of these could be the focus of an age-based analysis; a few of them have, in fact, been studied.

At the level of general ideology, the most popular image of the connection between age and political attitudes in American politics is that people in general get more conservative as they get older (Glenn, 1974). Indeed, some evidence suggests that older persons often take a more conservative position on such contemporary issues as school busing, abortion, legalization of marijuana, activism, women's rights, and protest politics (Cutler, 1974). There is also evidence that older persons are somewhat more conservative on such long-standing political issues as federal aid to education and federal activity in civil rights (Campbell, 1971). Another analysis employed party affiliation as a rough indicator of conservatism or liberalism and concluded that aging brought about a conversion to the Republican party (Crittenden, 1962). Older persons have also been found to be more "militaristic" or "hard line" in matters of foreign policy (Almond, 1960; Back & Gergen, 1963).

Yet in all of these examples, it is important to note that the specific issue and the specific way in which the attitude is measured in a given attitude survey or public opinion poll have an influence on the response and outcome. The particular nature of the civil rights or equality-of-opportunity issue or the particular aspect of foreign policy under consideration affects the response of all respondents in an opinion survey, and, hence, the generalizations that one draws concerning the role of age in these attitudes are also subject to modification.

In addition to the measurement, or "methodological," considerations that one must take into account, four additional parts of the puzzle deserve special attention.

First, although there are often differences in political attitudes along an age gradient, seldom are all young people (however *young* or *old* is defined) on one side of the issue and all old people on the other side. Age is but one of several character-istics of an individual that are relevant to attitudes—as we have seen, for example, in the data on voter participation. These other factors combine either to smooth out lines of conflict in political controversy or to provide bases of conflict other than age per se, although at times age differences have been so great as to be considered "gen-eration gaps" (Bengtson, 1970).

Second, the relationship between age and political attitudes may be selectively modified by various political agencies and institutions. The political party has been identified in much political science research (for example, Campbell, Converse, Miller, & Stokes, 1960) as being of great importance in organizing an individual's different political attitudes. Yet political party identification may only selectively combine with age in the association with attitudes. One analyst has argued that for issues that are relatively outside of the individual's own experience—such as issues of foreign policy or system-level economic policy—the political party, its candidates, and its platforms have a stronger influence on attitudes than on issues with which the in-dividual has more direct experience and personal interest—such as taxation, conscrip-tion, and social welfare issues (Foner, 1972). The nature of maturational age changes, as this argument continues, is likely to be quite different for these two general types of issues. Evidence germane to this argument was obtained in a research project that investigated age patterns in political attitudes at the family, community, and national levels. It was found that "the farther removed the political issue from the individ-ual, the less age will have a significant effect upon his attitude toward that issue" (Douglass, Cleveland, & Maddox, 1974).

Third, the meaning of *age* in any description of the relationship between age and political attitudes must be clearly understood. In social research chronological age differences are traditionally used to indicate maturational or developmental differ-ences (or changes) between old and young. Yet individuals of different chronological age do not simply represent individuals at different developmental stages in the life cycle; they also represent individuals born and raised in different historical contexts. Similarly, individuals of the same chronological age are not necessarily homogeneous with respect to the degree that age is salient to them as far as their political outlooks are concerned. Both of these examples illustrate the proposition that chronological age itself does not provide an automatic interpretation of patterns found in apparently age-concerned attitudes and behavior.

Fourth, one should not conclude that the conservatism of the aged on such issues as the federal government's involvement in the economy and society is an inevitable consequence of the aging process. On the contrary, in some instances it may be to the specific advantage of older persons to favor such federal activity. In a classic analysis of political behavior in the United States, a research team at the University of Michi-gan classified all voters as to the kind of issue orientation the voters implicitly ex-pressed in their attitudes. Four general categories were used: ideology, group benefits, nature of the times, and no issue content at all (Campbell et al., 1960). The modal category for the electorate was group benefits, into which 45% of all voters were classified.

Although the analysis did not present any information on age patterns in issue orientations, one could reasonably assume that older voters are just as group-benefits oriented as the rest of the electorate. More direct evidence of this is seen in a number of studies that have examined age patterns in attitudes toward a range of issues concerning federal involvement in social and economic programs. Analysis of data from the 1960 election (Campbell, 1962) indicated that there was little difference between old and young on issues of federal aid for school construction, federal involvement in guaranteeing fair treatment of blacks in jobs and housing, and the question of whether electricity and housing should be left totally to private enterprise. However, on two other issues in this general conservative-liberal cluster—governmental guarantees of full employment and government financial involvement in medical care programs—the old were substantially *less* conservative than the young.

A more complete analysis of this medical care issue has examined the age distribution of attitudes toward governmental support of medical care programs in four national surveys taken in conjunction with the presidential elections of 1956-1968; these data are presented in Table 19-3. The age distributions indicate quite clearly that "in all four studies, people aged 65 and over were the most likely of the four age groupings to favor a government program of medical aid" (Schreiber & Marsden, 1972, p. 98). Furthermore, more recent analysis has confirmed this age pattern (Weaver, 1976).

TABLE 19-3. Attitudes toward governmental medical aid program [a] (percentage in favor)

Age group	1956	1960	1964	1968
21–34	49	57	48	45
35–49	54	52	46	51
50–64	55	67	52	54
65+	63	74	58	59

SOURCE: Adapted from Schreiber and Marsden (1972), Table 2, p. 98.
[a] See Table 19-6 for the text of the questions asked each year.

When considering generalizations about age and political attitudes, therefore, one must take several processes into consideration. For some issues, age may be quite irrelevant to attitudes, or at least secondary to factors that are more salient. For other issues, the individual's attitude might be a reflection of a more general ideology, and this ideology, in turn, may be related to maturation and to such political factors as political party identification. For still other issues, the connection between age and attitudes may hinge on the fact that a particular age group may receive the benefits to be bestowed by a particular program or policy.

ALTERNATIVE MEANINGS OF AGE FOR POLITICAL GERONTOLOGY

In several places in the discussion we have noted that chronological age can have different meanings as far as analysis of political attitudes and behavior is concerned. This section presents two important alternatives to the meaning of *age*, that is, alternatives to the traditional approach in which chronological age is employed simply as an index of maturational or developmental change. The first approach presents age as an indicator of birth cohort membership; the second examines the implications of differences between an individual's chronological age and his or her subjective age identification.

Political generations and cohort analysis

Knowing that a person is, for example, 20 years old, we can assume to know two different clusters of data about the person: *maturational facts* and *generational facts*. Maturationally, we know that a person who is 20 years old has lived for two decades of what is an approximately six- to eight-decade life span. This person is at a more-or-less identifiable stage in the life cycle and has probably undergone certain experiences (family socialization experiences, high school, dating, and some planning for the future) and probably has not undergone others (completion of college, marriage, parenthood, and retirement). Of course, chronological age is an imperfect indicator of these social, life-stage events, and there is great variability across the population as to when any individual experiences one of the life events. Nevertheless, across the whole society, chronological age gives us a general idea of the developmental stage of the individual. To the degree that social and political attitudes are known to vary in terms of life stage or maturational age, knowing a person's age may give us clues about his or her attitudes.

Chronological age can be used to calculate when the individual was born and to know, in general, the social and political milieu in which the person was socialized. Thus in 1985 a person who is 20 years old was born in 1965 and experienced political socialization in a particular slice of national and world history. To the degree that direct exposure to political events and circumstances during the early and important years of political socialization has an effect upon attitudes, the individual's generational location can be quite important (Cutler, 1976; Jennings & Niemi, 1974).

The analytic problem in most studies that discuss age in chronological terms is that the person's age has *both* maturational meaning and generational meaning simultaneously. Both sets of factors can have an impact upon political attitudes, and thus one should be able to separate the two effects. Unfortunately, when a pattern of behavioral or attitudinal characteristics is presented along an age gradient, it is usually impossible to separate the maturational from the generational explanation.

To illustrate this ambiguity, consider a hypothetical age distribution, which we will assume is based on data collected in 1980 (see Table 19-4). These hypothetical data represent the way in which age patterns in opinion polls are often presented. Since the percentages are arrayed by age, the usual description would say that as age increases, the particular characteristic increases or decreases. Description, however, is not the same as interpretation, and often the interpretation is the more important contribution of the analysis. For example, if in these hypothetical data the characteristic was agreement with the policy of legalizing marijuana use, then the typical interpretation of the data might say that the older a person gets, the less likely he or she is to support the legalization of marijuana.

The problem with this example is that although the description is accurate (the characteristic indeed does decrease as age increases), the interpretation implies a

TABLE 19-4. Hypothetical age distribution in 1980

Group	Chronological age	Characteristic (%)
A	18–25	80
B	26–45	60
C	46–65	45
D	66+	30

maturational change occurring over the life cycle with causal implications about attitudes toward the legalization of marijuana. There are at least two possible fallacies in this kind of interpretation (Riley, 1973). First, since the hypothetical data are from a single year (a poll taken in 1980), there can be no evidence of the maturation of specific individuals over the life cycle. Second, the groups defined in terms of their chronological age represent different birth cohorts, each of which was born in a different historical period and, consequently, socialized in a different set of political circumstances. Thus, group A was born in 1955–1962, group B in 1935–1954, group C in 1915–1934, and group D before 1915. Certainly we might expect that people raised in the first decade of this century have different attitudes toward the legalization of marijuana than those born on the eve of the Vietnam War, and their different attitudes might be more related to the particular experiences of their cohort rather than to maturation per se.

We have suggested and attempted to illustrate here that the cohort or generational interpretation of age differences in characteristics is a plausible alternative hypothesis to maturational or developmental explanations of age differences. More simply, age differences do not always imply age changes (Schaie, 1965, and Chapter 7).

This argument can perhaps be made clearer by returning to our hypothetical data but considering a different characteristic. Assume that the characteristic under consideration is the educational attainment of the individual and that the percentages describe the proportion of each age group that has "high education"—at least a completed high school education. In this new view of the percentage distribution, the description would state that 80% of group A has achieved this educational level, but that only 30% of group D has achieved this level. The same summary description made for the data when they represented attitudes toward marijuana can be made here: as age increases, the characteristic decreases.

Although the description is the same (of course, it must be since we are dealing with the same data, only giving different hypothetical labels), the interpretation must be quite different. Consider how foolish it would be to argue, using the maturational interpretation, that as the person gets older his or her level of education decreases! Although an aging individual may appear to become less intelligent, the level of attained formal education cannot change; for each individual it is a personal historical fact. The most valid interpretation would be based on the idea of birth cohort in which each age group represents individuals born and raised in different historical periods; those born before 1915 did not have the same opportunity for educational attainment as those born after World War II.

The example of educational attainment, therefore, demonstrates that an age distribution of a characteristic does not always imply age changes produced by developmental or maturational processes. Whereas the maturational hypothesis may be quite appropriate for certain biological or physiological characteristics that may deteriorate or otherwise change with age, for a variety of psychological and sociological characteristics the generational or birth-cohort hypothesis may be the more plausible explanation. Furthermore, this may be particularly true for political orientations, since attitudes toward elements of the political system typically represent the joint contribution of the individual's psychological predispositions and the "objective" nature of political affairs (Greenstein, 1969; Renshon, 1974).

We have described at length the plausibility of the generational explanation for two reasons: first, because too often age differences in published studies and polls are automatically interpreted as maturational or developmental differences; and second, because the impact of the political environment on individual attitudes implies that people who are a part of different generations ought to be expected to hold different orientations toward various issues (Bengtson & Cutler, 1976). Another way to make this important point is to present actual examples of possible differences in interpretation of age distributions of political orientations.

We noted earlier that one of the more popular images (or myths) of political gerontology is that people get more conservative as they get older. In the United States this proposition has been tested by using identification or affiliation with the Republican party as the behavioral measure of individual conservatism. Crittenden (1962) examined the age distribution of Republican party identification in a series of national Gallup polls, 1946–1958. Looking at the vertical age distributions (ignoring the diagonal lines for now) presented in Table 19-5, Crittenden observed that in each year the younger age groups had lower percentages of Republicans, and the older age groups had higher percentages of Republicans; he further observed that this pattern was found in each of the national surveys.

TABLE 19-5. Age and party identification (percentage Republican)

Age intervals	Cohort labels	1946	1950	1954	1958
	A				
21–24	B	46	41	42	43
25–28	C	54	43	45	51
29–32	D	51	44	39	49
33–36	E	59	50	47	49
37–40	F	59	53	51	42
41–44	G	70	58	56	44
45–48	H	58	58	52	34
49–52	I	58	50	89	62
53–56		60	60	66	47
57–60		65	75	58	63
61–64		58	86	75	55
65–68		70	60	90	66
Total		57	51	50	48

SOURCE: These data are adapted from Cutler (1969, Table 1), which reanalyzed the data representing the high education group in Crittenden's (1962) analysis.

It should be noted that (without the diagonal lines) the structure of the age distribution given for each of the annual polls is similar to the hypothetical data presented previously. Crittenden found support in these data for the proposition that maturational processes bring about a conversion to Republicanism or conservatism as a function of aging.

The conclusion that aging brings a conversion to Republicanism was challenged in a reanalysis of the Crittenden data that employed the techniques of cohort analysis. The alternative hypothesis—that of generational or birth cohort differences—should also be considered as a plausible explanation. The diagonal lines in Table 19-5 were added in this cohort analysis to facilitate an evaluation of the data in a different way (Cutler, 1969). The logic of cohort analysis is that a given birth cohort can be traced over a series of national samples by simply looking at the appropriate age groups. Thus, for example, people who are 21 years old in 1946 represent the same generational birth cohort (that is, cohort A born in 1925) as the 25-year-olds four years later in a 1950 survey and the 29-year-olds in a 1954 survey. In short, cohort analysis is a technique (or set of techniques) by which a political analyst can see the degree to which the maturational hypothesis and the generational hypothesis of an age distribution of behavioral characteristics are useful in explaining a particular set of data (Cutler, 1977a, Evan, 1959; Glenn, 1977; Hyman, 1972).

The diagonal lines in Table 19-5 direct the observer's attention to the changes, across the 1946–1958 period, *within* the different cohorts, whereas the original investigation looked up and down the separate columns. In looking at the cohorts within the diagonals, it cannot be concluded that as a cohort of individuals age there is strong evidence of a "conversion" to conservatism or to the Republican party. Although there are indeed fluctuations, these seem to be reflections of the general political environment, and not the consequence of any "aging effect." Although older people in 1946 or 1958 may in fact be more Republican than younger people in those years, the answer is not in a maturational conversion but rather in the differences between generational birth cohorts—much like the explanation given earlier for the differences in educational attainment.

The Crittenden-Cutler cohort controversy, although interesting, did not provide the last word on this topic. Crittenden provided the initial data, Cutler published a reanalysis, Crittenden published a "Reply," and Cutler a "Rejoinder." The whole debate, in which neither analyst changed his mind, is reprinted in Kirkpatrick (1974) for the interested reader. It was not until later analyses by Glenn and Hefner (1972) and by Abramson (1976) that more definitive evidence was presented. Using a data base spanning 1945 through 1969, for example, Glenn and Hefner concluded:

> Therefore, the thesis that cohorts experience an absolute increase in Republicanism as a consequence of aging receives no support from our data. . . .the positive association of Republicanism with age, consistently revealed by the cross-sectional data gathered at various times during the past 30 years or so, reflects intercohort (or "generational") differences rather than the effects of aging. . . . [p. 35]
>
> This study should rather conclusively lay to rest the once prevalent belief that the aging process has been an important influence for Republicanism in the United States [p. 47].

A second example of the utility of applying cohort analysis to age distributions of political orientations can be taken from analyses of public attitudes toward governmental programs of medical care. You may recall from our discussion of the group-benefits orientation in American politics that older persons were more in favor of governmental involvement in medical aid programs than young persons. The data in Table 19-3 presented a series of results from each of four national surveys, each taken in a presidential election year. In each case the older respondents were more in favor of the medical aid policy than the younger respondents in the interview surveys.

The evidence in Table 19-3, however, does not answer the question of the maturational versus generational genesis of the age distribution of attitudes. Are older people more in favor of this policy because the processes of aging created a favorable orientation, or are older persons representative of generational cohorts that have been supportive of this policy throughout their lifetimes? A cohort analysis of this attitude (Bengtson & Cutler, 1976) reprinted in Table 19-6 presents at least preliminary evidence on this issue. Table 19-6 gives changes at the young end of the life cycle and at the old end of the life cycle. The change from 21-24 to 25-28 is given for those cohorts that were 21-24 years of age in four successive presidential election surveys. Similarly, the change from 61-64 to 65-68 is given for four cohorts, each of which was 61-64 years of age in one of the presidential surveys. Table 19-6 indicates the percentage of those in each cohort who support federal governmental programs of medical care and also indicates the changes that are associated with aging for each cohort.

There are, of course, ebbs and flows in the nation's attitudes toward this issue over the 1956-1972 period. Support for government involvement in medical aid

TABLE 19-6. Attitudes toward federal government medical aid programs[a] (percentage in favor)

Age group	1956	1960	1964	1968	1972
21-24	70	77	67	67	
25-28		69	62	56	56
Change		-1	-15	-12	-11
61-64	69	84	64	72	
65-68		85	73	76	69
Change		+16	-11	+12	-3
Total sample	70	77	65	67	61
Change		+7	-12	+2	-6

SOURCE: The data were made available by the Inter-University Consortium for Political and Social Research.

[a] The question read, for 1956 and 1960: "The government ought to help people get doctors and hospital care at low cost." For 1964 and 1968: "Some people say the government in Washington ought to help people get doctors and hospital care at low cost; others say the government should not get into this. Have you been interested enough in this to favor one side or the other?" For 1972: "There is much concern about the rapid rise in medical and hospital costs. Some feel there should be a government insurance plan which would cover all medical expenses. Others feel that medical expenses should be paid by individuals through private insurance like the Blue Cross. Which side do you favor?"

programs reached its peak in 1960 in conjunction with the Kennedy victory and just prior to the passage of Medicare. Yet even within the national pattern of changes, four generalizations describing support for federal medical care programs emerge from Table 19-6: (1) older people are more supportive than the nation as a whole; (2) older people are more supportive than younger people; (3) the increase in positive support at the older end of the life cycle is greater than the increase in support of the nation as a whole; and (4) the changes in support by the older people are by far more support-ive than the changes at the younger end of the life cycle. This is especially observable for the changes in 1964-1968. Note that although the population as a whole had virtually no change (2%), the younger group exhibited a 12% decline in support and people in their 60s exhibited a 12% increase in support.

Therefore, we may conclude that this particular attitude does appear to be strongly influenced by the aging process. Although the data of Table 19-3 suggested that such was the case, only in light of the cohort analysis presented in Table 19-6 do we have substantial evidence of the impact of the aging process. Thus, whereas in the case of Republican party identifications cohort analysis supported a generational interpretation, in the case of attitudes toward governmental medical aid programs, the cohort analysis tends to support the maturational explanation.

Subjective age identification

The second alternative to the meaning of *age*—as contrasted to "simple" chron-ological age—is that of subjective age or self-identification with age. Everyone has a chronological age, just as everyone, objectively, has a social class. But not everyone is aware or conscious of his or her social class; only in certain circumstances does class consciousness arise. Similarly, not everyone is age conscious; some people do identify themselves with an age group, but others do not think in age terms as far as their social and political attitudes are concerned.

Two interlinked questions for gerontologists flow from this distinction between chronological age and subjective age or age consciousness. First, what are the condi-tions producing age consciousness? Second, what are the consequences, in political and social terms, of age consciousness? The answer to the first question is a difficult one, but it might be answered, at least for contemporary society, in terms of analogy. Just as individuals have become conscious of their racial, ethnic, and sexual statuses, they have also become conscious of their age. Of course, it is not simply by analogy that people are becoming aware and conscious of their age and of the social and political power that collective action on the part of the aged might have. Govern-mental agencies (such as the Administration on Aging and the National Institute on Aging) as well as private associations (such as the American Association of Retired Persons and the Gray Panthers) serve in various ways to increase age consciousness.

The second of the two questions is, perhaps, more germane to this chapter: what are the political consequences of age consciousness? We have argued that simple chronological age is not, in and of itself, a sufficient explanation for many age distribu-tions of behavioral characteristics. The previous discussion of the generational cohort interpretation of age implies that individuals of different ages at a given point in time do not necessarily manifest differences due to the maturational effects of the aging process. When we speak of age consciousness, the question is turned around: are individuals of the same chronological age necessarily similar insofar as political orientations are concerned?

In an important essay on this issue, Riley (1971) draws an analogy between age consciousness and class consciousness. In certain periods of history, social class differences in a society give rise to class consciousness and in some circumstances to class conflict. Just as there is historical variation in class consciousness at the level of the whole society, so there is variation at the individual level: in any particular period, some individuals will be conscious of class differences, and for others class will not be a salient component of their orientation toward the world. All of these elements of the dynamics of class and class consciousness, Riley contends, are germane to the issue of age consciousness. In some historical periods and for some individuals, age identification and age consciousness are salient elements in social interaction and political debate.

For some analysts the issue is whether the elderly have the characteristics of a "minority group"—identifiable to the rest of society, discriminated against in economic and social interaction, and possessing common group-based needs and wants (Rose, 1965; Streib, 1965). Gerontologists and other students of the aging process have examined quite a number of factors that may lead to age consciousness of one form or another (as reviewed, for example, in McTavish, 1971; Peterson, 1971). Although we have some understanding of the genesis and social psychological attributes of age consciousness, there has been little research on the political consequences of such age identification (Cutler, 1981c; Gurin, Miller, & Gurin, 1980; Heilig, 1979).

Politically, age consciousness is potentially extremely important. As is indicated in greater detail in Chapter 2, there will be larger numbers of older persons in the near future with a potential for substantial political activity. Given this fact, a key question is whether such a group of older persons will, in fact, be involved politically as old people. Will people be conscious of their age status or position in society, and will there be political consequences of such consciousness?

We cannot, of course, make firm predictions about the political attitudes of tomorrow's older population. Yet we do have at least preliminary evidence of the political consequences of age identification. A national sample survey taken in conjunction with the 1972 presidential election included a series of questions by which each respondent in the survey could be classified as subjectively identified with "youth" or "old age." Using these attitudinal measures of youth and old age, we can classify every individual in the sample according to two characteristics: the person's subjective age identification and the same person's chronological age.

For purposes of the present discussion the important question is this: do older people who subjectively identify themselves as old have similar or different political attitudes from those older people who subjectively identify themselves as not old? Suggested answers to this important question can be seen in the context of three sets of political attitudes.

The data in Table 19-7 portray the chronologically older people (aged 60 and older) in the 1972 national sample as subdivided into those who expressed a subjective age identification as old and those who did not express such an old-age identification.

TABLE 19-7. Subjective age identification among older persons on selected social, political, and economic issues, 1972

Issue	Subjective age identification	
	As old	*As not old*
1. Government action on inflation		
Percent should act	97.9	89.5
2. Federal medical programs		
Percent in favor	71.7	51.9
3. Cuts in federal military spending		
Percent in favor	41.5	26.4
4. Self-identification as liberal or conservative		
Percent liberal	21.2	16.4
5. Personal financial condition, now vs. year ago		
Percent better now	44.0	59.6
6. Personal financial condition, now vs. next year		
Percent better next year	46.2	50.0
7. Abortion allowable under certain circumstances		
Percent agree	22.0	33.6
8. Government action against industrial pollution		
Percent in favor	67.6	73.0
All respondents aged 60+	38.1%[a]	54.5%

SOURCE: Data represent the responses of those respondents aged 60 and over in the University of Michigan Center for Political Studies national survey of the 1972 presidential election. The election survey was made available by the Inter-University Consortium for Political and Social Research; the age items were made available by Professor Gerald Gurin, Institute for Social Research, University of Michigan. Total N for the 1972 survey is 2705. More complete analysis of these data may be found in Cutler (1974).

[a] Not included here are the 7.4% of the 60+ group that identified as young.

These two subgroups are then compared in terms of traditional conservative-liberal issues (Issues 1-4), expectations as to the financial future (Issues 5-6), and what might be called contemporary issues of social conservatism-liberalism (Issues 7-8). The results of this research indicate that subjective age does indeed make a difference.

On the traditional issues the subjectively old are more liberal than the other older respondents; this is most dramatically seen on the issue of federal medical aid programs, which are much more strongly supported by the subjectively old (this, incidentally, is an interesting complement to the data presented in Tables 19-3 and 19-6 concerning this same issue). The subjectively old are somewhat more pessimistic with respect to their personal financial future. A smaller number of the subjectively old felt that financial conditions were better at the time of the interview than the previous year, and a similar pattern is seen when the present is compared with the immediate future. The last pair of items, however, indicates that the subjectively old are not always more liberal than those who do not subjectively identify themselves as old. The subjectively old are less in favor of abortion and are less in favor of government solutions or action in the area of industrial pollution.

Although the specifics of these and other issues that can be used to estimate the impact of subjective age identification are themselves interesting, the important point is that subjective age identification does distinguish among those who are chronologically old. Age clearly has a different meaning to different individuals who share the same general position in the life cycle—as indicated by the fact that 38% of those aged 60 and older do identify themselves as old while 55% do not. When considering the meaning of age differences in social and political attitudes, consequently, one must recognize the important interaction between the chronological age and such other meanings or interpretations of age as those suggested by the cohort analysis approach and consideration of subjective age identification. Additional aspects of subjective age identification will be presented as we consider the future of old age politics.

THE FUTURE OF AGE IN POLITICS

This chapter's final concern is the future role that age will play, or is likely to play, in the politics of the United States. We cannot predict with absolute certainty the degree to which older persons are likely to play a part in the politics of the future, or the specific issues around which political conflicts will emerge. Yet we can point to a number of factors that, when taken together, at least allow us to estimate tentatively that age is likely to play an increasingly significant role in the political future.

In particular, several areas of evidence collectively support the conclusion that age will be a salient factor in the politics of the near future. An important qualifying note, however, must be added to this "prediction." When we argue that age as an issue and the aged as a political constituency will be important in the politics of the future, we are not suggesting that all older persons or all organizations of the elderly will agree with one another on major issues; we certainly do not mean that old people will constitute a single voting bloc with a single mind and a set of social, economic, and political goals.

Some analysts have much too easily dismissed the old-age factor in future politics by suggesting that the aged will continue to be characterized by divisions on ethnic, social class, partisan, and other traditional lines of political cleavage. One prominent spokesman of this viewpoint is political gerontologist Robert Binstock, former president of the Gerontological Society of America and Director of the Program in Politics and Economics of Brandeis University. In a forceful essay on this subject Binstock (1974) argued that "there is no evidence to indicate that aging-based interest appeals can swing a bloc of older persons' votes from one party or candidate to another" (p. 203). He further suggested that "even a 100% increase in the proportion of chronologically aged voters during the next several decades would not likely, in itself, engender a cohesive aging vote that could determine the outcome of elections" (p. 203). Commenting further upon the likely impact of organized groups and organizations of older persons, Binstock recognized a probable growth in the number of such organizations, but concluded that "their political relevance would probably be negligible" (p. 210).

The position of this chapter is substantially different from Binstock's on several grounds. To argue, for example, that older persons do not and will not in the future constitute a single-minded voting bloc is to establish a "straw man" argument—that is, an unlikely argument that is easily defeated (Riemer & Binstock, 1978). The significance of the age issue in the future of American politics does not rest on the assumption of an old-age voting bloc. Indeed, the heterogeneity of older persons in ethnic, socioeconomic, and partisan matters is an observation with which we generally agree. The point, however, is that for a variety of reasons age will be an important facet of political life. Not all blacks and not all women agree with one another on all issues that are important to their positions concerning society and politics. Yet it would be foolish to deny that race and gender are quite salient aspects of contemporary politics. Similarly, we are suggesting that age is and will increasingly become a salient aspect of politics in the United States, even if all older persons and organized groups of older persons do not speak (or vote) with a single political voice.

Demographic factors

Chapter 2 in this volume is concerned with the demography of aging, and the pertinent facts need not be repeated in detail here. The basic demographic data relevant to gerontologists indicate that the size and proportion of the older population will continue to increase. By the year 2020, for example, the number of persons over the age of 65 will be in excess of 40 million, more than double the number of older persons in 1970. The percentage of older persons will continue to rise as well; by 2020 people over 65 will represent over 13% of the national population.

Chapter 2 also described the *dependency ratio*—a single number that represents the proportional relationship between the size of the working population and the size of the dependent old-age population. The dependency ratio has distinct political implications, since the question of the allocation of scarce economic resources, as in the case of Social Security and other retirement benefits systems, is, ultimately, a political question. In 1970 the old-age dependency ratio (those aged 65 and older divided by those aged 18–64) was .17; the projected old-age dependency ratio for the year 2020 is .24. The increase in this ratio indicates that a larger number of older persons will have to be economically supported by a relatively decreasing number of workers. The political implications of the dependency ratio are exacerbated by the fact that although the figures just presented use age 65 as the average retirement age, since the early 1960s—when the Social Security System allowed for early retirement— the actual average age of retirement has become closer to age 62 than age 65.

Political problems of retirement and related pension and economic programs arise because at any single point in time the current worker is largely paying the bill for current payments to the retired worker. Economists have referred to this situation in such terms as the "economics of intergenerational relationship" (Kreps, 1965) and the "intergenerational social contract" (Morgan, 1975). These terms imply a situation in which the worker of today contributes to the society's pension system on the expectation that future generations of workers will pay for his or her pension tomorrow.

Yet tomorrow's labor force, as indicated by the dependency ratio, will be relatively smaller as compared to the dependent, pension-receiving population. The political issue becomes magnified when we consider that the age of retirement is decreasing. This situation is made dramatically clear if we compute the dependency ratio using age 60 rather than age 65 as the definition of the dependent older population (Chapter 2, Table 2-18). For 1970, using this younger average age of retirement, the dependency ratio would increase from .17 to .29–already greater than the .24 predicted for the year 2020 using the age 65. It should be clear, therefore, that the mere facts of demographic change, in which the older population is increasing in both absolute and relative terms, will make age a salient factor of the politics of the future.

This is not to say, however, that early retirement will necessarily continue to be the major trend in the United States. In recognition of the impact of early retirement on Social Security and pension systems and the desire of many older persons to remain workers past the traditional retirement age of 65 (for example, Harris, 1975; Johnson & Higgins, 1979), Congress passed the 1978 amendments to the Age Discrimination in Employment Act of 1967, which raised the age of mandatory retirement in private sector employment to age 70 and eliminated such an age altogether for federal employment.

The potential impact of this change in public policy upon the demography and politics of old age is crucial. The retirement behavior of the baby boom of 1947-1962 will have a major impact upon what may be called the "politics of the dependency ratio." The federal Office of Management and Budget (OMB) has estimated that if the average retirement age of the baby boom is age 62–which approximates the current average retirement age–the dependency ratio in 2020 will be double that for 1970. On the other extreme, if the average retirement age of the baby boom increases to age 70, the dependency ratio in 2020 will remain about the same as it was in 1970 (Cutler, 1981a; Torrey, 1979).

With the 1978 ADEA amendments the average retirement age is likely to rise somewhat by the year 2020 and will be between age 62 and 70. Some persons will work longer, whereas others will want to retire as soon as it is occupationally and economically feasible. However, the raising of the legal age of retirement by itself will not automatically produce later retirement. People who have planned for their retirement based upon the traditional age of 65, or the availability of even earlier retirement benefits, will not change their planning overnight. More critical, however, is the availability of job opportunities for the older worker.

Indeed, in recognition of this opportunity factor, the United States Senate Special Committee on Aging in 1980 began a series of public hearings titled "Work After 65: Options for the 80s." In opening these hearings the committee's chairman argued that the legal raising of the retirement age was only the first step, and that before retirement decisions of older workers change, both the public and private sectors of the economy must respond with meaningful employment opportunities (Chiles, 1980).

Participation versus disengagement

Demographic issues by themselves predict that age will, in general, be a major issue in future politics. But we must still consider the issue of whether the aged themselves will be substantially involved in political affairs. Some theories investigated by gerontologists have suggested that as people age they naturally or inherently disengage from a variety of social activities–including political participation. Yet the evidence presented in this chapter indicates otherwise. The drop-off in voting and other forms of political participation among older persons have been seen to be influenced by generational and sex differences, as well as the relatively low socio-economic status of many older persons. It is a translation of the fact that poorer persons participate less, and that a disproportionately large number of old people are poor. But when the appropriate statistical controls for socioeconomic status are employed (Verba & Nie, 1972), older persons, on the average, do not necessarily disengage from political activity. In other words, age itself does not account for the lower rates of political participation among older persons. Thus, if and when other factors such as political interest, age consciousness, and generational/cohort differences become operative, we can expect older persons to be substantially politically involved.

Indeed, among older persons in recent years there is a substantial interest in political affairs—in contrast to what theories of old-age disengagement might predict. Table 19-8 presents the "political interest" question asked in the national 1976 presidential election survey conducted by the University of Michigan's Center for Political Studies. Each respondent was asked whether he or she was, in general, interested in politics "most of the time," "some of the time," or "hardly at all." Table 19-8 presents age patterns in the percentages of those who said they are generally interested in politics "most of the time." As discussed earlier, it is important that age patterns be arrayed against sex and education distinctions so as not to confound sex and education effects with age effects.

With the sole exception of the least educated females, the analysis makes it clear that strong interest in politics increases with age throughout the life cycle; indeed, political interest is at its highest level within the oldest age groups. For example,

TABLE 19-8. Self-reported interest in politics, 1976 (percentage indicating high interest)[a]

	Years of school completed			All educational levels
	0–8	9–12	13+	
Males				
18–34	— (9)[b]	18 (168)	45 (193)	32 (370)
35–64	34 (71)	42 (216)	73 (175)	52 (462)
65+	45 (82)	67 (51)	83 (23)	59 (156)
Females				
18–34	— (10)	16 (327)	39 (195)	24 (532)
35–64	23 (91)	32 (342)	57 (161)	36 (594)
65+	19 (111)	46 (103)	76 (49)	40 (263)

SOURCE: 1976 National Election Survey, conducted by the Center for Political Studies, University of Michigan. Data were made available by the Inter-University Consortium for Political and Social Research.

[a] Respondents were asked whether in general they were interested in politics "most of the time," "some of the time," or "hardly at all." This table gives the percentage of those responding "most of the time."

[b] Percentages represent the proportion of each age-sex education group that gave the "most of the time" response. The size of each group is given in parentheses; percentages not computed when the size was ten persons or fewer.

whereas only 18% of the 168 young males with some or completed high school education expressed a strong political interest, more than three times that many (67%) of the oldest high-school-educated males said they were interested in politics most of the time. This pattern is seen for both males and females and within each of the educational levels. Furthermore, looking at all educational levels combined, we again see that for both males and females strong political interest increases with advancing age. It may be noted, parenthetically, that the earlier edition of this chapter cited an analysis of the political interest question in a 1960 Gallup poll. The results of that study were identical to the 1976 results: political interest increased with age in both sexes and all three educational groups (Glenn & Grimes, 1968).

Education: A precondition for political participation

Although the data just described indicate that older persons are not necessarily disengaged from political activity, such information describes current or past groups of old people; our present discussion is concerned with the politics of age in the future. A major component of this chapter has concerned the concept of the birth cohort as a major interpretational tool for variations in age-linked political behavior. In this context, we may briefly examine the educational composition of the future cohorts within the electorate as part of a consideration of the possible and probable participation of tomorrow's older people.

A number of studies, many of which are summarized in Milbrath and Goel's (1977) inventory of research findings, have indicated that level of formal education is a major predictor of the degree to which an individual is likely to be involved in politics. Thus, an important question for consideration concerns the educational composition of the older portion of the electorate. Based on a sequence of presidential election surveys, each of which was national in scope, Table 19-9 presents the educational distribution of the electorate from 1952 through 1976. Each year is divided into "high" and "low" education, with completion of at least a high school education being defined as "high" education.

TABLE 19-9. Age composition in education

Age group	1952 Lo[a]	1952 Hi	1956 Lo	1956 Hi	1960 Lo	1960 Hi	1964 Lo	1964 Hi	1968 Lo	1968 Hi	1972 Lo	1972 Hi	1976 Lo	1976 Hi
21–24	45	55	33	67	39	61	30	70	19	81	14	86	1	99
25–34	47	53	34	66	36	64	29	71	21	79	22	78	3	97
35–44	58	42	48	52	36	64	34	66	34	66	26	74	8	92
45–54	67	33	59	42	47	53	50	50	39	61	40	60	13	87
55–64	76	24	65	35	68	32	62	38	55	45	55	45	24	71
65+	81	19	78	22	71	29	67	33	71	29	70	30	48	52
Total	62	38	51	49	48	52	45	55	41	59	38	62	18	82

SOURCE: Each year was taken from the University of Michigan Center for Political Studies presidential election national survey. The data were made available through the Inter-University Consortium for Political and Social Research.

[a] "Lo" Education is defined as no education through incomplete high school; "Hi" Education is complete high school (or equivalency) and higher.

We know that because of changes in the opportunity for education, the electorate has, in general, become more highly educated. This can be seen in the "total" row of the table. In 1952 only 38% of the electorate had a high education, whereas 82% had a high education in 1976. Our attention in the present discussion, however, is focused on those in the electorate over age 65. These individuals were born and educated in an earlier era when mass, free public education was not as widespread as it is today. Whereas in 1952 only 19% of the group aged 65 and older had a high education, by 1976 this had increased to 52%.

The important point for the future, however, is given by the data that describe the future cohorts of older members of the political system. The youngest group in the 1976 survey will all be at least age 65 by the year 2020. Therefore, by the year 2020, the 65 and older age group will be represented by a cohort that we already know to be highly educated. Whereas the 65 and older group in 1952 was divided 19%/81% in terms of high-low educational attainment, the 65 and older group by 2020 will not be divided at all—a rather substantial reversal. From the vantage point of political participation, tomorrow's older population will be better equipped for political participation and involvement than older people have been in the past.

Additional forms of political activity

An additional example of the political participation of tomorrow's cohort of older persons concerns "nonconventional" forms of political activity. Many of the studies of youth and political protest of the 1960s documented that new forms of political action became widespread and accepted as legitimate by substantial numbers of the younger cohort. It cannot, of course, be predicted with certainty that the forms of political activity supported by these younger people will continue to be supported when these same people become older. Yet we can at least know that the future cohort of older persons will include persons who, as part of their own political biographies, have participated in or approved of such activity. Illustrating this point are the data in Table 19-10, which portray the percentages among old and young in 1972 who approved of three forms of "nonconventional" political activity: protest politics in general, sit-ins, and civil disobedience.

The data in this table clearly indicate that the cohort representing tomorrow's older persons is substantially more approving of these three modes of political activity than contemporary older persons. Indeed, tomorrow's older persons are from two to

TABLE 19-10. Attitudes toward "non-conventional" political participation (percentage "approve")

	Age	
	18–35	*60+*
Protest politics	26.4%	10.2%
Civil disobedience	22.0%	9.3%
Sit-ins	10.8%	3.2%

SOURCE: Data are from the University of Michigan Center for Political Studies 1972 national presidential election survey. Data were made available through the Inter-University Consortium for Political and Social Research.

three times more supportive of protest politics, sit-ins, and civil disobedience. Although these data represent age differences between young and old in 1972 and cannot prove a continuity between the young responses of 1972 and the responses of the same cohort in future years, the substantial differences between old and young might be symptomatic of a large "gap" between the generations on this issue of political participation. To the degree that the approving attitudes of the young are even partially adhered to when these individuals mature, we can expect older persons in the future to be quite politically active.

Political role of organizations

Although the image of senior citizen sit-ins and protest politics is an intriguing one, such activities are likely to be engaged in by only a minority of any cohort. Table 19-10 was included primarily to indicate that future cohorts of older persons are likely to be at least congenial to a range of political activities. Voting will remain the main mechanism by which most people participate in the political process; and as previous tables in this chapter have illustrated, older persons exhibit high levels of political interest and voter turnout.

Voting will remain important, but recent political trends in the United States suggest questions about the basis on which future cohorts of older persons will make their voting decisions. Traditionally, political party identification has been the major psychological influence on most people's voting behavior. The accumulating evidence of a number of major studies, however, each based on different samples and surveys, documents the decline in partisanship in this country. Even more important, all of these studies suggest that the main characteristic of this decline is its *generational* origin. That is, it is the new generational cohorts entering the political system over the past few decades that have been most dramatically low in their levels of partisanship.

Glenn and Hefner (1972) examined a sequence of Gallup polls from 1945 to 1969. Jennings and Niemi (1975) interviewed a nationally representative sample of high school seniors and their parents in 1965 and reinterviewed the parents and the children in 1973. Abramson (1976) analyzed the University of Michigan data on presidential and congressional-year election surveys from 1952 through 1974. All these studies found that there has been a major decline in partisanship, and that the decline is clearly generational in nature. This suggests that those cohorts who are currently being socialized into patterns of relatively weak identification with the major political parties (Cutler, 1976), and who will be the senior citizens of the first decades of the 21st century, will be substantially less partisan than the older voters of yesterday and today.

What, then, is likely to replace or at least augment partisanship as far as political thinking and voting behavior are concerned? One very strong possibility is that of organizations. Over the past 20–30 years many large national organizations composed or supportive of older persons have emerged. To the degree that older persons either join these organizations or become familiar with their policy viewpoints, there is a distinct possibility that the decline of traditional partisanship will enhance the overall political influence of these organizations.

In our discussion of the political importance of organizations we shall consider two themes. First, at what might be called the "institutional level," we shall briefly note some of the characteristics of "aging organizations"—organizations that represent the interests of aging persons and contribute to their political influence. Second, at the "personal or behavioral level," we shall discuss the questions of whether older persons really do join organizations, and what political differences such association might make for the joiners.

The major reason that modern aging organizations are more successful than similar organizations in the past, according to the major analysis of this topic (Pratt, 1974, 1976), is their structure. In the past they tended to be structured around a single issue or a single charismatic leader. When the leader or the issue passed from the political scene, the significance of the organization, or the organization itself, also passed from the scene. Today, Pratt argues, the major aging organizations are concerned with broad ranges of issues and are organized bureaucratically with multiple leaders and internal suborganization; thus, they do not face the kinds of problems that precipitated the demise of organizations in the past.

From a political perspective the main functions of these organizations are functions that have traditionally been performed by political parties—that is, to "aggregate" and to "articulate" the political and policy preferences of the members and supporters (Almond & Coleman, 1960; Key, 1958). To aggregate simply means to bring together, often through accommodation and compromise, the diverse concerns of the (in some cases millions of) members. Few senators are likely to read all of the thousands of letters they receive expressing concern over the inflation-caused erosion of Social Security. Senators are more likely, however, to listen to the concern and proposals of leaders of major organizations representing the letter writers.

This latter point also illustrates the articulation function of organizational activities. The major purpose of most organizations in the political realm is to make their members' opinions, ideas, and policy preferences known, understood, and adopted by policymakers. This takes many forms and formats including magazines, newsletters, individual letters, and statements forwarded to congressional and presidential offices, conferences, and symposia; sponsorship of polls and research projects; drafting of legislative proposals; and testimony before various congressional and executive committes and commissions.

With the decline in importance of political parties, as well as the fact that issues of concern to older persons are likely to cut across traditional Republican-Democrat lines, the political role of organizations is enhanced. Furthermore, the existence of these organizations over time and across the country suggests that their activities of interest aggregation and policy articulation can and do take place at all levels of government.

This is not to argue that all such organizations agree with one another. But neither do all women's or civil rights organizations find themselves in total political agreement; yet it could hardly be argued that the diversity of groups within these "movements" decreases the importance and salience of issues concerning the rights of women, blacks, and minority groups. Indeed it may even be argued that the maturity of a political movement is signalled by the growth of organization and the diversity within it, and that public disagreement among the various organizations actually serves to maintain the visibility of the key issues in the public eye.

Such growth of organization and diversity in the area of aging is indicated not only by the number of such organizations but by the recent "organization of organizations." Kerschner and Reed (1980) describe the evolution of the "Leadership Council of Aging Organizations" over the 1976-1980 period. A listing of the more than 20 organizations that were part of the council as of January 1980 suggests the texture and diversity of aging organizations in contemporary American politics:

Urban Elderly Coalition
American Association of Homes
   for the Aging
AFL-CIO Social Security
   Department
Asociacion Nacional Pro
   Personas Mayores
National Indian Council on Aging
Association of Gerontologists in
   Higher Education
Concerned Seniors for Better
   Government
Gerontological Society
Gray Panthers
National Council of Senior
   Citizens
National Retired Teachers
   Association

American Association of Retired Persons
Western Gerontological Society
National Association of Area Agencies
   on Aging
National Association of Mature People
National Association of Retired
   Federal Employees
National Association of State Units
   on Aging
National Association of Title VII
   Project Directors
National Caucus of the Black Aged
National Council on the Aging
National Senior Citizens Law Center
United Auto Workers Retired Members
   Department

The functions of the council, as with an individual organization, are those of aggregation and articulation. Kerschner and Reed note, for example, that when the U.S. Senate was working on a major reorganization and consolidation of its own committee structure, the Special Committee on Aging was scheduled to be one of the committees to be eliminated. The aggregation of concern and the articulation of support for the maintenance of the Special Committee on Aging by the Leadership Council and its component organizations appears to be a major element in the survival of that committee.

Organizations and voluntary associations also play a role at the individual or behavioral level of analysis. Much recent research has demonstrated that older persons do join and take active roles in many kinds of organizations. The once prevalent view that "disengagement" from social involvement is an inherent and almost automatic component of the aging process is no longer accepted. Although not all older persons join political groups, neither do all younger persons. Thus, the question is not "Do old people join or don't they?" but "Under what circumstances do old people join, and with what consequences?"

It has long been recognized, for example, that socioeconomic status is a major influence upon both political participation and participation in voluntary associations (for example, Erbe, 1964; Hodge & Tremain, 1968; Milbrath & Goel, 1977). People with higher education and income levels tend to be more socially and politically involved. Among contemporary older people, we find, however, relative to the younger population, lower levels of education and income; consequently, older persons tend to have lower rates of membership and participation. But is this really an inherent consequence of aging itself? The study of political participation cited earlier demonstrated quite clearly that when appropriate statistical adjustments are made for the differential income and educational levels of different age groups, levels of political participation do not decrease with advancing age (Verba & Nie, 1972).

Thus, if today's older persons exhibit lower rates of involvement in organizations and in politics relative to younger age groups, it is due not to aging but to other factors—factors that are likely to be different for future cohorts of older persons. More specifically, as Neugarten's analysis (1974) has clearly demonstrated, the "young old" of the first decades of the next century will be much better educated and will have relatively higher income levels than people of the same chronological age at the present time.

An additional issue of relevance to the question of involvement in voluntary associations concerns the precise nature of the measurement of such involvement. If the concept of "voluntary association members" in general is the focus, then there is good reason to suspect that older persons will have lower membership rates since many kinds of organizations are concerned with interests that are of generally less relevance to older persons. National interview surveys typically include a dozen or more types of organizations in order to assess membership levels, and the dozen typically includes parent/teacher associations, professional and job-related organizations, and so on—in other words, the kinds of groups to which an older or retired person is not likely to join.

Our own research has focused on this issue and has attempted to disaggregate the typical set of organizational types into those that have relatively more appeal for younger versus older persons. When the appropriate classification of organizational types is identified and analyzed (for example, older persons tend to join religious, fraternal, and veterans organizations), the results clearly show that older persons are no less joiners than younger persons; the profile of which kinds of groups they join differentiates young from old (Cutler, 1981–82).

Finally, returning to the question of the political involvement of older persons, even the joining of nonpolitical groups, clubs, and organizations can have the consequence of increasing the individual's political interest and involvement. One study, for example, found that attendance at a senior center increased the political awareness of the older persons surveyed (Trela, 1971, 1972).

More direct evidence of this relationship was uncovered in an analysis of a national survey of political participation. Respondents were presented with a list of 14 types of groups, clubs, and organizations (excluding manifestly political organizations) and asked about their own membership. Those who indicated membership were further asked to estimate the degree to which the discussion of politics or public affairs took place within their organization—even if they had not personally engaged in such discussion. The respondents were then classified into three mutually exclusive categories: nonmembers, members of groups in which relatively less political discussion took place, and members of groups in which relatively more political discussion took place.

The research questions based on this set of procedures were as follows: "To what extent do nonpolitical organizations serve as a stimulus to political activity," and "To what extent do older people as well as younger receive such a political stimulus?" The research found that such basic forms of political participation as voting in presidential and local elections were indeed affected by such membership (Cutler & Mimms, 1977). More interesting, however, was the effect of membership on the more active or "elite" forms of participation such as attendance at political rallies and events and making financial contributions to political parties, candidates, and causes. Table 19-11 portrays the answer to these questions.

TABLE 19-11. The impact of membership in nonpolitical organizations upon two forms of "elite" political participation

		Members of groups with	
	Nonmembers	Less political discussion	More political discussion	Size of sample
Political meetings [a]				
21–35	13%	10	35	874
36–50	14%	19	32	803
51–64	15%	20	28	776
65+	9%	13	23	497
Political contributions [b]				
21–35	7%	7	18	874
36–50	17%	13	30	803
51–64	12%	16	24	776
65+	4%	9	15	497

SOURCE: Adapted from Cutler and Mimms (1977), based on the national survey conducted by Verba and Nie (1972). The data were provided by the Inter-University Consortium for Political and Social Research; the analysis above was supported by a grant from the NRTA-AARP Andrus Foundation of Washington, D.C.

[a] "In the past three or four years, have you attended any political meetings or rallies?" (% yes).

[b] "In the past three or four years, have you contributed money to a political party or candidate, or to any other political cause?" (% yes).

Although only a minority of the population engages in such elite forms of participation, the data clearly show that membership in organizations in which a relatively greater amount of political discussion takes place serves as a stimulus to political activity. Older persons are no different from younger persons in this regard. In the 65 and older age group, for example, almost twice as many members of the "high" as compared to the "low" political discussion clubs and organizations attended various kinds of political meetings (23% versus 13%) and made political contributions (15% versus 9%). Both categories of members were substantially more politically active in this regard than nonmembers. Thus, the participation of older persons in even nonpolitical voluntary associations and organizations represents a political resource.

Age consciousness

The final aspect of the future of the politics of aging returns to a concept introduced earlier in this chapter: age consciousness or subjective age identification. You may recall that one of the two major alternatives to the simple chronological meaning of age is the subjective meaning of age to people of different ages. As was noted, among persons aged 60 and above, some subjectively identify themselves as old and others do not. As Table 19-7 demonstrated, some notable attitudinal differences appear to exist between those who do subjectively identify as old and those who do not.

As we consider the factors that are conducive to the growing importance of the politics of old age, therefore, it is appropriate to conclude the discussion with a reconsideration of age consciousness. In doing so, we shall briefly consider three general questions: (1) Does age identification really exist as a "real-world" phenomenon, or is it simply the label that disappointed or unhappy old people use to describe their plight? (2) Is there any evidence of "how much" subjective age identification there is in the United States in recent years? (3) Is there any reason to believe that age consciousness will play a bigger role in future politics than has been the case in the past?

Real-world phenomenon or label. One of the major challenges to the importance of age consciousness is the view that it does not really exist in the real world of older people, but is instead nothing more than a surrogate or euphemism for the several negative or "disadvantaged" conditions that often accompany old age—such as poverty, widowhood, declining health, or forced retirement. Indeed, about 25 years ago one study went so far as to portray any individual who identified himself or herself as old as—by definition—maladjusted, on the grounds that a truly well-adjusted older person would not identify himself or herself as old (Phillips, 1957).

Although such a view may seem out of place in today's increasingly age-conscious society, it is nevertheless important to raise the question directly, and to evaluate scientifically the evidence germane to the question. Some recent research has suggested emphatically that age identification is quite distinct from the positive or negative evaluations that either an individual or society applies to that identification. That is, an individual may identify as old, and then feel either good or bad about it; the evaluation, however, is not synonymous with the identification itself. Similarly, the research suggests that age identification is distinct from such related concepts as self-esteem, which could be high or low, and stereotypes of old age, which could be positive or negative (Brubaker & Powers, 1976; Ward, 1977).

Other research has attempted to test directly the question of whether age identification is nothing more than a surrogate for the various disadvantaged aspects of old age. Although the statistical approaches employed by this research need not be detailed here, the results are clear. One study examined the degree to which the views of the subjectively old and the nonsubjectively old (that is, those chronologically older persons who did not subjectively identify themselves as old) held relatively consistent or coherent sets of attitudes with respect to such concepts as optimism and pessimism in financial matters, and the degree to which they thought they could plan and control their lives.

The research project, which was based on the 55–75 age group of a national sample of American adults, tested the "subjective-age-identification-as-surrogate" hypothesis using the following logic. The correlations among the various attitudes were first computed only in the context of the subjective age variable, and then computed using the subjective age variable along with measures of education level and income level (using first-order partial correlations). If in the second set of computations the correlations disappeared or were substantially reduced, then it could be concluded that subjective age identification was nothing more than a statistical replacement, or surrogate, for the education and income control variables. In fact, the results showed that the controls had no impact on the pattern or the magnitude of the attitude correlations (Cutler, 1975a); in other words, age identification itself, not education or income, affected the attitudes.

Another study used a more straightforward test of the same basic hypothesis. It was reasoned that if subjective age identification was nothing more than a surrogate for the disadvantaged statuses that often come with old age, then the combining of these "negative" statuses would equal, in a statistical sense, the measurement of subjective age identification itself. However, when the impacts of income, education, sex, retirement, widowhood, occupational status, and social class identification were combined in a single (multiple regression) analysis, all of these variables together could "explain away" less than 3% of the subjective age identification in the 50 and older age group of a national sample of the adult American population (Cutler, 1975b). In short, several studies have illustrated that subjective age identification is "real"—that is, it is not simply an empty label.

How much age identification?   Although the studies just noted (as well as others) have demonstrated that subjective age identification exists independently from other, closely related causes and concepts, to what extent is such age identification really present in contemporary American society? Fortunately, the national survey questions used in the measurement of subjective age identification were included in two large national surveys, in 1972 and 1976 (Cutler, 1981b). A straightforward descriptive analysis of age identification in these two surveys reveals three important results.

First, in both 1972 and 1976 the amount of subjective age identification increases with chronological age: the older the age group, the higher the percentage of the group that exhibits subjective age identification. In a sense this pattern is a check on the validity of the measure, since we would not expect that (in a nationally representative sample survey) the older people became, the less they subjectively felt old. Second, among the two younger age groups—50-64 and 65-74—there is actually an increase in the proportion of the age group exhibiting the subjective sense of age identification. This is to be expected since it is among these "young old" (Neugarten, 1974) people that we would expect an increasing recognition of both the personal concerns and the public issues of advancing age.

Third, although there is this observable movement in the direction of higher levels of subjective age identification, a more accurate characterization of the 1972-1976 "trend" is that of stability. There is a great similarity in the percentage of each age group, across the two surveys, that subjectively identifies itself as old. It is precisely because the two surveys were conducted independently from one another— that is, the same people were *not* interviewed in the two studies—and because these are both nationally representative samples, that we can have confidence that the research has in fact measured a real phenomenon within the older segment of the American population.

Future of age consciousness. We cannot predict with certainty if age consciousness will grow in the future, and to what degree such age consciousness is likely to
become intertwined with political action. All of the available indicators suggest, however, a virtually inevitable expansion both of age consciousness itself within American
society, and some political manifestation of that expansion. Two points should be
kept in mind in evaluating this statement of "inevitability." First, as discussed earlier,
age consciousness exists both at the level of the individual and at the level of the
society as a whole. Second, the inevitable growth of age consciousness does not mean
an inevitable acceptance of the claims and demands made by or on behalf of the older
population: an age-conscious society can be one characterized by a backlash against
expanding programs and budgets devoted to the older population (for example,
Ragan, 1977).

During the past two decades there has been a massive growth in age consciousness at every level of society in the United States: changes in Social Security benefits including increased equity for women; creation of Medicare and the Older Americans Act programs; extension of discrimination laws to older age groups; private
pension reform; cost-of-living increases in Social Security and public pensions; establishment of a National Institute on Aging; dramatic growth in gerontology courses,
textbooks, departments, programs, and schools; a historic break with the traditional
age of retirement; evolution of multimillion-member organizations of older persons;
and establishment of permanent committees on aging in both the Senate and the
House of Representatives. These are just a few of the more notable examples of the
growth of laws and institutions that reflect a society increasingly aware of—and in
most cases positively sensitive to—a growing older population.

The connection between age consciousness on the societal level and age consciousness at the individual level is not hard to uncover—especially as our comments
are directed toward the future. Recall the concept of the generational cohort explored
earlier in this chapter. Surely one of the most dramatic distinctions between the
cohort that is older now, and the generation that will be the older population in the
year 2020 is the degree to which each has—in its formative years and during its maturation—been raised in a society characterized by societal age-consciousness. To put it
another way, the cohort that will wear the mantle of old age in the year 2020 will
have grown up in an increasingly age-conscious society. This is rather unlike the
cohort that is in old age at the present time and that encountered the norms and
institutions of age consciousness in society only or primarily in its advanced age.

One dimension of increasing age consciousness is the possibility of a backlash.
Certainly some evidence of such a backlash has already appeared. Virtually every
month a major newspaper or magazine features a story about the wealthy elderly,
about retirees who receive more than one pension (so-called double-dipping), and so
on. Other kinds of stories are less concerned with examples of specific unsympathetic
individuals but rather with the overall size of the federal budget that is devoted to
aging programs—the "graying of the budget." Such stories are often connected to
estimates of what programs will cost as a consequence of demographic changes in the
age structure of the population, and it is probably not a coincidence that these stories
appear to increase in intensity and frequency in times of inflation, recession, and

budget constraints (Quinn, 1980). Even such a negative or antagonistic component of age consciousness, however, serves to validate the prediction of the inevitability of the growth of age consciousness and its potential political outcomes. From the vantage point of the structure of politics, a backlash suggests that there are at least two "political sides" to the issues, each of which is actively pursuing its philosophy and its political goals.

The evidence of the connection between age consciousness and political attitudes and action is just beginning to emerge. As age consciousness itself grows in the next decades, the connection can be expected to grow also. At the level of the individual, we have seen at least some evidence that those persons who subjectively identify themselves as old have somewhat different social, economic, and political attitudes compared with those who do not identify with age. At the societal level the connection between age consciousness and politics is even more apparent. The brief discussion of the Leadership Council of Aging Organizations illustrates the degree to which the organized elderly see the solutions to many problems through collective action, negotiation, advocacy, policy formulation, and analysis—in other words, politics.

In summary, this chapter has suggested that a sequence of factors leads to a prediction that age as an issue and the aged as a constituency represent an increasingly salient component of this nation's long-term political dialogue. As an increasingly greater proportion of the national population is old, as future cohorts of older persons have the educational resources and generational experiences conducive to political action, as political leadership and national and local organizations come to mirror the demographic changes in society, and as age consciousness continues to grow both within individuals and within social institutions, we should expect that age will play an increasingly important role in political affairs.

REFERENCES

Abramson, P. R. Generational change and the decline of party identification in America: 1952–1974. *American Political Science Review*, 1976, *70*, 469–478.

Almond, G. A. *The American people and foreign policy* (2nd ed.). New York: Praeger, 1960.

Almond, G. A., & Coleman, J. C. (Eds.), *Politics in the developing areas.* Princeton, N. J.: Princeton University Press, 1960.

Back, K. W., & Gergen, K. G. Apocalyptic and serial time orientations and the structure of opinions. *Public Opinion Quarterly*, 1963, *27*, 427–442.

Bengtson, V. L. The generation gap: A review and typology of social-psychological perspectives. *Youth and Society*, 1970, *2*, 7–31.

Bengtson, V. L., & Cutler, N. E. Generations and inter-generational relations in contemporary society. In E. Shanas & R. Binstock (Eds.), *Handbook of aging and the social sciences.* New York: Van Nostrand Reinhold, 1976.

Binstock, R. H. Aging and the future of American politics. *Annals of the American Academy of Political and Social Science*, 1974, *415*, 199–212.

Brubaker, T. H., & Powers, E. A. The stereotype of "old"—A review and alternative approach. *Journal of Gerontology*, 1976, *31*, 441–447.

Campbell, A. Social and psychological determinants of voting behavior. In W. Donahue & C. Tibbits (Eds.), *Politics of age.* Ann Arbor: University of Michigan Press, 1962.

Campbell, A. Politics through the life cycle. *Gerontologist,* 1971, *11,* 112–117.

Campbell, A., Converse, P. E., Miller, W. E., & Stokes, D. E. *The American voter.* New York: John Wiley and Sons, 1960.

Chiles, L. C. Chairman's opening statement for *Work after 65: Options for the 80s.* Hearing before the United States Senate Special Committee on Aging, Pt. 1, April 23, 1980. Washington, D.C.: U.S. Government Printing Office, 1980.

Crittenden, J. A. Aging and party affiliation. *Public Opinion Quarterly,* 1962, *26,* 648–657.

Cutler, N. E. Generation, maturation, and party affiliation: A cohort analysis. *Public Opinion Quarterly,* 1969, *33,* 583–588.

Cutler, N. E. *The impact of subjective age identification on social and political attitudes.* Paper prepared for the 27th Annual Meeting of the Gerontological Society, Portland, Oregon, 1974.

Cutler, N. E. *Chronological age, subjective age, and social welfare orientations: The organization of attitudes toward society, economics, and politics.* Paper presented at the Tenth International Congress of Gerontology, Jerusalem, 1975. (a)

Cutler, N. E. *Socioeconomic predictors of subjective age.* Paper presented at the 28th Annual Meeting of the Gerontological Society, Louisville, Ky., 1975. (b)

Cutler, N. E. Generational approaches to political socialization. *Youth and Society,* 1976, *8,* 157–207.

Cutler, N. E. Demographic, social-psychological, and political factors in the politics of aging: A foundation for research in "political gerontology." *American Political Science Review,* 1977, *71,* 1011–1025. (b)

Cutler, N. E. *The cohort analysis of cross-sectional data for social gerontology research.* Paper presented at the 30th Annual Meeting of the Gerontological Society, San Francisco, 1977. (a).

Cutler, N. E. The aging population and social policy. In R. H. Davis (Ed.), *Aging: Prospects and issues* (2nd ed.). Los Angeles: University of Southern California Press, 1981, 236–259. (a)

Cutler, N. E. Political characteristics of elderly cohorts in the twenty-first century. In S. B. Kiesler, J. N. Morgan, & V. Oppenheimer (Eds.), *Aging: Social change.* New York: Academic Press, 1981, 127–157. (b)

Cutler, N. E. Subjective age identification. In D. J. Mangen & W. A. Peterson (Eds.), *Research instruments in social gerontology.* Minneapolis: University of Minnesota Press, 1981, 437–461. (c)

Cutler, N. E. Toward an appropriate typology for the study of the participation of older persons in voluntary associations. *Journal of Voluntary Action Research,* 1981–82, *11,* 9–17.

Cutler, N. E., & Mimms, G. E. *Political resources of the elderly: The impact of membership in nonpolitical voluntary associations upon political activity.* Paper presented at the Annual Meeting of the American Political Science Association, Washington, D.C., 1977.

Douglass, E. B., Cleveland, W. P., & Maddox, G. L. Political attitudes, age, and aging: A cohort analysis of archival data. *Journal of Gerontology,* 1974, *29,* 666–675.

Erbe, W. Social involvement in political activity. *American Sociological Review,* 1964, *29,* 198–215.

Evan, W. M. Cohort analysis of survey data: A procedure for studying long-term opinion change. *Public Opinion Quarterly,* 1959, *23,* 63–72.

Flanigan, W. H. *Political behavior of the American electorate* (2nd ed.). Boston, Mass.: Allyn and Bacon, 1972.

Foner, A. The polity. In M. W. Riley, M. Johnson, & A. Foner (Eds.), *Aging and society, volume III: A sociology of age stratification.* New York: Russell Sage, 1972.

Glenn, N. D. Aging and conservatism. *Annals of the American Academy of Political and Social Science,* 1974, *415,* 176–186.

Glenn, N. D. *Cohort analysis.* Beverly Hills, Calif.: Sage, 1977.

Glenn, N. D., & Grimes, M. Aging, voting, and political interest. *American Sociological Review,* 1968, *33,* 563–575.

Glenn, N. D., & Hefner, T. Further evidence on aging and party identification. *Public Opinion Quarterly,* 1972, *36,* 31–47.

Greenstein, F. I. *Personality and politics.* Chicago: Markham, 1969.

Gurin, P., Miller, A. H., & Gurin, G. Stratum identification and consciousness. *Social Psychological Quarterly,* 1980, *43,* 30–47.

Harris, L. *The myth and reality of aging in America.* Washington, D.C.: National Council on the Aging, 1975.

Heilig, P. *Self-interest and attitude patterns among the elderly.* Paper presented at the Annual Meeting of the Midwest Political Science Association, Chicago, 1979.

Hodge, R. W., & Tremain, D. J. Social participation and social status. *American Sociological Review,* 1968, *33,* 722–740.

Hyman, H. H. Cohort analysis. In H. H. Hyman (Ed.), *Secondary analysis of sample surveys: Principles, procedures, and potentialities.* New York: John Wiley and Sons, 1972.

Jennings, M. K., & Niemi, R. G. *The political character of adolescence: The influence of families and schools.* Princeton, N. J.: Princeton University Press, 1974, 1316–1335.

Jennings, M. K., & Neimi, R. G. Continuity and change in political orientations: A longitudinal study of two generations. *American Political Science Review,* 1975, *69.*

Johnson & Higgins, Inc. *1979 study of American attitudes toward pensions and retirement.* New York, 1979.

Kerschner, P. A., & Reed, J. The leadership council of aging organizations: A capsule history. *The WGS Connection,* 1980, *1* (July), 1, 8.

Key, V. O., Jr. *Politics, parties, and pressure groups* (2nd ed.). New York: Crowell, 1958.

Key, V. O., Jr. *Public opinion and American democracy.* New York: Alfred A. Knopf, 1963.

Kirkpatrick, S. A. *Quantitative analysis of political data.* Columbus, Ohio: Charles E. Merrill, 1974.

Kreps, J. The economics of intergenerational relationship. In E. Shanas & G. Streib (Eds.), *Social structure and the family: Generational relations.* Englewood Cliffs, N.J.: Prentice-Hall, 1965.

McClosky, H. Survey research in political science. In C. Y. Glock (Ed.), *Survey research in the social sciences.* New York: Russell Sage Foundation, 1967.

McTavish, D. G. Perceptions of old people: A review of research methodologies and findings. *Gerontologist,* 1971, *11,* 90–101.

Milbrath, L. W., & Goel, M. L. *Political participation* (2nd ed.). Chicago: Rand McNally, 1977.

Morgan, J. N. *Economic problems of the aging and their policy implications.* Paper presented for the Gerontological Society Conference on Public Assessment of the Conditions and Status of the Elderly, Santa Barbara, Calif., February, 1975.

Neugarten, B. L. Age groups in American society and the rise of the young-old. *Annals of the American Academy of Political and Social Science,* 1974, *415,* 187–198.

Peterson, W. A. Research priorities on perceptions and orientations toward aging and toward older people. *Gerontologist,* 1971, *11,* 60–63.

Phillips, B. S. A role theory approach to adjustment in old age. *American Sociological Review,* 1957, *22,* 212–217.

Pratt, H. J. Old age associations in national politics. *Annals of the American Academy of Political and Social Science,* 1974, *415,* 106–119.

Pratt, H. J. *The gray lobby.* Chicago: University of Chicago Press, 1976.

Quinn, J. B. The affluent elderly. *Newsweek,* August 4, 1980, p. 53.

Ragan, P. K. Another look at politicizing of old age—Can we expect a backlash effect? *Urban and Social Change Review*, 1977, *10*(2), 6–13.

Renshon, S. A. *Psychological needs and political behavior: A theory of personality and political efficacy.* New York: Free Press, 1974.

Riemer, Y., & Binstock, R. H. Campaigning for the "senior vote": A case study of Carter's 1976 campaign. *Gerontologist*, 1978, *18*, 517–524.

Riley, M. W. Social gerontology and the age stratification of society. *Gerontologist*, 1971, *11*, 79–87.

Riley, M. W. Aging and cohort succession: Interpretations and misinterpretations. *Public Opinion Quarterly*, 1973, *37*, 35–49.

Rose, A. The subculture of the aging: A framework for research in social gerontology. In A. Rose & W. Peterson (Eds.), *Older people and their social world.* Philadelphia: F. A. Davis, 1965.

Schaie, K. W. A general model for the study of developmental problems. *Psychological Bulletin*, 1965, *64*, 92–107.

Schreiber, E. M., & Marsden, L. R. Age and opinions on a government program of medical aid. *Journal of Gerontology*, 1972, *27*, 95–101.

Streib, G. F. Are the aged a minority group? In A. W. Gouldner & S. M. Miller (Eds.), *Applied sociology.* New York: Free Press, 1965.

Torrey, B. B. *Demographic shifts and projections: The implications for pensions systems.* Washington, D.C.: President's Commission on Pension Policy, 1979.

Trela, J. E. Some political consequences of senior center and other old age group memberships. *Gerontologist*, 1971, *11*, 118–123.

Trela, J. E. Age structure of voluntary associations and political self-interest among the aged. *Sociological Quarterly*, 1972, *13*, 244–252.

U.S. Bureau of the Census. *Current population reports*, Series P-20, no. 322. Voting and Registration in the Election of November 1976. Washington, D.C.: U.S. Government Printing Office, 1978.

U.S. Bureau of the Census. *Current population reports*, Series P-20, no 344. Voting and Registration in the Election of November 1978. Washington, D.C.: U.S. Government Printing Office, 1979.

Verba, S., & Nie, N. H. *Participation in America.* New York: Harper & Row, 1972.

Ward, R. A. The impact of subjective age and stigma on older persons. *Journal of Gerontology*, 1977, *32*, 227–232.

Weaver, J. L. The elderly as a political community: The case of national health policy. *Western Political Quarterly*, 1976, *29*, 610–619.

Name Index

443

Subject Index